An Introduction to Film Studies

'Indispensable for the A-Level, degree student or lay reader in film communications or media courses . . . will indisputably be the standard text for many years to come . . . If I had to unreservedly tell a student at any level to buy one book, this is it: as close to the perfect film studies textbook as you're likely to see.'

John Lough, Senior Lecturer in Media Theory, University of Humberside

An Introduction to Film Studies is a comprehensive textbook for students of cinema. The book provides a guide to the main concepts used to analyse the film industry and film texts, and also introduces some of the world's key national cinemas.

Individual chapters introduce:

■ Cinema as institution
■ Film and technology
■ Film form and narrative
■ Genre, stars and auteurs
■ Documentary cinema
■ Animation
■ Women and film
■ Lesbian and gay cinema
■ British cinema
■ Soviet cinema
■ Indian cinema
■ New German cinema

Each chapter includes definitions of key terms, case studies of important films and suggestions for further reading and further viewing, and there is also a glossary of terms used in cinema studies and a bibliography. The book is richly illustrated with over 130 film stills and production shots.

Contributors: Lez Cooke, Chris Jones, Asha Kasbekar, Mark Joyce, Julia Knight, Searle Kochberg, Jill Nelmes, Patrick Phillips, Allan Rowe, Chris Webster, Paul Wells

Editor: **Jill Nelmes** is Head of Media and a Lecturer in Film and Media Studies at Pontypridd College.

'Very well set out and a pleasure to look at. Very easy to access information.'

R.J. Hand, Humberside University

'Clear, concise and comprehensive.'

Steven Hay, Barnsley College

'Clear, accessible, informative – an essential introductory reader.'

Alistair King, Portsmouth University

'The source book for all introductory levels – provides a pathway to more advanced levels of reading, viewing and research.'

J.E. Mair, Edge Hill College, Ormskirk

'To me it is simply the best introductory volume in the field so far.'

Jesus B. Sanchez, Castilla La Mongha University, Ciudad Real, Spain

'I loved the book. High readability of layout, excellent quality of images, wide range of case studies and topics. Wide range of theory, debates and concepts covered in depth using accessible language. Terminology clearly explained.'

Elaine Scarratt, Christ the King Sixth Form College, Lewisham

'This book is a treasure. Clear and very well presented. I shall recommend it.'

Francine Wetherill, Manchester University Institute of Science and Technology

An Introduction to Film Studies

Edited by Jill Nelmes

ROUTLEDGE

London and New York

First published 1996
by Routledge
11 New Fetter Lane, London EC4P 4EE

Simultaneously published in the USA and Canada
by Routledge
29 West 35th Street, New York, NY 10001

Reprinted 1996

Typeset in Monotype Neue Helvetica by
Florencetype Ltd, Stoodleigh, Devon

Text design by Secondary Modern

Printed and bound in Great Britain by
Clays Ltd, St Ives PLC

British Library Cataloguing in Publication Data
A catalogue record for this book is available from
the British Library

Library of Congress Cataloguing in Publication Data
A catalogue record for this book is available from
the Library of Congress

ISBN 0–415–10859–4 (hbk)
ISBN 0–415–10860–8 (pbk)

Contents

PART ONE: INSTITUTIONS, AUDIENCES AND TECHNOLOGY

PART FOUR: REPRESENTATION OF GENDER AND SEXUALITY

PART FIVE: NATIONAL CINEMAS

Contributors

Lez Cooke is a senior lecturer in Film and Media Studies at Staffordshire University, where he teaches courses on British cinema and television drama, among others. He has written for the journals *Movie* and *Screen* and has contributed chapters to several books on aspects of British cinema and television.

Chris Jones taught Literature, Theatre and Film Studies at Brooklands College for a number of years. He has participated in gay-related theatre and video work. In 1990 he completed an MA in Film and Television Studies at the University of Westminster. He is now living and writing in Toronto.

Mark Joyce is a lecturer in Film, Media and Communication Studies at West Kent College of Further Education, Tonbridge. He also lectures in Cultural Studies on the West Kent College/University of Greenwich BA Degree in Media and Communication. In the near future he is hoping to resume his Ph.D. in Film at the University of East Anglia.

Asha Kasbekar graduated from the National School of Drama in New Delhi, India, before studying French Drama at the Sorbonne in Paris. She was a film and drama critic for the *Indian Express* newspaper. She has taught Indian Cinema at the School of Oriental and African Studies, University of London, and works at the British Board of Film Classification as a film and video examiner.

Julia Knight is a senior lecturer in the Department of Media Arts at the University of Luton. She is the author of *Women and the New German Cinema* (1992) and has written for a number of film and video publications.

Searle Kochberg works as a senior lecturer in Film Studies at the University of Portsmouth, and is the co-ordinator of the mature students' foundation programme in Art, Design and Media at the same institution. He is currently an MA candidate in History of Art at University College London.

Jill Nelmes is head of Media and a lecturer in Film and Media Studies at Pontypridd College and Glamorgan Centre for Art and Technology, teaching a range of courses from Access to A-Level to HND. She has been assistant examiner for WJEC Media Studies for the last four years. She is currently researching into the relationship between art direction and mise-en-scène in film.

Patrick Phillips is head of Media Studies at Long Road Sixth Form College, Cambridge. He is also Curriculum Manager for Adult and Continuing Education at the College and is Course Director for the University of Cambridge Certificate in Film Studies. He is a senior examiner for both A-Level Film Studies and A-Level Media Studies.

Allan Rowe has lectured in Film, Media and Sociology since the mid-1960s. He has taught Film A-Level since the original consortium in 1984 and is an assistant examiner in Film. At present he combines these activities with directing Quality Assurance at Epping Forest College.

Chris Webster initially trained as a graphic designer and illustrator before beginning work in the animation industry. For ten years he worked as a traditional animator on adverts, children's series, specials and features before starting a small studio. He became a full-time animation lecturer in 1993. He continues to write on the subject while working alongside his son with computer animation.

Paul Wells is senior lecturer in Film and Media Studies at De Montfort University in Leicester. He has recently won a Sony Award for his BBC Radio series 'Spine-chillers' on the history of the horror film. He is the author of *Understanding Animation* (Routledge 1966) and is currently writing a book on situation comedy and the American way.

Acknowledgements

The following plates were reproduced with kind permission of their rights holders, wherever possible, and sources:

While every effort has been made to trace copyright holders and obtain permission, this has not been possible in all cases. Any omissions brought to our attention will be remedied in future editions.

I would particularly like to thank the contributors for their hard work as this book has been very much a team effort. My thanks also to the staff at Routledge for their professionalism and commitment to the project.

Finally I would like to thank friends, colleagues and family who gave me so much help and support whilst the book was in progress.

Chapter 1

Introduction

Jill Nelmes

We all enjoy watching films, whether in the cinema or on TV. Cinema attendance, after many years of decline, is now increasing and a new generation of film-goers are appreciating the pleasures of the 'big screen', a pleasure that even a 30-inch TV set cannot provide. The study of film is also increasingly popular and there are now many courses in film and media at the 16-plus and undergraduate level. Although film is often seen as a part of media studies it has particular qualities which separate it from the other media. How film is viewed, its history, conditions of production and the huge wealth of film available from not only Hollywood, but also countries such as India, Africa and the Caribbean, surely requires that film be seen as a discrete area of study. Yet film cannot be seen in isolation; films are shown on TV, satellite and video and are frequently referred to by the other media. Developments in computer technology and multimedia also affect film. How images are used, put together and understood is of relevance to all the visual media. Issues such as technology, ownership, representation and censorship of the media are often the subject of intense debate, not only in colleges, but within society as a whole.

There has been a huge expansion in the field of Film Studies and a wealth of useful resource material is now available. Yet much of this work is highly academic and 'difficult' for those who are new to the subject and who require an introductory text which gives an overview of film. This book hopes to fill the gap that exists by providing an approachable introduction to Film Studies, which will be useful for students, lecturers and those interested in increasing their knowledge and enjoyment of film. The range of the book is huge. It in no way attempts to be definitive, but rather hopes to stimulate an interest in further reading about and watching film. To some extent the WJEC A-Level Film Studies syllabus has been followed, giving a background to the history and development of film and an introduction to film theory and analysis.

At the end of each chapter a list of suggested further reading and viewing is given. Throughout the book key terms are emboldened in the text and explained in a marginal note. There is also a glossary of terms at the end of the book. A bibliography provides further background reading. Detailed reference is made to a wide range of films and this is furthered by the use of case studies in a number of the chapters, which suggest methods of analysing and discussing film. Many film stills are used, which not only provide visual referents but also the 'pleasure of looking'.

The book is divided into five sections, thirteen chapters in total, each providing an accessible background to the central ideas and theories appropriate to the area discussed.

PART ONE: INSTITUTIONS, AUDIENCES AND TECHNOLOGY

This part is divided into two chapters, the first of which explains how the film industry works as a complex organisation, an institution, having set rules and methods of working which have evolved from the early days of cinema through to the studio system to their present state. Case studies of mainstream and independent production are given. The relationship between the film industry, audience, control and censorship is also considered. The second chapter discusses the development of film as a technological medium, the implications for the future of film and the relationship between technology, art and society.

PART TWO: APPROACHES TO STUDYING FILM TEXTS

This part examines methods of interpreting and analysing film. 'Film form and narrative', Chapter 4, can be seen as an introduction to how film is constructed, shaped and formed; from its 'look', to editing, to sound and story. A close analysis of key films is given using examples from silent film, Hollywood and alternative forms of cinema. Chapter 5, 'Genre, star and auteur', examines each of the respective areas through the study of Hollywood cinema, again using a range of examples but particularly focusing on *New York, New York* as a case study to explain the role of the director (Martin Scorsese), the stars (Robert De Niro and Liza Minelli) and the film's placing as a musical in the genre system.

PART THREE: GENRE FORMS: REALISM AND ILLUSION

Part 3 examines two different categories or genre of film: documentary and animation. The documentary form aspires to record 'reality' as opposed to fiction, yet is very much a construction of events. Animation is literally created by the film-maker(s) and is not bound by a commitment to realism. Therefore it has great potential for innovation and experimentation. Often seen as merely cartoons, animation has an enormous range from Disney to the witty social commentary of Nick Park's *Creature Comforts*.

PART FOUR: REPRESENTATION OF GENDER AND SEXUALITY

The chapters in this part look at 'Women and film' and 'Lesbian and gay cinema'. Both chapters discuss representation and stereotyping in the media and cover the central theoretical developments in their respective areas. 'Women and film' examines the relationship between feminist film theory and film practice, focusing on films such as Marlene Gorris' *Question of Silence* and *Orlando* by Sally Potter. 'Lesbian and gay cinema' looks at representation in mainstream film and discusses films made by lesbians and gays, with detailed case studies of films such as Donna Deitsch's *Desert Hearts* and Isaac Julien's *Looking for Langston*. For further discussion of representation and national identity see Chapter 10, 'British cinema: representing the nation'.

PART FIVE: NATIONAL CINEMAS

In western society we tend to think of Hollywood as being the dominant form of cinema. This is arguable, when one considers other national cinemas, past and present, which have made an impact for many reasons, ranging from their productivity and popularity to their political and social value. British cinema has produced a diverse range of film, from the socialist inspired documentary film movement of the 1930s to the internationally successful *Four Weddings and a Funeral*. Chapter 10 focuses on representation in both mainstream and independent British cinema and may be linked with Part 4 of this volume for further discussion of representation. Soviet film of the 1920s, which is discussed in Chapter 11, emerged out of the Russian Revolution in 1917 as a propaganda form, spreading the message of socialism. Theories about the interpretation and construction of film were developed in this period by film-makers such as Eisenstein and are still influential today.

Indian cinema, often termed 'Bollywood', is even more prolific than Hollywood, producing over 900 films per year. Film is a central part of Indian culture, and Chapter 12 explores its history and development while looking at forms of popular Indian film. New German Cinema really only existed for a fairly brief period, from the 1960s to the early 1980s. Chapter 13 explores the reasons for its emergence, which is often attributed to the brilliance of auteur directors such as Wim Wenders and Werner Herzog, but this chapter argues that the social, economic and political conditions that existed in postwar Germany were also important factors.

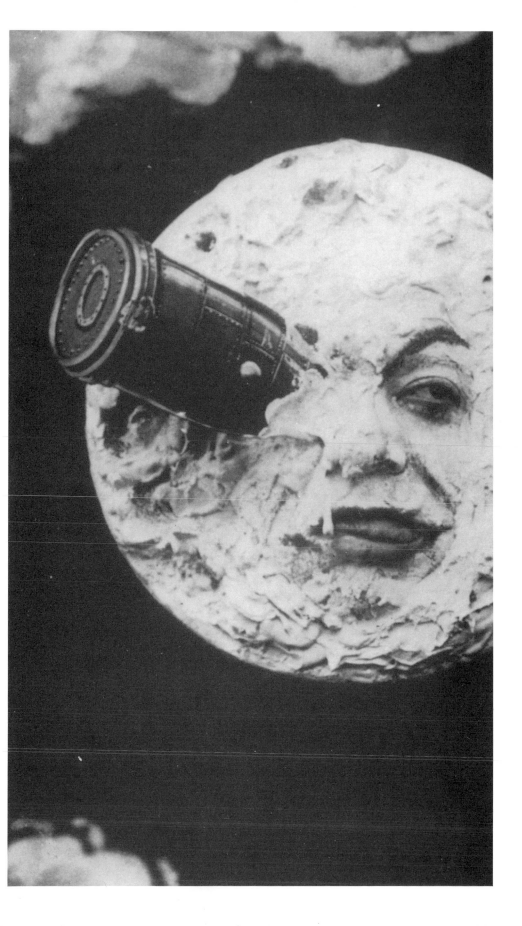

Part one

Institutions, audiences and technology

Chapter 2

Cinema as institution

Searle Kochberg

■ Cinema as institution

INTRODUCTION

Films do not exist in a vacuum: they are conceived, produced, distributed and consumed within specific economic and social contexts.

The chapter that follows is a journey through the institutional framework of mainstream film from the turn of the century to the present day. The American film industry has dominated all others this century and for this reason the section largely centres around it. I do not claim the itinerary to be definitive, but I have sought to cite some key issues and moments in the social and economic history of American and British film.

The origins and consolidation of the American industry are traced from 1895 to 1930 – a period which saw a fledgling industry harness new industrial practices and quickly grow into an important popular medium, organised into highly defined exhibition, production and distribution components.

The Hollywood studio era (1930 to 1949) is the next stop on the tour. Monopolistic practice and the finely tuned industrial organisation of the Hollywood 'factories' are discussed at some length. This section looks specifically at Warner Brothers as an example of a vertically integrated film company during the studio era.

There follows an exploration of the contemporary institutional framework of commercial film, starting with a review of the position of the 'majors' in the light of multi-media empires and mainstream independent US production. Mainstream UK film production is also reviewed. The production/distribution histories of *Jaws* (1975) and *Fellow Traveller* (1989) are taken as case studies.

The film-going habit is an important part of social history this century: the changing nature of UK and US audiences since the Second World War is reviewed.

The chapter ends with a review of the systems of censorship and classification that have operated in the US and UK since the 1920s. Both contemporary and historical case studies are looked at.

THE ORIGINS OF THE AMERICAN FILM INDUSTRY 1900–15

exhibition

Division of the film industry concentrating on the public screening of film.

distribution

Division concentrating on the marketing of film, connecting the producer with the exhibitor by leasing films from the former and renting them to the latter.

production

Division concentrating on the making of film.

The American film industry has been in existence as long as there has been American film. This section looks at how the film industry organised itself into three main divisions in the early years of this century, divisions that exist to this day – **exhibition**, **distribution** and **production**.

Exhibition until 1907

By 1894, the exhibition of moving pictures had been established in New York City with the introduction of the box-like **Kinetoscope**. This allowed an individual customer to watch a fifty-foot strip of film through a slit at the top of the machine.[1] In 1895, a **projector** called the Pantopticon was demonstrated, again in New York City, and for the first time more than one person could watch the same moving images simultaneously.[2]

Once projectors were available, single-reel films started to be shown in vaudeville theatres as novelties. Exhibition outlets began to multiply and by the first years of this century small high street stores and restaurants were being converted to small-scale cinemas or **nickelodeons**. As the name suggests, the cost of entry to these cinemas was 5 cents – an amount affordable to the (predominantly) working-class audiences of nickelodeons. By the end of 1905 there were an estimated 1,000 of these theatres in America and by 1908 there were 6,000.

Distribution until 1907

As the film industry expanded, exhibitors had a growing commercial need for an unbroken supply of films to show. To meet this need, the first **film exchange** was in operation by 1902 and acted as a go-between for the producers and exhibitors.[3] The exchanges purchased (later leased) films from producers and **distributed** films to exhibitors by renting to them. By 1907 there were between 125 and 150 film exchanges covering the whole of the US.

• Plate 2.1 A nickelodeon (5¢ entry fee) in New York City in the first decade of this century.
Converted high street stores like this one were typical of the first cinemas

Production until 1907

Until 1900 the average length of films was around 50 feet. Three major companies domi-nated production in the US: Edison, Biograph and Vitagraph.[4] Although filming on location was very common at this stage, as early as 1893 the world's first 'kinetographic theatre' or film studio was in operation. This was built by the Edison Company and called the 'Black Maria'.

kinetograph

Edison's first movie camera.

After 1900, films started to get longer, and by 1903, films of 300–600 feet were fairly common. The Edison Company's *The Great Train Robbery* (1903) was over 1,000 feet long[5] and is an example of early cinema utilising increased running time and primitive continuity editing to tell, for then, a fairly ambitious story. By this time there were several major film producers in the US, including (as well as the companies mentioned above) Selig, Kalem, Essanay and Lubin. These companies ensured their dominant position in the industry by holding patents in camera and projection equipment.[6]

The industrial organisation of film production until 1907 has been referred to as the 'cameraman' system of production.[7] As the name suggests, films were largely the creation of one individual, the cameraman, who would be responsible for planning, writing, filming and editing. Edwin Porter, working for the Edison Company, is a good example of such a craftsman.[8]

Thus, by 1907, the American film industry was already organised into three main div-isions: exhibition, distribution and production. The creation of these separate commercial divisions demonstrates pragmatic, commercial streamlining by a very young industry, which was designed to maximise profits in an expanding market.

The Motion Picture Patents Company and industry monopolies (1908–15)

In 1908, the Edison and Biograph companies attempted to control the fledgling film industry through the key patents they held in camera and projection technology.[9] They set up the Motion Picture Patents Company, a **patent pool**, which issued licences for a fee to companies on a discretionary basis.[10] Only licensed firms could legally utilise technology patented by or contracted[11] to the MPPC without fear of litigation. The MPPC was soon collecting royalties from all sectors of the industry, including manufacturers of equipment, film producers and exhibitors. The MPPC's ultimate ambition was to monopolise the film industry in the US. Its goal was a situation in which films would be shot on patented cameras, distributed through its general film company and screened on its patented projectors.

patent pool

An association of companies, operating collectively in the marketplace by pooling the patents held by each individual company.

Exhibition and audience during the MPPC era

An important contribution to the profits of the MPPC was from the licensing of projec-tion equipment to exhibitors. In 1908 the most important exhibition outlet was the nickelodeon.[12]

The year 1910 marked the peak of the nickelodeon theatre, with an estimated 26 million people attending the 10,000 'nickels' in the continental US every week.[13] The meteoric rise of the nickel theatres was remarkable and reflected the general expansion of popular entertainment during America's prosperous start to the twentieth century. Enormous expansion in film exhibition occurred throughout the US and inner-city loca-tions were particularly important due to their concentrated populations. The growth of the nickelodeon in large American cities has been well documented[14] and may in part be attributable to mass working-class immigration to the US at the time.[15]

The exhibition industry understood that its successful future lay in securing a wide audience base. It appears to have accomplished this, even in its nickelodeon years, by successfully positioning nickels in middle-class as well as working-class districts.[16] Exhibitors realised, however, that even greater profit lay in larger theatres and more ambitious narratives. As early as 1909, large movie theatres were being constructed.[17] Film producers were also being encouraged by exhibitors to provide films that would appeal to middle- as well as working-class audiences, including 'women's' stories and one-reel adaptations of literary classics.[18] This process continued to gather momentum in the final years of the MPPC era, when large luxurious theatres began to supplant the nickels in movie exhibition,[19] and audiences reached 49 million per week.[20] Feature-length films at an average length of four to six reels also became established.[21]

Distribution in the MPPC era

Soon after its inception, the MPPC turned its attention to film distribution and licensed 70 per cent of the film exchanges operating in the US.[22] By 1910, the MPPC had set up its own distribution company – the **General Film Company** – which soon had nation-wide cover through the purchase of forty-eight key exchanges in the US.[23] By 1911, the MPPC had constructed the first effective example of **vertical integration** in the film industry through a combination of takeovers and patent rights.

Changing conditions were soon to challenge the MPPC's supreme position in the industry. First, independent distributors, exhibitors and producers quickly and success-fully organised themselves in response to the MPPC's attempted monopoly.[24] Then, a charge of anti-**trust** violation was filed against the MPPC by the Department of Justice in 1912.[25] The outcome of the case (announced in 1915) was that it was ordered that the MPPC be split up. Ironically, by this time, other vertically integrated companies were being organised within the industry (see p. 12).

Production during the MPPC era

The years 1908 to 1915 were not only marked by the rise and fall of the industrial giant – the Motion Picture Patents Company – but also by the rise of the multi-reel feature film and the relative demise of the single-reel film.[26] Greater length and greater narra-tive complexity coincided with the application of scientific management principles to the industrial organisation of film production.

By 1908, the 'cameraman' system of production had already been discarded and replaced by the 'director system' (1907–9).[27] For the first time a **director** was respon-sible for overseeing a group of operative workers, including the cameraman. The director was central to the planning, filming and editing stages of film making. Production was centralised in a studio/factory, permitting greater control of production, thus keeping costs down. Around 1909, this system was in turn discarded in favour of the 'director–unit' system.[28] Directors were now in charge of autonomous production units within companies, each with a separate group of workers. Companies were subdivided into various departments, for ever greater productivity and efficiency (scientific manage-ment).[29]

By the end of the MPPC era, the 'central producer' system[30] had been introduced.[31] This was a fully structured hierarchical system, with a strict division of labour. Production line film-making was now the order of the day, all under the central control of a producer who used very detailed shooting scripts to plan budgets before giving the go-ahead to studio projects.[32]

vertical integration

Where a company is organised so that it oversees a product from the planning/development stage, through production, market distribution, to the end-user – the retail consumer. In the case of the film industry, this translates to a company controlling the production, marketing and exhibition of its films.

trust

A group of companies operating together to control the market for a commodity. This is illegal practice in the US.

Summary

During the first twenty years of its life, the film industry increased in size from a cottage scale enterprise to an established mass popular medium. Its rapid and enormous growth was largely driven by the explosion in exhibition, which in turn triggered a streamlining in distribution methods and the industrialisation of production. The predominant position of exhibition within the industry was also to be a hallmark of the studio era of American film.

THE STUDIO ERA OF AMERICAN FILM 1930–49

This section looks at the studio era of film production. By 1930 the film industry in America was dominated by five companies – all vertically integrated - known as the 'majors' or the 'Big Five': **Warner Brothers**, **Loew's–MGM**, **Fox**, **Paramount** and **Radio–Keith–Orpheum (RKO)**. Three smaller companies, the 'Little Three', were also part of the **oligopoly**: **Columbia**, **Universal** (both with production and distribution facilities) and **United Artists** (a distribution company for independent producers).

oligopoly

A state of limited competition between a small group of producers or sellers.

The origins of the studio era oligopoly

Vertical integration made sense to the power brokers of the film industry: companies with the financial resources to organise themselves in this way stood to dominate the marketplace through their all-pervasive influence and their ability to block out competition.

Despite the alarm bells of the MPPC anti-trust case in 1915, film companies continued to seek out legal ways to construct vertically integrated companies through mergers and acquisitions.[33] In December 1916 an industry merger occurred which became the cornerstone of the future Hollywood studio era. This involved the Famous Players and Jesse L. Lasky production companies and Paramount, a distribution company. By 1920 Famous Players–Lasky (as the new company was called) had established a pre-eminent position in the American film industry with the purchase of theatre chains throughout the US and Canada.[34]

The trend set by Famous Players–Lasky was soon copied elsewhere in the industry. In 1922 the distribution–exhibition giant First National became vertically integrated with the construction of a large production facility in Burbank, California.[35] By 1924 Loew's Incorporated, the major exhibition firm, had acquired both Metro Pictures (producer–distributor) and Goldwyn Pictures (producer-exhibitor). Henceforth, Loew's production subsidiary would be known as Metro–Goldwyn–Mayer (MGM).[36]

Exhibition during the studio era

Exhibition continued to be the most powerful and influential branch of the American film industry during the studio era. The reason for this was simple: it was where the money was made. Reflecting this, the majors channelled most of their investment into exhibition, which accounted for 90 per cent of their total asset value during the years 1930 to 1949.[37]

In spite of the fact that the majors owned only 15 per cent of the movie theatres in the US, they collected approximately 75 per cent of exhibition revenues in the US during the studio era.[38] This was possible because the **Big Five** film companies owned 70 per cent of the **first-run** movie houses in the US during this period.[39] Their numbers were relatively small, but the first-run theatres accounted for most of the exhibition revenue

first run

Important movie theatres would show films immediately upon their theatrical release (or their 'first run'). Smaller, local theatres would show films on subsequent runs, hence the terms second run, third run, etc.

because of their very large seating capacity (on average over 1,200 seats), prime locations (in key urban sites) and higher price of admission. The majors further strengthened their grip on exhibition by 'encouraging' the (30 per cent) independent first-run theatres to book their films, sight unseen, to the exclusion of competitors (see p. 14). By bowing to the wishes of the majors, the independents safeguarded their access to the majors' popular films. All in all, it was the majors' control of cinemas during the years of vertical integration that ensured their profits.

The successful theatre chains

By the 1920s, American innovations in national wholesaling and chainstore retailing had been absorbed into cinema exhibition methods. The introduction of scientific management methods and economies of scale led to the building up of chains of theatres, lower per unit costs, and faster, more efficient operations.[40]

Exhibition and Balaban and Katz

By far the most financially successful and innovative of the exhibition companies in the lead up to the studio era was Balaban and Katz[41] with corporate headquarters in Chicago. Its success influenced the whole exhibition industry, especially at the top end of the market. Key innovations of Balaban and Katz included locating cinemas in outlying business and residential areas as well as downtown, building large, ornate, air-conditioned movie palaces (trips to which were 'events' in themselves for movie-goers), and accompanying screen presentations with quality vaudeville acts.[42]

The 1930s and 1940s saw a continuation of the scientific management practices inaugurated by innovators like Balaban and Katz. Changes were made in exhibition during the studio era, some a direct result of the fall in attendance brought about by the Great Depression which followed the Wall Street Crash of 1929. Vaudeville acts were eliminated in all but the grandest of movie houses and replaced by talkie shorts,[43] new movie theatres were less elaborate,[44] double bills were introduced,[45] air-conditioning was more universally adopted[46] and food and drink stands – in the form of popcorn (pre-Second World War onwards) and Coke/Pepsi (post Second World War) – were introduced into foyers. These became major profit earners for exhibitors.[47]

The war years (1941–5) and the immediate postwar period were to mark the heyday of studio era exhibition in the US, with 1946 being the year of greatest profits for the Big Five.[48]

Distribution during the studio era

The distribution of films in America was effectively controlled by the Big Five during the studio era, even though the Little Three were also heavily engaged in the distribution business. The reason for this lay in the majors' complete domination of exhibition. To ensure access for their films to the nationwide cinema network controlled by the majors, the Little Three went along with the distribution system of the Big Five.[49] Areas were zoned by the majors, and theatres designated first-run, second-run, etc. The average period between runs, or clearance, was thirty days or more.[50]

When booking films into their own theatres, each of the majors ensured that precedence was given to their own product, followed by films of the other majors. Any exhibition slots still available would be allocated to the Little Three.

....

Block-booking

In distributing films to independent theatres, the Big Five and Little Three utilised a system of **advance block-booking**[51] (films booked *en masse* and in advance). Under this system, independent exhibitors were often forced to book a full year's feature-film output of an individual film company, sight unseen, in order to secure likely box-office hits.[52]

....

It is worth noting that genre films and star vehicles of the studio era owed their popularity with distributors and exhibitors to the fact that they were useful marketing tools for distributors and at the same time helped provide box-office insurance for exhibitors.

Production during the studio era

By the onset of the studio era, the major movie factories were each producing an average of fifty features per year to satisfy the voracious demands of the highly profitable exhibition end of the business. As in other areas of the film industry, production management was 'scientific': film studios were organised as assembly-line plants with strict divisions of labour and hierarchies of authority.[53]

As early as 1931, Hollywood majors had begun to move away from the central producer system which had dominated production since 1915. Columbia Pictures was the first company to announce the adoption of a producer–unit system in October 1931.[54] Under the new organisational framework, the company appointed a head of production to oversee the running of the studio. Several associate producers were then appointed under the head, and each had the job of supervising the production of a group of films and of delivering the films on completion to the head of production.[55]

Those firms that adopted the new system[56] were convinced that it was an advance in scientific management for two reasons. First, it was felt that the system saved money, since it allowed each associate producer to keep a closer control of individual budgets (overseeing far fewer films than a central producer). Second, the system was felt to foster 'better quality' films, and encourage specialisms in individual units, by investing in the creativity of the delegated associate producers.[57]

Certain production units were associated with particular genres: Jerry Wald's unit at Warner Brothers specialised in noir–melodrama, for example, *Mildred Pierce* (1945); Arthur Freed's unit at Metro–Goldwyn–Mayer specialised in the integrated musical, for example, *Meet Me In St. Louis* (1944).

Contracts and unions

It was standard studio practice during the 1930s and 1940s to employ personnel on long-term or permanent contracts.[58] Workers' unions had firmly established themselves in American film production by the early years of the Roosevelt administration (in the mid-1930s).[59] Ironically, by defining and enforcing rigidly delineated areas of responsibility

• Plate 2.2 An aerial view of Paramount's production facility in Hollywood in the 1930s
This studio was one of the most modern talking-picture production plants in the world. It covered an area of 26 acres, had fourteen sound stages on the grounds, and had a working population of 2,000 persons

for specific jobs to protect their members' jobs, the unions were directly instrumental in reinforcing the hierarchical structure of film production practice.[60]

Stars

Long before the 1930s, a whole subsidiary industry had grown up promoting the Hollywood 'dream factory', its films and its stars. This continued throughout the studio era, fuelled by the publicity machines of the film companies themselves.

Long-term contracts (normally lasting for seven years) secured the ongoing services of stars for the film companies. This was the key to the financial security of corporations since the acting ability and personality of stars generated significant value for the films in which they appeared. Stars helped differentiate films that were otherwise very standard in format. Their popularity re-inforced consumer brand loyalty for the films of individual film companies, and provided the majors with the necessary 'carrot' with which to entice independent exhibitors into booking blocks of films sight unseen (or 'blind').

Summary

During the Hollywood studio era, a small group of manufacturers-cum-distributors-cum-retailers controlled the film market between them. Smaller US producers were forced to make do with subsequent-run cinemas in which to show their films or to arrange distribution deals with the Big Five and Little Three. Likewise, foreign film-makers could not get a foothold in the US unless they too had arrangements with one of the eight US film companies comprising the oligopoly.

UK films and US distribution

Examples of UK production companies that had US distribution during the studio era were: London Films – distributing through UA, Imperator Films – distributing through RKO, and Rank Organisation – distributing through Universal.

It was not until after 1948 that the majors were forced to divest themselves of their cinema chains, as a result of the Supreme Court's decision in the Paramount anti-trust case (see p. 22).

☐ CASE STUDY 1: WARNER BROTHERS[61]

From its origins as a small production company in the mid-1920s, Warner Brothers rose to become one of the five major vertically integrated film companies by the end of the decade. This was largely achieved through debt-financing – expansion financed through loans.[62] Key to Warners' exponential growth were the following financial deals: its takeover of Vitagraph Corporation (with distribution and production facilities) in 1925, its exclusive licensing of Western Electric sound equipment for 'talking pictures' in 1926 and its purchase of the Stanley Company cinema chain with its associated film company, First National in 1928.

Vitaphone

Warner Brothers created a corporate subsidiary for its sound productions called Vitaphone Corporation in 1926. That year it premiered its Vitaphone 'shorts' and its first feature film with recorded musical accompaniment, *Don Juan*. The year 1927 saw the release of WB's first feature-length part-talkie, *The Jazz Singer*.

The Great Depression seriously weakened Warners' financial base. The company could carry its enormous debt-load while big profits were being generated at the box office. After 1930, however, box office takings fell off so sharply that the company began to

• Plate 2.3 The Warner Bros logo

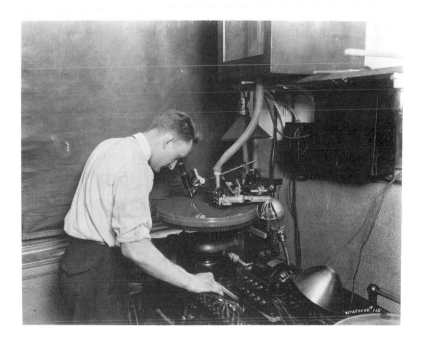

• Plate 2.4 The Vitaphone sound system: a sound-on-disc system
An engineer monitors the wax disc during a recording in the late 1920s

lose money and had difficulty meeting its loan commitments. Warners was not to show a profit again until 1935.[63]

Warner Brothers' response to its financial crisis was to sell off assets,[64] introduce production units (to help control film budgets) and to make feature films as cheaply as possible.[65] Its series of studio-bound, fast paced, topical films in the early 1930s were the direct result of this corporate policy.

By 1935, the fortunes of the company had improved sufficiently for it to return to profit again. As profits increased, so did film budgets. Studio genres changed too, with the entrenchment of the melodrama, biopic, Merrie England and film noir genres[66] in the late 1930s and early 1940s. As with the other majors, profits reached record levels for Warners during and immediately after the Second World War.[67]

Warners as **auteur**

The Warners' house style – cast, subject, treatment, technical standards – is a style discernible in the work of all of its contract directors and over a wide variety of genres.

Warners' style during the studio era

As discussed, film production during the studio era was all about standardised assembly-line manufacturing practice. This is why there is such impressive consistency in the physical makeup of the classic Hollywood film of the period. Individual film companies needed to differentiate their product, however, if they were to develop brand loyalty with their customers.

Senior management control over Warners' house style[68] is evident: staff workers were assigned projects by management, they did not choose them.[69] Management retained ultimate authority on all matters concerning its productions,[70] and the corporation had direct control over the final cut. This was extensively exercised, much to the chagrin of directors and stars.

Throughout the studio era, Warners' films articulated a populist, liberal ethos. Several productions of the early 1930s were particularly hard-hitting social critiques.[71] From 1933 onwards, though, Warners' films discarded their anti-government position and whole-heartedly supported the new Roosevelt (Democratic) administration and its **NRA programme**. The ultimate endorsement of the New Deal and Roosevelt must be *Footlight Parade* (1933), with its 'Shanghai Lil' dance routine incorporating images of the NRA eagle and Roosevelt, and its leading protagonist (played by James Cagney) apparently inspired by Roosevelt himself![72]

From the mid-1930s onwards, the radical streak in Warners' films may have been muted (due in part to a management eager for middle-class respectability),[73] but the company's films still retained an incisive edge not apparent in the films of the other majors.

Warners (like most of the major film companies of the studio era) specialised in particular genres. Until the mid-1930s, the company concentrated on low-budget contemporary urban genres[74] such as the gangster cycle,[75] the social conscience film[76] and the fast-talking comedy/drama.[77] The one costly genre that Warners specialised in during this period was the musical.[78] Later, from the mid-1930s onwards, new genres

---

auteur

French word meaning 'author'. Auteurs in cinema can be taken to be those creative individuals (usually directors) whose work over a body of films expresses a discernible world-view. We can use the term auteur in the case of Warner Bros because its studio-era management style discouraged individual authorship and imposed a house aesthetic – both visual and ideological – instead.

NRA (National Recovery Administration) programme

1930s government programme designed to rescue the American economy from the Great Depression (commonly known as the 'New Deal').

• Plate 2.5 Still from *Footlight Parade* (1933): James Cagney's character at the helm in this NRA-inspired musical

began to dominate: the Merrie England cycle,[79] the biopic,[80] the melodrama[81] and the film noir.[82]

As one might expect, Warners' roster of players during the studio era reflected to a large extent the studio's reputation for straightforwardness and toughness.[83] It is worth noting that Warners' stars tended to be very genre-specific: for example, Davis = melo-drama, Cagney = gangster film/musical, Bogart = gangster film/film noir.

The factory-like regimentation of Warners' production methods meant that its studio style inevitably overwhelmed the individual creative talents of its contract directors. Pressure of work and division of labour meant that there was little active collaboration on projects between director and editor, or director and writer.[84] Directors were assigned projects and as soon as their task was done they were moved on to others, leaving editors to complete the post-production work. It is thus particularly problematic to assign

Key films

gangster film

The Public Enemy (1931)
The Roaring 'Twenties (1939)

social conscience film

I am a fugitive from a Chain Gang (1932)
Wild Boys of the Road (1933)

fast-talking comedy/drama

Five-Star Final (1931)
Lady Killer (1933)

musical

42nd Street (1933)
Gold Diggers of 1933 (1933)

biopic

The Story of Louis Pasteur (1936)
The Life of Emile Zola (1937)

Merrie England cycle

The Adventures of Robin Hood (1938)
The Sea Hawk (1940)

melodrama

Jezebel (1938)
The Letter (1940)

film noir

The Maltese Falcon (1941)
The Big Sleep (1946)

● Plate 2.6 Production still from *Jezebel* (1938)
Bette Davis and Henry Fonda are directed by William Wyler (seated on the camera crane)

to Warners' contract directors, such as Michael Curtiz, William Keighley, Mervyn Le Roy and Raoul Walsh,[85] individual authorship of their films.

The cinematographic style of the company was very much in keeping with its tight budget policy. Studio cameramen such as Tony Gaudio,[86] Sol Polito[87] and Ernest Haller[88] were exponents of a visual style based on low-key lighting, incorporating many night scenes. This aesthetic strategy suited Warners' genres and also helped to disguise cheap sets.

Art direction

Warners' art direction reflected a low-cost policy: location work was avoided, films were designed around a studio-bound look and sets were regularly reused. Anton Grot,[89] a major art director at Warners during the studio era, typifies the studio's style. Grot not only designed sets, but also suggested camera angles and lighting for them.[90] His sets conveyed a mood. They were not literal reproductions of life, but instead were impressionistic, using shadow, silhouette and angular perspective. He is quoted[91] as saying, 'I for one, do not like extremely realistic sets. I am for simplicity and beauty and you can achieve that only by creating an impression.' The end result was art design that was both economic and atmospheric and in total sympathy with the studio's cinematography.

• Plate 2.7 Still from *Mildred Pierce* (1945)
This shot typifies the studio-bound cinematographic style and art direction of Warners during the studio era. The scene, photographed by Ernest Haller, is shot with low-key lighting; the art direction by Anton Grot conveys an impression of a quayside through its use of space, shadow, silhouette and perspective

Costume design at Warners was very much in keeping with the contemporary stories of the films. The studio's principal designers, Orry-Kelly for instance, designed modern clothes for ordinary people, in keeping with Warners' up-to-date urban image.

Warners' films of the studio era, particularly in the early to mid-1930s, had a particular 'fast' editing style. Narratives were developed in a rapid succession of scenes, with extensive classic Hollywood montage sequences. The overall effect was one of dynamism and compression of time.

Finally, the background music of Warners' films was highly individual, and typified by the work of Max Steiner[92] and Erich Wolfgang Korngold.[93] From the mid-1930s to the end of the studio era both composers created scores very much in the middle European tradition of romantic composition, using Wagner-like leitmotifs[94] throughout.

Warners' style of the 1930s and 1940s can thus be identified as a composite one, the product of its creative personnel working under the control and direction of corporate management. The various signifying elements that made up this style were reinforced film after film, year after year, producing what one now identifies as the studio era Warner Brothers' film.

THE CONTEMPORARY FILM INDUSTRY (1949 ONWARDS)

The late twentieth-century film industry is a very different affair from the system in operation during the studio era. This section looks at the contemporary institutional framework of film, first by examining the specifics within the film industry itself, and then by looking at the **wider media context** within which film exists today.

The 'Paramount' case

In the late 1940s an anti-trust suit was brought against the Big Five and the Little Three by the Justice Department of the United States (in the pipelines since the late 1930s).

Paramount and RKO were the first of the majors to agree with the US government to the terms of their **consent decrees**, putting to rest the government's charge against them of monopolistic practice in exhibition. The terms agreed were the divorcement of their cinemas.

consent decree

A court order made with the consent of both parties – the defendant and the plaintiff – which puts to rest the law suit brought against the former by the latter.

1949 to the 1990s – a brief review

The majors were finally forced to divest themselves of their theatres at the end of the 1940s as a result of the 'Paramount' anti-trust suit filed against them by the US government.[95] This divorcement of exhibition from production–distribution marked the end of the studio era.

The next few years saw a retrenchment of the majors. They no longer had a guaranteed market for their films and had to compete with independent producers for exhibition slots. The result was that they found their old studio infrastructure too expensive in the face of new market competition from the independents.

Meanwhile, for independents things had never been better, with the majors only too willing to rent them studio space and distribute their (better) films, and exhibitors eager to show them. The 1950s was to see an enormous explosion in independent production in the US.[96] By 1957, 58 per cent of the films distributed by the erstwhile Big Five and Little Three were independent productions that they financed and/or distributed.[97]

UA and distribution

In the 1950s, United Artists led the industry in the distribution of independent films. With no studios to restructure and no long-term contract players, UA was able to respond very quickly to the post-1949 reality. In the year 1957, for instance, only Columbia Pictures distributed more films than UA.[98]

Another shock to the film industry around the early 1950s was the exponential growth of television, a product of TV's own popularity and a postwar focus on the home and consumer durables: between 1947 and 1950, the number of TV sets in the US rose

• Plate 2.8 1953: the new pleasures afforded cinema-goers with the arrival of Cinemascope! (The still is from the first Cinemascope production of *The Robe*, directed by Henry Koster for Twentieth-Century Fox, 1953)

from 14,000 to 4 million[99] (see pp. 36–7). The film industry's response was twofold: differentiation from and collaboration with TV.[100]

In the 1950s, various film presentation strategies were introduced to emphasise the difference between the film-going experience and TV viewing in a bid to stave off the harmful competition from film's rival. Widescreen, colour, 3D and stereophonic sound were all introduced in the period 1952 to 1954. However, at the end of the day it proved expedient for the industry to collaborate with 'the enemy'. Film companies began to sell (and later lease) their films to TV,[101] to make films for TV,[102] and to merge with TV companies.[103] By the late 1960s, the futures of the two media industries were inextricably linked. The situation by the mid-1980s was more complicated. The two industries had become integrated into multi-media conglomerates where they represented just two of the many associated interests of their parent corporations.

Cinema exhibition today

Throughout the studio era and before, the most powerful sector of the film industry was exhibition. In today's film economy, however, distribution is the dominant sector (see p. 25).

Theatre ownership in the US is still dominated by a small number of companies. For example, in 1987, just twelve cinema circuits controlled 45 per cent of cinema exhibition in the US (and 29 per cent of the market was accounted for by the four leading circuits alone).[104]

Further, history does repeat itself. In spite of the Paramount case of 1948, the majors are once again among those companies with substantial interests in cinema chains.[105] By the end of 1987 they had acquired interests in 14 per cent of US and Canadian theatre screens.[106] By 1989, four film companies (Universal, Columbia, Paramount and Warners) were subsidiaries of parent companies owning 3,185 screens in the US and Canada.[107]

Theatrical presentation is no longer dominated by large, select first-run movie theatres as in the studio era. Individual theatres are now usually small mini-theatres (average seating capacity 200–300 seats), and mainstream commercial films distributed by the majors generally open simultaneously at a large number of these 'screens'.[108] Several screens are commonly housed under one roof – in multiplex theatres – where economies of scale (several screens sharing overheads) allow for low per-unit costs.

The multiplex theatre

This approach to exhibition was launched in the 1960s by American Multi-Cinema (AMC). The success of its multi-cinema formula was so great that by the 1980s AMC was one of the five largest cinema chains in the US. Based on the statements of AMC's senior management in 1983, its targeted audiences appeared to be the same as those of all exhibitors right back to the days of the nickelodeon theatres: 'we prefer to locate theatres in middle-class areas inhabited by college-educated families. . . . These groups are the backbone of the existing motion picture audience and of our future audience.'[109]

Another company notable for its development of the multi-screen concept is the Canadian company, Cineplex.[110] It opened its eighteen-screen Cineplex in Toronto's Eaton Centre in 1979, followed by a complex in the Beverly Centre, Los Angeles in 1982. After its purchase of the Odeon chain in Canada in the mid-1980s, it began its US acquisitions in earnest, so that by 1988 it was the largest theatre chain in North America.[111] Cineplex–Odeon's UK acquisitions began in May 1988 with the purchase of the ten-screen Maybox Theatre in Slough. Within a year its Gallery Cinema chain in the UK consisted of eleven multiplexes.[112]

From the mid-1980s, Cineplex–Odeon led the exhibition industry in its construction of several 'mini-picture palaces'[113] and the introduction of cafés and kiosks selling film-related materials.[114]

The company did find itself in a fragile financial position in 1989, a victim of debt-financing coupled with a growing recession,[115] but by then its style and innovation had set the tone for the mainstream exhibition practice of the 1990s.

Runs

It is worth noting that there are a variety of different types of cinema run in operation today. A run can be **exclusive**, **multiple**, or **saturation**. Combinations of runs are selected (largely at the discretion of distributors) on the basis of a film's likely perform-ance. For instance, the exhibition of a word-of-mouth 'sleeper' – a small budget film that does unexpectedly well at the box office – will usually begin with an exclusive run, until it has built up enough of a reputation to warrant a multiple run.[116]

exclusive run

Where a film is only screened in one movie theatre.

multiple run

Where a film is shown simultaneously at a number of cinemas.

saturation run

Where a film is shown simultaneously at an enormous number of cinemas (usually a minimum of 1,000 screens in the US/Canadian market), accompanied by heavy media promotion.

Distribution today

The role of the majors today embraces film production, distribution and (since the mid-1980s) exhibition. In the area of exhibition, the majors' participation is very significant but not completely dominant. In the fields of production finance and distribution, however, the majors rule supreme. Their names are all very familiar from the studio era: Paramount, Warner Brothers, Columbia, Universal, Disney and Twentieth-Century Fox.

Since the late 1940s consent decrees, the powerbase in the industry has shifted from exhibition to production finance and distribution, that is, from the powerbase of the pre-1949 majors to the powerbase of the post-1949 majors![117] This shift reflects the fact that film revenue is no longer purely a function of cinema receipts. With the increasing importance of other distribution 'windows'[118] and merchandising spin-offs, access to a major's worldwide distribution/marketing network has become the determining factor in a film's financial success. Through their domination of marketing and promotion, the majors ensure that it is their films that the public wants to see and that cinema-owners want to secure for their cinemas.[119]

Today, a major financier–distributor stands between the producer (if not directly producing the film itself) and the exhibitor. It will largely dictate the business terms which shape a film's finance and exploitation.

As noted by the ex-chairman of Cineplex–Odeon, Garth Drabinsky, in 1976:

> If, but only if, a distributor . . . decides that the picture merits release and the kind of expenditures necessary to get it off the ground, the distributor will enter into a distribution agreement with the producer to govern their relationship. . . .[120]

For the most part, the distributor dictates the terms of its deal with the exhibitor as well: the nature of the run, the length of the engagement, the advertising to be employed and the financial split of box-office receipts between the various parties.[121] It has also been reported that it is common practice for distributors to exploit their upper hand with exhibitors and insist on blind-bidding and block-booking.[122]

Distribution windows

Up to the mid-1970s, apart from the theatrical release, the only distribution windows were network and syndicated TV. The new age of film distribution began in 1975 with the introduction of Time Inc.'s Home Box Office cable pay TV (HBO) and Sony's domestic Betamax video cassette recorder (VCR). The following year, Matsushita introduced the VHS format for domestic VCRs. This soon became the industry standard.[123]

Today, a number of distribution windows play key roles in determining film profits. The most important is still the **theatrical window**. Failure to secure a theatrical release will severely restrict a film's profitability. Apart from the lost revenue, a film that has not secured a theatrical release cannot secure anything but poor deals for the other windows.[124] A typical distribution sequence for a major's film in the US will be an initial theatrical release of around six months, followed by a video window (which remains open for an indefinite period), followed by a pay/subscription TV window (for approximately one year), a network TV window and, finally, a syndicated TV window.[125] Because of the enormous importance of rental and retail home video software to film profits, the majors in recent years have increasingly marketed their own video labels, rather than sell the video rights of their films to video companies.

Marketing

One of the key roles of a financier–distributor is to successfully orchestrate the marketing of a film. The three main types of advertising[126] used in film marketing are: free publicity,[127] paid advertising[128] and tie-ins/[129]merchandising.[130]

Universal's UK marketing of Jurassic Park (1993)

Free publicity in the UK media included reports on such diverse subjects as Spielberg profiles, reports on the making of the film (particularly with regard to its special effects), the film's premières, genetic engineering, dinomania and the film's certification.

Paid advertising in the UK included promotion on TV, radio, billboards and in newspapers and magazines. The TV blitz the week before and the week of its opening is typical of saturation release patterns for 'big' movies.

Tie-ins in the UK included multimillion-dollar tie-ins with Macdonalds and selected hotels.

Merchandising in the UK included JP holographic watches, JP vinyl model dinosaur kits, JP fantasy balls, JP pinball machines, JP socks, JP briefs, JP Christmas cards and JP building bricks.[131]

The UK scenario

Distribution patterns in the UK mirror those in the US. However, in the case of TV-financed UK feature-film production (currently the dominant model for UK commercial production)[132] there can be the added impetus to curtail the theatrical and video windows and bring forward the broadcast TV window. This is because TV financiers may wish to show their product on TV as soon as possible. Factors such as critical and public response will, however, affect distribution patterns even for such films.[133]

Production today

Before examining those key players that dominate mainstream film production today – the majors, independent producers, agents and stars – it is useful to review the current industrial organisation of film production.

The industrial system in operation today is called the 'package–unit' system.[134] Under this system, the self-contained studio and long-term contract studio employee of the studio era have been replaced by rentable studio space and short-term contract employment. Today, individual producers are responsible for bringing together all the components of a film's production – finance, personnel, the 'property', equipment,[135] studio space – on a short-term, film-by-film basis.

Why package units?

The shift to the package-unit system from the mid-1950s onwards was a direct response to the combined effects of the 1948 consent decrees: the rise of independent production, cost-cutting and rationalisation at the majors' studios, and the majors leasing studio space to independent producers.[136]

Majors vs independents

Despite the growth of independent production in the 1950s after the consent decrees, the majors had reclaimed their domination in production by the early 1970s. The majors' hegemonic role in current film distribution (see p.25) and production is evidenced by the following statistic: between the years 1970 and 1987, films directly produced by the majors collected on average 84 per cent of the total US/Canadian box-office returns.[137]

In recent years, however, there has been some evidence to suggest that independent production is once again making inroads, at the expense of the majors' directly produced features. In 1991, films produced independently accounted for one-third of the summer box-office grosses in the US and Canada.[138] Despite this recent success for independents, their continued dependence on the majors for distribution makes their future financial performance somewhat uncertain.

Agents

The ending of long-term studio contracts for creative personnel[139] in the early 1950s meant that important stars, directors, writers and other talent could now negotiate very lucrative freelance deals with film companies.[140] Their increased negotiating power also strengthened the hand of their agents who negotiated the deals with the film companies. The most powerful agency at the time was MCA, controlled by Jules Stein and Lew Wasserman. So successful was the agency during the 1950s that it purchased Universal in 1959.[141]

Today there are three big talent agencies in Hollywood – Creative Artists Agency (CAA), William Morris and International Creative Management (ICM). Apart from these three, there are many smaller 'boutique' agencies[142] who handle a select number of important clients.

Agencies do occasionally get more directly involved in the production of film projects, as evidenced by the agency 'package', where big agents offer groups of creative personnel (with possibly a literary property as well) as a joint package to a production company for a single film or TV production.

Agency 'packages'

To date, Creative Artists Agency (CAA) leads in this area. Naturally, there are many critics of packaging who argue that it artificially inflates the cost of movie-making[143] and often forces film producers into artistic associations which are less than ideal for the productions.[144] Examples of CAA film packages include *Legal Eagles* (1986), *Rain Man* (1988) and *Ghostbusters 2* (1989).[145]

Stars

A star's association with a film project affects the ease with which it can be financed and marketed. A star's presence in a film is also held to be an important factor in a film's box-office performance. These three factors explain stars' huge salaries today.[146] However, some statistics suggest that stars are less a factor in a film's box-office success than was once the case.[147] Certainly, stars cannot ensure box-office success for films in which they appear (if they ever could), but their position within the current Hollywood economic structure is unassailable.

Arnold Schwarzenegger, star

Such is the popularity of this star that for *Total Recall* (1990) he was able to command a $10 million fee, plus 15 per cent of the gross takings of the picture. However, even Arnie cannot guarantee massive profits at the box office all the time, and his 1993 summer release, *The Last Action Hero*, was a major commercial failure in cinemas.

The UK production scenario

British feature films today are generally made on low to medium budgets (between £0.5 and £3 million) and are usually co-productions. The commissioning groups that have dominated UK film production in recent years have been the UK terrestrial TV companies. Typically they co-produce in association with any number of the following: British Screen,[148] the British Film Institute,[149] the Arts Council,[150] independent production companies (both UK and foreign), US film companies and American terrestrial, cable and satellite TV companies.

TV money for UK film production

At the very early stages in the financing of a UK production, TV money is usually sought. Channel 4 is the British channel most actively engaged in film production. Since its launch in 1982, it has participated in well over 100 films, for example, *A Room with a View*, *Mona Lisa* and *My Beautiful Laundrette*, all from 1986 alone. The BBC, under its policy of purchasing 25 per cent of its programmes from independent producers, also finances film production. Both Channel 4 and the BBC favour co-productions.[151]

A typical sequence of events for UK creative teams[152] developing and producing a feature film is as follows.[153] Applications are first made by the team for development money to produce a preliminary script and project budget: funding sources include the commissioning groups themselves and the European script fund.[154]

Having produced their preliminary script and budget, the creative team will now seek sources to fund the production proper. 'Pack-of-cards' financing typifies these

• Plate 2.9 Still from *My Beautiful Launderette* (1986): a film funded by Channel 4 in the UK

co-productions: each source of funding is dependent on the participation of the others. As each source of finance comes on board, the script is changed to fit in with the requirements of the specific investor. Once the budget is fixed, pre-production in earnest begins with the preparation of the final script.

It is worth noting that not all UK film is produced with the aid of TV finance. A recent trend among UK film producers seeking to escape from TV finance has been to arrange European co-finance, through initiatives like the Pan-European fund, Eurimages,[155] which makes loans to independent co-producers from its twenty-three member states.

□ CASE STUDY 2: A MAJOR US PRODUCTION, *JAWS* (1975)[156]

Script development and pre-production

The property, *Jaws*, started life as a novel by Peter Benchley. In July 1973, months before the book was published, Doubleday (the American publishers) opened the bidding for the film rights to the book. Richard Zanuck and David Brown, independent producers working out of Universal Pictures, acquired the screen rights for approximately US $200,000.[157] Under the terms of the deal, Peter Benchley was to produce a screenplay for the film.

The director for the project was selected by the producers after the completion of the first draft of the screenplay. Steven Spielberg joined the package-unit production just as the producers and Benchley started work on the second draft.[158] As is typical in mainstream production, several drafts of the script were produced: 'Benchley ultimately produced three drafts of his screenplay but all were considered unsuitable for filming. . . . The final script was written by Spielberg and Carl Gottlieb'[159]

During pre-production, the budget was set at $4 million, with a two-month shooting schedule.[160] Universal Pictures was the financier-cum-distributor of the film. Meanwhile, during this period before filming began, the success of the hardback sales of *Jaws* (the book) was greatly increasing the value of the film 'property' all the time.[161]

Production and post-production

The production stage commenced in April 1974. There were many publicised difficulties on location.[162] The budget had planned for a two-month location shoot on Martha's Vineyard (off Cape Cod, on the north-east coast of the US): this was extended to five and a half months. Costs escalated accordingly, from an original budget of $4 million to $8 million.[163] Nevertheless Universal continued to support the project despite the financial pressures alluded to by Richard Zanuck:

> Something has driven the budget up a bit. There are pressures that bear on you. . . . You're out there someplace using somebody else's [Universal's] money. We sign our names to the budget and agree to bring it in at a certain price. When that price starts escalating . . . pressures are applied. . . .[164]

During location shooting on Martha's Vineyard, Universal did not miss the opportunity to promote the film, and arranged free news junkets for the world's media:

> Murray Weissman, chief of the motion picture press department at Universal, estimated [that] media representatives conducted more than 200 interviews with actors, the director, the producers and others while the film was on location, 'three times the normal for even a big movie'. . . .[165]

In October 1974, filming shifted to Los Angeles for the last remaining scenes, including the final confrontation with the shark. The final underwater footage was shot 'In the waters of the Pacific off Catalina [island], and in one or two studio tanks, where lighting could be carefully controlled'[166]

Editing had commenced long before the completion of principal photography. The film's editor, Verna Shields, had assembled a rough-cut as the sequences were being

• Plate 2.10 Steven Spielberg on location during the filming of Universal's *Jaws* (1975)

shot. At the end of the production stage, only the rough-cut of the last third of the narrative was yet to be done.[167] Spielberg worked closely with Shields to deliver the 'first answer print'.[168] In March 1975 the film was handed over by the producers to Universal Pictures for audience test-previews and distribution.[169]

Universal retained the authority over the final cut of the film. But, in response to the excellent audience previews, only small changes were made by Spielberg and Shields.[170] June 20, 1975 was the date set by Universal for the opening of *Jaws*.[171]

Distribution and exhibition

For the film's distribution and exhibition, Universal devised and co-ordinated a highly innovative plan. Universal and Bantam (the paperback's publishers) had designed a logo which would appear on the paperback and on all film advertising.[172] Both publisher and distributor recognised the mutual benefits that a joint promotion strategy would bring. Such was the co-operation between the two parties that Zanuck and Brown 'embarked on a 6-city tour sponsored by Bantam books', to promote the publication of the paper-back and also the up-and-coming release of the film.[173]

At the beginning of April 1975, Universal invited blind bids from US and Canadian exhibitors.[174] Because of the enormous success of the paperback[175] and the film's excel-lent 'sneak' previews,[176] Universal was able to command very stiff financial terms from exhibitors.

June 1975 marked the dawn of a new era in the promotion and distribution of major releases. For the first time the exploitation of a movie incorporated saturation booking technique with simultaneous nationwide media promotion on a massive scale. The concept behind this strategy was to create maximum exposure for the film as quickly as possible, so as to recoup production costs as quickly as possible:

> *Jaws* has gotten a very massive release in about 500[177] theaters with a very intensive television campaign, probably the biggest, I would say, of all time. . . . It has become apparent to distributors today that they can get their money back faster and satisfy the demand to see a film by adopting a broader release pattern. . . .[178]

Coinciding with the nationwide opening of *Jaws*, was a media blitz which included approximately twenty-five thirty-second advertisements per night on prime-time network TV for the nights of 18, 19 and 20 June 1975.[179] Pre-opening promotion costs totalled $1.8 million, of which $700,000 went on this TV blitz campaign.[180]

The strategy paid off: '*Jaws* made 14 million dollars its 1st week in release. . . . Production costs were totally recouped within the first 2 weeks of release. . .[and] as of September 5, 1975, Universal declared *Jaws* the all-time box-office champion.'[181]

Universal also exploited very profitable tie-ins/merchandising to help promote the film:

> In eight weeks, over a half million *Jaws* t-shirts, 2 million plastic tumblers, and 2 hundred thousand soundtrack record albums were sold. *The Jaws Log*, a quickly produced paperback about the making of the film, sold over 1 million copies in the first month. . . .[182]

By December 1977, the worldwide gross for *Jaws* was over $250 million.[183]

Jaws was made before the era of domestic video and pay TV, so it did not benefit from these lucrative distribution windows at the time. However, US network TV (ABC) did pay $25 million in the late 1970s for three screenings of it and *Jaws 2*.[184]

☐ CASE STUDY 3: A LOW- TO MEDIUM-BUDGET UK PRODUCTION, *FELLOW TRAVELLER* (1989)

This film was co-produced by the British Broadcasting Corporation (BBC), Home Box Office Showcase (HBO) in the States and the British Film Institute (BFI).

Fellow Traveller has been chosen as a case study because it is an example of the TV co-production feature which has dominated UK film production in the recent past. The project was conceived and written by Michael Eaton whose interview with myself[185] forms the basis of the case study.

Script development

The project began life in 1987 and was originally conceived as a TV play by its creator, Michael Eaton. He brought his idea to Colin MacCabe, then head of the production division at the BFI, who suggested that he write an outline and submit it to the BFI's production board to see if it would qualify for the (then) new scheme of monies for script development. On the basis of his 'pitch' document, Eaton received a modest sum to develop the script.[186]

Eaton prepared the first draft of the script on the basis of it being a low budget (under £0.5 million) studio-shot telefilm. This script was rejected by the BBC and ITV companies, but was enthusiastically received[187] when seen by HBO[188] in New York City. As a result, Eaton met with HBO in early 1988. He was given a similar sum to that received from the BFI to develop a second draft of the script (modified to suit an enlarged budget,

• Plate 2.11 Still from *Fellow Traveller* (1989)

at HBO's request).[189] HBO indicated that if they liked what emerged from the second draft, they would co-finance the project.

Eaton arrived back in the UK to work on the TV movie[190] script, which was completed very quickly.[191] The BBC then became interested in the project and agreed to co-finance with HBO.[192] Like HBO, the BBC also made some suggestions regarding the script content.[193] With both co-producers now coming from TV, it was looking less likely that the property would ever have a theatrical run, something Eaton was very keen on.

Pre-production

The next stage was assembling the production team and moving to pre-production. This began in earnest in autumn 1988. The BBC producer, Michael Wearing,[194] was brought on board to produce, with Philip Saville as director.[195]

HBO was very enthusiastic about the production team selected for the film. During pre-production, its main area of activity was in the casting of the principal parts.[196]

Production

Production began in the new year, 1989. Most of the film was shot on location, except for the 'Robin Hood' scenes which were shot in a studio. The production schedule was five weeks in the UK and ten days in the US (Florida). Last minute funds contributed by the BFI enabled the film to be shot on 35 mm.[197] This gave the film's mise-en-scène its very high visual clarity and definition.

Distribution/exhibition

The film received a theatrical première in New York City before HBO put it out on their cable channel. Although Time–Warner owned the rights to the film outside the US and the UK, the film was hardly exhibited theatrically outside Britain.[198]

The film's distribution history in the UK is a little more extensive! Originally, the BBC had wanted to put the film on TV very quickly.[199] However, the film's reception at its première at the Edinburgh film festival[200] in August 1989, and at the London film festival a few months later, was so positive that it was decided to give the film a limited theatrical window in the UK. *Fellow Traveller* was shown at the Metro cinema in central London very successfully in early 1990.[201] It was also shown at the Cannon, Tottenham Court Road (London) and at regional BFI theatrical houses.

Eighteen months[202] after first appearing at the Edinburgh film festival, *Fellow Traveller* was premièred on BBC2.

In summary, the UK distribution windows for *Fellow Traveller* were as follows:

Film festival première
Edinburgh Film Festival, August 1989
and
First commercial theatrical exhibition
Metro cinema, January–March 1990

Video release date, November 1990

TV première Screen 2 (BBC), February 1991

Multi-media empires

Today, it is not adequate to consider the film industry in isolation, for it is only one part of a network of media, entertainment and communications industries controlled by **vertically and laterally integrated** multi-media conglomerates, 'each company controlling a vast empire of media and entertainment properties that amounts to a global distribution system.'[203] Examples of such organisations are Time–Warner,[204] News Corporation[205] and Sony Corporation of Japan.[206]

At present, Time–Warner is the biggest media company in the world,[207] with interests in film and TV, publishing, cable and satellite systems and the music industry.[208]

Rupert Murdoch's News Corporation is the world's second largest media conglomerate.[209] As an example of its **synergy strategy** – a strategy central to all multi-media conglomerates – we need only look at its UK Sky satellite service, which utilises press,[210] magazines[211] and film and TV production companies[212] owned by News Corporation to help boost its turnover.[213]

Sony Corporation of Japan purchased Columbia Pictures entertainment in 1989 for $5 billion. Underlying this purchase also was a synergy strategy.[214] Sony bought Columbia to boost sales of its home electronics hardware and to achieve synergy between its

synergy strategy

Combined or related action by a group of individuals or corporations towards a common goal, the combined effect of which exceeds the sum of the individual efforts.

software and hardware enterprises.[215] Since it acquired Columbia, Sony has used the studio to showcase its electronic high-definition technology.[216]

UK scenario

The global media conglomerates already have footholds in the UK as elsewhere, for example, News Corporation and Time–Warner.[217] UK-based broadcasting organisations have been slow to join the global multi-media bandwagon. This is largely a result of their retrenchment in the light of the Conservative government's under-financing,[218] deregulation and re-franchising[219] of British broadcasting in the 1980s, all of which has hardly left surviving companies fighting fit.

However, in 1991 the BBC launched its twenty-four-hour satellite news service – **World Service Television**. WSTV was expanded in March 1993 with the setting up of a joint-venture between the BBC and ABC TV (of the US) to form the world's biggest radio and TV news-gathering operation. WSTV is proving to be a popular alternative to CNN (Cable News Network), the US-based global satellite news service.[220]

UK producers do have a vested interest in a globally fit and healthy BBC. Some would argue that with it rests the ongoing sponsorship of UK media production.

Summary

In a few years we could be looking at an integrated digital combination of TV, cable descrambler, personal computer, camcorder and radio and phone set, which plugs into a telephone outlet.[221] Products like these will revolutionise the communications business – of which film is a part.

The communications revolution is being orchestrated by only a handful of global players. Unless properly regulated, these few companies stand to enjoy an oligopolistic power not dreamed of in the far-off days of the MPPC and the studio era.

FILM AUDIENCES

Fundamental to the study of cinema as institution is a study of cinema audience. This section reviews the changes in cinema audience patterns/profiles from the end of the Second World War to the present day, and considers their likely causes. The section ends with a review of how film companies attempt to build audiences for their films.

The 1940s: cinema-going as recreation

Before the 1950s, cinema-going was a very major recreational activity. According to one official report,[222] film-going was the number one recreational activity for most people in wartime US. The year 1946 marked the peak in cinema-going in the United States, unsurpassed to this day: in that year, the average weekly attendance[223] in US cinemas was 95 million.[224]

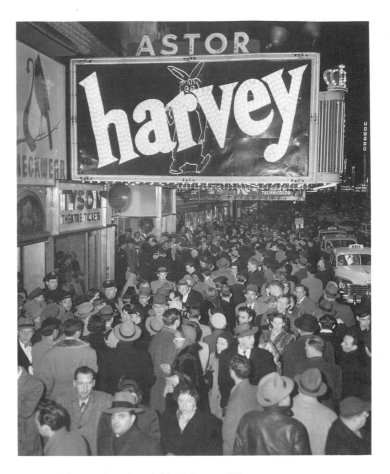

• Plate 2.12 Cinema-going at the end of the studio era, *c*.1950

The late 1940s to the present

Studies of the composition of audiences in the 1940s identify certain key trends. Although men and women registered the same average monthly picture attendance,[225] a greater percentage of men were very high frequency cinema-goers.[226]

Age was the major determinant in the frequency of attendance. All surveys of the 1940s point to the fact that young people attended much more frequently than older persons.[227]

Statistics from the 1940s also indicate that expenditure on motion pictures increased with annual income, and that those with higher levels of education (that is high school and/or college) were more frequent movie-goers than persons with only a grade school education.[228]

By the 1950s, cinema attendance was in rapid decline. Average weekly attendance figures had dropped in 1950 to 60 million (from their 95 million peak four years earlier), and by 1956 the number had slipped to 46.5 million.[229] What happened to bring about this sudden decline? Two reasons are most often cited: the first is the change in living patterns of Americans after Second World War, and the second is the establishment of TV.

'Being at home' explains the drop in cinema attendance after the peak of the mid-to late 1940s. There was a radical change in social trends in the US after the war: 'Home ownership, suburbanization[230] of metropolitan areas, traffic difficulties, large families, family-centred leisure time activities, and the do-it-yourself movement'. These new trends put the focus firmly on domestic lifestyle, to the detriment of 'outside-the-home'[231] film entertainment.

The early days of TV

The number of TV sets in America grew from 250,000 in 1947 to 8 million by 1950 and to 42.2 million by 1956.[232] TV's rise was directly proportional to the demise of movie theatres, particularly those situated in the residential neighbourhoods. It is thus logical to assume that the audiences who previously frequented local theatres were now at home watching TV instead.[233]

The 1960s and 1970s saw an enormous growth in the leisure industry in the US. Yet, despite this, film-going continued to decline.[234] A gallup poll taken in 1977 underlined the dominance of home-based leisure pursuits as a 'favourite way to spend an evening'.[235] The survey also confirmed the long-standing trends of movie-going being more popular with younger persons,[236] those with higher incomes and those who were college educated.

The 1970s and 1980s saw the expansion of home-based, 'TV-related media' entertainment in the form of VCRs, subscription cable and satellite services and video games, all of which weakened movie-going as a commercial leisure activity.[237]

UK scenario

The history of cinema attendance in the UK since the Second World War mirrors US statistics to a large degree. As in the US, 1946 marked the peak for UK cinema-going. That year, the average weekly cinema attendance was 31.5 million,[238] and as in the US, high-frequency cinema-going in the 1940s was predominantly the habit of the young.[239] However, unlike statistics in the US, working-class people went to the cinema significantly more often than others.[240]

Attendance figures fell dramatically in the 1950s: by 1956 weekly attendance was down to 21.1 million and by 1960 to 9.6 million.[241] As in the US, the precipitate drop corresponded with the dramatic rise in the number of TV sets in circulation.[242] This phenomenon was symptomatic of a much larger social change in the 1950s: the growth of outlying residential areas[243] and the subsequent establishment of a home-based consumer culture. The decline in attendance among the frequent cinema-going age group (16–24 years) might also be attributable to the sudden appearance of a distinct youth culture in the 1950s, which led to new forms of recreation for teenagers.[244]

By the early 1970s, cinema-going was just one of many options in the expanding leisure industry. The long decline continued through the 1970s, so that by the mid-1980s weekly attendance had plummeted to just over 1 million.[245] Other changes were apparent too: by the early 1980s the percentage of working-class people attending cinemas had declined significantly for the first time.[246]

• Plate 2.13 Queue outside the Odeon Leicester Square, London, in the late 1940s
The years immediately following the Second World War were to be the last ones where film held the position as number one mass medium of entertainment

Recent and future trends

Although the under-30s still account for the largest number of yearly admissions at movie theatres,[247] in recent years the percentage of the movie audience over the age of 30 has climbed significantly. For instance, between 1979 and 1987, the percentage of over-30s (in the US) in the total movie audience increased from 24 per cent to 38 per cent.[248] This trend is expected to continue. The figures will, of course, be affected by fluctuations in age distribution within the population.

There has long been evidence supporting the claim that increased education translates to increased frequency of cinema-going. If, and it is a big if, the number of college-educated individuals continues to rise, as it has in recent years, we can suppose that movie attendance may also go up.[249]

Currently, film-going is enjoying a renaissance with the public, with local multiplexes offering the 'supermarket' convenience of choice and car-parking facilities. But new films are also being delivered to their audience via pay TV and domestic VCRs. In the end, movie-going will continue as a social practice as long as the public and film industry show a willingness to support it.

Building an audience

Since the earliest days of the film industry, there have been attempts by makers, distributors and exhibitors to build audiences for their films. In today's film industry, building an audience is a sophisticated business: audience profiling, psychological testing and advertising (see p. 26) are all incorporated to help 'deliver' an audience for a film.

• Plate 2.14 Still from *No Down Payment* (1957)
The film industry in the 1950s would certainly have wished this fate on all domestic TV sets!

Audience profiling

Audience profile data – age, sex, income level, education, etc. – are influential in determining the kinds of films that are financed and the shape the projects take.[250]

Audience data is sought by film 'backers' seeking evidence of potential audiences for
films. For instance, in recent years the percentage of the total movie audience over the
age of 30 has increased significantly (see p. 38). The effect of this statistic has been to
spur Hollywood producers on to make more films that appeal to a wider range of audiences than just the teen market. The summer 1993 releases reflect this policy – films
like *The Firm*, *In the Line of Fire*, *Sleepless in Seattle*, *The Fugitive* and *Rising Sun*.

Psychological testing

Elaborate psychological test systems have been used in market research to help producers determine what audiences care to see or not to see in films. An early (and extreme) example of this was Sunn Classic Pictures who, in the late 1970s, identified a huge 'untapped audience for movies – working-class families that attended films only once or twice a year'.[251] By carrying out extensive market research on the narrative and formal elements that would appeal to this target audience,[252] and by then submitting the data to computer analysis, the company was successful in creating a substantial audience for its low-budget nature movies, for example, *The Life and Times of Grizzly Adams*.[253]

Advertising

This topic has already been covered on p. 26. However, it is important to restate that advertising is an essential tool in building audience interest for films; consequently, advertising budgets for mainstream films tend to be very high.[254]

TV promotion

Since *Jaws* (1975), concentrated national TV promotion (allied with saturation booking of theatres) has proven the most effective way of exploiting big-budget films: it is important that a lot of money is made in the first week of a film's theatrical release, before potentially bad reviews and word-of-mouth reduce the returns. *Jurassic Park* (1993) is a case in point: 'after taking $50 million in its first American weekend in June, [it] took half of that in weekend three'.[255]

Particularly in the case of the 'big' pictures, the majority of a film's advertising budget[256] will be spent the week preceding and the week following its theatrical release. During this period, TV saturation advertising is predominant, though the printed media does play a key role in film advertising after this two-week period.

Summary

Film as communication is not uni-directional, with the producer presenting the consumer with a fixed diet of consumables. Quite the contrary. Increasingly, information technology allows market analysts to access accurate information about movie-goers – information which is used to determine production decisions. Whether these decisions can help to sustain the recent renaissance of film-going remains to be seen.

CENSORSHIP AND CLASSIFICATION

Embarking upon a review of censorship, even when limiting the discussion to films, is a daunting task given the size of the topic. For this reason the content of this section is limited to a brief discussion of contemporary censorship in the US and the UK, followed by a look at specific historical examples of censorship in both countries.

Advocates vs critics of censorship

Those who argue in favour of censorship claim that it reflects and protects standards of morality generally held in society. Those who argue against it say that, rather than reflecting standards, it imposes them. There are strong arguments on both sides: advocates argue that depiction of graphic violence and sex on film 'shapes'[257] social behaviour, especially in young people, and that therefore its circulation needs to be controlled.[258] Critics, on the other hand, argue that film censorship is only one example of where ideals and morals are imposed on the public by powerful groups within society.

The contemporary US scenario

Since 1952, film has been protected under the first amendment to the constitution of the US, along with other communication media such as newspapers and magazines.[259] Under American law, individual states have the power to censor adult material, but only if it is deemed 'obscene'.[260] However, where children are concerned state censors have extended[261] legal powers[262] to **classify** (or to **rate**) films as well.

The introduction of the ratings system in 1968 is usually explained as an attempt by the film industry to offset the extended powers of state and municipal censors granted them that year by the Supreme Court which ruled that local authorities had the legal right to classify films for the protection of children.[263]

The ratings system is the film industry's 'voluntary' self-regulation system, and is administered by the Motion Picture Association of America (MPAA).[264] The ratings in current use are **G**,[265] **PG**,[266] **PG-13**[267], **R**,[268] and **NC-17**.[269]

Motion Picture Association of America (MPAA)

Administers the classification (ratings) system in the US.

Some observers argue that there is little censorship in the US, only classification. However, can one really argue that position with any confidence when film-makers are contractually obliged to deliver films to distributors that do not exceed an R rating, because exclusion of the pre-17 – frequent film-going – audience will mean that the films will do less well commercially? When this happens, as it does, censorship is in operation.[270]

Other serious issues are raised by the current ratings system. First, what are the MPAA board's criteria for determining what children should and should not see? Second, do major film companies, as the backers of the MPAA, receive preferential treatment, as has been suggested?[271] Issues such as these need to be raised and discussed if we are to fully understand the motivation behind the promotion of certain moral positions in films seen in the US and the suppression of others.

The contemporary UK scenario

In matters of censorship and classification, the UK does share many similar strategies to the US: the only legally recognised censor bodies in the UK are local authorities, the nation's law cites 'obscenity' as a major reason for film censorship, and there exists a universally adopted system of film classification, administered by an industry-supported board – the British Board of Film Classification (BBFC) – which argues that the primary role of classification is the protection of children.

British Board of Film Classification (BBFC)

Responsible for *both* classification and censorship of film shown in the UK.

The BBFC operates a system of classification for film releases as well as video releases.[272] For the cinema, the ratings are: **U**,[273] **PG**,[274] **12**,[275] **15**,[276] **18**,[277] and **R18**.[278]

For the video industry, an additional classification exists: **U**$_c$.[279] Video releases are classified separately from cinema releases. BBFC policy means that classification categories for videos are more rigidly imposed than for film releases, because videos are intended for home consumption, a 'sacrosanct . . . protected place'.[280]

Unlike the US, however, films intended for adult consumption are subject to broad legal censorship as well as classification, and this job also falls to the BBFC.[281] Such is the widespread legality of censorship in the UK that a charge of obscenity, or any of the following will likely result in cuts:

> Sexual violence, . . . emphasis on the process of violence and sadism, . . . glamor-isation of weapons that are both particularly dangerous and not already well-known in Britain, . . . ill-treatment of animals or child actors that breaks the Cinematograph Act 1937 or the Protection of Children Act 1978, . . . details of imitable, dangerous or criminal techniques, . . . blasphemous images or dialogue. . . .
> (From BBFC's (Ferman and Phelps) *A Student's Guide to Film Classification and Censorship in Britain*)

The BBFC claims to be 'independent' of government and industry influences. But can this be fully justified, given its involvement with them? The organisation is funded entirely by the film industry, and 'the appointment of the president and director have tradition-ally required the agreement of the local authorities, the industry trade associations, and the Home Secretary of the day'.[282] Given this, just whose interests does the BBFC represent?

There is no doubt that there is widespread support for the BBFC's role where the protection of children is concerned. However, its function in the censorship of films intended for adult consumption provokes a far less clear response. In the US, freedom of speech is guaranteed. No such position exists in the UK with the result that the BBFC can feel free to voice this statement on the population's behalf:

> In the USA, freedom of speech takes precedence over all other considerations. This [is] not the case in this country where we argue that one freedom (e.g. to own a gun) may limit another freedom (e.g. to stay alive without fear of being shot). . . . There is far more violence in the USA and American society is evidently prepared to accept more violence in its media. We do not feel there is any great pressure for us to follow suit. . . .[283]

☐ CASE STUDY 4: US – THE HAYS CODE

For a period of approximately twenty years, from the early 1930s to the early 1950s, American commercial film was subject to rigid regulation from within the industry itself. The Production Code, or Hays Code, laid down specific ideological and moral principles to which all films shown commercially in America had to subscribe.

Will Hays and the Production Code

The history of the Production Code dates back to 1922, and the appointment of Will Hays[284] as president of the new, industry-sponsored, Motion Picture Producers and Distributors of America. He was an ideal front man for the organisation, having been a senior Republican – the ex-Postmaster-General. Hays' brief was twofold: to improve the public image of Hollywood (following a series of very public Hollywood scandals around that time[285] – the film industry feared a backlash from state censors), and to protect Hollywood's interests in Washington and abroad, through his strong ties with the Republican Party.

Throughout the 1920s, Will Hays, as president of the MPPDA, saw to it that the influence of his organisation increased steadily within the industry. In the first few years of his appointment, Hays focused his energies on heading off state censorship boards,[286] under the banner of free speech. In 1924, the MPPDA introduced advice to film-makers on 'the suitability for screening of current novels and stage plays'.[287] In 1927, it produced a small document called 'The Don'ts and Be Carefuls'[288] for producers. With the coming of 'talking pictures', a more formal code was announced (in 1930) – the **Production Code**.

The code proved difficult to enforce until 1934, because producers, faced with falling box-office receipts brought about by the onset of the Depression, would not adhere to its principles.[289] Film producers saw sex[290] and violence[291] as box-office insurance. The Hays office was not yet powerful enough to force the issue.

The decisive year proved to be 1934. State censors, women's groups, education groups and religious groups were demanding action. The Roman Catholic Church formed its 'Legion of Decency', whose oath of obedience not to attend condemned films was recited by millions across the country during Sunday mass.[292] In this climate of threatened mass boycott of Hollywood films, the MPPDA could now rely on the complete support of the majors in implementing the Production Code.

Universal implementation of the code was finally assured with the arrival of the 'Production Code Administration' (PCA) that year, whereby the industry agreed that no film would be distributed or exhibited in the US that did not carry a PCA seal.[293]

Thus, from 1934 until just beyond the end of the studio era, the code defined the ideological limits of the classic Hollywood film.

The content of production code[294]

The production code stated that when depicting crime, producers were not allowed to include scenes on how to commit a crime, inspire the audience to imitate the crime, or make criminals seem heroic or justified. *The Public Enemy* (1931), for instance, with its glorification of the gangster, would in all likelihood not have been granted a PCA seal after 1934.

The code, in keeping with its project of pacifying the religious groups in the country, took a hard line on religion. No film could 'throw ridicule on any religious faith'. Ministers of religion could not be depicted as villains or comics and religious ceremonies had to be handled respectfully.

Under the terms of the code, representation of foreign countries and foreigners had to be respectful.[295] 'The history, institutions, prominent people and citizenry' of other nations had to be represented fairly.

Key films

exceeding the provisions of the code:
in its depiction of sex –
Red Dust (1932);
in its depiction of violence –
Scarface (1932)

Overt depiction of sex was banned of course. Other taboo subjects were sexual perversion, white-slavery, miscegenation and sex hygiene! In the depiction of gender relations, films had to be sympathetic to marriage as an institution. 'Impure love' could not be represented as attractive, it could not be the subject of comedy, it could not be presented so as to 'arouse passion or morbid curiosity' in audiences, and it could not be portrayed as permissible. 'Compensating moral values' were required where the scenario depicted 'impure love': that is, characters had to suffer in the scenario as a result of their behaviour.

Under the rules of the code, no adult nudity was permissible. Bedrooms had to be treated with the utmost discretion, because of their association with 'sexual life or with sexual sin'. Vulgarities, obscenities and profanities[296] of any kind were all banned. Producers could not depict dances which suggested 'sexual actions'.

With so many restrictions, it is a wonder that Hollywood was able to dispense any 'pleasure' from its dream factories during the studio era!

Key film

compensating moral values
Back Street (1941)

□ CASE STUDY 5: UK CENSORSHIP – INTERWAR AND SECOND WORLD WAR

The British Board of Film Censors[297] was founded by the film industry in 1912 to neutralise the effect of local authority censorship (see p. 41). From its inception, the BBFC operated a system of classification. It issued two categories: **U**,[298] and **A**.[299] These categories were advisory until 1921, when the London County Council decided to adopt them. (An **H** category was introduced in 1933 for horror films.[300])

Although not an official censor, the BBFC protected ruling values and interests. Indeed, its personnel had established links with government. For instance, Baron Tyrrell – the president of the BBFC from 1935 to 1947 – had been head of the Political Intelligence Department and Permanent Under-Secretary of State at the Foreign Office before taking up his post at the BBFC.[301]

During the interwar years, most local authorities accepted a BBFC certificate as validation of a film's moral rectitude and therefore as fit for exhibition. Up until the end of the Second World War, the BBFC maintained a formal code of practice, like the MPPDA in the US. The BBFC was nothing if not conscientious in its crusade and, predictable censor fodder aside (that is, sex[302] and crime[303]), made sure that any filmic material that was in any way 'sensitive' did not get passed.[304] To quote Julian Petley, in his essay 'Cinema and State':[305]

With its bans on the great Russian [Soviet film] classics,[306] on . . . newsreels critical of Nazi Germany and Fascist Italy, on 'references to controversial politics,'[307] 'relations to capital and labour,'[308] 'subjects calculated or possibly intended to foment social unrest or discontent,'. . . it is perhaps hardly surprising that in 1937 Baron Tyrrell could say to the exhibitors association: 'We may take pride in observing that there is not a single film showing in London today which deals with any of the burning questions of the day'. . . .

Examples of films banned by the BBFC in the UK
during the 1920s and 1930s

Film	Reason for ban
Battleship Potemkin (1925)	pro-revolutionary propaganda
Mother (1926)	pro-revolutionary propaganda
La Chienne (1931)	an unrepentant prostitute was the central character
The Public Enemy (1931)	subversive depiction of crime and gangsterism

With the start of the Second World War, the state took a direct role in film censor-ship. The Ministry of Information was set up to control the flow of public information, for the sake of national security. In other words, it became the official censor. (The BBFC's role during wartime was vastly reduced as all films were first submitted to the MoI.) It was also responsible for presenting 'the national case to the public at home and abroad' and for 'the preparation and issue of national propaganda'.[309] Under the leadership of Jack Beddington (1940–6), the **Films Division** of the MoI conveyed the 'dos and don'ts' to commercial film-makers, among others.

Around 1942, Jack Beddington initiated an **Ideas Committee**, included in which were eminent writers and directors of UK commercial film.[310] It operated as a forum for dis-cussion, a kind of proactive censorship group, where the wartime ideological (propaganda) strategy was formulated. A film that definitely was not a product of the ideas committee, and seems to have 'slipped through the net' during the Second World War, was *The Life and Death of Col. Blimp* (1943). Winston Churchill, no less, attempted to stop the pro-duction, because he felt it was 'propaganda detrimental to the morale of the army'.[311] Despite his attempts, the film was made and shown: the Ministry of Information deemed it could not impose a ban on the film because it did not pose a threat to national security.[312]

☐ CASE STUDY 6: UK CONTEMPORARY – *PLATOON* (1986)[313]

A review of the BBFC's handling of the classification of the 'Vietnam' film , *Platoon*, reflects a board which has abandoned a formal code of practice (eliminated after the Second World War), and which appears sensitive to social attitudes, with a willingness to reflect them. (That is, not merely to impose standards – as witnessed in the previous case studies.)

After screening the film,[314] many BBFC examiners and members of the board felt it should carry an 18 certificate, but expressed regret that the age group 15–17 'would be barred from a film that they were likely to find interesting'.[315] When the UK distributor was notified of the Board's likely decision – that the film would receive an 18 classification – it appealed on the basis that the film was not a 'comic book war' film,[316] but rather a serious discourse on the meaning of war (and no doubt on the basis that an 18 certificate would have seriously limited the audience for the film and its box office!).

After further screenings and discussions, the film was given a 15 certificate, with the stipulation that there be a **test screening** for 15–17 year olds, to ensure that they understood that the film was not glorifying violence and war. Their response supported the decision to grant the film a 15 certificate. A point worth raising, however, is whether the film of a small independent production company would have been shown quite the same consideration by the BBFC.

Summary

There is no question that in the past, dominant groups in society were able to impose a strict code of values on films consumed by US and UK film-goers. Today, however, media penetration and accessibility (for example, through satellite), and the democratisation of culture make a mockery of any attempt to fashion such a dogmatic policy. Nevertheless, the shaping of film texts to prescribed notions of what is 'suitable for children' or what is 'obscene' still goes on. It must be left to society to debate the correctness and appropriateness of such a policy.

CONCLUSION

This chapter has centred on the insitutional framework of mainstream film, and the historical relationship between **text** and **context**. Any change in production, exhibition or distribution practice, in communication technology (both hardware and software), in audience demographics or in censorship will have repercussions for the films we see and how we see them.

Films and their socio-economic contexts are part of a much broader history, that of twentieth-century culture in general. The purpose of this overview has been to go some way towards illuminating this point.

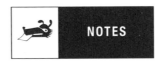 NOTES

Full bibliographical details of references cited in the notes section can be found on pp. 439–40.

1 T. Balio (ed.), 1976, pp. 23–4.

2 ibid., p. 28.

3 ibid., p. 14.

4 ibid., p. 7.

5 ibid., pp. 7–9.

6 ibid., p. 16.

7 D. Bordwell, J. Staiger and K. Thompson, 1985, pp. 116–17.

8 ibid., pp. 116–17.

9 J. Staiger, 1990, pp. 189–91.

10 The trust issued licences to produce films only to its members – including Edison, Biograph, Essanay, Kalem, Lubin, Méliès, Pathe, Selig and Vitagraph. This safeguarded the group's dominant position in the industry. See Balio (ed.), 1976, p. 103.

11 In 1908, the MPPC signed an exclusive contract with Eastman–Kodak for the supply of raw film stock in the US. See Staiger, 1990, p. 192.

12 The great increase in profits for film companies, with the coming of the nickelodeon era (post 1905), provided a major impetus for the holders of film patents to attempt an industry monopoly. Note that by 1908 there were 6,000 'nickels' in the US. See Balio (ed.), 1976, p. 62.

13 ibid., p. 63.

14 R. Allen and D. Gomery, 1985, pp. 202–5.

15 D. Gomery, 1992, p. 21.

16 Allen and Gomery, 1985, p. 204.

17 The 900-seat Princess Theatre (1909); see Gomery, 1992, p. 32.

18 Balio (ed.), 1976, pp. 73–4.

19 ibid., pp. 76–7.

20 ibid., p. 75.

21 ibid., pp. 74–5. Also Staiger, 1990, p. 201.

22 ibid., p. 192.

23 Staiger, 1990, p. 193.

24 Immediately after the formation of the General Film Company, independents began operating their own distribution company – the Motion Picture Distributing and Sales Company (May 1910). This was superseded by the Film Supply Company of America, the Universal Film Manufacturing Company and Mutual Films in 1912. Later, the introduction of feature-length films further weakened the MPPC, when many of its own members began dissociating themselves from the GFC and distributing their features through alternative distribution organisations. See Staiger, 1990, pp. 194–6, 201.

25 ibid., p. 198.

26 ibid., p. 198.

27 See Bordwell, Staiger and Thompson, 1985, pp. 113–20.

28 ibid., pp. 121–7.

29 For instance, the Solax Company in 1912 was organised into the following departments: executive, production, direction, art, wardrobe, small properties, electrical, mechanical, laboratory, sales, publicity, shipping, accounting. See ibid., p. 124.

30 ibid., pp. 128–41.

31 This was to dominate until the start of the Hollywood studio era around 1930.

32 By the mid-1920s the physical form of films had been totally standardised in the name of production efficiency – i.e. the classic Hollywood film format.

33 See Staiger, 1990, p. 204, for an early case of vertical integration – Triangle Film Incorporated (1915).

34 D. Gomery, 1986, pp. 26–8.

35 Balio (ed.), 1976, p. 114. NB, In 1928, First National was purchased by Warner Brothers Film Company.

36 Gomery, 1986, pp. 54–5.

37 ibid., p. 14.

38 ibid., pp. 12, 18.

39 The other 30 per cent of first-run theatres were owned by non-affiliated 'independent' exhibitors.

40 Gomery, 1992, pp. 34–6.

41 The company merged with Famous Players–Lasky in 1925, to form the new corporation Paramount Publix. See ibid., p. 43.

42 ibid., pp. 40–56.

43 In part a reaction to the coming of sound to exhibition in the late 1920s, for example, Paramount–Publix's elimination of stage shows from their theatres in Alabama, Texas and Louisiana in 1928. See ibid., p. 58.

44 ibid., p.73.

45 Or 'two-movies-for-the-price-of-one' see ibid., pp. 77–9.

46 ibid., p. 77.

47 ibid., pp. 80–1.

48 The immediate postwar era also marks the peak of attendance in UK cinemas.

49 Gomery, 1986, p.18.

50 Gomery, 1992, p.67.

51 An early form of block booking had existed during the days of the MPPC called standing orders. See Staiger, 1990, p. 193.

52 Gomery, 1992, pp. 67–9.

53 Producer-unit system: modelled after the manufacturing process introduced into automobile production during the 1920s. See Gomery, 1986, p. 15.

54 Bordwell, Staiger and Thompson, 1985, p. 321.

55 ibid., p. 321.

56 NB: this system was not universally adopted nor did companies refrain from changing production systems periodically. Taking 1941 as an example, it is interesting to note that the three most financially successful companies, in terms of box-office receipts, were all operating different production systems:
    • United Artists had a system of director-units and producer-units.
    • MGM operated a producer-unit system.
    • Twentieth-Century Fox used a central producer system.
    See ibid., pp. 320–9.

57 ibid., p. 321.

58 That is, executives, producers, directors, actors, screenwriters, cameramen (plus other production unit personnel), art directors, editors, musicians, special effects people, wardrobe people, casting people, publicity people, carpenters and others.

59 Through the National Recovery Act (NRA) and the Wagner Act. See Gomery, 1986, p. 10.

60 Bordwell, Staiger and Thompson, 1985, pp. 311–13.

61 For a detailed description of Warner's corporate history during the studio era see Gomery, 1986, pp. 101–23.

62 In Warner's case, this was arranged through the Wall Street investment merchant bank Goldman Sachs.

63 See WB's balance sheet for the studio era, Gomery, 1986, p. 102.

64 WB theatres were sold off (or leases terminated) to help meet its debts: see ibid., p. 110.

65 In 1932, the average production cost per feature was US $200,000 at WB, whereas at MGM it was $450,000. See R. Campbell, 1971, p. 2.

66 See N. Roddick, 1983.

67 D. Gomery, 1986, p..102.

68 Warners can be considered an 'auteur' in the same way as a director is. However, this model is not

without its problems: for instance, the ascription of authorship to the Warners/Howard Hawks film, *Sergeant York* (1941).

69 Staff members were largely on long-term or permanent contracts which offered no creative independence.

70 For example, Darryl Zanuck, WB's head of production 1931–3, specified that no scripted dialogue was to be changed on set without the authorisation of the production office. See R. Campbell, 1971, p. 2.

71 For example, *The Public Enemy* (1931). *I am a Fugitive from a Chain Gang* (1932).

72 See M. Roth, 1981.

73 Campbell, 1971, p. 3.

74 To the price sensitive Warners, genre film-making was a crucial part of its production strategy: genre films were very cost-effective and profitable, repetition allowing for assets to be reused again and again (for example, genre stars, sets, scripts).

75 Most typified by the films of Edward G. Robinson and James Cagney, for example, *Little Caesar* (1930), *The Public Enemy* (1931), *Taxi!* (1932), *Bullets or Ballots* (1935), *Marked Woman* (1937, starring Bette Davis), *Angels with Dirty Faces* (1938), and *The Roaring 'Twenties* (1939).

76 For example, *I am a Fugitive from a Chain Gang* (1932), and *Wild Boys of the Road* (1933).

77 *Five-Star Final* (1931), *Hard to Handle* (1933), *Lady Killer* (1933) and *Jimmy the Gent* (1934).

78 Usually with musical numbers designed by Busby Berkeley, for example, *42nd Street* (1933), *Gold Diggers of 1933* (1933) and *Dames* (1934).

79 That is, the films of Errol Flynn, for example, *Captain Blood* (1935), *The Prince and the Pauper* (1937), *The Adventures of Robin Hood* (1938) and *The Sea Hawk* (1940).

80 Most typified by the films starring Paul Muni, for example, *The Story of Louis Pasteur* (1936), *The Life of Emile Zola* (1937) and *Juarez* (1939).

81 Characterised by the films of Bette Davis, for example, *Jezebel* (1938), *Dark Victory* (1939), *The Letter* (1940) and *Now Voyager* (1942).

82 For example, *High Sierra* (1941), *The Maltese Falcon* (1941), *Mildred Pierce* (1945) and *The Big Sleep* (1946).

83 Stars like James Cagney, Edward G. Robinson, Bette Davis, Joan Blondell, Humphrey Bogart, Ruth Chatterton, Glenda Farrell, John Garfield, Paul Muni, George Raft, Joan Crawford. (A glaring exception among the roster of players is Errol Flynn.)

84 Campbell, 1971, p. 2.

85 For a discussion on the relationship of this director and Warners' studio style see E. Buscombe, 1974.

86 See *The Adventures of Robin Hood* (1938).

87 See *Now Voyager* (1942).

88 See *Jezebel* (1938) and *Mildred Pierce* (1945).

89 See the films *The Sea Hawk* (1940) and *Mildred Pierce* (1945).

90 See drawings for *Mildred Pierce* sets in D. Deschner, 1975, p. 20.

91 ibid., p. 22.

92 For example, *Now Voyager* (1942), *Casablanca* (1942) and *Mildred Pierce* (1945).

93 For example, *The Adventures of Robin Hood* (1938), *The Sea Hawk* (1940), *King's Row* (1941).

94 That is, a recurring melodic phrase used to suggest a character, thing or idea.

95 Orders making the decrees law were then issued by the court in 1948–9. See Balio (ed.), 1976, pp. 316–17, 347.

96 For a full account see ibid., pp. 348–54.

97 See ibid., table 2 p. 353.

98 And 30 per cent of Columbia's releases were also produced by them. See ibid., table 2, p. 353.

99 See ibid., p. 315.

100 See Balio (ed.), 1976, pp. 320–5, 'Responding to Television'.

101 The first major film company to sell its film library to TV was RKO, in December 1955. See ibid., p. 322.

102 From the late 1940s onwards, film companies began producing programmes for TV, for example, Warners' weekly series for ABC TV, *Warner Bros. Presents* (1955). By the early 1960s, producing TV shows was standard film industry practice and a major source of its revenue. Shortly afterwards (from the mid-1960s onwards), TV networks began commissioning made-for-TV films from major studios and independent producers. ibid., p. 322–4.

103 For example, in 1956, United Paramount Theatres (ex-exhibition arm of Paramount) merged with ABC TV. See ibid., p. 324.

104 See G. Jowett and J. Linton, 1989, p. 43.

105 The majors started buying theatres again in the mid-1980s. The US government's view on this was that vertical integration was not such a threat to competition as in the studio era because of the diversified nature of the industry infrastructure – i.e., independent production, pay TV, video and the general increase in theatres outside the direct ownership of the majors. ibid., p. 46.

106 ibid., p. 46

107 See *Variety*, 6 December 1989, p. 3.

108 The pattern of exclusive first-run releases having been broken with *The Godfather* in 1972. See Jowett and Linton, 1989, p. 59.

109 N. Fellman and S. Durwood, 1972, p. 221.

110 See Gomery, 1992, pp. 105–14 for a good account of 'The rise of Cineplex–Odeon'.

111 Jowett and Linton, 1989, p. 47.

112 *Screen International*, No. 750, 31 March 1990.

113 See Gomery, 1992, pp. 109–10, where comparisons are made between the centralised management style and innovation of Cineplex in the 1980s, and Balaban and Katz in the 1920s.

114 See *Variety*, 12 December 1989, p. 3; and Jowett and Linton, 1989, p. 47.

115 Much the same problems as Warners in 1931.

116 Jowett and Linton, 1989, pp. 48–9.

117 See D. Gordon, 1976, pp. 458–67.

118 For example, video, TV, satellite and cable subscription/pay TV.

119 As witnessed by the reaction of public and exhibitors to the beat of the distributors' tom-tom, on the saturation releases of *Batman* (summer 1989) and *Jurassic Park* (summer 1993).

120 G. Drabinsky, *Motion Pictures and the Arts in Canada: The Business and the Law*, Toronto: McGraw-Hill Ryerson, 1976. Quoted In Jowett and Linton, 1989, p. 56.

121 Jowett and Linton, 1989, p. 48.

122 ibid., pp. 43–4.

123 Balio (ed.), 1990, pp. 319–22.

124 Video, TV, etc. rely on the publicity of a theatrical release to promote a film. Without one, the film is a far less valuable commodity to them.

125 Balio (ed.), 1990, pp. 321–2.

126 See Jowett and Linton, 1989, p. 58.

127 Free coverage of subjects the media feel newsworthy.

128 Promotion on TV, radio, billboards and in newspapers and magazines. In the late 1980s, it was estimated that 50–60 per cent of the negative cost of a film was spent on advertising. See S. Donahue, *American Film Distribution: The Changing Marketplace*, Ann Arbor, Mich.: UMI Research Press, 1987. Cited in Jowett and Linton, 1989, p. 58.

129 A tie-in between the film and a consumer product and/or personality. See Jowett and Linton, 1989, pp. 63–7.

130 Where manufacturers pay a film company to use a film title or an image from its film on a product.

131 Reported in 'The Sunday Review', *Independent on Sunday*, 11 July 1993, p. 15.

132 Examples of such films include *Fellow Traveller* (1989) (see pp. 32–4), *Truly Madly Deeply* (1990), *Howards End* (1992) and *The Crying Game* (1992).

133 Nevertheless, when showing their features, UK TV companies abide by the agreed time limits for the showing of UK features on terrestrial TV:
   • two years minimum for films with budgets higher than UK £4 million
   • eighteen months for films with smaller budgets.
   See J. Dibie, 1993, p.138; and case study 3 of *Fellow Traveller* (pp. 32–4).

134 Bordwell, Staiger and Thompson, 1985, pp. 330–7.

135 The unit will lease or purchase equipment – that is, costumes, cameras, special effects equipment, lights, recording equipment, etc. – for a particular project from production studios and/or an array of support firms.

136 See Bordwell, Staiger and Thompson, 1985, p. 331.

137 Jowett and Linton, 1989, p. 38.

138 US $600 million of the summer's $1.8 billion gross. The independent productions that were major box-office winners were: *Terminator 2* (Carolco Productions), *Robin Hood* (Morgan Creek Productions), *City Slickers* (Castle Rock Productions), *Backdraft* (Imagine Productions), *Point Break* (Largo Productions). Reported in P. Biskind, 1991, p. 6.

139 A consequence of the rationalisation by the majors of their studios after the consent decrees.

140 In 1950 James Stewart's agent, MCA (Music Corporation of America), arranged for him to be paid 50 per cent of the net profits of the Universal film, *Winchester '73*, in lieu of his normal salary of $250,000. This arrangement would not have been possible under the terms of his MGM contract during the studio era. See N. Kent, 1991, p. 86.
   Percentage deals for stars were very rare during the studio era: one exception was Bette Davis – MCA arranged a deal for her in 1943 which brought her 35 per cent of the net profits from the movies she made for WB. See Kent, 1991, p. 100.

141 MCA's agency monopoly ended in 1962, when it voluntarily closed down to concentrate on production. This decision pre-empted an anti-trust suit that was to be brought against it by the US government Justice Department. ibid., pp. 216–19.

142 ibid., p. 221.

143 The agents ensure for themselves very high commissions for such packages.

144 ibid., p. 231.

145 See ibid., pp. 210–45.

146 See ibid., p. 242.

147 A *Variety* study of the annual top grossers between the late 1950s and early 1970s revealed that whereas 80 per cent of the films in the late 1950s featured bona fide stars, by the early 1970s this figure had dropped to only 50 per cent. Quoted in Jowett and Linton, 1989, p. 39.

   A more recent audience survey (1989) reported that the presence of stars is *not* an important factor in movie attendance decisions, but only important as a means of publicising a film. See B. Austin, 1989; cited in Jowett and Linton, 1989, p. 39.

148 A private company, partly financed by the DTI, which endeavours to support the creation of low- to medium-budget features.

149 A public body subsidised by the Department of National Heritage. It has a production department which finances feature films.

150 A public body funded by the Department of National Heritage. It puts money into films that enhance British culture.

151 See Dibie, 1993, p. 139.

152 In the form of writer/producer teams, writer/producer/director teams and unattached writers.

153 Information supplied by Laura Hastings-Smith, independent writer/director/producer.

154 The European script fund (part of the EC Commission initiative, Media 95) loans money to producers, directors and writers for the development of film and TV fiction.

155 A support fund to develop the European cinematographic and audiovisual industry. The fund was instituted by an agreement between the twelve member states of the Council of Europe in 1988. The UK joined in April 1993. To qualify for funding, the film must be a co-production involving at least three independent producers from the fund's (now expanded) twenty-three member states. Eurimage projects involving UK producers in 1993 included *In the Hollow of the Deep Wave* (director: J. Dehlavi) and *The Bishop's Story* (director: R. Quinn).

156 A detailed review of the (production) distribution and exhibition history of this film is to be found in D. Daly, 1980. The chapter on *Jaws* in Daly's book forms the basis of the following account.

157 For details see ibid., pp. 106–09.

158 See interview with Zanuck and Brown, 'Dialogue on film', 1975, p 40.

159 Daly, 1980, p. 107. NB, changes were made to the script during production.

160 ibid., p. 111.

161 The hardcover version of *Jaws* was on the *New York Times* bestseller list for forty-five consecutive weeks. See ibid., p. 109.

162 'Stolen equipment, labor troubles, and problems in getting "Bruce," the 24-foot $150,000 mechanical shark, to perform'. See ibid., pp. 110–11.

163 ibid., p. 111.

164 See 'Dialogue on film', 1975, p. 43.

165 Daly, 1980, p. 110, from comments reported in *Los Angeles Times*, 28 September 1975, Section VII, p. 1.

166 See C. Gottlieb, 1975, p. 204.

167 ibid., p. 206.

168 That is, the director's first cut:

> He [Spielberg] has to bring the film in within a certain length, and it's got to get a certain rating [classification]. . . . He [Spielberg] cuts the picture. We [the producers] work closely with him after he has presented his first cut [first answer print]. If there are discrepancies and differences of opinion, they are flushed out in previews. . . .
>
> ('Dialogue on Film', 1975, p. 42)

169 See Gottlieb, 1975, p. 213.

170 ibid., pp. 213–14.

171 Daly, 1980, p. 115.

172 That is, 'The open-mouthed shark rising toward a lone female swimmer': ibid., p. 113.

173 See ibid., p. 114.

174 ibid., p. 115.

175 By mid-March 1975 the paperback had sold 5 million copies. See ibid., p. 119.

176 To test audience response to the film – a standard industry practice. Films will often be re-edited to comply with audience comments on preview cards, which are filled out after 'sneak' previews.

177 Actually 464 theatres. By 15 August 1975, 954 theatres were showing *Jaws*. See Daly, 1980, pp. 124–5.

178 R. Zanuck's comments in 'Dialogue on Film', 1975, pp. 51–2.

179 Daly, 1980, p. 122.

180 ibid., pp. 122–3.

181 ibid., pp. 124–5.

182 ibid., pp. 137–8.

183 Reported in *Variety*, 10 December 1977, p. 5 and quoted in Daly, 1980, p.138.

184 Reported by D. Pringle, *TV Guide*, December 1979, pp. 39–40. Quoted in Jowett and Linton, 1980, p. 125.

185 2 April 1993.

186 According to sources within the industry, BFI development money for projects of this type in 1994 was in the region of £5,000 plus.

187 With its theme of a black-listed American writer working in exile in England during the early mid-1950s.

188 Via the BFI.

189 According to Eaton (interview 2 April 93),

> [the HBO development officer] told me, 'In this next draft is there any chance you can make it more like a movie?' . . . It was the opposite position I'd always been in in the past, which is like, 'Can you make this script cheaper?'. . . In the move from the 1st draft to the 2nd draft, I . . . put a lot more [of] America in there. . . .

There was to be a big shift between drafts one and two, a shift from a TV studio drama to a TV film conceived entirely in terms of cinema.

190 Eaton knew that to enter a deal with HBO would, by definition, limit the project to cable exposure in the US:

> One knew that they [HBO] would want to put it out on their cable movie channel as soon as it was finished. So, therefore, to go in with HBO was really to jettison any idea of a theatrical deal in the USA. . . .

191 With the assistance of John Amiel (UK TV director), acting in the capacity of script editor.

192 Eaton's project was an ideal US/UK co-production, with its narrative involving both countries' media histories: that is, the McCarthy witch-hunts of Hollywood personnel in the late 1940s-early 1950s and the startup of commerical TV production in the UK in the mid-1950s.

193 > He [Michael Wearing, producer] had a few things to say about the script, all of them sensible. . . . At this point [pre-production] the script becomes collective property. . . . The suggestions that people made for the most part made this a better script. . . .
>
> (Eaton, 2 April 1993)

194 Then Head of Drama at the BBC studios at Pebble Mill, whose previous credits had included *The Boys From the Blackstuff*.

195 The transformation of the final draft of Eaton's script into the camera (or shooting) script was the job of the director.

196 > They [HBO] have this incredible market research. It's done by another office than the development office. They know their market very very well. They know which faces have recognition value within that [TV cable] market and they suddenly become extremely active at the time of casting. . . .
>
> (Eaton, 2 April 1993)

197 With the quid pro quo that they would have theatrical distribution rights in the UK.

198 It has been seen in international film festivals.

199 'on "Screen Two" . . . they [the BBC] had just put all this money into this picture. They wanted to put it out straight away' (Eaton, 2 April 1993).

200 Including a very favourable piece by Philip French in the *Observer*.

201 Between 5 January 1990 and 14 March 1990, the film was seen at the Metro (a small art-house cinema) by 16,357 people and grossed £60,455. This was a very good run for the cinema.

202 See the section on 'Distribution today: the UK scenario', on p. 26.

203 'Plenty of fish in pond Time–Warner wants to swim in', *Wall Street Journal*, 7 March 1989, p. B1; cited in Balio (ed.), 1990, p. 315.

204 Owner of Warner Communications since 1990.

205 Owner of Twentieth-Century Fox.

206 Owner of Columbia Pictures since October 1989.

207 Sales of $14 billion in 1992. See P. Koenig, 1993, p. 2.

208 > [Time–Warner] owns Lorimar, the largest TV production co in the US. . . . It put out the *Lethal Weapon* and *Batman* films. It recently produced *JFK*, *Malcolm X* and *The Bodyguard*. Along with Madonna . . . it numbers amongst its music acts Simply Red, Genesis . . . Natalie Cole . . . and The Cure. As a book publisher it markets Sidney Sheldon and PD James. It owns the copyright to Superman. . . .
>
> (ibid., p. 2)

209 With sales of US $12 billion in 1992: ibid., p. 2.

210 For example, *Sun*, *News Of The World*.

211 For example, *TV Guide*.

212 Twentieth-Century Fox and Fox TV (in the US).

213 The printed media promote Sky TV and the US film/TV companies provide programming for it.

214 N. Perry, 1991.

215 Sony Corporation is convinced that its Betamax videotape format would have had greater success in the late 1970s if Sony had owned a studio and had thus secured for itself software for its hardware. (VHS succeeded as the standard format because it was promoted by European manufacturers – the first important domestic VCR market – and Hollywood studios adopted it as their standard format.) See ibid.

216 Sony is developing high-definition TV, and interactive multimedia videogames which combine

music, film, graphics, and special effects so that videoholics can become part of a movie by watching real footage, listening to the soundtrack (Sony's music company is the ex-CBS Records), and interacting with the characters. Of course, to program such a game one needs film and music. . . . Do you begin to get the picture?

(ibid.)

217 Although its January 1993 bid to operate Britain's Channel 5 (with Thames TV) was rejected, it is a partner in Classic FM, and has a small stake in UK Cable TV (reported in Koenig, 1993, p. 4). One can safely assume that Time–Warner will continue in its attempt to infiltrate British media companies – ultimately to the detriment of companies trying to produce and deliver UK programming to UK consumers.

218 Of the public sector BBC.

219 Of private company (ITV) broadcasting licences.

220 *Sunday Telegraph*, 4 July 1993. p. 2.

221 See M. Frankel and C. Wall, *et al.*, 1993, pp. 28–35. (The above scenario no doubt underlies the News Corporation/British Telecom partnership announced on 1 September 1993.)

222 Report by the US Department of Labor entitled, *Family Spending and Saving in Wartime*, Bulletin no. 822; quoted in L. Handel, 1950, p. 104.

223 That is, the average number of tickets sold.

224 Source: *Film Daily Year Book*; quoted in Handel, 1950, p. 96. As a comparison, attendance figures for 1940 (pre–Second World War) were 80 million/week, and around 85 million/week for 1945 (end of the Second World War). See B. Austin, 1989, p. 36.

225 Women: 3.75 times per month; men: 3.7 times per month. Source: L. Handel, *Studies of the Motion Picture Audience*, New York, December 1941. Cited in Handel, 1950, p. 100.

226 Defined as attending ten times a month or more: figures for men were 11.8 per cent, as opposed to only 7.5 per cent for women. Source: Handel, cited in *Studies*, ibid., p. 100.

227 For example, in a state-wide survey conducted in Iowa In 1942, 31 per cent of men and 24.9 per cent of women aged 15 to 20 attended cinemas over five times per month, as opposed to only 11.4 per cent and 7.6 per cent respectively of those aged 21 to 35 Years. Source: F. Whan and H. Summers, *The 1942 Iowa Radio Audience Survey*, Des Moines, 1942. Cited in Handel, 1950, p. 103.

228 NB: in actual numbers, persons with higher levels of education were a minority among cinema-goers in the 1940s. See ibid., pp. 104–8.

229 Source: *Film Daily Year Book*; quoted in I. Bernstein, 1957, p. 2.

230 In the 1950s, suburban families accounted for around one-fifth of the nation's population. Their

spending power was considerable, earning as they did 70 per cent above the national average for families (see Austin, 1989, p. 37).

The rise of outdoor drive-in theatre in the early 1950s can be linked with post-war suburbanisation and economic prosperity. By 1954, there were 3,800 drive-ins in America whose box-office grosses accounted for 16.2 per cent of the total US box-office receipts. (Source: Department of Commerce's Census of Business for 1954; cited in Bernstein, 1957, p. 5.) Quote from Bernstein, 1957, p. 74.

231 See ibid., p. 74.

232 Source: *Film Daily Year Book*; quoted in ibid., p. 73.

233 ibid., p. 73.

234 The average weekly cinema attendance in the US for 1960 was 40 million, for 1970 17.7 million, and for 1975 19.9 million. See Austin, 1989, p. 36.

235 Thirty per cent of those surveyed cited watching TV as their favourite way to spend an evening. Only 6 per cent of those surveyed cited going to the movies. Source: *The Gallup Opinion Index*, report 146, pp. 14–15, September 1977; quoted in Austin, 1989, p. 40.

236 Defined in this survey as persons under the age of 30.

237 Average weekly movie attendance for 1980 was 19.7 million, Austin, 1989, pp. 36, 40–1.

238 D. Docherty, D. Morrison and M. Tracey, 1987, pp. 14–15.

239 In a 1948 Gallup Poll, 79 per cent of people surveyed between the ages of 18 and 20, and 76 per cent of those between the ages of 21 and 29 had been to the cinema within the last three weeks: this declined to 57 per cent for those aged 30–49. Source: Gallup, cited in ibid., p. 17.

240 In a survey in 1949, 19 per cent of the working-class people surveyed (that is, those persons with low levels of income and education) went to the cinema (at least) twice a week, as opposed to 13 per cent of middle-class people interviewed, and 8 per cent of upper-class people surveyed. Source: Hulton Research. cited in ibid., p. 16.

241 ibid., pp. 14–5.

242 'There was an increase in TV licences from 343k in 1950 to 10 million in 1960' (ibid., p. 23).

243 Partly a product of 1950s prosperity and a move towards greater owner-occupation, and partly the result of the Town and Country Planning Act of 1947 which 'led to the clearing of slums, the growth of new towns . . . and, crucially, the resiting of large sections of the working class . . . around the edges of cities' (ibid., pp. 25–6).

244 ibid., pp. 26–7.

245 ibid., p. 29.

246 Dropping from half the total audience to one-third between 1977 and 1983 (ibid., pp. 30–1).

247 For example, for the year 1987, US 12–15 year olds accounted for 11 per cent of yearly admissions; 16–20 year olds, 21 per cent; 21–24 year olds 15 per cent; 25–29 year olds 15 per cent. Source: Motion Picture Association of America 1987; cited in Jowett and Linton, 1989, p. 90.

248 Source MPAA; cited in ibid., p. 90.

249 The US adult population with some college training increased from 15 per cent of the adult population in 1960 to 25 per cent in 1975, and by 1990 it is expected that over 1/3 of the adult population will have a year or more of college level work. . . .

(ibid., p. 134)

250 That is, the budget, script, cast, etc.

251 See Jowett and Linton, 1989, p. 106.

252 Potential movie-goers were questioned 'On unusual ideas, newspaper articles, current books, or anything that might get them out of the house and into the theatre' (P. Morrisroe, 'Making Movies the Computer Way', *Parade*, vol. 16, 3 February 1980; quoted in ibid., p. 106).

253   Every element of this heart-warming drama [*Grizzly Adams*], from the hair and eye colouring of the actors to the type of animals they frolic with, was pre-tested. . . . Your family's every 'ooh' and 'ahh' was anticipated in tests taken by other families demographically identical to yours.

                                                                            (Morrisroe, 1980)

254 In the 1980s, it was noted that marketing expenses for US mainstream films were approximately 25 per cent of a film's total revenue: Jowett and Linton, 1989, p. 58.

255 Quoted from *Independent on Sunday*, 11 July 1993.

256 Eighty per cent; see ibid., pp. 58–60.

257 NB: there is *no* decisive proof that films actually *cause* copy-cat acts of violence and sex.

258 See N. Andrew, 1993.

259 See Balio (ed.), 1976, p. 432.

260 ibid., p. 438.

261 Following two 1968 decisions by the Supreme Court – cases *Interstate v. Dallas* and *Ginsberg v. New York*.

262 See S. Byron, 'Letter to Editor,' *Film Comment*, vol. 22, issue 5, October 1986, p. 74.

263 'The choice was not between a rating system and no rating system. It was between an industry rating system and 50 state classification boards (more if you add municipalities such as Dallas)' (Byron, ibid., p. 76).

264 Headquartered in Los Angeles. The names and backgrounds of the board are kept secret. All that is known of the 6 board members who classify the films is that they are all parents and that one of them is nominated by the California Parent Teacher Association. See L. Sheinfeld, 1986, p. 11.

265 General audience.

266 Parental guidance suggested.

267 Parental guidance suggested; some material is not suitable for under-13 year olds.

268 Persons under the age of 17 must be accompanied by a parent or adult guardian.

269 No one under 17 admitted.

270 See C. Taylor, 1990–1, pp. 14–15.

271 See Sheinfeld, 1986, p. 14.

272 As a result of the Video Recordings Act 1984, the BBFC now exercises for the first time a 'statutory function on behalf of central government' whereby it is the **designated authority** appointed by the Home Secretary to classify videos. See J. Ferman and C. Phelps, 1993a.

273 Suitable for all.

274 Parental guidance advised.

275 Restricted to persons 12 years and over.

276 Restricted to persons 15 years and over.

277 Restricted to persons 18 years and over.

278 Restricted distribution only, through sex shops, specially licensed cinemas, etc.

279 Particularly suitable for children.

280 See J. Ferman and G. Phelps, 1993b.

281 Although statutory power to censor remains with the local authorities, the board's decisions are generally accepted.

282 Ferman and Phelps, 1993a

283 Quoted from BBFC n.d.: a. NB: although the statement suggests otherwise, there is *no* decisive proof that films cause violence.

284 See C. Champlin, 1980, p. 42.

285 That is, the Fatty Arbuckle scandal (rape and murder trial), the murder of William Desmond Taylor and death (through drug addiction) of Wallace Reid. See ibid., p. 42.

286 'Reformer-inspired censorship legislation' was on the rise at that time in more than half the states in the US. See Balio (ed.), 1976, p. 304.

287 ibid., p. 308.

288 See Champlin, 1980, p. 42.

289 Despite the introduction of mandatory script submission by producers to the Hays office in 1931.

290 For example, *Red Dust* (MGM 1932), *She Done Him Wrong* (Paramount 1933) and *Baby Face* (Warner Brothers 1933).

291 For example, *Public Enemy* (WB), *Scarface* (H. Hughes Productions).

292 Champlin, 1980, p. 44.

293 ibid., p. 44.

294 L. Leff and J. Simmons, 1990, pp. 283–92.

295 As early as 1922, the Mexican government negotiated with the MPPDA, over the representation of Mexicans in American films.

296 The dialogue, 'Frankly my dear, I don't give a damn' was allowed in *Gone With The Wind* (1939), after a special appeal by the producer to the Hays office.

297 As it was called until 1985.

298 Universal.

299 Adult, denoting that the film was more suitable for adults.

   NB: in 1921, the classification **A** was modified to stipulate that children under 16 had to be accompanied by a parent or guardian. See R. Falcon, 1994, part 2, p. 4.

300 See J. Robertson, 1985, p. 58.

301 C. Barr (ed.), 1986, p. 44.

302 For example, *La Chienne* (1931), in which a prostitute is a central character, was banned in 1932. See Robertson, 1985, p. 62.

303 For example, *The Public Enemy* (1931) was initially banned by the BBFC in 1931: ibid., p. 78.

304 Originally the code was based on 'temporary' rules introduced during the First World War.

305 Barr (ed.), 1986, p. 44.

306 For example, both *Battleship Potemkin* (1925) and *Mother* (1926) were banned by the BBFC for being pro-revolutionary Bolshevik propaganda (in 1926 and 1928 respectively). See J. Robertson, 1985, pp. 37–51.

307 *Spanish Earth* (1937), a left-wing, highly anti-Franco documentary dealing with the Spanish Civil War, was severely cut in 1937. See ibid., p. 106.

308 For example, a ban was imposed on the scenario, *Love on the Dole*, until the outbreak of the Second World War. In 1940, the project was given the go-ahead.

309 I. McLaine, *Ministry of Morale*, London: Allen and Unwin, 1979; quoted in A. Algate and J. Richards, 1986, p. 18.

310 Including (at various times): M. Balcon, M. Powell, S. Gilliat, L. Howard, C. Frend and A. Asquith.

311 From Prime Minister's Personal Minute M.357/2, 10 September 1942; reprinted in I. Christie (ed.), 1978, p. 107.

312 However, the film was cut at the request of the MoI before an export licence (for America) was granted for it. See ibid., p. 110.

313 Based on information contained in Falcon, 1994, part 3, pp. 25–9.

314 In January 1987; ibid., part 3, p. 26.

315 ibid., part 3, p. 26.

316 Like *Rambo*.

FURTHER READING

Algate, A. and Richards, J., *Britain Can Take It*, London: Basil Blackwell, 1986.

Austin, B., *Immediate Seating: A Look at Movie Audiences*, Belmont, Calif.: Wadsworth Publishing Company, 1989.

Balio, T. (ed.), *The American Film Industry*, Madison: University of Wisconsin Press, 1976.

—— (ed.), *Hollywood in the Age of Television*, Boston: Unwin Hyman, 1990.

Barr, C. (ed.), *All Our Yesterdays*, London: British Film Institute, 1986.

Bernstein, I., *Hollywood at the Crossroads: An Economic Study of the Motion Picture Industry*, Los Angeles: Hollywood Film Council, 1957.

Bordwell, D., Staiger J. and Thompson, K., *The Classical Hollywood Cinema*, London: Routledge & Kegan Paul, 1985.

Daly, D., *A Comparison of Exhibition and Distribution Patterns in 3 Recent Feature Motion Pictures*, New York: Arno Press, 1980.

Docherty, D., Morrison, D. and. Tracey, M., *The Last Picture Show?*, London: British Film Institute, 1987.

Falcon, R., *Classified! A Teacher's Guide to Film and Video Censorship and Classification*, London: British Film Institute, 1994.

Ferman, J. and Phelps, G., *A Student's Guide to Film Classification and Censorship in Britain*, London: BBFC, 1993.

Gomery, D., *The Hollywood Studio System*, London: Macmillan, 1986.

—— *Shared Pleasures*, London: British Film Institute, 1992.

Handel, L., *Hollywood Looks at its Audience*, Urbana: University of Illinois Press, 1950.

Jowett, G. and Linton, J., *Movies as Mass Communication*, Newbury Park, Calif.: Sage Publications, 1989.

Kent, N., *Naked Hollywood*, London; BBC Books, 1991.

Leff, L. and Simmons, J., *The Dame in the Kimono*, New York: Grove Weidenfeld, 1990.

Robertson, J., *The British Board of Film Censors: Film Censorship in Britain, 1896–1950*, Beckenham: Croom Helm, 1985.

Roddick N., *A New Deal in Entertainment*, London: British Film Institute, 1983.

Chapter 3

Film: the place where art and technology meet

Chris Webster

■ Film: the place where art and technology meet

INTRODUCTION

We are in the midst of a storm, a technological maelstrom. We have the ability to weather this storm, to harness and use its power for the good of humankind or we can allow it to engulf us.

Film is as much a science as it is an art form and, since its early days, cinema and technology have been inseparable. Cinema has been a forum for the public exposure of, not only new film technologies, but other associated areas such as computers. The rate at which some of these changes and developments have come about is so fast that this book, indeed any publication, is almost out of date by the time it reaches its readership. This beggars the question; how new is a new technology? In this chapter we will look at some of the more important developments in film technology, how they have shaped cinema and what effect this has had on the way in which we 'read' film, the financial and political implications and how our expectation of cinema has altered.

Most people will be familiar with computers of one form or another and by and large we take them for granted in our everyday lives. Using satellite communications people can engage in telephone conversations and even video conferencing with people on the other side of the world. Since the end of the Second World War a huge technological revolution has taken place in the way in which we communicate with each other. At that time radio was still quite primitive, televisions were a rarity, computers unheard of and as for satellites – the only place they were orbiting was in the fervid imagination of a few boffins. The rapidity of this change has never before been experienced, even during the days of the Industrial Revolution. The way in which forms of new technologies, such as electricity, washing machines, televisions and the computer are introduced to our society and become part of its fabric changes the way in which that society behaves. Computer technology will even affect our society and its cognitive and learning processes for ever.

The increasing speed at which new developments and breakthroughs occur is creating a self-perpetuating atmosphere of 'techno fever' and fostering an ethos of newer, faster, smaller. In the past, new technologies were developed in response to evident needs and as solutions to very real and tangible problems such as shortcomings in industrial production methods. However, we are now seeing the development of computer software in advance of any such need and in search of an application. It is far from certain that the age of the microchip will bring about the techno renaissance of the adman's dream of creating a Brave New World. It may, in reality, turn out to be nothing more than technological mayhem causing a major headache for companies trying to offload such goodies as upgrades, memory, faster chips, better graphics, more colours, digital sound, interactivity, CD technology and artificial intelligence.

SIMMS, MIPS, ROM, RAM, CD-i, CDR, VR, CPU, VDU, GIF, TIF and PICT are the mantras of those initiated into the new cyber religions. Purposely unintelligible, such jargon creates an impenetrable world for those believers and is used by them as a weapon against those not 'of the faith' to keep them out of temple. Why should this be? Could it be that all this technological wizardry capable of creating cyber worlds in full glorious three-dimensional technicolour complete with digital quadraphonic sound is in some measure a substitute for original thought and creativity? Are ideas out and a disposable facile techno gloss in? This would certainly appear to be the case in the film industry where content and script development are being noticeably ousted by bigger and bolder explosions, computer animation and alien technology. Somehow directors seem to be happier to depend on the latest gimmick from Technotrash plc than to work out *original* ideas for themselves. But surely the use of animation techniques, pyrotechnics and weird camera effects (with a liberal sprinkling of computer graphics over the lot) cannot be the solution to a bad script. In the hands of an incompetent these techniques become a crass representation of what Hollywood *thinks* the public wants. Our attitude towards and relationship with new technologies has historically been a complex one. On the one hand, we reap great benefits from them, while, on the other hand, we are terrified of the disrupting effect they have on our world. In the early days of aviation it was thought by some scientists that it would be harmful for women to fly, as the altitude and speed would cause their wombs to explode. This illustrates very well the unease that is generally felt about new inventions and theories.

As the popularity of computer games first began to grow in the late 1980s and early 1990s similar unease began to be expressed. Moral panic ensued from those who had little or no understanding of computer games and their possibilities. They cited cases of computer addiction and objected to a perceived subversion of more traditional learning methods. Thankfully this attitude is on the decline as the benefits that computers bring with them are becoming self-evident.

IN THE BEGINNING

Cinema, by its very nature, has always been closely linked with technology. We take for granted the level of technological wizardry that we see nightly on our TV sets. Almost every programme, no matter how modest, is preceded by the, now obligatory, flying logo and usually contains aspects of computer aided design of one sort or another. Cinema, and by this term I include the early **magic lantern** shows, has always been a marriage of entertainment and technology, of the aesthetic and the industrial: the place where science and art meet.

Shadow puppets

The earliest known form of visual entertainment/experience using the elements of artificial light and objects in an attempt to create a synthetic 'other' reality that could, in some way, be described as 'cinema' was happening several thousand years ago in the form of shadow plays. Shadow puppet characters were constructed from thin pieces of stiffened leather, heavily decorated with intricate patterns of perforations that allowed light through. These were attached to rods of cane which enabled the puppet operator to work the jointed arms and legs. These performances were usually accompanied by orchestral music and narration. Throughout the late Middle Ages the popularity of such plays had spread through the Middle East and to Europe. Later, the use of optical devices was to bring about the change in approach to the projection, and ultimately the recording, of images.

Early opticals

In the early seventeenth century a number of individuals were carrying out experiments with the separate components that go to make up basic elements of photography, that is, light source, subject and lens. In a document published in 1646 by the Jesuit, Athanasius Kircher, various methods of projecting images by the use of lenses were discussed. These first experiments are considered to be the forerunners of magic lantern technology.

magic lantern

An early form of slide-projector usage. More advanced models used three separate lenses and were capable of optical effects such as dissolves and mixes. Some slides were capable of achieving simple animation sequences.

Probably the most famous of all lanternists was the Belgian Etienne Gaspard Robert. Known as Robertson, he took his very spectacular lantern show, Phantasmagoria, across Europe, thrilling audiences with a display of macabre sensationalism. With the use of a variety of lenses, screens and movable lanterns he was able to achieve a wide range of effects:

- Zooms   This is a technique whereby the image appears to advance towards or recedes away from the viewer.
- Track and pans   A process that enabled the image to move horizontally or vertically across the screen.
- Dissolves and fades   Where one image would fade from view to be replaced by a separate image. When this is done with two images simultaneously the effect is known as a mix or a dissolve.

Quite a feat considering the date, 1798.

The simple magic lantern show was soon improved by the introduction of dual lenses, triple lenses and devices to achieve mixes, fades and even very basic forms of animation and special effects.

During the nineteenth century a variety of optical devices, little more than toys, began to appear. The first, the **Thaumatrope**, was a simple disc of card with images on both sides which was spun by using twisted cords attached to opposite edges. As the card revolved at high speed both images were seen simultaneously creating the illusion of a single image. The popularity of this quaint optical trinket ensured that other devices quickly followed. The **Phenakistoscope**, the **Zoetrope** and the **Praxinoscope** all found favour with a public that sought novelty, though few of them could have been aware of the importance of these trivialities and where they would lead to.

The Praxinoscope, invented by the Frenchman Emile Reynaud was to be the forerunner of his famous Théatre Optique. Utilising the lantern technology of the day and a series of transparent picture bands he projected whole sequences of animated images lasting up to twelve or fifteen minutes. Unlike other lantern shows Reynaud's device was placed behind a translucent screen which was set into a proscenium arch reminiscent of theatres of the day. The first public showing, greeted with great public acclaim, was in Paris in October 1892. Though popular at the time Reynaud found increasing competition from the photographic moving image which would ultimately bring about the demise of this charming form of entertainment. The public, ever eager for new forms of 'realism', found it in photography and particularly cinematography. Increasingly the Théatre Optique began to look like something belonging to a bygone age and in February 1900 the final show took place. It was the end of an era.

From toys to tinseltown

As a result of the experiments first carried out around 1800 by Thomas Wedgwood and later by Nicéphore Niépce, Louise Daguerre and William Henry Fox Talbot, by 1840 it had become possible to make a permanent photographic image. However, photography was still in its infancy and it remained impractical to create sequences of photographic imagery. It was Edward Muybridge who was to make the breakthrough in the sequencing of photographic imagery. Using banks of individual cameras connected to each other, so that each spring-loaded shutter mechanism was fired in sequence at split-second intervals, Muybridge found it possible to record the action of a galloping horse. In the years that followed Muybridge made over 100,000 sequential photographs of all kinds

Thaumatrope

Attributed to the London physician Dr John Ayrton, this was made in Paris in 1826. It consisted of a disk of card on either side of which were separate images. With the use of twisted threads that were attached to opposite edges of the disk, a spinning motion was achieved. This enabled both images to be viewed simultaneously.

Phenakistoscope

Invented by a Belgian physicist, Joseph Plateau, in 1832. An optical device consisting of a disk with slots cut into its edge. When rotated, images on one side could be viewed with the aid of a mirror, the resulting stroboscopic images gave the illusion of movement.

Zoetrope

Forerunner to Praxinoscope.

Praxinoscope

An advanced version of the Zoetrope. Invented by the Frenchman Emile Reynaud in 1878. Utilising mirrors and its own discrete light source, this was the forerunner of Reynaud's Théatre Optique.

of subjects, animals and people. To this day his work is used as an invaluable source of reference, by artists and animators alike, and remains a milestone in the history of photography and cinematography.

Cinematography

While Muybridge was conducting his work using many cameras his French counterpart, Etienne Jules Marey, was struggling with the similar problem of recording animals in motion. He was experimenting with a device that could record a number of sequenced images using a single camera. The 'Photographic Gun', designed by Marey in 1882, was light and portable enough to be used much in the same way as a conventional gun. It was capable of capturing a series of twelve exposures in one second on a single plate that revolved through the gun's stock with the aid of a clockwork mechanism. Though Marey's 'Photographic Gun' was a direct forerunner of the cine-camera, it was not until he built more reliable apparatus capable of much faster shutter speeds that the necessary equipment for the recording of motion photography was available. Their improved mechanisms enabled him to achieve film speeds of 100 pictures per second. Others were to succeed him with improved and more reliable cameras and projectors, and over the following few years a great many such devices were to appear.

Few did as much to popularise the new 'art form' as the French brothers Auguste and Louis Lumière. Not only were they the first to achieve a satisfactory system for recording and projecting motion pictures, they were a major influence in developing the cinema as a form of mass entertainment. Long queues began to form at all of their shows at which they presented a number of films such as *Feeding the Baby*, *Workers leaving the Lumière factory* and *Delegates at the Photographic Congress*.

Only ninety-five years had elapsed from Wedgwood's first tentative experiments with light-sensitive materials to the birth of what was to become an industry. Cinema had arrived.

Trick film

During these early years of cinema the public demand for new films far outweighed supply, and this led to a major growth in the number of film producers. One such producer was the wealthy shoemaker's son, Georges Méliès. His initial interest was in magic and illusion, and after selling his share in the family business, he opened a theatre of illusion at which he gave regular performances. He also began to make and show short cinematic subjects as part of his theatrical illusion programmes. This was in an effort to compete with the increasing popularity of Cinematographs that were opening throughout Paris.

Because of the increasing prices demanded by producers for such films Méliès began to create his own, but while shooting a sequence of a street scene in Paris his camera jammed. By the time he had rectified the problem and was able to continue filming the pedestrians and traffic had moved on about their business to be replaced by other vehicles and individuals. The resulting footage gave the illusion of carriages and people suddenly turning into different vehicles and people. This 'mistake' was to give him the inspiration to carry out a series of experiments based on his interests in illusion and magic. Méliès began to make films using his 'substitution technique' and experimenting with multiple exposures, matte techniques and dissolves. Both an accomplished artist and film-maker, with a flair for solving the technical problems involved in creating his cinematic illusions, his work became ever more ambitious and popular. At the height of his career Méliès had a large studio employing many people turning out a number of films each year, of which the most famous was *Le Voyage dans la lune*, probably the earliest sci-fi movie.

• Plate 3.1 *Le Voyage dans la lune/A Trip to the Moon* (George Méliès, France 1902)
Partly inspired by Jules Verne's science fiction work, *De la terre à la lune* (1865) and H.G. Wells' novel *The First Men in the Moon* (1902), the film was an immediate success, mixing traditional stagecraft with special effects

trick film

The generic term for the development of early cinematic special effects, the development of which is generally attributed to the Frenchman George Méliès.

The amazing special effects developed by George Méliès became collectively known as **trick film**. This could be said to be the direct forerunner of animation and other stop motion techniques as well as the more elaborate technical effects that we are familiar with today. His legacy lives on in *Star Wars*.

Animation

The English-born artist J.S. Blackton, while working at the Vitograph film company in New York, began to make films using the trick film techniques of Méliès. In 1906 he made a film utilising his skills as a 'lightning cartoonist', a term he used to bill himself in his vaudeville act. This short film, *Humorous Phases of Funny Faces* created on a blackboard using chalk, is the most likely candidate for the title of earliest drawn animation. Hot on the heels of Blackton was one of the most noted pioneers of early animation, Emile Cohl. Born in Paris, 1857, Cohl began his career as a cartoonist and political satirist. His work in the sequencing of drawings in strip cartoon form led to his interest in film. His first film *Fantasmagorie*, made in 1908, while owing a lot to the work of Blackton, created even more interest in this new technique. Gaumont, for whom Cohl worked at the time, had him make a colossal amount of footage, turning out one film

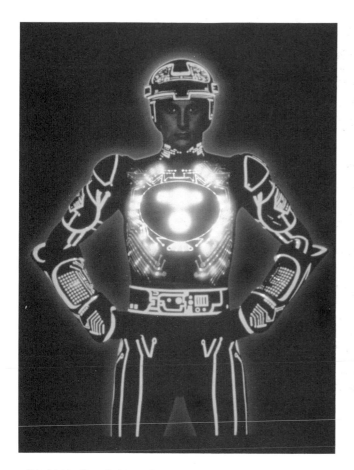

• Plate 3.2 *Tron* (Bruce Boxleitner, US 1982)

a month. Even in their simplest form this is an astounding achievement. While Blackton and Cohl are credited as being the first to create animation using sequential drawings and puppets, it was the work of the American cartoonist, Winsor McCay, that did the most to popularise the medium of animation. Whereas Cohl and Blackton thought it necessary to simplify their drawing styles in order to complete the necessary amount of drawings for animation, McCay did not. His animation displayed all the detail of his cartoon work, for which he was already famous. The film, *Gertie the Dinosaur*, was to ensure him of a place in the annals of animation and cinematic history.

COMPUTER ANIMATION AND COMPUTER-GENERATED IMAGERY

Computer-generated imagery and computer animation are used and appear within film in two very distinct and separate ways. First, as a way of improving technical and design processes and replacing some of the labour-intensive tasks previously carried out solely by human hands. This is usually the case with certain traditional animation techniques and processes. Second, as a way of making imagery within a computer environment. The manner in which such images are made makes them inseparable from the medium used for their creation. This lends them a validity, a separate and distinct integrity from the *reason* they were made.

The recent introduction of this type of computerised image has enabled a broadening of the filmic language that has been with us since the early days of cinema. If the suspension of disbelief is the aim of cinema, to make the impossible plausible, then the introduction of new technologies has created a whole new version of reality – a pseudo reality, a **virtual reality**.

virtual reality

The term used for an artificial 3-dimensional computer environment that can be experienced through the use of a special visor linked directly to the computer enabling a degree of interactivity.

Computers within cinema

From the early days of film man's schizophrenic love–hate relationship with the Brave New World of technology has been part of the cinematic experience. In Fritz Lang's *Metropolis* we are witness to man's celebration of technology. Its beautiful possibilities and its potential for disaster and misery, like a roller-coaster ride, are at once thrilling and frightening. Were the audience seeing this film for the first time aware of this new

• Plate 3.3 *Metropolis* (Fritz Lang, Germany 1927)
Said to be the most significant utopian film of the silent era, Lang projects his ideas about the possible future organisation of society

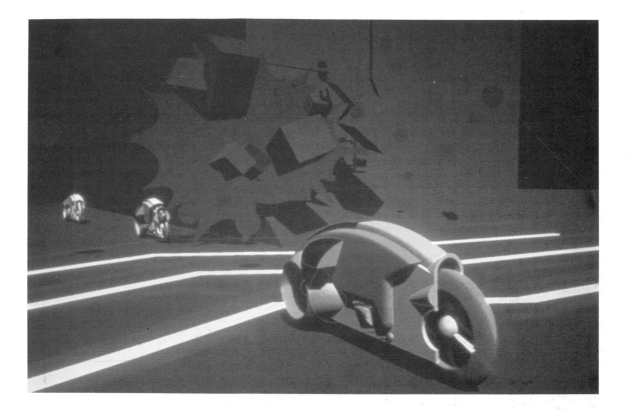

• Plate 3.4 *Tron* (Bruce Boxleitner, US 1982)
A complete computer environment

electronic modernity extending beyond the images on the silver screen? Did they perceive that cinema was an example of this modernity and, by their very presence in the theatre, that they were part of that 'technological future'? Perhaps this is overstating the effect cinema had on the public consciousness.

Computers began to appear in films in a small way. This was in part due to the large amounts of money involved in creating even the simplest of computer animation sequences. One of the earliest examples was *2001: A Space Odyssey*. A sequence involving a space ship docking with an orbiting space station used a degree of computer animation for the control consoles on the flight deck. Seen in wire frame (three-dimensional shapes, with neither surface colour or texture, illustrated through a pattern of interconnecting lines, literally a framework of 'wires' on a two-dimensional surface – the computer screen), basic shapes represented the converging craft. At the time of release the sequence was state of the art entertainment and was reputed to have cost a small fortune. By today's standards it looks simplistic bordering on the primitive, certainly not representative of the computer technology of the year 2001. More important than the actual appearance of computer technology in this film was the role played by the computer as *an actor*. In some measure it reflected the current way in which new computer technologies were still perceived as dangerous and very much the prerogative of

the military and research scientists. No longer something relegated to the fervid imagin-
ings of directors of sci-fi B movies, computers had started to become part of society.

By the time *Alien* was released the computer entertainments industry was well under
way and the public's understanding of computers had begun to be established. As with
2001, *Alien* did little more than use computers for the creation of certain elements of
set design, such as control panels, and while 'Mother', the spaceship's computer, had
a degree of characterisation it lacked the degree of sophistication of HAL in *2001*. It
was not until 1982, with the release of *Tron*, that computer animation took a major leap
forward, with the film becoming a landmark in the way computers were used in a cinematic context. More than that it gave a deeper insight into the world of computers, its
imagery and terminology. Not only did *Tron* use computers as a story-telling vehicle,
but its entire world was one of technology, its very substance electronic and binary, set
as it was *within* the computer.

Despite its lack of commercial success *Tron* initiated a development in the role of the
the computer-generated image. The computer image in *Tron* was not only used for the
creation of control panels, but had become a central characteristic of the film.

Ten years later, with the release of *The Lawnmower Man* in 1992, another step forward
was made in the way computers were used as part and parcel of a cinematic experience. *Lawnmower Man* relies heavily on our perception and understanding of computers,
their language and environments. Not only do computers appear as computers, they
are used to generate an entire environment within cyberspace, a place where people
become computer-generated images. The film begins to question our perception of
ourselves as beings occupying a given space within a three-dimensional world. The
distinction between people and computer software, between the actual and the virtual
becomes unclear. In the film this notion is taken to its logical conclusion, such that the
man experimenting with virtual reality no longer exists on a physical plane but is incorporated entirely into the computer system, existing only as information. The creation of
artificial cyberspace landscapes as depicted in *Tron* and *Lawnmower Man* leaves us
feeling that we know more about these places.

Computers were used to create another kind of reality in 1993 in the film *Jurassic
Park*. Prehistoric animals that had roamed the earth millions of years ago were brought
back to life with the aid of computer wizardry. On their own the computer graphics are
very impressive; when used in conjunction with go-motion (a development of stop-motion
animation) and combined with live action footage the results are sensational. One of the
problems the special effects artists encountered in *Jurassic Park* was how to create a
surface for the computer-generated dinosaurs that would give the impression of skin.
Replicating man-made substances, such as plastic or chrome, is relatively easy with a
computer, and convincing to the viewer, but until *Jurassic Park* no one had ever
attempted anything quite as complex as this. The final result was achieved by several
layers of textured mapping which produced the colouring and texture required to imitate
the animals' reptilian skin. Working with live action and model animation generates an
effect of hyper-realism. The computer techniques behind the creation become transparent, merely part of the process. The audience are no longer watching computer
graphics, they are viewing wildlife footage of extinct creatures. *Jurassic Park* must be
the finest example to date of how computers can be used as an integral part of the
on-screen entertainment, creating animation sequences that go far beyond the imitation
of live action. To all intents and purposes it *is* live action.

The integration of computer animation with more traditional methods of animation is
probably best exemplified by the 1994 Disney release, *The Lion King* . The Disney studios

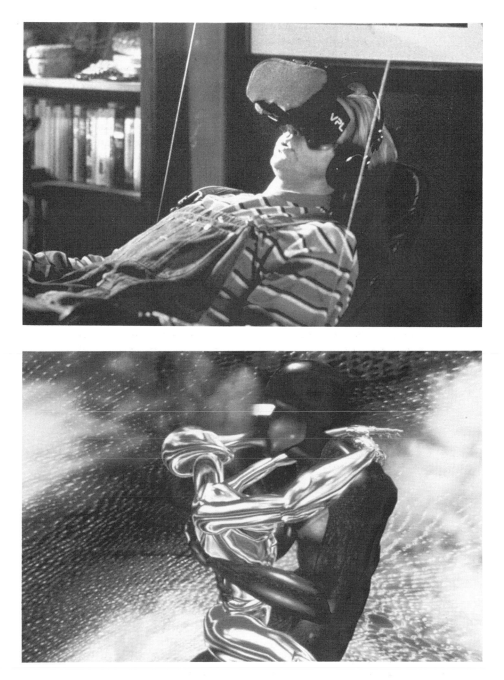

• Plate 3.5 *The Lawnmower Man* (First Independent/Allied Vision, US 1992)

have for some time used computer-generated sequences for backgrounds in such films as *The Rescuers*, *The Rescuers Down Under* and *Beauty and the Beast*. The use of computer-generated animation within an otherwise traditionally animated film took on a different aspect with *Aladdin*. Computers were used to generate not only backgrounds but also animated effects and character animation. With *The Lion King*, Disney took computer-generated imagery even further, creating huge herds of stampeding wildebeest and zebra – footage that would be almost impossible using solely traditional hand-drawn methods. Having said that, traditional methods are still found to be the best way of animating an individual animal. The Disney animators found that by creating an animated sequence of a single wildebeest and then digitising those drawings into a computer it was possible to reproduce them many times. To avoid all the animals looking the same the computer animators then grouped together small numbers of animals as a kind of 'sub-herd'. The timing of the individual animals within a 'sub-herd' was varied to give the impression of individuality. Each of these 'sub-herds' was then assigned a path of action that it would follow across the screen. Other 'sub-herds', all with their own animation timings, were then in turn animated along separate paths. The whole effect was of a mass of animals running at various speeds along their own paths yet following the general direction of the herd. Finally, to further enhance the illusion of hundreds of individual animals, each wildebeest was painted a slightly different colour enabling the eye to follow one particular animal within the larger herd. To contemplate animating such a sequence using wholly traditional methods would be to run the risk of giving the producer a coronary. While other animated films have used computer-aided animation in this 'invisible' manner, while maintaining the traditional appearance, *Aladdin* and, more noticeably, *The Lion King* have taken these techniques to new levels of accomplishment.

Dead actors live again

When you are in the middle of shooting a multi-million dollar movie and your lead actor dies on you from an exotic concoction of artificial stimulants, do you throw your arms up in despair and set out to join him there in the cinematic Valhalla? Of course not. You get in a bunch of computer whiz kids and create your own superstar: one who will not confuse chemical degradation with a pathway to enlightenment.

With the untimely death of Brandon Lee in 1993, killed in a tragic shooting accident on the set of *The Crow*, the producers were faced with a terrible dilemma. They could scrap the film and start again or they could try to finish the film without Lee. Fortunately, a good deal of the principal photography was already in the can, but for the film to work it did require more footage of Lee. The answer was to approach an effects company who used digital photo compositing processes to create the necessary scenes. Using this technology they were able to take an image out of one frame and then place it and animate it within another piece of film. In at least two scenes action shots were filmed using Lee's double for the required extra footage, and Lee's face was then superimposed on the double's body using photo imaging software. The designers had to painstakingly create mattes for each frame by hand in order to make a perfect match on the composited film. The new footage then had to be colour-enhanced to match the rest of the scenes. Such techniques have been used in other films to great effect. In the film *In The Line Of Fire* Clint Eastwood plays the role of a secret service agent detailed to the bodyguard of the US president. In this film, Eastwood, playing a man of around 50, experiences flashbacks to a time when he was much younger and assigned to guard US President Kennedy and his wife, Jackie. We see Eastwood, as a member

• Plate 3.6 *Jurassic Park* (Spielberg, US 1993)

• Plate 3.7 *The Crow* (Brandon Lee, US 1994)

of the presidential entourage, and the Kennedys on screen together, seemingly filmed alongside each other.

For this illusion to work successfully it was necessary to create an atmosphere of authenticity. It was decided that utilising original footage of the Kennedys, including film of that fateful day in Dallas when the president met his death in a hail of assassin's bullets, would be the answer. This was then married together with footage of Eastwood as a young actor, taken from an earlier production. Using computers and image photo-compositing software the two individual films were integrated on a single separate reel of film. This was then visually enhanced to ensure that both sets of footage 'sat well' together. Further treatment of the composite footage was then needed to give the appearance of the quality of newsreel footage of the day.

OTHER WAYS OF SEEING

As with television, the film industry seems to be mesmerised by the development of new technologies. Digital sound, computer-aided video editing and an ever increasing number of film and video formats including the huge **Imax** and **Omnimax**.

Imax

Similar to the Omnimax, though the Imax covers a narrower vertical field of vision, the image of which is projected on to a large, horizontally curved surface.

Omnimax

A specialist format of cinematography requiring specific recording and projection equipment and facilities. It enables the recording of images at a far greater lateral and vertical field of vision. The aim is to achieve the projection of images on to a concave surface that extends into and beyond the peripheral field of human vision.

35mm

70mm

Imax

• Figure 3.1 Image size comparison: Imax, 70mm and 35mm formats (not actual size)

The Imax and Omnimax cinemas are quite a distinct experience from the cinema of the high street. The underlying principle behind both these systems is to utilise, to the maximum, the human field of vision. Images of such large proportion are projected on to a curved screen that extends beyond the range of peripheral vision – wrap-around vision. This means that to view certain areas of the screen it is necessary to turn one's head to focus on the action. The effect of this is seemingly to envelop the viewer within the film imagery. Physically, the format of the Imax negative is much larger than the 35mm or 70mm formats used for 'standard' cinematic releases.

This obviously necessitates not only special cameras and lenses when shooting the footage but also a completely different projection system. In the case of Omnimax this entails the use of a huge curved screen that not only extends well beyond the lateral range of vision but the vertical range as well. The nature of this large format medium lends itself well to film subjects involving large and impressive geographic shots such as the Grand Canyon, the Great Barrier Reef, the Taj Mahal and the Great Wall of China. It has also been used to great effect to film 'activity' shots, such as shooting the rapids on the Colorado River, surfing in Hawaii and aerial stunts such as wing walking. One film even depicts astronauts space walking in orbit above the earth.

Imax has certain advantages over other types of cinema. It presents exhilarating footage beyond the scope of 'standard' cinema and as such has a huge novelty factor attached to it. This type of cinematography, while very spectacular, does have its drawbacks. It tends to depend on the 'spectacle' without the involvement of emotional or intellectual elements to be found in drama. Directors have found that the format creates problems when trying to sustain a subject involving character action, dialogue and relationships. The very size of the screen makes it difficult to use the same filmic language that is used to create cinematic storytelling. Edits between scenes need longer intervals for the viewer to register the image properly, so quick cutting is out. Close-ups can create strange images and bring with them problems of picture quality – due to the size of the screen there is low tolerance of grainy images.

Presently there are only a few of these cinemas throughout the world. Because the Imax experience is such a different one from the cinematic 'norm' the marketing potential has yet to be fully explored.

There is no doubt in my mind that such technological advance should be pursued in order to maximise the audience's cinematic experience and entertainment and to widen the realm of film.

Computer games

Far from being a hindrance to a child's development, computers and computer games can greatly enhance the level of and opportunities for varied learning situations – particularly within a classroom environment. Interactive games can be likened to reading or playing chess as they involve similar thought processes. Alternative worlds and scenarios can be created by children, enabling them to make their own stories and games.

To dismiss computer games as nothing more than a high-tech version of 'Snakes and Ladders' would be to misinterpret them entirely. Maybe it is even time to consider computer games featuring characters and distinct story-lines as part of the development of a new form of folk tale: thus following on from the oral tradition with a binary one.

The comparative sophistication of children's awareness of television and film techniques may give some indication of how such technologies are incorporated into the fabric of society. My childhood experience of a televisual future in the form of *Doctor*

Who and the terrifying Daleks only brings about derisive laughter from my own children. Brought up on *Star Wars* and *Terminator* they expect more from their robots.

The increase in popularity of computer games is having a knock-on effect on other aspects of the media and in particular on the cinema. There are now computer games of many blockbuster films: *Batman*, *Aliens*, *Terminator 2*, *Robocop* and *Predator*. With the making of the film version of *Street Fighter* it is obvious that there is two-way traffic in the spread of influence. It may be the case that the large studios are making films with a view to the merchandising of computer games and that the special effects within a film are in some way linked to this. If this is so what kind of effect will this have on the script and will it mean that character development will follow strong stereo-types?

Computer art

During the late twentieth century we have seen the very notion of art, what it is and is not, being questioned by the advent of the **postmodernist** movement. Nevertheless in the public eye 'art' is still seen to be very much involved with the creation of paintings and sculpture. The idea of art as something alive, and not merely to be made for the confines of the gallery, has not really been taken on board by the public at large. The role of the computer within art has been something of a misnomer to date, the popular perception of computer art being an 'applied' art, usually relegated to the movie industry. Computer 'art' is usually restricted to strange images evolving or growing on screen. As an art form in its own right it has yet to spawn its own heroes and villains or to make an impact on the public consciousness. It is still very much in its infancy and only time will tell if computer art will offer an alternative to the established arts of painting and sculpture.

Miniaturisation of cinematography

The miniaturisation of video equipment, in particular the video camera, has made major inroads into the fields of both science and entertainment.

For a number of years it has been possible to photograph micro-organisms and even capture video footage of bacteria within laboratory conditions. But the new developments in miniature cameras, image enhancers and fibre optics have made possible the use of cameras in delicate examinations of the internal organs. This breakthrough has been of great benefit to patients and an aid to doctors and surgeons in their diagnosis. Indeed it has become almost standard procedure in the treatment of heart complaints involving bypass surgery.

The use of cameras in sport has long been a method of bringing a wide variety of entertainment to the homes of millions. Recently we have seen the use of cameras integrated within the very process of the sporting event. Cameras are now so small and light that it is possible to mount them on formula one racing cars and high performance motor cycles with no perceptible effect on their racing capabilities. In the more passive sport of cricket the cameras are even incorporated into the stumps, giving a whole new look to the televisual experience of the test match. However, this is not just to enhance the audience's experience of these events. We are witnessing the use of instant play-back video in the decisions being made by the umpires. Is this an example of the 'art' of the sport, with all its hit and miss, nuances being eroded by a more technological precision? Some would decry the introduction of the third umpire in cricket, preferring to leave things as they were, and hoping that somehow the bad decisions would balance

postmodernist

A term used to describe many aspects of contemporary cultural production from architecture to music. Characteristics include eclectic borrowing from earlier styles (see **bricolage**) to produce witty new combinations. Postmodernism involves the playful manipulation of **paradigms** and the exploitation of **intertextuality**.

themselves out. This might have been acceptable when cricket was a gentlemen's game, but in these days of big prize money and the economic success of teams riding on the results, the introduction of such measures seems inevitable.

Probably the most spectacular use of the miniaturisation of video technology we have witnessed was those remarkable images that played nightly to the western world during the Gulf War. The miniature cameras placed in the nose cones of those 'smart bombs' gave us some idea of the horrific efficiency and the destructive power of modern weaponry.

FILM AND POLITICS

Image manipulation and propaganda

The development of technologies that can be used to alter video footage and stills photography has serious political implications. The wiping out of people from history, the altering of history itself, is not something that merely belongs within the pages of George Orwell's *1984*. Many countries throughout the world are guilty of at some time having falsified documents, fabricated evidence and arranged for individuals to be 'disap-peared'. Most notoriously the totalitarian states of Soviet Union, Nazi Germany, China, and certain Latin American countries. The creation of ever more sophisticated image manipulation systems makes this kind of activity even easier.

The manipulation of imagery, the altering of photographic records, for political ends is nothing new and goes back to the work of the German artist John Heartfield. He used photomontage to great effect, creating images of such potent political satire and importance, that they annoyed the Nazi Party. So much so that he ended up on Hitler's death list and had to flee his own country.

While Heartfield made work that was obviously contrived (one of his pieces depicts Hitler with a gullet crammed full of gold coins), there are other types of political propa-ganda that passes itself off as being the 'real thing'.

Hitler's own propaganda machine was a superb example of the manipulation of truth and the perpetuation of myths and the creation of new ones. At the head of this organ-isation was Joseph Goebbels, a man who claimed that Disney's *Snow White* was one of his favourite films. A brilliant film-maker in his own right, Goebbels understood only too well the power of the cinema which he used with all his guile. He attempted to create not only fear and hatred in the hearts of the German population, as he spread his own poisonous anti-Semitic views across the cinema screens, but a belief in Germany as the guardian of the pure Aryan ideal. In a film that purports to be a document of the idyllic, sickeningly titled *The Führer Gives the Jews a New Home*, the Jews are seen to be settling into a new homeland where they can thrive and be prosperous, away from the ravages of war. The Jews' 'new home' was, in reality, one of the many death camps scattered throughout Europe as part of the Nazis' mass extermination programme. The film was actually shot within the confines of one such camp in Czechoslovakia, Theresienstadt (Terezin), though well away from the ovens designed to dispose of 190 victims of the gas chambers at a time.

More recently, the activities and covert operations of the CIA (Central Intelligence Agency, a US governmental organisation dedicated to espionage and information gath-ering) have demonstrated clearly the importance the Agency places on film as a means to fabricate its own brand of reality, presenting visual evidence to discredit undesirables or to massage the truth into a more palatable form. Photographs of US President J.F.

Kennedy as he lay dead in a Dallas hospital, the result of a brutal assassination, were altered to obscure the true extent of the head injuries caused by a marksman's bullets. Allegations were levelled against the CIA claiming complicity, if not direct involvement, in this bloody affair. It was only years later, well after the commission investigating the events had published its findings, that the undoctored images came to light.

By its very nature film is malleable. Long after the camera has ceased rolling the images it has captured are changeable and therefore open to the manipulation of truth. Film is not just a manifestation of an optical illusion, it is the fabrication of 'factual illusion'. Some of the most authenticated examples of film footage have had doubts cast upon their veracity.

Is it any longer necessary for us to experience current footage of famine victims as part of a news broadcast, or will stock footage of a similar but earlier event suffice to illustrate the horror? The children may be different but the horror remains the same; after all as long as public sensibilities are moved enough to help alleviate the situation one image of a starving child is much the same as any other. Or is it?

It has long been said that the first casualty in any war or conflict is truth. A recent example of this 'massaging of truth' occurred during the Gulf War. In 1990 Iraq, under the despotic leadership of Saddam Hussein, invaded the small neighbouring state of Kuwait. It was not long before the might of the western world leapt to the defence of this oil-rich independent state. For months we were treated nightly to a 'Hollywoodised' version of the conflict – Scud missiles being intercepted by Patriot missiles, part of Israel's ground to air defence systems, regular launches of Cruise missiles from the American fleet, mass air attacks including hardware that looks more at home in the *Star Wars* trilogy in the shape of the Stealth bomber. If this was not enough, we were also treated to a bombs' eye view via the miniaturised cameras on the nose cones of the 'smart' bombs. It all became mesmerising. Sanitised and safe. We could all assure ourselves, at the behest of those top brass public relations men running the press conferences, that the only real damage being done was of the *collateral* type. Unfortunately, along with this new technological war came a new use of language where collateral meant anything but property. Although the use of technology meant these events were presented to us through nice neat bloodless images, we would do well to remember that wars are fought by people and that the innocent also suffer. The nightly screenings were not about journalism but about sensationalist entertainment. The broadcasters could not have hoped for a better soap. In such an atmosphere it becomes too easy to recreate heros and villains for political reasons.

Digital images

It is now possible to capture imagery in a digital form through such devices as a stills video camera. This equipment does away altogether with film and replaces it with recordable discs, rather like a computer floppy disc. Such an innovation has meant that the reshaping of 'reality' has become much easier to achieve – and easier to disguise. Images of this nature can be easily imported on to a computer's hard disk, and, once there, seamless alterations can be made. The colour range can be balanced for printing purposes, images can be cropped to make a better layout and the combination of two or more images is made possible. This kind of image manipulation for production purposes seems reasonable enough, but where does this tweaking end? With the photographic process physical evidence, in the form of a negative, exists and may give some veracity of the actuality of events. If the negatives can be traced, that is. With the introduction of digital imagery there are no originals, only copies. The only 'original' exists in cyberspace as information. Malleable in a million different ways, each permutation, each new alteration, has as much authority as any other. Each 'truth' is just as complete, just as valid as any other.

With image manipulation technology for printing processes used as a standard practice the question is no longer whether to manipulate but what to manipulate and why. While it would be a gross exaggeration to claim that the sole reason for altering images is for cynical political purposes, such manipulation, by its very nature, must have an effect on 'truth'. Is truth to remain as an accidental casualty or does it become a legitimate target in its own right? The initial and necessary target for those with a vested interest in perpetuating fear, hate and greed? And does such technology make that target an easier one?

SHAPING SOCIETY

Cultural imperialism

The spreading of the cultural traditions of one society to another is a natural process usually brought about by exposure to one another through trade or conflict. The forced imposition of one culture on to another is something quite different. Historically, centres of world power have forced their beliefs and practices on others, often in the name of religion, but mostly for profit. In recent times advances in telecommunications have made this cultural invasion much simpler. War is out of date. It's messy, it's time-consuming and above all it's expensive. Not only that, but it can have the effect of destroying millions of potential customers. Consumers of all those little disposable items of modernity that multinationals are continuously trying to offload on societies that can not afford them. A harsh cynical view perhaps, but for television stations in some of the poorer countries, faced with the dilemma of creating their own expensive programmes or buying up large amounts of cheap American soap operas for next to nothing, the choice is easy. And what effect does this kind of exposure have? The sales of hair straightener and skin lightener seem to be going from strength to strength in some African countries as they are 'encouraged' to aspire to western (American) values. The same is true of the Australian soap *Neighbours*, which completely denies the existence of its own native aboriginal heritage, preferring to emulate its Western counterparts.

As a form of mass entertainment, education and information television has no equal – it not only reflects society but does much to shape it. Unfortunately, because the financing of television broadcasting is driven by market forces we are witnessing a gross misuse of this wonderful and very powerful tool. Broadcasters are forced to fill air time with the cheapest form of programme possible, which usually means wall to wall game shows, chat shows, reruns of old movies and cheap cartoons, a lot of which is imported. Television now seems to be most concerned with such issues as better reception, clearer images, stereo sound, wrap-around sound and more and more channels. The quality of the image seems to be the aim, with the emphasis being on *how* we see things rather than on *what* we see. With viewing figures being uppermost in the station controllers' minds, producers are finding it increasingly difficult to make documentaries, particularly of the investigative journalism type, and quality drama, though there are exceptions to this.

Hollywood appears to be concentrating its efforts on making films for a young audience with a disposable income. The tendency is away from script and content and towards a technological veneer of computer-generated effects, explosions and pubescent sexual fantasising. In the 1970s films were crammed full of the then obligatory car chases. During the 1980s the move was towards gore – the more blood the better. In the 1990s technology (preferably alien) in the form of robots, weaponry and vehicles is the order of the day, with just enough female flesh showing throughout the film to titillate the audience. With the majority of money for these ventures coming from the USA it is not surprising to find that a lot of these films reflect the current interests of the American youth culture. With our own film industry not exactly dead but on a life-support machine, it is no wonder that the films we are accustomed to are all American, depicting American values and an American attitude towards the rest of the world.

Our own impoverished film industry can do little to counter this tendency or to give us a sense of our own identity and our own culture, whatever that is. In France there is a policy that 40 per cent of films shown in cinemas should be home-grown. This not only makes for a lively film industry but for a cinematic tradition that is recognisably French. It does not attempt to compete with Hollywood in the type of film it makes, but instead relies on its own special qualities, appealing first and foremost to a home market. In the UK we seem doomed to a diet of McDonald's and *RoboCops*.

Sex and violence/stereotype and discrimination

To expect these new technologies to herald a new era would be asking far too much of them. The use of new technologies sometimes just serves to perpetuate old prejudices and entrenched bigoted attitudes, but how else should we expect this to be? Computers are man-made not heaven sent. Rubbish in – rubbish out. With the computer's capacity for information storage, image and sound creation and communication, immense possibilities for the furthering of man's creative urges are opened up. This seems somehow at odds then with the tendency for computers to be confined to just another means of creating and distributing pornography and interactive violence in the form of computer 'beat'em ups'.

World economics and new technologies

As with other forms of industry the cost of film production is on the increase. As a measure to improve profits and maintain production values, studios and producers are ever on the look out for new ways to cut costs. Within the traditional drawn animation studio system, exploitation of labour, particularly where the unskilled tasks are concerned, is nothing new. Most notable of these is the use of paint and trace. After the animation at the drawing stage is completed the images are transferred on to clear sheets of celluloid, either by hand or by photocopying. These are then individually painted by hand: a very expensive but necessary element of the production. When unemployment is high it is easy to find people willing to train to carry out this semi-skilled task. During the 1980s a lot of this work moved away from the UK-based studios and went to Ireland and Spain where labour costs were low and where studios existed that were able to complete the work. By the late 1980s even this option was unacceptable to many producers and more work began to move out to the Far East. The Chinese, in particular, were not slow to take advantage of the West's desire for cheap paint and trace, and work began to pour into their newly created 'economic zone'. As the work heading east began to increase they became involved in other areas of production: layout, animation and camera. The developing areas of the Far East are now the heartland of this end of production. With a massive, easily renewable workforce willing to work for extremely low wages and with no union representation, the lure of the east is far too much for profit-hungry producers to resist. The introduction of electronic paint systems is set to completely revolutionise animation production. Not only will wages be even lower than the work-hungry Koreans are willing to accept, but it will mean that production can be carried out in the country of origin. This will enable the producers to keep a closer eye and a tighter rein on the production schedule. As for other aspects of traditional animation production, we are likely to see a move towards the development of a computer **lightbox** that does away with the need for paper at all.

If such a system were linked to a telecommunications network using a satellite facility there would be no reason why animators could not work from their own small work stations at home, wherever that may be. This scenario would have a major effect on a studio system that has been in place since the 1920s. It would also drastically affect the level of employment within the industry, doing away with the need for assistant animators, inbetweeners, animation checkers, line test camera operators and a large paint and trace department. One thing is certain, not everyone will benefit from these new innovations.

VIRTUAL REALITY

Robertson's *Phantasmagoria* created a sensation in the eighteenth century as did the Lumière Brothers' *cinématographe* shows in the nineteenth century. *King Kong* and the broadcast of Orson Welles' radio production of *War of the Worlds* did much the same in the twentieth century. The live broadcast of the *War of the Worlds*, which was produced using a semi-journalistic style, with on-the-scene reporters and complete with sound effects, had a particularly devastating impact on the public consciousness. So convincing was it that panic broke out among some of the audience listening at home. Some people called the police for help and advice, others jumped in their cars and took to the hills in fear of their lives. There is even one account of a farmer blasting holes in a water tower with his shotgun as he mistook it for an alien war machine in the evening gloom. These major events did much more than extend our understanding of cinematic language or new communication 'languages' – they raised our expectations of those forms of communications. In a very real way the responses they elicited were symptomatic of the rapidly changing pace of communication systems and our inability to adapt easily to them. Although still in its infancy, virtual reality is already with us and, as we head for the twenty-first century, it may well take up the running in the expansion of the cinematic experience. It may even redefine the parameters of cinema into a literally three-dimensional space. Direct parallels can be drawn between our response to virtual reality and the early days of cinema. The unsophisticated audiences of the nineteenth century were happy to witness what was by our standards mundane footage of everyday Parisian life or scenes from the seaside. Few of them could have imagined in their wildest dreams where the art form was to lead. The same is true of virtual reality – the truth is that we simply do not yet know the true extent of the impact virtual reality will have on society.

What is virtual reality?

Virtual reality is a computer system whereby the operator, or perhaps it would be truer to say the experiencer, is in direct communication with the computer via a head set. Three-dimensional graphic images are viewed through a visor at the front of the helmet while stereo sound is experienced via built-in headphones. As the user turns their head

lightbox

A lightbox is an animator's drawing desk. An adjustable angled surface, rather like any draughtsman's desk, it has a ground glass or perspex disk cut into it. This is illuminated from below to enable two or more separate drawings to viewed at the same time when laid over one another. At its simplest a lightbox enables the animator to create a number of drawings while viewing each of them as part of a sequence.

electronic lightbox

While not in existence as yet, such a device would enable the animator to create drawings directly on to a computer via a graphics drawing table and a stylus, replacing paper and pencil. Software is already available that will allow the inbetweening (the drawings between the major key positions of a movement or action) to be carried out by computer. With the use of touch-sensitive screens and electronic painting, also available, an animator should be able to draw directly on to the screen, creating finished animation to be stored directly on to the hard drive.

to the left or right the computer can trace the headset's spatial relationship to the computer via sensors in the helmet. It then processes this information and returns modified images to the visor that give the impression that the wearer of the headset has turned their head within the computer-generated three-dimensional cyberworld. Other spatial information can be collected through the use of data gloves, which incorporate sensors that behave in a similar manner to those within the helmet. Pressure pads within the gloves, linked to the computer, enable the user to experience an illusion of picking up and moving virtual objects within this computer-generated world.

Presently, the application of virtual reality has, by and large, been an industrial one. Architects and designers have used it to create three-dimensional representations of their proposals before committing to the costly process of manufacture. The military have also used virtual reality as a training tool, simulating armoured vehicle control and fighter aircraft flight in combat situations.

The real potential for the entertainments industry and particularly the film industry has yet to be explored. Imagine a time when 'films' are made to be experienced not only in two dimensions, within the confines of a cinema, but on another level altogether. Wild fantasy? Maybe, but it was not that long ago that the Lumière Brothers were amazing all and sundry with their footage of *Feeding the Baby*. We have come a long way since then. Recent developments within virtual reality technology have meant that it is possible to screen virtual worlds for a group audience. Although still in development, this could lead to another form of interactive cinema.

Another aspect of virtual reality 'entertainment' being experimented with is cybersex. Participants wear data suits, elaborate versions of the data glove, incorporating a multitude of sensors to give the impression of touch – which enable 'physical' (virtual) involvement with the computer-generated images. As this type of usage becomes more widespread and cybersex becomes increasingly trendy serious questions of morality will be raised. Is cybersex open to misuse? Are women at risk of exploitation? What dangers are there to children? And could crimes such as murder or rape be acted out with impunity? Are 'crimes' committed only in the 'virtual' still crimes? There may be situations where two or more people are involved in a common interactive virtual reality although physically separated by many miles. If crimes are committed against real people in cyberspace are they out of the jurisdiction of the law? Along with the development of virtual worlds will we need to develop a virtual morality? Along with new technologies come a new set of problems.

Our infatuation with the creation of 'other' realities and 'virtual' worlds seems a little odd coming at a time when mankind appears to be ill equipped to deal with the actual realities of our physical world.

It is interesting to note that Timothy Leary, the psychedelic guru of the 1960s who used mind-altering drugs, most notably LSD, in his experiments into the spiritual, psychological and metaphysical aspects of humankind, is currently exploring these same virtual reality themes. Will he once again be urging us to turn on, tune in and drop out?

Coe, Brian, *The History of Movie Photography*, Westfield, NJ: Eastview Editions, 1981.
Hayward, Phillip and Wollen, Tana, *Future Visions: New Technologies of the Screen*, London: British Film Institute, 1993.
Mealing, Stuart, *The Art and Science of Computer Animation*, Oxford: Intelect, 1992.
Robinson, David, *George Méliès: Father of Film Fantasy*, London: British Film Institute, 1993
Smith, Thomas G., *Industrial Light and Magic: Ther Art of Special Effects*, London: Virgin, 1991.

The Last Machine (television series, 1995)
The Abyss (James Cameron, 1989)
Bram Stoker's Dracula (Francis Ford Coppola, 1992)
Mask (Chuck Russell, 1994)
Lawnmower Man 2 (Forhard Mann, 1995)

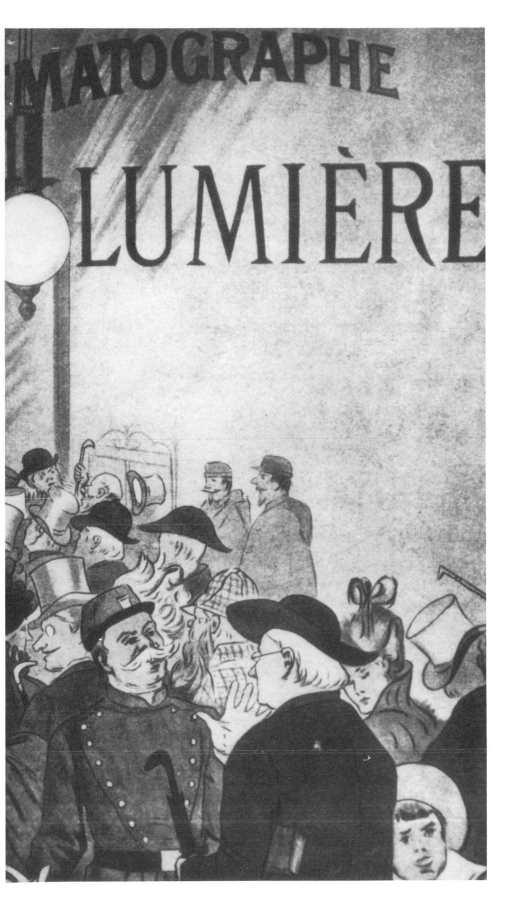

Part two

Approaches to studying film texts

Film form and narrative

Allan Rowe

Film form and narrative

INTRODUCTION: THE ACT OF VIEWING

The experience of watching films – particularly in the cinema – is an intense one. We are sitting in near-darkness, in rows of seats directed towards a screen, separated from one another, but sharing an experience with the rest of the audience. We are viewing large images – allowing a closeness to the figures on the screen not afforded in everyday life, and often seeing things that we do not usually see. There is a co-ordinated, concentrated and often loud soundtrack, further directing our attention if it threatens to wander. It is small wonder that the viewers of the Lumière Brothers[1] took evasive action as that train first pulled into the station. Elvis Presley is alleged to have been concerned with the script of his first movie. He was required to hit a woman, and that was 'against his nature'. He could not be convinced that what occurred on screen did not actually have to take place. Yet we are ultimately aware of the fantasy nature of what we see – Edward G. Robinson went on to make many more films after the 'end of Little Rico' in *Little Caesar*[2] without provoking doubts or outcry among his fans. What occurs is a process of 'suspension of disbelief' whereby we seem to accept temporarily the reality of what appears in front of us, while having the capacity to switch off this belief at a moment's notice, if someone talks to us or the celluloid breaks.[3]

It is this capacity to switch on and off, rather than the poorer quality of the visual image, that accounts for the reduced potency of a horror film when watched at home with the remote control at hand. It is not the fidelity of image and sound that creates the illusion of reality for us. The early viewers of film accepted the shades of grey that appear in a black and white film. Viewing these films today, we find it hard to accept the illusion of films made in a period with different technical standards – the **noise** gets in the way. The mere recording of events in front of the camera – and the use, for instance, of everyday speech by non-actors in a **drama-documentary** – often appears strange to us. The 'illusory reality' of **mainstream** cinema is created for us by a number of devices, involving the use of camera, microphone and lighting. These devices are not fixed – a 'correct' way of recording the truth – but conventions developed over a hundred years of cinema. These are ingrained in us as viewers – and we can feel disturbed or cheated if these conventions are broken. If we are 'duped' by this – we are willingly duped. We participate in this process of suspension of disbelief as a price for the pleasures we get from film viewing – including that of 'surviving' being scared by a horror movie.

However, our role in this process is not merely a passive one. We work actively at making sense of the individual scenes and particularly at predicting the story. To do so we retain an awareness of the conventions of film and are able to retain a critical distance from what we see. I would maintain this is not a capacity possessed solely by 'film students', but rather is integral to the act of viewing.

noise

In the film industry, it refers to any barrier to successful communication.

drama-documentary

Any format which attempts to re-create historical or typical events using performers, whether actors or not.

mainstream

Feature-length narrative films created for entertainment and profit. Mainstream is usually associated with 'Hollywood', regardless of where the film is made.

☐ CASE STUDY 1: *ROBOCOP*

The process of making sense of a movie is initially produced at the beginning of a film when we are first drawn into its world. We will explore the film *RoboCop*[4] to see how this process works. This film operates in an area between that of comic strip construction – a recently deceased policeman transformed into an indestructible robot – and the environment of police precinct work. This is a form recognisable from both TV fictions and news programmes, of an uncontrollable urban area and a political climate of privatisation. For the film to 'work' there is a need to absorb the impossible into the all too probable. The film's popular and critical acceptability suggests that this has worked.

After an initial aerial shot showing a modern, sky-scrapered city, with the film title (maybe suggesting that this could be any modern city), we are presented with a sixteen picture grid – dominated by images of urban violence, followed by a shot of a male and female facing directly to the camera. Before they start talking, a voice-over addresses the unseen TV audience, which in effect is us, the viewers of the film; 'This is Media – you give us three minutes – we give you the world.'

We are aware that this is a TV news item. Apart from TV lights and the studio backdrop – there is a direct address to the audience. In doing so the shot acknowledges the presence of a camera and by implication an audience. As a strategy, this has been denied to mainstream fictional cinema, since the early days. Although this is not an identifiable TV station, and we are viewing a fictional film, the film-maker presumes our capacity to read the **conventions**. This first news item, a nuclear threat in the besieged white city-state of Pretoria, suggests a future, but not too far future, scenario; the second, a jokey news item on the Star Wars Initiative, suggests a comic element – but also a world without clear moral values. A commercial for artificial hearts follows. On first viewing we cannot place these. However we 'trust' the narrative to make sense of them, as it does with the construction of the artificial policeman within the corrupt environment. Nothing in a mainstream narrative is there by accident.

The final item relates directly to the narrative of the film: the killing of three policemen, the taking over of policing by a private corporation and the introduction of two villains – the corporate boss Jones, in an insensitive interview, and the crime boss Boddicker, through a soft focus newspaper shot. The TV introduction is not only an economical introduction to the narrative but authenticates the reality of the situation. It also places us at a distance from those in authority.

The next scene – in the police precinct – is constructed with long moving shots using Steadicam,[5] overlapping dialogue and a high level of verbal violence, all familiar as the style of TV police series such as *NYPD Blues*. However, the futurist nature of the scene is implied by the unremarked upon unisex locker room. There is a newcomer to the precinct, who is seen taking the place of a murdered policeman. We **read** this through his action in taking over a locker and replacing the name. He joins up with a partner, Lewis, who in a stock scene, subverted by her gender, proves herself in a fight. The two ascend in the car to the 'real world', he driving the car, she blowing her bubblegum in his face.

The film cuts, without an **establishing shot**, to the inside of an ascending lift in the corporation building, suggesting a link organisationally if not physically between the two buildings. The locations show similarities, but also contrasts.

Uniforms are worn in both buildings – the dark blue bullet-proofing of the police and the mid-grey of the 'suits', the walls are predominantly single coloured, a grubby light green at the precinct and light grey at the corporation building, clutter at the precinct,

conventions

Conventions are established procedures within a particular form which are identifiable by both the producer and the reader. The implication of the idea of conventions is that a form does not naturally mean anything, but it is an agreement between producer and user.

reading a film

Although films are viewed and heard, the concept of 'reading' a film implies an active process of making sense of what we are experiencing.

establishing shot

A shot using distant framing, allowing the viewer to see the spatial relations between characters and the set.

space at the corporation, a blackboard at the precinct and a high-tech bank of TV screens at the corporation.

The focus of this scene, used widely in the marketing of the film, is the presentation by Jones of a robot 'Future of Law Enforcement, ED, 209'. This robot is shot predominantly from below, indeed from ground level, initially dominating the frame of the open doors leading from the boardroom, with corresponding **high angle** shots of the terrified executives. The robot's movements are heavy, metallic and jerky – and are accompanied by a high volume soundtrack. Its appearance with large bulky 'legs' and 'arms' suggests something subhuman – particularly when compared later with the human-based RoboCop. The crude mechanical 209 proceeds to destroy a junior executive in a demonstration of its power, failing to recognise that he has disarmed. This reflects the attitude of corporation, 'It's life in the Big City.'

The first few minutes of the film have established its **reality** – part drawn from contemporary images, such as the boardroom, but with an invented technology like the robot inserted in it. However, the construction of this reality is not just through a selection of the world outside, but rather through the judicial use of existing images and conventions that have already been **mediated** through film – or other related forms. We understand the film through our experiences and comparisons with other films or media products. These in turn assure the film of its authenticity. We believe in the world of *RoboCop* because it has been validated by a spoof of recognisable TV news programmes. We can 'place' the film as we can identify both the images and the way they are presented from images and representations with which we are already familiar.

The reading of film

RoboCop rests therefore on a number of cultural readings of the content by the viewer, but also on a reading of the film and its conventions. It is relatively easy for us to read such a film; it has been made recently, and for people like ourselves, and there is general

high angle

A shot from a camera held above characters or object, looking down at them.

reality

The concept of the 'real' is problematic in cinema, and is part of the focus of this chapter. The concept is generally used in two different ways.

First, the extent to which a film attempts to mimic reality so that a fictional film can appear indistinguishable from documentary. Second, the film can establish its own world, and can by consistently using the same conventions establish the credibility of this world. In this later sense a science fiction film such as *RoboCop* can be as realistic as a film in a contemporary and recognisable world such as *Sleepless in Seattle*.

mediation

A key concept in film and media theory, it implies that there are always structures, whether human or technological, between an object and the viewer, involving inevitably a partial and selective view.

• Plate 4.1 *RoboCop* (Paul Verhoeven, US 1987)
ED 209, the future of law enforcement

agreement among members of the audience as to what it is about, what is happening. The reading of an early film, made a hundred years ago, appears on first sight to be easier. The language of the films of Lumière and Méliès[6] appears simpler – the visual equivalent of children's picture-books – and it is tempting to regard the early film-makers and their audiences with condescension. The conception of a 'Primitive Mode of Representation'[7] (Noel Burch), applied to the first two decades of film-making, encourages us to read these as the first faltering steps to the irresistible final product of the modern Hollywood movie.

Although the first extant movies are documentary records of either public or private events, such as the Lumières' home movie of feeding a baby or the reconstruction of events as in Edison's early boxing Kinetoscope[8] pictures, the normal format soon became fictional narrative. The earliest films are the so-called 'tableau' films, including most of the work of Georges Méliès. These films are characterised by a succession of scenes recorded in long shot square on to the action. Each scene begins with a cut to a black and is replaced by another scene in a different (later) time and place. Characters walk on and off either from the side of the frame, or alternatively through 'stage doors' in the frame, like the 'crew' walking into the space ship in Méliès' *Voyage to the Moon*. These films draw strongly on a theatrical tradition. They appear to be shot from the 'best seat in the stalls', and represent a series of scenes, albeit short ones, without the need to wait for the scene to be shifted.

Such films can still be enjoyed as 'spectacle' – the special effects, the hard painted colour, the sets and costumes. These are connected by a narrative linking each shot to the whole, and usually each shot to the next one, by a pattern of cause and effect. However, the narrative is hard to follow for the contemporary viewer. This is in part due to the absence of **close-up** or identification with character. However, in a number of instances Méliès relies upon our knowledge of the narrative. *Ali Baba* (1905 Méliès from the BFI early cinema video) depends on the audience's pre-knowledge of the story. The individual tableau appears to be operating as illustrations of the narrative rather than driving it.

The shift to a cinematic narrative and formal structure occurs fairly swiftly, so that by the mid-1910s most films are recognisable to a contemporary audience as fiction films. While there may be some dispute about who 'invented' the language of film – with most accounts ascribing to D.W. Griffith[9] a major role – it is generally accepted that changes that had occurred by the end of the decade make the films of the late silent period resemble modern films more than the 'primitive' cinema.

close-up

Normally defined as a shot of the head from the neck up.

□ CASE STUDY 2: BEGINNING OF KEATON'S FILM *THE GENERAL*[10]

This is an example of the **Institutional Mode of Representation (IMR)** (Burch), that is, despite being a silent film it has a complex narrative structure based on identification with character.

The credits prioritise Keaton as both star and co-director. It starts with a title establishing place, 'Marietta Ga' and time '1861' a device that continued into the sound era. This is followed by an establishing long panning shot of the train, cutting to a medium shot to identify Johnny Gray (Keaton) as driver and continuing to track forward to identify 'The General' – the name of the train. It then cuts ahead to the arrival of the train in the station.

IMR

The Institutional Mode of Representation is a broad categorisation of systems of film form and narrative characterising mainstream cinema from around 1915 onwards. It was perceived as replacing the Primitive Mode of Representation (a set of conventions used in early film between 1895 and 1905) as a gradual process in the first twenty years of cinema.

• Plate 4.2 *The General* (Buster Keaton, US 1925)
Johnny Grey (Keaton) and admirers

There is then a reverse shot of the other side of the train. As Johnny descends he is admired by two children and checks with a colleague the time of the arrival of the train (implying the high status of the job and his proficiency).

This is followed by an inter title – 'There were 2 loves in his life his engine and . . .' – and a cut to a close-up of a portrait of a young woman which he has in his cab.[11] Keaton walks off towards frame right. The following fade to black implies a different place or time and cuts to Annabelle (Marion Mack) who is identifiable as the woman in the portrait. She is looking away to frame right, the opposite direction from Johnny and receives a look from an unseen admirer(?) (The viewer can read that this is not Johnny.)

Keaton is discovered walking from left to right followed by the two children (the same direction as he left the previous frame and the same direction as the train). Annabelle hides and deceives him by following the children (parallel to her deception of him with the admirer). She ends the joke and invites him in, with the children following. This creates a 'family', but not a real one and Johnny has to tell them to leave. (This parallels her trick on him and suggests a similarity between them – they are a 'proper couple'.) He gives her a picture of himself standing in front of the train (a parallel of her portrait, but significantly different: he is a driver and The General).

There is a cut to an older man in a different room who, after looking off frame to the right, moves into the sitting room and a younger man enters from the door (right). The exchange that followed is 'in depth' and in a different plane to the 'lovers'. The first speech title appears announcing the war and the wish to enlist. After the two men leave we get a subjective shot from Annabelle to Johnny, who is left alone and uncomfortably framed on the sofa (due to her absence they are no longer a couple).

As he leaves to try to enlist we are shown his awkwardness and inexperience; she kisses him and he tries to hide his embarrassment, he waves to an imaginary person over her shoulder and falls over.

There is no fade to black before the recruiting office scene, thus implying the speed of the action. This scene is largely in long shot. After his initial rejection, we pull away from Keaton and discover the reason for it. We know why he has been rejected; he doesn't. However, he remains the centre of the narrative and we identify with him in his attempts to make sense of his rejection. For instance, he is placed next to a very much taller man in the queue and we realise before him(?) that he would consider this the reason for his rejection. We also admire and identify with his attempts to trick his way in (there is a slightly strange cut where he appears on opposite sides of the frame in consecutive shots taken from the same angle thus breaking the 30° rule[12] and thus confusing us as to where he actually is).

In the following scene there is a false 'eye-line'[13] match from Johnny sitting on the side of the engine to Annabelle looking from the gate (we 'know' this is false from the journey Keaton takes to get to the house early in the film). His absence is stressed by the arrival of her father and brother who have enlisted and are where Johnny ought to be (both physically and in the narrative).

In the final scene she accuses him of not trying to enlist and therefore being a coward. We know (because we have seen it) that this is untrue. Our identification with the unjustly treated Johnny is therefore complete. In the final shot the train accidentally takes him away, establishing that he is not in control. The dilemma is set and we know, first, he must regain control, second, he must prove to be a hero and, third, he must gain the love of Annabelle.

This sequence, although not cinematically complex, shows a strong sense of narrative and **identification** and is **economically presented**. All elements are used to develop our knowledge of the narrative, including the use of **mise-en-scéne** (the photographs), Keaton's body language, framing of shots and the continuity of editing. There even appears to be a **modernist** editing with a false cut. Although we cannot assume that the contemporary audience would read all into the sequence that we have done, any more than a modern audience would, to make sense of the sequence does presume an understanding of film language. It is also a 'self-contained text' in that it is possible to understand the film without any previous knowledge of, for instance, the American Civil War. This contrasts to Méliès tableaux films like *Ali Baba* which do not make sense without a pre-knowledge of the narrative.

CINEMATIC CODES

With the addition of sound to film in 1927, the 'message' coming from film was relatively complete – strange experiments like 'sensorama' or the 'smellies' not withstanding. In normal film viewing we experience simultaneously a number of codes: visual, sound and the codes controlling the linking of one sound or image to another. The division of the components we use in reading film are relatively arbitrary, but it will help in analysis to theoretically separate them.

MISE-EN-SCÈNE

This term derived from the French, literally 'having been put into the scene', is used to describe those visual aspects that appear within a single shot. The term has been used

identification

The process of identification allows us to place ourselves in the position of particular characters, either throughout or at specific moments in a movie. The devices involved include subjectivity of viewpoint (we see the world through their eyes, a shared knowledge, we know what and only what they know), and a sharing in their moral world, largely through narrative construction.

economic presentation

All the components are designed to help us read the narrative. An examination of the first few minutes of almost any mainstream fictional film will reveal a considerable amount of information about characters, their social situation and their motivation.

modernist

Any device which undercuts the invisible telling of the story. A modernist device draws attention to itself and makes us aware of the construction of the narrative. It would be unclear in this instance whether the device is a consciously modernist one or a primitive one which unconsciously draws attention to itself.

differently by writers about film – some limiting it to those elements that are needed by the camera – objects, movements, lighting, shadow, colour and so on – while others have included the art of recording itself, the focusing of shots and the movement of the camera. In the former sense mise-en-scène is limited to some kind of 'pro-filmic event'; those elements that are there before we start filming. In documentary films such events are perceived to have a 'real world' existence and hence appear not to be 'encoded', or at any rate only coded to the extent that the elements in the real world are. For instance, we may only expect certain categories of people with appropriate dress to be found in a hospital theatre. Not surprisingly, early cinema either used pre-existing events – the workers leaving a factory[14] – or alternatively it constructed events, such as the early boxing scenes used by Edison in his Kinetoscope showings. Subsequent developments involved the use of theatrical performance, vaudeville turns, even performances of plays, albeit silent and much condensed. This history, however, reinforced a 'common-sense' notion that filming was solely the recording of reality or theatrical performance.

The concept of mise-en-scène was developed by those theorists interested in issues of authorship, in the role of participants, and particularly directors in constructing the meaning of film.[15] During the classic period of the Hollywood studio the control of the director was limited to those processes that were recorded during shooting. The overall narrative was clearly established, and the script would be written before the director was even engaged.

Similarly the editing of the film, and the post-dubbing of the soundtrack, were taken out of the control of the director, sometimes involving a re-cut to meet the needs of the studio, or the responses of an audience at a preview. It was therefore the capacity to control what happened on the set, and the way this was recorded by the camera, which was the sign of filmic art as displayed by the director. The quality of a director's work could be read through his style, his control over the mise-en-scène.

SETTING

In the context of studio shooting, the predominant form in the 1920s–1940s, all elements in front of the camera were controlled and chosen; even if sometimes the director took over a set, already existing on the back-lot, an inheritance maybe from a more highly budgeted film. While settings are usually perceived as a signifier of authenticity, the place where the events are happening, they are nevertheless a constructed setting for action. This becomes clear if we examine the different 'look' of the West in films such as *Shane, My Darling Clementine*, and *Johnny Guitar, A Fistful of Dollars* and *The Unforgiven*. Although each of these is recognisable as 'the West', they emphasise different kinds of settings: the wilderness, the small town and the large ranch.

Most viewers have no concept of the nature of the historic West against which the images the films are to be judged, although films have been defined as more realistic at particular moments in time. The landscape and settings of a western are probably better read against the conventions of the western.

Jim Kitses in *Horizons West*[16] describes the western in terms of the opposing focus of wilderness and civilisation, 'the contrasting images of Garden and Desert'. These oppositions permeate through the themes of the western, the definition of characters and the status of particular settings and locations. The Starrett homestead in George Stevens' *Shane* is presented as an isolated place, overlooked on one side by the mountains, from where Shane comes and where he goes, with the town, a scene of danger and evil, on the other.

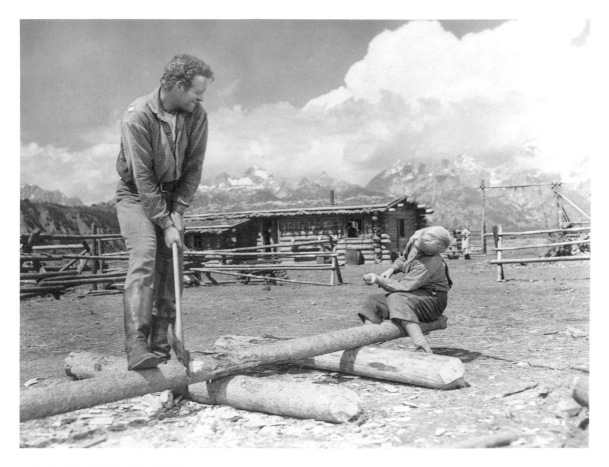

• Plate 4.3 *Shane* (George Stevens, US 1953)
A romantic view of the west

The setting can also function to place the performers. In *The Cabinet of Doctor Caligari* the characters are enclosed in a two-dimensional set, with expressionist 'lighting' pointed over the backdrop and the stage. The setting constantly suggests danger and paranoia which is revealed, at the end of the film, to be a relocation of the interior world inhabited by the 'crazy' narrator. Similarly in Frank Capra's *It's a Wonderful Life*, George Bailey (James Stewart), on the point of suicide, is taken by his guardian angel away from the middle American world, where he has grown up with its model estate that he has helped to build, to a neon-lit 'modernist' rebuilt town which would have existed but for his help. Similarly, in *Blade Runner* Ridley Scott invents a futurist location that does not exist anywhere – a dystopia[17] that we can recognise, possibly as much from other films as from extensions of a contemporary inner-city location.

Locations can not only be recognised and help us to place the characters within a film, but can also through the film itself create their own space and meaning. In Douglas Sirk's *All that Heaven Allows*, the principal action takes place in a family house, lived in by a family whose father is dead before the film begins. While we learn little directly

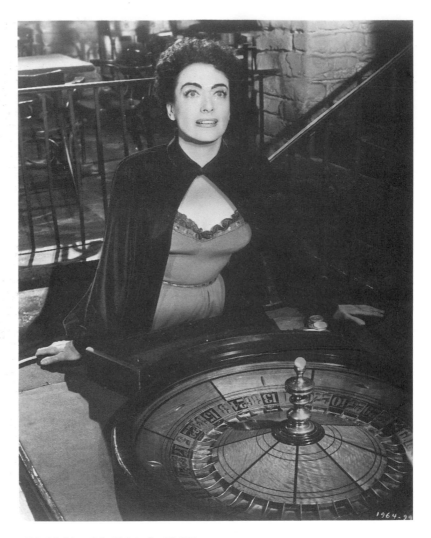

• Plate 4.4 *Johnny Guitar* (Nicholas Ray, US 1954)
A darker view of the west

about this man, his presence lives on in the house, his trophies over the mantelpiece. The house with its oppressive lighting becomes almost the 'tomb' in which his widow – Cary (Jane Wyman) – is obliged to live out the rest of her life. The main room is divided up by screens. These divide Cary from her children, and particularly the son. Throughout the film he resists any attempt to change the house from the way it was when the father lived, and most particularly resents the presence of other men in the house. However, after he decides to leave it is the house, and the implied memory of the father, that 'gets in the way' of a new relationship with his mother.

• Plate 4.5 *All that Heaven Allows* (Douglas Sirk, US 1956)
The father still dominates the home even after his death

PROPS

Films are also dependent on 'props' as a device for conveying meaning. In a familiar
sense, props are definers of genre – particularly weapons in 'action' genres, or the arcane
paraphernalia of the horror films – garlic and crosses. However, props can also become
unique signifiers of meaning in a particular film. While all scenes are constructed around
a number of props – to make the sequence 'look right' – by the use of close-up, and
dialogue, our attention can be drawn to particular objects. This in itself suggests the
significance of particular objects – we know that such objects will be of importance in
the narrative. In Hitchcock's *Strangers on a Train* a lighter changes hands from Guy, the
'innocent' tennis player, with a wife he would rather be rid of, to Bruno, the plausible
psychotic whom he meets on the train. The lighter is decorated with crossed tennis
rackets, and the initials of Guy and his lover. The crossed rackets signify a number of

• Plate 4.6 *Strangers on a Train* (Alfred Hitchcock, US 1951)
A significant icon

'crossings' within the movie, the initial 'crossed lovers', the offer of an exchange of murders by Bruno, the choices offered to Guy in the initial exchange, and so on. However, the lighter remains the significant 'icon' throughout the movie; it represents Bruno's threat to expose Guy if he does not keep his side of the bargain, its temporary loss delays Bruno's attempt to frame Guy, and its presence in the dying Bruno's hand at the end of the movie releases Guy from the hold that is upon him.

Props can also be used to 'anchor'[18] characters into particular meanings. In the complexities of possible ways in which an individual character may be read an object may be used to clarify meaning. While Hannibal Lector in *Silence of the Lambs* may appear increasingly civilised, even charming, in relation to his fellow inmates and guards, the danger from his mouth, whether in terms of his speech or more obviously in his capacity to bite, is exemplified by the face guard placed over him when he is being transported. The significance of this guard is that it denies the viewer full access to him in the way that we are permitted in the earlier exchanges through the reinforced glass.

In *Godfather 1* the entire film is suffused with props relating to family life. At the key moment when the Corleone family 'go to the mattresses' to prepare for the shoot out, the domestic world, exemplified by the cooking of a pasta sauce, is taken over by the men, exemplifying the contradiction of these family-centred and very traditional men who are prepared to murder to preserve family honour.

COSTUME

Costume is a variant of the prop, but of course tightly connected to character. Minor characters are often primarily identified on the basis of costume, which uses the codes of everyday life, such as uniforms, or the cinematic codes, say the wearing of white and black, to signify virtue and villainy in the early westerns. Subtle changes in the costume of a single character can be used to signify changes of status, attitude and even the passing of time. In many 1930s gangster movies such as *The Roaring 'Twenties* and *Scarface*, the rise of the gangster, and his increasing separation both from his roots or from 'acceptable society', are exemplified by a change into clothes that are signifiers of affluence, if not taste. In *Mildred Pierce* we see the process in reverse. Our initial viewing of Mildred Pierce is as a smart, rich and powerful woman in a fur coat. In the first flashback we are introduced to the same character wearing an apron, in a clearly suburban domestic setting. We are presented with an 'after and before', raising for us not only the dominant issue of the storyline at the moment – who killed Mildred's husband – but also the more complex issue of how this transformation has taken place.

Costume can also be used to signify mismatches. We bring to a costume a series of expectations, which are then subverted by the action. The 'false policeman' is regularly used as a plot device – either simply a robbery device, as in *The Wrong Arm of the Law*, or alternatively in films such as *The Godfather* where police act or speak in ways that we deem to be inappropriate.

A further example of mismatch is cross-dressing, usually a male in female clothing. Normally such devices are humorous: *Some Like it Hot* and *Tootsie*, where our expectations of appropriate behaviour and that of the male characters in the film, given the signifying props, are a mismatch with our knowledge of the gender of the character. In *The Crying Game* our knowledge is at least problematic, and the mismatch only appears retrospectively.

In *Desperately Seeking Susan*, rather than using a uniform, Roberta, a suburban housewife with aspirations to a more exciting lifestyle, acquires a jacket belonging to Susan, a woman with bohemian and underworld connections. This distinctive jacket, allegedly previously worn by Jimi Hendrix, allows Roberta to be 'misread' by other characters as Susan, but equally allows the viewer to place her in her aspirational world.

PERFORMANCE AND MOVEMENT

Probably the richest source of mise-en-scène is the performance of actors. While there is more to consider in performance, it may help to consider the performer – whether human or animal – as an object for the cameras' gaze. As with costume there is a strong coded element in the facial expressions and body positions held by performers. These codes, broadly referred to as 'body language', are of course part of everyday life. While there are cultural and temporal variations in body language, due to our familiarity

• Plate 4.7 *Mildred Pierce* (Michael Curtiz, US 1945)
Joan Crawford translated from housewife (above) to businesswoman (right)

with Hollywood the body language of American film has become almost universally understood. Indeed one of the consequences of the spread of film has been the global penetration of particular aspects of language such as the 'thumbs up' sign.

The presentation of characters by actors using body language is a key element in the creation of a 'performance'. It is perhaps significant that the much-vaunted performances of recent years – Dustin Hoffman in *Rain Man*, Tom Hanks in *Forrest Gump* – have been characterised by bodily styles, conventionally associated with marginal figures in society. Again body movements can be used to express both change of emotion and change of time. In *Citizen Kane*, the decline of Kane can be identified from the animated young man to the almost robotic, lumbering figure who smashes up his second wife's room when she threatens to leave him.

While early film was often dependent on the kind of exaggerated body movements that in the theatre were recognisable from the upper gallery, with the development of the close-up, meaning can often be expressed by the slightest movement, whether the

• Plate 4.8 *Mildred Pierce* (Michael Curtiz, US 1945)

wringing of hands in D.W. Griffith's *Intolerance* or the maintenance of facial expressions to be observed in almost any contemporary film. In an acting master-class, Michael Caine, that most minimalist of screen actors, ably demonstrates what can be conveyed by the flickering of the eye, the raising of the eyebrows or the turning of the lip.

Finally, and briefly, the performer, and particularly the 'star' brings to the film a meaning derived merely from their presence. While some performers such as Jennifer Jason Leigh deliberately appear to present themselves differently in the films that they make, the majority operate with a high degree of consistency both in terms of appearance and type, a consistency which will usually be reinforced in terms of non-filmic appearances. As such, stars will bring in with them a level of expectation and an implied meaning from their previous films. This becomes obvious when performers attempt to take parts that move away from type, often with disastrous effect at the box office. It may be useful therefore to consider the (known) performer as part of the language of film, having a meaning that can be stretched and reused, but only to a limited extent.

'PUTTING INTO THE SCENE'

Having assembled other components of our shots, the next procedure involves a process of recording these elements. However, such a distinction between content and form is an artificial one, in that we have already had to have recourse to concepts of close-up in order to describe individual constituents. Nevertheless, it is helpful to separate the processes, and hence those codes that characterise them from the codes of the objects themselves. While the latter are related to wider cultural artefacts and the meanings they have – like the meanings of ways of dressing – the former can be either perceived as strictly cinematic codes, or at any rate strongly related to the codes of other representational forms, painting, drawing and of course photography.

LIGHTING

Lighting of film is the first of the 'invisible' codes of cinema. While there are apparent sources of light within a shot, the lighting of a shot is off camera, and even with an outside location is used to guarantee that the light level is adequate both to produce a sufficient level for recording and also to highlight particular aspects of the image. This activity is not separate from the shooting of the film, but is integral to it – and hence the term 'lighting cameraman', which is applied to the principal operator within the camera crew.

Whereas early cinema relied on a relatively flat field of action, with the development of faster film stock it became possible and indeed desirable to establish a source of depth in the action. This, coupled with a small aperture lens, has enabled the camera to record over a number of fields of action. The French theorist André Bazin[19] argued that such a form of shooting was both more 'realist' in the sense that the shots closely resemble the capacity of the eye to recognise objects across a wide depth (or at least to rapidly adjust focus to do so) and also more 'dramatic' in allowing the viewer the capacity to choose, within a given shot, where to direct attention. In practice, deep focus shots and, in particular, a number of shots in *Citizen Kane*, such as the attempted suicide of Susanne Alexander, with a close-up of the sleeping draught and the distance shot of Kane breaking in through the door, allow little choice of attention. The planes of action are immediately joined as Kane rushes to the bed.

Lighting involves choices of level and direction of light. Classic Hollywood lighting involves a strong level of lighting on the main objects of a shot with fill lighting designed to eliminate shadows. The set is then back lit to enable those elements at the front of the set to be distanced from that which appears at the back, to give an illusion of diversion. However, lighting is also characterised by its absence.

Light and shade can be used to direct our attention to a particular part of the frame. This is most usually done by the movement of characters through a variously lit set. A more dramatic variant can be seen in Sergio Leone's *Once Upon a Time in the West*. In an early scene in the trading post a mysterious character, 'Harmonica' (Charles Bronson), is identified as present only through his characteristic theme music. He is dramatically exposed by 'Cheyenne' (Jason Robards) who propels an oil lamp on a horizontal wire across the room, producing a **low-key image** of Harmonica. This, the first meeting of these characters, who maintain an ambiguous relationship to one another, is both sudden, the characters revealed from out of the dark, and is followed by the flashing on and off of the light as a 'consequence' of the swinging of the oil lamp.

Sometimes, however, lighting can be used as a characteristic of the style of a whole film or over a number of scenes – rather than just a specific light to light a specific

low-key image

Light from a single source producing light and shade.

set. The classic realist film is usually characterised by a full lighting effect – high key lighting – seemingly as a device to ensure that we see all the money that has been spent on constructing the effect. However, widespread use of shadows can be used to convey their own meaning. The use of reflective light scenes, and the often apparently dominant use of shadows, originated in German Expressionist cinema, but was incorporated into a Hollywood style of lighting in the 1940s and 1950s which later became known as **film noir**. This was largely to be found in films within the detective/thriller genre, and was characterised by a world of threat and danger, but also one where characters' motivations were hidden from one another, and by implication from the viewer. Lighting effects usually appear to be 'motivated', in that they come from sources, like table lamps, that are in the shot. In an early scene in *Mildred Pierce*, the leading character Mildred 'frames' an old acquaintance Wally for a murder that she appears to have committed. The scene commences in a nightclub where the low level of lighting together with Mildred's wide-brimmed hat creates shots in which the face is half in shadow, with the eyes in particular in darkness. Later, returning to the beach house, where the murder was committed, the interior is a kaleidoscope of lighting from the low table lights and the seeming dappled effect on the ceiling which is implicitly caused by reflections from the sea. It is within this scene that Wally is apparently trapped by the shadows that cut across him at every turn. The style of film noir is one of few formal characteristics that have come to be widely recognised, and indeed it survives into contemporary films such as John Dahl's *The Last Seduction*. This perhaps can be in part explained through its seeming difference from the visual effects of realist film, usually fully 'high key' lighting and its connection with a particular genre. The style of film noir is linked in an obvious way with themes of paranoia and alienation and other characteristics such as *femme fatale*, a woman who is not what she immediately appears to be. In this instance the use of lighting enables the knowing viewer to be one step ahead of the protagonists within the film.

CAMERA AND CAMERA MOVEMENT

Having created the pro-filmic event and lit it, the next set of choices surround the positioning of the camera. Early cinema was largely characterised by a steadily held camera, at least as steady as hand-cranking permitted, and by the predominant use of the long shot incorporating all the action. Technological developments up to the Steadicam, permitted greater flexibility and choice, both of movement and angle, as well as offering the option of different ratios with the variety of wide scene formats operating since the 1950s. This 'progression' has not necessarily been continuous, particularly at the point of the introduction of sound when the cameras were initially installed within sound-proofed booths. However, the 'language' of the camera had to be both developed by film-makers and 'learnt' by the audience.

Drawing primarily from the already existing art forms of photography and theatre, the camera was held static, with movement being derived from the actors in front of a scene. The camera was placed in the 'best seat in the stalls', square on to the action, with actors moving in and out of the shot as if from the 'wings'. The development of alternative camera positions and movements evolved in the first decade of the century. Probably the best introduction to this process and its effects can be gleaned from Noel Burch's *Correction Please* which combines early cinematic footage with a period narrative, progressively filmed using a range of methods. Within the capacities of focus the camera is able to move anywhere from the extreme close-up to the use of wide-screen

film noir

A term developed by French film critics in the postwar period to describe a number of films produced in the 1940s. It has subsequently become a marketing device used to describe films with some of the lighting and narrative conventions of the period.

• Plate 4.9 *The Last Seduction* (John Dahl, US 1994)
The style of film noir survives in contemporary films

shots limited to pairs of eyes, as in the final shoot-out in *Once Upon a Time in the West*, to the extreme long-shot of the field hospital in *Gone with the Wind*. The close-up has a particular place in the development of film, however, permitting us to 'know intimately' the faces of leading characters, and hence by implication to read their thoughts and feelings. This operates without needing to use either the knowing subtitle of the early cinema, or even the voice of the narrator to take us into the character.

It is also necessary to decide on the angle of the shot[20] and the relative height of the camera to the object being filmed – a low-angle shot looking up to the object or a high-angle shot looking down. Conventional accounts suggest that low-angle shots imply the power of the object – usually a human figure – and a high-angle shot its weakness. Such a rule can be seen to operate in many exchanges between characters – such as those between Kane and Suzanne Alexander in *Citizen Kane*, as she pieces together her jigsaw puzzle and he looks down on her. However, such rules cannot be applied to read off automatically the meaning of an individual shot. After the assault by the birds on the Brenner household in Hitchcock's *The Birds*, there is a tracking shot of the three members of the family taken from a very low angle. The suggestion is of their dominance; the birds have indeed disappeared, yet the anxious look on their faces and their isolation from one another suggest an alternative meaning. Our experience throughout the film suggests that danger comes from above – and indeed we are soon to discover that the birds have broken into the house and are waiting in an upstairs room.

While the camera is normally held level, it can also be tilted to one side. Such a shot is read as an indication of instability, that either of the characters, or of the situation that the shot is recording. In an early scene in Nicholas Ray's *Rebel Without a Cause* there are a series of shots on the staircase where James Dean's family are rowing. The shots are sharply tilted – an effect exaggerated by the cinemascope screen.

While shots are classically in sharp focus, a soft focus can be used either to enhance the romantic effect of a scene or alternatively to expose the incapacity of a character to register the world around him.

Finally, the camera is able to move. The earliest moving shots were dependent on the movement of objects – cars or trains – so shots mimic the experience of viewing. Similarly pans (horizontal movements) and tilts appear to reproduce eye movements and are motivated by the action that is occurring. Shots can also be developed to reproduce the movements of the characters within the set, originally using rails, hence the tracking shot, or in a more liberated way using a hand-held or a Steadicam camera, walking the action. These shots give a strong sense of identity and place. For instance, in Scorsese's *Goodfellas*, when Henry displays his power by entering a popular restaurant through a side entrance and impresses both his girlfriend and us, by his capacity to walk through the back passages, and the kitchen, acknowledged only by the most important figures.

While such shots are perceived as naturalistic, and replicate the natural movements of the eye, the use of the crane moves beyond this to display a degree of control by the director of the world of the film. Such shots are in positions and involve movements that are inaccessible to us on a day-to-day basis. Crane shots can take us from the wide panorama of a scene to focus in on the object of our attention. In Hitchcock's *Marnie* a crane shot at a party takes us from Marnie's point of view on the landing above the expansive entrance hall of her husband's mansion to a close-up of her previous employer, Strutt, who has the potential to expose her earlier misdeeds. While this shot bears no relationship to any possible human movement towards Strutt, it reflects the sense of powerlessness and inevitability felt by Marnie at that moment. The crane can also be used to dramatically reveal what has previously been hidden. In *Once Upon a Time in the West* there is a connection between Harmonica and the villain Frank, although this is not known by Frank. Only at the moment of death is this link established. In a flashback, Hormonica is revealed as a boy in close-up, with the camera craning back first to reveal his elder brother standing on his shoulders, and then literally suspended by a noose from a ruined archway in the desert, waiting for the boy to weaken and plunge the brother to his death, and finally Frank laughing. A similar effect is produced in John Carpenter's *Halloween* where, following a lengthy Steadicam shot from behind a mask where the 'camera' searches through a house and discovers and kills two lovers, the mask is removed revealing a small boy. The camera cranes back and upwards stressing both the vulnerability of the child and the judgement of the local community.

While there has been a concentration in the preceding pages on some of the more obvious effects of the camera, the predominant style of Hollywood film-making is the use of a camera which is largely invisible, with a predominance of shots within the medium distance, 'le shot American', using very slight variations from the horizontal shot, and involving limited camera movement, usually motivated by the action or the interest of the characters. Yet every shot is selected from a range of possibilities, even when it continues to appear to be the 'natural', the only, one.

EDITING

Having established the codes contributing to our understanding of the single shot, we can now look at the combination of shots which construct a film flowing over time. While most of the characteristics of film shot are related to codes developed in still photography, the joining of strips of films is specific to cinema, and as such has been seen as the component that is the essence of cinematic art. The Soviet film-maker Lev Kuleshov[21] engaged in a number of 'experiments' linking shots and 'proving' that with adept editing it was possible to create alternative readings of the same facial expression – or to bring together cuts occurring in completely different locations. However, notions of the essential nature of film are certainly unfashionable and probably unhelpful in any attempt to read the meaning into sequences of film.

Historically, the first editing was between scenes, with individual extreme long shots recording a self-contained sequence at a particular time and place followed by a cut to black. This device, drawing on the theatrical black-out, could easily be read by the early audiences, although for a contemporary audience a pre-existing knowledge of the story-line seems necessary in order to understand the narrative flow (see pp. 115–16). In the first twenty years of cinema a 'vocabulary' of linking devices between scenes was established and largely attributed to D.W. Griffith. In particular, this involved the distinction between 'slower' devices: the fade to and from black and the dissolve between the image and the cut. While the fade implied a change of scene and the change of time, the cut was used within a scene or, in the case of cross-cut[22] editing, signified that two events although separated by space were happening simultaneously. This device was used particularly by Griffith to build up suspense in the rescue scene in *The Birth of a Nation*. Other devices such as the 'wipe', 'push off', the 'turn over', while popular in the 1920s and revised as a relatively simple technique of the TV vision mixer, have largely been reduced to comic effects. The revival of linking devices by French New Wave directors such as Truffaut in *Tirez sur la pianiste* extended the use of the devices, in particular the use of the dissolve within a sequence to suggest the passing of time. The fade to black, which after time becomes almost an invisible device, was replaced by a dissolve to white, drawing attention to the uncertain status of the narrative in *Last Year in Marienbad*, and to other colours with specific emotional readings. However, the inventiveness of the New Wave directors, far from creating a universal language of the linking device, gave a number of alternative readings that had to be anchored through the mise-en-scène. The passing of time, for instance, would normally be doubly signified by use of mise-en-scène, the movement of characters, facial expressions, consumption of food and drink or even the movement of the hands of the clock. New Wave directors felt free to ignore these conventions if the viewer was able to identify the passing of time through what was happening in the narrative.

While the linking devices described above have the function of signifying to the viewer the discontinuity of the action – the change of time and place – the major development in film editing has been to minimise the sense of disruption. Unlike studio TV, film is shot with considerable breaks, with changes of set, positioning and lighting. As a consequence film-makers are rarely able to record more than two–three minutes of usable stock in the course of a full working day. Those separate shots designed to be in the 'ideal' viewing place, for instance, a close-up on the speaker, have the potential to disrupt the viewers' attention. A system of conventions governing editing developed in the first two decades of cinema (although there were some changes following the introduction of sound) and these have become known as the 'rules of continuity editing'. A full account can be found in Karl Reisz and Gavin Millar's *The Technique of Film Editing*, but also can be traced in any beginner's guide to film editing. The intention of the rules is to produce a system to tell a story in such a way as to set out the action of the narrative and its position in space and time so that it is clear to the viewer, but also unobtrusive. In particular, the storytelling should do nothing to draw attention to itself, the apparatus of cinema, in the physical sense of equipment, but also so that strategies employed should appear to be 'transparent' to the viewers, in the sense that they would not be aware of their existence.

These rules can be briefly summarised as follows. A scene will normally start with an 'establishing shot', a long shot which enables the spectator to orientate her- or himself to the space of the scene, the position of the performers and objects, as well as reorientating from the previous scene with a different space. All subsequent shots can therefore be 'read' within the space already established. Such a shot, a 'master shot', can of course be reintroduced in particular moments in the scene, whether to re-establish the space or to show significant movements of characters.

The 180° rule involves an imaginary line along the action of the scene, between actors involved in a conversation or the direction of a chase. The 'rule' dictates that this line should be clearly established and that consecutive shots should not be taken from opposite sides of the line. The consequence of this is the establishment of a common background space (either implicitly or explicitly) in static shots, and a clarity of direction of movement when, for instance, characters are running towards or away from one another. An extension of this is the principle of the 'eye-line match'. A shot of a scene looking at something off-screen is then followed by the object or person being looked at. Neither shot includes the viewer and the object, but on the basis of the established space we presume their relationship.

The 30° rule proposes that a successive shot on the same area involves at least a 30° change of angle, or at any rate a substantial change of viewpoint. Although this involves a reorientation for the viewer, it does not involve the noticeable 'jump' of objects on the screen, which would produce a 'jump-cut'. Again assuming the establishment of the narrative's space the viewer is able to place the action.

Finally, the movement of actors and the reframing of the camera is so arranged and planned that the movement of the camera does not 'draw attention to itself'. This involves, for instance, the cut on action, so that the cut anticipates the movement to be made, a long shot of a character standing up say, or a cut to the person talking. The cut both takes the viewer where she/he as reader of the narrative wishes to be, and implies the control of the film-maker over the narrative. The cut appears to be 'motivated' by the need to tell the story.

This style of editing, including as it does decisions on the placement of camera and characters, is integral to the Hollywood classical realist text, a film that 'effaces all signs of the text's production and the achievement of a invisibility of process'. As such it is very hard to cite examples of the operation of the rules, or indeed to be aware of them when they are happening, although there is a full account of a scene in the *Maltese Falcon* in Bordwell and Thompson's *Film Art*.[23] However, we are made aware of these conventions when they are broken or in any way subverted. It is not unusual to commence a sequence with a close-up. In the post-sequence scene in Scorsese's *Goodfellas* we have an extreme close-up of the adolescent Henry before the reverse shot and pan reveals the gangsters across the road as the object of his gaze. Henry's voice-over stresses this boy's eye view of the action, 'They were able to stay up all night playing cards', rather than an objective narrative viewpoint. The initial close-up thus reinforces the subjective reading of the action before it is presented to us. The 180° was perhaps most forcibly broken in John Ford's *Stagecoach* as the Indians attack the coach, seemingly riding from both directions. However, the strength of the narrative line, and the clear visual distinction between the Indians and the cavalry present us with no problems in identifying narrative space. In *Who's That Knocking at My Door?*,[24] the concluding dialogue between Harvey Keitel and Zina Bethune, the breaking of an 'impossible' relationship, again breaks the 180° rule as the camera plays on the invisible line. The effort is disturbing, but only reflects the concern we have about how to 'place' ourselves emotionally in the sequence. The jump-cut was used widely by the French New Wave directors, notably Jean-Luc Godard in *A Bout de souffle*. The device used within conversations and during car journeys has the consequence of producing an ellipsis – the reduction of time spent on a sequence. Such a process is a necessary part of feature film narrative – films rarely operate in 'real time', equating the time of the action with what we see on the screen. However, the usual form of continuity editing hides this process by making the sequences within say a car journey appear continuous. It is not that Godard's use of the jump-cut makes the film's narrative incomprehensible, – but rather it draws attention to the process of selection that has taken place.

While continuity editing dominates classic narrative, other strategies have been used – and were perhaps more formally developed in the silent era before the requirements of continuity in both sound and image restricted, at least temporarily, the expressive-ness of successive images. The 'montage' sequence entailed a number of shots over a period of time to demonstrate a process of change. In *Citizen Kane*, the disintegration of Kane's first marriage is shown in a scene of breakfast, with the couple eating in silence hiding behind rival newspapers. A similar device is used in *The Godfather* where a sequence of killings occurs in different locations, while the baptism of Michael Corleone's child is taking place. In the sequence the soundtrack of the church service is held over the images, not only contrasting the pious words of the protagonists with their actions, but also establishing the contemporaneity of the action.

An alternative form of editing is the so-called 'non-diegetic insert'[25] which involves a symbolic shot not involved with the time and place of the narrative to comment or express the action in some alternative way. Eisenstein in *Strike* uses the image of a bull in a slaughterhouse to represent the killing of strikers by the mounted soldiers. The primacy of realist narrative has made this kind of device less prevalent in 'Hollywood'[26] cinema, although such coded inserts proved useful as devices to circumscribe censor-ship in earlier eras. Hitchcock used the clichéd train entering the tunnel as an expression of the consummation of Roger Thornhill's marriage at the end of *North by North West*. The irony, however, is that they are on the train and the shot is an expression of narra-tive space. In *Goodbye Columbus*, the 'seduction' of the daughter in the attic is similarly expressed by an abrupt cut to the carving of roast meat at the family lunch.

The cutting of film stock can also be expressive in itself. While the speed of cutting appears, particularly in dialogue sequences, to be determined by the pro-filmic event, the meaning of action sequences can be determined by editing. The length of a shot is in part determined by the amount of information within it. However, rapid or slow cutting can convey meaning in itself. Rapid cutting reflects the degree of excitement with a sequence, and cutting speeds can be accelerated to convey mood, so that the viewing of individual shots becomes almost subliminal. Perhaps most famously, the *Psycho* shower scene exemplifies the use of rapid and highly fragmented images to present a climactic moment. The viewer, including the original American film censor, may often claim to see things that were not originally there.

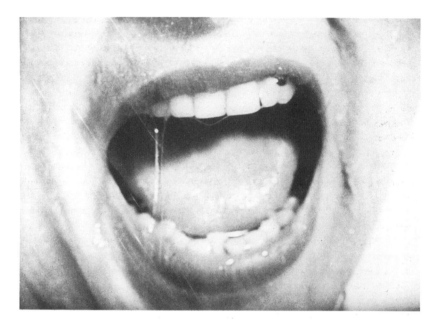

• Plate 4.10 *Psycho* (Alfred Hitchcock, US 1960)
Highly fragmented images

SOUND

The final element in constructing the 'image' of a film is the soundtrack. Sound as an integral part of a film only developed after 1927. While films were rarely seen in silence (they were sometimes accompanied by a speaker, a piano, organ or small orchestra) the nature of the sound was rarely in the control of the originators of the film and certainly not for all showings of the film. Unlike other innovations, colour and wide screen for instance, sound, once introduced, became a virtually universal format in a very short period of time. Ed Buscombe argues that the speed of this innovation arose from the need for a more realistic narrative. Certainly, while Warner Brothers saw music as being the appealing part of sound, it was the talking element that attracted the first audiences. The role of the soundtrack was seen as one of reproducing the sounds that would normally be associated with the images, whether the unenunciated words in almost any 'silent movie' or the silent but ringing alarm in Porter's *Life of an American Fireman*. In this sense sound is perceived as diegetic, arising from objects in a scene either inside the frame, or logically related outside the frame – say for instance, the sound of knocking on a door heard within a house.

However, it would be unwise to assume that a soundtrack can merely be read off from the visual image. Soundtracks are equally 'sound images', constructed and selected in much the same way as the visual image is created. Components on the soundtrack may be simulated at the moment of shooting, but rarely except in a documentary is the soundtrack laid down at the same time. With the development of sound mixing the quality of the track is constructed over a period of time, whether the sound is diegetic or a music track laid over the top of it. A visual image tends to be simplified, Bazin's theory of deep focus notwithstanding – the eye tends to take in different aspects of the image sequen-tially, whether within or between shots. The ear, by contrast, is able to absorb a number of distinct sound sources simultaneously. Early sound films tended to display a relatively unilateral soundtrack – with dialogue, sound effects and music operating successively. Sound effects, in particular, were only included because they were integral to the narrative (in much the same way as visual effects). By the 1960s, Robert Altman, in particular, was developing soundtracks using the mixing devices available for music sound recording to produce dialogue where individuals interrupted or spoke over other actors (overlapping dialogue), but which also used locations such as the mess-hall in *MASH*, where conver-sations could be picked up apparently at random. The logical extension of this were sequences in *Pret-à-Porter*, when, using multi-camera and microphones, the sound and image appear to be collected almost randomly on the set.

Sound can be used to reinforce the continuity of the action. While the image is frag-mented by the cuts from one shot to another which we 'know' can hide temporal ellipsis, a character not shown crossing a room for instance, an unbroken soundtrack signifies a continuity of time. This is perhaps best illustrated by an example that deceives the spectator. In an early scene in Scorsese's *Mean Streets*, Charlie (Harvey Keitel) climbs on the stage to perform with an exotic dancer. The soundtrack playing the Rolling Stones' 'Tell me, (you're coming back)' appears to be running continuously, and yet Charlie appears in consecutive shots to be on the stage and then to be in the audience viewing the dancer, thus challenging the 'reality status' of one of the shots. Our understanding of the narrative certainly suggests on subsequent viewings that the first part is Charlie's fantasy.

Sound also has a continuity role in establishing links across scenes. Orson Welles, draw-ing from his radio experience, used sound to bridge between sequences. In *Citizen Kane*, Welles uses Thatcher's 'Merry Christmas' as a bridge between Kane's boyhood greeting and adulthood. Such extravagant devices do not, however, disguise transitions in the way of continuity editing, but rather celebrate it. More commonly soundtracks marginally precede the visual image as a preparation for what we are about to see. Sound can also access experiences not immediately evident to the viewer. In *Psycho*, Marion Crane 'remembers', while driving along, the demands of her boss to deposit the money which she has purloined. More problematically she also 'hears' the discovery of the theft of the money and the reaction of her boss and the man she has robbed. The latter sound must at the moment of hearing be a projection of the sound which she could not in reality possibly hear, as she dies before the office is opened.

Sound can also be used to direct us into the past through the use of the voice-over as in *Mildred Pierce*, where Mildred takes us back on three occasions as part of her confession in the police station. Voice-overs, while seemingly a useful device to accel-erate storytelling, to comment on the action and to admit us into the thoughts of the protagonists in the way of a novelist, are rarely used in feature films and even then sparingly. A flashback sequence once introduced is normally allowed to return to a conventional mode in which the visual narrative is dominant. Martin Scorsese maintains a voice-over throughout *Goodfellas*, in keeping with its presentation as a 'true life' filmic representation of the life of a sub-Mafia wise guy. Yet the voice-over narrative appears often to be contradicted by the visual narrative, at the very least suggesting Henry's explanation and indeed control of the narrative is partial. At one stage he even loses control of the voice-over, which is taken over by his wife.

A predominant form of sound, and indeed the original function of soundtracks, is the use of non-diegetic music. Primarily music is used to inform the audience of appropriate emotional responses or, having established a response, to enhance it. The emotional pull of music and its high level of connotative meaning allow these processes to operate almost subliminally. While the impact of the *Psycho* shower scene can be attributed to the rapid cutting described on pp. 108–9, it can equally be attributed to Bernard Hornmann's 'shrieking strings', not least because they are a magnified reprise of Marion Crane's growing hysteria as she drives the car in the heavy rain. With the general denial of the use of voice-over to provide 'inner thoughts', and given the stress on the surface reality of the classic realist film, music appears to give us direct access to the emotions of the characters.

Music also plays the role of 'confirming' the emotional response of the spectator, seemingly leading us to a particular way of seeing a sequence, or at any rate editing a 'preferred reading' of the image. As such it can be seen as a way of anchoring meaning, eliminating ambiguities of response. In this sense music is often seen to be a final track. Indeed the adding of the sound on to a pre-existing image and diagetic soundtrack, whether Miles Davis improvising to *Lift to the Scaffold* or a 'classical' orchestra playing a carefully choreographed score, is the more common method of construction. However, music, whether the final soundtrack or similar music, may be used at the editing state as a rhythmic device to inform the pace of the cutting. Sergio Leone describes the cast and crew of *Once Upon a Time in the West*, 'throughout the shooting schedules, listening to the recording [Morricone's score] acting with the music, following its rhythms and suffering its aggravating qualities, which grind the nerve'.

Sound effects are normally perceived as part of the narrative realism, authenticating the images and informing the narrative attention. At the beginning of *Mildred Pierce* we hear the gunshots while viewing the exterior of the beach house, only to cut to the consequential dying body of the victim. The denial of the image of the murderer, either at the moment of shooting or the subsequent reaction shot, is a key to the remaining narrative when the murderer is revealed. Increasingly, sound effects have come to be used to evoke mood. Peripheral sound can be used to establish the wider environment. Hospital or police precinct movies will normally feature telephone rings, not as a cue to the protagonist lifting the receiver and furthering the narrative, but to create other unseen and unrecorded narratives occurring at the same time, or simply to invoke the busyness of the location. David Lynch in *Eraserhead* extends this to a non-specific industrial background sound, permeating a number of interior domestic scenes and establishing without elaborate visual images the quality of the environment. The distinction between non-diagetic music and sound effects can become blurred with the electronic production of both. At the beginning of *Nightmare on Elm Street* we are presented with a dream sequence involving a chase among the furnaces. What sounds to be modernist horror film mood music also includes human sighs, muffled screams and the mechanical sounds relating to the working of furnaces, all integrated into a seamless music/soundtrack, and only loosely linked to the visual images.

Music may also be used to identify character, for example, themes associated with particular performers in *Once Upon a Time in the West* and *Dr Zhivago*, locations and time. In *Goodfellas*, Scorsese uses an elaborate soundtack with some forty-two tracks, a mixture of American commercial ballads and rock music, Italian opera and traditional songs. The music is used to contrast the Italian-American from the American-Italian and to identify age distinctions between the protagonists. It is also used to delineate the time of the action in a movie telling a story with a twenty-five year time span, but using only limited changes in the appearance of the characters.

NARRATIVE

Throughout our consideration of the components and coding that make up film, there has been explicit the idea of a **narrative**; that films have a primary function of telling a story. The images are organised and are made sense of around this function. This is particularly true of the feature film, which is developed, given a 'treatment' in terms of its plot line, and this is perceived as being what a film is 'about'. However, documentaries and TV news 'stories' show many characteristics of film narrative. Equally the cinema has often drawn its plots and, to some extent, its storytelling strategies from literature, most notably the novel. Work on film narrative has therefore often drawn from work on other media, notably literary criticism expressing an interest in the similarities and differences in the ways stories are told in various media.

At the simplest level, narrative analysis is concerned with the extent to which those things that we see make sense. It is assumed that those elements that we see cohere in some way, that they are part of a whole. While all elements of an image will not be of equal importance, and indeed one aspect of the detection narrative is the attempt to determine the important components, the 'clues' as against the 'red herrings', there is a supposition that if a film draws attention to something, it will have a consequence in the development of the story. In *North by Northwest*, Roger Thornhill lights a cigarette for Eve Kendall, using a personalised match-book 'ROT'. The significance of this artefact is marked by a conversation – 'what does the "O" stand for?', 'nothing' – signifying a man with nothing at the centre. Yet at the level of the story – the match-book re-emerges at the end when Thornhill uses the matches to alert Eve of his presence in the villain VanDamm's house. In general terms all that is of significance in the narrative has a subsequent consequence. Narrative develops on the basis of a chain of cause and effect. An event happens and is shown to have (likely) consequences. As experienced film-goers, we learn to expect and anticipate this chain, or any rate to recognise the causal links when they are made. At the simplest level these links are consecutive, the effect from one cause becoming the cause of the next link, as for instance the succession of trials facing Indiana Jones in the search for the holy grail in *Raiders of the Lost Ark*. However, the example from *North by Northwest* illustrates that causal links can operate over a longer period with other plot devices intervening.

Narrative involves the viewer in making sense of what is seen, asking questions of what we see and anticipating the answers. In particular, narrative invites us to ask both what is going to happen next and when and how will it all end. It operates on the tension between our anticipation of likely outcomes drawn from genre conventions and the capacity to surprise or frustrate our expectations. Some sixty minutes into *Dirty Harry* we appear to have the final link of the cause/effect chain as Inspector Callaghan arrests the serial killer Scorpio after a chase across a football field. Yet the force entailed in the arrest becomes, in turn, the cause of Scorpio's release, and the beginning of a new cause and effect chain leading to an apprehension from which Scorpio can never be released.

While film narrative can be viewed as a number of cause and effect links, it may also be perceived in terms of larger structures incorporating the entire film. Todorov sees the start of narrative as a point of stable equilibrium, where everything is satisfied, calm and normal. This is disrupted by some kind of force which creates a state of disequilibrium. It is only possible to re-create equilibrium through action directed against the disruption. However, the consequence of this reaction is to change the world of the narrative and/or the characters so that the final state of equilibrium is not the same as the initial state. Although this analysis is a simplified one, it is a useful starting-point – delineating the differences between individual films or genres.

• Plate 4.11 *Vertigo* (Alfred Hitchcock, US 1958)
A disruptive act

The initial equilibrium state of the film is often very brief, little more than an establishing shot, or at most an establishing sequence. Our expectation of narrative disruption, together with our capacity to 'read' the equilibrium state rapidly, has led to shorter and shorter equilibrium sequences. The beginning of *Jaws* involves a brief scene of teenagers on a beach enjoying a night-time party before two of their number engage in a swim dramatically interrupted by the shark attack. Horror films, in particular, have become increasingly characterised by immediate disruption, as for instance in the dream sequence at the beginning of *Nightmare on Elm Street* referred to on p. 111. Even when they return to a temporary equilibrium, the girl wakes up, this is an unstable state capable of easy disruption. *Vertigo* commences with a particularly disruptive act, a chase across the rooftops, culminating in Scottie's loss of nerve and consequent retirement from the police force. If there is a stable equilibrium state, it is implicit and occurs before the movie begins.

Initial equilibrium states are also particularly unstable in melodrama. It is clear from the beginning of the flashback sequence in *Mildred Pierce*, in effect the beginning of the narrative, that this is not a harmonious family setting, despite the iconography of the mother baking cakes and wearing an apron. The nature of Mildred's relationship with Vida suggests that trouble is in store, quite apart from the somewhat incongruous image of Joan Crawford as a petit bourgeois housewife. As a consequence the seeming cause of the disruption, Bert's decision to leave the family, is in no way an unexpected disruption to a stable state.

Equally in the 'romance' genre, the initial equilibrium is signified by an absence or a 'lack' (of a partner) by one, Richard Gere in *Pretty Woman*, or two, Billy Crystal and Meg Ryan in *When Harry Met Sally*. The initial equilibrium is perceived as integrally unstable to be resolved within the movies, and the 'disruption' involving the first meeting of the characters, usually disharmoniously, in which the misunderstandings of motive are the beginning of the resolution.

Disruptions similarly are variable, although they tend to be genre specific. Action genres are often disrupted by an external threat or raid, for instance the raid of the Indians in *The Searchers*, or the arrival of the vengeful Max Cady in *Cape Fear*. The leading characters may be forced to disrupt their normal lifestyle due to a chance experience – for example, Jack Lemmon and Tony Curtis viewing the St Valentine's Day massacre in *Some Like It Hot*. Within the genres the disruption may be equally important to the characters and their drive towards some particular goal. Travis Bickle in *Taxi Driver* is not so much driven into disequilibrium by external events, his meetings with Betsy, the appearance of Iris and Sport in his cab, as by his determined drive to transform the world.

The actions to restore equilibrium, of course, become the narrative drive of the movie. Such re-equilibrating processes are resisted, whether by the protagonists or by chance events. The pleasure associated with conventional narrative is, at least in part, related to our recognition of the strategies employed to delay the pleasure. Opposition to equilibrium can be attributed to the 'villain', a function within the narrative, and the stronger the 'villain', the greater the pleasure in the triumph of the 'hero'. This will often involve a number of moments where there appears to be a temporary equilibrium – involving the seeming defeat of the hero, the 'cliff-hanger', or more rarely of the villain. Since the 1970s the horror film has developed the temporary equilibrium state of the defeat of the villain at the end of the movie, only for him to reappear in subsequent movies (for example, the Hammer *Dracula* series and *Halloween, Friday 13th*). The struggle to resolve, while usually explicit in say the revenge movie, in other genres may be present and obvious to the viewer, but not to the protagonists. In the romantic comedy (*Bringing up Baby, What's Up Doc, When Harry Met Sally*) the resistance to an early resolution comes from the characters themselves who are unaware of the mutual attraction (of opposites) that is 'obvious' to the viewer.

The final resolution again differs between films. There is a drive towards the 'happy ending' – we assume that Hugh Grant and Andie MacDowell will end *Four Weddings and a Funeral* in domesticity rather than death. Films often end with an 'establishing' long shot which is similar to the one with which they began – even where this involves other characters with no place in the new equilibrium 'riding off into the sunset' (*Shane, The Searchers*). Occasionally such an ending appears ironic, the conflicts within the movie are seen as ultimately unresolvable in the way that conventional narrative demands. At the end of *All that Heaven Allows* a relationship between Rock Hudson and Jane Wyman,

• Plate 4.12 *The Searchers* (John Ford, US 1956)
No place in the new equilibrium

separated by age and class and resisted by family and community, is allowed to develop, but at the cost of a fractured leg. However, the film ends with a kitsch shot of a baby deer playing in the snow, suggesting that the resolution is no more than the false harmony of a traditional Christmas card. The 'happy ending' of *Taxi Driver* similarly strains belief. The European art movie and American 'independent' cinema, while ending with a resolution, is more often associated with character development and a recognition by protagonists of the inevitability of an unsatisfactory state of affairs.

A more elaborate analysis of narrative structure has been associated with the work of Vladimir Propp. Drawing on an analysis of Russian folk-tales, he concluded that regardless of individual differences in terms of plot, characters and setting, they would share common structural features. There were the functions of particular characters: 'the villain', 'the donor', 'the helper', 'the princess', 'her father', 'the dispatcher', 'the hero' and 'the false hero'. There were also thirty-one narrative units descriptive of particular action, for instance: 'a member of a family leaves home', 'a prohibition or rule is imposed on the hero', 'this prohibition is broken', etc. The characters were seen as stable elements from story to story, despite individual variations of appearance or idiosyncrasies of personality. The narrative units were sufficient to describe all of the stories, although not all units appear in all of the stories, but when they do appear they are in the prescribed order. While it might appear that such narrative structures are specific to a given genre or culture, the model has proved adaptable to Hollywood movies, such as *Sunset Boulevard*, *Kiss Me Deadly* and *North by Northwest*. They inevitably had to be 'translated' from the original. For instance, in Peter Wollen's article on *North by Northwest*, Eve Kendall, a double agent, becomes a princess. However, the accounts do have a degree of credibility, and at the very least have the function of making the analysis of a narrative 'strange'. The very force of narrative often makes it difficult for even the trained viewer to stand back and observe what is really going on.

The Proppean analysis does, however, depend on the existence of a single narrative operating in a linear way. The examples chosen to illustrate the analysis are characterised by a strong central story-line – although one of them, *Sunset Boulevard*, does have a framing device. Even mainstream movies have tended to develop a system of subplotting, often with a 'romantic' subject subservient to the action plot. While this is recognised within Propp – the resolution involves a wedding as a result of the success the hero has had in the action plot – the main plot and the subplot often exist in a state of tension. Police movies have increasingly stressed a tension between the demands of the job, the successful solution of a crime and the satis-faction of the hero's romantic and domestic needs. The very principle of a linear narrative is being increasingly challenged – and not merely outside the mainstream. Robert Altman's *Short Cuts* combines a number of short stories, but with many of the characters appearing in more than one story, who have, in Proppean terms, alternative character functions. Quentin Tarantino's *Pulp Fiction* extends this, using three stories with overlapping characters, but also inserts the final resolution – Bruce Willis with girlfriend riding off on his motor bike, the final moment in the time of the narrative – around two-thirds of the way through the film. *Pulp Fiction* does not conform to mainstream narrative structure, and it is only comprehensible because we as viewers hold on to an understanding of narrative and formal conventions through our experience of the mainstream.

Todorov and Propp's work stresses the simplicity of film narratives which are media specific. In particular, the classic realist text appears to narrate itself. Despite the example of *Goodfellas* quoted on p. 110, the film does not usually appear to have a narrator, an 'I' who tells the story. Novels can either have a 'teller', a character or observer within the text, or an author, who by implication has privileged access to some of the characters. Similarly, in much television news or documentary coverage there is either a voice over or a presenter who operates as the authoritative voice. In the absence of a presenter, the narrative itself is seen as the embodiment of the truth of what is happening, no matter how far-fetched.

☐ CASE STUDY 3: *IF* – AN ALTERNATIVE TEXT

This chapter began with an account of a movie, *RoboCop*, clearly within the mainstream Hollywood tradition. Although originating from within American cinema, the codes, conventions and narrative patterns have come to dominate entertainment cinema and fictional TV the world over. However, the forms and conventions are by no means static, but are affected by cross-cultural, cross-media and technological influences or even by the impact of particular talented directors with their own style. There are also films which are constructed to work against the conventions, either for artistic or political reasons.

In 1968, Lindsay Anderson, after working in the subsidised theatre, as a film critic and producing both documentaries and 'social realist' fiction films, made *If*. It was financed by a major studio, Paramount, who at that stage were interested in investing in British film-makers. Although based on an existing book, *Crusaders* by David Sherwin, it is nevertheless a highly personal film using for its locations and backdrop Anderson's own public school background. Furthermore, the film draws upon Anderson's interest in Brechtian theatre, and is an attempt to explore the 'alienation effect' in a cinematic setting. The film,

• Plate 4.13 *If . . .* (Lindsay Anderson, UK 1968)
A mixture of filmic styles

• Plate 4.14 *If . . .* (Lindsay Anderson, UK 1968)
Do we believe what we see?

however, was targeted at a commercial audience, and rested upon the understandings of a mainstream audience. Far from producing a detached, analytical spectator, the film produced in its contemporary audiences an involved and committed response.

There are two immediately strange devices, disturbing for a viewer inbred in realist text. The film is divided up into sections, each with a heading rather like the chapter heading of a book. Since the coming of sound such disruption is rarely to be seen except as a comic effect. More speciously, however, the film stock changes from colour to black and white at frequent intervals within the film. Normally these changes are between scenes, but sometimes occur within sequences. Such shifts provoke a need in the viewer to explain, possibly to discover the 'code'. Anderson's explanation at the time was simply that of budgetary constraints, not enough money to film in colour throughout. Whatever the status of that explanation, the consequence is to foreground the process of film production throughout the film.

I would like to briefly consider the sequence 'Ritual and romance' that occurs about halfway through the film. The sequence in plot terms involves the transgression of school rules – not to attend the house rugby match, to escape out of bounds, to steal a motor bike and to meet a young woman in a transport café.

The sequence involves an approximate balance of colour and black and white shots, but also a mixture of filmic styles. Although narrative cinema has involved a range of stylistic practices, a Frank Tashlin/Jerry Lewis comedy, spaghetti westerns, British drama-documentary, there is normally a characteristic unity of style within a film. However, even within this sequence we get a black and white documentary realist sequence in the school chapel, predominantly long shot; an accurate slow-motion sequence with a boy performing on parallel bars from the admiring gaze of his lover; a colour sequence of a performance on a motor bike by three characters to popular music; a long shot 'candid camera' sequence; as well as sequences filmed with conventional narrative strategies involving continuity editing and eyeline matches. There are also variable uses of sound, a variety of microphone positions sometimes giving 'tight' sound designed to clearly pick up dialogue, but elsewhere a distant and echo-ey sound as if from a documentary. Music is fragmented and inter-cut with silence. Sound is overlaid from one scene to another in such a way as to draw attention to itself – yet at the same time the narrative appears to be constructed along a conventional cause and effect chain. The rebels are instructed to attend the game; cut to the game, and they are not there; cut to the town where they are seen drifting, cut to motor cycle shop where they steal a bike; cut to the open road where they escape; and cut to the transport café. The transport café scene commences with narrative continuity. They continue to behave in the boorish and chauvinist way we have learnt to expect from the narrative so far. The female waitress responds by slapping the face of Travis as a response to his advances. He turns to the juke box on which he plays or maybe does not the African mass which he has on his record-player back at school. In the following sequence the waitress appears to make her own animal advances and after a jump-cut they appear naked play/fighting/loving on the café floor. They then appear fully clothed and, unfazed by their experience, resume drinking the still warm cup of tea.

This scene problematises the 'reality status' of what we see. Do we accept the truth of what appears in front of us despite both the improbability and the continuity breaks, or do we read the sexual encounter as 'only a fantasy'? However, if we attempt to read this as a fantasy then the status of the rest of the scene is thrown into question. Given that there is no consequence from the theft of the bike is this also a fantasy, despite its realistic depiction? If this scene is a fantasy how do we read the subsequent scenes where the young woman appears within the school setting? While the sequence subverts the process of the classic realist narrative, it is none the less only comprehensible on the basis of our knowledge of this process.

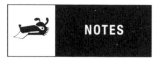

NOTES

1   Auguste and Louis Lumière are credited with developing a lightweight movie camera and a system of projecting moving images on the screen. They gave their first public projection of single-shot films on 28th December 1895.

2   Warner Brothers 1929.

3   For a full account of the process of viewing film and its parallels with the process of dreaming, see John Ellis, *Visible Fictions: Cinema, Television, Video*, London: Routledge, 1982; chapter on 'cinema as image and sound'.

4   Directed by Paul Verhoeven, it is available as a Virgin video.

5   A technical development from the late 1970s which permits the use of a camera held by hand and walks with the action, but with the steadiness of a camera moving on rails.

6   Georges Méliès, a pioneer of film, developed short narrative films as an entertainment within magic shows.

7   See Noel Burch, *Theory of Film Practice*, London: Secker & Warburg, 1973; also the film *Correction Please* and the accompanying booklet, published by the Arts Council of Great Britain, which reconstructs the development of film language in the first decade of the century.

8   Thomas Edison developed a peepshow system of viewing moving pictures which predated the Lumière system of projection.

9   Griffith directed about 400 single reel (eleven-minute) films between 1908 and 1913 and subsequently developed the full-length feature film with *The Birth of a Nation* (1915).

10 *The General* (1925), directed by Buster Keaton. Available on video.

11 This title would seem to suggest an external narrative commentary – a 'primitive' device that was destined to disappear, though see *Goodfellas* on p. 110. In the IMR the narrator is absent – the story 'tells itself'.

12 See section on editing, pp. 105–9.

13 See section on editing, pp. 105–9.

14 One of the original Lumière shorts.

15 There are a number of examples of work relating to mise-en-scène, particularly by those critics involved in *Movie* magazine. One example that may be accessible is Victor Perkins, 'The Cinema of Nicholas Ray', I.F. Cameron (ed.), *Movie Reader*, London: November Books, 1972.

16 Jim Kitses, *Horizons West*, London: Thames & Hudson, 1969.

17 A world of the future where everything has gone wrong.

18 The concept of anchorage was developed by Roland Barthes and has been particularly used to show the way that captions are used in magazines to limit the choice of meanings of a particular photographic image.

19 See André Bazin, *What is Cinema*, vol. 1: *Ontology and Language*, Paris: Editions du Cerf, 1958. There are also a number of summaries of Bazin on realism, for instance, Andrew Tudor, *Theories of Film*, London: Secker & Warburg for the BFI, 1974.

20 For a straightforward account of the 'grammar' of film shots see John Izod's *Reading the Screen: An Introduction to Film Studies*, Harlow: Longman and Beirut: York Press, 1984.

21 Lev Kuleshov (1899–1970) attempted to prove that the meanings of shots could be changed by altering the juxtaposition of shots. This involved a close-up of an actor playing a prisoner, which was then linked to two different shots: a bowl of soup and the open door of freedom. The audience were said to be convinced that the actor's expression was different even though the same shot was used.

22 For an account of cross-cut editing and parallel editing in the early cinema see D. Bordwell, J. Staiger and K. Thompson, *The Classical Hollywood Cinema*, London; Routledge & Kegan Paul, 1985.

23 K. Bordwell and K. Thompson, *Film Art*, New York: Knopf, 1990.

24 *Who's That Knocking at My Door?* directed by Martin Scorsese was released under a number of titles between 1965 and 1970. The reference is to the 1969 version.

25 Diegesis refers to the world of the narrative. In this sense anything that is not 'happening' within the story, whether an image or a sound used as a commentary of what is going on, is 'non-diegetic'. See below for the use of non-diegetic music.

26 Quotation marks around Hollywood are often used to indicate commercial American cinema which is not necessarily produced at a particular geographical location.

FURTHER READING

Bordwell, K. and Thompson, K., *Film Art*, New York: Knopff, 1990, is probably the most comprehensive text, with a wide range of examples.

Bordwell, D., Staiger, J. and Thompson, K., *The Classical Hollywood Cinema*, London: Routledge, 1985, an encyclopaedic and scholastic look at the development of film and narrative in Hollywood. Its wide set of references to films of the first fifty years of cinema is daunting but stimulating.

Cook, D., *History of Narrative Film*, New York: Norton, 1991, fluctuates from detailed analysis of particular 'significant' films to lists of films outside Hollywood mainstream.

Ellis, J., *Visible Fictions*, London: Routledge, 1982, a provocative account of film and TV which requires a full read rather than dipping in.

Three introductory texts of increasing level of difficulty.

Turner, G., *Film as Social Practice*, London: Routledge, 1988.
Andrew, D., *Concepts in Film Theory*, Oxford: Oxford University Press, 1984.
Lapsley, R. and Westlake, M., *Film Theory: An Introduction*, Manchester: Manchester University Press, 1988.

FURTHER VIEWING

In a sense almost any viewing would be applicable to work on this chapter. Nevertheless, the 'non-obtrusiveness' of much of mainstream cinema creates difficulties in observing the processes whereby meaning is created. This suggests that initial work on form and narrative is perhaps most productive with work characterised by 'excess'.

At the risk of appearing to be an unreconstructed auteurist, this might suggest the work of the following directors as a possible way in: Altman, Argento, Bertolucci, Bresson, Coen brothers, Fuller, Hitchcock, Jamusch, Lynch, Minelli, Murnau, Ophuls, Powell and Pressburger, Ray, Scorsese, Sirk, Sternberg, Tarantino, Vidor and Welles.

A more austere approach would extend this list to include perhaps more self-consciously 'modernist' directors: Anderson, Bunuel, Eisenstein, Godard, Oshima, Potter, Resnais and Straub.

Chapter 5

Genre, star and auteur: an approach to Hollywood cinema

Patrick Phillips*

■ Genre, star and auteur: an approach to Hollywood cinema

INTRODUCTION

Ways of approaching Hollywood

New York, New York is a film produced in Hollywood in 1977 by United Artists. It contains 'bankable' elements around which a characteristic Hollywood deal could be struck by producers Irwin Winkler and Robert Chartoff: a director (Martin Scorsese) and two stars (Liza Minnelli and Robert De Niro). Previous remarkable collaborations between Scorsese and De Niro, most recently *Taxi Driver*, further guaranteed the project. What was less certain was the box-office potential of a film dressed up as classic **studio system** musical. However, the confidence of the backers was clear; they agreed to a budget of $9 million. In return they got a film 153 minutes long costing $11 million. Any film of this length has exhibition problems, but in fact the film was first released in a version of (only) 136 minutes and got longer on re-release. The director had enough power to insist that what he considered a crucial scene – one which cost $350,000 to shoot – be included despite a general perception that the narrative needed to be tighter rather than more expansive. *New York, New York* was a commercial failure although it has been passionately defended by some critics and audiences.

A study of *New York, New York* could elaborate on some of the stark details outlined in the previous paragraph. The film could be seen in relation to the institution which produced it, in this case, the Hollywood industry, as it was operating in the second half of the 1970s. *New York, New York* is very much a product of the 'New' Hollywood of independent producers, powerful directors and autonomous stars drawn together in speculative one-off projects. The study could focus on the financing of the project, the power-broking involved during the different stages of production. The marketing, distribution and exhibition of the film would, perhaps, consider the particular challenges presented to the industry in handling a musical – and one of such length. Of particular concern might be the perennial conflict between financial restraint and artistic license; a conflict which would reach its high point with Cimino's *Heaven's Gate*, five years after *New York, New York*, which brought United Artists to financial ruin. Beyond this, the more fundamental debate about production under the 'new' Hollywood compared with production under the studio system might be generated; a debate with unusual significance in this particular case where a deliberate attempt was made to recreate what appears at least on the surface to be the quintessential studio system product in a very different production context.

A different approach to *New York, New York* would be one that focuses less on institutional issues and more on *film form*, the organisation of narrative, the use of mise-en-scène, editing and cinematography. For example, the narrative of this fictional musical melodrama/bio-pic is conventionally linear, one event follows the preceding one in a chronological way conveying in the process a cause→effect→cause→effect pattern. Much more unusual, by comparison, is the film's use of very long sequences, partly the result of an improvisational, documentary-style approach. In editing, the rejection of the master shot, that is one which provides an overview of the setting and the

---

* By request, Patrick Phillips's key terms (in bold type) do not appear as marginal notes but only in the glossary (see pp. 429–37) [Ed.].

place of the characters within it, in favour of a rhythm of tracking shots creates a distinctive visual style. Most obviously there is the challenge contained in the film's anti-naturalism.

Scorsese has said:

> In the city streets I'd seen in MGM and Warner Brothers musicals, New York kerbs were always shown as very high and very clean. When I was a child, I realised this wasn't right, but was part of a whole mythical city, as well as the feeling of the old three-strip Technicolor with lipstick that was too bright and make-up even on the men.[1]

One pleasure of this film is precisely in its contrast between this nostalgic artificiality of the film's look and the edgy improvisational acting of its stars, especially Robert De Niro. (This type of acting which involves actors engaging very intensely with their roles is referred to as the 'Method' and more will be said about this on pp. 144–6.)

In summary, one can describe *New York, New York* in relation to genre, star performance and director: the 'Method' meets the MGM musical through the distinctive visual style and thematic preoccupations of the film's director.

Studies in **genre, star** and **auteur** (a director who brings distinctive and recognisable stylistic or thematic characteristics to a film) have developed as the most common critical approaches to Hollywood film.

Genre, star and auteur approaches can be applied to the principal areas of film studies, helping to make sense of, for example:

1   the production and marketing practices of the *industry*;
2   the meaning systems at work within the *film text*;
3   the range of expectations which determine *spectatorship*.

For reasons of length this chapter cannot possibly consider the full complexity of genre-star-auteur across industry-text-audience. The focus elsewhere in this book on industry and spectatorship means that the most appropriate focus here is on assessing the value of these critical approaches to understanding how genre, star and auteur contribute very significantly as 'meaning systems' at work within the film text.

Discourse and structure

In the interplay between industry-text-audience, genre, star and auteur critical approaches perform two essential roles, both of which are primarily communicative:

- they function as **structures** to be deployed by those making the film;
- they function as **discourses** for those who wish to talk about the film, make sense of it.

To take the second of these first. A discourse is a mode of speech which has evolved to express the shared human activities of a community of people. So, for example, there is the distinctive discourse of the medical and legal professions and there is the discourse of different academic disciplines. Film Studies has, like other disciplines, developed its own language – its own discourse system – to make possible the identification and structuring of that area of human activity and experience with which it is concerned. In addition to narrative and realism, genre, star and auteur are fundamental discourse systems working within the larger discourse system we call Film Studies.

Any language system allows us to:

1 *identify* through isolating phenomena and naming them; and
2 *construct meaning* through organising the otherwise shapeless and random into some sort of system.

In applying a generic or star or auteurist approach we are attempting just this with regard to film.

Thinking of a genre or a star or an auteur as a structure allows us to understand how it contributes to the overall meaning we are able to discern in the film. A structure is a combination of elements, this combination governed either explicitly or implicitly by 'rules' which can be identified as a result of study. The elements available for inclusion in a particular structure are limited by convention or common sense. They are referred to in what follows as **paradigms**.

For example, a western like *Stagecoach* (1939) has a characteristic set of paradigms (locations, characters, costumes, etc.) which operate according to a code, a 'rule' of combination. The star of *Stagecoach*, John Wayne, also has a characteristic set of paradigms (voice, mannerisms, character types, etc.) which are combined in a way which constructs Wayne's very distinctive screen persona. The director of *Stagecoach*, John Ford, similarly brings to the films he directed a characteristic set of paradigms (theme, characterisation, visual style) which possess a 'rule' of combination which allows us to recognise both the individuality of Ford's film and the way this individuality contributes to the overall impression the film makes on us.

The figure below represents in simple outline form the relationship between paradigms and their 'rule' of combination. This structure provides a common approach to the study of genre, star and auteur.

```
paradigm
(choice from
conventional
range of
options)              paradigm     paradigm
————— | ————— | ————— | ————— 'rule' of combination
```

The immediate objection to this '**structuralist**' approach is that it seems too abstract and appears to convert the life of a film into a set of lifeless formulae. However, if we accept that genre, star and auteur each provide a set of meanings which are central to our understanding of a Hollywood film and our response to it, then it is important to consider how these meanings work as 'systems'; what are their components and how they work. It is very useful to think of the 'meaning systems' of different genres, stars and auteurs as *communication structures*. And since there are other key structures working within a film as well, most obviously the narrative structure, then it is particularly important to develop the ability both to distinguish between them and to recognise how they work in conjunction with one another.

In fact the major problem with a structuralist approach is not its abstraction but its power. As tools, structures can dominate our thinking, indeed do our thinking for us. We need to be critically self-aware about the ease with which it is possible to force a film or a series of films into a generic, auteur or star 'structure'. Ultimately we need to be alert to the possibility that in constructing an argument around a particular genre, auteur or star, we may be producing a neatly organised overview – but we may also be constructing a fiction every bit as credible but every bit as contrived as the narratives of the films themselves. For example, having identified common features across two or three films directed by the same individual, it is reasonable to organise these features into an auteur 'structure' which represents this person's work and allows us to talk intelligently about it. We then encounter a film which does not seem to fit the auteur 'structure' we have created. The temptation to force the film into the framework we have constructed, by the most convoluted of means if necessary, is great. Neatness will have been prioritised over genuine complexity and truth. As with other forms of language study, a descriptive rather than a prescriptive approach is to be recommended, that is one which honestly respects what is actually there rather than one which tries to side-step the messy reality of what is in front of us. A structuralist approach is only a means to an end; our goal is to appreciate the film being studied as well as we can.

☐ CASE STUDY PART 1: *NEW YORK, NEW YORK*

Consider these three statements:

New York, New York is a musical. It has a generic identity.
New York, New York is dominated by two stars who define much of the film's identity.
New York, New York is directed by an auteur, someone who brings to the film a very distinct identity.

The need to identify, the need to be identifiable, are vital for audience and industry respectively. Concepts and categories are constructed through naming: a musical, a Scorsese film, a Scorsese-De Niro film, a Minnelli vehicle. An audience will be sold a product on the basis of expectations offered, guarantees promised in the perceived identity of the film text. Hollywood sometimes creates this identity, sometimes exploits it after it has emerged in popular culture. These identities are mobilised in the whole social practice surrounding Hollywood cinema, including advertising, media treatment and ordinary conversation, entering freely into circulation as 'common sense' shared by industry financiers and publicists, critics, journalists and audiences.

The fact that disagreements arise over identification opens up critical debate and encourages more detailed analysis. In the case of *New York, New York* a major difficulty arises over its generic identity. Is it a musical? Could it be better described as a melodrama involving musicians? If it is a musical, which of the various subgenres of the musical does it most obviously conform to? Is it a celebration or a **deconstruction** of the MGM musical with its refusal of a happy ending? (The dismissal by Jimmy Doyle (De Niro) of the lavish *Happy Endings* film within a film as 'sappy endings' will be touched on in the next section.) These questions are all interesting and worth pursuing and are all premised on the notion of generic identity. The ability to agree in some definitive way is less important than the much more basic fact that a critical approach through genre allows the discussion to take place at all, in the process heightening our awareness of the film's complexities and ambiguities.

The presence of Liza Minnelli brings a number of elements associated with her star image. What precisely are we to make of the fact that the film is consciously re-creating

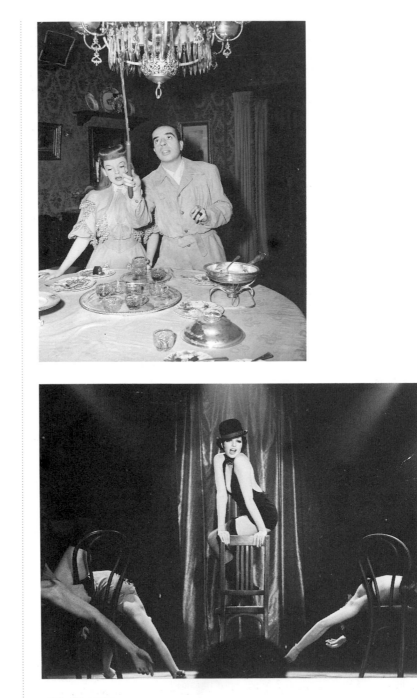

• Plates 5.1 and 5.2
Mother, father, daughter: 5.1 Vincent Minnelli directs Judy Garland on the set of *Meet Me in St Louis*
(US 1944); 5.2 Liza Minnelli in *Cabaret* (US 1972)

the look of her father's MGM musicals or that her onscreen vulnerability is possibly informed by knowledge of her mother, Judy Garland? Perhaps neither of these things is important as the final third of the film becomes a vehicle for Minnelli to 'do her thing', belt out numbers in her distinctive style. Perhaps it is the sassiness which is most important – first established in her Sally Bowles role in *Cabaret* (1972) – and the provocation this provides the De Niro character. The latter is equally easily identifiable as the inarticulate, aggressive male-in-crisis we associate with so many of his collaborations with Scorsese (especially between 1972 and 1982). In arriving at some critical understanding of Minnelli or De Niro's contribution to *New York, New York* a fundamental point has to be acknowledged: that it is star study which allows us to enter into such a potentially interesting and revealing inquiry at all.

An understanding of *New York, New York* is very much enhanced by an appreciation of the identity Martin Scorsese's auteurism brings to the film. With no awareness of his thematic and stylistic preoccupations in films either side of *New York, New York*, it may appear a far less interesting work. Reference has already been made to his conscious 'hommage' to the musical, on the one hand, but his rejection of its easy optimism, on the other. Also, reference has been made to the deliberate conflict between improvisational and documentary realist techniques, on the one hand, and the pure artifice of studio sets, on the other. The excess and abundance normally associated with the classical Hollywood musical has become an introverted and dark melodrama of threatened masculinity. Scorsese is one of relatively few directors working in Hollywood today who can unambiguously be described as an auteur. The assembled identity of the auteur, built up through careful viewing of several films in which the individual is clearly the controlling presence, informs analysis and discussion of the film text in potentially very useful ways.

Put very simply, the combination musical-Scorsese-De Niro-Minnelli will produce a film distinctive from one in which any of these four elements are changed. In analysis, knowledge of the identity of each will inform understanding of the other three.

Audiences, students, critics, film historians, marketing executives, actors and directors themselves create identities by selecting significant elements and putting them together into coherent structures. In *New York, New York* we have available an auteur 'structure' (Scorsese), a star 'structure' (De Niro or Minelli) and a genre 'structure' (the musical) each made up of observable characteristics.

Sometimes these structures may be over-elaborate, sometimes over-crude as critical tools – as much of the rest of the chapter will go on to investigate. However, they provide the principal means by which we talk, both critically and conversationally, about Hollywood films.

GENRE

How to approach genre?

Genres are formal systems for transforming the world in which we actually live into self-contained, coherent and controllable structures of meaning. Genres can thus be considered to function in the way that a language system does – offering a vocabulary and a set of rules which allow us to 'shape' reality, thus making it appear less random and disordered. Transforming the experience of living into a set of *predictable conventions* provides a number of pleasures. These include anticipation of these predictable features and satisfaction when expectations are fulfilled. (At the same time the 'mix' of elements is slightly different each time thus providing just enough uncertainty for the spectator to be held by anxious curiosity.)

At an ideological level, genre offers a *comfortable reassurance*, closing down the complexities and ambiguities of the social world we actually inhabit, replacing them with patterns of order and continuity deriving from the conventions of genre itself.

Genre and specific generic forms have evolved through the history of Hollywood so that industry and audience alike have learnt to speak through them and have their thinking done by them.

The most common-sense approach to genre is through **iconography** – the props, costumes and settings. In the terminology of semiotics these are signs, visual **signifiers**, which can immediately alert us to the generic identity of a film. The visual signifiers of a western, like *Stagecoach*, are clearly different from those of a techno-thriller such as *Terminator* (1984). Each genre has a limited number of characteristic elements, paradigms (see p. 124). Each paradigm has a limited range of signifiers. We cannot dress or arm or transport a western hero, a city detective and the commander of a space station as we please. Decisions are determined by the limited range of paradigms associated with each genre. Similarly, verbal and musical signifiers, in the form of dialogue and soundtrack, are often closely associated with particular genres.

As formal systems genres have recognisable paradigms made up of signifiers. These are deployed according to rules of combination and the 'structure' which results is one which is highly conventional, highly recognisable. For example, we find in the mise-en-scène of a genre film such as a Warners' gangster film of the 1930s a number of signifiers which, in combination, communicate important aspects of generic identity. The figure below can be used as a template for listing the conventional characteristics of any genre.

The gangster generic structure

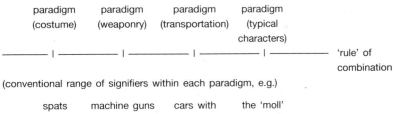

One feels an infringement of these 'common-sense' rules if the choice is made of a signifier which does not seem to be on the 'list' of paradigms established by convention. The often quoted example of the introduction of a motor car, and even more disconcertingly a camel, into Peckinpah's western *Guns in the Afternoon* (1962) illustrates well the dramatic effect of going outside the accepted paradigms. This strategy of deliberately selecting inappropriate signifiers has become more common since the mid-1980s and is well illustrated by a film like *Back to the Future III* (1991). More will be said about this on pp. 133–6.

This structural approach helps in tracing continuities and changes within a genre over time. If you try to list the major paradigms of the gangster film and the characteristic signifiers within each of these paradigms, you will become aware of the need to

• Plates 5.3 and 5.4 Paradigms of dress as illustrated here from two gangster movies, *Public Enemy* (Warner Bros, US 1931) and *Goodfellas* (Martin Scorsese, US 1990), may help identify a genre – but not always. We often need to look beyond iconography

differentiate in some respects a Warners' product of the early 1930s such as *Public Enemy* (1931) from *Goodfellas* (1990).

Many genre films cannot be immediately identified by their visual signifiers. A contemporary comedy, a thriller and a melodrama may look identical (though verbal and musical signifiers may help to distinguish them). This leads us to consider whether in identifying the characteristic features of a genre we might more usefully look to the **narrative conventions** of different genres.

Within Hollywood cinema genre manifests itself in narrative. However, the work of theorists such as Propp and Todorov[2] has emphasised that narratives can be remarkably similar across a range of different genres. Genres which are clearly different from one another in terms of visual, verbal and musical signifiers actually operate according to the same overall narrative structures. It is worth mapping out the major narrative elements of, say, a western, a science fiction adventure and a police thriller to investigate the extent to which this is true. At the most obvious level films classifiable into different genres because of their visual signifiers are simply 're-costuming' narratives which function just as effectively in other genres. *Star Wars* (1976) is often referred to as a western in disguise. Carpenter's *Assault on Precinct 13* (1977) is a reworking of Hawks' *Rio Bravo*, a western of 1959. A study of the opening sequences of Siodmak's *The Killers* (1947) and Siegel's *The Killers* (1964) raises more subtle questions about transitions and transformations between related genres, film noir and the gangster.

If generic identity is simply a superficial if effective way by which film texts multiply a relatively small number of basic narratives, then it is clear that genre study must go beyond these 'superficial' elements if it is to be anything more than just a means by which films are classified. Genre study must reach across its own classification borders if it is to offer real insight and understanding of core elements of mainstream Hollywood cinema.

But where to go if the study of generic signifiers is in itself a 'superficial' form of analysis and if we accept that there is only one narrative structure with a very limited number of variants? One possibility is to consider the different thematic preoccupations of different genres and the contrasting ways different genres manage the same thematic issues. For example, the western or the police thriller are concerned with issues of law and order, contested space, the individual hero and handle them in very similar ways. The musical or the romantic comedy are more centrally concerned with issues of class, status and sexuality but may handle them rather differently.

The relationship between genres and cultural myths is particularly strong. Mythical representations of the nineteenth-century American West or the 'mean streets' of the American city in the 1930s and 1940s are obvious examples. Across this range of myths there are certain recurring figures and situations which dramatise fundamental ideological values and which 'negotiate' shifts in the culture.

In a particularly imaginative study, Frank McConnell[3] offers just four character types and four genres which correspond to the four-stage historical cycle of a culture:

The King – establishing the state – the epic;
The Knight – consolidating the state – the adventurous romance;
The Pawn – trapped in the institutionalised state – the melodrama;
The Fool – responding to the madness of the state – the satire.

Beyond this McConnell posits a fifth stage in the cycle – apocalypse – a breakdown which leads back to the beginning and the initiation of a new cycle.

It is possible to consider how Hollywood has been particularly preoccupied with, for instance, the 'knights' of westerns and science fiction, the 'pawns' of noir crime and melodrama and the perceptive 'fool' who from Chaplin through the Marx Brothers to Steve Martin comments on the pretension and institutionalisation of contemporary life.

This kind of 'archetypal' criticism attempts to construct broad patterns to break down distinctions which appear in a genre classification system based primarily on contrasting visual, verbal and musical signifiers. Applying McConnell's model we are encouraged to see the ideological interrelationships that exist, for example, across a range of genres where characters are essentially 'pawns' with a sense of entrapment within an oppressive, institutionalised society. It is also possible to identify different tendencies and emphases within a genre by reference to McConnell's cycle: for example, we find in the western not only the four archetypes listed above but the tensions between them.

If what may be seen as a large number of genres actually represent a relatively small number of fundamental ideological/mythical/thematic concerns and if, in commercial Hollywood cinema, they manifest themselves in a remarkably small number of basic narratives, then it seems sensible to look towards forms of classification which emphasise similarity and overlap.

One such model has been provided by Thomas Schatz in his definitive study, *Hollywood Genres* (1981). He adopts a thematic and ideological approach which identifies only two genres: the genre of order and the genre of integration.[4]

Genres of Order	*Genres of Integration*
(Western, gangster, sci-fi, etc.)	(Musicals, comedies, domestic melodramas, etc.)
Hero	
Individual (male dominant)	Couple or collective (e.g. family) (female dominant)
Setting	
● Contested space (ideologically unstable)	● Civilised space (ideologically stable)
Conflict	
● Externalised (expressed through violent action)	● Internalised (expressed through emotion)
Resolution	
● Elimination (death)	● Embrace (love)
Thematics	
● the hero takes upon himself the problems, contradictions inherent in his society and acts as redeemer	● the romantic couple or family are integrated into the wider community, their personal antagonisms resolved
● macho code of behaviour	● maternal – familial code
● isolated self-reliance (either through his departure or death, the hero does not assimilate the values/lifestyle of the community – but maintains individuality)	● community co-operation

131

• Plates 5.5 and 5.6 Genres of order. Is it possible to see two genre films, which at face value appear completely different from each other, as having important things in common? Plate 5.5 *Stagecoach*, Plate 5.6 *RoboCop*

One value of Schatz's approach is that it allows *Rio Bravo* and *Assault on Precinct 13* to be discussed together, and not only in order to identify a similar narrative structure but also shared ideological themes and effects. The combination of different ideological themes with the standard narrative (disruption of equilibrium → overcoming the resulting crises → restoration of equilibrium) makes possible complex critical analysis. The kinds of disruption which trigger the narrative in different genre films can be compared. What is the nature of the disruption in *My Darling Clementine*? How does it compare with the disruption in *Meet Me in St Louis*? Equally, the means by which narrative resolutions are sought can be compared. What are the principal means used in *RoboCop*? How do they compare with those employed in *Sister Act*? Perhaps most pertinent is to look at the characteristic ways in which narratives in different genres come to a point of closure. To take two notorious recent examples: how is *Fatal Attraction* brought to a point of closure? How does this compare with the closure in *Thelma and Louise*? How can these films separately, together, be linked to ideological themes established over time in several different Hollywood genres?

Schatz's model also encourages the exploration of films which fall between the binary opposites of order/integration presented in his model. Certain films with female protagonists reveal their ideological contradictions precisely in the crossover area between order and integration. Where do we place *Mildred Pierce* or *Thelma and Louise*?

A study of genre which allows, say, *High Plains Drifter* and *Terminator* to be compared collectively to, say, *Desperately Seeking Susan* and *Fried Green Tomatoes* will be significantly more incisive than one which retains its focus exclusively within traditional generic categories such as the western and the comedy. Indeed it can be argued that the latter approach is circular and self-fulfilling: the critic starts off with a notion of the 'essential' elements of some archetypal form called the western and then proceeds to identify them within particular films.

Like the genre itself, this critical approach produces a formal containment and closure of the world it represents, a world reduced to a set of conventions. A genre's apparently freestanding existence in which it appears to make reference only to itself discourages the spectator from thinking beyond the fictional world to the reality which exists outside the cinema. From an ideological perspective it can be argued that tying the spectator into the 'closed' world of the genre closes down the possibility of critical engagement with ideological issues which may be at the heart of the film. It is interesting, for example, to look at a range of Hollywood Vietnam War movies in relation to the extent to which each absorbs ideological issues into the conventions of the war genre.

Western, musical, techno-thriller, pyscho-thriller, road movie. If genre study is of value it is in encouraging a marauding approach to the *whole* of Hollywood. Genre study can easily become the kind of 'strait-jacketing' exercise, warned against on pp. 124–5, which only succeeds in locking the film into the structure which the student imposes on it. What is required is a flexible rather than a pedantic approach to generic classification which encourages creative and productive comparisons to be made across formal generic boundaries such as is encouraged, at least to some extent, by the application of Schatz's model. In fact a 'marauding' approach to genre is best exemplified today from within Hollywood, from film-makers and scriptwriters.

Playing with genre

Genre production in the **'New' Hollywood** is very different from the way it was under the Studio System of production. In the 1930s and 1940s an efficient and quality production system was able to turn out films which conformed unproblematically to formulae and satisfied audience expectations. The conventional wisdom of film historians states that the production of standardised generic product was transferred to television in the 1950s. Those genres which remained in production were increasingly determined, first, by social and demographic changes which led to a pandering to the American teenager and, second, by the 'deal' method of putting together a film project which worked to the disadvantage of traditional genre production in favour of the one-off 'concept' or series film. Stars, who under the studio system had further stabilised genre production, were, with notable exceptions, less willing to tie their star image too closely to a specific genre, while the rise of the auteur drove the Hollywood film further into the realms of the 'distinctive' and 'different' and further away from any comfortable acceptance of the generically conventional.

However, the **Studio System** period of genre film production is still central to an appreciation of Hollywood film today. Even, and arguably, especially, films which are preoccupied with transformation and 'hybridisation', have their roots in this earlier period. Accessibility to the standard genre films of the studio period has never been greater. Whether screwball comedy or film noir, they exist alongside the product of the 'New' Hollywood in the continuous present tense of reception – on television and video. The auteurs of the New Hollywood from Scorsese to Tarantino are steeped in classical Hollywood genre and the contemporary cultural condition which they work to reflect and explore includes the 'still-present' of so many past Hollywood films. Hollywood genres make possible transformations precisely to the extent that they are reference points, sites of order, coherence and stability to contemporary culture.

Awareness today of genre among both film-makers and audiences is such that it has become a defining characteristic of what is often referred to as **postmodern** Hollywood.

John Belton, in his excellent *American Cinema/American Culture* (1994), identifies three characteristics of postmodernist cinema:[5]

- First, it is based on pastiche of traditional generic material.
- Second, much of this imitation is of images from the past offered as a nostalgic substitute for any real exploration of either the past or the present.
- Third, this referencing the past reflects another problem the artist faces today: not being able to say anything that has not already been said.

The postmodern artist struggles to make meaning from what appear as the meaningless assembly of the details of contemporary culture. As Belton says (p. 309), 'in transmitting the reality of their social and cultural context, they reproduce only its incoherence'. This can produce work which is superficially exciting, both thematically and stylistically, but which begs questions about any substantial meaning. The Coen Brothers' work is most often cited to illustrate postmodern Hollywood – *Barton Fink* (1991) providing a particularly good example.

'**Bricolage**' – the playful mixing of elements from different artistic styles and periods – finds its manifestation in Hollywood film in the self-conscious use of references, especially generic references from the vast storehouse of images and memories of film accumulated through the viewing and reviewing of films from the past. The access to this storehouse through television, and particularly video, has created a genre-literate culture of considerable sophistication. Reference was made earlier to Peckinpah's shocking use of a motor car and a camel in *Guns in the Afternoon*. The use of these signifiers is motivated by the desire to introduce in a startling way the theme of the

• Plates 5.7 and 5.8 *Raising Arizona* (Coen Bros, US 1986): this baby has genre problems!

West as a place of transition and change. In pastiche and parody films like *Airplane* and *Dead Men Don't Wear Plaid'*, there is clearly an exploitation of genre for comic effect and the joke depends on a knowledge of genre shared by film-makers and audience.

The postmodern goes well beyond this. Jim Collins[6] describes the contemporary Hollywood text as a narrative which now operates simultaneously on two levels:

- in reference to character adventure
- in reference to a text's adventure in the array of contemporary cultural production.

The 'text's adventure' can be described as being in large part the free use of generic signifiers, dissociated from their conventional paradigmatic deployment in stable narratives. *Raising Arizona*, the 1986 Coen Brothers film, provides a vivid illustration of this playfulness. Its overall hybrid generic identity – comic melodrama, social satire, thriller – is intensified by its exploitation of signifiers from an even broader range of genres. The Mad Max biker figure and the escaped convicts come from other generic worlds; the comedy their presence creates is shadowed by other associations, capable of inducing anxiety, even terror in an audience.

In returning to the figure on p. 128 to illustrate the highly stable, conventionalised world of the genre film, we must now take on board the freeing of signs from their generic structures, of signifiers – visual, verbal and musical – available for use anywhere within cultural production. (The music video and advertising provide both the strongest impetus and most vivid illustrations – consider the appropriation of such films as *Metropolis*, *Citizen Kane* and *Casablanca*.)

The generic 'hybrid': some features of *Raising Arizona*

```
    paradigms from       paradigms from        paradigms from
  (screwball comedy) (prison escape thriller)    (Mad Max)
——————— | ————————————— | ————————————— | ——————— playful combination
                                                        ('bricolage')
(potentially any signifier
from the vast range put
into circulation by genre)
```

The 'playfulness' is dependent on pre-existing generic forms which, in the case of Hollywood, after nearly a century are able to offer a 'vocabulary' rich in association shared across industry-text-audience.

Not only in relation to the hybrid but to the generically unambiguous film, audiences and film-makers are bringing a heightened awareness of genre which is altering the viewing experience and making available different forms of pleasure. Coppola's *Bram Stoker's Dracula* (1992) uses the signifiers and structures of a particular genre in a highly conventional way – elaborated on by some blockbuster budget special effects and an understated AIDS theme. By contrast, Scorsese's *Cape Fear* (1991) exploits a range of 'vocabularies' within the psychological thriller format. However, in both films there is a 'knowingness', a complicity between film-maker and spectator as they produce meaning in the deployment and reading respectively of the film's generic signifiers. Both film-maker and audience are aware of their revisiting of generically constructed worlds which increasingly are perceived as having their own history, their own independent reality. The self-conscious 'knowingness' is also clearly present in the performances of Hopkins' Von Hessling and De Niro's

GENRE, STAR AND AUTEUR

Max Cady and in the 'excess' in visual style. Both are further characteristics of postmodern Hollywood and characteristics of postmodern cultural production in general.

The foregrounding of production values, the straining for auteurist signature in the visual style, mark both Coppola and Scorsese's 'performances' as auteurs. (More will be said about the signifiers of performance with regard to stars on pp. 143–4 and with regard to auteurs on p. 153.)

In contrast to the 'new eclectic film' defined in terms of such films as *Blade Runner* (1982), *Who Framed Roger Rabbit?* (1988), *Wild at Heart* (1990) and *Back to the Future III* (1990), Jim Collins[7] identifies a counter-tendency in films such as *Field of Dreams* (1989), *Dances with Wolves* (1990) and *Hook* (1991). These films, in different ways, are reasserting authenticity, some sense of value and clarity of definition in worlds which, however fictional, are underpinned by a simplicity and reassurance which genre production in Hollywood traditionally provided. Certainly the extravagant reception given to more traditional genre films in 1992 such as Eastwood's *The Unforgiven* or Franklin's low budget *One False Move* suggests, at the very least, a nostalgia for the Hollywood structures to which they conform. However, this same nostalgia which informs the making and the viewing of such films is itself a form of self-conscious knowingness, a variant on the sensibility characteristic of the postmodern condition generally, 'serious', respectful but only a short remove from 'play'. *Reservoir Dogs*, for example, negotiates this border area in a striking way.

To return again to the analogy between genre and language made at the start, it can be said that just as we inherit language so we *inherit genre* with all its accretions through history. At the same time it can be said that just as we inhabit a language which structures the way we process our world so we *inhabit genre*. As film-maker, as spectator, the more appreciation of the inheritance, the more understanding of the habitation, the more creativity will be shown by both film-maker and spectator in the making of meaning. Film-makers like Scorsese, Lynch, the Coen Brothers and Tarantino are steeped in genre traditions but use their knowledge in creative and exciting ways.

Genre criticism has the potential to be equally bold, prepared to demonstrate that 'the construction and criticism of genres is itself an important cultural process'.

☐ CASE STUDY PART 2: THE PROBLEMATIC MUSICAL – *NEW YORK, NEW YORK* AS GENRE FILM

In returning to *New York, New York* I wish to consider the potential of genre study for opening up a specific film for discussion and analysis.

The spectator is first confronted with the problem of classification. A range of visual and musical signifiers indicate that this is a musical, although it is to be noted that there are four sorts of musical, four subgenres present. Most remarkable for a film of 1977 is the hommage to the clearly artificial studio sets of the Vincente Minnelli and Stanley Donan-Gene Kelly MGM musical of the late 1940s, early 1950s. However, the performances themselves refer, on the one hand, to the big band era which preceded the great MGM musicals and, on the other, to the modern individualistic star celebration incarnated in the 1970s by Liza Minnelli's *Cabaret* and various Streisand vehicles. In narrative development the film most resembles the musical biography popular in the 1940s and 1950s, though integrating narrative and set-piece elements from the other subgenres referred to here.

The musical numbers occur as part of the narrative, as an actual stage performance – or, in the *Happy Endings* sequence as a film performance – rather than leaving behind the surface realism and going off into another dimension of fantasy and artifice as was the convention in Busby Berkeley Warner Brothers or MGM musicals. Further, these numbers are nearly always fragmented as rehearsals or snatches of performance without the usual production values and with no choreography (except in the *Happy Endings* film-within-the-film).

Like *Cabaret*, it is probably most appropriate to describe *New York, New York* as a melodrama with music. Its main themes revolve around marriage and personal relationships. Scorsese has said:

> It could have been a film about a director and a writer, or an artist and a composer. It's about two people in love with each other who are both creative. That was the idea: to see if the marriage would work.[9]

Although there is some complexity, the generic description, as presented so far, allows us to place the film within Schatz's 'Genre of Integration' which includes the musical and the melodrama. The identification of contrasting and potentially conflicting musical subgenres at work within the film is useful in terms of trying to 'name' the film. But this in itself can only be regarded as a means to an end – a delineation of the contours of the film so that greater understanding of the whole might become possible.

However, the description is not yet complete. Richard Dyer[10] identifies the distinctive 'product' of the classic MGM style musical as feeling – abundance, energy, community. Dyer demonstrates how these qualities of the musical provide imaginary solutions to a real world of scarcity, exhaustion, dreariness, manipulation and fragmentation. *New York, New York* singularly lacks this 'feel-good' factor, does not attempt a 'utopian solution' to the problems of living in a real social world. The sets have an eery, often barren quality to them, their obvious artificiality is used expressively to convey distance, disconnectedness, alienation. This may not quite be the world of *Taxi Driver*, but it certainly suggests the world of film noir. The further underlying ideological issues are explored – issues of masculinity, individualism, contested space – the deeper we travel into that set of descriptors which Schatz drew up to describe not the Genre of Integration but the Genre of Order.

Three moments:

- Jimmy (De Niro) alone observes a sailor dancing with a girl late at night. The couple are alone and there is no music. This is less an 'hommage' to *On the Town* (Donen, 1949), than a re-enactment of the kind of alienation and male-angst associated with the period immediately following the end of the Second World War and which is generally referred to by students of film noir as a formative element in the development of that genre.
- Jimmy impulsively decides to marry Francine (Minnelli) – in the middle of a snowy night (of studio-set artificiality). He drives her to the registry office without having proposed or even explained his actions. The scene that follows has elements of both comedy and romance, but it is uncomfortable, at times embarrassing to watch. Neither the comedy nor the romance promises any kind of 'integration'.
- Jimmy and Francine have divorced. Francine is now a movie star. Jimmy goes to see her latest film, *Happy Endings*, which contains Busby Berkeley style choreography

• Plate 5.9 *New York, New York* (Martin Scorsese, US 1977)
Robert De Niro and Lisa Minnelli breakfasting in the opening scene

and exuberant display (highlighting in its extravagance and joy the starkness of the musical called *New York, New York* which contains it). Afterwards Jimmy lightly dismisses the sequence as 'sappy endings' – in so doing dismissing the film's own hommage to the classical musical. This is followed by the closure of narrative in which no reconciliation between Jimmy and Francine occurs – no happy ending.

What is going on in this film?

Genre is being employed as one of the principal components of the film's discourse system through which the particular themes of the film can be articulated. This is not the simple communication of an unproblematic set of conventional signifiers operating according to a stable and therefore predictable rule of combination. Rather it is a complex exploitation of different genres developed through the history of Hollywood. As described earlier, film-maker and spectator alike inherit and inhabit genre, but in the making of meaning they also constantly work to expand genre.

The generic pleasure of *New York, New York* is partly that of recognition, the connection that is established with other texts of pleasure from the history of Hollywood cinema. However, the most common form of generic pleasure – the pleasure of expectations fulfilled – is replaced by the potentially more thrilling but also potentially disconcerting interrogation of those expectations. Andrew Sarris wrote in *The Village Voice*: 'What is it like? people ask me . . . it is mixed moods and delirious dialectics – two crucial ingredients for box office poison.'

Like Scorsese's *The King of Comedy*, and for similar reasons, the film did indeed do badly at the box office. Delirium is far too dangerous a state of pleasure for the spectator keen to receive the conventional reassurances of Hollywood entertainment. The value of genre study in this particular case is that it allows us to both experience and understand that delirium.

STARS

Where do we find the star?

The star is found in two places – in the *roles* s/he plays in films and in the *media* exposure s/he receives as a consequence of this and which will in turn contribute to the meaning she brings to her next role.

The film is often a *vehicle* for the star, offering her the opportunity to display whatever is specific to her star persona. Dyer identifies the following:[11]

- a character role;
- a situation;
- a context for doing her 'thing' – be it dancing, singing or whatever.

In addition, the star's appearance within the film may have certain recurring elements which lead to a high degree of predictability and associated audience expectation. Again Dyer identifies three:

- iconography;
- visual style;
- placement within the structure of the narrative.

It will be seen from the above that the star can be approached as a formal structure. As in a generic structure there is a definable set of paradigms which will be the principal means of repetition and differentiation from one film to the next. These include the star's appearance, voice, gestures, movement and other distinctive characteristics. Like a generic structure, a star structure provides a communication system capable of generating complex meanings.

The star persona often evolves through the vehicle provided by a particular genre and in the process creates something distinct, for example, Clint Eastwood's work both as the Man with No Name and as Dirty Harry. However, the measure of this distinctiveness can only be made in relation to the generic and narrative conventions which precede the star. Thus stars depend heavily on genre as a system through which their persona finds expression.

At the same time it should be acknowledged that a genre may well rely upon the availability of a star to embody the archetypal roles associated with that genre. The exchange of stars within a genre and the movement of a star across several genres are each extremely interesting points of focus for the film student. Genre study can be advanced through a focus on stars (as an example, one could look at the shifting dynamic of the western as chartered by the star personae of Wayne, Cooper and Eastwood). Star study can in turn be advanced through a focus on genre (as an example, one could compare James Stewart's star persona in Hitchcock thrillers and Mann westerns). Edward G. Robinson's defining role in *Little Caesar* in January 1931 and James Cagney's in *Public Enemy* three months later raise questions about the simultaneous development of generic and star paradigms.

The following version of the figure on p. 141 illustrates how the star structure, for example, James Cagney, exists in a complex relationship with the generic structure of the Warners' gangster movie:

The gangster generic structure

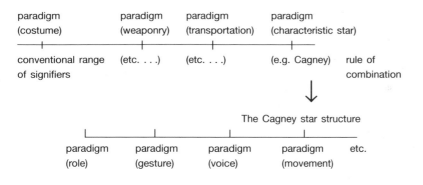

In addition to the vehicle, the star is 'accessed' through the exposure her constructed image receives in forms other than film itself. Dyer differentiates between *promotional material*, produced by the industry (including the agency acting on behalf of the star) and *criticism and commentaries* which function to 'voice' the response of the public. In practice each can both construct and alter the star image while circulating it within culture.

In practice, of course, the second of these may be highly determined by the first. Nevertheless, the actual ways in which spectators 'use' stars and seek 'gratification'[12] from them are far more varied than a deterministic model of star production–consumption would suggest. In reality the star image is **polysemic**, that is having many different meanings, and its study can lead into a much broader exploration of popular culture in which their images circulate, embodying (literally) the fantasies, desires and myths – often otherwise repressed – of ordinary people.

A useful way of drawing together these opening remarks is by reference to Christine Gledhill's identification of the four components which make up the star:[13]

1 The real person.
2 The characters/roles – which are generally fixed by fictional and stereotypical conventions.
3 The persona – the combination of the first two – the predictable in role, the 'unique' in self.
4 The image – circulating in subsidiary media forms such as TV interviews, magazines, etc.

In public actors begin to project themselves as though these four categories collapse into one another. In a sense one can say that the image becomes a character, but not a character in a narrative film, rather a character within the institution of cinema. The complexities of this are increasingly exploited in postmodern Hollywood. For example, Arnold Schwartzenneger plays not so much himself as his own cinematic image within the narrative of *Last Action Hero* (1993).

Richard Dyer offers an analysis of Julia Roberts[14] which employs many of the ideas so far outlined. What is exemplary about this short study – whether or not one wishes to dispute the detail – is the way it moves across the four components of the star construct in a way which emphasises their complex interdependence. He describes 1991 as 'the moment' of Julia Roberts and asks what precisely constituted her as star, the first female star for twenty years whose name alone was enough to sell a movie.

The subsidiary forms of circulation and the roles she plays coalesce around the crucial quality of 'authenticity'. The stories told about Julia Roberts in the media, about her relationships with the male leads in her films, convey the idea that she is just being herself. The characters she plays have a powerful mixture of strength and vulnerability which suggests that these roles are personifications of a real person. The spectator is presented with the classic paradox of stardom: the star is known or knowable, accessible, ordinary and yet, at the same time, extraordinary and only attainable in the everyday world of the spectator in forms of desire and fantasy.

The 'real' person, Dyer says, is likeable, attractive and talented – but this only begs the question, why *this* particular likeable, attractive, talented young woman?

One explanation Dyer offers is in terms of charisma: the fact that some people naturally 'glow'. 'We often talk about people whom the camera loves . . . Perhaps it is not so much that the camera loves some people as that some people love the camera.' The star displays herself, as Roberts does in sequences of *Sleeping with the Enemy* which have no motivation other than display. Both this film and *Pretty Woman* include the sheer enjoyment of trying on different images.

An alternative explanation is simply that Roberts was lucky enough to be the one from many young women with virtually identical attributes chosen to be hyped by the marketing machinery of Hollywood. But hype in itself cannot guarantee stardom. The history of Hollywood is littered with examples of actors who did not reach stardom despite having huge amounts of money invested in them.

Dyer concludes that to become a star 'you have to be the right person in the right films at the right time'. This involves a complex mix of real person-role-persona-image which structures and gives coherence to moods, feelings, desires in the culture at that particular moment. Dyer suggests that Roberts embraces feminism in as much as it is no longer credible to be a bimbo or a housewife for a female audience. At the same time she is not so far prepared to suppress the bimbo or the housewife that she fails to appeal to the male spectator. She's no pushover, no victim in the parts she plays, and yet 'there are some of the disturbing implications of female desirability – she's vulnerable, that's to say eminently hurtable'. Dyer concludes his analysis as follows:

> Julia Roberts is so sexy and yet so very much her own woman that she's the very embodiment of the so-called post-feminist woman. She's prepared to allow herself to be sold as a sex object and yet at the same time she gives the impression that she's in charge of her image. . . . Playing with your own image, shopping is the only thing worth doing; these are very 80s images – but Julia Roberts is just soft and old-fashioned enough to reconcile them with what we flatter ourselves are the more caring attitudes of today. And she does light up the screen.

Dyer synthesises a set of observations by reference to the way the star functions as a signifying system communicating a range of meanings – some of which reinforce accepted cultural myths (here of appearance, sexuality, lifestyle) – and some of which represent specific cultural tensions and contradictions within or between these myths and idealisations. The complex meaning structure called Julia Roberts can be considered to function very much as genre was described as doing in the previous section: embodying dominant values and reconciling or closing down contradictions.

To borrow from Pam Cook's *The Cinema Book*, stars thus offer 'insurance value' to the industry, a 'production value'[15] to the film-makers and a 'trademark' value to potential audiences.

Impersonation or personification?

Inasmuch as the stars operate as signifiers within narrative and genre their meaning is controlled and predictable, providing the pleasures of recognition and expectations fulfilled. However, inasmuch as the star signifier operates not just within narrative and genre but as an image within culture, it is potentially much less stable. Their polysemic potential is such that they can open up rather than close down the fracture lines between opposing values and attitudes in culture. The critical industry which has grown up around the persona-image of Madonna illustrates well the conflict between the star seen as suturing or 'stitching together' contradiction and the star as subversive, working away at those contradictions, forcing us to pay attention. She is scarcely, if at all, 'confined' by the textual system into which she is placed. For an audience of today the same could be said of Marilyn Monroe – in a particularly interesting way. The very fact of her 'confinement' in generic roles contributes to the way we read her wider cultural image which includes the way she has come to signify, in an archetypal way, the objectification and exploitation of a talented woman by an industrial complex.

Nothing so obviously or so frequently challenges the fictional illusion of a Hollywood film than the presence of the star. However much the conventions of Hollywood narrative realist cinema are intent upon rendering invisible the constructedness of its product through, for example, naturalistic mise-en-scène and continuity editing, the star presence has the potential to undo this. The spectator is consciously aware of, for example, Schwartzenneger-in-performance. Although this does not undermine the pleasure of the text, indeed it can intensify it, the act of spectatorship must negotiate the potential conflict between star presence and the fiction's attempt to persuade us that we are watching 'life' rather than a Hollywood construct. Why is it that the illusion 'gap' opened up by star in performance rarely provides a real problem for the spectator?

One explanation has to do with the way an audience is invited to approach the reading of a film. The narrative and generic structures of Hollywood film provide pleasure both through the illusion of reality they offer and through their self-containment as forms which have no existence outside themselves. The latter pleasure is that of the safety hatch – it's only a film . . . it's only a horror movie – after having been scared witless. The star structure, working within the larger structures of narrative and genre is handled in the same way. 'It's just a movie' is a statement which acknowledges that a 'gap' exists and yet uses this knowledge as a means of escape from the film's more demanding thematic and ideological implications.

Often the 'gap' is made invisible by the casting to type of star (signifier) in role (signified). The relationship between the star and the part s/he is playing appears 'common sense' whether it be Harrison Ford as the law enforcer or Sharon Stone as the *femme fatale*. The pleasure of reassurance felt by the audience comes from a perceived 'natural' connection between star and role which, in some respects, is a reassurance based on the confirmation of cultural myths, of ideologically-based stereotypes.

Thus a second possible answer to the question involves looking at the nature of star performance itself.

Acting involves either impersonation or personification.[16]

Impersonation, involves the actor creating a role from the range of skills and imagination she possesses. Successful impersonation involves disappearing into the role and leaving the 'real' self behind. The actor as impersonator is evaluated in relation to the range of roles s/he can successfully take on and the degree to which they are perceived as psychologically realistic. It is most often associated with serious acting in the theatre.

Personification involves the actor stepping into a role by virtue of her physical appearance and behaviour patterns conforming to the 'type' of that role. The actor as personifier is evaluated in terms of what s/he is – rather than what s/he can do. It is most often associated with cruder forms of melodramatic theatre – and with popular cinema.

Hollywood star acting has traditionally been dependent on a very high degree of personification. Bogart personifies the noir private eye. Flynn personifies the swashbuckling hero. Sometimes it is difficult to describe a typical role at all: Garbo or Dietrich or Madonna primarily personify themselves.

It is this merging of person-persona-image and role through the process of personification which provides a second more tentative answer to the question of why the star in performance does not encourage, by her presence, a deconstruction of the film's realist illusion.

Having said this, the 'gap' remains real, the site where the so-called 'seamless' text is most easily exposed as a fictional construct. And this is equally true of star performances today as it is of those produced under the studio system. The tendency since the breakdow of the studio system, through the early Method performances (see p. 123) of, for example, Brando and Steiger, to the star-as-actor phenomenon of the new Hollywood, well exemplified by a star-as-actor such as Meryl Streep, is to claim for the star personifier the skills of impersonation.

However, the American Method as originated by Lee Strasberg, while giving performance the appearance of impersonation, is in practice a more intense form of personification. Unlike the process of character construction advocated by Stanislavski[17] which encourages the actor to work from the imagination, the process advocated by Strasberg demands that actors work from within their own person, their own conflicts and personal experiences. It can lead to the painful self-exposure of Brando in *Last Tango in Paris*, the literalness of physical identification of De Niro in *Raging Bull*. The Method can be seen as a more sophisticated and intense kind of personification. Whereas the latter requires that the star physically embodies the role in appearance, gesture and movement, the former adds to this the requirement that a star psychologically 'becomes' the role.

Method acting, far from closing the 'gap' between star (signifier) and role (signified), actually emphasises it. One is often more aware of Hoffman or Streep or Pacino 'doing their thing' the more they strain towards impersonation.

Personification can be described as a relationship between star (signifier) and role (signified) which is so highly motivated as to render signifier and signified almost identical. It is for this reason that the *commutation test* is particularly applicable to star study. Substitute one actor for another in a particular role and see if it makes any significant difference (for example, try Hoffman, Cruise, Robbins and Costner as Tom Hank's Forrest Gump).

The principal value of a commutation test (besides its fun) may appear to be descriptive: it can lead to a more precise description of what is indeed unique in one persona over another measured in terms of their potential for personifying a 'type'.

A variation on the commutation test is to look at a *star in transition* from one persona and image to another. A spectacular and interesting example is offered by Jane Fonda whose career has represented major transitions which include, rather crudely, a range from bimbo to left-wing political activist to one of the most successful businesswomen

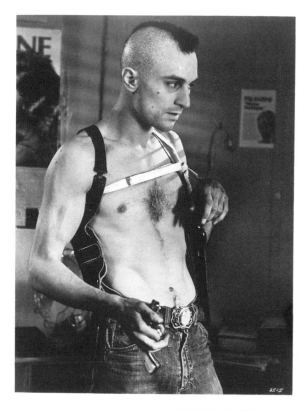

• Plates 5.10, 5.11 and 5.12 The Method actor: De Niro in *Taxi Driver* (Martin Scorsese, US 1976) (left) and as both the young and fit middleweight boxing champion La Motta (above) and the middle-aged, 60-pound heavier La Motta (below) in *Raging Bull* (Martin Scorsese, US 1980)

in America. A study will reveal the extent to which a 'core' persona holds across these changes. (In Fonda's case, a 'core' persona including voice, gesture, mannerism and other aspects of the body consistently applied in Method performances and beyond this, qualities of sincerity, independence, competence and vulnerability.)[18]

It is especially useful to study Fonda's 1972 participation in Godard's *Tout Va Bien*. It provides an interesting and rare example of star deconstruction. She offers herself to the film in an act of pure personification – she signifies her own star persona – within a film with a strong left-wing polemic. As in Brechtian theatre, the audience is constantly aware that they are watching actors in a constructed performance. Fonda's presence is one of the means by which this awareness is communicated.

The star and the ideology of individualism

Collectively, narrative, genre and star provide a highly conventionalised form of communication which makes available to an audience two forms of fantasy pleasure.

One is the artificial security created by the formal organisation of the film; we know the real world is far less comprehensible and manageable than that constructed by narrative and genre (see p. 127). The second is the intense personal potential for the resolution of crisis embodied in the star; we know the real world cannot be acted upon so directly, so effectively by the individual.

The fact that the star is a 'maximised type', that is, as perfect an embodiment of a set of characteristics as can be imagined, allows the culture to perpetuate its myth, be they of forms of masculine heroism or forms of female beauty. Inasmuch as western consumer capitalism is built on the cult of the person, the development of a unique individualised identity through image, the ideological reinforcement provided by the star image is very powerful.

Take, for example, the 'maximised types' personified by Kevin Costner and Whitney Houston in *The Bodyguard*. Both star personae are displayed doing 'their thing', action hero and singer, with narrative clearly subordinated to spectacle. Neither star creates character so much as embodies 'type' traits which, at the same time, have a uniqueness deriving from who they are as stars. On the one hand, then, are their generic roles, highly conventionalised and predictable. On the other, there are all the meanings each star image possesses for the spectator who has encountered them in a vast range of subsidiary forms of circulation. The star is recognisable yet unique, caught in a melodramatic narrative but free to assert individuality, enclosed within a recognisably naturalistic world and yet able to exist as an autonomous self which can gain a significant degree of control over this world.

Thus the pleasure the star provide us with includes that of *ideological reinforcement*, a renewed image of the importance of the self as an agent able to act upon and make a difference to the world s/he inhabits.

As an aside to this discussion, it is ironic to observe that in practice Hollywood does not offer the individual-as-star the mythic freedom to act on her world which has just been described. Stars have, in economic terms, an 'exchange value'; they are forms of capital strategically employed in order to create profit. Equally, stars have a 'use value' which is what they bring as signifying systems, as meaning structures to a narrative. In both their exchange and use values, that is in their existence as forms of capital, on the one hand, as raw material available for refinement within narrative and genre, on the other, stars are far from free agents. In their willingness to function as signs, actors surrender control to those responsible for the construction of image – both in film production and in publicity. The extent to which a contemporary star is significantly more

• Plate 5.13 *The Bodyguard* (Warner Bros, US 1992)
The movie as star vehicle

in control of their image than a star working within the studio system is debatable. No less than during the studio system period, to the extent that a star offers herself as a bearer of meaning, a 'semiotic commodity', she exposes herself to the shifting require- ments of the market and those who try to manage that market.

☐ **CASE STUDY PART 3: *NEW YORK, NEW YORK* – CLASH OF THE STARS**

If *The Bodyguard* offers a fine 'old-fashioned' example to illustrate how star study can be productive in the analysis of a film text, *New York, New York* puts into play a more complex combination of elements.

The two stars, Robert De Niro and Liza Minnelli, perform within the terms of melo- drama discussed above. *New York, New York* in focusing so exclusively on a relationship by reference to psychology and emotion illustrates Hollywood's typical avoidance of other determining factors – social, cultural, political. However, the film is unusual in demonstrating so vividly two contrasting tendencies in star performance. First, how the application of a Method performance to a melodramatic scenario can produce charac- terisation of depth. De Niro's Jimmy Doyle is not one-dimensional as is often the case in melodrama. Second, how this is countered by a much more old-fashioned and extremely powerful form of star performance from Minnelli. The relationship has a genuine complexity arising from each star persona's interrogation of the other and from the very different resources each brings to the screen.

De Niro and Minnelli bring their star personae to bear in extremely powerful ways. De Niro's role as Jimmy Doyle presents uncompromising yet self-doubting masculinity; a struggle to control and channel his violent energy; an inability to articulate verbally so that communication must take the form of physical action; a lack of social competence which can be both humorous and embarrassing. This is a persona developed through *Mean Streets* and *Taxi Driver* and which is therefore rich in associations from those films. However, it is also important to point out that at this time in his career De Niro had scarcely any image in subsidiary forms of circulation – except the entertainment media's reference to him as 'Garbo' in his successful attempt to keep his private life private. More significant is De Niro's role-by-role commitment to the Method. He devoted eight months to learning how to play the saxophone as he had spent two weeks driving twelve hours a day around the streets of New York in preparation for *Taxi Driver* and as he would spend a year in training for his boxing role in *Raging Bull*.

Unlike De Niro, Minnelli brings with her to the film a persona constructed in her performances as Liza Minnelli, singer, as well as in earlier screen performances – most obviously *Cabaret*. Much more than De Niro, she brings with her an image constructed in other media, an image which includes her personal background and problems, as well as her characteristic style as singer in performance. She is able to personify a star- in-the-making who is self-confident, seeking independence and who, while vulnerable (how often this word comes up in describing Hollywood female star personae!) is able to survive and succeed through her own qualities rather than through the 'prop' of a man. She brings the power and charisma of her image to bear throughout the film and not only in her on-screen performances. The explosion of energy after the divorce when she achieves stardom is contained from the beginning in the 'promise' of Lisa Minnelli superstar.

Thus a principal source of interest lies in the interplay between a star (Minnelli) whose personification in the role of Francine Evans is based on traditional roots in a star image and De Niro's Method 'entry' into role.

If the De Niro and Minnelli roles are informed both by the 'baggage' they bring with them and by their particular mode of performance, this is a common enough phenomenon with stars (very similar to Costner and Houston, for example). However, the way these meaning systems are allowed to interact is far from usual. They are not tightly managed and controlled (as the Costner and Houston personae are), but rather they probe each other in scenes whose excessive length by Hollywood standards can be justified in terms of the excess, the *surplus of meaning* which is generated. (A 'surplus' of meaning is meaning in excess of what is required to fulfil the functional requirements of the narrative; a 'surplus' includes the ambiguities and imaginative associations which leave us with a sense of wonder.) In discussing the film in the previous section (p. 139) the idea of generic 'play' leading to 'delirium' was used. Here, it is possible to use the same words to talk about the way – in some scenes at least – contrasting star performances offer an audience much to engage with.

Certainly with regard to the problem of the star presence threatening to undermine the fictional illusion of the film, *New York, New York* offers a valuable case study. De Niro's Method and Minnelli's virtual self-personification both draw attention to themselves. The spectator is simultaneously drawn into the intensity of the melodramatic conflict and consciously aware of two very different star presences and performances in the process of self-activation. The fact that this is done on sets of stunning artificiality, counterpointing performance style and visual style in a complex revisiting of an old Hollywood genre, further confirms the film as one which is operating through multiple levels of meaning.

Scorsese has said, 'we were just doing it – rewriting, improvising, improvising, improvising until finally twenty weeks of shooting had gone by and we had something like a movie'.[19] It is uncommon in Hollywood commercial cinema for narrative development to be so dependent on the way character evolves through improvisation.

This Method approach to character creation is a demand made on both De Niro and Minnelli. However, inasmuch as this is a performance mode more suited to De Niro playing a character who foregrounds extreme emotions, especially aggression as a means of overcoming repression, Jimmy Doyle appears to dominate much of the film. What is remarkable about *New York, New York* is the balance between a masculine Method performance and Minnelli's much more traditional form of personification as Francine Evans. However, it has been argued[20] that the film privileges the male point-of-view, even in the latter part of the film when Minnelli appears strong, since she is seen through and judged from a male perspective.

Star study, like genre study, can help to explain the textual operations of a Hollywood film – as well as locate those textual operations within the wider context of Hollywood cinema as a whole. In turning to auteur study one is drawn away to some extent from the concept of broadly based meaning systems rooted in the whole Hollywood industrial process towards notions of individual creativity and control.

AUTEUR

The auteur contrast

The director in modern Hollywood can function much like a star in offering an *insurance value* to the industry and a *trademark value* to an audience. Increasingly films are bought and sold on the basis of a director's name, which takes on the function of a sign. This sign will carry much information of significance concerning the popular and critical 'credit' of the director based on his previous work and the kind of promise offered by a new film bearing his name. The auteur sign, by contrast, is much more precise and specific. It will signify a set of stylistic and thematic features which, it is anticipated, will be identifiable in the text of a film bearing the auteur name. In other words, an auteur possesses a *sign(ature)* marking out his own individuality which is legible in a film over which he has enjoyed sufficient creative control for that sign(ature) to permeate the film. In practice the auteur sign, like the star sign, can be approached as a structure made up of a set of paradigms working in distinctive rules of combination.

Issues of definition and classification which are encountered in studying genre and stars are at least as problematic in Hollywood auteur study. Since the late 1950s, following the work of critics in France, it has been considered both possible and necessary in film studies to distinguish **the auteur** in Hollywood cinema from what they called the **metteur-en-scène**, that is to distinguish a director who brings to a film the signs of his own individuality as the dominant creative force in the film's production from the director who 'merely' brings competence to the particular specialist role of directing. It is difficult to determine in many instances where on a continuum the qualities of a metteur-en-scène become those of an auteur, and this is especially so as the Hollywood industry markets films increasingly in terms of a name, in the process collapsing distinctions students and critics may want to make.

This last point is particularly significant. In previous sections it has been apparent that genre and star are phenomena of importance to audiences; a genre or a star signifies myths and desires which circulate at the heart of popular culture. By contrast, the presence of an auteur structure is neither so easily 'felt' nor, as a consequence, so direct a focus for response. If genre and star study can be said, in broad terms, to have been developed out of the lived experience of Hollywood cinema, auteur study is a construct of criticism. As such its centrality within film studies has long been a cause of dispute. This is compounded not only by problems of definition touched upon above, but by fundamental questions surrounding the very idea of 'authorship'.

The auteur structure

Early auteur theory pursued what might reasonably be described as a cult of the personality in which a film text under close examination might reveal the 'essence' of its director – and hence invite the granting of auteurist status. This approach did not so much ignore factors such as narrative and genre, or the fact that film making is a co-operative enterprise, as suggest that the auteur somehow rose above these 'restraints' to personal expression. The underlying 'politics' of the *Politique des Auteurs*, the name given to the movement in France in the 1950s to promote Hollywood directors as 'authors' of their work, included the admirable desire to have Hollywood cinema taken more seriously. However, in pursuing the idea of the individual creative figure, conceived as romantically fighting against the odds to impose his unique mark on the text, much more was lost than gained:

- Directors whose work did not reveal the marks of some essential underlying personal force were relegated to the status of metteurs-en-scène – and their work relegated with them.
- The evaluation of a film was carried out in terms of whether or not it possessed an auteurist identity – leading to some absurd conclusions. (A bad film by an auteur was 'better' than a great film by a non-auteur.)
- The 'Genius of the System' in Thomas Schatz's words,[21] the industrial production of quality entertainment through the formal means of narrative and genre, far from advanced by early auteur theory, was underestimated even further – the system was regarded as that which the great creative individual struggled against.
- The attempt to raise the status of a popular cultural form by reference to one of the characteristics of high culture – the individual genius – ignored the specific ways in which Hollywood cinema produces meaning across industry – text – audience.
- Instead of broadening the study of film into wider political and cultural debates, auteur theory led inwards towards pedantic and trivial debates about who was and who was not an auteur and what precisely were the features that constituted the auteur signature.

Perhaps the most telling indictment on early auteur theory was its failure to be endorsed by many of the very directors who were assigned auteurist identity by film criticism. Directors like Hawks, Ford and Wilder were eager to place their work within a description of film production which emphasised collaboration by a significant number of creative individuals within a profit-driven industrial system.

However, auteur study has made two profound and fundamental contributions to film studies:

- In the most general sense it encouraged the serious study of popular Hollywood cinema.
- More specifically, it did so by demanding a close analysis of mise-en-scène – as the principal site of the auteur identity.

'Excavating' a film is an activity already referred to in relation to star 'persona' and genre. Certainly there is some continuity between auteur study and the study of genre and stars. As with genre 'excavation', it is necessary to identify in auteur study the characteristic range of paradigms employed across a range of films and the characteristic rules of combination for these paradigms across two or more films directed by the same individual. Like a star, an auteur can be regarded as a 'persona', similarly made up of a combination of a real person and the films in which he exists as sign(ature). The principal difference, of course, is that the auteur does not appear in films (with notable exceptions like Woody Allen and Spike Lee) so that whereas the star-in-role is visible, functioning as icon, the auteur-in-role must be excavated by critical analysis.

The development away from the auteur as individual to *auteur as structure* (a development particularly associated with the work of Peter Wollen in the late 1960s)[22] did not get rid of the idea of an author but it radically redefined the nature of this authorship in Hollywood cinema. The emphasis shifted to a study of the recurring features operating in films bearing the name of a particular director. Although these recurring features were identified in terms of an individual (a 'Hawks' structure, for example), there was no requirement to go looking for a person called Howard Hawks whose essence was waiting to be revealed beneath this structure. These recurring features form what might be called a 'meaning structure' operating in addition to those of narrative, genre and star across the body of a film. This is not to say that biographical information about the auteur is irrelevant. It may be useful in helping to confirm observations made about the distinctive 'presence' communicated by the auteur structure. The sign(ature) is a set of formal elements – the choice remains for the student as to whether to engage in character analysis based on this signature.

Consider the problem of reconciling the concept of the auteur with that of film production as co-operative enterprise involving the contributions of an assortment of creative personnel. In specific scenes the work of one or more of these may be particularly foregrounded – the actor, the set designer, the scriptwriter, the editor, the music composer – but the controlling creative authority and deployment of these contributions is that of the auteur director. The contributions of others are expressions of specific aspects of the auteur's overall imaginative vision and to that extent they become inscribed with the auteur's identity. For example, disputes as to whether Saul Bass's scenario or Bernard Hermann's music constituted the crucial creative contributions to the shower scene in *Psycho* become irrelevant if we accept that these elements exist only as 'potential' until mobilised and made coherent within a meaning structure with a unitary identity – in this case something called 'Hitchcock'.

What this suggests is in fact something of a compromise between early auteur individualism and a purely structuralist conception. The auteur structure called 'Hitchcock' leaves room not only for the individual called Alfred Hitchcock to be seen as a 'catalyst' but as the final determining creative force. In addition, this does not preclude the possibility of a 'combination' structure, in which a text is 'authored' by different codes working together in an identifiable, recurring form: the Ford–Wayne–western structure for example.

Certainly the identification of a single 'author' has been embraced by all those who must classify and catalogue films. The listings produced both by other media and by academia embrace the single name – perhaps as much as anything for convenience. However, this simple justification sidesteps the contested reading of this name: as originating genius, as catalyst, as structure. And convenience or not, it is difficult to accept uncritically a discourse which so powerfully diverts attention away from the collaborative and complex creative relationships between a large number of people which are at the heart of Hollywod cinema.

The auteur's habitat

Under what circumstances does the auteur flourish? In the security of a studio system or the wheeler-dealing of the new Hollywood? In the formal conventions of narrative and genre or in the 'free play' of postmodernism referred to on pp. 134–7?

Both these questions tempt answers formulated in terms of establishing what might be considered optimum conditions for individual expression. Much of the critical writing on auteurism is preoccupied with, for example, the extent to which Ford or Hawks were able to work through the conventions of genre in order to produce films marked with their distinctive thematic preoccupations and characteristic signifiers, or the extent to which either of these men benefited from working within the studio system.

Perhaps the most satisfactory response to the 'problem' of the auteur working within Hollywood conventions is to regard these conventions as facilitating expression. A system of rules provides both security and the opportunity for inventing variations. Indeed it is possible to argue that Hollywood narrative and generic norms provide the ideal frame-work for creative expression. The auteur enjoys both a safe anchorage within an artistically self-enclosed world and the incentive to constantly push against the edges of this world to discover new possibilities.

However, Francis Ford Coppola acknowledges the reality of Hollywood box-office pressure:

> The problem is I have a double life and I work for the commercial film industry, which basically wants to take old formulas and make them with new actors. It's like Boeing – they have to make planes that will fly. They can't make one that flies on its side, even though that might be a good idea. . . . People are particular about films, they don't want to be put into an incredibly unusual situation. It's like the little kid who says 'Tell me the story of the Three Bears again.'[23]

In fact the tension between auteurist innovation and commercial requirements continues to sustain a romantic view of the 'heroic' embattled creative artist. Consider, for example, the tension in the following between acknowledging the power of Hollywood discourse and the need to retrieve the individual figure working within and through it. Dudley Andrews writes that:

> to 'begin' a project is not to originate a work, but rather to deflect a flow, to branch off in a direction. This limited sense of novelty retains the power of individual effort and critique while recognizing the greater power of the social system within which anything that makes a difference must begin. . . . Why not apply [this view] in some degree, to a Ridley Scott, whose attempt to branch out from the road picture in *Thelma and Louise* seems more *heroic* for its collapse in the film's final chase sequences.[24]

At the same time, in pursuing debates about the pressures imposed on the auteur in the new Hollywood by the deal system of one-off film production, it is necessary to take on board the opposite pressure to the one Coppola refers to: the increasing expec-tation in audiences of *textual 'excess'* in production values and stylistic flourishes. A young director wishing to be noticed must leave his calling card on screen. All directors must aspire to the status of auteur in the new Hollywood while prioritising audience requirements (box office) over their own individuality. Maybe this is the way it has always been but the current Hollywood system exposes the conflict particularly starkly (Altman's *The Player* captures these issues with sharp ironic humour).

Coppola is also an interesting point of focus in relation to debating the benefits or otherwise of working within a studio system. His attempt to make films with an auteur signature across a range of genres and to enable others to do the same under the new Hollywood dispensation led him to create in 1969 a 'studio' (Zoetrope) which would offer the kind of security and continuity creative personnel had not been offered since the end of the studio system. (It is worth comparing Coppola's *One from the Heart* with *New York, New York* – both are auteurist attempts to do something new while exploiting the conventions of the 1950s studio musical and melodrama – and both were box office failures.)

Under whatever production system and regardless of the film form in vogue, the auteur needs to enjoy a significant level of control and independence in the various stages of production if the auteur structure is to assert itself on the screen. To refer back to an earlier point, his *'catalyst' function* must be secured. This is equally true of those working on mainstream commercial projects, directors like Steven Spielberg, Oliver Stone, Clint Eastwood and Spike Lee, as it is for those working in the low-budget 'independent' sector such as John Sayles, Jim Jarmusch, Gus van Sant and Hal Hartley. In this regard the de facto producer role of the director is fundamental. In the studio system directors such as Howard Hawks and John Ford enjoyed either actual or de facto producer power. However, it is difficult to precisely define the amount of control a director needs to enjoy before he can be considered sufficiently enabled to impose his sign(ature) on a film. Using right to the final cut as a benchmark of an auteur's controlling presence within the film is to go too far. Clearly *The Magnificent Ambersons* would have been the better for Welles retaining control through to final cut, but the film in the form in which it survives is still very visibly marked by the Welles' auteur presence. Is Sluitzer's Hollywood remake of his own Dutch-language *The Vanishing* with an entirely different ending an example of loss of auteur control? The case of *Blade Runner – the Director's Cut* raises the interesting idea that it is possible to become the auteur of a film ten years after its original release through being granted additional power. At what point precisely did Ridley Scott make the transition from metteur-en-scène to auteur?

This example of the foregrounding of Ridley Scott in the re-release of *Blade Runner* also indicates the extent to which the industry is keen to promote directors to the auteur ranks for marketing reasons. 'A film by ——' or 'A —— film' is a typical feature of film promotion today even when the director clearly has not enjoyed the producer power described above (for example, *Fatal Attraction* – an Adrian Lynne film?). Thus for marketing purposes all directors seem to have assumed or had thrust upon them auteur status. Is this to fatally undermine the auteur concept or does it highlight how absurd it has been all along to try to make meaningful distinctions between those who 'direct' and those who 'create'?

Beyond this, one may ask whether the producer himself can be regarded as auteur with recurring characteristics observable across a range of films. This might be particularly appropriate in looking at groups of films from the studio system produced by men with characteristic personal visions – like Thalberg or Selznick or Freed. In contemporary Hollywood Spielberg is, arguably, as much an auteur in his role as producer as he is in films which he personally directs. And still further, should one regard the studio as auteur; the Warners gangster film, the MGM musical, for example, represent meaning structures with characteristic paradigms.

And what of the star as auteur? The vehicle can be so controlled by the star that he becomes the producer–star determining the stylistic as well as the thematic content of the film. Is Schwartzenneger or Stallone an auteur? A claim can be made for Kevin Costner as auteur not only in his role as director–star in *Dances with Wolves* (including a 'Director's Cut') but in his role as producer–star in *The Bodyguard*.

If there are more questions than answers here, this is because traditional auteur theory stands on insecure ground in relation to the whole issue of origination. Its undoubted value is in putting in place another meaning structure, another creative dimension (whether deriving from auteur–director, auteur–producer or even auteur–studio) to intersect with those of genre and star already discussed, thus enabling a closer interrogation of the film text. However, before proceeding to an application of auteur structuralism to *New York, New York*, it is necessary to touch upon two further issues regarding origination, identity and the 'politics' of classification.

The spectator as auteur?

Meaning is only created in the act of reading – an encoded message (text) remains only as potential meaning until it is decoded by a reader (or spectator). Further, different readers come to a text with their own specific social, culture and psychological formation as individuals. The logical deduction from this is that the text is 'authored' by the reader rather than by the text's originator. Roland Barthes, for example, talked of the 'death of the author' and the 'birth of the reader'.

In practice, however, spectatorship is not as autonomous as the above would suggest. There are not literally as many readings of a text as there are readers – far from it. The range of responses within an audience will be made relatively homogeneous as a result of

1 *hegemony* – the conventional 'common-sense' political, social and cultural ways of seeing the world shared, more or less, by the vast majority of spectators;
2 *language* (in the broadest sense of signs working in structures and including non-verbal languages) which, to emphasise the point again, 'does our thinking for us'.

This can be illustrated clearly by examining the range of response to genre or star. Each is brought into consciousness through the act of reading but in that moment powerful conventional ways of thinking and decoding impose themselves on what might otherwise be a very personal, idiosyncratic reading.

As with any other meaning structures, an auteur structure is brought into consciousness in the act of reading, decoding. However, as has already been pointed out, a crucial difference exists between this and genre or star structures in that the latter exist much more obviously and vibrantly as discourses within popular culture. An auteur structure is rendered visible and therefore readable by the invention of the auteur in a much more critically willed manner than is the case with genre and star. Once named (and thus capable of identification) it imposes its own power on the reader.

A 'Douglas Sirk' film will be read in response to knowledge about the 'Douglas Sirk' auteur structure and if that knowledge is absent, the auteur structure will not be read at all – it will be a meaning 'potential' left untouched by the reader. Sirk was thought of in the 1950s as a director of traditional melodramatic 'weepies' set in a bourgeois world. Only with auteur critic Andrew Sarris at the end of the 1960s was a different view of Sirk's work put forward: that he was in fact offering a scathing critique of the world depicted in his films. Sarris argued that in visual style and in his 'narrative attitude' Sirk was a remarkable auteur – delivering films to Universal as per contract which appeared to be standard genre product but which were characterised by an individual way of seeing and telling. One of Sirk's celebrated films, such as *Written on the Wind*, may well appear of little or no special interest unless the spectator is aware of the Douglas Sirk auteur structure. The claims made for it as a 'subversive' text rather than as a regular 1950s melodrama and star vehicle require validation through reference to the determining additional meaning structure – 'Sirk' – operative within the text. In other words, the film can only be read as a text of significance if mediated through the process of criticism.

On a more basic level, even if the spectator is ignorant of the auteur structure, the simple power of *naming* remains significant. The classification which the auteur name allows means that texts can be differentiated from one another, most particularly in terms of the status which can be conferred upon them. The act of spectatorship will be

• Plate 5.14 *Written on the Wind* (Douglas Sirk, US 1956)
Rock Hudson and Dorothy Malone: early American soap or auteur masterpiece?

influenced by the power of the name. This returns us to the auteur as 'guarantee' and 'trademark'. It also returns us to the observation that in contemporary Hollywood nearly all films have placed upon them the name of an auteur whether or not any auteur structure has been established behind that name. The name exists purely as a name-tag on a commodity – indeed the name-tag is itself a commodity: 'Spielberg'.

The attempt to establish a recognisable set of thematic and stylistic features (a signified) for the auteur name (the signifier) is, in a self-reflexive way, increasingly taken on by the bearer of that name, that is the director himself. Thus we can trace a transition from the late 1950s when critics constructed an auteur meaning structure out of a body of films put in place more or less intuitively by a director in active collaboration with other creative individuals within enabling institutional structures to the situation today where a director often strives, self-consciously, to impose a recognisable auteur structure to verify the commercial and critical existence of the name s/he bears.

☐ CASE STUDY PART 4: SCORSESE AND *NEW YORK, NEW YORK*

Finally, it is worth returning to another idea introduced earlier: that of 'surplus' meaning. An auteur critical approach, described here as an 'excavation' of the text, may reveal meaning which is 'surplus' to what is required for the text to make basic narrative sense but it is precisely in surplus meaning that the text marks itself as having a distinct identity. It is in surplus meaning that much pleasure, possible 'delirium', has its source. As with a star study, auteur study confirms the presence of some of this surplus, identifies its mechanisms and explains the pleasure which is its product.

Some of the surplus of meaning contained in *Written on the Wind* (1956) can be confirmed by reference to its stars, much more by reference to the 'Sirk' auteur structure – and the same can be said of *New York, New York* when an additional level of 'coding', the 'Scorsese' auteur structure, is examined.

The Scorsese auteur structure is assembled deductively from the films Martin Scorsese has directed. (The extent to which this structure is also the result of inductively applying biographical information about the person Martin Scorsese is more debatable and will be touched on below.) The structure is then applied to the text under scrutiny.

Concern over the circularity and self-fulfilling character of this procedure must be considered – even as it is put into practice. There is clearly the danger of locking the film into a formalist system in the same way as was commented on earlier with regard to the application of a genre structure (see p. 125). There is a fine line between determining and overdetermining the meaning of a film text. A structuralist approach provides the student with valuable tools, but they are tools which must be used with intelligence and flexibility. If the film can be regarded as an object, the purpose is not to package and make it conform to some standard but precisely the opposite: to unpack its meaning and in the process identify what is distinctive in the particular combination of elements.

The Scorsese auteur structure can, at least in part, be deduced from films which lie chronologically either side of *New York, New York* in which Martin Scorsese enjoyed the kind of producer–director control discussed on p. 151. Thus *Who's That Knocking at My Door?*, *Mean Streets*, *Raging Bull* and *King of Comedy* offer themselves as texts to be searched for the kind of recurring features which will allow us to construct an auteur structure. *Boxcar Bertha* and *Alice Doesn't Live Here Anymore*, films over which Scorsese did not exercise such personal control, are excluded from consideration. (But should they be? Perhaps they are in some respects the most interesting; projects where the director had to 'negotiate' a relationship, an identity with the material.)

We discover the following principal thematic preoccupations in two or more of Scorsese's 'auteur' films:

- a strong focus on masculinity: on male friendship, on male sexuality and on the ways in which these are threatened or experienced as areas of personal crisis;
- more specifically: the male attitude to women as 'other', as unknowable, definable as 'whores' or 'virgins', as the source of the threat to masculinity, as the cause of male paranoia, and consequently as objects of abuse within relationships where the male seeks to assert dominance;
- explicitly or implicitly the male character is placed within a framework of guilt, sin, retribution, redemption;
- the male existing within a closed world, either a community (Italian New York) or a mental state of alienation and reality distortion;

- this reality distortion is sometimes linked to wider forms of reality distortion within American culture (*Taxi Driver* and *King of Comedy*);
- generally the resolution of internal conflict by means of external violence;
- as an extension to this: the dominance of the physical over the verbal – male characters are characteristically inarticulate but physically expressive;
- a representation of blacks which reflects either the overt or implicit racism of the protagonists.

We also note the following features of form and style recurring in two or more of the above-named films:

- documentary-style realism in Method performances and locations;
- the expressive use of mobile camera, lighting, editing and sound which works against the documentary realism, placing it within a stylised artificiality;
- thus point-of-view is a complex interaction of the spectator's observations of an 'objective' world and the character's 'subjective' perception of that world;
- the primary role assigned to soundtrack in the creation of meaning;
- the adoption (and subsequent problematising) of generic forms and, in particular, the ambiguity and perplexity of the films' closures.

These paradigms, these features observable within the films can be amplified by reference to biographical information concerning Martin Scorsese. So, for example, his close identification with Little Italy in New York City with its distinctive social formation may be cited. More specifically, his Catholic background provides useful corroborating evidence, and some (overly neat?) personal statements such as that in which he says that as a boy he wished to be either a priest or a gangster. His immersion from a very early age in film culture helps to explain something of the rich repertoire of styles and images he is able to bring to the screen. His interest in the films of Powell and Pressburger, as well as the more obvious homage to the MGM classic musical, may, for example, advance our appreciation of *New York, New York*.

Keeping Scorsese-the-person at arm's length by working with Scorsese-the-structure in order to make meaning out of *New York, New York*, may appear absurdly purist. Biographical information such as that outlined in the previous paragraph clearly contributes to the composite auteur-structure which we are applying to the film. However, the question must be considered: what kinds of biographical detail are useful? For example, during the filming of *New York, New York* Scorsese was having a relationship with Minnelli while his nine-months pregnant wife, co-screenwriter Julie Cameron, stalked the set. There were also strong rumours of on-set cocaine use. When considering the improvisational approach used throughout the film, is it necessary to probe the madness in this Method?

Nevertheless, whether the focus is Scorsese or Hitchcock or Woody Allen, an emphasis on the biographical, and especially the more speculative forms of the biographical, takes us into the 'essentialist' distraction – that a text is a site for excavating the 'essence' of a person, albeit the film's principal creative force. The emphasis in this section and throughout the chapter has been firmly on the film text and how it operates as a meaning system.

In placing *New York, New York* within an auteur structure called 'Scorsese' it is possible to identify more sharply both stylistic and thematic elements and in so doing move towards a more complex understanding and appreciation of the film.

• Plate 5.15 *New York, New York* (Martin Scorsese, US 1977)
'Happy endings' or 'sappy endings'?

One of the themes which is amplified by application of the auteur-structure is the male struggling to find expression and identity within a heterosexual relationship. For example, Jimmy Doyle's saxophone as phallus is most dramatically referred to in a scene with Francine just before the birth of their baby when he accuses her of provoking him to smash it.

One of the stylistic features which is amplified by the application of the auteur-structure is the placing of Method performance against the artificiality and visual excess of its studio-bound locations. At the same time, the film does not demonstrate some of the key elements of other Scorsese films such as the placing of the central character within a Catholic theological context of guilt and redemption (the rejection of *Happy Endings* actually makes this a less 'redemptive' film than those apparently much bleaker films made on either side of it). The fact that there is not a perfect 'match' between auteur-structure and film is perfectly reasonable. To repeat the point: the structure is a tool not a strait-jacket.

This superficial sketch of auteurist features of *New York, New York* nevertheless allows some evaluation of the use of auteur study as a critical approach to Hollywood cinema. Most obviously, elements of theme and style become foregrounded, confirming what might otherwise remain a spectator's tentative interpretation of the film's meaning. Perhaps new significance can be read into detail and a richer appreciation becomes possible of aspects of the film's form.

While remaining philosophically and methodologically suspect, an auteur approach offers an additional layer of coherence to the text and explicates some of the text's important 'surplus' meaning. The more auteur structures/identities that enter into general circulation, the more expectations are raised and fulfilment sought by audiences always on the look out for patterns of repetition and variation as part of the pleasure of cinema.

FILM, AUDIENCE, DIALOGUE

A structuralist approach to film study can be very useful. It allows a *common approach* to be adopted not only to a large number of apparently very different films but also to different critical discourses within the subject – such as genre, star and auteur. It also allows for sufficient *containment of all the surface variables* that make every film different from every other film for a study of a film text or a group of film texts to become manageable.

However, these advantages – a 'common approach' and 'containment' – can also be regarded as disadvantages, *overdetermining* how a film is read and critically 'processed' (see again pp. 134–6). Also, comment has been made throughout this chapter on the increasing *difficulty or desirability of containment*, of limiting for the purpose of study all the meanings in play.

In relation to genre, star and auteur, the chapter has emphasised the loosening of traditional categories:

> The range of paradigmatic features 'permissible' within a genre film has been freed up considerably with the text cross-referencing paradigms from the whole of Hollywood cinema (see pp. 144–6).

> In relation to star study, the shift from 'star' to 'actor' has made it much more difficult to fix in place a set of recurring characteristics, in relation to either roles or persona (see pp. 155–6).

> With the industry's incorporation of many directors into the ranks of auteurism, if only for marketing purposes, and with the free movement by auteurs between 'personal' and 'commercial' projects (Scorsese provides an obvious example over the past ten years), it is as difficult as it has always been to agree what might actually constitute an auteur in Hollywood cinema (see pp. 156–7).

All those elements which cannot be contained and which, with reference to *New York, New York*, have been described as 'surplus meaning' or 'excess' or even 'delirium', are the very things we might most want to explore. Particularly intense forms of pleasure and meaning are precisely in those aspects of the film which escape structural containment. The film illustrates not only the rich complexities of **intertextuality**, of the 'dialogue' which is going on between this film and a whole Hollywood history, rich in association, but also how much internal 'dialogue' is going on within and between the different paradigmatic elements, genre, star and auteur, which the simple musical bio-pic narrative (just about) holds together. The imposed logic of structuralism needs to be balanced by a sensitivity to these forms of 'dialogue'.

To continue the analogy made throughout with language, a finite set of rules and a limited vocabulary can generate an infinite number of meanings. It is very useful to learn the vocabulary and the structures, but the purpose of doing so is to participate in the real world of communication. In the real world of interaction between film industry–film text–film audience, a limited vocabulary in the form of paradigms, structured in ways which are sufficiently conventionalised to be called 'rules' are capable of producing an infinite number of meanings. Pleasure is to be found both in the artificial containment of the real world in structured forms and in the 'play' which these structured forms allow.[25]

For this reason the formal study of genre, star and auteur must be balanced by a very different approach to film studies which emphasises reception and the actual uses to which a film text is put by specific groups of people differentiated by gender, class, race or age at the particular historical moment of viewing. A film is a text with complex internal structures put into circulation as a commodity by an industry. But it is also an experience, a cultural event in which the commodity form of the film can be appropriated by an audience as part of their own cultural production. (For example, the meaning of Schumacher's vigilante thriller *Falling Down* for lower middle-class white American urban audiences; the appropriation of Lisa Minnelli's mother, Judy Garland, by gay audiences.) This is where the exploration of genre and star in particular must move along the continuum from textual to *cultural studies*, from structuralism to *ethnography*, from theories to the way people actually watch and use films within their lives.[26]

NOTES

1   D. Thompson and I. Christie (eds), 1989, p. 69.

2   See J. Fiske, 1987, ch. 8.

3   See F. McConnell, 1979.

4   See T. Schatz, 1981, pp. 29–36.

5   See J. Belton, 1994, pp. 305–10.

6   J. Collins, 'Genericity in the Nineties', in J. Collins, *et al.* (eds), 1993, p. 254.

7   ibid., pp. 257–62.

8   See J. Cawelti, 1976, ch. 1.

9   Thompson and Christie (eds), p. 72.

10 R. Dyer, 'Entertainment and Utopia', in R. Altman (ed.), 1981.

11 R. Dyer, 1979, pp. 68–72.

12 For a simple exposition of Uses and Gratification Theory, see J. Fiske, 1990, pp. 154–6.

13 See C. Gledhill (ed.), 1991, chs 13–16 have provided the basis for pp. 143–7.

14 This is taken from Richard Dyer's piece on Julia Roberts broadcast on BBC's *The Late Show* in March 1991.

15 See P. Cook (ed.), 1986, pp. 50–2.

16 See B. King, 'Articulating Stardom', in Gledhill (ed.), 1991.

17 The Russian Stanislavski and the American Strasberg developed, arguably, the century's two most influential theories and practices of acting. Whether they are as opposing to one another as is commonly thought is open to debate.

18 See Dyer, 1979, pp. 72–98.

19 Thompson and Christie (eds), p. 72.

20   See the articles by R. Lippe and L. Cooke, in *Movie*, vol. 31–2, winter 1986.

21   See T. Schatz 1988, an excellent study of the studio system.

22   P. Wollen, 1972.

23   See *Guardian*, 21 January 1993.

24   See D. Andrews, 'The Unauthorised Auteur Today', Collins *et al.* (eds), 1993, pp. 82–3 (emphasis added).

25   See, for example, ch. 12 of Fiske, 1987.

26   See J. Basinger, 1993, for a very entertaining example of how genre and star study can be refocused on how audiences actually 'use' films.

FURTHER VIEWING

If you wish to engage in a detailed study of *New York, New York* the following are some of the films that will place it in context:

Scorsese:

Who's That Knocking at My Door (1969)

Mean Streets (1973)

Alice Doesn't Live Here Anymore (1975)

Taxi Driver (1976)

New York, New York (1977)

Raging Bull (1980)

King of Comedy (1982)

The musical:

On the Town (Donen/Kelly, 1949)

The Band Wagon (Minnelli, 1953)

A Star is Born (Cukor, 1954)

The Glenn Miller Story (Mann, 1954)

Funny Girl (Wyler, 1968)

Cabaret (Fosse, 1972)

It is also useful to compare Scorsese's film with Coppola's *One from the Heart* (1982) in relation to its hommage to the studio film.

The study of genre, star and auteur invites list-making. Over sixty films are referred to in this chapter. You may find it useful to use some of them as the basis for constructing such lists. These lists may be based on conventional generic or star or auteur identities: a list of westerns, for example; a chronological list of films by star or auteur. However, it is in the construction of more imaginative lists which go across these obvious categories that critical discussion is opened up. This may be along the lines of Schatz's 'Genres of Order' and 'Genres of Integration' (p.131) or Collins' 'eclecticism' and 'authenticity' (p. 136). It may be in terms of grouping stars by their leanings towards impersonation or personification (pp. 143–6). The vital thing to remember is that criticism is a creative act and the construction of shapes and patterns within film studies is merely a particular example of the way we engage in complexities of all kinds, attempting to disentangle and make sense through language.

Part three

Genre forms: realism and illusion

Chapter 6

The documentary form: personal and social 'realities'

Paul Wells*

- **What is documentary?**
- **Some developments in non-fiction film**
- **From travelogue to authored documentary**
- ☐ Case study 1: Robert Flaherty
- **From social commentary to propaganda to poetic actuality**
- ☐ Case study 2: Humphrey Jennings
- **Propaganda as documentary myth**
- ☐ Case study 3: Leni Riefenstahl
- **From documentary bias to direct cinema and cinéma vérité**
- ☐ Case study 4: Frederick Wiseman
- **From radical documentary to television and diversity**
- **Notes**
- **Further reading**
- **Further viewing**

■ The documentary form: personal and social 'realities'

> I hate the word 'documentary', I think it smells of dust and boredom. I think 'Realist' films much the best.
>
> Alberto Cavalcanti[1]

> One of the things that has fouled up the discussion of documentaries, I think, in recent years has been the identification of documentary with information or even instruction. Maybe, it's a word that's outlived its usefulness, because I think that it no longer has a very clear significance.
>
> Lindsay Anderson[2]

In the first instance, the documentary form may be perceived as unappealing to the average viewer, somehow 'dry', unexciting, bound up with ordinary, everyday reality. This in itself may be a reflection upon the way that documentary as a form has been introduced to and received by new audiences. Often it has been viewed as a poor relation to mainstream cinema, local and mundane, rather than universal and spectacular. More to the point, its primary concern with recording 'reality' seems in direct opposition to the seemingly more appropriate capacity film possesses to create 'fantasy'. What is the point, one may ask, of recording the very things that many people are immersed in all the time, and wish to escape from by seeing a film? What, in short, is the 'point' of documentary?

This kind of response to the form, of course, represents the very narrowest kind of thinking, and misrepresents the purpose of the documentary enterprise. While documentary calls to mind terms like 'factual', 'objective' and 'informative', this is to categorise such films in a way that sometimes alienates certain audiences. These very terms must be subjected to close scrutiny, for under closer inspection they become relative and ambiguous in the production of most documentary films. If audiences expect to be merely 'educated' by documentaries, they may be surprised by their capacity to entertain, provoke, persuade and move.

It is often the case that documentary is believed to be the recording of 'actuality' – raw footage of real events as they happen, real people as they speak, real life as it occurs, spontaneous and unmediated. While this is often the case in producing the material *for* a documentary, it rarely constitutes a documentary in itself, because such material has to be ordered, reshaped and placed in sequential form. Even in the shooting of the material, choices have been made in regard to shot selection, point of view, lighting, etc., which anticipate a certain presentation of the material in the final film. Andrew Britton extends this point by suggesting,

> In the first place, truly great documentaries are analytical, in the sense that they present the corner of reality with which they deal not as a truth there to be observed, but as a social and historical reality which can only be understood in the context of the forces and actions that produced it. Secondly, they are engaged, in the sense that they lay no claim to objectivity, but actively present a case through their structure and organisation of point of view.[3]

---

* By request, there are no key terms in this chapter [Ed.].

It is important to stress then that, just like any 'fiction' film, the documentary is *constructed* and may be seen not as a recording of 'reality', but as another kind of representation of 'reality'. The documentary form is rarely 'innocent' and is defined in a number of ways, ranging from direct cinema through to propaganda. It is the intention of this chapter to look at documentary practice and address its codes and conventions, focusing upon its history and intentions, suggesting, perhaps, that documentary shares a much more common bond with mainstream cinema than audiences might initially think.

Most people see many documentaries on television and are so familiar with their techniques that those techniques have become invisible and not subject to interrogation. Audiences regularly watch documentaries characterised by the use of voice-over, a roll-call of experts, witnesses and opinionated members of the public, an apparently 'real' set of locations, footage of live events and 'found' archive footage. All of these recognisable conventions have a particular history and place in the development and expansion of the documentary as a *cinematic* form. Documentary was film before it was television. This is an important point to stress because in many ways, the documentary form has been neglected and marginalised as a film art because it has been so absorbed by television.

The documentary tradition and approach is still a profoundly significant and influential form. This is largely, of course, because cinema itself is still characterised by ongoing debates about representations of what is 'real' and what constitutes different modes of 'realism', topics right at the heart of any discussion about documentary, and those to be addressed later in this chapter. Having relocated the documentary form in its cinematic context, I will now suggest certain ways of analysing and understanding this complex and often contradictory medium.

WHAT IS DOCUMENTARY?

John Grierson first coined the term documentary in a review of Robert Flaherty's film *Moana* (1925), indicating the ability of the medium to literally produce a visual 'document' of a particular event. Grierson, though fiercely committed to the educational and democratic capabilities of the documentary form, clearly recognised that film itself was a relative form and, in typically combative style, suggests 'Cinema is neither an art nor an entertainment; it is a form of publication, and may publish in a hundred different ways for a hundred different audiences.'[4]

The documentary form is one method of cinematic 'publication' which in Grierson's terms is defined by 'the creative treatment of actuality'.[5] Supporting Britton's earlier point, Grierson acknowledges that the filming of 'actuality' in itself does not constitute what might be seen as the 'truth'. He recognises that 'actuality' footage must be subjected to a creative process to *reveal* its 'truth'. This apparent manipulation of the material is both a recording *of* 'reality' and a statement *about* 'reality'. Clearly, though, the nature and extent of the manipulation in using footage of 'actuality' is absolutely central to any discussion which seeks to define documentary in its purest form. It is probably the case, though, that for every documentary film-maker, there will be a specific attitude about, and deployment of the form, and it is necessary to examine some case studies to trace differing yet related trends in the documentary field.

A useful starting-point is Richard Barsam's list of categories which constitute and define what he generically terms the non-fiction film.[6] This list effectively demonstrates the different types of film which have often been perceived as documentary, and clearly share some of its possible codes and conventions. The categories include

- factual film
- ethnographic film
- films of exploration
- propaganda film
- cinéma vérité
- direct cinema
- documentary.

Barsam essentially locates the documentary itself outside the other categories because he suggests that the role of the film-maker is much more specific in determining the interpretation of the material in these types of film. In other words, he views the documentary as a medium which, despite its use of 'actuality' footage, is still what we may term an 'authored' form. This view, of course, may be challenged by some, dismissed by others, but it provides a useful distinction by which we may view the other categories in order to determine common characteristics and divergent methods.

Barsam's categories attempt to distinguish different uses of 'actuality' footage. We may view this footage as 'raw' footage, which, although subject to processes of selection as it is photographed, may be viewed as an unmediated recording of an incident, an event, an interview, etc., *as it happened*. This footage then becomes subject to specific compilation and organisation which defines its context. In its turn that footage can then become,

> the Newsreel (record of current events), the Travelogue (description of a place, often for the purposes of promotion or advertising), the Educational or Training film (to teach an audience how to do or understand something), and the Process film (to describe how an object or procedure is constructed).[7]

These films, having determined their context, that is, their purpose and perspective, are then constructed in a specific way. John Corner suggests that we may address these films and their claim to be defined as documentary by looking at three key areas which inform all non-fiction films.[8] These are,

1 technological factors;
2 sociological dimensions;
3 aesthetic concerns.

Clearly, technological developments have been absolutely intrinsic to the changing styles and approaches that characterise the non-fiction film. Advanced technology essentially enables advanced technique. Light, hand-held cameras capable of recording sound and using sensitive film stocks and able to record footage for a considerable length of time, will obviously produce a different kind of film to that produced by a static, heavy camera unable to record sound or photograph material for more than a few minutes.

The sociological dimension of these films is important because the documentary medium is a specifically social form. In attempting to record certain aspects of 'reality' in a particular time and space, the documentary implicitly and explicitly locates itself in the historical moment and focuses on the personal and cultural codes and conventions of that time.

It is in the aesthetic concerns of documentary that there is considerable debate, because it is largely in creating an aesthetic approach that documentaries and other non-fiction films begin to challenge, distort and subvert notions of documentary 'truth' and 'authenticity'. The aesthetics of a piece determine its proper context. It may be argued that the more unmediated the footage is (that is, the less 'manipulated' the material) the more it resembles the kind of film which impartially reveals the 'truth', the 'facts', 'reality' as it is. Whether this defines documentary is another matter, however, and the subject of the rest of this chapter.

Having established these criteria I am going to address certain developments in the history of non-fiction film, analysing specific examples and concluding with some points which distinguish documentary film from its kindred forms.

SOME DEVELOPMENTS IN NON-FICTION FILM

The history of the non-fiction film has its origins in the development of the earliest motion pictures. Following on from still photography, and motion studies like those photographed by Edward Muybridge, and yet further extending a trend in the arts to record 'reality' in the most accurate way,[9] 'actualities' or 'documentaires' filmed by the Lumière Brothers in 1895 constitute some of the first non-fiction films. These films included *Workers Leaving the Lumière Factory* and *Arrival of a Train at Ciotat Station*, and are merely examples of simple everyday events recorded with a static camera. Audiences were astonished by the images because they were seeing moving pictures of 'reality' for the first time. Similar short films were recorded by Edison in America and soon the phenomenon spread worldwide with examples emerging from Spain, India and China.

Perhaps the first major examples to characterise the documentary form were the films emerging after the Russian Revolution of 1917, and particularly the work of Dziga Vertov, who edited a newsreel series called *Kino-Pravda* (literally, *Film-truth*), and developed an approach to film called 'Kino-eye', characterised by twelve major theoretical points. In the space available here, I only intend to stress three of the points, but they are representative of the highly politicised and, indeed, highly aestheticised view Vertov had of the cinematic medium as a documentary tool:

> The Cameraman uses many specific devices to 'attack' reality with his camera and to put facts together in a new structure; these devices help him to strive for a better world with more perceptive people.

He continues,

> Knowing that 'in life nothing is accidental', the cameraman is expected to grasp dialectical relationships between disparate events occurring in reality; his duty is to unveil the intrinsic conflict of life's antagonistic forces and to lay bare the 'cause and effect' of life's phenomenon,

and concludes,

> All this is necessary if kinoks want to show on the screen 'Life-as-it-is' in its essence, including the 'life' of the film itself – the process of cinematic creation from shooting and laboratory, through editing, up to the final product i.e. the film being projected to the audience in the movie auditorium.[10]

Vertov's use of the film medium is a highly creative one, stressing simultaneously the importance of the art of film and the politicised 'reality' it records. It is this tension between revealing the 'form' of recording (that is, the unusual use of the camera, complex editing, etc.) and the 'content' it shows which confuses the notion of the films as documentaries, especially in regard to his later and most renowned work, *The Man with the Movie Camera* (1929). Cinéma vérité director Richard Leacock says that Vertov's newsreels were persuasive, even if they were superficial in their recording of famine or disaster, but adds,

> [Vertov] . . . went on to film *The Man with the Movie Camera*, which was accused of being formalistic, and to me it was. It was tricks, games, and I don't see that it really has any connection with his expressed desire to show life as it is.[11]

It is Vertov's aesthetic sense which in Leacock's mind ultimately distances him from the true spirit of the documentary enterprise in showing 'reality' as it is, unhindered by 'formalist' principles. A similar kind of formalism occurs in what became known as the City Symphony documentaries which include *Rien que les heures* (1926), directed by Alberto Cavalcanti, and Walter Ruttman's *Berlin, Symphony of a Great City* (1927), both of which were characterised by avant-garde and surrealist techniques. The films were essentially impressions of each city, using footage of real locations to reveal the disparity between rich and poor. Despite their formalist pretensions, the films succeed in making social comment, and are influential in their achievement in using images of everyday people, objects and locations for symbolic and political effect.

FROM TRAVELOGUE TO AUTHORED DOCUMENTARY

In America, the non-fiction film had essentially been defined and sustained by the 'travelogue' (a term coined by Burton Holmes), which was footage shot in foreign lands and shown at lectures and slide-shows to introduce audiences to different cultures and exotic locations. In 1904, at the St Louis Exposition, George C. Hale's *Tours and Scenes of the World* was particularly successful, but did not reach the mythic proportions of the footage from President Teddy Roosevelt's African safaris or Robert Scott's expedition to the South Pole. These kinds of travelogues appealed to the American public because they demonstrated the American spirit of enterprise and adventure, supporting the view that the American consciousness was characterised by a pioneering spirit and an enduring sense of 'the Frontier'. This informs a Romantic tradition of film-making which begins with travelogue footage of real cowboys and Indians and comes to its apotheosis in the films of Robert Flaherty. Special mention must be made though of Merian C. Cooper and Ernest Schoedsack who shot *Grass* (1925), a film about Iranian nomadic tribes searching for fresh pasture land, and *Chang* (1927), which followed a Thai family's experiences in the jungle, and included scenes of predatory animals attempting to kidnap women and children, which had a profound influence on Cooper and Schoedsack's most famous feature film, *King Kong* (1933).

It is Robert Flaherty, though, who most embodies the development of the documentary form as an ethnographic (the scientific study of other races from a position 'within' the community) and anthropological tool.

☐ CASE STUDY 1: ROBERT FLAHERTY

His films were travelogues to places that never were.

(Richard Barsam)[12]

Flaherty's films are not just moving pictures. They are experiences, similar in a geographic sense to visiting Paris or Rome or seeing the dawn rise over the Sinai desert. Flaherty is a country, which having once seen never forgets.

(Arthur Calder-Marshall)[13]

Sponsored by fur company Revillon Frères, Robert Flaherty made *Nanook of the North* (1922), a study of the Inuit Eskimos of northern Canada, which is acknowledged as one of the most influential films within the genre. It perhaps provides us with all the clues we require to define both the documentary and its acceptable limits. As is indicated above by Barsam and Calder-Marshall, Flaherty's films are 'authored' films with a specific intent; an intent that we might characterise as not merely the desire to record the lives of the Eskimos, but to recall and restage a former, more primitive, more 'real' era of Eskimo life. This nostalgic intent only serves to mythologise Eskimo life and to some extent remove it from its 'realist' context, thus once again calling into question some of the inherent principles that we may assume are crucial in determining documentary 'truth'.

Though Flaherty was an advocate of the use of lenses that could view the subject from a long distance so as not to affect unduly the behaviour of the Eskimos, and deployed cinematography (using long uninterrupted takes) instead of complex editing, it is Flaherty's intervention in the material that is most problematic when evaluating *Nanook* as a key documentary. Flaherty was not content merely to record events; he wanted to 'dramatise' actuality by filming aspects of Eskimo culture which he knew of from his earlier travels into the Hudson Bay area between 1910 and 1916. For example,

• Plate 6.1 *Nanook of the North* (Robert J. Flaherty, Canada 1922)
Filmed August 1920–August 1921 in the area around the Hudson Strait, Canada, and along the shore of the Hopewell Sound, Quebec

• Plate 6.2 *Nanook of the North* (Robert J. Flaherty, Canada 1922)

he wanted to film Eskimos hunting and harpooning seals in the traditional way, instead of filming them using guns, which was their regular practice. Similarly, he rebuilt igloos to accommodate camera equipment, and organised parts of the Eskimo lifestyle to suit the technical requirements of shooting footage under these conditions. In *Moana*, Flaherty staged a ritual tattooing ceremony among the Samoan Islanders, recalling a practice that had not been carried out for many years, while in *Man of Aran* (1935) shark-hunts were also staged which did not characterise the contemporary existence of the Aran Islanders.

John Grierson argues that Flaherty becomes intimate with the subject-matter before he records it and, thus, 'He lives with his people till the story is told "out of himself"' and this enables him to 'make the primary distinction between a method which describes only the surface value of a subject, and a method which more explosively reveals the reality of it'.[14] This seems to legitimise Flaherty's approach because *Nanook*, *Moana* and *Man of Aran* all succeed in revealing the practices of more 'primitive' cultures – cultures which in Flaherty's view embody a certain kind of simple and romanticised utopianism.

Clearly, then, Flaherty essentially uses 'actuality' to illustrate dominant themes and interests that he is eager to explore. In some ways Flaherty ignores the real social and political dimensions informing his subjects' lives, and, indeed, does not engage with the darker side of the human sensibility, in order to prioritise larger, more mythic and universal topics. There is almost a nostalgic yearning in Flaherty's work to return to a simpler, more physical, pre-industrial world, where humankind could pit itself against the Natural world, slowly but surely harnessing its forces to positive ends. Families and communities are seen as stoic and noble in their endeavours, surviving often against terrible odds. Flaherty obviously 'manipulates' his material and sums up one of the apparent ironies in creating documentary 'truth' by suggesting 'Sometimes you have to lie. One often has to distort a thing to catch its true spirit.'[15]

FROM SOCIAL COMMENTARY TO PROPAGANDA TO POETIC ACTUALITY

If Flaherty established a tradition of documentary which emerged out of the travelogue and aspired to celebrate humankind, then it was John Grierson in Britain who defined the documentary on more politicised terms. Grierson theorised the documentary, produced a number of films (all influenced by his political stance) and created a distribution network for them. His outlook suited a period in which the mass media (film, radio and the press) and advertising industries were having considerable impact, while the idea of mass political democracy was emerging in a way that necessitated the education of ordinary people in its principles.

Enamoured by the view that documentary could serve the processes of democracy in educating the people, Grierson pursued his aims with characteristic zeal. He was influenced by the ideas of Walter Lippmann (who believed that the complexity of modern life prohibited ordinary individuals from participating in a society to a proper extent) and the works of Sergei Eisenstein (whose film *Battleship Potemkin* (1925) (see pp. 343–4), Grierson admired as 'glorified newsreel' and thus organised a showing of it in England). Grierson wanted the documentary to be more sociologically aware and less formally aesthetic than the work of Vertov. Grierson's documentary film unit was initially sponsored by the Empire Marketing Board, under the leadership of Sir Stephen Tallents, who sought to reach Commonwealth nations both in a commercial and ideological sense. (Tallents sought to promote Britain as much as its trade.) The unit came under the auspices of the General Post Office in 1933 and finally became the Crown Film Unit in 1940, predominantly working with the Ministry of Information on wartime propaganda.

The films produced by Grierson fall into Dennis De Nitto's definition of the social commentary film, which he divides into three distinct subgroups:

> The documentary of *Social Description* has its primary purpose to present to an audience social conditions, particularly how an environment and institutions affect the lives of people. Any criticism of these conditions is oblique, implied rather than stated.

> In a documentary of *Social Criticism*, the director is less objective, and his intention is to make audiences conscious that something is wrong in their society and should be remedied.

> When a director is angry about a situation and wishes to induce outrage in his audience and even provoke them to action, he creates a documentary of *Social Protest*.[16]

Most of Grierson's output falls largely into the first category, beginning with *Drifters* (1929), the only film actually directed by Grierson, and concerned with herring fishermen in the North Sea. Other significant films followed: *Granton Trawler* (1934), directed by Edgar Anstey, also about fishing; *Song of Ceylon* (1934), directed by Basil Wright, which featured the first attempt to counterpoint sound to visual images rather than use music or dialogue; *Housing Problems* (1935), co-directed by Anstey and Arthur Elton, which deployed a journalistic newsreel style in interviewing ordinary people living in slum housing conditions; *Nightmail* (1936), directed by Basil Wright and Harry Watt, which features music by Benjamin Britten and poetry by W.H. Auden in its highly lyricised view of the night-time mail train on its journey from London to Glasgow; and *North Sea* (1938), produced by Alberto Cavalcanti, and directed by Harry Watt, which tells the story of ship-to-shore radio, using dramatised reconstructions.

Inevitably, the work of Grierson's documentary unit changed during the war period. The emphasis of the films shifted from the mode of record to the mode of propaganda. It may be suggested that the documentary genre as a whole may be viewed as consistently propagandistic in the sense that it constructs a particular point of view about a particular situation in the hope that such a point of view is accepted, believed and utilised. The conscious construction of a point of view is often informed by an overtly political intention. Even when the point of view is not constructed with such a bias in mind, it will still carry political implications. Propaganda, then, is fundamentally about the specificity of intention and the emphasis involved in constructing a particular position within a film. This is a complex issue and can extend to using both fictional and documentary forms. Simply, in order to analyse and assess 'propaganda' we must ask the question:

WHO says *WHAT* to *WHOM*, *WHEN*, *HOW*, and *WHY*, and with *WHAT* effect?[17]

During the Second World War, the Ministry of Information appointed Jack Beddington as the film liaison officer to work with Grierson's newly christened 'Crown' film unit to produce works of documentary information and propaganda. These films addressed domestic and strategic issues and were characterised by the desire to educate the public and invoke a consensus among the people in the conduct of the war at the personal and social level. Films like *Squadron 992* (1939), *Dover Front Line* (1940) and *Target for Tonight* (1941) established Harry Watt as one of the most important film-makers of the period, but it is the work of Humphrey Jennings which represents some of the finest aspects of British documentary film-making.

□ CASE STUDY 2: HUMPHREY JENNINGS

Having read English at Cambridge University, and become interested in theatre and costume design, Humphrey Jennings immersed himself in the arts and joined the GPO film unit in 1934. He designed sets for Cavalcanti's *Pett and Pott* (1934) and directed *Post Haste* and *Locomotives* in his first year. By 1936, he was part of the organising committee for the International Surrealist Exhibition in London, and working on ideas concerning an 'anthropology of our own people' which would be the catalyst for the Mass Observation Movement, principally taken up and established by journalist and anthropologist, Tom Harrison. Mass Observation sought to observe and record detailed

• Plate 6.3 *A Diary for Timothy* (Humphrey Jennings, UK 1945)
With a commentary written by E.M. Forster and spoken by John Giegud, and 'produced with the help of people
all over Great Britain, among them Dame Myra Hess', it represented the condition and mood of Britain in the final
stages of war

aspects of human behaviour, including the 'shouts and gestures of motorists', 'Bathroom
Behaviour', 'Distribution, diffusion and significance of the dirty joke' and 'Female taboos
about eating'.[18] Clearly, this reflects some of the aspirations of Jennings' work as a
documentarist, particularly in his film following the journey of a picture postcard, *Penny
Journey* (1938) and his record of working-class communities' leisure pastimes, *Spare
Time* (1939).

When war broke out, Jennings made two films, *The First Days* (1939) and *Spring
Offensive* (1939), but his first major achievement was in collaboration with Harry Watt.
Entitled *London Can Take It*, the film dealt with how the British people survived the Blitz,
demonstrating their indefatigable spirit and endurance. The film was especially made to
appeal to markets in the Empire and in the United States. *Heart of Britain* (1940) followed,
but it was *Words for Battle* (1941) that established Jennings as a distinctive film-maker
not afraid to develop aspects of the form that he was working within. In a letter to
Cicely Jennings in March 1941, he defends the technique he employed to heighten the
emotional impact of Britain's purpose in fighting the war:

> I have been accused of 'going religious' for putting the Hallelujah Chorus at the end
> of 'This is England' [Words for Battle]. This of course from Rotha and other of
> Grierson's little boys who are still talking as loudly as possible about 'pure docu-
> mentary' and 'realism' and other such systems of self-advertisement.[19]

Jennings simultaneously demonstrates a sceptical view of documentary and signals a more poetic and emotive approach to emotional realism. *Words for Battle* is composed of seven sequences, each with a commentary by Laurence Olivier, each demonstrating a juxtaposition of images with a specific piece of poetry or public oratory – these include William Blake's 'Jerusalem', Rudyard Kipling's 'The Beginnings', Winston Churchill's speech made on 4 June 1940 and Abraham Lincoln's Gettysburg Address. Jennings effectively poeticised 'actuality', effectively rehistoricising public monuments and buildings and elevating the human worth of ordinary people as they stoically endured the hardships of the war. This redefined the documentary as a genre which not merely recorded events and locations but appropriated them as illustration for the poetic muse.

Listen to Britain (1941) and *Fires were Started* (1942) continue this approach which attempts to lyricise and celebrate ordinary working practices, previously ignored until their importance was heightened and their value was acknowledged during the war. It was suggested by certain distributors and critics based at Wardour Street in London that *Fires were Started* should be cut further. This drew a response from Jennings which is revealing about his position on documentary: 'Well, of course one expects that from spineless well known modern novelists and poets who have somehow got into the propaganda business – who have no technical knowledge and no sense of solidarity or moral courage.'[20]

Significantly, Jennings rejects the idea that his films are propaganda, and, indeed, that they fit easily into any Griersonian category of documentary achievement. Moreover, he aligns himself with the power of film itself to *evoke* and *provoke* consensus through moral and emotional empathy. *A Diary For Timothy* (1946) completes Jennings' war cycle, and is perhaps his finest achievement in this mode of documentary film-making, for it anticipates the baby Timothy's growing up in postwar Britain. With a script by E.M. Forster, read by John Gielgud, the film has an elegiac and ambiguous feel because Jennings' normal emotional optimism has become emotional uncertainty. Documentary 'actuality' has been imbued with the inconsistency of 'feeling' rather than the consistency of 'fact'.

PROPAGANDA AS DOCUMENTARY MYTH

A European tradition of documentary film-making would necessitate a chapter in its own right, but figures like Joris Ivens (Holland) and Henri Storck (Belgium) contribute a great deal to the understanding of prewar Europe in their films. Ironically, one of the greatest European documentary film directors, Leni Riefenstahl, emerges from a more sinister context, in that she was responsible for Nazi propaganda film, and created what has become acknowledged as one of the greatest films, documentary or otherwise, of all time. In 1935, Riefenstahl made *Triumph of the Will*, a record of the 1934 Nuremberg Party rally, and with this one film initiated an enduring debate. Should such a film, which so effectively promotes and endorses the Nazi Party, be elevated to the notion of 'art' and championed as one of the finest examples of documentary? Only by addressing the approach of Leni Riefenstahl can one posit an answer.

☐ CASE STUDY 3: LENI RIEFENSTAHL

Leni Riefenstahl began her career as an actress, most commonly in Arnold Fanck's 'mountain' movies, which featured aspirant climbers scaling alpine ranges in search of spiritual truth and mythic grandeur. Riefenstahl herself directed and starred in a 'mountain' movie entitled *The Blue Light*. This served to confirm her as an emergent talent which had already been acknowledged by Hitler himself. The themes of the 'mountain' movie – the search for purity and higher knowledge, the pursuit of personal excellence in the face of the elemental and primitive, notions of physical self-discipline and spiritual purpose – were curiously similar to the politicised High Romanticism of National Socialism, later distorted into the perverse criminal agendas of Nazi policy. This inherently 'fascist' genre clearly informs Riefenstahl's later work.

Riefenstahl made *Triumph of the Will* after she completed *Victory of Faith* (1933), celebrating Hitler's first National Socialist Party Congress, and *Day of Freedom: Our Army* (1934), a tribute to the discipline and regimented efficiency of German soldiers. *Triumph of the Will* essentially combines these two themes and develops them into the notion of documentary propaganda as myth. Seemingly fully supported by Hitler and Goebbels, and given full co-operation and funding by government agencies, Riefenstahl deployed some 120 crew members and over thirty cameras in the shooting and construction of the film. The rally itself was staged to accommodate the film and essentially operated as a highly artificial, closely planned piece of theatre. This directly refutes Riefenstahl's claim that *Triumph of the Will* is direct cinema or cinéma vérité, because as Susan Sontag indicates, 'In *Triumph of the Will*, the document (the image) is no longer simply the record of reality; "reality" has been constructed to serve the image.'[21]

This construction of documentary 'myth' corresponds to the fascist aesthetics Sontag outlines in her evaluation of Riefenstahl, where she indicates that the 'ritual' of the Nuremberg Rally is characterised by 'domination' and 'enslavement' and this is reflected symbolically in,

> the massing of groups of people; the turning of people into things; the multiplication of things and the grouping of people/things around an all-powerful, hypnotic leader figure or force. The fascist dramaturgy centres on the orgiastic transaction between mighty forces and their puppets. Its choreography alternates between ceaseless motion and a congealed, static, 'virile' posing. Fascist art glorifies surrender, it exalts mindlessness: it glamourises death.[22]

Sontag usefully shows how a film like *Triumph of the Will* constructs its 'actuality' around consciously conceived choreographic principles which recognise and deliberately deploy symbolic relationships. Documentary 'actuality' acts as a set of metaphors which are informed by rich mythical and political associations. An examination of the opening sequence of the film supports this view because it begins with the emergence of a plane from parting clouds, which casts its shadow over Nuremberg as it flies over excited crowds staring up towards it in anticipation. Needless to say, this is Hitler's aircraft, which serves the symbolic function of defining Hitler's Godhead as he descends from the heavens, literally overshadowing his people as he arrives to dispense his glory and wisdom. Hitler is constantly looked up to in the film and individualised and elevated above the dehumanised masses of both people and soldiers.

In making the film in this fashion, Riefenstahl uses film form in a sophisticated way to construct power relations and define Hitler's mystical identity in the light of faceless,

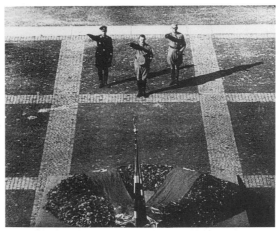

• Plates 6.4, 6.5 and 6.6 *Triumph des Willens* (*Triumph of the Will*) (Leni Riefenstahl, Germany 1935)
Filmed 4–10 September 1934 in Nuremburg at the Nazi Party Congress. Winner of the National Film Prize of
Germany, 1935, and the Venice Biennale Gold Medal, 1936

highly regimented groups of undifferentiated 'ordinary' people. Hitler becomes an icon
which is apparently authenticated and naturalised by the 'realism' inherent in the documentary form. It is only by understanding that 'actuality' may be extensively manipulated
that we can understand the relativity of documentary practice and question the whole
notion of documentary 'truth'. The combination of Riefenstahl's compositional skill and
the specific choreography of the proceedings succeed in making a great film 'fiction'.
'Actuality' is not actual; the filmic record of the event is highly mediated; the material
is edited not to reveal the 'truth' but a set of symbolic relationships with a specific
political purpose; the rally in becoming an illusion of 'reality' becomes 'documentary
myth'.

FROM DOCUMENTARY BIAS TO DIRECT CINEMA AND CINÉMA VÉRITÉ

Propaganda is essentially overtly politicised film-making which exhibits its bias in a number of complex and sometimes contradictory ways. Riefenstahl's film-making practice idealised fascist principles, combining right-wing ideology with an approach to film-making that made the two indistinguishable – her achievement in documentary may be characterised as the use of film form (that is, the construction of mise-en-scène, the uses of different kinds of cinematography, etc.) to dramatise 'actuality' within the framework of particular political ideas about power, status and divinity.

Another kind of approach to political documentary informed the work of The Workers' Film and Photo League of America (1930–5). Overtly left-wing in its outlook, it championed the ordinary working people of America, and sought to educate, inform and politicise blue-collar groups in securing better pay and conditions. Griersonian in spirit, the League recorded key historical moments of the Depression, which included protest marches about unemployment and pictures of families in bread-lines. The League's work was later overshadowed by the emergence of 'Nykino', who were also dedicated to socialist principles and a commitment to support union activity in working environments. Dutch documentarist Joris Ivens, while working in America, was influential upon the group's political film output, particularly in Nykino's newsreel *The World Today*, which was essentially a left-wing version of the popular mainstream newsreel *The March of Time*[23] (satirised in Orson Welles' *Citizen Kane* (1941)). Though not a left-wing sympathiser, Pare Lorentz, another key figure in American non-fiction film-making, made two important films in the style of Nykino, employing a number of the group's key personnel. These films were entitled *The Plow that Broke the Plains* (1936) and *The River* (1937), and were both sponsored by the government and attempted to sustain 'the American Dream' in spite of less than ideal social realities. In principle, Lorentz tried to create films that provided ideological justification for potentially unpopular or difficult to understand programmes of reform which necessitated a high financial commitment by the government.

The River was a thirty-minute documentary made on 16mm film, designed to be shown in farmhouses, schoolrooms and any suitable venue, in order to educate the people of the Mississippi Valley in the disastrous effects of flooding and 150 years of exploitation of the land's resources. The documentary centres on the experience of one poverty-stricken family and clearly attempts to create sympathy for the people on emotional terms, suggesting that they are 'ill clad, ill housed, ill fed' and 'a share of the crop their only security'. It is suggested that the people lack 'a frontier'; they have no new continent to build, they have to be instrumental in saving their land – 'the greatest river valley in the world'. Roosevelt's 'New Deal' administration had already established the Tennessee Valley Authority and the Farm Security Administration in 1933, and successfully justified state intervention in that area. The film attempts to prove that state intervention in this instance had rehabilitated the land, so that it might gain the support of Mid-Western audiences in financing further state reform in the Mississippi Valley.

Significantly, the family that the film focuses on is white, when it is more likely that a black family would be working in the area, and thus be more representative. It is possible that 'the argument' of the film may have been strengthened by showing a black family, and engaging 'race' sympathy. Any film's 'argument' is targeted to specific audiences, however, and it is clear that Lorentz was using his film to engage white power elites, legislators and voters in order to secure change. In short, the film was not for black audiences, though, of course, many black families were affected by the situation. Here, it is important to note that 'actuality' is once again subjected to politicised choices and adjustments. The film attempts to relate a 'national' issue through a regional policy; thus it makes specific decisions about which audiences it can *initially* speak to, even if its intentions are more democratic and universal. Documentary film is here used as a specific tool in the process of communication between government and its people. In the American tradition of documentary, it is this very premise that over thirty years later American film-makers were to reverse. New leftist film-makers wanted to directly intervene in the process of communication between government and its people by revealing how government created institutions which oppressed and misrepresented its people in the name of democracy.

If American wartime propaganda had been characterised by the consensus of patriotic folksiness, civilian education and the efficiency of military strategy and resource, especially in the films of Willard Van Dyke and Frank Capra's 'Why We Fight' series, then the postwar period saw a shift in emphasis. The use of the atomic bomb at Hiroshima and Nagasaki illustrated the means by which the world might annihilate itself. Suddenly, the means by which 'democracy' could be secured seemed extreme and at odds with 'peace'. It was the first great contradiction that informed an American society that was to fall prey to a number of contradictions and crises that profoundly challenged American politics and the consensus of belief in the American Dream. The rise of television temporarily replaced the film documentary as the vehicle by which 'record' and 'analysis' could take place. The American public witnessed the legitimised witch-hunts of the McCarthy era and the sustained Cold War paranoia over communism; they also saw the effects of the Korean War, the emergence of 'the juvenile delinquent' and the demise of American optimism and innocence, all of which anticipated the radical agendas of the 1960s. It was in this climate that cinéma vérité or direct cinema emerged and flourished, once more matching a particular documentary style to a certain kind of revolutionary intention.

The phrase cinéma vérité (literally 'cinema truth') emerged from the film-making practice of Jean Rouch in France,[24] who explains,

> it's really in homage to Dziga Vertov, who completely invented the kind of film that we do today. It was a cinema of lies, but he believed simply – and I agree with him – that the camera eye is more perspicacious and more accurate than the human eye. The camera eye has an infallible memory, and the film-maker's eye is a multiple one divided. . . .
>
> The one thing I want to say about cinema-verite is that it would be better to call it cinema – sincerity, if you like. That is, that you ask the audience to have confidence in the evidence, to say to the audience, 'This is what I saw. I didn't fake it, this is what happened. I didn't pay anyone to fight, I didn't change anyone's behaviour. I looked at what happened with my subjective eye and this is what I believe took place.'[25]

This view of documentary practice is important in that it acknowledges the 'subjectivity' of the film-maker because the film-maker cannot help but have a 'multiple' eye, that is, the ability to see, acknowledge and understand numerous images and perspectives. The film-maker, in short, must make choices. Having made those choices, Rouch suggests that the camera can record 'actuality' in a truthful and unmediated way. He also insists though that it is the integrity of the film-maker which essentially distinguishes the intention of the documentary. In other words, the 'author' of the film and the style and approach adopted reveal the documentary as 'propaganda', 'myth', 'reconstruction', 'poetic realism', etc. Documentary is thus seen in direct relationship to the person or persons who produce it without sacrificing the idea that what an audience is seeing is 'actuality'. It is merely acknowledged that this 'actuality' is necessarily mediated through the camera and is defined as a particular kind of 'truth' by its construction and the uses to which it is put. Simultaneously, a film is a 'record of events' and a subjective set of choices in relation to this record.

The re-emergence of direct cinema in America in the early 1960s was also accompanied by the necessary developments in technology which enabled a different approach to film-making. Light, portable, technically sophisticated equipment, able to achieve good quality sound and vision, meant that the film-maker need not be studio-bound, but in principle could make a film anywhere, under any conditions. Also, by being able to move the camera a greater intimacy could be achieved with the subject or event, thus heightening the idea that 'reality' is being directly observed. This provides the sensation for the viewer of an immediate involvement with 'reality' because the viewer is perceiving the experience as directly and unmediatedly as possible.

This has specific effects which effectively redefine the approach to documentary film-making as previously discussed. In rejecting more normal approaches, the film-making has a less controlled style, recording ordinary people in everyday situations. The films are not scripted or directed, and do not anticipate a particular end, thus heightening the ambiguity of 'meaning' a viewer may see in the film. The film concentrates on the 'experience' of reality and the sense of spontaneity of the action which prioritises observational rather than narrative techniques. A particular kind of 'storytelling' is resisted and voice-over is not used, but intervention is prioritised in the editing of material. Frederick Wiseman (see case study 4, p. 186) recognised that it was important to edit material in a way that did not simplify a context or situation but also did not distort the material to fit a specific ideological position. He felt that editing was not a totally rational procedure, but essentially 'a process of dreaming', which involved taking a great deal of time to respond intuitively and imaginatively to the enormous amount of footage taken in any particular project. Such an approach attempts to let self-evident relationships and social processes emerge in a coherent form but without any manipulation or resolution.

Robert Drew headed the television production section of Time Inc. and worked with key direct cinema directors, Richard Leacock, Donn Pennebaker and Albert and David Maysles, initially within the context of ABC TV. The company were at first responsive to Drew's fresh approach to news and current affairs coverage, but scheduled his programmes unfavourably, still prioritising a more mediated style of 'talking head' analysis. Ironically, the most influential film by Drew and his associates was made before joining ABC TV. Called *Primary* (1960), it followed Hubert Humphrey and John F. Kennedy on the Democratic Party campaign trail at the Wisconsin primary election, and attempted to view the proceedings through the candidates' eyes. Using shoulder-mounted camera work, the film echoes the candidates' experience and proves very revealing in its concentration on the 'liveness' of the event. This style greately influenced the 'fly-on-the-wall' documentary style adopted by many British TV documentary directors. Its intimacy and immediacy appeared to record 'actuality' in a way that seemed to demonstrate historical authenticity and accuracy. Documentary could provide 'documents' which appeared to offer veracity.

Upon leaving Drew Associates, Pennebaker pursued his interest in the popular culture of the period, making *Don't Look Back* (1966), a film of Bob Dylan's tour of England in 1965, and *Monterey Pop*, featuring performances by The Who, Simon and Garfunkel and Jimi Hendrix. Pennebaker, like his colleague Leacock, seemed to have an affinity with music as a barometer of popular attitudes and communal energy. Pennebaker viewed his films in a less political light than his direct cinema colleagues. He says, 'They're not documentaries. They weren't intended to be documentaries, but they're records of some moment.' He continues,

> My definition of a documentary film is a film that decides that you don't know enough about something, whatever it is, psychology or the tip of South America. Some guy goes there and says, 'Holy shit, I know about this and nobody else does, so I am going to make a film about it.'[26]

Pennebaker views documentary as the use of film for exploratory, investigative and analytical purposes. He sees his own films merely as films of 'record', free from these agendas. Once more, the definition of documentary seems to be related to the intention of the film-maker and the nature and emphasis of the 'intervention' in finally producing the film. Films like Pennebaker's 'records' of popular culture became the staple of non-fiction film-making and continued to test traditional views of the documentary form and make controversial statements about the era.

• Plate 6.7 *Woodstock* (Mike Wadleigh, US 1970)

This may perhaps be most significantly illustrated by comparing *Woodstock* (1970), made by Mike Wadleigh (with the sing-along 'bouncing ball' sequences directed by a young Martin Scorsese), and *Gimme Shelter* (1970), made by the Maysles brothers. If *Woodstock*, a record of the most famous rock festival of all time, was a celebration of the spiritual value of peace, love, community and the use of mind-expanding drugs, then *Gimme Shelter*, a record of the Rolling Stones' American tour, featuring a murder

• Plate 6.8 *Woodstock* (Mike Wadleigh, US 1970)

which takes place at the band's Altamont concert, policed by Hell's Angels, suggests this era is over.

The Maysles made many documentaries about popular cultural figures, for example, The Beatles in *What's Happening!: The Beatles in the U.S.A.* (1964), Marlon Brando in *Meet Marlon Brando* (1965), Mohammed Ali and Larry Holmes in *Mohammed and Larry* (1980) and visionary artist Christo, who wraps certain geographical landmarks like islands, valleys and bridges in silk, in *Christo's Valley Curtain* (1974), *Running Fence* (1976) and *Islands* (1986). One of their most important films, though, is *Salesman* (1969), which follows four members of the Mid-American Bible Company in their attempts to sell bibles. The Bible, of course, is more than 'a book', more than 'a commodity', so what the film ultimately becomes about is a tension between commercial and spiritual values. In order to buy or sell a bible it is necessary to address what you have 'faith' in, and Paul Brennan, 'the Badger', whom the film mainly focuses on, clearly exhibits an inner crisis in doing his job. As well as prioritising the direct cinema approach, the Maysles also looked to different methods of recording or deploying 'the interview', for example, contextualising the footage of the murder in *Gimme Shelter* by asking Mick Jagger and Keith Richard to observe and comment upon the incident and its inclusion in the film. This raised issues about the nature of documentary, in that the film seemingly distances itself from the stabbing of a black man by a white youth, and does not prioritise raw 'actuality' as enough to substantiate a viewpoint. Once more, the 'relativity' of documentary was called into question – a relativity never denied by one of its greatest exponents, Frederick Wiseman.

☐ CASE STUDY 4: FREDERICK WISEMAN

> I think this objective–subjective stuff is alot of bullshit. I don't see how a film can be anything but subjective.[27]

Ex-lawyer Frederick Wiseman, though committed to the filming of 'actuality', recognised the role of the film-maker as intrinsic to the purpose and ultimate creation of documentary. Rather than trying to make a film with a certain ideological position, Wiseman wished to make socially conscious films, which essentially established his own position about the people and events he was encountering. At the same time, he attempted to work in a style that enabled his audiences to do the same. Wiseman resisted the kind of documentary approach that prioritised figures or events in popular culture. He was more concerned with a particular kind of film-making which involved the viewer in the everyday life of American institutions. Wiseman said,

> What I am aiming at is a series on American institutions, using the word 'institutions' to cover a series of activities that take place in a limited geographical area with a more or less consistent group of people being involved. I want to use film technology to have a look at places like high schools, hospitals, prisons and police, which seem to be very fresh material for film.[28]

• Plate 6.9 *High School* (Frederick Wiseman, US 1968)

Wiseman wished to address these institutions because they operate as part of the intrinsic structure of a democratic society yet seem so integrated in that society that their activities remain unexamined and uninterrogated. By not concentrating on an individual story with an imposed 'narrative', Wiseman created a 'mosaic' of events, interactions and working processes revealing patterns of behaviour, which ultimately reflected the morality of the institution, and the social values of the society that established and defined the role of that institution. In order for an audience to recognise and interpret the material it was viewing, it was important that they were not 'passive' viewers but actively engaged in perceiving the world they, like Wiseman, were encountering. Consequently, Wiseman did not use voice-over or music to guide the viewer's understanding of the film. Although Wiseman clearly wished the audience to make up its own mind, he also wanted the audience to make the imaginative leap in understanding that any institution is a model of society, and its activities serve as symbols and metaphors for some bigger themes about power and authority.

Wiseman has made many films. Some of the most important include *Titicut Follies* (1967), *High School* (1968), *Basic Training* (1971), *Model* (1980) and *Central Park* (1989). *Titicut Follies*, Wiseman's first film, perhaps remains his most controversial, as it is about the Bridgewater State Hospital for the criminally insane in Massachusetts. Effectively banned for over twenty-five years because of continuing legal action, the film created considerable controversy in its revelation of the conditions and treatment the inmates had to endure. The film, named after the annual revue staged by the staff and patients, shows the inhumane attitudes and actions of authorities and the lack of proper care for seriously disturbed patients. It is the first example of one of Wiseman's key themes, which is the attempt by any one individual to preserve their humanity while in apparent conflict with institutional rules and regulations which have a dehumanising effect.

High School, concerning the NorthEast High School in Philadelphia, illustrates the theme in another form by showing how pupils are forced to conform unquestioningly to the rigid principles of the school. Blind obedience and a lack of personal identity are seen as practical and valuable in the school's understanding of a proper induction to the institutional frameworks operating in society as a whole. The film concludes with a sequence of Dr Haller, the school's principal, reading a letter from ex-student Bob Walter, who requests that his GI insurance money be given to the school if he is killed in Vietnam. In the letter, he says 'I am only a body doing a job', and this in many ways serves as Wiseman's position about the school, and, indeed, the army which the boy is to serve in, a context Wiseman took up in his film, *Basic Training*. Once more illustrating the effects of the processes of dehumanisation, Wiseman shows the initiation of recruits at the Fort Knox training centre in Kentucky. Key questions are raised about the humiliation of certain soldiers (the film was later an influence on Stanley Kubrick's *Full Metal Jacket*) and the regimentation achieved through manipulative strategies which focused on the fears of individuals and the perceptions they had of their own masculinity.

Ultimately a liberal humanist, Wiseman raises questions about the assumptions of, and conduct within, 'institutional' life. The irony inherent in Wiseman's approach is that it is simultaneously an intimate portrait of an institution, operating very close to its 'real' interaction, yet his style remains remote. At one and the same time, Wiseman is completely *present* in making the film, but *absent* in its ultimate completion. This achievement in itself creates documentary in a spirit which refuses to take sides, blame particular people or offer solutions to problems, but still operates with a forceful commitment. These documentaries are 'comments' but not 'opinions'.

FROM RADICAL DOCUMENTARY TO
TELEVISION AND DIVERSITY

The cinéma vérité school in America was significantly opposed by film-maker Emile De Antonio, who felt the ambition of such film-making – an unmediated, apparently unbiased version of 'reality' – was naive and unachievable. De Antonio embued his films with Marxist politics and fierce intellectual criticism of American institutional hypocrisy. This meant that he was monitored by J. Edgar Hoover, the FBI and the CIA throughout his career. His films are largely 'reconstructions' compiled from footage taken by a number of sources, particularly a great deal of film taken but not used in network news coverage. He deliberately made films which created an alternative view of American culture as it had been mediated through television and government agencies. These films included *Point of Order* (1963), which showed the demise of Senator McCarthy at the Senate army hearings of 1954; *Rush to Judgement* (1967), which was the first major documentary to challenge the findings of the Warren Commission in regard to the assassination of John F. Kennedy in 1963; *In the Year of the Pig* (1969), an uncompromising view of American conduct in the Vietnam War; and *Milhouse: A White Comedy* (1972), a satirical portrait of Richard Nixon. De Antonio feels that his work is a necessary antithesis to bland and highly censored news reporting on the main television networks, which have sanitised current affairs and documentary. He suggests this occurred most particularly in the coverage of the Vietnam War:

> The democratic approach is nullified in the United States by the most powerful of the media, television. The news on television is built upon the newscaster as star. And it's not the real news. Nothing is clearer than something that happened a long time ago, and that the networks to this day defend. They said that the war in Vietnam was the only war that was shown on TV everyday. True. But what was being shown was the media doing their own thing.[29]

De Antonio believes that ABC TV constructed a sensationalised view of the war, which misrepresented the Vietnamese people, did not show illegal American activity and privileged media personnel as key figures. He also condemns the idea that coverage was placed between commercial breaks, thus trivialising the horrors of war and desensitising audiences. He says, 'Television did that to us because it never took a stand.'

It was television that essentially absorbed the documentary form in the 1970s and 1980s, enabling a number of film-makers to work in the field, but probably with less distinction and innovation than the directors of earlier periods. Diversification has meant that film-makers from minority groups with marginalised interests have gained the opportunity to use the documentary to privilege specific voices with particular concerns. This is important because it confirms that the documentary is still a necessary social vehicle, demonstrating democratic principles. Clearly, the growth and accessibility of video has enabled more and more film-makers to make documentaries and extend the possibilities of the genre. Many of these film-makers are extremely cine-literate and have extensive knowledge of the documentary work that has preceded their own efforts. Important feminist non-fiction films have emerged that directly challenged the predominantly male concerns and outlook of the documentary form. These included Kate Millett's *Three Lives* (1971), Donna Deitch's *Woman to Woman* (1975), Connie Field's *Rosie the Riveter* (1980) and Michelle Citron's *Daughter Rite* (1978). These films sought to both reclaim 'film language' and express the historical, social and personal concerns of women.

Similarly, lesbian and gay film-makers have found a voice in documentary, for example, in *Before Stonewall: The Making of a Gay and Lesbian Community* (1984) by Greta Schiller, John Scagliotti and Robert Rosenberg and, most movingly, in Robert Epstein's *The Times of Harvey Milk* (1984), about the murder of Harvey Milk, the gay and lesbian rights campaigner and official in San Francisco. Further, black film-makers have used documentary to reclaim history and identity, perhaps most notably in Henry Hampton's *Eyes on the Prize* (1989). Oppressed or under-represented groups have been enabled to tell their 'truth', demonstrate their 'fact' and illustrate their experience with their 'actuality', and in this the ironic flexibility of the documentary form has served them well.

Increasingly, the documentary has become a hybrid of forms, often erring towards the cinematic vocabularies of narrative 'fiction' to apparently present 'fact'. More documentaries are being made on video and more documentaries fill the ever expanding television schedules. The study of documentary in schools, colleges and universities as well as specialist festivals dedicated to non-fiction films have promoted the form and recovered its history. Important works like Claude Lansmann's *Shoah* (1986), a nine-hour epic of interviews with survivors of the holocaust, Errol Morris' *The Thin Blue Line* (1988), a study of a roadside murder case in which Randall Adams, the man imprisoned for the crime, was proved innocent and Michael Moore's *Roger and Me* (1990), an employee's eye-view of betrayal by the Ford Company, were all internationally successful, an indication of the documentary form's continuing power in the contemporary era. Literally thousands of documentary films have been made throughout the world. This chapter can only touch on a few of them. The documentary is a constantly evolving form, crucial to the understanding of ourselves and others. At all times it has attempted to break down the frontiers of 'realist' cinema to find the 'truth' inherent in all contexts and situations. It is this fundamental purpose that defines the documentary form as intrinsic to democratic and humanist cultures.

NOTES

1 Cited in E. Sussex, *The Rise and Fall of British Documentary*, Los Angeles: University of California Press, 1976, p. 52.

2 Cited in G. Roy Levin, *Documentary Explorations*, New York: Doubleday, 1971, p. 62.

3 A. Britton, 'The Invisible Eye', *Sight and Sound*, February 1992, p. 29.

4 F. Hardy (ed.), *Grierson on Documentary*, London: Faber & Faber, 1979, p. 85.

5 J. Grierson, 'The Documentary Producer', *Cinema Quarterly*, vol. 2, no. 1, p. 8.

6 R. Barsam, *The Non-Fiction Film*, Bloomington and Indianapolis: Indiana University Press, 1992, preface, p. 1.

7 D. De Nitto, *Film: Form and Feeling*, New York: Harper & Row, 1985, p. 325.

8 J. Corner (ed.), *Documentary and the Mass Media*, London: Edward Arnold, 1986, pp. xiii–xx.

9 See Barsam, 1992, pp. 13–17.

10 V. Petric, 'Dziga Vertov as Theorist', *Cinema Journal*, vol. 1, autumn 1978, pp. 41–2.

11   Cited in Roy Levin, 1971, p. 202 (interview with Richard Leacock).

12   Barsam, 1992, p. 53.

13   A. Calder-Marshall, *The Innocent Eye: The Life of Robert J.Flaherty*, New York: Harcourt Bruce Jovanovich, 1966, p 229.

14   Cited in Hardy (ed.), 1979, p. 148.

15   Cited in Calder-Marshall, 1966, p. 97.

16   De Nitto, 1985, p. 330.

17   Quoted from S. Hall, *Art and Society: Film Propaganda*, Open University Broadcast, BBC, June 1989.

18   M.L. Jennings, *Humphrey Jennings: Film-maker, Painter, Poet*, London: BFI., 1982, p. 17.

19   ibid., p. 27.

20   ibid., p. 35.

21   S. Sontag, 'Fascinating Fascism', in B. Nichols (ed.), *Movies and Methods*, Los Angeles: University of California Press, 1976, p. 34.

22   ibid., p. 40.

23   For information on the American newsreel series 'March of Time', see Barsam, 1992, pp. 163–5.

24   For information on Jean Rouch, see ibid., p. 301; and Roy Levin, 1971, pp. 131–47.

25   Cited in Roy Levin, 1971, p. 135.

26   Cited in ibid., p. 234–5 (interview with Jean Rouch).

27   ibid., p. 321.

28   A. Rosenthal, *The New Documentary in Action*, Los Angeles: University of California Press, 1972, p. 69.

29   E. De Antonio, *Sight and Sound*, summer 1982, p. 183.

FURTHER READING

Barnouw, E., *Documentary: A History of Non-Fiction Film*, Oxford: Oxford University Press, 1974.
Barsam, R., *The Non-Fiction Film*, Bloomington and Indianapolis: Indiana University Press, 1992.
Corner, J. (ed.), *Documentary and the Mass Media*, London: Edward Arnold, 1986.
Hardy, F. (ed.), *Grierson on Documentary*, London: Faber & Faber, 1979.
Roy Levin, G., *Documentary Explorations*, New York: Doubleday, 1971.
Rosenthal, A., *The New Documentary in Action*, Los Angeles: University of California Press, 1972.
Sussex, E., *The Rise and Fall of British Documentary*, Los Angeles: University of California Press, 1976.

FURTHER VIEWING

These films are important documentaries not particularly stressed in the text but worth viewing in the light of the points raised:

Olympia (1936) (Dir.: Leni Riefenstahl)
The Spanish Earth (1937) (Dir.: Joris Ivens)
The Power and the Land (1940) (Dir.: Joris Ivens)
Chronicle of a Summer (1961) (Dir.: Jean Rouch)
Woodstock (1970) (Dir.: Mike Wadleigh)
The Sorrow and the Pity (1970) (Dir.: Marcel Ophuls)
Shoah (1985) (Dir.: Claude Lansmann)
The Thin Blue Line (1988) (Dir.: Errol Morris)
The Times of Harvey Milk (Dir.: Robert Epstein)
Night and Fog (1955) (Dir.: Alain Resnais)

Chapter 7

Animation: forms and meanings

Paul Wells

■ Animation: forms and meanings

INTRODUCTION

For many years, the animated film has been seen only as another aspect of live action cinema. This is mainly because the history of the animated film has been intrinsically bound up with the development of the moving image and the creation of 'cinema' itself. It is the intention of this chapter, though, to demonstrate that the animated film is a discrete type of film with its own codes and conventions.

Initially, I will define what animation actually is, and how it relates to the early developments in motion pictures. I will then show the progression of the animated film in its own right, addressing the key *forms* of animation and how the viewer may determine *meanings* in these often neglected films – films that have been dismissed as only children's entertainment or relegated to filling spaces in the television schedules.

WHAT IS ANIMATION?

A working definition of animation is that it is a film made frame by frame, providing an illusion of movement which has not been directly recorded in the conventional sense. Though this is a definition which serves to inform conventional cel, hand-drawn and model animation, it has proven insufficient in the description of other kinds of animation, particularly the kinds of animation that have been facilitated by new technologies, chiefly those images which are computer-generated or subject to other kinds of pictorial manipulation. I will address these issues later in the chapter, but in the first instance it is useful to consider the definition of Norman McClaren, one of the medium's acknowledged masters: 'Animation is not the art of drawings that move, but rather the art of movements that are drawn. What happens *between* each frame is more important than what happens on each frame.'[1] McClaren is suggesting that the true essence of animation is in the manipulation of movements between frames. Animators of the Zagreb School, however, seek to develop this definition by stressing the creative and philosophic aspects of the craft: 'To animate : to give life and soul to a design, not through the copying but through the transformation of reality.'[2]

Although recognising the importance of animation as a technical process, the Zagreb film-makers wanted to emphasise the creative aspect of literally 'giving life' to the inanimate, revealing something about the figure or object in the process which could not be understood under any other conditions. They wanted to transform reality, and resist the kind of animation created by Walt Disney, which for all its personality and comic energy, conforms to a certain kind of reality, which in turn conforms to a dominant ideological position. As if to confirm this point, British-based animators John Halas and Joy Batchelor posit the idea that, 'If it is the live-action film's job to present physical reality, animated film is concerned with metaphysical reality – not how things look, but what they mean.'[3]

Implicit in the animated form is the notion of how 'meaning' is released by the unique vocabulary available to the animator which is not the province of the live-action film-maker. Czech surrealist animator, Jan Svankmajer, perceives this vocabulary as liberating, original and potentially contentious:

> Animation enables me to give magical powers to things. In my films, I move many objects, real objects. Suddenly, everyday contact with things which people are used

to acquires a new dimension and in this way casts a doubt over reality. In other words, I use animation as a means of subversion.[4]

Svankmajer's view probably most articulates the real possiblities available to the animator, in the sense that he stresses how animation can redefine the everyday, subvert our accepted notions of 'reality' and challenge the orthodox understanding of our existence. Animation can defy the laws of gravity, challenge our perceived view of space and time, and endow lifeless things with dynamic and vibrant properties. Animation can create magical effects – a point well understood by pioneer film-makers like Georges Méliès and early animators, J. Stuart Blackton, Emile Cohl and Winsor McCay.

EARLY ANIMATION

The development of the animated form is specifically related to the early experiments in the creation of the moving image. As early as 70 BC there is evidence of a mechanism that projected hand-drawn moving images on to a screen, described by Lucretius in *De Rerum Natura*. In the sixteenth century, 'Flipbooks' emerged in Europe, often containing erotic drawings which, when riffled, showed the performance of sexual acts. (So much for those 'stickman' drawings of footballers and weightlifters I drew in the margins of my textbooks!)

In 1825, Peter Mark Roget wrote about what was later to be called the *persistence of vision* theory. This theory determined why human beings could perceive movement, that is, the human eye saw one image and carried with it an after-image on to the image that followed it, thus creating an apparent continuity. This is of the utmost importance in watching moving pictures in general, of course, but is particularly significant in legitimising the kind of animated cinema that was to be achieved frame by frame.

With developments like the Phenakistoscope (two rotating discs appeared to make an image move) in 1831, the Kinematoscope (sequential photographs mounted on a wheel and rotated to create movement) in 1861 and the Praxinoscope (a strip of images which when mounted in a revolving drum and reflected in mirrors became animated) in 1877, there was the eventual emergence of the cinematic apparatus. Still intrinsic to the understanding of these developments was the idea of the moving image as essentially magical – something colourful, playful and 'miraculous' in its manipulation of still images.

Also in place by the 1890s was the comic strip form in the American print media industries. This is important because the comic strip was to help provide some of the initial vocabulary for the cartoon film: characters continuing from episode to episode, ongoing narrative sequences, comic structures emerging from visual jokes, etc. By 1893, the *New York World* and *New York Journal* were using colour printing in their strips, and these may be seen as prototypes of later animated forms.

At the centre of the development of 'trick effects' in the emergent cinema was Georges Méliès. His accidental discovery of the 'dissolve' (that is, when one image fades into another) when his camera accidentally jammed, led him to pioneer a whole number of other cinematic effects that have become intrinsic to the possibilities available to animators. These included stop-motion photography, split-screen techniques, fast and slow motion and the manipulation of live action within painted backdrops and scenery. Méliès was also a 'lightning cartoonist', caricaturing contemporary personalities, speeding up their 'construction' on screen by undercranking the camera.

By 1900, J. Stuart Blackton made *The Enchanted Drawing*. He appeared as a 'lightning cartoonist', drawing a man smoking a cigar and drinking some wine. By the use

proto-animation

Early live-action cinema demonstrated certain techniques which preceded their conscious use as a method in creating animation. This is largely in regard to stop-motion, mixed-media and the use of dissolves to create the illusion of metamorphosis in early 'trick' films.

of stop-motion, one drawing at a time is revealed and the man's face is made to take on various expressions. Various similar films had preceded this, including *The Vanishing Lady* (1898) and *A Visit to the Spiritualist* (1899). These films can be classified as **proto-animation** as they use techniques that are used by later animators, but are not strictly and wholly made frame by frame. Blackton achieved full animation of this sort in *Humorous Phases of Funny Faces* (1906). Though using full animation in key sequences, the film was still essentially a series of tricks. Primitive notions of narrative animation followed in the early work of famous comic strip artist, Winsor McCay, who under Blackton's supervision at the Vitagraph Brooklyn Studio made an animated version of his most celebrated strip, *Little Nemo in Slumberland* in 1911. Blackton's influence in general cannot be understated as he is responsible for distinguishing the concept of the animated film as a viable aesthetic and economic vehicle outside the context of orthodox live–action cinema. His film, *The Haunted Hotel* (1907), a simple narrative piece with impressive supernatural sequences, was instrumental in convincing audiences and financiers alike that the animated film had an agenda and position all of its own, unique in its form and unlimited in its potential.

The Haunted Hotel had been released in the United States and France, where French animator Emile Cohl completed his *Fantasmagorie* in 1908. Cohl returned the compliment when his later film, *En Route*, was released in the United States in 1910. Cohl employed a technique in line-drawing where lines would fall randomly into the image and converge into a character. This technique was borrowed by McCay in *Little Nemo*, and informed his other key works as he translated his comic strip style into the newly emergent animated form. Based on one of his 1909 comic strips, 'Dream of the Rarebit Fiend', McCay made *The Story of a Mosquito* (1912), a mock horror story of a mosquito graphically feeding on a man until it is so bloated with blood that it explodes! McCay's

• Plate 7.1 *Gertie the Dinosaur* (Winsor McCay, US 1914)

most significant contribution to the animated form, however, is the development of **personality** or **character animation** through his creation of *Gertie the Dinosaur* (1914). The playful dinosaur, Gertie, gleefully hurls a mammoth into a lake in the film and clearly displays an attitude. This **anthropomorphism** (the endowment of other creatures with human attributes, abilities and qualities) informs the work of Walt Disney who, of course, has become synonymous with and the embodiment of animation in general.

While McCay can claim to have created the first colour cartoon (he hand tinted at least one of the prints of *Little Nemo*), and produced a cel-animated film, *Winsor McCay Makes his Cartoons Move* (1911) (using rice-paper cels), it was John R. Bray who pioneered the cel-animation process using translucent cels in 1913, and made a film called *The Artist's Dream*. Bray Studios then released a series of cartoons with a continuing character, *Colonel Heeza Liar*, and demonstrated the viability of animation as a commercial industry capable of mass production. Cartoons emerged into the marketplace in the United States at the same time that more experimental abstract animation was beginning to emerge in Europe, particularly through film-makers like Oskar Fischinger and Walter Ruttmann. Rapid advances in film-making technology encouraged the emergence of a variety of organisations making films, including Walt Disney Productions founded in Los Angeles in 1923. Key figures like the Fleischer Brothers, who later made 'Betty Boop' and 'Popeye' cartoons, initially worked at Bray Studios, and then created their own organisation with an efficient streamlined animation process. It was Disney, of course, who became most prominent in the establishment of a studio ethos. Although a considerable team of established artists and animators produced his films, they were always 'Disney' films defined by a particular attitude towards **realism**. Even though Disney dealt with an abstract, non-realist form, he insisted on verisimilitude in his characters, contexts and narratives. He wanted animated figures to move like real figures and to be informed by a plausible motivation. To this end Disney accelerated the process of innovation in the animated form.

By 1927, Disney began working on his 'Oswald the Rabbit' series of cartoons and during this process he developed 'the pencil test', that is, photographing a pencil-drawn sequence to check its quality of movement and authenticity before proceeding to draw it on cels, to paint it, etc. In 1928, Disney premièred *Steamboat Willie*, featuring Mickey Mouse, which was the first synchronised sound cartoon. Following continuing experiments in the use of sound effects and music in differing relationships to the visual images, the cartoon began to standardise itself as a form which moved beyond the illustration of different kinds of music into one which accommodated narrative and a series of related jokes. Disney introduced technicolor, the three colour system, into his Silly Symphony *Flowers and Trees in 1932*, which later won an Oscar. All Disney's animators undertook programmes of training in the skills and techniques of fine art in the constant drive towards ever greater notions of realism in his cartoons – animals had to move like real animals, but it was important that the complexity of this movement must be unnoticeable, a condition achieved through the dexterity of the artist's skill in drawing the creatures.

This level of reality was further enhanced by the development of the multi-plane camera. Traditionally, in the two-dimensional image the illusion of perspective had to be created by the artist. As the camera approaches an image – for example, cattle grazing outside a farmhouse on a moonlit night – the image loses its perspective as the elements merely enlarge and the moon becomes as big as the farmhouse or the cattle. The multi-plane camera stops this from occurring by painting the image in perspective on different panes of glass that are placed directly behind each other but have the ability to move.

character animation

Many cartoons and more sophisticated animated films are still dominated by 'character' or 'personality' animation which attempts to present human traits in an expressive form that directs attention to the detail of gesture and the range of human emotions and experience.

anthropomorphism

The tendency in animation to present creatures with human characteristics. This can redefine or merely draw attention to characteristics which are taken for granted in live-action representations of human beings.

realism

Live-action cinema has inspired numerous debates about what may be recognised as 'realism';that is, what may be considered as the most accurate representation of what is 'real' in the recording of the concrete and tangible world. Clearly, the animated form in itself resists 'realism' and prioritises 'fantasy'. Disney, however, still aspired to **hyper-realism** in his films, by making his characters correspond as closely as possible to the 'real' world in their movement and context while allowing for fantasy elements in character and narrative.

To use my example, the cattle would be painted in the foreground, the farmhouse behind the cattle in the field and the moon in the background, so that when the camera moves *through* the image all the elements stay in perspective. Disney's Silly Symphony *The Old Mill* (1937), successfully demonstrated this technique, but it found its most advanced and persuasive use in the first full-length animated feature, *Snow White and the Seven Dwarfs* (1937).

The animated film had reached maturity, and in doing so had established Disney as synonymous with animation. This has led to animation being understood in a limited way. Disney perfected a certain language for the cartoon and the full-length feature which took its model from live-action film-making. This overshadowed other kinds of innovation and styles of animation which have extended the possibilities of the form and enabled other kinds of film to be made. Disney's art remains the dominant language of animation and we can term this **orthodox animation**. This kind of work must be compared though to two other areas of the form which we may classify as **developmental animation** and **experimental animation**. These areas reflect certain styles and approaches and characterise the particular objectives and intentions of some leading animators.

ORTHODOX ANIMATION

Cel animation remains the most convenient technique for the mass production of cartoons. These kinds of films are usually storyboarded first, after the fashion of a comic strip, and corresponding to a prerecorded soundtrack. 'Key drawings' are then produced indicating the 'extreme' first and last positions of a key movement which are then 'in-betweened' to create the process of the move. After 'pencil-testing' (now often done on computers), the images are drawn on separate sheets of celluloid, painted and photographed frame by frame against the appropriate background. The music, dialogue and effects can then be synchronised with the images. This process enables a large number of animators to be involved and facilitates an industrial process.

Aside from the Disney Studios producing Silly Symphonies, Harman and Ising created the first of the Looney Tunes in 1930, entitled *Sinkin' in the Bathtub*. In the same year, the Fleischer Brothers introduced Betty Boop in a Talkartoon called *Dizzy Dishes*, and two years later translated Popeye from comic strip to cartoon. Harman and Ising moved to MGM and created the Happy Harmonies, while Warner Brothers created the Merrie Melodies. Walter Lantz, later creator of Woody Woodpecker, was appointed as head of Universal studio's animation team, and coincidentally, like Disney, chose to create an Oswald the Rabbit series. In many ways this period can be seen as the beginning of the golden era of cartoon animation, where all the major figures who were involved were not merely furnishing the demands of an industrial process, but were evolving the language of the medium, which in turn became its orthodoxy.

This orthodoxy was characterised by a number of dominant elements which I will now discuss.

Configuration

Most cartoons featured 'figures', that is, identifiable people or animals who corresponded to what audiences would understand as an orthodox human being or creature, despite whatever colourful or eccentric design concept was related to it. Thus Donald was recognisable as a duck whether he wore a sailor's suit or khaki togs and a pith helmet!

Specific continuity

Whether a cartoon was based on a specific and well-known fairy tale or story or on 'riffing' (a sequence of gags developed around a specific situation), it had a logical continuity even within a madcap scenario. This was achieved by prioritising character and context. For example, Goofy was perpetually trying to succeed at a task and consistently failing. He is thus contextualised in the continuing attempts to complete the task, and creating slapstick comedy through his failure, but simultaneously he creates sympathy for, and understanding of, the fundamental aspects of his character.

Narrative form

As an extension of the previous point, it is necessary to stress the importance of narrative form. Most early cartoons echoed or illustrated the musical forms which provided their soundtracks. The soundtrack suggested a possible proto-narrative before particular visual scenarios or sight gags were developed. Most often, these were based on character conflict and chase sequences, where common environments became increasingly destabilised as they were subjected to (accidentally) destructive forces. However notional, the idea of 'a story' was essentially held in place by following the principle of establishing a situation, problematising it, creating 'the comic' and finding resolution, mainly through the principal character whom the audience has been encouraged to support and sympathise with.

Evolution of content

The orthodox cartoon rarely draws the audience's attention to its construction (though Chuck Jones' masterpiece *Duck Amuck* (1953) is an obvious exception to this). Rarely also does it tell the audience of its interest in the colour and material of its making. Instead it prioritises its content, concentrating specifically on constructing character, determining comic moments and evolving the self-contained narrative.

Unity of style

The formal properties of the animated cartoon tend to remain consistent. Cel-animated or hand-drawn cartoons remain in a fixed two-dimensional style throughout their duration and do not mix with three-dimensional modes as later more experimental animation does. Visual conventions echo those of live-action cinema in the deployment of establishing shots, medium shots and close-ups, but camera movement tends to be limited to lateral left to right pans across the backgrounds or up and down tilts examining a character or environment. However, one consequence of camera movement across a drawing can be the illusion of a change of perspective or angle to facilitate an unusual context for the character. This often happens, for example, when Wile E. Coyote chases Roadrunner and finds himself in an impossible predicament. An apparently safe rock formation suddenly presents itself at an impossible angle and becomes a dangerous landscape that defeats him once more. Story conventions like these inform most cartoons which mainly operate on the basis of a repeated formula and, most obviously, the chase. The chase informs the pace of these narratives, privileging speed and frenetic action and creating conventions like visible movement lines around moving limbs and the blur of fast moving bodies.

Sound conventions like 'the crash', 'the bo-ing' or the ascending and descending scale are also instrumental in determining a specific kind of film language in the cartoon. Although dissolves and fade in/fade out often provide the mechanism for scene changes, there is also the emergence of one of the most important terms in an animator's

metamorphosis

The ability for one creature or object to make the transition into another form by the manipulation of the material in which they were created, that is, pencil-drawn characters, by a reduction into line and colour, may be re-formed into another shape. Similarly, clay may change from one form into another by first degenerating into a mass before being moulded into a new form.

vocabulary, **metamorphosis**. The animator can thus tell the story by evolving the image rather than cutting from one image to another. While using all these conventions, colour, scenic design and character formation remain consistent.

Absence of artist

Some later animation signals its codes and conventions and thus reveals the presence of the individual artist in creating the work. Conventional cartoons prioritise their characters and style and at no point privilege the artist or signal the process of their creation.

Dynamics of dialogue

Even though the fundamental appeal of the cartoon lies in its commitment to action, character is often defined by key aspects of dialogue. This was a particular feature of the characters created at Warner Brothers Studio for the Looney Tunes and Merrie Melodies cartoons. Bugs Bunny's laconic sense of superiority is established by his carrot-munching proposition, 'What's up, doc?', or by his call to arms when his current adversary temporarily gains the upper hand when he confirms, 'You realise, this means war!' Specifically based on the verbal dexterity of Groucho Marx, Bugs also qualifies any minor error in his plans by claiming 'I should have taken the right turn at Albuquerque!' Equally, Daffy is characterised by his persistent babble, arrested only when he has experienced complete humiliation and when he lispily claims 'You're despicable!' Elmer Fudd always insists upon quiet as he is hunting 'wabbits', while Yosemite Sam overstates his position when he says 'I'm seagoing Sam, the blood-thirstiest, shoot-em firstiest, doggone worstiest, buccaneer that's ever sailed the Spanish Main!' All these verbal dynamics served to support the visual jokes and create a specific kind of 'noise' that is characteristic of these films. Philip Brophy suggests that the Disney soundtrack moves towards the *Symphonic* while the Warners soundtrack embodies the *Cacophonic*. The Symphonic is informed by classical aspirations towards the poetic, balletic and operatic, while the Cacophonic is more urban, industrialised, beat-based and explosive in its vocabulary.[5]

☐ CASE STUDY 1: *DUCK AMUCK* (1953)

deconstruction

All media 'texts' are constructed. To understand all the components within each construction it is necessary to deconstruct the text and analyse all its elements. For example, the cartoon is made up of a number of specific elements which define the cartoon as a unique cinematic practice.

Although in a sense untypical of the kind of style and unity I have described in orthodox animation, *Duck Amuck*, directed by Chuck Jones, is the perfect example of a cartoon which is wholly self-conscious and reveals all the aspects of its own construction. This is known as **deconstruction**. As Richard Thompson points out,

> It is at once a laff riot and an essay by demonstration on the nature and conditions of the animated film (from the inside) and the mechanics of film in general. (Even a quick checklist of film grammar is tossed in via the 'Gimme a close-up' gag).[6]

Daffy begins the cartoon in anticipation that he is in a musketeer picture and swash-buckles with due aplomb until he realises that he is not accompanied by suitable scenery. He immediately recognises that he has been deserted by the context that both he and we as the audience are accustomed to. He drops the character he is playing and becomes Daffy, the betrayed actor who immediately addresses the camera,

• Plate 7.2 Daffy Duck from *Bugs Bunny* (Walt Disney, US 1953)

acknowledging both the animator and the audience. Perceiving himself as an actor he localises himself within the film-making process, and signals its mechanisms, all of which are about to be revealed to us.

Trouper that he is, Daffy carries on, adapting to the new farmyard scenery with a spirited version of 'Old Macdonald had a Farm', before adjusting once again to the arctic layout that has replaced the farmyard. The cartoon constantly draws attention to the relationship between foreground and background, and principally to the relationship between the character and the motivating aspects of the environmental context. Daffy's actions are determined by the understanding of the space he inhabits. These tensions inform the basic narrative process of most cartoons: all Daffy wants is for the animator to make up his mind!

Each environment is illustrated by the visual shorthand of dominant cultural images – the arctic is signified by an igloo, Hawaii by Daffy's grass skirt and banjo! The white space, however, becomes the empty context of the cartoon. Daffy is then erased by an animated pencil rubber and essentially only remains as a voice. However, as Chuck Jones has pointed out, 'what I want to say is that Daffy can live and struggle on in an empty screen, without setting and without sound, just as well as with a lot of arbitrary props. He remains Daffy Duck.'[7] This draws attention to the predetermined understanding of Daffy as a character, and to the notion that a whole character can be understood by any one of its parts. Cartoon vocabulary readily employs the **synecdoche**, the part that represents the whole, as a piece of narrative shorthand. Daffy can be understood through his **iconic** elements, both visually and aurally. No visual elements of Daffy need be seen for an audience to know him through his lisping voice, characterised by Mel Blanc. We need only see his manic eyes or particularly upturned beak to distinguish him from Donald Duck and other cartoon characters, who all have similar unique and distinguishing elements in their design.

synecdoche

The idea that a 'part' of a person, an object, a machine, etc. can be used to represent the 'whole', and work as an emotive and suggestive 'shorthand' to the viewer, who invests the 'part' with symbolic associations.

iconic

The iconic is defined by the dominant signs that signify a particular person or object – Chaplin, for example, would be defined by a bowler hat, a moustache, a cane and some old boots, while Hitler would be defined by a short parted hairstyle and a small moustache.

Upon the point when Daffy asks 'Where am I?', even in his absence the audience know of his presence. When he is repainted by the anonymous brush as a singing cowboy we anticipate, of course, that Daffy will sing, although the genre probably prohibits him singing 'I'm Just Wild about Harry', which remains one of his favourites! Initially, Daffy finds there is no sound and holds up a small sign requesting 'sound please', thus drawing the audience's attention to the explicit vocabulary of sound necessitated by the cartoon form, and one immediately familiar to the anticipated viewer. When Daffy attempts to play the guitar, it sounds first like a machine gun, then a horn, then a donkey, thus simultaneously showing the necessity of sound and image synchronisation for narrative orthodoxy, and the creation of comedy through the incongruous mismatching of sound and image. This is developed after Daffy breaks the guitar in frustration – a standard element of the cartoon is the process of destruction – and attempts to complain to the animator about his treatment, especially as he considers himself 'A Star'. He is given the voice of a chicken and a cockatoo, and just when he is at his most hysterical in his attempt to speak, he is allowed his own voice, but at increased volume. Daffy is visibly humiliated and his attitude once again reveals to an audience his helplessness in the face of the power of the animator. The animator is at liberty to manipulate the image completely and create impossible and dynamic relations which need not have any connection with orthodox and anticipated relations.

This manipulation of Daffy's image and identity also tells an audience about his essential character traits – egotism, ambition, frustration, anger and wilfulness – which are constantly challenged in most of the narratives through the resistance offered by the world around him. In *Duck Amuck*, he is also defeated by the animated context he exists within. He pleads with the animator for orthodoxy and is greeted with a child's pencil drawing for a background, slapdash painting for the scenery and an absurd reconstruction of his own body in wild colours and a flag tied to his newly drawn tail indicating that he is a 'screwball'. Despite protestations that he has fulfilled his contract, Daffy continues to be treated with contempt. Just when he seems to have been granted the legitimacy of 'a sea picture' – an obvious reference to both Donald Duck and Popeye – Daffy is subjected to the standard cartoon gag of recognising that he is temporarily defying gravity by standing in mid-air only to drop into the sea the moment he realises. Seconds later he is on an island, but the image is merely a small frame within the normal frame, this time drawing the audience's attention to the compositional elements of the cartoon and, indeed, of film language itself. We can hardly hear Daffy as he calls for a close-up, and receives one at rapid speed, only showing us his eyes.

Once again calling upon the audience's recognition of the frame as a potentially three-dimensional space, Daffy then tries to cope with the sheer weight of the black background scenery which falls upon him like a heavy awning. He eventually tears up the 'screen' in sheer frustration and demands that the cartoon start, even though it has already been going several minutes. A screen card with 'The End' comes up accompanied by the Merrie Melodies theme. Daffy then attempts to take control of the film by returning to the key notion of himself as an entertainer performing a vaudevillian soft-shoe shuffle. He is trying to reclaim the idea of the cartoon as a medium for entertainment rather than deconstruction. His song and dance routine is interrupted, however, by the slippage of the frame as it appears to divide the screen in half and expose the frames of celluloid the film is supposedly composed of. The two frames, of course, reveal two Daffys, who immediately start to fight and disappear in a blur of drawn lines – the fight merely becomes a signifier of cartoon movement, a symbol of kineticism unique in embodying character and signifying form.

Narrative life improves for Daffy as 'the picture' casts him as a pilot. This is merely a device, however, to demonstrate a series of conventional cartoon gags, including an off-screen air crash, the appearance of the ubiquitous anvil as a substitute for Daffy's parachute and an explosion as Daffy tests some shells with a mallet – by this time, however, he is a gibbering heap, devoid of dignity or control, the two qualities Daffy most aspires to. As he tries to assert himself one last time, Daffy demands to know 'Who is responsible for this? I demand that you show yourself!' The frame as we under-stand it is then completely broken as the scene changes and the camera pulls back to reveal the drawing board and 'the animator' – Bugs Bunny, Daffy's arch-rival. As Thompson remarks, 'Duck Amuck can be seen as Daffy's bad trip; his self-destruction fantasies and delusions, with their rapid, unpredictable, disconcerting changes of scene and orientation, are the final extension of ego-on-the-line dreams.'[8] This is an important point in a number of respects. It locates Daffy as a character firmly in a relationship between form and meaning. Each narrative establishes and develops the vocabulary which defines the underpinning imperatives of both character and the form the character inhabits. This leads to the cartoon animation embodying a number of **ideological** positions. Disney's films, for example, often play out an orthodox narra-tive form to reinforce an ideological status quo. In other words, Disney's films support and illustrate what Robert Sklar calls 'the spirit of social purpose, the re-enforcing of old values'.[9] This idealised world is often challenged by the anarchic worlds of Tex Avery[10] and Chuck Jones, and, indeed, other kinds of animation which send complex and often subversive messages even when deploying the orthodox conventions I have outlined. An example of this would be Joanna Quinn's 1986 short entitled *Girl's Night Out* (see Plate 8.15).

ideological

Although a complex issue, ideology may be seen as the dominant set of ideas and values which inform any one society, but which are imbued in its social behaviour and representative texts at a level that is not necessarily obvious or conscious. An ideological stance is normally politicised and historically determined.

☐ CASE STUDY 2: *GIRL'S NIGHT OUT* (1986)

Joanna Quinn's *Girl's Night Out* tells the story of Beryl, an ordinary Welsh housewife, who goes out for a 'quiet drink with the girls' and ends up enjoying a striptease routine by a male stripper. Quinn is careful to prioritise character and encourage our empathy with Beryl by stressing the mundaneness of her existence. The soundtrack is a constant babble of conversation as the film opens, simultaneously defining factory life and sexual titillation by focusing upon the image of a passing conveyor belt line of cakes as they are being individually topped with bouncing cherries. By the subtle implication of breasts, and the chorus of chatter, the factory, and indeed the narrative form of the animation, is gendered feminine. This is important as the film is attempting to reclaim the language of film which is predominantly gendered as masculine.

The sheer vitality of the film is expressed by endowing objects and figures with an excess of drawn movement – telephones shake and jump when they ring, drinks rattle fervently on a tray matching Beryl's bouncing bosom, figures literally blur into shapes which embody the visual dynamics of excitement and laughter. This energy drives the narrative and underpins the sexual agenda of the film. Beryl, for example, fantasises that the macho man of her dreams 'will take her away from all this' and make love with her on a desert island. These fantasies which are projected in the thought bubbles of the comic strip, become a whirling blur of lines and shapes as Beryl kisses her dream man, exhibiting not merely sexual frenzy but uninhibited joy. This is juxtaposed with the static images of domestic boredom as Beryl's couch-potato husband and the family cat sit drowsily and unmoving in front of the television. Quinn skilfully keeps the scene static while giving it a visual interest by changing the look of the image through the use of the flickering light of the television set. Beryl's husband ignores her when she tells him she is going out, and, clearly, the audience's sympathy and encouragement lie with Beryl.

She speeds off in a car that leaps across a street map representing the town where she lives. This juxtaposition of images is a good example of narrative and visual **condensation**. Quinn also deploys metamorphosis to provide this kind of condensation in the evolving passage of one scene into another. As Beryl speeds along, the pub sign of 'The Bull' swings in anticipation, and provides punctuation in the construction of her journey. When she arrives at the pub, Beryl buys her drinks and the image, in concentrating on the 'wobble' of her body, stresses her size, especially when she settles her large bottom on a creaking bar-stool. In a similar way to Daffy in *Duck Amuck*, the audience is invited to inspect and interrogate Beryl's body, in the spirit of acceptance, a point Quinn develops in a later film about Beryl entitled *Body Beautiful* (1989). Beryl is an ordinary working-class woman with a pedestrian existence who is looking for some excitement in an otherwise dull and oppressive life. The film is suggesting that the audience see life from Beryl's point of view by sharing Beryl's point of view. This is made explicit when the male stripper is made the obvious subject of the female gaze, a reversal of the dominant orthodoxy of women being the subject of the male gaze that characterises mainstream film.[11]

Beryl's body is set against the stereotypical ideal of the macho body as it is expressed through the stripper. Clad in a black vest and leopard skin G-string, the moustachioed, muscle-bound stripper reveals his hirsute chest and rotates his hips as the image concentrates on his bulging codpiece, toying with the idea of the exposure of his penis. The soundtrack consists of screams of delirium and encouragement – 'Get 'em off!' roars Beryl, as she sprouts horns of bedevilment and mischief. The girls enjoy both their excitement and their embarrassment as the stripper operates with increasing confidence and physical bravura. The film endows him with status over the women – he possesses an impossible physical dexterity as he bends over and wobbles his buttocks or moves across the stage balanced on one finger! His shadow looms over an initially terrified Beryl, who offers him a drink – the drink in essence being offered to the camera, and the mechanism by which Beryl's actions are disguised as she tugs at the stripper's G-string. Once more, in a frenzy of 'reaction' lines drawn around the stripper's face and body, the film stresses its agenda as a woman's film. The audience has identified with the heroine and enjoys how she undermines the sexual posturing of the stripper (which by extension is a metaphor for arrogant, oppressive masculinity) by tearing off his G-string, exposing a small penis.

The stripper is humiliated and the women, chiefly Beryl, feel empowered by the moment. She gleefully swings the G-string around after the fashion of the stripper himself, and clearly enjoys her moment of triumph and difference. Temporarily, Beryl, in the symbolic act of challenging male dominance as it is coded through the stripper's sexual confidence and sense of superiority, undermines patriarchal norms. What Beryl achieves in the narrative, Joanna Quinn achieves in her manipulation of film form – a subversion enabled by the reclaiming of a cinematic language in the animated film, a language *not* wholly colonised by men, and often deployed by an increasing number of female animators creating a feminine aesthetic in the medium.[12]

condensation

The compression of a set of narrative or aesthetic agendas within a minimal structural framework.

UPA and Zagreb studios

Before addressing the concepts of developmental animation and experimental animation, it is important to note two studios who largely developed key aspects of orthodox animation. As a consequence of the strike at Disney studios in 1941, Canadian animator Stephen Busustow left the company and established United Productions of America (UPA). He, along with other talented animators, John Hubley, Pete Burness, Bob Cannon and Bill Hurtz, wanted to pursue a more individual style that the Disney 'look' could not accommodate. This led to work that was less specifically 'realist' in its approach, and, as Ralph Stephenson has suggested, 'the cynicism, the sophistication, the depth of adult attitudes are not ruled out'.[13]

Ironically, this 'sophistication' was achieved through non-naturalist, fairly unsophisticated technical means. These included minimal backgrounds, 'stick' characters and non-continuous 'jerky' movements. The **squash and stretch** conception of movement in conventional cartoon characters, based on a design where the body is thought of as a set of circles, was replaced by the representation of a body as a few sharp lines. Backgrounds, which in Disney animation were positively voluptuous in their colour and detail, were defined by a surrealist minimalism, where stairs led nowhere and lights hung from non-existent ceilings. This kind of development expanded the vocabulary of the animated film and served to define its potential in one particular style.

Most surreal, both in its design and its soundtrack, was Bob Cannon's *Gerald McBoing Boing* (1951), where a little boy speaks only through incongruous sounds. More popular was the *Mr Magoo* series, featuring a short-sighted old man, voiced by Jim Bacchus and based on W.C. Fields, who had endless encounters based on mistaking the people and objects he saw for someone or something else. UPA established a new style and liberated many artists, despite economic limitations and the initial resistance to a new aesthetic principle, an agenda which was fuelled by economic as well as aesthetic necessity, an agenda shared by the Zagreb studios in the former Yugoslavia.

Influenced by UPA's *Gerald McBoing Boing* and *The Four Poster* (1952), designed by John and Faith Hubley, the Zagreb animation industry developed around the two key figures of Dusan Vukotic and Nikola Kostelac. Initially making advertising films, the two progressed to making cartoons deploying **reduced animation,** which is described by Ronald Holloway:

> Some films took an unbelievable eight cels to make, without losing any of the expressive movement a large number of cels usually required. Drawings were reduced to the barest minimum, and in many cases the visual effect was stronger than with twice the number of drawings.[14]

Liberated from the limitations of orthodox animation, these films increased the intensity of suggestion located in the images and moved towards a more avant-garde sensibility without neglecting key aspects of the vocabulary outlined above.

DEVELOPMENTAL ANIMATION

Developmental animation may be described as the intermediary stage between orthodox and experimental animation, and it is in this category that the majority of animation is located.

It may be defined as the kind of animation which deploys but extends the principles of orthodox animation using other materials, that is, models, puppets, clay/plasticine,

squash and stretch

Many cartoon characters are constructed in a way that resembles a set of malleable and attached circles which may be elongated or compressed to achieve the effect of dynamic movement. When animators 'squash' or 'stretch' these circles they effectively create the physical space of the character and a particular design structure within the overall pattern of the film.

reduced animation

Animation may be literally the movement of one line which, in operating in time and space, may take on characteristics which an audience may perceive as expressive and symbolic. This form of minimalism constitutes reduced animation which takes as its premise that 'less is more'. Animation is created at its sparest level to suggest more to its audience. This may enable the film to work in a mode which has an **intensity of suggestion.**

objects and cut-outs, etc. These films are made frame by frame but extend the vocabulary into the three-dimensional and visually innovatory sphere. Each methodology clearly creates its own agenda for analysis as the possibilities determined by the use of other materials becomes as large as the number of films made. In illustrating some of the types of animation in this category, I will suggest ways in which orthodox animation has been redefined and reformulated.

□ CASE STUDY 3: *CREATURE COMFORTS* (1990)

Nick Park's Oscar-winning *Creature Comforts* essentially develops the anthropomorphic tendencies of the Disney cartoon into three dimensions by using plasticine models of zoo animals. They are voiced by real people talking about their own living conditions and those of animals in a zoo. This ambiguity is played out in the responses of each character as they are being interviewed by an unseen microphone-wielding film-maker, not unlike Park himself. The film emerges as a hybrid of the cartoon and a mock documentary.

The humour of the film derives from the tension between the very ordinariness of the varied verbal responses on the soundtrack and the visual jokes, first, created by the design of the character, and second, by the activities which take place in the background or alongside the main character speaking. These include a hippo doing 'number twos' while another is interviewed, a highly coloured bird having its beak 'twanged' as if it were a paper cone on an elastic band around someone's face, or a beach ball, which comes from off-screen, bouncing on a surprised tortoise's head! These visual jokes are directly drawn from Park's enjoyment of *It'll Be Alright on the Night*, which is

• Plate 7.3 *Creature Comforts* (Nick Park, UK 1990)

a programme composed of 'out-takes' from other programmes, featuring mistakes and unexpected situations. Park found particular amusement in those 'out-takes' where a reporter is talking about a serious subject, only to be unknowingly undermined by an animal copulating or defecating in the background!

The soundtrack is characterised by different age groups speaking in different dialects, and these voices are skilfully matched to the appropriate animal. An old lady's voice, for example, is matched to a koala bear as it perches precariously on a eucalyptus tree. The koala is endowed with large glasses to foreground its large eyes and its difficulty in seeing. This reinforces the vulnerability and 'cuteness' of the creature and the old lady it represents, especially when she says that she feels just secure just at the moment when the branch creaks before breaking!

While prioritising a more static image system than orthodox animation to focus on small details, especially in its jokes, *Creature Comforts* does localise its interest in characters and an evolving 'content' (making points about meat-eating, housing conditions and the benefits of double glazing along the way!). It also possesses a unity of style, but it is a style that enables Park to use a wider filmic vocabulary 'like camera movements, effects of lighting and complex sets that exist in real space'.[15] He uses a conventional soundtrack for the zoo/jungle 'atmos' and sound effects to accompany jokes, but instead of deploying the 'dynamics of dialogue' he prefers the 'dynamics of monologue', carefully editing juxtapositional voices together.

It is clear, then, that Park uses the conventions of orthodox animation, but adjusts them to his own specifications. The result of this is to bring an intrinsic 'Englishness' to the piece in its irony and gentle reserve. Though informed by the influence of *The Beano* and the work of Terry Gilliam,[16] Park dilutes the craziness and surreality of these 'cartoon' forms, preferring an unpretentious whimsical style that highlights the eccentricities of the everyday, and a nostalgic belief in the uncommon and unaddressed aspects of the ordinary.

☐ CASE STUDY 4: *NEIGHBOURS* (1952)

Norman McClaren is probably the most experimental film-maker in the animated field. He has explored a number of different styles, including direct animation (drawing directly on to celluloid), paper and object animation (stop-motion frame-by-frame constructions of movement with objects and cut-outs, etc.), evolution works (the gradual evolution of a pastel or chalk drawing) and multiple printing works (where movements are recorded as they evolve through the multiple printing of each stage of the movement). McClaren, then, is strictly an experimental film-maker, and many of his works would be rightly included in the final category I have defined. *Neighbours*, however, sits neatly in the developmental animation category in its use of **pixillation** in the redefinition of the orthodox form.

As Cecile Starr has noted, 'His films are enriched with an abundance of childish playfulness, artistic subtlety, psychological insight and human concern.'[17]

In *Neighbours*, these qualities are played out, revealing McClaren's insight into how the language of the cartoon could readily be applied to a form that manipulated live action, the consequence of which would be to create a commentary on the representation of violence in cartoons and the presence of violent impulses in human nature. McClaren combines 'the childish playfulness' of the cartoon with a specific contemplation of aspects

pixillation

The extreme editing of rehearsed and deliberately executed live action movement to create the illusion of movement impossible to achieve by naturalistic means; that is, figures spinning in mid-air or skating across grass.

● Plate 7.4 *Neighbours* (Norman McClaren, UK 1952)

of the human condition, bringing to that agenda an artistic sensibility that reworks the codes and conventions of orthodox animation.

Employing pixillation, *Neighbours* works as an affecting parable. Two neighbours, seated in deckchairs, smoking their pipes, reading newspapers with the headlines, 'War certain if no peace' and 'Peace certain if no war', become involved in a territorial dispute over the ownership of a wild flower. This dispute escalates rapidly, horrible violence takes place and the pair eventually end up killing each other. The method by which this simple yet telling narrative takes place reveals as much about orthodox strategies of animation as it does about the inevitability of human conflict and, indeed, confirms that conflict is the key underpinning theme of the orthodox animated narrative.

McClaren alludes to the two-dimensional cartoon by employing this in his scenery. He creates the illusion of two neighbouring houses in the middle of a real field by erecting two hand-painted cartoon-like housefronts. He then concentrates on establishing **symmetry** in his frame before disrupting it with the chaos, first of ecstatic responses by the men to the fragrance of the flower, and second, of their conflict. The wild exaggeration of their movements successfully parodies the dynamics of movement in the orthodox cartoon.

Similarly, the electronic soundtrack echoes the role of sound effects in such films, creating mood, accompanying actions and replacing words. The effect of using these conventions but reinventing the means to create them is to draw attention to them. This in turn signals that to reinterpret the conventions is to reinterpret the meanings inherent within them. To create cartoon conventions *showing* violence is to ignore that the conventions are *about* violence too. It is this very point that McClaren clearly understands, taking the exaggeration of cartoon violence to its logical extreme and showing the audience primitive barbarism. Two men die, two families die, and by implication two

symmetry
Direct balance of imagery in the composition of the image using parallel or mirrored forms.

nations die, thus illustrating the futility and tragedy of war. If the close reworking of the cartoon in another kind of animated form has not done enough to signify the presence of the artist, then the final multilingual sequence of titles saying 'Love thy neighbour', certainly does, in the sense that the moral and didactic purpose of the film has been revealed.

☐ CASE STUDY 5: *DADDY'S LITTLE BIT OF DRESDEN CHINA* (1987)

Karen Watson's graduation film, *Daddy's Little Bit of Dresden China*, is another good example of developmental animation. As in the other examples that I have dealt with, this film takes some general principles of orthodox animation as I have defined it and adds or revises some key elements.

Watson sophisticatedly blends two- and three-dimensional animation in a powerful address of child abuse that took place in her own family life. As she suggests, 'For me, *Daddy's Little Bit of Dresden China* acted as a form of therapy, enabling me to express feelings I could not have expressed otherwise. Feelings I didn't have words for, and forbidden feelings such as anger.'[18]

Animation offers the film-maker the opportunity for total control over the material in a film in a way that is rarely seen in other areas of film-making practice. This enables the animator to express ideas and feelings through the work in an intimate and personal way. Watson created the means by which she could deal with a profoundly personal issue in deploying and extending the vocabulary of the animated film. This kind of work proves that animation can be the vehicle for serious issues and challenges the received view of animation as only for children and only the context for comedy.

While Park configures in clay and McClaren pixillates real people, Watson uses three-dimensional models, which operate with a greater complexity than normal puppet or model figures in the sense that they are composed of materials which have symbolic connotations. The father figure in the film is constructed out of metal with glass for a head and razor-blades for a mouth. He is clearly coded as cold, remote and dangerous, in order to alienate an audience, as he, of course, is responsible for the abuse of his daughter. She is a small figure composed of feathers and bandages, with a china vase for a head, to suggest her vulnerability and fragility. Her mother is made from dried flowers and has a wooden spoon for an arm. The dried flowers represent the loss of Nature and fertility while the wooden spoon connotes her domestic role.

These figures are located in the artificial setting of the theatre, illustrating the polite façade of domestic life, which once the curtains are closed hides a multitude of sins. This has already been signalled by a prologue which deploys the fairy tale as a narrative form, casting mother, father and daughter as King, Queen and Princess Snow White. The voice-over concludes this initial piece of storytelling with the ominous words, 'Unfortunately, for Snow White, no-one ever questioned the King's love for her. The mother was blamed, the father forgiven and the daughter silenced.'[19] This kind of use of the fairy tale form returns it to its more complex and sinister origination, reclaiming it from the ideological and censorial manipulation it has often been subjected to, particularly in its use in the dominant orthodox animation created by the Disney studios.[20]

By not choosing a unity of style, and using scratched film, drawn animation, collage manipulation and models, Watson draws the audience's attention to various styles, not merely for pictorial variety but, most importantly, for narrative and thematic purposes. The 'content' evolves in not merely illustrating the personal crises of child abuse and domestic violence, but politicises the piece by showing the broader social context of the hypocritical attitudes of men in regard to their treatment of women, particularly in regard to sexual harassment and the assumption that women are sex objects and commodities. This is mainly addressed through collage work which both stylistically and thematically frames the domestic scenarios done in model animation. Using storytelling, voice-overs of real victims of sexual abuse and music that reflects the sinister and forbidding aspects of fairy tale, as well as considerable silence, the film's soundtrack resists dialogue. The film lets its conflicting images tell the tale and create the emotional response, drawing further attention to the personal aspect of the piece. Animation facilitates this kind of subjectivity and informs the exploratory work that I will now address, which we may term experimental animation.

EXPERIMENTAL ANIMATION

avant garde

The practice of innovative and inventive use of the cinematic form outside the codes and conventions of mainstream film-making (that is, classical Hollywood narrative).

Experimental animation embraces a number of styles and approaches to the animated film which inevitably crossover into areas which we may also term **avant-garde** or **art** films, which may only partially display aspects of animation in the form I have previously discussed. Of course, there has been experimentation in all areas of animation, but I am prioritising animation which has either been constituted in new forms (computer, photocopy, sand on glass, direct on to celluloid, pinscreen, etc.) or resists traditional forms. As in my definition of orthodox animation, I would suggest that there is another set of dominant strands to experimental animation which I will define as the signposts for analysis in this type of film.

Abstraction

This kind of animation tends to resist configuration in the ways audiences most often see it, that is, as an expression of character through the depiction of a human being or creature. Experimental animation either redefines 'the body' or resists using it as an illustrative image. Abstract films are more concerned with rhythm and movement in their own right as opposed to the rhythm and movement of a particular character. To this end, various shapes and forms are often used rather than figures.

Specific non-continuity

While initially seeming a contradiction in terms, the idea of specific non-continuity merely signals the rejection of logical and linear continuity and the prioritisation of illogical, irrational and sometimes multiple continuities. These continuities are specific in the sense that they are the vocabulary unique to the particular animation in question. Experimental animation defines its own *form* and *conditions* and uses these as its distinctive language.

Interpretive form

The basis of experimental animation is aesthetic and non-narrative, though sometimes, as I will illustrate, aesthetics are deployed to reconstruct a different conception of narrative. Predominantly, though, experimental animation resists telling stories and moves towards the vocabulary used by painters and sculptors. Moving away from the depiction of conventional forms and the assumed 'objectivity' of the exterior world, animation, in enabling shapes and objects to move, liberates the artist to concentrate on the vocabulary he/she is using *in itself* instead of giving it specific function or meaning. As Leopold Survage wrote,

> I will animate my painting. I will give it movement. I will introduce rhythm into the concrete action of my abstract painting, born of my interior life; my instrument will be the cinematographic film, this true symbol of accumulated movement. It will execute 'the scores' of my visions, corresponding to my state of mind in its successive phases. . . . I am creating a new visual art in time, that of coloured rhythm and of rhythmic colour.[21]

This kind of subjective work has therefore necessitated a different response from audiences. Instead of being located in understanding narrative the audience is asked to bring its own interpretation to the work.

Evolution of materiality

The experimental film concentrates on its very materiality, that is, the forms in which it is being made, and the colour, shape and texture which is being used in the creation of the piece. These colours, shapes and textures evoke certain moods and ideas, but once again, film-makers of this type are suggesting that these aspects should give pleasure in their own right without having to be attached to a specific meaning or framework. Experimental animation thus privileges the literal evolution of materiality instead of content, showing us, for example, how a small hand-painted dot evolves into a set of circles, where the audience recognises the physical nature of the paint itself, the colour of the dot and its background, and the shapes that emerge out of the initial design. This sense of 'materiality' goes hand in hand with the emergent technologies which have liberated more innovative approaches to animation.

Multiple styles

If orthodox animation is characterised by a unity of style, experimental animation often combines and mixes different modes of animation. This operates in two specific ways: first, to facilitate the multiplicity of personal visions an artist may wish to incorporate in a film, and, second, to challenge and rework orthodox codes and conventions and create new effects.

Presence of the artist

These films are largely personal, subjective, original responses, which are the work of artists seeking to use the animated form in an innovative way. Sometimes these 'visions' are impenetrable and resist easy interpretation, being merely the absolutely individual expression of the artist. This in itself draws attention to the relationship between the artist and the work, and the relationship of the audience to the artist as it is being mediated through the work. The abstract nature of the films insists upon the recognition of their individuality. Sometimes, however, individual innovation is localised in more accessible ways that have a relationship with dominant forms, however tenuous the link. It may be, for example, that the experimental animation will try to create something aspiring to the condition of the dream-state, which, of course, has its own abstract logic, but conforms to a common understanding of 'the dream'. Dreams may be the vehicles for personal visions but they possess a universalised dimension.

Dynamics of musicality

The experimental animation has a strong relationship to music, and, indeed, it may be suggested that if music could be visualised it would look like colours and shapes moving through time with differing rhythms, movements and speeds. Many experimental films seek to create this state, and, as I have already suggested, some film-makers perceive that there is a psychological and emotional relationship with sound and colour which may be expressed through the free form that animation is.

Sound is important in any animated film, but has particular resonance in the experimental film as it is often resisting dialogue, the clichéd sound effects of the cartoon or the easy emotiveness of certain kinds of music. Silence, avant-garde scores, unusual sounds and redefined notions of 'language' are used to create different kinds of statement. It may be said that if orthodox animation is about 'prose' then experimental animation is more 'poetic' and suggestive in its intention.

☐ CASE STUDY 6: *A COLOUR BOX* (1935)

Len Lye's *A Colour Box* is a completely abstract film in that it is created with lines and shapes stencilled directly on to celluloid, changing colour and form throughout its five minute duration. It has dominant lines throughout, with various circles, triangles and grids interrupting and temporarily joining the image, until it reveals its sponsors, the GPO film unit, by including various rates for the parcel post, that is, 3lbs for 6d, 6lbs for 9d, etc.

The dazzling, dynamic images are set to a contemporary jazz–calypso score which has the effect of bringing further energy and spontaneity to the piece. Lye believed that this kind of work should be seen as *composing motion* as it reveals the 'body energy' which connects the music and the images.[22]

☐ CASE STUDY 7: *THE NOSE* (1963)

Alexander Alexieff invented the pinscreen technique in animation. This involved a 3 foot by 4 foot board into which a million headless pins, with the capability of being pushed backwards and forwards, have been placed. Black and white images were created by graduating the pins in the fashion required and lighting them in a specific way. Each image was created and photographed frame by frame. Hard black, bright white and various tones of grey could be achieved and as images dissolved and metamorphosed one into another a unique sense of dreamlike continuity and mood was created.

The Nose is a free adaption of Nikolai Gogol's surreal short story of a barber who finds a nose in his loaf of bread (a nose that wants a life of its own) and a noseless young man. It is the very 'unnaturalness' of the story and images which appealed to Alexieff in the creation of his free-flowing animated film. Animation can create 'the unnatural'. Alexieff shows a sofa metamorphosing into a rowboat in a dream sequence and also a street light becoming a policeman. Objects disappear, the nose transforms in size and shape, and time speeds up and slows down, all in the spirit of resisting 'story' to create mood and atmosphere. The film was made as a silent film, but music was added later to punctuate aspects of it rather than to create a specific emotional response.

☐ CASE STUDY 8: *DEADSY* (1990)

David Anderson's *Deadsy* is an example of the combination of xerography and puppet animation. Xerography, in this particular instance, involves the filming of a live perform-ance by an actor, followed by the transfer of still images of his performance on to videographic paper. These images are photocopied and enlarged, and then rendered and drawn on before being refilmed on a rostrum. The effect is to distort and degrade the image to give a haunting and hallucinatory quality to 'the character' known as Deadsy, a symbol of apocalyptic despair aligned with shifting sexual identity.

Deadsy is located as one of the 'Deadtime Stories for Big Folk', thus signalling its relationship to the vocabulary of the dream-state and, most particularly, the nightmares experienced by adults. The film creates the dream-state of deep sleep and reveals profound anxieties about the fear of death and the instability of gender and sexuality in its central character, Deadsy, who oscillates between being represented by a skeletal model and a distorted human figure. The film continually blurs lines in regard to its representation of life and death, masculinity and femininity and the physicality of sex and violence. Particularly effective in reinforcing this uncertainty and ambiguity is the use of writer Russell Hoban's monologue for Deadsy, which echoes the corrupted nature of the images by creating a post-apocalyptic language which slurs and mixes words together, for example:

> When Deadsy wuz ul he like din do nuffing big He din do nuffing only ul ooky-pooky Deadsy Byebyes like he do a cockrutch or a fly
> He din do nuffig big. He werkin his way up tho after wyl He kilia mowss o yes my my.

This kind of language *suggests* meaning; it does not formally fix meaning in the way that English-speaking peoples might readily understand it. It alludes to the escalation of violent behaviour in the development of humankind and the inevitability of the apoca-lypse. Deadsy as a character becomes aligned with the personality of a rock star motivated by inner voices and instinctive drives, and aroused by the spectacle of destruc-tion. This sense of arousal either inspires or informs the shifting gender positions Deadsy represents. Anderson shows the phallic relationship between male genitals ('sexothingys') and missiles, illustrating the masculine imperative to violence. Deadsy has a desire to change sex, however, to justify these actions. Deadsy assumes that if he becomes fem-inised, that is, 'Mizz Youniverss', then 'ewabody will luv me'. These gender shifts become symptomatic of the complex relationship between sexuality and violence and the socially unacceptable thoughts and feelings each individual may experience and repress. Anderson is suggesting that this kind of complexity underpins the fundamental anxiety that humankind will inevitably destroy itself.

The film is clearly trying to break into the viewers' preconceived ideas both about animation as a form and gender, death and global politics as a set of issues. Anderson is attempting to re-engage an audience with an abstraction of visual and verbal languages which reflect an anti-rational stance. Deadsy is a notional configuration but is charac-terised by differing representations as a form (that is, as a photographed image and a model) and in regard to gender and expression. Dialogue is abandoned in favour of voice-over monologue, but only to privilege a corrupted language that is difficult to understand. Styles are mixed, narrative and continuity are blurred and ambiguous, some-times resisting interpretation, and even the artist, while clearly present, is elusive too.

This is an attempt to create the post-apocalypse dream-state in the only form that could properly facilitate it.

CONCLUSION

Animation can create the conditions to express new visions by creating a vocabulary which is both unlimitedly expressive and always potentially progressive because it need not refer to or comply with the codes and conventions that have preceded it. Orthodoxy, developmental and experimental animation are constantly changing.[23] Computer technology, for example, is enabling a new generation of animators to work with a different tool in order to both use traditional methods and invent fresh approaches to the animated form. Science, art and the moving image are conjoining to create a new digital cinema, enabling both a redetermination of the animated film and the enhancement of special effects in mainstream movies. From the early experimental uses of computer animation at NASA and the Massachusetts Institute of Technology, the film exercises of James Whitney senior and junior, the work of Stan Vanderbeek (*Poemfields* 1967–9), Lillian Schwartz (*Pictures from a Gallery* 1976) and Peter Foldes (*Hunger* 1973), and the output at the PIXAR company, there is already a tradition of animation in computing that is continually developing a vocabulary that is extending the limits of the form. Ironically, it is ex-Disney animator, John Lasseter, who has created some of the best computer-animated shorts – *Luxo Jnr* (1986), *Tin Toy* (1990) and *Knick Knack* (1991) – by emulating the character animation of Disney and the 'gag' structures of Warner Brothers and MGM cartoons.

Yoichiro Kawaguchi, in Japan, has sought to be more abstract and experimental in his computer-generated films – *Eggy* (1990), *Festival* (1991) and *Mutation* (1992) – by emulating organic forms and developing random systems which create different shapes, forms and colour combinations. It is clear in movies like *Terminator 2* (1991) and *Jurassic Park* (1992) that computer animation can create unbelievable 'naturalistic' effects, another ironic echo of Disney's demands for a hyper-realism in his films.[24]

Even without new technological apparatus animators are finding unique ways to express their individual vision. It is the intrinsic nature of animation itself which enables this to happen and animators to continually amaze, shock and amuse with their films.

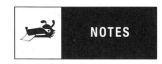

NOTES

*This chapter is dedicated to Jo for her love and patience.

1   Quoted in C. Solomon, 'Animation: Notes on a Definition', in *The Art of the Animated Image*, Los Angeles: AFI, 1987, p. 11.

2   Quoted in R. Holloway, *Z is for Zagreb*, Cranbery, NJ: Tantivy Press, 1972, p. 9.

3   Quoted in T. Hoffer, A*nimation: A Reference Guide*, Westport, Conn: Greenwood Press, 1981, p. 3.

4   Quoted in *The Magic Art of Jan Svankmajer*, BBC2, June, 1992.

5   P. Brophy, 'The Symphonic Experience', in A. Cholodenko (ed.), *Illusion of Life*, Sydney: Southwood Press, 1991, pp. 73–112.

6   R. Thompson, 'Pronoun Trouble', in D. Peary and G. Peary (eds), *The American Animated Cartoon*, New York: Dutton, 1980, p. 221.

7   ibid p. 233.

8   ibid p. 233.

9   R. Sklar, 'The Making of Cultural Myths – Walt Disney', in Peary and Peary (eds), 1980, p. 61.

10 Tex Avery, in being vehemently anti-Disney in his style, essentially extended the vocabulary of the animated cartoon by exposing and extending the conventions of the cartoon, in a similar way to those described in my analysis of *Duck Amuck*. Using alienation devices (methods by which the viewer is made to remember that he/she is watching a cartoon), he broke the frame of the cartoon, showing the audience characters running past the edge of the celluloid, crossing from the end of technicolour into black and white, acknowledging an audience by directly talking to them, etc. He changed the pace of the cartoon, making it frenetic and surreal, and he prioritised the zaniest of gags which foregrounded adult concerns like irrational fear, status and power and, most particularly, overt sex and sexuality. For a full analysis of Avery's work, see J. Adamson, *Tex Avery: King of Cartoons*, New York: De Capo, 1975.

11 For a full discussion of this issue, see L. Mulvey, 'Visual Pleasure and Narrative Cinema', in *Popular Television and Film*, Oxford and London: Oxford University Press and British Film Institute, 1981, p. 206.

12 See J. Pilling (ed.), *Women and Animation: A Compendium*, London: British Film Institute, 1992.

13 R. Stephenson, *Animation in the Cinema*, London: Zwemmer Ltd, 1969, p. 48.

14 Holloway, 1972, p. 12.

15 Quoted in R. Buss, 'Creatures Great and Small', *Independent on Sunday*, 7 November 1993, review section, no page numbers.

16 ibid.

17 C. Starr, 'The Art of Animation', in Starr, *Discovering the Movies*, New York: Van Nostrand Reinhold Co., 1972, p. 111.

18 K. Watson, 'Drawing on Experience', in Pilling (ed.), 1992, p. 96.

19 ibid. p. 97.

20 See, for example, Peter Brunette's essay on Disney's version of '*Snow White and the Seven Dwarfs*', in Peary and Peary (eds), 1980, p. 66.

21 Quoted in R. Russett and C. Starr, *Experimental Animation*, New York: Da Capo, 1976, p. 36.

22 From D. Curtis, 'Len Lye', Exhibition Catalogue Watershed, 24 October–29 November 1987, London: Arts Council, 1987, p. 5.

23 Obviously, in a chapter of this length, no justice can be done to the many kinds of work in the animation field, nor the gifted animators who make it. While one could mention Svankmajer, Norstein, the Quay Brothers, Pitt, de Vere, Neubauer, Driessen and Rbycynski as important names, this already neglects many others, and it is hoped that the chapter raises a general awareness of the field in order that students will seek out new work and cultivate tastes and preferences.

24 An overview of special effects and aspects of computer animation is given by the same author in *An Introduction to Special Effects* (with accompanying video), London: British Film Institute/MOMI, 1994.

FURTHER READING

Adams, T.R., *Tom and Jerry*, New York: Crescent Books, 1991.

Adamson, J., *Tex Avery: King of Cartoons*, New York: Da Capo, 1975.

Beck, J. and Friedwald, W., *Looney Tunes and Merrie Melodies*, New York: Henry Holt and Co., 1989.

Brion, P., *Tom and Jerry*, New York: Crown Publishers, 1990.

Cabarga, L., *The Fleischer Story*, New York: Da Capo, 1988.

Canemaker, J. (ed.), *Storytelling in Animation*, Los Angeles: AFI, 1989.

Cholodenko, A. (ed.), *The Illusion of Life*, Sydney: Power Publishers, 1991.

Hollis, R. and Sibley, B., *The Disney Studio Story*, New York: Crown Publishers, 1988.

Klein, N., *7 Minutes*, London: Verso, 1993.

Maltin, L., *Of Mice and Magic*, New York: NAL, 1987.

Peary, D. and Peary, G. (eds), *The American Animated Cartoon*, New York: Dutton, 1980.

Russett, R. and Starr, C., *Experimental Animation*, New York: Da Capo, 1976.

Solomon, C. (ed.), *The Art of the Animated Image*, Los Angeles: AFI, 1987.

FURTHER VIEWING

Here are some key models of animated film which repay viewing and analysis:

Asparagus (1978) (Dir.: Suzan Pitt)

Bad Luck Blackie (1943) (Dir.: Tex Avery)

Binky and Boo (1989) (Dirs: Derek Hayes and Phil Austen)

Body Beautiful (1990) (Dir.: Joanna Quinn)

Dimensions of Dialogue (1982) (Dir.: Jan Svankmajer)

Elbowing (1981) (Dir.: Paul Driessen)

Ersatz (1961) (Dir.: Susan Vukotic)

Fatty Issues (1990) (Dir.: Candy Guard)

Great (1974) (Dir.: Bob Godfrey)

The Hand (1965) (Dir.: Jiri Trnka)

The Hat (1964) (Dirs: John and Faith Hubley)

Knick Knack (1991) (Dir.: John Lasseter)

The Nose (1963) (Dir.: Alexander Alexieff)

Pas De Deux (1967) (Dir.: Norman McClaren)

Popeye the Sailor meets Sinbad the Sailor (1936) (Dir.: Dave Fleischer)

Red Hot Riding Hood (1949) (Dir.: Tex Avery)

Springer and the S.S. (1946) (Dir.: Jiri Trnka)

The Stain (1991) (Dirs: Christine Roche and Marjut Rimmenen)

The Street (1974) (Dir.: Caroline Leaf)

Tale of Tales (1979) (Dir.: Yuri Norstein)

Tango (1981) (Dir.: Zbigniew Rybczynski)

Three Little Pigs (1933) (Dir.: Walt Disney)

What's Opera, Doc? (1957) (Dir.: Chuck Jones)

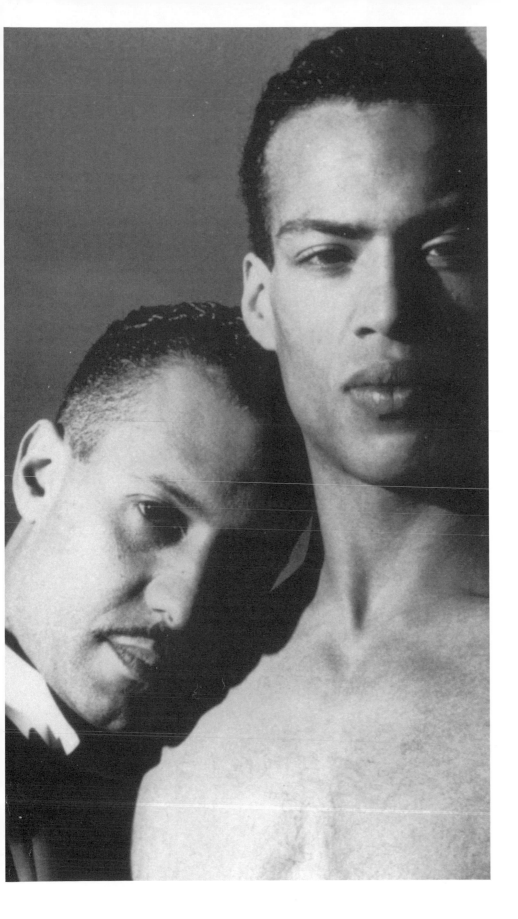

Part four

Representation of gender and sexuality

Chapter 8

Women and film

Jill Nelmes

■ Women and film

This chapter looks at the role of women in film-making and film theory, with particular reference to the relationship between feminist film practice and feminist film theory from the late 1960s to the present day.

The emphasis is on giving a background to British women film-makers and film theorists although reference will be made to American and European films and film theory – it would be difficult to ignore the contributions made by film-makers such as Lizzy Borden and Marlene Gorris, and the more recent contributions made to film theory by Teresa De Lauretis and Tania Modleski.

First, a broad background history traces women's place in film-making and focuses on the difficulties women had gaining positions of authority and control in the industry.

feminism

This is based on the belief that we live in a society where women are still unequal to men; that women have lower status than men and have less power, particularly economic power. Feminists argue that the media reinforces the status quo by representing a narrow range of images of women; for instance, woman as carer, as passive object, as an object of desire. Many feminists now argue that the range of representations for both male and female is limited and slow to change. In recent years feminism has become fragmented and it is difficult to argue that feminism is a complete area of study; but gender and power relations in society can be seen as central to feminist thinking. For an interesting discussion on this area see Liesbet van Zoonen 1994.

Second, the rise of **feminism**, the development of feminist film theory and the parallel rise of feminist film-making is discussed; in the 1970s feminist film theory and practice seemed to converge, but by the 1980s the links had become more tenuous. Many film-makers felt that they were being marginalised and needed to gain a wider audience; the concept of pleasure in watching a film that had been seen as fundamental to mainstream, conventional cinema had been denied in aspects of feminist film theory and practice. A number of women wanted their voice to be heard and felt that aspects of feminist film were in danger of alienating their potential audience.

Third, by the 1990s an increasing number of women in Britain and America had made mainstream films, yet the film and video workshops which had done so much to encourage women in film were in decline, mainly because of lack of funding; so although there has been a rise in the number of women directing bigger budget movies such as Beeban Kidron and Sally Potter in Britain and Penny Marshall and Nora Zephon in America, conditions in the small budget, independent sector seem to be worsening.

Finally, a selection of case studies of differing aspects of women in film is given.

NO JOB FOR A WOMAN – A HISTORY OF WOMEN IN FILM

The first years

From the beginnings of the film industry in the late nineteenth century women were generally excluded from the film-making process, although it was traditional for women to work in non-technical areas such as continuity and make-up or as a production assistant. Recent research, though, seems to suggest that woman's role has not been as silent as once thought and some women did, both directly and indirectly, exert their influence as directors, producers, editors and scriptwriters.

The only recorded early women film-makers were in France and America – there were apparently none in Britain. Two well-known Hollywood movie actresses, Mary Pickford and Lillian Gish, both directed films but did not want this known for fear of harming their image.

France can claim to have raised the first woman director, Alice Guy Blaché, who gained access to equipment because she worked for Gaumont, a company that manufactured cameras. Her career began in 1896 with a one-minute short called *The Good Fairy in the Cabbage Patch*, which Blaché believed was the first narrative film ever made. After eleven years of working in the industry in France she left for America and the greater opportunities it would give her. There she wrote, directed and produced many films including *In the Year 2000*, a film where women ruled the world. Blaché found working conditions in the US much easier than in France, where a working woman was frowned on. Her daughter, Simone Blaché, explained in an interview that: 'Mother was really cherished in the US. She used to say that people treated her so wonderfully because she was a woman, because she was a woman in film. The situation in France was quite the reverse' (Smith 1975: 6).

In the early 1900s there was an enormous expansion of the American film industry, which was making large profits because of the vast audiences attracted to the new medium. Although the new industry was cut-throat and competitive, it was also much more receptive and open to change than the European film industry and there was significantly less discrimination against women. It has been estimated that there were at least twenty-six women directors in America before 1930, but there were probably many more who directed and acted or were screenwriters and not credited with these roles.

Lois Weber was the first female American film-maker and probably the most famous, often writing, producing and starring in her films, many of which dealt with social issues such as abortion and divorce. Weber directed over seventy-five films.

By the end of the 1920s silent movies were on their way out and talkies had arrived which, indirectly, brought about the demise of many women in film. Only the bigger studios could survive because of the expensive equipment needed in the change-over to sound, and it was generally the many small, independent companies (who employed the majority of women) that had to close down, and so with them went many jobs for women in the industry.

Only one woman director, Dorothy Arzner, really survived the transition to talkies. She went on to make many famous movies such as *Christopher Strong* (1933) with Katherine Hepburn and *Dance Girl Dance* (1940). At one time Arzner was ranked among the 'top ten' directors.

Somewhat ironically, the changes in America drove directors like Elinor Glynn and Jacqueline Logan to Britain and Europe, which had an extremely poor record of women working in film.

Britain did not seem to have given much encouragement to its indigenous women film-makers; the earliest woman known to have directed British films was Dinah Shurey, though very little is known about her other than that she made two films, *Carry On* (1927) and *Last Port* (1929).

Until the Second World War, hardly any women could be termed film-makers, but some had key roles in the film-making process: Alma Reville, married to Alfred Hitchcock, assisted him in many films such as *The 39 Steps* (1935) and *The Lady Vanishes* (1938). She also helped to write other scripts such as *Suspicion* (1941) and *Shadow of a Doubt* (1943). Mary Field worked in documentary from 1928 and became executive producer of children's entertainment for J. Arthur Rank from 1944 to 1950. Joy Batchelor worked mainly in animation from 1935 and co-directed the first British feature-length cartoon, *Animal Farm* (1954), continuing to make animation films until the 1970s.

Women working in documentary film

The British Documentary Film Movement, of which John Grierson was the founder, had a huge influence on British film and has continued to exert its influence to the present day. Grierson's sister, Ruby, worked alongside him on a number of films and was involved in making films herself, such as *Housing Problems* (1940).

Many film-makers involved in the early documentary movement went on to make propaganda films during the war. This was one area of film where a few women could be found working as directors and assistant directors. Some women were taken on in

• Plate 8.1 *Blue Scar* (Jill Craigie, 1950)
Miners being attended to by the women

roles usually only open to men because of the increased demand for documentary propaganda film in wartime Britain and the shortage of available manpower.

Kay Mander is one woman film-maker who initially worked in continuity and was then
able to work as a director, partly because of the increased opportunities the war gave
to women. Her career as a film-maker is varied, having worked in both documentary
and feature film-making, originally directing films for the Shell Film Unit and then working
for the Department of Health, winning a British Film Academy award in 1949. Mander
explained that she lost her desire to direct and eventually went back into continuity
when she was told by a renowned feature film producer that: 'Women couldn't control
film crews', and the job was given to a man.[1]

Reflecting on the lack of women film directors and technicians, Mander felt that there
were so few because the way of life was very different then; women had different expectations, many of the women involved in film had husbands or brothers or fathers whom

• Plate 8.2 *To Be A Woman* (Jill Craigie, 1951)
An early documentary short arguing that women should be an essential part of the labour force

they assisted, and for a woman to work in film 'you had to be desperate to do it, in those days you had to have some sort of special drive'.[2]

Other women film-makers such as Yvonne Fletcher and Budge Cooper directed documentaries for Paul Rotha. Mary Marsh directed educational films and Marjorie Deans started Touchstone Films in this period.

Jill Craigie continued the tradition of women making documentaries about social conditions, writing and directing a number of films such as *The Way We Live* (1946–7), *Blue Scar* (1950) and *To Be A Woman* (1951), a documentary short about women's employment, which promoted women as part of the labour force, arguing that they had a right to equal pay and should not be treated as cheap labour.

Very few women in Britain have directed fiction film, but two women who made a number of films in the 1940s and 1950s, Muriel Box and Wendy Toye, gained an international reputation. The lesser-known Wendy Toye made such films as *Raising A Riot* (1957) and *We Joined The Navy*, with Dirk Bogarde and Kenneth More.

Muriel Box – an outstanding career in film

Muriel Box is regarded as one of the outstanding British film-makers of the 1940s and 1950s, and possibly the most successful woman director to date. Her career in film began as a script girl but really took off in a husband-and-wife partnership with Sydney Box when they worked on films together from 1939 to 1964. The *British Film Guide* (1979) says of Box:

> One of only two women directors regularly employed in British features . . . sister in law of our only British producer Betty Box. . . . Her own films are for the most part 'women's pictures'. . . . They are part of the magazine fiction of the screen and no less competently organised than most magazine fiction.
>
> (cited in Heck-Rabi 1984: 10)

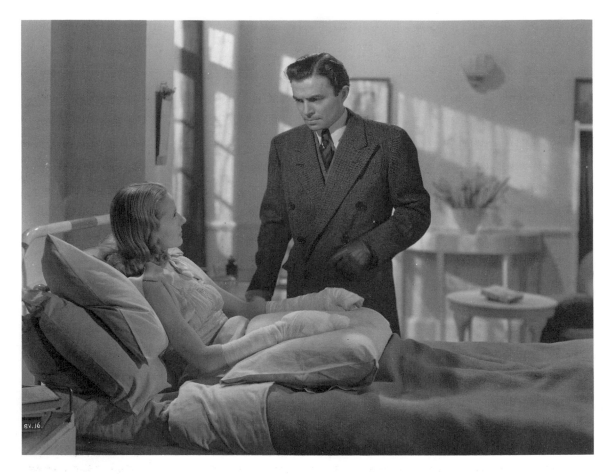

• Plate 8.3 *The Seventh Veil* (Muriel Box, 1945)
A hugely successful melodrama

Critical opinion of Box's work was not, as the above quote suggests, high. *Movie Magazine* placed her in the bottom group of directorial talent, yet her films can be seen as part of the strong tradition of melodrama passed down from the Victorian and Edwardian theatre.

The Box team made profitable, popular, mass entertainment films and Muriel Box was a highly respected film-maker and scriptwriter who wrote and directed more than thirty films. Probably her most famous film, which she scripted, is a melodrama, *The Seventh Veil* (1945), which received international acclaim and was a great box-office success.

By the 1960s the number of women directors could be counted on one hand – Muriel Box made her last film in 1964, *Rattle of a Simple Man*. Mai Zetterling, the Swedish actress married to a British film-maker, made a few documentaries such as *Polite Invasion* (1960) and *Visions of Eight* (1973) and Joan Littlewood directed *Sparrows Can't Sing* (1963). There seemed to be little reason for women to be hopeful of an expanding role within the British film industry which unfortunately was in a state of decline. By the end of the 1960s the American money that had helped support the British film industry in the boom decade had been pulled out. The film industry could not provide for the men and few women already working in it, let alone produce conditions that were conducive to the acceptance of more women film-makers:

> The British film industry has, since the end of the First World War, staggered from crisis to crisis (with occasional very brief periods of health) because the British market is not large enough to support a film industry built on the classic laissez-faire model.
>
> (Auty and Roddick 1985: 5)

Very few women film-makers existed in Britain before 1970 and even fewer could be termed commercially successful, Muriel Box being the outstanding exception. Yet the strong tradition of documentary film in this country did give women like Kay Mander, Jill Craigie and Yvonne Fletcher the opportunity to acquire film-making skills. It was virtually unheard of for women to work in technical areas like sound or camera, although women art directors and film editors were not so unusual – Ann V. Coates worked on Box's film *The Truth About Women* (1958) and David Lean's *Lawrence of Arabia* (1962). In general, though, it was rare for a woman to have a key role in film-making and, it could be argued, the rise of feminism in the 1960s was to be the great catalyst for change for women in film. This will be discussed in the next section.

FEMINIST FILM THEORY AND PRACTICE IN BRITAIN

The feminist revolution

The women's movement did not suddenly arrive; since the days of the suffragettes an increasing number of women had seen the need for equality with men. A new political and social climate was evolving in the 1960s and early 1970s which questioned the established order, encouraged radical reform and produced conditions that were conducive to the rise of the feminist movement. Although this radical dissatisfaction with contemporary society began in America its message soon spread to Britain and in both countries there was a questioning of woman's role in society. Betty Friedan's book, *The Feminine Mystique*, was published in 1963 and touched a chord in many discontented women. The time was ripe for the spread of the feminist movement,[3] as Friedan explained:

> the absolute necessity for a civil rights movement for women had reached such a point of subterranean explosive urgency by 1966 that it took only a few of us to get together to ignite the spark – and it spread like a nuclear chain reaction.
>
> (cited in Banner 1974: 247)

Representation and stereotyping of women in the media

Feminists generally believe that the media is a contributory factor in perpetuating a narrow range of **stereotyped** images of women. How women are **represented** in the media may encourage particular expectations of women that are extremely limiting; for instance, that women are always based in the home, that they are inferior to men, that they like men who are violent, are just a few of the myths that are arguably perpetuated by the media. As Molly Haskell points out:

stereotyping

A quick and easy way of labelling or categorising the world around us and making it understandable. Stereotypes are learned but are by no means fixed, yet are often resistant to change. They tend to restrict our understanding of the world and perpetuate beliefs that are often untrue or narrow. For instance, the concept that only thin women are attractive is a stereotype promoted by much of the media in the late twentieth century (though there are some exceptions like comediennes Dawn French and Roseanne); yet in other eras the opposite has been true. Stereotyping is not always negative, but tends to be very much concerned with preserving and perpetuating power relations in society. It is in the interests of those in power to continue to stereotype those with lower status in a negative light, thus preserving the status quo.

representation

The media *re*-presents information to its audience, who are encouraged by the mainstream media to see its output as a 'window on the world', as reflecting reality. Yet the process of representing information is highly complex and highly selective. Many feminists argue that the way notions of gender are represented by the media perpetuates and reinforces the values of patriarchal society; for instance, men tend to take on strong, active roles, while women are shown as passive and relying on their attractiveness.

There are exceptions to such narrow stereotyping, the 'strong' woman shown by Ripley in the Alien trilogy and the two heroines in *Thelma and Louise* could be seen as positive, although rather more cynically they could be seen merely as 'role reversal' films and so having purely novelty value. Representations often make use of stereotypes because they are a shorthand, quick and easy way of using information. It could be argued that the media production process encourages the use of stereotypes because of the pressure of time and budget.

Many feminists point out that because so few women hold key positions in the media hierarchies representations of women are bound to be from a male perspective.

patriarchal society

A society in which it is men who have power and control. Women are generally disadvantaged and have lower status.

From a woman's point of view the ten years from, say, 1962 or 1963 to 1973 have been the most disheartening in screen history. In the roles and prominence accorded to women, the decade began unpromisingly, grew steadily worse, and at present shows no sign of improving. Directors, who in 1962 were guilty only of covert misogyny (Stanley Kubrick's *Lolita*) or kindly indifference (Sam Peckinpah's *The High Country*) became overt in 1972 with the violent abuse and brutalisation of *A Clockwork Orange* and *Straw Dogs*.

(Haskell 1973: 323)

Film, particularly in the early feminist period, was seen as one area of the media that would become a battleground for the women's movement. Film would be used as an ideological tool, which would counteract the stereotyped images of women presented by the male-dominated media and raise women's awareness of their inferior position in **patriarchal society**, where women generally take a subservient role. For instance, in film, women, as the historical section indicates, have usually taken supportive roles rather than key, decision-making ones.

The influence of alternative, independent and avant-garde film

Alongside the expansion of feminism and the women's movement **alternative** and **avant-garde cinema** was flourishing. **Independent cinema** could, at its simplest, be divided into two forms: documentary and avant-garde. British film has a strong documentary tradition, which was to some extent socialist-influenced, and feminist film initially saw documentary as a way of presenting the 'truth' about the lives of women. During the 1960s American, avant-garde film-makers produced many innovative and controversial films, some of the most well known being 'gay' and 'camp' films that challenged traditional stereotypes of gender roles such as Andy Warhol's *Lonesome Cowboys* (1968) and Kenneth Anger's *Scorpio Rising* (1965). Also in Europe, avant-garde film had been taken up by a number of film-makers, Jean-Luc Godard and François Truffaut being its most famous exponents. Although gender roles in European films tended to be stereotypical, some feminist film-makers saw the potential of avant-garde film as a means of breaking away from the constraints of traditional cinema.

The expansion of independent film-making in Britain encouraged the formation of a number of workshops, which aimed to make film-making available to all and to destroy the elitism often found in the industry. Many workshops made films that were outside the sphere of mainstream film and television, often being concerned with areas that were considered radical in politics or content. Cinema Action was one of the earliest workshops. Formed in 1968, it toured the country screening films aimed at a working-class audience. Amber Films, based in Newcastle, began in 1969 and The Other Cinema opened in London as a distribution agency (an essential outlet for the distribution of independent films). Perhaps the best known of the workshops is the London Filmmakers Co-op, which is still in existence today.

The late 1960s and early 1970s was a period of great academic and cultural vitality. The government supported the arts and there was a commitment to film-making; in 1968 the Regional Arts Associations began funding individual films and in 1972 the Arts Council did likewise.

The first women's film group

The combination of the expansion of the women's movement and the rise of independent film-making brought about the conditions in which feminist film could thrive. In 1972 the first women's film group in Britain was formed, The London Women's Film Group, which aimed to spread ideas about women's liberation and enable women to learn film-making skills otherwise unavailable to them.

The London Women's Film Group, apart from making films by women, also campaigned for equal opportunities for women in the industry, and was instrumental in initiating the examination of the role of women within the ACCT (The Association of Cinematographers, Television and Allied Technicians). Without acceptance by the union it was, and still is, virtually impossible to work in the industry. In the 1970s there were no more women working in high-grade jobs in the film and television industry than there had been in the 1950s. Demystification of the learning of technical skills was considered vital, but it was also necessary to make women familiar with all the stages in the film-making process so that they had a large pool of knowledge, which they would never have been able to obtain in mainstream film. Many film groups worked co-operatively, giving all members an equal say in the production process and rejecting the strict hierarchy of roles used in mainstream film production.

The feminist film movement was intentionally political, aiming to give all women, but especially working-class women, a chance to work in film. The films were often shown to trade unions, in factories and housing estates, and it was hoped they would help to raise women's consciousness about their place in society. Many of the early feminist films fitted into the black and white documentary realist tradition, the dominant mode of alternative, political film-making in this country. Linda Dove, of the London Women's Film Group, explained in an interview:

> We tended to reject commercial films wholesale as the ideological products of capitalist, sexist, racist society. . . . Originally our aim was to change the context in which a film is seen – we wanted to break down the audience passivity by always going out with films and discussing them when they were shown.
>
> (Dove 1976: 59)

Film as a 'window on the world'

Left-wing documentary films had been seen as presenting the 'truth' and a form of reality, but the viewpoint that the visual media presented a 'window on the world' came under question in the early 1970s. The media, it could be argued, are manipulated by the ruling patriarchal ideology and what is seen as natural, as clear-cut and obvious, is in fact a concept produced by our society. The ambivalence about the meaning of film suggests its interpretation by the audience may be different to that intended by the film-maker. For instance, *Women of the Rhondda* (1972) has a naturalistic style with no voice-over and the images are intended to speak for themselves, but the message is somewhat ambiguous for a non-feminist audience because there are so many possible readings (this multitude of possible readings has been termed a polysemic text). This awareness resulted in a number of radical documentary film-makers becoming more didactic in their approach: for instance, *The Amazing Equal Pay Show* (LWFG, 1972) experimented with film conventions, developing links with avant-garde cinema, as does *The Night Cleaners* (Berwick Street Collective, 1972) which was concerned with better pay for office cleaners but used unconventional editing techniques.

---

alternative cinema

Provides an alternative to the codes and conventions of mainstream, narrative cinema, often both thematically and visually.

avant-garde cinema

Essentially non-narrative in structure and often intellectual in content, working in opposition to mainstream cinema. Avant-garde film is often self-concious and frequently makes use of devices such as cuts to the camera crew, talking to the camera and scratching on film.

Independent cinema

May be divided into two areas: first, independent mainstream cinema, such as HandMade Films, which aims to compete with the big studios, although without any large financial backing finds it difficult to survive. Palace Films was one such casualty; the success of *The Crying Game* came too late to save its demise. Second, the term is used to describe film-making outside the mainstream sector, for instance, film workshops, avant-garde film, feminist film. The boundaries between these two areas are not always clear and may overlap.

Many feminist film-makers in the 1970s appropriated ideas from avant-garde art cinema and applied them to discuss questions that were of concern to the women's movement, such as representation. The avant-garde had always been male-dominated and narrow in its representations of women (see, for instance, Jean-Luc Godard's films such as *Breathless* (1960), *A Married Woman* (1964) and *Weekend* (1968)). But the avant-garde's political/anarchist basis gave an alternative form to the traditional use of realism in both fiction and documentary film. This influence was most profound in film-makers like Laura Mulvey and Sally Potter, whose films are discussed on pp. 249–53.

Early feminist film theory

A key year for the women's film movement and the development of a feminist film theory and practice was 1972. In August, a women's event was held for the first time, in conjunction with the Edinburgh Film Festival, and proved to be very successful. In early 1973, Claire Johnston organised a season of women's cinema at the National Film Theatre.

The ideological sense of purpose and political debate behind feminist film-making ensured the development of a film theory. Feminist film theory was, in the early period, especially concerned with representation and sexuality and its relation to the dominance of the male power structure within a patriarchal society. A number of women, often from an academic background, encouraged this development, but it was perhaps Laura Mulvey and Claire Johnston who were the progenitors of feminist film theory. Both wrote seminal articles that were to have a huge impact on the study of film and the media and will be discussed in this chapter.

Developing a counter-cinema

Claire Johnston's *Women's Cinema as Counter-Cinema* (1973) is one of the earliest articles on feminist film theory and practice. Johnston shows how women have been stereotyped in film since the days of the silent cinema, and argues for a cinema that challenges such narrow conventions but which will also be entertaining. In mainstream cinema woman is seen as an extension of a male vision and Johnston criticises the narrow role she is given in film: 'It is probably true to say that despite the enormous emphasis placed on woman as spectacle in the cinema, woman as woman is largely absent.' (Johnston 1973: 214).

The work of two female Hollywood directors, Dorothy Arzner and Ida Lupino, is considered by Johnston, who suggests that their films partially subvert the patriarchal viewpoint. An understanding of how these films work could be important for feminist film practice in breaking through and challenging the ruling ideology.

Johnston argues for a woman's cinema that will work both within and outside mainstream cinema, and that will work collectively in groups with no hierarchical structure but also more conventionally, using film as a political tool and an entertainment.

The importance of developing a film practice that questions and challenges mainstream dominant cinema and its patriarchal basis is stressed by Johnston. She terms it a counter-cinema movement which will have links with avant-garde and left-wing film.

Pleasure, looking and gender

Psychoanalytic theory, particularly the theories of Freud and Lacan, has been instrumental in the development of a feminist film theory, although **structuralist** and **Marxist theories**[4] have also been influential to a lesser extent. Laura Mulvey's article 'Visual

psychoanalytic theory

Based on the theories of Freud and, more recently, Lacan. Feminists argue that aspects of psychoanalysis are questionable because they are based on patriarchal assumptions that the woman is inferior to man. Freud found female sexuality difficult and disturbing. Lacan argues that the mother is seen as lacking by the child because she has no phallus. Uncertainty about the role of the female in psychoanalytic theory has been picked up on by a number of feminists such as Mulvey, De Lauretis and Modleski, who question the inevitability of Freud and Lacan's theories which emphasise the importance of the phallus, penis envy and patriarchal supremacy.

structuralism

This was founded on the belief that the study of society could be scientifically based and that there are structures in society that follow certain patterns or rules. Initially, most interest was centred on the use of language; Saussure, the founder of linguistics, argued that language was essential in communicating the ideology, the beliefs, of a culture. Structuralists have applied these theories to film, which uses both visual and verbal communication, and pointed out that the text conveys an illusion of reality, so conveying the ideology of a society even more effectively.

Pleasure and Narrative Cinema' (first published in 1975) emphasises the importance of the patriarchical viewpoint in the cinema; that the pleasure gained from looking (called scopophilia) is a male pleasure and that 'the look' in cinema is directed at the male.

Scopophilia can be directed in two areas: first, voyeurism, that is scopophilic pleasure linked to sexual attraction, and, second, scopophilic pleasure that is linked to narcissistic identification. Mulvey argues that this identification is always with the male, who is the pivot of the film, its hero, while the female is often seen as a threat. Film reflects society, argues Mulvey, and society influences our understanding of film. This viewpoint is linked with psychoanalytical theory to demonstrate the influence of patriarchal society on film. Patriarchy and phallocentrism are intrinsically linked; the phallus is a symbol of power, of having (note how guns are used in film: guns = phallus = power). The woman has no phallus, she is castrated, which relates back to Freudian theory that the woman is lacking and therefore inferior because she has no phallus.

Freud's theories on scopophilia centre around voyeurism and the desire to see the erotic and the forbidden, yet this desire is male-centred. The cinema provides a perfect venue for illicit voyeuristic viewing because the audience is in a dark enclosed womb-like world. Mulvey argues that the power cinema holds is so strong it can act as a temporary form of brainwashing (an argument which is still very much alive today!).

The woman in Freudian theory represents desire, but also the castration complex, and so there is a tension, an ambivalence towards the female form and her 'look' can be threatening. As the male is the controller, taking the active role, the female is reduced to the icon, the erotic, but at the same time is a threat because of her difference.

Mulvey argues that woman has two roles in film: erotic object for the characters in the story and erotic object for the spectator. More recent feminist theory, though, seems to suggest that the representation of women is far more complex, and later theory, including Mulvey's, looks at films where women do have a key role as subject rather than object. Melodrama is one such area (see Mulvey 1981).

Mulvey refers to Hitchcock because of the complicit understanding in his films that the audience gains a voyeuristic pleasure from watching a film, from looking: 'In *Vertigo* (1958) in particular, but also in *Marnie* (1964) and *Rear Window* (1954), the 'look' is central to the plot oscillating between voyeurism and fetishistic fascination' (Mulvey 1975: 813).

The denial of pleasure

Mulvey points out that devices used in the traditional Hollywood narrative film have trapped film-makers into using certain codes and conventions that place the female in a subordinate, passive position, making her role as erotic object extremely limiting. Mulvey criticises the narrowness of this role and argues that to change woman's position in film a revolutionary look at cinema needs to be taken and the denial of cinematic pleasure be given a priority. The exclusion of woman as object, as provider of voyeuristic pleasure will then free her from the narrow limits she has been allocated in cinema. This may seem an extreme reaction to mainstream, narrative cinema, but in the early 1970s feminists felt the only way to change female representation was to take extreme measures; a new radical cinema was needed, an alternative to the 'magic' of narrative cinema.

A new language

The importance of the creation of a female subject and the development of a new language is central to early feminist film theory, which argued that spoken, written and

Marxist theory

Argues that those who have the means of production have control in a capitalist society. The dominant class have control of the means of production and have an interest in perpetuating the dominant ideology. More recently exponents of Althusserian Marxism, particularly post 1968, have argued that mainstream narrative cinema reinforces the capitalist system and that a revolutionary cinema is needed to challenge the dominant ideology.

visual languages all placed women in a subordinate position and reflected a patriarchal ideology. A film theory and practice that had its own codes and conventions would replace the dominance of patriarchal cinema. Christine Gledhill echoes this desire in her article, 'Some Recent Developments in Feminist Criticism' (1985):

> A feminist filmmaker then, finds the root of patriarchy in the very tools she wishes to employ to speak about women. So what is required of her is the development of a counter-cinema that will deconstruct the language and techniques of classic cinema.
>
> (Gledhill 1985: 841)

Classic cinema was based on ideas that had been passed on from the old literary/ realist tradition and many feminists felt that the realist tradition perpetuated a way of seeing, of understanding the world, that belonged to dominant patriarchal society and that feminists should break with this tradition.

Avant-garde feminist film

Film-makers like Mulvey and Potter were interested in a film theory and practice which worked together and would produce a new feminist language. Avant-garde film was the ideal vehicle for these ideas because it broke the normal rules and conventions of main-stream cinema; its political/anarchist basis gave an alternative form to the traditional use of realism in both fiction and documentary film. Mulvey's article 'Film, Feminism and the Avant-Garde' (1979) explores this relationship, suggesting that both forms of film can be mutually beneficial, working towards similar goals. Mulvey's films, for instance, actively avoid any sense of being constructed for the male spectator, confronting the lack of representation of women in film; they are a mixture of avant-garde, melodrama and psychoanalytic theory. Mulvey has put her theories into practice, providing an alternative cinema in which:

> pleasure and involvement are not the result of identification, narrative tension or eroti-cised femininity, but arise from surprising and excessive use of the camera, unfamiliar framing of scenes and the human body, the demands made on the spectator to put together disparate elements.
>
> (Mulvey 1989: 125)

Paenthesilea (1974) discusses how women have been excluded from the dominant culture. The film is composed of a number of sections, avoiding traditional narrative structure; the first part is about the Amazons resisting patriarchy; other sections examine issues around language, and the final section is seen from one woman's viewpoint, the suffragette trying to persuade people that a woman's right to vote is a class issue also. *Riddles of the Sphinx* (1977) continues to question women's lack of voice, but through the exploration of the role of the mother. *Amy* (1980) is perhaps the most accessible of Mulvey's films and is about the life of Amy Johnston who completed a round-the-world solo flight in 1930. She stands out as a strong, independent woman and role model who gave up her career for marriage. The film is a mix of fiction and documentary but the spectator is forced into an awareness of woman traditionally being the object of the male gaze.

(For further analysis of avant-garde, feminist film see Case study 3 on Sally Potter's films.)

The need for an audience

Avant-garde was limiting as a form in achieving feminist aims of reaching a mass audience precisely because of its upturning of the codes and conventions of mainstream cinema. Many avant-garde films were termed 'difficult' and only attracted a small audience which tended to be those familiar with 'art film'. Even though avant-garde-influenced film-makers, like Mulvey, did much to aid the understanding of their films by producing hand-outs and giving lectures, some feminists felt that avant-garde film was elitist and would be of no interest to a mass audience of women. Mulvey's and Johnston's theories, they suggested, would be more useful for the development of a feminist film theory than as a guide on how to make feminist films. Kaplan (1983), for example, points out that it makes more sense to use familiar and recognisable cinematic conventions to explain that the 'realism' of mainstream cinema is a fabrication.

Questioning representation

The need for a strong feminist film practice which provided an alternative view other than the gender stereotype was voiced by feminists. There had been a shift in attitude by the end of the 1970s when it was acknowledged that representation was a complex area and there need not necessarily be a direct link between media representations of women and their changing place in society. If the media does not represent a 'window on the world' it would therefore be naive to assume that changes in representation in the media would automatically result in changes in society. Mulvey comments on the dangers of an over-emphasis on representation and suggests that to bring about change by working within the conventions of patriarchal production could be counter-productive.

A period of optimism and defiance

Johnston's article 'The Subject of Feminist Film Theory/Practice' was published in a spirit of optimism when the women's movement was still strong and the Feminism and Cinema Event had been successfully held at the Edinburgh Film Festival in 1979. Johnston points out that feminists had achieved much in a short time span, and 'We are now at a stage when it is becoming possible to theorise a conception of ideological struggle within feminist film theory and practice more concretely' (Johnston 1980: 28).

Feminist film theory and practice in the early period up to 1980 had been a joint ideological struggle; film theory analysed the patriarchal conventions that mainstream film worked within and film practice was physically able to break these rules. Yet there was only a limited audience for feminist film in this period, even though there was an increasing interest in academic circles in feminist film theory. In the strongly male-dominated world of film-making women were not seen as artists or film-makers, and feminist art was seen as a possible challenge to patriarchal society.[5] As Johnston explains, the female within patriarchy is seen as the 'other' and feminist art challenges these narrow conceptions of gender:

> Feminist art, on the other hand, which asserts a woman's discourse about her position and ... the subjective relationships which constitute her a female subject in history, is far more problematic and far less easily assimilated into the conception of woman as irrevocable 'other' by which patriarchy is maintained.
>
> (Johnston 1980: 34)

By the end of the 1970s a feminist film theory and practice had been established, giving many women a new-found confidence and a belief that society could change. In the

• Plate 8.4 *Thriller* (Sally Potter, 1979)
Explores the lack of female voice in society

previous decade a number of influential articles on feminist film theory and practice had been written. A body of work had been formed by feminist writers and academics, Mulvey and Johnston being the founder writers that were to influence a generation of film and media critics. Janet Bergstrom, in 'Rereading the Work of Claire Johnston', explains how Johnston laid the groundwork for 'a recognition of the importance of an understanding of feminist criticism and theory, feminist filmmaking' (Bergstrom 1988: 83)

Films were being made by women and about women. More women's film groups had been formed. Sheffield Film Co-Op, for instance, was formed in 1975 by a group of socialist feminist film-makers who made documentary and drama-documentary films about women in the local community, such as *A Woman Like You* (1976) and *Jobs for the Girls* (1979). Films such as Clayton and Curling's *Song of the Shirt* (1979) and Sally Potter's *Thriller* (1979) were received with interest and some acclaim.

Making feminist film accessible

Feminist film practice generally saw itself as separate from mainstream film. Yet in the next decade this was to become an area of debate. Strategies for gaining a larger audience for feminist ideas would be hotly argued. Lack of money and very tight budgets did not appear to have caused real frustration and the main concern was to develop a feminist film practice. Sally Potter, for instance, felt that although it was desirable to gain a larger audience, her ideological position excluded her from becoming involved in the mechanisms of the mainstream film industry: a feminist film would have little marketability and be a huge risk for a distributor. Potter argues that pleasure can be revolutionary:

> I think that working for a wide audience is not a matter of compromise at all . . . and that pleasure need not be an ideological acceptance of a patriarchal society. . . . There is pleasure in analysis, in unravelling, in thinking, in criticising the old stories. That was the premise from which *Thriller* worked.
>
> (Cook 1981: 27)

While Sally Potter was developing fictional film and seeking a wider audience, a significant strand of feminist film, more Marxist-influenced than avant-garde/structuralist, was developing a documentary style aimed at working-class women with the intention of making feminist film more accessible. These documentary film-makers felt that there should not be just one authorial voice, a sole director, and a number of films were made co-operatively. Clayton and Curling's *The Song of the Shirt* (1979) was one such project. This was initially instigated and researched by a feminist history group and then brought to the film-makers for completion. Clayton in an interview comments on the transient nature of debate around feminism and film, showing an awareness of the polysemic nature of a text and the variety of meanings that can be obtained:

> Women's cinema is something different from what it was in 1979 when we finished it (the film). The context of everything is changing so that there is going to be a point when all of us, not just the people who made the film, but everybody will have moved on from these specific debates. And the film will become something different. It will become, if you like, a document of its own.
>
> (Lehman and Mayne 1981: 72)

At the beginning of the 1970s the focus was on representation in film and the media, but by the end of the decade attention was being diverted to the concept of 'pleasure' and whether this should be denied in film. Some feminists expressed the concern that by denying the pleasures of mainstream cinema feminist film-makers might alienate their audience. Yet feminists generally agreed that feminist film theory and practice had an important role to play in raising conciousness as to the marginalisation of women in a patriarchal society.

Some feminists still called for a counter-cinema and a deconstructive cinema in the early 1980s. Ann Kaplan and Annette Kuhn argued that there is a need to break down the dominant forms of cinema, and that the audience should become active rather than passive, gaining pleasure from learning rather than the narrative. Feminist counter-cinema can be broadly divided into three types of film: first, those films that look at the absence of a female voice in film and women's marginalisation in a phallocentric language and image system. Mulvey's films are an example here. Second, films that have points in common in their use of Lacanian psychoanalytic theory, and demonstrate that women have been used as an empty vessel, an extension of the male voice; Sally Potter's

Thriller, for instance. Finally, films that are concerned with writing women into history and the problems of depicting women's role in society. Clayton and Curling's *Song of the Shirt* comes into this category.

Both Kuhn and Kaplan and film-makers like Sue Clayton were aware of the problems of using a cinema which rejects the mainstream, that is anti-conventional, and may therefore alienate its audience. Kaplan suggested that a way forward would be to work within and manipulate the conventions of mainstream cinema.

Moving towards mainstream narrative cinema

A number of feminists feared that certain areas of feminist film practice had become so entrenched in promulgating a theoretical viewpoint that a barrier had been created between film and audience, and felt that to appeal to a mass audience traditional narrative structures and conventions might have to be used.

In fact, by the early 1980s more films by women were working within mainstream film conventions. Alongside experimental films like *The Gold Diggers* (1983) and *An Epic Poem* (1982) more traditional narrative and documentary forms were being investigated by feminists such as Dutch film-maker Marlene Gorris, who made the excellent but somewhat controversial, at the time of release, *Question of Silence* (1982) (see Case study 4, p. 247), and Lizzy Borden who made *Born in Flames* (1983), a mix of documentary and science fiction. Both films were received with interest and seemed to indicate a new way forward for feminist narrative film.

By the mid-1980s the documentary was being used to considerable effect by women's film groups such as Red Flannel, giving a voice to women's issues (see Case study 1, p. 244). Formed in 1984, it benefited from the advent of Channel 4 (in 1982) which gave financial assistance to a number of film groups and provided a wider audience through the mass medium of television. The feminist Sheffield Film Co-Op continued to make films with strong representations of working-class women like *Red Skirts On Clydeside* (1983) which is a documentary concerned with reclaiming key points in women's history, in this case the 1915 Rent Strike in Glasgow.

Reassessing feminist film theory

Feminist film theory was going through a similar period of reassessment that also seemed to suggest that feminist ideas could be expounded using mainstream cinema. In 1981 Mulvey published a 1980s response to her 1970s article 'Visual Pleasure and Narrative Cinema', which was so fundamental to the development of feminist film theory, entitled 'Afterthoughts on Visual Pleasure and Narrative Cinema' (1981). In the article Mulvey develops two lines of thought: first, examining whether the female spectator can gain a deep pleasure from a male-orientated text, and second, how the text and the spectator are affected by the centrality of a female character in the narrative. 'Afterthoughts' does seem to mark a shift in attitude, a move away from representation to studying the female response, to asking how women watch films and questioning the role of melodrama, which has traditionally been viewed as the woman's genre.

Feminist film theory has been especially influenced by psychoanalytic theory and particularly Freud and Lacan. Mulvey acknowledges her debt to Lacan who, she explains, has 'broadened and advanced ways of conceptualising sexual difference, emphasising the fictional, constructed nature of masculinity and femininity' (Mulvey 1989: 165).

Not all feminists supported a feminist film theory based on psychoanalytic theory. Terry Lovell in *Pictures of Reality* (1983) criticised Lacanian theory because of its emphasis on the individual rather than the collective and argued that gaining pleasure from the text is rather more complex than a simple attribution to sexual desire.

In the latter part of the 1980s Freud's work had been re-examined by many feminists because of its phallocentric basis. Tania Modleski, for instance, in her book *The Women Who Knew Too Much* (1988), asks for a less male-centred version of spectatorship and calls for the development of a feminist psychoanalytic theory that is challenging and inventive. Penley, in the introduction to *Feminism and Film Theory* (1988), states that much feminist film criticism questions the patriarchal roots of current psychoanalytic theories, especially those of Freud and Lacan.

Modleski applies her ideas to an analysis of Hitchcock's films, which have been of great interest to feminists because of his extreme use of voyeurism and the 'look'. Reassessing earlier theory, Modleski points out that Mulvey's article 'Visual Pleasure and Narrative Cinema' (1975) does not allow for the complex nature of representation and raises questions about the stereotypical, passive female object and the active male. Modleski states: 'What I want to argue is neither that Hitchcock is utterly misogynistic nor that he is largely sympathetic to women and their plight in patriarchy, but that his work is characterised by a thoroughgoing ambivalence about femininity' (Modleski 1988: 3).

Many of Hitchcock's films are seen from the point of view of a female protagonist: *Blackmail* (1929), *Rebecca* (1940), *Notorious* (1946), for instance, or when the hero or heroine is in a vulnerable or passive, female position as in *Rear Window* (1954).

Modleski suggests that aspects of Mulvey's work need to be re-examined, especially the suggestion that the patriarchal order has banished a strong female presence. In *North by Northwest* (1959), Cary Grant's role is that of hero and sex object, the desirable male; in *Marnie* (1964), Sean Connery plays a similar role, which also serves to heighten the irony that Marnie, the heroine and his wife, is frigid. In Hitchcock's films both male and female can become objects of the 'look'.

The strong and powerful female can exist within mainstream film, yet Hitchcock is patently not a feminist film-maker and his films tie in with Freud's assertion that the male contempt for femininity is an expression of the repression of their bisexuality – woman is a threat who must be destroyed: 'the male object is greatly threatened by bisexuality, though he is at the same time fascinated by it; and it is the woman who pays for this ambivalence, often with her life itself' (Modleski 1988: 10).

Towards the end of the 1980s there was a certain ambivalence regarding the role of feminist film theory and practice; the close ties that had worked together and argued for a counter-cinema were now divorcing, theorists and practitioners felt that to work within mainstream cinema was possible, if not essential, to gain a wider audience. Teresa De Lauretis in her article, 'Guerilla in the Midst – Women's Cinema in the 1980s' (1990), suggests there are two distinct areas in which women film-makers may work: the alternative 'guerilla' cinema that is locally based, and mainstream film aiming at a nationwide or worldwide audience.

Women in the mainstream film industry

Although the number of women working in key roles in the film industry was still very small, by the late 1980s an increasing number of women were entering these areas after

• Plate 8.5 *North by Northwest* (Alfred Hitchcock, 1959)
Cary Grant – irresistible to women

receiving training in a film school or gaining experience in the growing number of film workshops. The National Film School, for instance, increased its intake of female students from one out of twenty-five when it first opened in 1971 to around 30 per cent by the mid-1980s. In an interview, camerawoman Belinda Parsons explains how important a thorough preparation and training was in a male-dominated workforce: 'As a woman one was going to have a lot of other problems and I didn't need confidence problems on the technical side; so from that point of view film school was brilliant' (Fitzgerald 1989: 193).

By the 1990s more women were working in previously male-dominated areas like directing, camera, sound and lighting.[6] Diane Tammes, Sue Gibson and Belinda Parsons are all respected camerawomen; Diana Ruston and Moya Burns work in sound.

• Plate 8.6 *Orlando* (Sally Potter, 1993)
An elegant gender-bender

Surprisingly, they have come across little sexism and feel that with more and more women coming into the industry men have no choice but to accept them. Moya Burns comments in an article entitled 'Women in Focus':

> The industry has changed a lot in the last ten years, there are not so many hard-boiled areas, like big-budget features. The features that get made today are financed differently, a lot of the money seems to be coming from bodies like Channel 4. They have a different emphasis on the type of film they want to make, and this filters right down to the type of crew they want to employ.
>
> (Burns 1992: 4)

In the field of directing women film-makers are now beginning to break into mainstream film, often from the independent and workshop sector. Lezli-Ann Barrett made the 'arty' feminist film short, *An Epic Poem*, in 1982 and went on to make the political but more conventional *Business As Usual*, starring Glenda Jackson, in 1987; Zelda Baron had a minor success with *Shag* (1988) and then worked in America; Beeban Kidron directed *Vroom* and then made the highly acclaimed TV series *Oranges are Not the Only Fruit*. In 1992 she worked in America on *Used People*, starring Shirley Maclaine, and completed *Great Moments in Aviation History* with John Hurt and Vanessa Redgrave in

• Plate 8.7 *Dream On* (Amber Films, 1992)
A supportive community of women

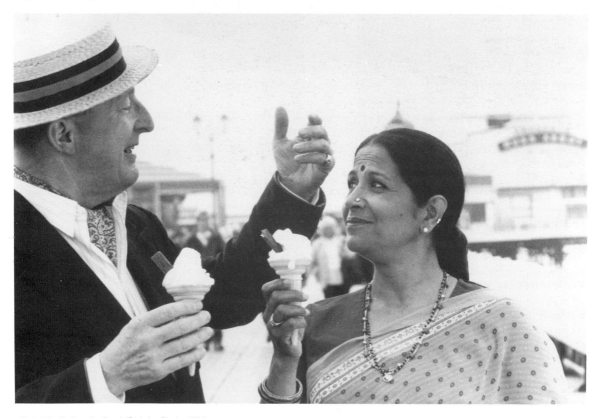

• Plate 8.8 *Bhaji on the Beach* (Gurinder Chada, 1994)
Received a BAFTA nomination for best film

• Plate 8.9 *The Unforgiven* (Clint Eastwood, 1992)

1993. Kidron looks set to have an international career in directing. Sally Potter moved from the avant-garde *The Gold Diggers* (1982) to *Orlando* (1993), a film based on a Virginia Woolf novel. Although the film is art-based in form, it is coherent enough in style to have gained a wide audience and much praise and attention from film critics in Britain and America (see Case study 3, p. 251). One of the most striking films to come out of the workshop sector is Amber Films' *Dream On* (1992), focusing on a group of women who live on a Tyneside estate. Gurinder Chada's most recent film takes a wry and witty look at life for Asian women in Britain today. *Bhaji on the Beach* (1994) is a rich and colourful film that deserves to be seen by a wide audience.

The advent of Channel 4 in 1982 proved beneficial for women and film. Apart from funding a number of film and video workshops the company also employed women in

• Plate 8.10 *Thelma and Louise* (Ridley Scott, 1992)

key positions who in turn encouraged a programme of work by women (Caroline Spry, for instance, is a commissioning editor for Channel 4). In 1990 Channel 4 screened a series of films by women from all over the world. Entitled 'Women Call the Shots', this was a response to the wealth of cinema made by women that is rarely seen by a large audience. More recently, though, Channel 4 has dramatically cut back on its workshop funding,[7] including financial support for Red Flannel and many other innovative workshops which provided a vehicle for women to gain work and experience in film and video without being part of the mainstream industry. The whole of the workshop sector is having to cope and remain solvent in the 1990s post-Thatcher recession and with growing competition from other independent film and TV companies.

Fragmentation of the feminist movement

Many women in film seem to have distanced themselves from the feminist movement, and, although retaining sympathy for its ideals, question what feminism and feminist film really means. The term post-feminism has frequently been referred to, suggesting that we are past feminism. Feminism certainly seems to have become fragmented, yet Jane Pilcher argues that many women, especially those under 30, are aware of the term in its widest sense: 'However, they also described feminism as being concerned with a

• Plate 8.11 *The Piano* (Jane Campion, 1993)

wider range of issues, including, for example the sexual objectification of women or the politics of appearance. Others described feminism as being a wide ranging "philosophy of ·life" ' (Pilcher 1993: 4).

Pilcher also came across the 'I'm not a feminist, but' syndrome in her research, women who were sympathetic to feminism but did not want to be associated with extremism. This is a dilemma that confronts women who work in film. As film-maker Sally Potter points out, in an interview with David Ehrenstein, to acknowledge being a feminist is problematic:

> So if I said, 'Yes I'm a feminist', it would slot in with their definition, which was a cliche of a protesting radical – everything they fear. You've got to be clever. You've got to speak freshly with nice juicy words that intoxicate – not trigger jargon words that turn people off.
>
> (Ehrenstein 1993: 17)

Perhaps a new term, 'feminist realism', should be applied to women working in film, who have to be sensitive to the demands of the mainstream film industry if they are to get backing for their films, especially in such a competitive industry when production funding for both men and women is so difficult to obtain.

A number of support agencies for women film-makers have been established which aim to provide the female equivalent of the 'Old Boys' Network'; 'Women in Film and TV' helps women in the mainstream sector and in the independent and workshop sector, groups like 'Real Women' hold regular seminars and screenings, while 'Networking' provides information and support for all women interested in film and video.

So much of the future for women in film seems to be dependent on funding; in the independent sector on government support for the arts, and in the mainstream sector on confidence and continued investment in the industry. Possibly, in a British film industry that is so reliant on television, there may be more openings for women film-makers there (Beeban Kidron, for instance, gained experience working in television drama and documentary before moving on to TV-funded films).

Whether changing attitudes towards women working in the film industry will produce more positive representations of women in film is open to question. Feminism has perhaps changed the way we look at film, and there is a greater awareness of how gender is represented in the media, yet many films, particularly genre films, still display woman as erotic object or passive and incapable (see Clint Eastwood's *Unforgiven* (1992)). *Thelma and Louise* (1992) was hailed as a feminist film (directed by Ridley Scott, but scripted by a woman, Callie Khouri), although a more cynical analysis reveals that the women are filmed quite conventionally, as objects of 'the look'.[8] As more women work in mainstream film, though, it does seem likely that there will be a widening out of representations of women both visually and thematically. Films like Sally Potter's *Orlando* (1993) and Jane Campion's *The Piano* (1993), for instance, have both had successful releases yet are concerned with subject-matter that would not normally be considered mainstream. They are also both exquisitely photographed and sensual films that offer an alternative world-view to the Hollywood norm.

□ CASE STUDY 1: RED FLANNEL

Red Flannel is a women's film and video production group based in South Wales. It was formed in 1984, partly as a result of working together on film projects during the miners' strike of 1984–5. The group was originally envisaged as providing a workshop where women could acquire training in film and video, but that it would also provide media education, produce films and videos and be a facility for hiring equipment. Red Flannel was provisionally franchised by the ACTT (the union for the film and TV industry) in 1985 and was fully franchised in 1987, when it also gained Channel 4 funding. At present there are six women involved with Red Flannel, three full time workers and three who have continued links.

The group has always been particularly concerned with portraying the lives of women in South Wales. Members define themselves as being socialist, feminist and Welsh. The political slant to their work ensures that issues are examined from a women's perspective, drawing attention to areas that are often ignored by the mainstream media.

In an interview with Red Flannel, it was pointed out that working for a feminist film and video group enabled its members to gain invaluable experience and training: 'We could make mistakes and not have to defend ourselves from the male onslaught.

These sorts of organisations are very important because women tend not to have much confidence in our industry.'[9]

The group emphasised how male dominated the industry still is. From Hollywood downwards there is a lack of representation of women's ideas and issues. Even though the situation has improved over the last ten years there is much room for progress.

At present Red Flannel are surviving in a climate that is difficult for all small production companies. The loss of funding from Channel 4 in 1992 affected their ability to exist as a workshop. Channel 4 funding had enabled Red Flannel to operate with an enormous amount of freedom, they provided an everyday running budget (to include wages), a generous budget to produce one documentary a year and money for community work, which Channel 4 encouraged. Since the funding cuts the group have kept busy, making a number of programmes over the last two years, but are still under enormous financial pressure and are running from commission to commission. Each commission provides a film budget and production fee of between 7 and 10 per cent of the budget (the production fee includes the running costs and wages). To remain solvent Red Flannel need to complete at least four productions a year, and these are generally made on a much lower budget than previously; most of their films are local commissions costing around £1,000 a minute (about half the London budget).

In 1993–4 Red Flannel put in twenty film proposals to television companies (HTV, BBC and Channel 4), approximately half of which were focused on women's issues. The response was positive; the BBC was interested in five of the proposals, HTV and Channel 4 in one each. However, an interest in a proposal still does not mean a production is guaranteed and this causes some uncertainty. Red Flannel are competing in a recession when the government is committed to deregulating the television industry. Indeed, they are one of the few women's film and video groups to have survived the early 1990s, yet are cautiously optimistic about their future as an independent film and video company.

As a feminist and socialist group, Red Flannel have tried to work co-operatively whenever possible. This has been most successful in documentary programmes where everyone can be involved in the research side, rather than an individually conceived, expressionistic piece like *Otherwise Engaged* (1991) where an author is needed. *Mam* (1988) was devised by the group and worked well as a collective film: 'There were very long discussions about what should go in, right up to the editing stage, but in production we had a specific role.'[10] The next film, *If We Were Asked* (1989), was a less successful collaboration and after that, partly because of pressure of time, collective working became a less realistic option. Projects now tend to become the overall responsibility of two people, with others giving comments at 'report-backs' on a film's progress.

☐ *MAM* (1988)

Mam is a documentary film that uses a mix of archive footage and interviews to give an historical account of the role of the Welsh mother in the working-class mining communities of South Wales. The film explores how the 'mam' is a concept originally imposed by early Victorian patriarchy, when the morals of Welsh women were put under question by a report from three Anglican commissioners who investigated the state of education in Wales. Among other points made, the report stated that Welsh women were lacking in morals and domestic skills. It resulted in the 'Blue Book' which said women should be based in the home and serve their husbands and children. Many women had worked

● Plate 8.12 *Mam* (Red Flannel, 1988)
Women working on the production

in the heavy industries such as coal and iron, which then became exclusively male preserves, emphasising the divide between male and female that was to continue well into this century.

The harshness of life for women in the early 1900s is evident from statistics that show there was a higher mortality rate for women in childbirth than there was from working in the pits. Women made enormous sacrifices for their families, doing without food, always putting husband and children first. Girls took second place in the family and while a boy's education was considered important, a girl's was not.

Many women worked in factories and industry during the Second World War which gave an increasing sense of independence and confidence, opening up women's lives. After the war, women were encouraged to go back into the home, but a new lifestyle had been revealed and factories such as GEC continued to employ women (often as cheap labour), quite a few of whom became involved in trade union life, and so were politicised.

The nationalisation of the mines in 1946 continued to change women's lives; better working conditions and pit-head baths meant less cleaning and washing in the home.

The film focuses on the community in a state of change. By the early 1980s the pits had nearly all closed and the 1984 miners' strike was a catalyst for a number of women who became actively involved in protecting the future of the community and providing a positive role for women within it.

Women in the Valleys often work for pin money, are frequently isolated and lacking in confidence. Training is suggested as a way forward, as a means of empowerment. Shirley Powell, for instance, explains how she is part of a workers' clothing co-operative that was formed when the company she worked for 'went bust'.

In a series of short 'talking heads' interviews women discuss why the male/female divide has been so strong in the Valleys, and why the 'mam' has endured. It is argued that mothers tend to reinforce these stereotypes. One woman suggests that it is the 'mam' herself who is to blame and sons should do more in the home; another points out that the Valleys' man is twenty to thirty years behind the average male in his attitude to women.

The film has a fairly conventional structure, although there is no single linking voice-over. This style developed from the influence of the British Documentary Movement on independent film, ranging from early films like Humphrey Jennings' *Listen To Britain* (1942) to the later *Women of the Rhondda* (1972) made by The London Women's Film Group (a film well worth looking at in conjunction with *Mam* because of the similarity of style and content). The style is often referred to as 'the storytelling technique' when the visuals and interviews explain the narrative – there is no omniscient narrator to explain how the film should be read. This method can produce ambiguity, but often leads to a livelier, more creative work.

☐ *OTHERWISE ENGAGED* (1991)

The film is a fairly light-hearted look at Valleys' life through the eyes of different generations of women enjoying themselves on a night out. The focal point of the film is the toilets, where women have traditionally met to gossip, put on make-up and chat about men. Women in different clubs, from the working-men's club to the youth-orientated night club, are interviewed and talk about their lives, women's issues, their careers and relationships with men.

The difference in outlook between the generations is highlighted; the younger women, for instance, seem to be split between those who want to marry and have children and those who want to have careers and travel. The older women seem to envy the freedom of youth. A general point made is that women can relax and enjoy themselves more with other women than with men, feeling that they don't have to put up a front and 'behave'.

Otherwise Engaged records a way of life that is changing, a community that is changing. The working-men's clubs are a part of a mining community that no longer exists; jobs are scarce and many women are now having to move from the area to find work.

☐ CASE STUDY 2: *A QUESTION OF SILENCE* (1982)
Director: Marlene Gorris

A Question of Silence is an unusual and still topical film that gained some notoriety when it first came out because many men found its central subject-matter offensive.

The plot, at its simplest, tells the story of three women who are charged with murdering the male manager of a boutique. The story has an investigative structure that gradually reveals information about the murder, as the female psychiatrist assigned to the case attempts to find out why the murder took place.

The narrative is in certain aspects fairly conventional; it is the discourse of the film that is most disturbing to the audience, the acceptance of a 'logically' motiveless murder. Yet showing this film to male and female students in the 1990s generally elicits a response of interest tinged with amusement. This perhaps suggests a shift in attitude over the last decade: the film is not seen as threatening and there is an awareness of its black humour and playfulness, the poking fun at the ridiculousness of patriarchy. Masculine constructions in society such as the court system, for instance, are satirised in the film.

A Question of Silence challenges male authority, rendering it absurd and pointless, and examines women's lack of power and voice in a patriarchal society. It has been argued that the film supports a feminist separatist existence, a world apart from men; indeed, the film has no positive male characters. Even the psychiatrist's husband, originally presented as a liberal thinking 'new man', gradually reveals his underlying authoritarian, patriarchical values.

Jeanette Murphy argues that the murder is generally seen as a metaphor, a symbol of woman's oppression, but could also be seen as a literal device to show women's anger and frustration with patriarchy: 'How else to expose the insidious and deeply hidden forces of male dominance? How else to express the depth and degree of women's anger?' (Murphy 1986: 105).

The form of the film is often elliptical and only partly fits into the mainstream, although the investigative plot makes the form more acceptable and great pleasure is gained from the gradual revelation of events (Barthes named this the 'enigma' code). Alternative cinema can use this form to attract an audience who may have antipathy towards anything other than mainstream cinema.

The film begins about half way through the timescale of events and is interspersed by flashbacks which reveal more and more about the events building up to the murder, which is then only partly shown to the audience. The murder is confusing and disturbing because there is no obvious motivation – a logical reason for murder is part of the expectation of the conventional narrative structure. Gorris makes fun of narrative expectations, often with a strong sense of irony; for instance, the murder weapons are everyday objects familiar to women, coat-hangers and shopping trolleys. The bizarreness of the plot creates a sense of the surreal, of wicked black humour which is particularly pointed against men and is continued after the murder when the three women show no sign of remorse: Christine goes to the funfair, Ann has a feast of fine food and Andrea prostitutes herself.

All three women are presented as being very ordinary, having little power or control over their lives, and their frustration is made clear: Ann, a barmaid, has to put up with sexist insults; Christine is a mother and housewife whose husband treats her like a servant; and Andrea, the most confident and assertive of the women, is an indispensable secretary, but patronised by her male bosses.

Janine Van Der Bos, the psychiatrist, initially represents authority and middle-class, patriarchal values. We see events through her eyes, and so how her role changes from inquisitor to supporter. As Janine begins to understand the women so she questions her role in society and her marriage, becoming distanced from her husband. The distance between them is heightened when he rapes her in their bedroom, a scene which is intercut with images of the women standing over the murdered boutique manager. Janine now identifies with the women.

Heterosexual sex is not presented as pleasurable for a woman – Janine's relationship is on her husband's terms, and Andrea coldly and unemotionally sells her body. Although the relationship between the women is not directly presented as sexual, there seems to be a mutual understanding that is almost telepathic. This is most evident when Andrea outlines Janine's body with her hands, in an emotional and potentially sexual scene which emphasises their closeness. There is certainly a hint that a lesbian relationship may be more satisfactory than a heterosexual one.

The final court scene begins with a wide shot of the court emphasising the all-male exclusiveness of those in power. At the same time a voice-over of the prosecutor represents the pompous and convoluted language of patriarchy that is designed to intimidate. Many feminists, particularly in the early 1980s, believed that a new language should be devised that would be sympathetic to women (at its simplest, words like history would become herstory). Throughout the film, language is problematic; Christine refuses to talk, the murder is carried out through a play of silent looks, as in the court scene when Janine communicates with the women by a series of looks, a more effective means of communication than language. Laughter is seen as an alternative to patriarchal language, as being able to subvert patriarchal authority, and is used to confuse the judge and undermine the court scene. The ripple of laughter that spreads across the women and finally to Janine effectively disrupts the seriousness of the court, making the legal process look ridiculous.

Janine's insistence that the accused are sane is received with disbelief because this does not make the crime understandable and rational. If the women were insane then the crime would be explainable. Janine's judgement is questioned by the prosecutor, who tries to ridicule and patronise her. After Janine walks out of court in solidarity with the others, her husband waits for her impatiently by the car, but we know that she will not go back to him, and there is even a repetition of the music motif from the murder scene which suggests he may be the next victim.

☐ CASE STUDY 3: SALLY POTTER, FILM-MAKER

Sally Potter is probably best known for three films: the film short *Thriller* (1979), the feature-length *The Gold Diggers* (1983) and her most recent film, the much-acclaimed *Orlando* (1993). Potter worked in dance and performance for many years and in the 1980s worked in television. Her work has been termed avant-garde, yet *Orlando*, although having many of the qualities of an 'art' production, has a strong narrative drive.

Potter's earlier films could be termed feminist, but in more recent years she has found the term problematic and in an interview with Penny Florence explains, 'I can't use the word anymore because it's become debased' (Florence 1993: 279).

Whether Potter will be able to continue to make films with a strong personal vision, as Peter Greenaway and the late Derek Jarman have done, will depend very much on funding, but Potter is optimistic that there has been a change in attitude towards women film-makers, that they are now seen as just directors. *Thriller* (1979) is a feminist reading of Puccini's opera *La Bohème* (1895). Linking together feminist, Marxist and psychoanalytic theory, the film is a critique of the constraints of patriarchy, the lack of female voice and woman as object and victim. The film was funded by the Arts Council, and although avant-garde in style received much interest from quite a wide audience, though it was by no means a mainstream success. Ann Kaplan explains why the film aroused such interest: 'It is, first, an imaginative intervention in the dominance of a certain kind of classical narrative (the sentimental romance and the detective story) making a critique of such narratives into a alternative art form' (Kaplan 1983: 161).

□ *THE GOLD DIGGERS* (1983)

The Gold Diggers is a full-length film made with a grant from the British Film Institute (BFI). The film explores the relationship between women and power, money and patriarchy: developing and continuing themes from *Thriller*. The film has two main characters, both women: the early nineteenth-century heroine (Julie Christie), and the modern heroine (Colette Lafone). Potter purposefully and ideologically chose an all-women crew to work on the film, including women musicians.

On its release in 1983 the film was poorly received, partly because of its complex yet plotless narrative that seemed to exemplify some of the problems of art and avant-garde cinema in the early 1980s – a lack of awareness of audience.

Potter has discussed the problems of the film, explaining the difficulties of working collaboratively with others (which was the case with *The Gold Diggers*). She said that the film 'came out of a practice in the theatre of going with the moment, incorporating ideas, and not being completely text-bound (Ehrenstein 1993: 3)

Imagery in the film is visually arresting, often verging on the surreal, but the script is stilted, elliptical and difficult to follow, being almost a series of vignettes. A shorter, tighter script might have been more effective in retaining an audience.

The modern heroine in the film plays the part of investigator and observer of events, an observer of patriarchy, which is seen as disempowering women. Patriarchy is threatening, bureaucratic, intimidating and ultimately ridiculous (compare with *A Question of Silence*). In the scene when Colette is working at a VDU in an office with other women, the only male is the manager who imperiously surveys the scene. Colette asks him to explain what the information is on the screen, to which he patronisingly replies, 'Just do your job.'

• Plate 8.13 *The Gold Diggers* (Sally Potter, 1993)
A search for identity

The Gold Diggers was filmed in black and white, and is a bleak film suggesting that woman is either revered or reviled by man. *Orlando*, in contrast, is full of colour and optimism.

☐ *ORLANDO* (1993)

Potter's most recent film is an adaptation of a Virginia Woolf novel and is made by her own company, Adventure Pictures, formed with *Orlando*'s producer Christopher Sheppard. The film budget was £2 million, making it a medium-size British film, though the quality of the production gives it the look of a much more expensive film. In contrast to *The Gold Diggers*, in which the crew was all-female, a mixed crew worked on *Orlando*.

After the experience of *The Gold Diggers*, Potter took great care to ensure that the script was just right, doing endless rewrites until she was happy with it. The developmental process took years rather than months but ensured a clear narrative that drives the film powerfully forward.

The film is concerned with two central ideas: the concept of immortality and the changing of gender. Orlando travels 400 years, from the Elizabethan age (Queen Elizabeth is played by Quentin Crisp, introducing the theme of playing with gender) to the present day, changing sex in 1700. The mise-en-scène is sumptuous and exotic, richly coloured and textured, enhanced by the camera work; the scene when Orlando moves into the Victorian age, for instance, is full of movement and dynamism, the gorgeous costumes swirl forward into the future.

Aspects of feminism, gender, imperialism and politics are part of the narrative discourse – areas that are often anathema to a film's success. Yet *Orlando* has been received with much acclaim: David Ehrenstein in *Film Quarterly* compares the film to Orson Welles' *The Magnificent Ambersons*: 'Like no other film of the moment, it demonstates that art and pleasure are not mutually exclusive categories of experience' (Ehrenstein 1993: 2).

• Plate 8.14 *Orlando* (Sally Potter, 1993)

• Plate 8.15 *Girl's Night Out* (Joanna Quinn, 1986)
Animation by women is thriving

Potter is more concerned with gender than feminism, although the vulnerability of women is a key theme: when Orlando becomes female she loses her home, her financial power. She then only has her body, her femaleness to bargain with, which she refuses to share in marriage with the archduke, who sternly reminds her she has nothing and will suffer the ignomy of remaining a spinster.

The film has a strong sense of playfulness, from the knowing looks that Orlando gives to the audience to the confusion of sexual identity. When Orlando becomes female in a beautifully filmed metamorphosis, she boldly states to the camera, 'same person, just a different sex'. Potter explains:

> I don't think the book so much explores sexual identity as dissolves them, and it's that kind of melting and shifting where nothing is ever what it seems for male or female that I think is the strength of the book and which I wanted to reproduce in the film.
>
> (Florence 1993: 283)

Potter put much thought into the development of Orlando's character. This led her to consider what it means to be 'male' and the dangers and difficulties of being masculine. At times gender differences are de-emphasised, for instance, the clothing worn by the young Orlando is not much less constricting than that worn by the female. However, when Orlando returns to Britain as a woman, her dress is used as a powerful symbol of her womanhood and the constraints and limitations that imposes. As a woman in the seventeenth century, Orlando must curb her sense of adventure and her inquiring mind. Orlando is offered the final insult when told that she may as well be dead as be a woman and has to endure the threat of house and wealth being taken away from her.

Orlando rebelliously enters the Victorian age, a heroine of melodrama ready to be rescued by a handsome, romantic hero who becomes her lover, and fathers her daughter. Although Orlando has lost her home and refuses to follow her lover, she retains her independence and moves forward in time to successfully negotiate life in modern Britain.

The film finishes on a positive note. There is hope for the future in the form of a child and we are told 'ever since she let go of the past she found her life was beginning'. Orlando is at peace.

Orlando, in style, has moved away from the avant-garde towards the mainstream without being conventionalised by narrative form. Potter's film is a stimulating and rich attack on the senses and has a discourse that, although concerned with gender, seems to suggest a blending of the sexes rather than a separation, which many of the earlier feminist films like *A Question of Silence* (1982), *The Gold Diggers* (1983) and Lezli-Ann Barrett's *An Epic Poem* (1982) seemed to encourage.

NOTES

Full details of works cited in the Notes section can be found in the bibliography beginning on p. 439.

1   From an interview with Kay Mander, film-maker, July 1990.

2   ibid.

3   Suggested further reading: on the early feminist movement, K. Millett, *Sexual Politics* (1969), and G. Greer, *The Female Eunuch* (1971); and, more recently, M. Maynard, 1987, p. 23.

4   Structuralism and Marxism have been, and still are, important concepts in the application of film theory and to some extent have affected film practice, particularly in the independent and workshop sector. For a good general background to these viewpoints read chs 1 and 2 of Robert Lapsley and Michael Westlake, 1988.

5   For further discussion of woman's lack of place in art see Griselda Pollock and Roszika Parker, 1981. Rosemary Betterton, 1987, is a useful and interesting collection of essays about images of women in art and the media.

6   For further information on women working in the media read A. R. Muir, 1988. Also of interest is the article by J. Arthur, 1989.

7   For a discussion of Channel 4's involvement with the workshop sector see Alan Lovell, 1990.

8   See Donald and Scanlon's article on whether *Thelma and Louise* (1991) is a feminist film, Donald and Scanlon, 1992.

9   Interview with Red Flannel, December 1993.

10   ibid.

FURTHER READING

Berger, J., *Ways of Seeing*, London: Penguin, 1972.

Betterton, R., *Looking On: Images of Femininity in the Visual Arts and the Media*, London: Pandora, 1987.

Brundsen, C. (ed.), *Films for Women*, London: British Film Institute, 1986.

Cook, P. and Dodd, P. (eds), *Women and Film: A "Sight and Sound" Reader*, London: Scarlet Press, 1993.

Haskell, M., *From Reverence to Rape*, London: New English Library, 1973.

Kaplan, E.A., *Women and Film: Both Sides of the Camera*, London: Methuen, 1983.

Modleski, T., *The Women Who Knew Too Much*, London: Methuen, 1988.

Mulvey, L., *Visual and Other Pleasures*, London: Macmillan, 1989.

Penley, C., *Feminism and Film Theory*, London: Routledge/British Film Institute, 1988.

Pilling, J. (ed.), *Women and Animation: A Compendium*, London: British Film Institute, 1992.

Pollock, G., *Vision and Difference*, London: Routledge, 1988.

Zoonen, L., *Feminist Media Studies*, London: Sage, 1994.

Women: A Cultural Review, vol. 2, no. 1, spring 1991 (the whole issue is devoted to women and the media).

Periodicals are extremely useful to refer to for further reading; they tend to be more topical and 'up-to-date'. Look out for articles on women and film in the following: *Feminist Review*, *Women: A Cultural Review*, *Sight and Sound*.

FURTHER VIEWING

This chapter has focused mainly on women in independent film in Britain and is therefore a selective view, having only touched on cinema by women in other countries such as the US and the Netherlands. Worldwide women's cinema is rich and varied – countries as small and culturally diverse as New Zealand and Tunisia have contributed to this upsurge. As more women enter the film industry and take on key roles, the number of mainstream films by women will hopefully increase. Films to look out for in this category which would provide interesting discussion regarding representations of men and women are: *Wayne's World*, Penelope Spheeris (US 1991); *The Piano*, Jane Campion (Australia/France 1993).

Other chapters in this book refer to films by women; see Chapters 7 and 9. Unfortunately, many films by women are dificult to obtain. The BFI and Cinenova (a film and video distributor that promotes films by women) hold a number of titles for rental. The latter's comprehensive catalogue is well worth looking through. The following films can all be hired through Cinenova at 113 Roman Road, London E2 0HN, telephone 0181 9816828: *To Be A Woman*, Jill Craigie (UK 1953); *Women Of The Rhondda*, Esther Ronay (UK 1972); *A Comedy In Six Unnatural Acts*, Jan Oxenburg (US 1975); *An Epic Poem*, Lezli-Ann Barrett (UK 1982); *Born In Flames*, Lizzie Borden (US 1983); *Mam*, Red Flannel (UK 1988); *Otherwise Engaged*, Red Flannel (UK 1991).

The following films are all available for rental from the BFI and provide stimulating viewing: *A Question of Silence*, Marlene Gorris (Holland 1982) (see Case study 2, p. 247); *Orlando*, Sally Potter (UK 1993) (see Case study 3, p. 251); *Wayward Girls And Wicked Women*, vols 1, 2 and 3 (1992) (various women animators, often witty, poignant and hard-hitting); *Sweetie*, Jane Campion (Australia 1989) (better than *The Piano*, it's anarchic, funny and strange!); *Dream On*, Amber Films (UK 1992) (focuses on women on a north-east estate, realistic, hard-hitting with some lighter moments); *Bhaji On The Beach*, Gurinder Chada (UK 1994) (a film I really enjoyed, why didn't it get more publicity? Perhaps being nominated for a BAFTA will change this). An Asian women's group go to Blackpool! A sharp script takes on race, culture, gender and family in contemporary Britain.

Chapter 9

Lesbian and gay cinema

Chris Jones

- **Representation**
- **Definitions and developments – homosexual and gay**
- **Audiences**
- **Lesbian and gay film festivals**
- **Gay sensibility**
- **Lesbian and gay film study**
- **Critical rereadings**
- **Some films with gay themes**
  - ☐ Case study 1: *Victim* (Basil Dearden, UK 1961)
  - ☐ Case study 2: *Desert Hearts* (Donna Deitsch, US 1985)
  - ☐ Case study 3: *Looking for Langston* (Isaac Julien, UK 1988)
  - ☐ Case study 4: *The Living End* (Gregg Araki, US 1993)
- **Conclusion: A queer diversity**
- **Further reading**
- **Further reading for teachers**
- **Further viewing**
- **Useful addresses**

Lesbian and gay cinema

REPRESENTATION

Representation is a social process which occurs in the interactions between a reader or viewer and a text. It produces signs which reflect underlying sets of ideas and attitudes. In her essay, 'Visual Pleasure and Narrative Cinema' (1988), Laura Mulvey suggested ways in which a viewer of classic Hollywood films is addressed as male by being encouraged to adopt the viewpoint, the 'look' of the male protagonist. Although she later adjusted these ideas to cater for such female-orientated Hollywood genres as the melodrama, Mulvey's argument is based on the traditional psychoanalytic notion of male/female definitions and oppositions. Nowhere does she take into account the extent to which her argument is geared towards a **heterosexual** look. Nevertheless, her ideas about the positioning of the film spectator and film-maker within the **gender** system have been very influential. They have led to much constructive critical investigation into how different kinds of film-makers and viewers affect meaning–making processes according to their race and **sexuality**, as well as gender. Such investigation has also started to take into account a variety of viewing formats based on video and the TV screen.

An integral part of the process of reading a film is the use of stereotyping, the depiction of characters according to their perceived membership of a certain social group such as Asians, mothers-in-law, businessmen, lesbians. This is a form of shorthand; a few visual or sound cues give the audience a view of a certain type of person which is widely accepted. The nature of this view is generally shaped by the dominant groups in a society.

In film, representation is organised through the signs of mise-en-scène, editing, sound and narrative patterns. The final part of this chapter will deal with the representation of gay people in a selection of postwar films.

DEFINITIONS AND DEVELOPMENTS – HOMOSEXUAL AND GAY

Men and women who relate sexually to members of their own **sex** have always existed, but the modern term 'homosexuality' was invented in 1869 by a Swiss doctor. It was not commonly used in the English language until the 1890s, the decade that saw the birth of cinema. The term **homosexual** was partly inherited from nineteenth-century ideas of disease. Previously, same-sex relations had been predominantly characterised by notions of sin inherited from the medieval period. These commonly-held associations continued into this century as German film-makers produced a number of works campaigning for more enlightened attitudes in sexual and social matters. *Different From the Others* (*Anders Als Die Andern*, 1919) was a success on first release. Even though the main character, a homosexual musician, finally poisons himself, the dour storyline is strongly countered by sections of the film in which Dr Magnus Hirschfield puts forward an affirmative view of homosexuality. Hirschfield was a sexual researcher and social reformer whose world-renowned institute was later destroyed by the Nazis. Within a year of its release the film was subject to censorship and now exists only in fragments, although these have since been assembled and shown. *Girls In Uniform* (*Mädchen in Uniform*, Leontine Sagan, 1931) can still be seen today as a major portrayal of anti-authoritarianism, with the love of its two female protagonists for each other triumphing over the oppressive regime of their boarding school.

heterosexual

A word used to name and describe a person whose main sexual feelings are for people of the opposite sex.

gender

A name for the social and cultural construction of a person's sex and sexuality. Gender, sex and sexuality can overlap but are by no means an exact match; it is this 'mismatch' which has generated a fascinating body of film production and criticism.

sexuality

The name for the sexual feelings and behaviour of a person. When applied to groups of people (for example, heterosexuals) ideas of social attitude and organisation are implied.

sex

A word used to denote and describe a person's physical type according to their genital make-up. In academic discourse, this is primarily a scientific term.

homosexual

A word used to name and describe a person whose main sexual feelings are for people of the same sex. Mainly, but not exclusively, used in reference to males.

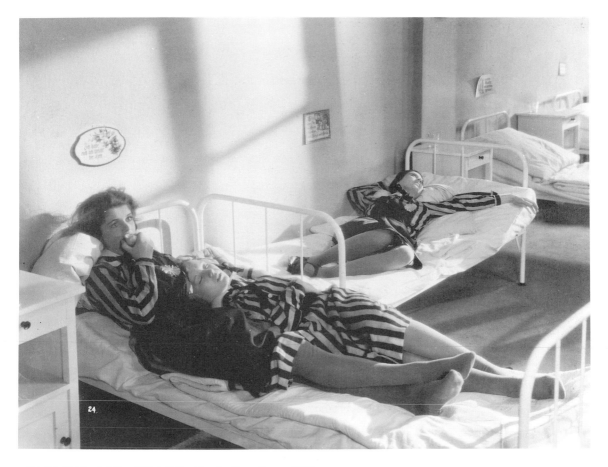

• Plate 9.1 *Mädchen in Uniform* (*Girls In Uniform*) (Leontine Sagan, Germany 1931)
Based on the play by lesbian poet Christa Winsloe, the film portrays the friendship and support given to the main
character, Manuela, in her love for her teacher

During the Second World War, with the movements of population and large numbers
of servicemen and women being thrown closely together in same-sex barracks, many
people became aware of homosexuality on a personal and social level. This resulted in
two parallel and contradictory developments in North America and Europe during the
1950s: increasing growth among communities of homosexuals and lesbians in big cities,
and systematic attempts by those in authority to prevent and eradicate homosexuality.

These communities began to demand and develop wider networks of meeting-places
and entertainment, including film. Early examples of films made with such audiences in
mind are the physique films of Dick Fontaine, who worked in San Francisco from the
late 1940s. Such film activity mainly took place within the art-film world, and involved
small-budget production and viewing in clubs and homes. Jean Genet's *Un Chant
D'Amour* (1950), with its sexually-charged images of handsome male prisoners, became
a cult film, as did Kenneth Anger's *Fireworks* (1947), a young man's sexual fantasy
involving sailors. From the 1960s the **homoerotic** films of Andy Warhol and George

homoerotic

A description of a text – prose,
poem, film, painting, photograph,
etc. – conveying an enjoyable
sense of same-sex attraction.

• Plate 9.2 *Chant D'Amour* (Jean Genet, France 1950)
Genet's erotic imagery has inspired generations of film-makers

gay

A description of strong, positive
sexual love and attraction between
members of the same sex, used by
extension to describe cultural
products, such as film and video,
concerned with similar themes.
Mainly referring to males, it can
also be used for any person.

lesbian

A word used to name and describe a
woman whose main sexual feelings
are for other women. Coined as a
medical term in the late nineteenth
century, the word has been invested
post-Stonewall with new ideas of
openness and liberation. It can also
be used to describe cultural
products, such as film and video,
dealing with lesbian themes.

Kuchar began to find wider audiences. It was during this period that the word **gay** began
to be used to both denote and describe a male homosexual person.

In 1969, for the first time in modern history, homosexuals in a small New York bar
called the Stonewall Inn fought back against a police raid. A major riot ensued and the
New York Gay Liberation Front was immediately formed, soon to be followed by similar
organisations across the world. Members of the new movement adopted the word 'gay'
for its positive connotations of happiness, and because they wanted to use a term to
describe themselves that had not been chosen by outsiders. For them, the term represented a way of demonstrating pride in their identity, the power of political organisation
and a distinct culture. The term was initially conceived as describing both men and
women, but women soon began to feel marginalised within the movement, and the term
lesbian came back in general use during the 1970s to signal the distinctness and
strength of women.

It is the very different emotional connotations of these varying terms which led critic
Vito Russo to say, 'There never have been lesbians or gay men in Hollywood films. Only
homosexuals' (Russo 1987: 245).

AUDIENCES

Gay men, like men in general, have on average more spending power than women,
despite equal opportunities legislation in many countries. With gay liberation came a
greatly expanded network of related commercial goods and services; nightclubs, shops,
clothing, books and magazines, the majority of which were aimed at men. The same

conditions apply in the developing structures of film and cinema aimed at lesbians and gays. Men constituted the main organised audience for film and video production. Even those films with non-commercial financial backing, such as the work of Derek Jarman and Isaac Julien, tended to attract funds partly because of the perceived existence of this established gay male audience.

Lesbian film and video developed in parallel with the emerging women's movement, almost always with less finance than its male equivalent, and found a base in film clubs and workshops. The American film and video artist Su Friedrich actively prefers this type of outlet as a way of reaching lesbian audiences with films such as *Damned If You Don't* (US 1987). As a result of this production and viewing background, and the modest financial levels this involves, many lesbian films are less than feature length. *Home Movie* (US 1972) by Jan Oxenberg is a modest but highly effective twelve-minute film, which edits home-movie footage from the director's own childhood with scenes of her adult life as a lesbian to make the viewer amusingly aware of the conventions of family life. Her *Comedy in Six Unnatural Acts* (US 1975, twenty-six minutes) presents six short, staged scenes dealing with the foibles of lesbian life, and debunking a few myths about **butch/femme** role-playing.

LESBIAN AND GAY FILM FESTIVALS

After 1945, film festivals became recognised across Europe and America as serving several useful functions. They act as a marketplace for film distributors to view and possibly buy new product, and allow producers, scriptwriters and others to gather and discuss new projects. Critics attending festivals alert wider audiences to new and interesting work. Audiences can view and enjoy a wide range of films they would not normally see in the cinema.

Since the 1970s a worldwide circuit of lesbian and gay film festivals has grown up. San Francisco was the first to start operating, followed by London, Paris, New York, Toronto, Berlin and others. These events, often accompanied by lively lectures and discussions, serve all the purposes already mentioned for lesbian and gay producers, directors, critics and audiences. Their development has gone hand-in-hand with the flowering of gay political consciousness; Rosa Von Praunheim's early gay liberationist film, *It is not the Homosexual who is Perverse, but the Situation in which he Finds Himself*, was typical of the kind of work that found a viewing base in such festivals. In particular, these festivals have helped to bring small-scale film and video work and feature films from the Third World to the attention of wider lesbian and gay audiences. An example of the latter is the work of Lino Brocka from the Philippines, whose treat-ment of homosexual themes contains messages of tolerance and democracy not always acceptable to established authorities in his own country. Recent festivals have included work from Israel, Taiwan, Mexico, India and Japan.

Another form of film-making given wider distribution through the festival circuit is the feature-length documentary. *The Times Of Harvey Milk* (Robert Epstein, US 1985) chron-icles the rise to power, and tragic assassination, of the San Francisco city supervisor who was one of the USA's first openly gay elected politicians. *Before Stonewall: The Making of a Gay and Lesbian Community* (Greta Schiller, US 1985) vividly recalls gay and lesbian lives in the years during and following the Second World War. All these films weave together interviews, contemporary newsreel film and photographs. Through fostering cultural and historical consciousness, such films as these aided the growing self-awareness of lesbian and gay communities in the USA and elsewhere.

butch

The description of behaviour patterns – such as aggression, sexual dominance – traditionally associated with masculinity.

femme

The description of behaviour patterns – such as gentleness, sexual passivity, concern with dress and appearance – traditionally associated with femininity.

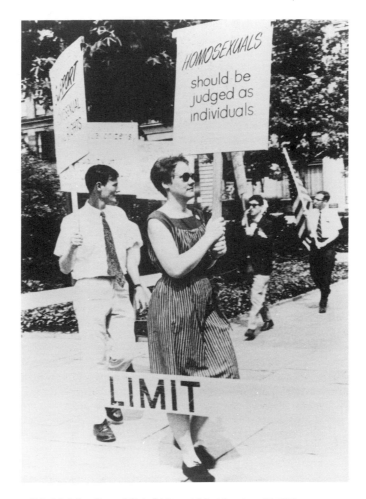

• Plate 9.3 *Before Stonewall* (Greta Schiller and Robert Rosenberg, US 1985)
A full-length film documentary about the gay and lesbian movement in the US from the 1920s to the 1960s. This film vividly evokes lesbian and gay life in the US before gay liberation and forms part of a growing body of work on lesbian and gay history

As the AIDS crisis arose in the 1980s, this newly developed network of audiences and exhibition venues was particularly receptive to the wide variety of film and video work created around this topic, such as Rosa Von Praunheim's *A Virus Knows No Morals* (Germany 1986). Short videos such as John Greyson's *The ADS Epidemic* (Canada 1986) boosted morale by warning in a jokey way against ADS (Acquired Dread of Sex) while reminding people about safe sex. Bill Sherwood's outstanding independent film *Parting Glances* (US 1986) presents a mature, low-key portrait of a group of New Yorkers in the late 1980s. A central character of the group is Nick, who has AIDS. The character is portrayed with gentle humour and his condition is accepted and supported by those around him. *Common Threads; Stories From The Quilt* (Robert Epstein and Jeffrey Friedman, US 1989) is a full-length documentary chronicling the stories of a group of

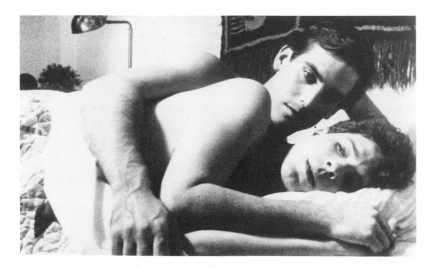

• Plate 9.4 *Parting Glances* (Bill Sherwood, US 1986)
The two lovers live through their ups and downs with credible warmth and humour

people who have lost loved ones to AIDS and contributed panels to the memorial quilt. We see moving interviews with, among others, the parents of a haemophiliac boy, the lesbian spouse of a gay man by whom she has had a child, the widow of a drug addict struggling to bring up her children and Vito Russo talking of the death of his lover. The final scene, with acres of quilt laid out in the grounds adjoining the White House in Washington, is an inspiring tribute to human solidarity in a crisis.

GAY SENSIBILITY

In a book published by the British Film Institute to coincide with the first ever Lesbian and Gay Film Festival at the National Film Theatre, London, in 1977, the critic Jack Babuscio wrote:

> I define gay sensibility as a creative energy reflecting a consciousness that is different from the mainstream; a heightened awareness of certain human complications of feeling that spring from the fact of social oppression; in short, a perception of the world which is coloured, shaped, directed and defined by the fact of one's gayness.
>
> (Babuscio 1977)

In a key essay, 'Rejecting Straight Ideals; Gays in Film', Richard Dyer (Steven 1985: 286) challenged Babuscio's emphasis on oppression as a mainspring for gay sensibility. He says this sensibility must be understood as 'something that has been and is produced and praised in history and culture' (Dyer 1985: 287). For Dyer, oppression 'merely provides the conditions in relation to which oppressed people create their own sub-culture and attendant sensibility' (Dyer 1985: 287) and is not the defining factor as Babuscio perceives it.

In his essay, Dyer makes a convincing and clear argument based on the idea of what he calls 'the sexual **ideology** of our culture' (Dyer 1985: 294); that is the idea that society

ideology

A set of ideas and attitudes held so much in common by most members of a society that they are seen as part of the natural order.

camp

A critical attitude which involves looking at texts less as reflections of reality than as constructed sets of words, images and sounds at a distance from reality. The attitude often involves irony or detachment when considering this distance. See Susan Sontag 1983.

and culture, through structures such as the family and artefacts such as film, impose a particular view of what they consider correct sexual behaviour. This view includes a dominance of the heterosexual viewpoint and antipathy towards the homosexual one. Homosexuality, according to Dyer, is predominantly seen from a heterosexual viewpoint in most mainstream films. As examples he cites the image of homosexuality as a sickness and a problem in *Victim* (Basil Dearden, UK 1961) and an endless succession of gay and lesbian characters as vampires, psychos and criminals which still continues. However, as Dyer points out, ideology is contradictory and ambiguous, full of what he calls 'gaps and fissures' (1985: 294) through which film-makers and audiences can make new, alternative meanings. This process sometimes involves an attitude of conscious, ironic distancing on the part of a spectator known as **camp**, traditionally associated with gay audiences. Critic Susan Sontag describes camp as 'a certain way of seeing the world as an aesthetic phenomenon, not in terms of beauty, but in terms of degree

• Plate 9.5 *The Boys in the Band* (William Friedkin, US 1970)
This pre-liberation film contains an array of stereotypes, sometimes hilarious, often controversial

of artifice, of stylization' (1990). The concept is useful when considering how lesbian and gay audiences cope with mainstream representations.

Critical awareness and discussion of gay sensibility and established sexual ideology, a concept that was later labelled 'heterosexism', started to be shared by increasing numbers of people: audiences, critics and film-makers. Film production in this area continued to take place mainly within the structures of alternative or art cinema, although Hollywood made occasional attempts to exploit what was seen as an increasingly open gay audience and a greater interest in gay themes by non-gays. Examples of such products are *The Boys in the Band* (William Friedkin, US 1970), which exploited the sensationalistic stereotypes of emotional trauma, and *Making Love* (Arthur Hiller, US 1982), an over-sweet romantic treatment of male love. *Cruising* (William Friedkin, US 1980) equates homosexuality with pathological violence. These, and many other mainstream films such as Jonathan Demme's *Philadelphia* (US 1993), could profitably be examined using Dyer's notion of sexual ideology.

As a concept useful in the study of film, gay sensibility can be defined as a developed awareness of sexual variation. This does not automatically mean that a film-maker or viewer has to be gay or lesbian to be able to present or appreciate themes and issues connected with gay people, but such awareness can open up rich creative possibilities. David Cronenberg's films, such as *Dead Ringers* (Canada 1988), make viewers uncomfortably aware of the fragile limits of conventional masculinity. While one can debate what exactly constitutes a 'lesbian film' or a 'gay film', gay sensibility can enrich film production and appreciation for gays and non-gays.

LESBIAN AND GAY FILM STUDY

The following elements can be identified as constituting lesbian and gay film study:

1 Rereadings of films by lesbian and gay audiences and critics, often producing meanings and messages that were not consciously intended by their original makers.
2 Film and video work dealing sensitively and/or positively with lesbian and gay themes, characters and issues, often, but not exclusively, made by and/or for gay people.

These elements are centrally concerned with the issue of representation. At times these two elements can overlap, as will be shown, for example, in the reading of *Victim* (see p. 271).

CRITICAL REREADINGS

The possible meanings of a film, as with all signifying practices, reside in the interaction between the viewer and the text. Much work has been done in recent years on how subgroups within the wider popular audience arrive at their own particular meanings when watching a mainstream film. Lesbian and gay critics have been at the forefront of such 'rereadings'. Here are some examples.

Vito Russo

Russo's work as a film critic and journalist included articles for *The Advocate* in the US and *Gay News* in Britain during the 1970s and 1980s. Parker Tyler's book, *Screening the Sexes:*

• Plate 9.6 *Rebel Without a Cause* (Nicholas Ray, US 1955)
The star images of Dean and Mineo were strong precursors of later gay images

Homosexuality in the Movies (1993) opened up the field of study and analysis of lesbian and gay cinema when it was first published in 1972, but Russo's *The Celluloid Closet – Homosexuality in the Movies* is now regarded as a major landmark. First published in 1981 and revised in 1987, the book has continued to influence later critical work in this area.

Russo combines a historical view of lesbian and gay people's contribution to Hollywood cinema with an awareness of representation and audience. Although it deals mainly with Hollywood product, in contrast to Tyler's work, Russo's book is packed with examples and ideas which have formed the basis of further research by new generations of critics and academics. He traces the images of lesbians and gay men in Hollywood film from relatively open portrayals in the silent and early sound eras. He outlines the development of what he calls 'the sissy image' as a coded portrayal of gay men after the introduction of the Production Code in 1934 and goes on to outline how 'as an outlet for unspeakable ideas, then, the sissy often became a monster or an outlaw'. One example of the new insights Russo has to offer is his interpretation of the monster in the horror films of gay director

James Whale. He sees *Frankenstein* (US 1931) and *The Bride Of Frankenstein* (US 1935) as images of unnameable experiences and feelings outside normal society.

Using cogently-argued examples, Russo outlines gay invisibility in the Hollywood films of the 1950s, followed by marginality and violence in the 1960s and 1970s: 'in twenty-two of twenty-eight films dealing with gay subjects from 1962 to 1978, major gay characters onscreen ended in suicide or death' (Russo 1987: 52). At the same time, he makes out a powerful argument about how gay men derived particular subcultural messages from *Rebel Without a Cause* (Nicholas Ray, US 1955) when empathising with the relationship between Jim (James Dean) and Plato (Sal Mineo). Among the few positive examples he cites from this period are some British films. *The Family Way* (Roy Boulting, 1966) and *The Leather Boys* (Sidney Furie, 1964) are seen as illuminating portrayals of the way in which fear of homosexuality limits the feelings between men. He praises *The L-shaped Room* (Bryan Forbes, 1962) for its sensitive portrayal of an elderly lesbian music-hall artiste, and sees the character Geoff in Tony Richardson's *A Taste of Honey* (1961) as relatively sympathetic.

The emergence of neurotic, shadowy gay characters is discussed using *The Boys in the Band* (William Friedkin, US 1970) and *The Killing of Sister George* (Robert Aldrich, US 1968). Russo's final argument, in the revised 1987 edition, is that worthwhile gay and lesbian cinema can only be developed and encouraged outside the traditional Hollywood power structures, and he outlines a range of examples of such positive work.

Richard Dyer

Richard Dyer has been lecturing and writing about lesbian and gay film for about twenty years, and currently teaches at the University of Warwick. His book, *Now You See It: Studies in Lesbian and Gay Film* (1990) is a comprehensive academic survey of the German films outlined earlier in this chapter, as well as the work of Jean Genet and Kenneth Anger. It contains a particularly useful introduction to lesbian film and video-making in the postwar period.

Dyer is the author of many illuminating essays. His work on sexual ideology has already been mentioned, but he is perhaps best known for his work on stars. In *Heavenly Bodies – Film Stars and Society* (1987) Dyer investigates the cultural associations between Judy Garland's star image and gay male audiences from the 1950s onwards. He shows members of this audience strongly allying themselves with Garland's much-vaunted ability to fight back against oppression and the status of outsider which her behaviour and personality often conferred on her.

As part of his study of the film noir, *Gilda* (Charles Vidor, US 1946), Dyer teases out the film's homoerotic subtext, the sexually-charged dockside meeting between the Glen Ford character and the casino-owner which leads to the two men working closely together and pledging the firm friendship with 'no women' that is subsequently destroyed by the appearance of the *femme fatale*, played by Rita Hayworth. He relates this subtext to film noir traditions and the dominant postwar view of sexual relations. His essay 'Homosexuality in Film Noir' (in Dyer 1993a) coherently shows how gay characters in this classic Hollywood genre were negatively portrayed in both appearance and behaviour. This is an important topic to investigate because, as Dyer points out, 'Some of the first widely available images of homosexuality in our time were those provided by the American film noir' (1993a: 52).

Dyer's later studies of star image include a seminal essay on Rock Hudson in relation to public perceptions of sexuality, both before and after Hudson's homosexuality became public knowledge (Dyer 1993b). Dyer cogently argues how knowledge of Hudson's

• Plate 9.7 *All That Heaven Allows* (Douglas Sirk, US 1955)
Rock Hudson becomes a wish-fulfilment figure for both Jane Wyman and the audience

sexuality greatly enriches a viewer's appreciation of the gender-play in the 1960s sex comedies in which he starred. He shows how such knowledge gives extra depth to Hudson's star performances in the famous sequence of 1950s melodramas directed by Douglas Sirk, such as *All That Heaven Allows* (US 1955).

Andrea Weiss

The work of Andrea Weiss, like that of other writers on lesbian film such as Mandy Merck, B. Ruby Rich and Judith Mayne, was nurtured within the feminist movement. Weiss works primarily as a film-maker. She was chief researcher on the documentary feature *Before Stonewall* and has produced an equally well-researched book on lesbians in film, *Vampires and Violets* (1993).

In her book, Weiss clearly tackles the critical problems associated with identification and representation for lesbians. She states that

THE H. B. M'S

"IT'S THE SIGN OF THE HARD-BOILED MAIDENS'~ NIFTY, WHAT?"

• Plate 9.8 *The Wild Party* (Dorothy Arzner, US 1929)
The energetic college girls have such a fun time together that being paired off with the males at the end comes almost as an anti-climax

identification involves both conscious and unconscious processes and cannot be reduced to a psychoanalytic model that sees sexual desire only in terms of the binary opposition of heterosexual masculinity and femininity; instead it involves varying degrees of subjectivity and distance depending upon race, class and sexual differences.

(Weiss 1993: 40)

This judgement reflects the questioning of Laura Mulvey's ideas on cinematic looking referred to on p. 258, a critical practice that has grown steadily since the 1980s. Weiss gives her readers a fascinating set of studies to show how lesbian audiences of classic Hollywood cinema have used their own interpretations to empower themselves, and how lesbian film-makers have been able to make their own images. These studies range across Dorothy Arzner's *The Wild Party* (US 1929), star performances by Greta Garbo and Marlene Dietrich in the 1940s, lesbian vampire films, and 1970s radical lesbian films by Barbara Hammer. She offers fascinating, oppositional interpretations of the way in which lesbian audiences gained positive messages from the otherwise bleak and tragic

Dorothy Arzner

The work of the only woman to pursue a career solely as a director in classic Hollywood is currently undergoing reassessment by critics of lesbian film. Here are some key films.
The Wild Party (1929)
Christopher Strong (1933)
The Bride Wore Red (1937)
Dance, Girl, Dance (1940)
To explore Dorothy Arzner's films in greater depth, Judith Mayne's book (Mayne 1994) is highly recommended.

lesbian characters and relationships in *The Killing of Sister George* (Robert Aldrich, GB 1968) and *The Children's Hour* (William Wyler, US 1961).

Weiss clearly outlines the ongoing critical debate about the difficulties of representing autonomous female sexuality in a system of representation which continues to be focused on the male heterosexual look. A major part of this debate for lesbian film centres on the problems of producing scenes of woman-centred intimacy and love-making that remain satisfying for lesbian audiences while not falling into the traditional function of being a turn-on for heterosexual men.

Bearing in mind ideas of dominant heterosexual ideology, Weiss points out how Dolly, the lesbian character played by Cher in *Silkwood* (Mike Nichols, US 1983), is marginalised, made to look childlike and seen predominantly through the eyes of the heterosexual characters – what she deftly calls the 'happen to be gay' approach to the depiction of lesbians and gays in film. That is, the character is gay or lesbian but is presented within a completely heterosexual framework and outlook and is therefore found to be lacking. In a similar fusion of ideology and representation, she shows how the central lesbian relationship between Celie and Shug in Alice Walker's novel *The Color Purple* is downgraded and put under male control in Steven Spielberg's film version (US 1985).

In her section on the lesbian aspect of art film, Weiss uses some key films to show how their directors have dealt in various productive ways with the male heterosexist narrative and viewing strategies of this kind of film tradition. In this context she gives clear readings of films such as Chantal Akerman's *Je, Tu, Il, Elle* (Belgium 1974) and *Joanna D'Arc of Mongolia* by Ulrike Ottinger (Germany 1988). She points out how Marlene Gorris's *A Question of Silence* (The Netherlands 1983) sees lesbian relationships as part of a continuum of relations between women, which are privileged over those with men.

Weiss finishes her book with a look at the viewing strategies of recent film-making by and for lesbians. She has positive praise for the focus on racial and sexual diversity among women, as well as the fluid viewpoints used, in Lizzie Borden's *Born in Flames* (US 1983). On the other hand, she analyses a well-known lesbian film of the 1980s, Sheila McLaughlin's *She Must be Seeing Things* (US 1987), and sees it as being so caught up in conventional viewing strategies that it denies any positive pleasure or viewpoints for lesbian viewers. Finally, she rightly cautions against a simplistic view of lesbian film as progressing from hidden signs to liberated images, pointing out that 'the cinema has been and continues to be a contested terrain in which people and groups with often opposing interests have staked their claims' (1993: 163).

SOME FILMS WITH GAY THEMES

Stereotypes and characters

In his book, *The Matter of Images* (1993a), Richard Dyer has pointed out the dangers inherent in thinking rigidly in terms of **stereotypes** when dealing with representation: 'a stereotype can be complex, varied, intense and contradictory, an image of otherness in which it is still possible to find oneself' (1993a: 74). Stereotypes, he points out, are not always or necessarily negative, although some, such as the black mammy of Hollywood, are very limiting. The process of stereotyping involves power; the power of dominant groups to mould the accepted social view of themselves and of those groups that they perceive as marginal. This view can change and develop as certain social groups, such as gays and lesbians, grow in self-awareness, expression and power, so that dominant

stereotype

A set of commonly-expected behaviour patterns and characteristics based on role (for example, mother) or personal features such as race, age or sexuality. In society and cultural products, the depiction of a stereotype becomes a form of communicative shorthand, and often reflects the attitudes of dominant social groups.

groups have to modify their available images. As an example, Dyer cites the 'sad young man' stereotype common in popular film and literature of the 1940s and 1950s, an image of the passive, unhappy, sexually troubled outsider which grew into the ambiguously attractive and strong image of the social rebel as embodied in James Dean and Montgomery Clift. Are there any stereotypes in the films listed below that that could be interpreted in several ways?

Dyer also suggests that replacing stereotypes with the traditional idea of a 'rounded' character can be an advance of sorts. However, he points out (Dyer 1985) that the 'well-rounded character', as advocated by theorists such as E.M. Forster, is in itself a limiting concept, for, in its strong preoccupation with individuality, it can obscure awareness of the social groups to which that character belongs. A really useful study of representation can only take place within an overall awareness of the dominant ideology, the chief component of which, for the purposes of this chapter, is the assumption of heterosexuality as a dominant, structuring outlook and viewpoint.

The following film analyses are intended as sample case studies for an approach which can be applied to other films, to indicate ways in which wider ideolological meanings and values can be examined.

Compare and contrast E. M. Forster's novel of *Maurice* with the James Ivory film version (UK 1987) bearing in mind Dyer's ideas about rounded characters.

Examine the ways in which the characters and situations of *The Torch Song Trilogy* (Paul Bogart, US 1988) and *La Cage Aux Folles* (Eduard Molinaro, US 1978) reflect heterosexual models of male/female roles and relations.

☐ CASE STUDY 1: *VICTIM* (BASIL DEARDEN, UK 1961)

Genre, star and theme

Victim has a solidly crafted script in the thriller/detective genre, with the reasons for the suicide of 'Boy' Barrett gradually coming to light through the investigations of barrister Melville Farr supported by his wife. The black and white cinematography recalls film noir in its depiction of urban bedsitters, pubs and clubs, and the key investigator is not the police but a private individual. Tense music evokes mystery and urban spaces. In the tradition of the genre hero, Farr not only uncovers the reasons for the young man's suicide but makes a heroic stand against injustice.

As well as genre, the film utilised the British star system of the time with Dirk Bogarde, a male sex-symbol of the 1950s, playing the lead. The element which makes this film unusual for its time is not only its main theme of homosexuality, but the fact that some of its character portrayals are relatively sympathetic, given the era and social climate in which the film was made.

Victim was produced by the Rank Studios at a key period of social change in British attitudes towards gay people, and was unique in being specifically seen, at the time of its release in 1961, as a liberal film campaigning against the legal oppression of male homosexuals. In 1957, a government report had recommended a limited reform of the laws that then existed against male homosexual relations. These changes became law in 1967, and the intervening period was one of widespread debate in the British media about homosexuality, a central theme of which was the vulnerability of homosexuals to blackmail. A very high proportion of gay men were blackmail victims.

The construction of images

American film noir, the genre which 'Victim' echoes, often featured homosexual characters. The insinuatingly weak Cairo in *The Maltese Falcon* (John Huston, 1941) and the mean, manipulative Waldo Lydecker in *Laura* (Otto Preminger, 1954) are two

Victim (Basil Dearden, UK 1961)

This film contains both positive and negative elements, but is definitely a milestone in the mainstream depiction of gay themes (available on Rank Video: VC 3080).

Key European films

These films by major European auteurs are also important as gay texts and as such will reward further study:

Beauty and the Beast (*La Belle et la Bête*) (Jean Cocteau, France 1946)

Theorum (*Teorema*) (Pier Paolo Pasolini, Italy 1968)

Fox and His Friends (*Faustrecht Der Freiheit*) (Rainer Werner Fassbinder, Germany 1975)

• Plate 9.9 *Victim* (Basil Dearden, UK 1961)
Boy Barrett (right) is a tormented character driven to suicide, despite the presence of a sympathetic detective
inspector (seated behind)

examples. A major generic element of film noir was that it dealt with characters, themes
and settings that were considered abnormal, corrupt or deviant in some way, and *Victim*
makes use of this tradition in its creation of a secretive, oppressive homosexual underworld whose only solace seems to be the pub with its unsympathetic landlord.

As Farr uncovers more victims of blackmail, we see a succession of nervous, oppressed
men paying money to the blackmailers in order to protect their jobs and social standing,
which in that era would be destroyed by revelations of then-illegal homosexual relations.
The film deliberately depicts a wide social cross-section of men. Among the sadder homosexual characters the film presents is the bookseller Harold Doe, a self-effacing, nervous
man. On hearing of the death of Jack Barrett, known as 'Boy', Mr Doe is contrite. He
blames Farr for interfering in his life and reveals his deep feelings for Boy, saying that he
offered to share his life and the running of the bookshop with Boy. The film's most pathetic
minor character is Eddie Henry, the barber. He is jumpy and defensive in conversation
with Farr, where he reveals that he has been to prison four times as a result of his homosexuality. Apologetic for his own existence, he is subsequently attacked by the thuggish
blackmailer, and dies of a heart attack. Throughout the film minor characters express
various types of anti-gay prejudice, and the words 'Farr is queer' are painted on the Farrs'
garage door in large letters.

Liberal arguments

So far, the representations dealt with in this film have been predominantly negative in
that they indicate secretiveness, oppression and misery. They tie in with an underlying

social view at that time of homosexuality as some sort of unfortunate affliction. Critics have pointed out this negativity. In his essay 'Victim: Hegemonic Project' (in Dyer 1993a), Richard Dyer argues that the whole film promotes an attitude of pity for homosexuals as pathetic outsiders. At the same time the film arguably reflects the discrimination and distress experienced by many gay men in the late 1950s and early 1960s. By pointing out these conditions as unjust, the film itself formed part of a wider discourse about the need for change.

A key figure in pointing out legal injustice is the sympathetic, worldly-wise detective inspector. The film is punctuated by office discussions which, although over-wordy at times, serve to make the audience aware of the main argument of the film. The inspector says that it is unjustifiable for the police to interfere in private behaviour between consenting adults and concentrates his anger against blackmailers who make the lives of homosexuals a misery. As the film unfolds and the audience witness this misery, a classic build-up of narrative expectation is brought into play by the inspector's heart-felt assertion that if only one blackmail victim had the courage to come forward, he could do something.

New attitudes

The film was an important precursor of newer attitudes towards homosexuals which were to culminate a decade later in the gay movement. The character of Melville Farr epitomises these changes. At the start he is secretive and ashamed, refusing to see Boy or even speak to him on the phone. He later admits, 'I thought he was trying to blackmail me.' It takes the knowledge of Boy's motivations to galvanise him into posi-tive action. He finds out through Boy's friend that Boy has in fact been trying to shield him from blackmail by stealing money from his employers to pay the blackmailer for the negative of a photograph of the two of them together. Boy's last action before being apprehended by the police was to attempt to destroy his collection of press cuttings about Farr, which Boy's friend has retrieved and brought to Farr.

Both Boy and his friend are attractive, ordinary-looking young men, a very important point for positive representation. Boy has stolen a large sum of money in what is seen as a brave but futile attempt to buy off the blackmailers. The half-burnt pile of press-cuttings attests to Boy's continuing devotion to Farr. Boy's suicide when he thought Farr was rejecting him is yet more evidence of the depth of his feelings, as well as his courage in not betraying the 'secret'.

Once Farr takes the decision to act positively, his character is seen to develop in courage and moral responsibility. Jolted by the injustice of Boy's death, Farr is clearly prepared to risk his career and marriage to expose the blackmailers' injustice. He enlists the help of Boy's friend, saying 'fear is the oxygen of blackmail', and asking the friend to 'watch for signs of fear' among his circle. The friend clearly points out to Farr that his actions will bring him down.

The emotional impact on Farr's wife, Laura, of seeing the newspaper headline about her husband's involvement with the suicide leads to a climactic confrontation where she draws her husband out into declaring his true feelings. The audience, significantly, never see the blackmail photograph so pivotal to the plot. Instead, we see various people's reactions to it, mainly Laura's. On seeing the photo she asks, 'Why is he crying?', and Farr replies, 'Because I just told him I couldn't see him again.'

The ensuing conversation imbues Laura's character with strength and psychological credibility. She does not hesitate to point out the pain and emotion on both men's faces in the photo, and makes her husband come clean and declare, 'I stopped seeing him

How do you think audience reactions to *Victim* have changed since the 1960s?

because I wanted him.' To which she replies, 'You don't call that love?' Her subsequent courageous declaration that she will stand by her husband gives Farr courage to continue his pursuit.

Melville Farr has other supporters in his quest for justice. The inspector admires and supports him. Boy's friend advises him and makes inquiries on his behalf in London's homosexual community. It is this friend who notices that Eddie Henry is looking harassed and has decided to sell his business and move out, thus enabling Farr to home in on one of the blackmail suspects. Once the case starts to become public, Farr feels he must inform his long-serving assistant, William, who expresses loyalty and respect for Farr as a man and a barrister.

Ambiguous messages

Certain figures in the film are presented in such a way as to reverse conventional audience expectations, a recognised genre tactic in the thriller/detective tradition. The bowler-hatted man in the pub who seems to be trying to pick other men up turns out to be a plain-clothes police officer on the track of the blackmailers. When Doe's secretary and her thuggish accomplice are eventually tracked down, the case is thereby solved and genre expectations are clearly satisfied.

On the other hand, the ending of the film is ambiguous on the level of its homosexual theme, and has been much discussed. Perhaps this ambiguity is a suitable reflection of the era in which the film was made. Farr insists that Laura leave him for the duration of the difficult period ahead, when, as he points out, terrible things will be said about him and he could not bear to see her implicated and hurt. This is a brave act on his part, and Laura reluctantly agrees. The audience is left with several questions: will Laura and Mel get back together again, and what kind of relationship might they have if they do? Should Laura pursue her own life? Melville Farr's final act is to tear up the photo of himself and Boy and throw it in the fire. What does this indicate about his attitude towards his own homosexuality, or his relationship with Jack Barrett? The film's final image is of Dirk Bogarde/Melville Farr leaning on the mantelpiece in a pose that conveys despair and dejection. What kind of feeling does this leave the audience with about Farr, and perhaps about homosexuals in general? Does the film as a whole portray homosexual men as sad cases or does a feeling of hope for the future emerge from the brave stand of Melville Farr and his friends?

Compare and contrast *Victim* with a similarly liberal-minded American production, *The Detective* (Gordon Douglas, US 1968).

□ CASE STUDY 2: *DESERT HEARTS* (DONNA DEITSCH, US 1985)

Critical attitudes

The film concentrates closely on the psychological world of its two central female characters, and their love is seen to grow and realise itself in a natural progression. Black lesbian film-maker Michelle Parkerson, on the other hand, sees the film as part of what she calls the 'easy heterosexist niches for homosexuality on the silver screen' negotiated by Hollywood (Parkerson 1993). The relationship portrayed is easy in the sense of being an idealised one between two beautiful, socially well placed white women, and the male characters are too good to be true. On the level of the film's production history this comment seems less warranted, since Donna Deitsch spent nearly ten years

Desert Hearts
(Donna Deitsch, US 1985)
Beautiful scenery, big cars and an engaging lesbian romance (available for hire in video shops).

• Plate 9.10 *Desert Hearts* (Donna Deitsch, US 1985)
Cay (left) never loses the support of her friend Silver

trying to persuade reluctant financial backers to support this film adaptation of Jane Rule's novel. It was eventually made independently on a very small budget by Hollywood standards.

Plot patterns

The opening scene is signalled with a caption, 'Reno, Nevada, 1959' and shows a woman, Vivian Bell, tentatively descending from a train and welcomed by Frances, in whose house she is staying as a paying guest. Most American viewers know that people come to Reno to gain divorces and we subsequently see Vivian consulting her lawyer. Driving Vivian to the house, Frances talks of her 'wild' daughter who, she says, is just like her dead father. We see the wide-ranging desert scenery glide past. Vivian makes it clear that she is from the city and unable to cope with such space. 'Just sit back and let it clean out the impurities', says Frances.

Frances' daughter Cay zooms up in her car, Buddy Holly blasting on her radio. She recklessly drives on the wrong side of the road in order to converse with Frances, who introduces her to 'Professor Bell'. After Cay zooms off, narrowly missing an oncoming car, Vivian asks if she can smoke, confides in Frances that she feels shaky and that 'I can't really face being one of the gang right now.' She later emerges from her room and talks with some of the other women seeking divorces who are staying at Frances' house. She starts to get to know Cay, who produces sculpture and works at one of the casinos. The two are soon discussing ambitions and plans.

In keeping with its genre pattern of romance, this film follows a simple plot whereby Vivian and Cay gradually come together, fall for each other and, towards the end, make passionate love. The generic plot complications consist of the very different person-alities and backgrounds of the two women, and the neurotically possessive nature of Frances which is gradually revealed. She is not Cay's natural mother but lived for ten years with Cay's father and is the mother of Cay's half-brother Walter. We learn that Cay's father died young, that Frances still loves and adores him and that she has a voracious need to keep Cay near her as a reminder of him. When she dances with Cay at the engagement party of Cay's friend Silver, Frances talks of how special the memory of Glen, her lover, is to her 'because he reached in and put a string of lights around my heart'. She tells Vivian, 'I got what I wanted. I had a love of my own.' Vivian's reply, 'You had more than most people dare hope for', sets up the main dramatic expectations of the plot as we gradually learn about Vivian's conformist marriage from which she is escaping. She tells her lawyer, 'I want to be free of what I've been.'

Character patterns

The differences between Vivian and Cay are clearly signalled through dress and behaviour. Vivian wears a steel-grey, precisely cut 1950s skirt-suit with a matching cloche hat. Her blonde hair is up in a neat, business-like style which matches her stiff, formal movements. She is ten years older than Cay. She lectures in English Literature at Columbia University, and makes frequent references to what she calls her 'circle'. In terms of representation in American films, this brings into play a whole set of stereotypes in the contrast between the more intellectual, snobbish easterner and the more physical westerner. Cay shows off her long brown legs in skimpy denim shorts and cowboy boots. Her medium-length black hair flows freely. A representational tradition of associating blonde hair with aloof coolness and dark hair with a lively, passionate nature is being brought into play.

Cay is open and positive about her love of women. The first time Vivian visits Cay in her cottage she is disconcerted to glimpse another woman, Gwen, in Cay's bed. Vivian accepts Cay's offer of a lift into town, but is evidently awkward sitting between Gwen and Cay. Cultural differences are underlined when Cay replaces the blaring pop music on the radio with another station playing Prokoviev, whereupon Vivian recognises the music and says she likes it. Gwen makes snide remarks about the music. When Cay says, 'Oh come on, Gwen, we all have our sensitive side', Gwen's reply, 'I didn't hear you talk about your sensitive side last night', angers Vivian into switching the pop music back on.

This exchange indicates an important point about the portrayal of Cay. Although undeveloped in her education, she is open to new ideas and cultural influences, and it is for this reason that Vivian later wants to take her to New York. Cay is strong-minded, and tells Frances firmly, 'One of these days I'm gonna meet somebody that counts.' We see her resisting various social pressures to 'settle down' with Darrell, the male supervisor at the casino. When Silver tells Cay of her engagement to Joe and suggests a double wedding with Cay and Darrell, Cay rejects the idea. She makes it clear to Silver that she wants to be accepted for what she is, and Silver declares her continued friendship.

Later, Silver tells Cay she has been looking glum and invites her over. We see the two in the bath together as Joe serves them drinks, Silver professing delight at having near her the two people she loves most. Cay tells Silver that she is very much in love with Vivian, but does not know whether anything will come of it. Darrell is shown protecting Cay from the unwanted advances of a client at the casino, and is polite and patient with her. His offer to 'look the other way' about Cay's affairs with women evokes her exasperation, and shows his complete misunderstanding of who Cay is.

It is Cay who makes most of the moves in bringing herself and Vivian together. She makes Vivian laugh, offers to go riding with her, takes her to the cowboy clothing shop to equip her with jeans, shirt and boots, and insists, much to Frances' annoyance, on her coming to Silver's engagement party. Cay's brother Walter, a good-looking, gently understanding, rather idealised figure, offers to accompany Vivian to the engagement party, thereby calming the confrontation with Frances that arose when Cay insisted on Vivian coming along.

At the motel, when Vivian, on the opposite side of the door, asks her to go away, Cay replies, 'I can't, honest.' Once she has let Cay into her room, Vivian turns round to find Cay naked in her bed, and Cay succeeds, once again, in relaxing Vivian by making her laugh.

Vivian slowly develops a more relaxed outlook. She adopts a looser hairstyle, wears jeans and visits the casino. As she watches a rodeo, we see a close-up of her slipping her wedding ring off her finger, symbolising a new life. Lucille, another guest at Frances' house, tries to warn Vivian against getting too close to Cay, informing her that Cay was kicked out of college for 'unnatural acts': 'I'm definitely out to lunch when it comes to queers', she declares. Vivian shows her contempt for Lucille's attitudes. When she finally gets her divorce, the lawyer remarks that Vivian has found a 'pen-pal' in Reno. Her reply, 'I've found much more than that, Mr Warner', is strong and confident.

Sex and the spectator

A key scene in advancing the couple's intimacy occurs when Cay is driving Vivian home after the party, during which Silver's performance of her loving country song is accompanied by shots of the two looking at each other. Cay tells Vivian that she can only find real love with a woman. When Vivian, continuing to wrap her reactions in a cloak of academic tolerance, says, 'Are you trying to shock me?', Cay replies calmly, 'No, I was only telling you the truth.' Unnerved, Vivian takes refuge in the car, closing the door against Cay. Cay walks to the vehicle and, knocking gently on the glass, coaxes Vivian into winding down the window. She leans in to caress Vivian's cheek with her lips. Vivian's desire for Cay becomes clear as their lips meet. The romantic convention of the first kiss is made dramatic and memorable by the heavy shower that is drenching Cay, and the unusual positioning of the lovers.

The lovemaking scene at the motel raises the vexed question of erotic voyeurism. We have a woman directing a scene of woman-to-woman love-making which generally avoids angles or shots which could echo those traditionally associated with images directed at heterosexual males. Helen Shaver, as Vivian, conveys pleasurable sexual awakening and a nervousness that is carried into the next scene. In a restaurant, the two declare their love for each other, but Vivian is uncomfortable and her lack of 'points of reference' leads to a quarrel and the reconciliation with her lover.

Given the 1950s setting, remarkably little **homophobia** is encountered by the two lovers in this film. Lucille's prejudice and Darrell's incomprehension are balanced by the tolerant support of Silver and Walter. Frances' attitudes remain ambiguous and perhaps more credible given the era in which the film is set. Frances kicks Vivian out of her house and books her into a motel. This act is partly aimed at hanging on to Cay, although she says 'at least I'm normal'. The act backfires, and Cay moves out to stay with Silver. In her final conversation with Cay, Frances displays mystified antagonism: 'I just don't understand it. Women together.' Cay uses Frances' words to explain: 'She just reached in . . . put a string of lights around my heart' and earns a reluctant blessing and a hug, an action marred by Frances' comment that people will be talking about her.

Vivian needs to get back to New York, but Cay refuses to have dinner with her, saying 'being with you is beginning to hurt'. She agrees to see Vivian at the station, where Vivian invites her to New York, saying she would benefit there from being with somebody who realised how wonderful she was. Cay holds back, talking of loose ends, but agrees to accompany Vivian on the train to the next stop, forty minutes away. The

Consider the love-making scene in *Desert Hearts* in relation to critical ideas about spectatorship.

homophobia

Irrational prejudice and hatred against a person because of her or his homosexuality.

fragility of this lesbian relationship across class, regional and educational differences is echoed by the question posed narratively at the end as the train pulls away – will it be just forty minutes, or will Cay stay on the train?

CASE STUDY 3: *LOOKING FOR LANGSTON* (ISAAC JULIEN, UK 1988)

Poetic meditation

Subtitled *A meditation on Langston Hughes (1902–1967) and the Harlem Renaissance*, this film is a tribute to the American poet Langston Hughes, who lived in New York and whose writings formed a key part of the flowering of black culture in that city during the 1920s, known as the 'Harlem Renaissance'. It is less than an hour long and was funded by Britain's Channel 4. As the word 'meditation' suggests, the work is structured in a non-narrative way around a collage of visual images and a soundtrack of poetry by Hughes, Essex Hemphill and Bruce Nugent. It is dedicated to another outstanding American writer who was also gay and black, the novelist James Baldwin.

The film opens with newsreel footage of Hughes' funeral. A female voice-over delivers an oration about the struggle of opposition, which no one undertakes easily. Later on, this idea of opposition is underlined when we see a modern article on Hughes entitled 'Black and Gay', and when we see a gang of fierce-looking skinheads attempting violence on the nightclub space occupied by the men. The skinheads are white, and when they invade the space they are seen to do so with white police officers looking on and doing nothing. The funeral footage immediately cuts to a modern re-creation, in sensuously crisp black and white, of the funeral, with large white lilies and the body laid out in its coffin. The black and white cinematography continues throughout the film as a homage

A collage-style meditation on the life of poet Langston Hughes, *Looking for Langston*, is available on the *Gay Classics* video in the Connoisseur Video Collection (CR052).

• Plate 9.11 *Looking for Langston* (Isaac Julien, UK 1988)
The beauty of this film's images form a vivid tribute both to Hughes as an artist and to the culture that nurtured him

and reference to famous gay images. The lilies recall the photography of Robert Mapplethorpe.

Male, black and gay

Images of the funeral recur and evoke respectful homage. They are interwoven with images of a nightclub peopled by handsome men dancing, drinking, talking and laughing together, images of enjoyment, sensuality and cultural solidarity. The men are in formal evening clothes and dancing to music which recalls the 1920s. One of the men is white and is later seen in intimate, loving surroundings with his black lover after displaying jealousy in the club. Later, the music and dancing become disco-style in a mix between 1920s and modern styles and scenes, a mix which recurs throughout the film to evoke the continuity of both black and gay culture.

The central figure in the club is a handsome man with a moustache who sees another very good-looking man. The two are attracted to each other, and the middle part of the film presents sensuous fantasy sequences of the two of them together. The man with the moustache is seen relected in a pond in a spacious moorland setting. He comes across the other man, who is naked. His firm, well-made body is revealed to the viewer from behind, gradually, from the legs up. The poetry on the soundtrack talks of the man's 'dancer's body' and makes clear that this man is the figure of Beauty: 'Beauty's lips touched his. . . . How much pressure does it take to awaken love?' The shots of Beauty culminate in a scene of him lying naked in bed with the other man, their bodies intertwined. This memorable image recalls a famous photograph by George Platt Lynes, thus once again paying homage to a major figure of gay culture.

Cultural continuity

Fantasy elements underline the sense of meditation about Hughes and the cultural tradition of which he formed part. The nightclub is first seen with the men in still poses. Male angels, one of whom is played by the singer Jimmie Sommerville, watch over the nightclub. At one point, a beautiful young angel is seen holding a large picture of Langston Hughes, then the camera pans slowly to a large picture of James Baldwin. At another point, the camera rises from the nightclub to a scene of funeral mourning situated on the balcony above. This establishes a spatial relationship between the two main movements and moods of the film, and the words of the poem on the soundtrack, 'Let my name be spoken without effect, without the ghost of shadow on it', show that we are invited to celebrate with joy, not mourn with sadness, Hughes and the culture he represents. Nightclub images of kissing, dancing and talking are then followed by the slow pan of the camera sideways along the bar, past more posters of Hughes and Baldwin, to a young man with a flower.

Archive footage underlines cultural continuity. There is footage of Hughes reading his poetry in a TV programme, literary gatherings, jazz bands in Harlem, a football team, references to poets and anthologies and to the first production of the play, *Amen Corner*, by James Baldwin. A sequence which evokes the milieu of Harlem in the 1920s is accompanied by a poem on the soundtrack which tells how black artists at the time were expected to produce something called 'black art', a ghetto concept which was supposed to keep them in their place. Black artists were not supposed to concern themselves with wider ideas such as modernism. The poem tells how black art later went out of fashion with collectors: 'History as the smiler with the knife under her cloak.'

Throughout the film, Julien juxtaposes image and sound in order to provoke thought and emotion. Later, as a young man walks into the club, the song lyric rings out,

You're such a beautiful black man,
But you've been made to feel,
That your beauty's not real.

To accompany this we see footage of a black sculptor working on a sculpture of a naked black man. The lyric, the footage of the sculptor at work and the preceding homage to Beauty as a black man, provide a critique of sexual and aesthetic attitudes towards black men in a society dominated by ideas of beauty as white. Sound and image in collision are used to provoke questions and thoughts about how black men are sexually used by whites, black men as both objects and users of pornography and the use of pornography for safe sex.

As the man with the moustache leaves the nightclub, the street is dark, he is in shadow and we see barbed wire. There follows a sequence about men cruising each other in public places. The poem on the soundtrack talks of 'stalking' and we see men walking through trees and bushes. There is a foot-to-head shot of two men in leather, one black and one white, who meet and kiss. Then, in a typical time-jump, we are back with the man in evening dress walking over cobblestones. What both the modern and the 1920s scenes have in common is a sense of danger for gay men in public spaces, outside the safety of places like the club, but at the same time a sense of going out into, of braving those public spaces.

Strong, positive attitudes

This film tackles several controversial issues, including interracial sex and the questioning of the nature of black masculinity, and deals with them in an accomplished and stylish way. Such glamorously eroticised male images are, as Andrea Weiss points out (1993, p. 148), very different from the low-key approach taken by lesbian film-making, as in the film she and Greta Schiller made about the black lesbian jazz artist Tiny Davis, *Tiny and Ruby; Hell Drivin' Women* (US 1988).

The final and dominant mood of *Looking for Langston* is upbeat. The club dancers become more expansive and expressive. Two women are seen dancing together. A male couple is seen to leave the club and walk across Waterloo Bridge in contemporary London. While a train passes and they look at each other the voice-over poem is wistful: 'I love my friend. He went away from me. There's nothing more to say.'

But life goes on, the angels overlook scenes of love and celebration, and a poem refers to Hannibal, Toussaint and other strong figures of black history. As the gang of skinheads advances down the street, the club erupts with disco music and we see the dancers enjoying themselves. The editing rhythm increases as it cuts between the skinheads and the clubbers. Menacing shots of police with truncheons alternate with shots of men laughing and making love, a mirror ball, glasses dropping and smashing, police and thugs advancing up the stairs and entering the building. The expected clash is undercut when we see the police and thugs enter the club only to find it empty, followed by a shot of a laughing black angel. Is this a comment on the invisibility and/or oppression of black gay culture? Is it a demonstration of how prejudice and oppression can and will be deflected and dissipated? The final upbeat note is sounded when footage of the old TV programme is shown with Hughes reading

Sun's a risin'
This is gonna be my song.

Compare and contrast this film with Isaac Julien's feature, *Young Soul Rebels*, in terms of representations of race and sexuality, and of narrative structure.

☐ CASE STUDY 4: *THE LIVING END* (GREGG ARAKI, US 1993)

Genre and anarchy

Gregg Araki began his film-making career in 1987 producing quirky short films which directly challenged the conventions of classic narrative. *The Living End*, his first feature-length work, follows more conventional narrative patterns. However, the film uses traditional genre elements of the road movie, with comedy and romance, in unusual, offbeat and sometimes outrageous ways.

In the opening shot of the film we see Luke, a gorgeous young man in torn jeans, leather jacket and Ray Ban sunglasses, spraying 'fuck the world' on a wall, an image which sets the anarchic tone of the film. We immediately cut to the other main character, Jon, writing 'the first day of the rest of my life' in his diary, an entry explained for us by the mechanical-sounding voice-over of the doctor explaining to Jon that he is HIV positive. The doctor's continuing drone about antibodies, safe sex and healthy living is contrasted with a shot of Jon throwing up in the toilet, the film thus making its own comment on conventional medical attitudes. The film's offbeat attitude to HIV and death

The Living End **(Gregg Araki, US 1993)**

Araki's road movie features two contrasting characters, both HIV positive, on an anarchic and often hilarious journey to fulfilment (available for sale on Pride video).

• Plate 9.12 *The Living End* (Gregg Araki, US 1993)
The characters Luke (left) and Jon form an oddly-matched couple. Here they are, seen with director Araki.

281

is indicated when Jon says, 'Live fast, die young, leave a beautiful corpse – yeah right. Death is weird.'

Jon's friend Doris is seen hugging him, comforting him and offering help. Throughout the film she worries about him, even as she is breaking up with her boyfriend, but we see little indication of her state of mind other than her nervously playing with an executive toy. That, and the scene of her concentrated work on her painting, indicate the similarity of her world and Jon's. Her feelings for Jon are portrayed as warm and concerned, but she has a limited role within the film as foil and support for Jon.

Later, Jon picks Luke up in his car. Their conversation reveals Jon's conventional attitudes and Luke's anger. Jon invites Luke home to his apartment. Andy Warhol posters, a large blow-up dinosaur and the word processor indicate a playfully arty lifestyle. Luke casually looks round and is obviously uninterested in hearing about Derek Jarman and the article Jon is writing about 'The Death of Cinema'. Jon starts clearing his things away and Luke points out that he is being paranoid. The differences in personality and outlook between the two young men are further underlined when Luke asks if he can shower and immediately strips in front of an embarrassed Jon.

When Luke and Jon begin to make love, Luke shows himself to be sensitive to Jon's uptightness. Jon falteringly starts to explain, 'I just found out this afternoon that . . .'. Luke's tone is firm and affectionate: 'If you're trying to say what I think you are, don't worry about it.' With a kiss, he says, 'It's really no big deal.' He switches off the light and says, 'Welcome to the club, partner.'

Later, over breakfast, this tone of relaxed acceptance of each other and of their HIV positive status is given a harder edge as the two men talk of how they are going to die. Jon declares that he does not want to get fat and old, and describes his generation as 'victims of the sexual revolution', forced to pick up the tab for the previous generation who had all the fun. When Luke talks of genocide and neo-Nazi Republican plots Jon comments jokily, 'and you're calling me paranoid'. Luke goes on to point out that there must be millions of people like them walking 'with this thing inside them', that he, Jon and people like them have nothing to lose, are totally free and can do whatever they want, whereupon he produces a credit card which he says is his uncle's.

Luke's forceful attitude is underlined and perhaps magnified by the experiences which the audience have already witnessed. He escapes a grisly death at the hands of Daisy and Fern, the lesbian serial killers who have given him a lift, by stealing their car. After a kinky sex-scene with a tennis racket and a bisexual man he has picked up, Luke witnesses the man's murder at the hands of his wife. He is then confronted with three baseball-wielding thugs: 'Prepare to swallow your teeth, faggot, it's cosmetic surgery time.' He stops them in their tracks when he takes out a gun. First, he calmly shoots the one who tries to run away, then the other two.

Audience reactions

These scenes evoke conflicting audience reactions of outrage and laughter. Daisy chats Luke up in order to anger her girlfriend, calling him 'a sexy slab of hunk beefcake'. Fern stops the car and threatens to blow Luke's face to smithereens. The script pushes the man-hating lesbian stereotype to comic extremes with Daisy's descriptions of the painful deaths she and Fern have inflicted on previous victims, right to the point where Fern says, 'You got me so agitated with all this talk, I gotta pee.' She tells Daisy not to kill Luke until she gets back 'and no more flirting'. Daisy's line, 'I love it when she gets jealous', caps their over-the-top comic dialogue. The two women are strong foils for each other, and Daisy cares enough for Fern to run to her aid when she calls, thereby giving Luke the opportunity to steal their car.

The outrageous humour continues as we see the wife of the bisexual man bursting into the bedroom where he is sleeping with Luke. She informs her husband bitterly that 'It's not the seventies any more when being married to a bisexual was fashionable.' We see a low-angle shot of her holding a large knife in both hands and producing a tarzanic scream, then cut to a splash of blood hitting Luke's face and a series of unexpected shots which culminate in Luke leaving the house, chased by the dog. The combination of skilful editing and offbeat subject-matter make for unsettling comedy.

The scene where Luke shoots the three queer-bashers could well represent a form of wish-fulfilment. Luke becomes a liberating hero figure through expressing his anger, from spraying graffiti to bashing a skinhead who makes a gross AIDS joke. Jon's life is trans- formed once he commits himself to Luke, but his commitment only comes gradually. He goes along with the mad credit card spending spree, but throws Luke out after the skinhead-bashing incident, only to discover that he cannot live without him.

Motivation and character

The motivation for the two lovers hitting the road is typical of the road movie genre: a crime from whose consequences they need to flee. In this case, Luke admits that he has killed a policeman and they set off for San Francisco. Still, Jon has times when he wishes he was at home listening to his Smiths CDs, and the contrasts between the two characters surface comically. As with much comedy, traditional stereotypes lurk near the surface. Jon is the prissy queen and Luke the butch, streetwise hustler. Luke breezily confesses to having no licence when Jon comments on his adventurous driving, and calls Jon a 'princess' because of his precise bathing habits. Jon is reluctant to be touched while he drives and declares he is fed up with Luke's 'Clint Eastwood act with the gun'. Meanwhile, the familiar genre imagery of open spaces viewed from a speeding car embodies Jon's ever-growing distance from his old life. Doris, checking his apart- ment back home, finds an ansaphone full of unanswered messages and a dead goldfish. Luke writes 'Jon and Luke – Till Death Do Us Part' on a phone box, and Jon confides by phone to Doris, 'I don't know how to describe it. Nothing is the same any more. Everything has changed.'

A romantic ending?

The final sequence is both disquieting and romantic. Luke angrily destroys a bank machine, and in reaction Jon is determined to leave Luke and return home. He comes back from phoning Doris to find Luke has cut his wrist to examine his own blood, the source of his HIV anxiety. 'Just looks like boring old blood', he says. Jon is angry and ready to leave, but still binds Luke's wound. Luke points his gun at Jon, caressing him with it in an image replete with sexual overtones, saying 'you'll never find anyone who cares as much about you as I do'. He fires the gun to one side, they fight and Luke knocks Jon unconscious with the gun.

The final scene takes place on the beach. Jon comes to and finds he is tied up. Luke declares, 'Can't you see? I love you more than life.' Keeping the gun in his mouth, Luke rubs himself between Jon's legs in a desperate act of affirming his feelings for Jon. After Luke has finished we cut to a shot of the two from a distance, with a view of the deserted beach, as Luke throws the gun away. Jon frees himself, slaps Luke and walks away. There is a long pause, then Jon's crucial final act is to return to his lover and put his head on Luke's shoulder.

Compare and contrast the treatment of HIV and AIDS in *The Living End* with that in other fictional features such as *Parting Glances*, *An Early Frost* or *Longtime Companion*.

The final long-shot is of the two together peacefully on the beach with just the sound of the sea, a shot which implies a peaceful equilibrium achieved in a fragile relationship. The playful waywardness of this film, its gleeful man-killers, unsafe shower sex, amoral attitudes and discomforting treatment of AIDs, make it a central text of the New Queer Cinema. To what extent do Araki's unusual methods of comic exaggeration make viewers aware of the tensions, anger and survival strategies associated with being young, gay and HIV positive?

CONCLUSION: A QUEER DIVERSITY

Critic B. Ruby Rich has described 1992 as 'a watershed year for independent gay and lesbian film', not only because of the number of shorts and features being made and shown, but because of the surge in critical interest which has accompanied them. The recent crop of film and video activity is being called the 'New Queer Cinema'. Lesbian and gay activists, critics, film-makers and audiences are imbuing the previously negative term **queer** with a range of new, exciting, positive meanings in politics, literature, art and film-making. This process of an oppressed group reclaiming and reshaping a previously negative word or idea is known as **reappropriation**; it has happened with

• Plate 9.13 *Edward II* (Derek Jarman, UK 1991)
The love between Edward (left) and Gaveston evokes mixed audience reactions

the word 'black'. Critic Amy Taubin (1993, p. 176) said 'American queer cinema has achieved critical mass' with the release of features such as *My Own Private Idaho* (Gus Van Sant, 1991), utilising the Hollywood star system with Keanu Reeves and River Phoenix, and Tom Kalin's *Swoon* (1992).

The key idea behind the New Queer Cinema is diversity; a range of homosexualities manifested through a variety of character, situation, race, gender, sexual practice and film language. Film-makers are questioning the attitude, developed in the 1970s, that one must promote only positive images of lesbian and gay characters and situations. Although debate rages around what many lesbians and gays see as negative images in mainstream Hollywood films such as *The Silence Of The Lambs* (US 1990) and *Basic Instinct* (US 1992), lesbian and gay film-makers see such ideas as constraints on creativity in an era where a much wider variety of lesbian and gay images is available. Gus Van Sant's *My Own Private Idaho* dramatises the hopeless love of a teenage male hustler for a straight college boy. In *Swoon*, Tom Kalin examines the infamous Leopold/Loeb case of 1924, where two rich, Jewish 18-year-olds kidnap and murder a 14-year-old boy. Unlike previous film versions, such as Hitchcock's *Rope* (US 1948), Kalin concentrates on the homosexual relationship between the two young men, and the hold which the pathological Leopold had over Loeb. In an interview, Kalin stated, 'We're in a sorry state if we can't afford to look at "unwholesome" lesbian and gay people.' Derek Jarman's *Edward II* (UK 1991) does not hesitate to portray England's monarch as weak and vacillating, while his male lover, Gaveston, is scheming and slimy. What Kalin's and Jarman's films do, in their very different ways, is make the audience aware of the political dimensions of homosexuality.

New techniques of expression

Diversity and experimentation in film language has characterised recent lesbian and gay film. John Greyson mixes history in *Urinal* (Canada 1988) as famous figures of gay culture, including Langston Hughes and the Russian director Sergei Eisenstein, help to investigate police harassment of gays. In *Edward II*, following a style he had already used in *Caravaggio* (UK 1986) to point up the continuing relevance of its sexual and political themes, Derek Jarman deliberately mixes and clashes the fourteenth century and the 1990s. We see Annie Lennox singing a Cole Porter song, vicars in dog-collars spitting on Gaveston after his banishment and gay activists with placards invading the king's palace and wearing pink triangles, the symbol allotted to homosexual prisoners in Nazi concentration camps (see Marshall 1991). In *Blue* (UK 1993), Jarman's one-colour screen counterpoints the emotional range of the soundtrack's meditation on his life with, and approaching death from, HIV.

The documentary work of Stuart Marshall is challenging in subject-matter and form. *Bright Eyes* (UK 1984) presents the viewer with ever-relevant parallels between Nazi treatment of gays, Victorian medical practice and media coverage of the AIDS epidemic. *Desire* (UK 1989) deals with the lives of lesbians and gay men in Germany under the Nazis, building up a picture of fear, oppression and survival through low-key interviews with young historians of lesbian and gay life, paralleled with people who lived through those times telling their stories. The strength of Marshall's films lies partly in the way he lets the camera linger over a photograph, a building or a woodland scene to allow the viewer to take in and connect the past with the present.

Rosa Von Praunheim's *I Am My Own Woman* (Germany 1993) presents a portrait of Charlotte Von Mahlsdort (born Lothar Berfelde), a famous lifelong transvestite who is also gay. As well as using direct interviews with him, the film dramatises scenes from

queer

Originally a negative term for (mainly male) homosexuals, this word has been recently reappropriated by critics, artists and audiences to describe a challenging range of critical work and cultural production among lesbians and gays, with an emphasis on diversity of race, nationality and cultural experience.

reappropriation

The process whereby a previously oppressed group takes a negative term and turns it around to invest it with new meanings of power and liberation. Examples include 'black', 'virago' and 'queer'.

Derek Jarman

Painter, writer, activist and acclaimed British gay auteur. Derek Jarman was a provocative figure and an inspiration for younger artists and film-makers. Here are some key films:
Sebastiane (1976)
Jubilee (1978)
The Tempest (1979)
The Angelic Conversation (1985)
The Last Of England (1987).

• Plate 9.14 *Khush* (Pratibha Parmar, UK 1991)
The title of this memorable film is the Urdu word for 'ecstatic pleasure'. In her look at some Asian lesbian and gay lives, Parmar mixed pleasurable dream sequences with interviews which recall oppression

his life, including his anti-Nazi work during the Second World War. At the end of many of these dramatised scenes, he himself walks on to the set and is questioned by the actors about his thoughts and motivations, a productive distanciation effect.

Film genre and film style are mixed creatively in New Queer Cinema. Tod Haynes' *Poison* (US 1991) mixes 1950s B film sci-fi and zombie elements with a homoerotic section styled as a homage to Genet. In *Caught Looking* (UK 1991), Constantine Giannaris takes the viewer on a journey through a spectrum of gay viewpoints with a character participating in an interactive video fantasy. John Greyson's *Zero Patience* (Canada 1993) subverts the conventions of the Hollywood musical to investigate attitudes to AIDS, once again using a figure from the gay past, the Victorian explorer Richard Francis Burton, in creative and amusing ways.

Gender, race and queer cinema

Monika Treut's feature-length *Virgin Machine* (Germany 1985) accompanies its heroine on a sexual odyssey in New York City, but the inequality of funding for men's and women's work means that many lesbian film-makers continue to produce shorter films and videos. In *The Meeting of Two Queens* (US 1992) Cecilia Barriga has taken images of Garbo and Dietrich and edited them together to produce a provocatively sensual play of eye contact and undressing between two screen goddesses. The video work of Sadie Benning, such as the ten-minute *Jollies* (US 1991), intimately explores her own body, thoughts, memories and sexuality with a bold use of camerawork intricately interacting with the soundtrack.

Pratibha Parmar is a British film-maker and critic of Asian origin who helped found the first group in Britain for black lesbians. For her, as for Julien Isaac, race is as important an issue as sexuality, and the intervention of both film-makers contributes to the new kind of diversity within queer cinema, although one only has to compare Julien's feature film, *Young Soul Rebels* (UK 1991), with the short pieces produced by Parmar to be aware once again of the gender inequality in funding. Parmar is concerned to disrupt and change the conventional images of Asians prevalent in British society. Her 1990 documentary, *Flesh and Paper*, on Indian lesbian poet and writer Suniti Namjoshi, was, as Parmar herself said, 'the first time that British television audiences saw an Indian woman in a sari talking about being a lesbian and Indian in a way that was not apologetic or explanatory' (in Gever, Greyson and Parmar (eds) 1993: 45). *Khush* (UK 1991) is a television film she made for Channel 4 about the experience of being Asian and lesbian or gay. In this piece, interviews are interwoven with images of two women in saris relaxing and dancing together, and a classic Indian musical film is provocatively re-edited so that the dancing girl's glances interplay with those of another woman.

With videos such as *Orientations* (Canada 1985), Richard Fung helps give voice to North American lesbians and gays of Chinese origin. Marlon Riggs' feature-length poetic meditation on the lives of black gay men in the US, *Tongues Untied* (US 1989), is a beautifully constructed work.

The continuing queer cinema debate

Amy Taubin has called *Tongues Untied* and *The Living End* (see Case study 4, p. 281) 'heedlessly misogynistic' (1993: 179), the first because of its exclusion of any idea of lesbian presence and the second for its two-dimensional female characters as mere male appendages. *Paris is Burning* (US 1990), Jenny Livingston's documentary about the black gay drag scene in Harlem, New York, is regarded by some as condescending in its viewpoints. Such criticism and debate is healthy, and is set to continue along with the wide, creative and growing range of lesbian and gay film- and video-making, work which will surely benefit anybody who seeks to widen and enrich her or his viewing experience.

Consider the varying ideas and attitudes associated with the words homosexual, gay and queer. To what extent can these terms be used to describe various kinds of film-making?

 FURTHER READING

Babuscio, Jack, 'Camp and Gay Sensibility', in Richard Dyer (ed.), *Gays and Film*, London: BFI, 1977. An essay which presents pioneering insights.

Cook, Pam and Dodd, Philip, *Women and Film – a Sight and Sound Reader*, London: British Film Institute, 1993. An excellent section entitled 'Queer Alternatives' contains B. Ruby Rich's essay on queer cinema, Pratibha Parmar's response, Amy Taubin's lively criticisms and an essay on Monika Treut.

Dyer, Richard, *Now You See It: Studies on Lesbian and Gay Film*, London and New York: Routledge, 1990. A detailed academic study, best tackled in individual sections, mainly on early German film, Genet and developments in America.

—— *The Matter of Images – Essays on Representation*, London: Routledge, 1993. Dyer illustrates the power and complexity of images across a range of films, including film noir, *Victim*, *Papillon* and *A Passage To India*.

Gever, Martha, Greyson, John and Parmar, Pratibha (eds), *Queer Looks – Perspectives on Lesbian and Gay Video*, Toronto: Between the Lines, 1993. A wealth of new insights, including a look at gay punk video-maker Bruce LaBruce, new interpretations of Fassbinder's films and a superb essay by Thomas Waugh on gay spectatorship.

Jarman, Derek, *Dancing Ledge*, London: Quartet, 1984. Britain's foremost gay auteur. The critically-acclaimed artist's account of his formative years, which cover the making of *The Angelic Conversation*, *Sebastiane* and *Jubilee*. The first of a number of fascinating writings he has produced, which include books to accompany *Caravaggio*, *War Requiem* and *Edward II*.

Russo, Vito, *The Celluloid Closet – Homosexuality in the Movies*, New York: Harper & Row, 1987. The classic introduction to this area.

Steven, Peter (ed.), *Jump Cut – Hollywood, Politics and Counter Cinema*, Toronto: Between the Lines, 1985. Useful essays include viewpoints on lesbian spectatorship, Richard Dyer on stereotyping and sexual ideology.

Weiss, Andrea, *Vampires and Violets – Lesbians in Film*, Harmondsworth, Penguin, 1993. Key films and the main debates clearly presented.

Wood, Robin, *Hitchcock Revisited*, London: Faber & Faber, 1989. This volume includes Wood's original auteurist essays on Hitchcock with challenging new rereadings in the light of gay critical perspectives.

FURTHER READING FOR TEACHERS

The following book titles are recommended for further reading on historical background and critical theory.

Historical background

Dyer, Richard, *Now You See It: Studies on Lesbian and Gay Film*, London and New York: Routledge, 1990.
Lauritsen, J. and Thorstad, D., *The Early Homosexual Rights Movement*, San Francisco: Times Change Press, 1974.
Weeks, Jeffrey, *Coming Out – Homosexual Politics in Britain, from the Nineteenth Century to the Present*, London: Quartet, 1983.

Critical theory

Bad Object Choices (ed.), *How Do I Look? – Queer Film and Video*, Seattle: Bay Press, 1991.
Boffin, Tessa and Gupta, Sunil (eds), *Ecstatic Antibodies – Resisting the AIDS Mythology*, London: Rivers Oram Press, 1990. See especially Stuart Marshall's essay, 'Picturing Deviancy', on sexuality and photographic representation.
Fuss, Diana (ed.), *Inside/Out: Lesbian Theories, Gay Theories*, New York and London: Routledge, 1992. See especially Richard Dyer's essay on gay authorship.

FURTHER VIEWING

Before Stonewall (Greta Schiller, US 1985). A rich documentary of ordinary lesbian and gay lives in 1940s and 1950s USA (Pride: PR1 11012).

The Best of 'Out' and 'Out On Tuesday'. A diverse compilation from Channel 4's 'Lesbian And Gay' series, including Pratibha Parmar's *Khush*, a documentary meditation about Asian lesbians and gays in Britain (Connoisseur: CRO51).

Blue (Derek Jarman, UK 1993). Jarman's most artistically audacious film. The soundtrack explores death, AIDS, Jarman's own fight against blindness and many connotations of the vivid blue that fills the screen (Artificial Eye Video: ART 082).

Born in Flames (Lizzie Borden, US 1983). Radical science fiction. A sexually and racially diverse group of women fight to express themselves (available for hire on video).

Caravaggio (Derek Jarman, UK 1986). Jarman's view of this famous painter's life. An eye-catching blend of art, gay history and modern sensibilities (Connoisseur: CRO84).

Gay Classics (Genet/Julien/Kwietniowski, UK). Three major, thought-provoking works by gay men: Genet's *Un Chant d'amour*, Julien's *Looking for Langston* and Richard Kwietniowski's stylish drama, *Flames of Passion* (Connoisseur: CRO52).

The Killing of Sister George (Robert Aldrich, US 1968). A tragicomedy about a soap opera actress whose homely on-screen image clashes with her off-screen dyke persona. Oppressive stereotypes or liberating humour? Worth watching to make up your own mind (ABC Video: SPT 71067).

Law of Desire (Pedro Almodovar, Spain 1987). A gripping gay melodrama by one of Spain's leading contemporary directors (Tartan Video: TVT 1016).

Lesbian Lykra Shorts (UK). A rich international compilation which highlights the diversity of recent lesbian film-making. (Dangerous To Know: DTK 002. Contact Dangerous To Know for information about *Lesbian Leather Shorts* and *Lesbian Lace Shorts*)

Maurice (James Ivory, UK 1987). A visually rich story of gay love which crosses the class barriers of Edwardian England, based on the novel by E.M. Forster (Curzon Video).

My Beautiful Laundrette (Stephen Frears, UK 1986). A quirky and entertaining look at modern multicultural London, centred on a happy, generally relaxed relationship between a white skinhead and a young Asian businessman (available for hire on video).

Nighthawks/What can I do with a Male Nude? (Ron Peck/Paul Hallam, UK 1978). One of the first UK gay feature films. Centred on the life of a gay teacher, it presents a refreshingly non-stereotyped view of London gay life in the 1970s. The second piece is a short film questioning erotic representation in photography (Connoisseur: CRO83).

North of Vortex (Constantine Giannaris, UK 1992). Two men and a woman, a poet, a crook and a waitress, meet by chance and take off across America together in this evocative, erotic road movie. Winner of the 1992 *Gay Times* Jack Babuscio Award. A troubling text of the New Queer Cinema (Western Connection: WEST 008).

No Skin Off My Ass (Bruce LaBruce, Canada 1992). New Queer Cinema with all its rough edges and unusual cinematic strategies; a punk hairdresser seduces a skinhead (available for purchase from Out On A Limb).

Parting Glances (Bill Sherwood, US 1986). A beautifully made depiction of a group of people, gay and straight, in New York City (available on Pride Video).

Queen Christina (Rouben Mamoulian, US 1933). Despite all Hollywood could do to suppress it, the lesbian subtext rings clear and true through Garbo's performance and Salka Viertel's script (Warner Brothers Video).

The Rocky Horror Picture Show (Jim Sharman, UK 1976). A radical, entertaining gender-bender (Fox: 1424S).

Young Soul Rebels (Isaac Julien, UK 1991). A gay murder is solved. In the process, two young DJs, one gay and one straight, find romance and promote their brand of music. A vivid evocation of the London club scene of the late 1970s, with a lively soundtrack (Braveworld: STV 2195).

USEFUL ADDRESSES

Video availability is very variable. All the following organisations offer helpful, up-to-the-minute catalogues and brochures of currently available material.

Connoisseur Video, 10A Stephen Mews, London, W1P 0AX: Connoisseur has a video series entitled 'Home Video For The Gay Connoisseur' which includes titles by outstanding directors such as Pasolini, Cocteau, Kuchar and Jarman as well as recent works such as Tom Kalin's *Swoon*.

Western Connection, another distributor at the same address, offers exciting contemporary works such as Constantine Giannaris' *Caught Looking*.

Dangerous To Know, PO Box 1701, London, SW9 0XD: this distributor offers a rich variety of contemporary lesbian and gay work on video, such as *Oranges Are Not The Only Fruit*, *My Own Private Idaho*, *Salmonberries* and *Pink Narcissus*. Contact DTK for information about their collections *Lesbian Leather Shorts* and *Lesbian Lace Shorts*.

Pride Video Productions Limited, PO Box 179, Pinner, Middlesex, HA5 2TU: Pride has a variety of material available on video: feature films, documentaries and safer sex guides.

Out On A Limb, Battersea Studios, Television Centre, Thackeray Road, London, SW8 3TW: This collective distributes material on both film and video for educational and club viewing. Its catalogue includes the films of Monika Treut, a variety of documentaries, experimental and short fiction, and material dealing with HIV and AIDS.

Part five

National cinemas

Chapter 10

British cinema: representing the nation

Lez Cooke

■ British cinema: representing the nation

INTRODUCTION

This chapter will seek to explore the ways in which British cinema has, at different times, inflected images of the national culture – the aim being to explore how representations of class, gender, race, sexuality, regional and national identity are manifested in different kinds of British film at different historical moments and to examine how these images have served to represent the nation to itself and to the world. In order to do this we need to consider the relationship between films, culture and society in Britain at any particular historical moment and to examine the ways in which different kinds of British film – mainstream and independent, documentary and art cinema – have projected different images of 'Britishness'.

A chapter of this length cannot hope to consider the entire history of British cinema. Instead it is proposed to consider three different historical moments, beginning with a brief look at some films from the often neglected early years, before 1910, when British cinema was not yet established as an industry. Second, consideration will be given to a range of British films from the 1930s, by which time cinema had become established as the predominant form of mass entertainment with 20 million people going to cinemas in Britain every week. Despite the dominance of Hollywood films at the British box office, the 1930s was a productive time for both mainstream and alternative forms of domestic film production and a variety of British films of the period will be discussed. After a linking section considering notions of independence in British cinema, the third historical moment to be considered will be that of the 1980s. This period saw the British film industry struggling to survive in the absence of government support. Despite severe financial difficulties, however, a wide variety of commercially successful and artistically challenging British films were made during this time reflecting, in their different ways, the social, racial and political divisions of the decade presided over by Margaret Thatcher's Conservative government.

By concentrating on these three periods, plus issues of independence and representation, whole chunks of British film history have inevitably been overlooked. Needless to say, this is not because there is nothing of value to discuss in the periods not covered: the Second World War has often been described as a 'golden age' for British cinema, and a wide variety of interesting films were made in the 1950s and 1960s. On the whole, however, these periods have been well documented elsewhere and the concern here has been to consider some less familiar films (alongside a few very familiar ones) within a more conceptual framework.

While this approach may be somewhat idiosyncratic, there has been a deliberate attempt to strike a balance between the popular and the obscure, between mainstream and alternatives, in the examples selected for discussion. In doing so some care has been taken to ensure that the films discussed are available for further study, but there can of course be no guarantee that a film will remain in distribution. A list of further viewing has therefore been provided to supplement the range of films discussed in the chapter.

Similarly, a select list of essential reading on British cinema has been given, together with a more detailed bibliography, to facilitate further study, not only of the films and film-makers discussed here, but also of those areas of British cinema which this chapter has not been able to consider.

Before proceeding with the main task of exploring how British cinema inflected images of the national culture in these three different periods it may be useful first of all to define a few terms. For example, what exactly do we *mean* by 'British cinema'? What *is* 'a British film'? What do we understand by 'the nation' and 'national culture'? And how might we define the central concept of 'representation'?

WHAT IS BRITISH CINEMA?

British cinema is a broad term which could be seen to encompass the network of production, distribution and exhibition of films in Britain. But we immediately come up against a problem here in that, just as films made in Britain are not only shown in Britain, films that are distributed and exhibited in Britain are clearly not just British films. In fact, since 1915, the majority of films that have been shown in British cinemas have been American – British films have been in the minority. By the 1920s the number of British films being shown in British cinemas had fallen as low as 5 per cent and it was because of this that the government introduced legislation designed to increase the representation of British films on British screens. The Cinematograph Films Act of 1927, therefore, set a quota for the number of British films which had to be shown in British cinemas (initially 5 per cent – the quota was to increase by stages to reach 20 per cent by 1936). For the purpose of administering the Act certain criteria were devised for classifying a film as British:

> A British film was defined as one made by a British subject or company. The definition did not specify that control had to be in British hands, but only that the company had to be constituted in the British Empire and that the majority of the company directors should be British. All studio scenes had to be shot in the Empire, and not less than 75 per cent of the labour costs incurred in a film production, excluding payments for copyright and to one foreign actor, actress or producer, had to be paid to British subjects, or to persons domiciled in the Empire. The 'scenario' – a term never clearly defined, so that the provision became a dead letter – had to be written by a British subject.
>
> (Dickinson and Street 1985: 5–6)

These criteria have been adjusted over the years and the quota has fluctuated, being fixed at a high point of 45 per cent in 1948 (although the highest figure actually achieved was 37 per cent). After a long and troubled history the quota system was finally killed off in 1982, at a time when it had become untenable, not simply because of the small number of British films being made, but because exhibitors were unwilling to show British films because of their poor commercial potential. As a consequence, the criteria for classifying a film as 'British' are no longer as rigid as they once were and different sources give different classifications according to their own, often somewhat subjective, interpretation of the circumstances of finance and production. For example, a spokesman for the trade paper *Screen International* informed me that they mainly use *financial* criteria for deciding whether a film is British or not, so that a film such as Richard Attenborough's *Chaplin* (1993) would be classified as American, because the finance for the film came from an American company, whereas a film that was *partly* financed by British money would be considered a co-production. On the other hand, a spokesman for *Screen Finance* told me (surprisingly given the financial orientation of the publication) that they would classify *Chaplin* as British because it was made by a British production company and British personnel were involved, even though the money spent on British production resources and personnel was barely half of the film's total budget of £16.67 million, which was provided entirely by an American company, Carolco.[1]

Using the production company and/or British production base as the criterion would explain why – before the 1985 Films Act ended the need to register films which had been initiated by the 1927 Act – such apparently typical 'Hollywood' films as *Superman* (1978) and *Alien* (1979) were registered as British, because they were filmed in British studios using British personnel. The definition of 'British' here is a purely economic definition. It is, as John Hill notes, important from the viewpoint of the British film industry and British film production, but it does not necessarily help us in seeking to explore the relationship between British films and British culture:

> It is from this industrial standpoint that films like *Flash Gordon*, the *Superman* movies, *Insignificance* and *Full Metal Jacket* have qualified as 'British' films while, conversely, such a typically British film as *Shirley Valentine* is registered as American. This is not, of course, to say anything about the relative merits of these films but simply to note that economic arguments regarding the value of a national film industry do not necessarily guarantee a national cinema characterised by national preoccupations.
>
> (1992: 11)

What we are concerned with here then is not the film *industry* as such but British cinema as it is characterised by 'national preoccupations'. And these national preoccupations will, as we shall see, manifest themselves in terms of varying definitions of 'Britishness' defined through the representation of class, gender, race, sexuality, regional and national identity in a range of British films.

THE NATION, NATIONAL CULTURE AND NATIONAL CINEMA

It will become apparent as we explore these representations that notions of 'national culture' and 'the nation' are by no means unproblematic. What, for example, do we mean by 'the nation' in relation to British cinema when the nation is in fact made up of four countries? The growth of Scottish and Welsh nationalism in recent years has resulted in attempts to develop indigenous Scottish and Welsh cinemas as part of the endeavour to promote national cultures which are distinct from 'English' culture. The question of Irish national culture and Irish nationalism is complicated by the division between north and south, Protestant and Catholic, Unionism and Republicanism in Ireland, making it even more difficult to subsume Irish film culture within a concept of 'British' cinema. Any discussion of British cinema and national culture therefore must be sensitive to the claims of the 'peripheral' nations within the nation state of the United Kingdom to have their own national cultures and national identities. Even within England, regional, class and ethnic differences have led to the development of very different ways of life and the pursuit of very different cultural activities within one country of the nation state. These different communities have different identities which cannot be easily subsumed within a unitary national identity.

All of this makes it very difficult to talk about a unitary national culture and a uniform national cinema. Any discussion of British cinema as national cinema needs to take this heterogeneity into consideration – which is an argument for considering representations of class, gender, race, sexuality and regional identity as different facets of a heterogeneous national identity. Better perhaps to talk of national *identities*, national *cultures* and national *cinemas* in the plural rather than the singular.[2]

CONTEXTUAL AND COMPARATIVE ANALYSIS

To some extent, then, the representations of class, race, regional and other identities that we shall consider will be bound up with questions of national identity and national culture. It will only be possible to disentangle them by considering them within their particular social and historical contexts. The meaning of films, or their representations, is never immanent or self-contained, but needs to be analysed in relation to the specific conditions of production and consumption pertaining at any particular historical moment. Our analysis, therefore, will need to consider the representation of class in relation to the class structure in Britain as it existed at the time at which the film is set, at the time at which the film was made and at the time at which the film is viewed. Each of these may be different and will have a bearing on how audiences make sense of the representation of class in a film. In addition to this we will need to consider the representation of class in any one film in relation to representations of class in other films, both fictional and non-fictional, commercial and independent.

The issues here are complex because they are often interdependent. It is often not possible to dissociate the representation of class in a film from questions of gender or regional identity, just as it is not always possible to dissociate race from questions of national identity. Furthermore, the production context will often set the terms for our discussion. A commercial film produced for profit and with a view to entertaining its audiences will not often be concerned to challenge or question dominant views about how the world is or should be represented. Whereas an independent film made outside of the mainstream and targeted perhaps at a different audience may foreground the politics of representation and challenge dominant images in a way that a mainstream film might never consciously seek to do. (The definitions of 'commercial', independent', 'mainstream' and 'alternative' will be elaborated below, together with the notion that independent films may be more 'progressive' in their representations than mainstream, commercial films.)

These different contexts need to be taken into consideration in exploring forms of representation within British cinema, so that the textual analysis of individual films can be placed within a contextual analysis which considers the variety of ways in which social, political, cultural, economic and institutional forces may impinge upon the production and consumption of individual films. This is a complex task and cannot hope to be exhaustive without limiting our discussion to just one or two films. It is hoped, however, that different kinds of comparative analysis can be offered here, each within a limited contextual analysis.

One form of comparative analysis would be to compare the representation of one concept (for example, class) in a range of different kinds of film produced at a certain time (for example, in the 1930s). Another form of comparative analysis would be to consider several different aspects of representation in relation to a limited number of films produced within a certain historical **conjuncture** (for example, the Second World War). Each of these approaches would require attention to the historical context within which the films were produced, and the latter approach would, because of its focus upon a particular conjuncture, make the placing of the films within their social and historical context essential. A third form of comparative analysis might be one in which a particular aspect of representation (for example, race) is considered in films produced

conjuncture

A combination of events – social, political, economic – occurring at a particular historical moment.

at different historical moments (for example, the 1930s, 1950s and 1980s). This would allow for historical comparison and changes over time in the representation of race (for example) to be taken into consideration. Clearly the need for historical contextualisation here would be just as important as with the first two forms of comparative analysis.

REPRESENTATION, IDEOLOGY AND HEGEMONY

This brings us to the question of 'representation' which has already been used here in differing senses. There is clearly a difference, for example, between talking about 'the representation of class' and 'the representation of British films on British screens'. The former is concerned with the ways in which a particular social group is portrayed in the visual media through being photographed or filmed and thus re-presented to us as an image. The latter refers to a different notion of representation which is concerned with the numbers of British films being shown in British cinemas and the extent to which this adequately represents the national interest in the face of foreign, particularly American, competition. This latter meaning is analogous to talking about members of parliament 'representing' us when we vote for them, but it is not the same as talking about the representation (or portrayal) of a member of parliament in a film like *Scandal*.

It is useful to hold on to the notion of representation as the *re-presentation* of the world because it foregrounds the fact that film-making is a process of construction. In cinema (or television for that matter) there is no such thing as unmediated access to the real world. No matter how 'real' the representation of the world may appear to be on screen, decisions have been taken about how to re-present to us the 'reality' which lies before the camera. Sometimes, as in a historical drama, the staging or re-presentation of an event is evident from the period setting, costumes, props, etc. At other times, as with a cinéma vérité-style documentary, the staging of the film may be less obvious, but decisions have none the less still been taken about what to film, how to film it and how to edit together the filmed material, during the process of which a certain view of the subject-matter has been constructed, the 'reality' before the camera has been re-presented to us in the form of a film.

It is in this process of construction, of re-presenting the world for our consideration, that questions of **ideology** become important. For it is in the decision-making process that ideological values come into play as those responsible for making the decisions, consciously or unconsciously, bring their own moral, political and cultural values to bear upon the particular representation of the world which they are in the process of constructing. Sometimes, as in the case of overt propaganda films, the ideology will be self-evident. At other times, and this may apply equally to fiction and non-fiction films, dramas and documentaries, the ideology may be less evident, even 'invisible'. Yet it is at such moments that ideology is most effective in reproducing and reinforcing the values of the dominant groups in society, thus ensuring, by a process that because of its 'invisibility' seems 'natural', that the unequal relations in society between dominant and subordinate groups continue without the dominant groups needing to resort to coercion to maintain their control and without the subordinate groups recognising the degree of their subordination.

The significance of ideology and **hegemony** to the representation of class, gender, race and other identities in British cinema may not seem immediately apparent. But it will be the purpose of this chapter to explore how the representation of social groups

ideology

A system of ideas, values and beliefs held by individuals or groups within society. Ideology can be highly visible, as in 'racist ideology' or 'sexist ideology', where the racist or sexist beliefs of individuals or groups are self-evident; it can also be 'invisible' in the sense that it is something we take for granted in our everyday lives. Ideology permeates social institutions such as the media, education and the family, but we are often not conscious of it because of the manner in which ideology 'naturalises' values and beliefs, making them seem like 'common sense' (for example, ideology operates to make the servicing role of the housewife and mother appear natural, rather than being a consequence of patriarchal ideology).

in British films relates to the reproduction of ideologies of class, gender, race, sexuality, regional and national identity in British society. In doing so we shall consider to what extent these representations might serve the interests of certain groups in society while contributing to the subordination of others, and whether such representations can be utilised to challenge the status quo.[3]

FOUR ASPECTS OF REPRESENTATION

With these aims in mind, it is useful to ask the same questions of British cinema that Richard Dyer posed when considering the different connotations of the concept of representation in an article on popular television:

> What sense of the world is this programme [film] making?
> What does it claim is typical of the world and what deviant?
> Who is really speaking? For whom?
> What does it represent to us, and why?
>
> (1985: 45)

The first question refers to the concept of representation as construction, re-presenting the world to us in the form of recorded images. We need to analyse these images (these films) to see what sense they make of the world – whether, and how, they are defining and determining how *we* make sense of the world.

The second question refers to the way in which representations can set the agenda for what is considered 'normal' and 'natural' in our society and what is considered beyond the pale. This notion of 'typicality' is central to discussions of stereotyping, a process whereby particular groups in society are defined in a highly simplified manner, and which can contribute to the marginalisation and subordination of these groups, identifying them as in some way socially 'deviant'.[4]

The third question asks who is responsible for the representations which appear onscreen, and whether the people responsible for producing them are really *representative* of the people for whom those representations are being produced. Given the dominance of white, mainly middle-class, men as directors, producers, screenwriters, etc., throughout the history of British cinema, this question is clearly pertinent to any consideration of how women, the working class, and ethnic minorities are portrayed onscreen.

The question of for whom these images are being produced brings us to the fourth aspect of representation which we need to consider: the audience. It would be as much of a mistake to leave the audience out of consideration when analysing representations of social groups as it would be to ignore the social, economic and historical context within which those representations are produced. This leads us into a difficult area, however, for how do we know what audiences thought of representations of class and gender in British films in the 1930s, for example? To some extent we are dependent here upon research which has been undertaken by film and social historians. As we move nearer to the present such research is more readily available and can even be undertaken ourselves. In other cases we may need to hypothesise as to the possible responses of audiences to the films under consideration. However, this is preferable to ignoring the audience altogether or considering them as a homogeneous mass on whom films have exactly the same effect regardless of the class, gender or ethnic composition of the audience. We need to ask, therefore, what a film or particular representation means, or might have meant, for its audience.

hegemony

A concept developed by the Italian political thinker Antonio Gramsci to explain the process by which the dominant classes or groups in a nation maintain power over subordinate classes or groups. Hegemony can be achieved by coercion (through 'repressive' state institutions like the police, the penal system, the army) or it can be achieved by consent, operating *ideologically* through the institutions of civil society, for example, the media, the family, the education system. Ideology is therefore central to the maintenance of hegemony in capitalist societies.

• Plate 10.1 *Buy Your Own Cherries* (UK 1904)
Defining class difference through mise-en-scène

REPRESENTATIONS OF CLASS IN EARLY BRITISH CINEMA

Let us begin by considering some examples from the early years of British cinema, returning to a moment before film-making had become industrialised, before the feature-length film, before America had achieved its dominance in world cinema. The first ten years of British cinema was a time of innovation and experiment, and it is now generally recognised that the pioneer British film-makers were at the forefront in the development of film technique in these early years. While some of these pioneers had experience of photography and the optical lantern, they were not primarily artists but craftsmen – inventors and manufacturers who in some cases turned to film-making simply to demonstrate and sell the equipment they were manufacturing. Robert Paul was one such early British film-maker. An inventor, manufacturer and businessman who progressed from making 'actualities', usually single-shot documentaries filmed with a static camera like his recording of *The Derby* in 1896, to staged films like the four-minute, seven-shot narrative film *Buy Your Own Cherries*, filmed in 1904. This was a scene-by-scene reproduction of a nineteenth-century lantern slide show about the dangers of drink which tells the story of a family rescued from the ruinous effects of alcohol when the father is persuaded to join a temperance society by a Methodist preacher. After joining the Independent Order of Good Templars the father is transformed from an alcoholic into an upright and responsible family man who is able to resist the temptations of the gin house and instead buys cherries to take home to his wife and children.

From the point of view of representation, the film is interesting in terms of its class perspective. At the beginning of the film the father, seen drinking in the gin house, is

• Plate 10.2 *Rescued by Rover* (UK 1905)
The privileged classes dread of the lower depths

clearly defined by his clothing as working class in relation to the other man drinking there whose top hat and coat, not to mention his superior attitude, identifies him as upper middle class. When the father goes home the plain decor of the house and simple clothing of his wife and children confirm the family's impoverished working-class status. But after the father has been 'saved' by the preacher and has joined the temperance society the transformation which takes place in his life is immediately evident from the **mise-en-scène**, as well as from his action in resisting the lure of the gin house. When he goes home to his family the second time the decor and clothing suggest a comfortable middle-class household rather than the working-class household of the earlier scene, and the **embourgeoisement** of the family is completed by the gifts which the father produces for his wife and children.

The ideological implications of *Buy Your Own Cherries* are not difficult to identify. As in its previous life as a magic lantern show, the story is designed to warn the lower orders of the dangers of drink and to show how their lives might be transformed as a result of abstinence. It is worth noting here that although the early cinema had quickly become a form of entertainment for the working classes the films that were being made for their consumption were being produced by film-makers like Robert Paul, middle-class men who had most likely been producing moralistic lantern slide shows like *Buy Your Own Cherries* in the late nineteenth century. This tradition of the middle classes providing moral guidance for the masses was continued when these lanternists turned to making films.

The class perspective is equally transparent in Cecil Hepworth's famous *Rescued by Rover*, made in 1905 and directed by Lewin Fitzhamon. This six-minute film is a classic

mise-en-scène

A theatrical term usually translated as 'staging' or 'what has been put into the scene'. In film, mise-en-scène refers not only to sets, costumes and props but also to how the scene is organised, lit and framed for the camera. Mise-en-scène is one way of producing meaning in films which can be both straightforward and extremely complex, depending upon the intentions and skill of the director (the *metteur-en-scène*).

embourgeoisement

A sociological term describing the adoption of middle-class (bourgeois) values and attributes by members of the working class as a result of increased affluence.

301

of the early cinema. It is also a classic piece of middle-class film-making conveying what Noel Burch has described as 'the privileged classes' dread of the lower depths'[5] with its story of the abduction of the baby of a respectable middle-class family by an unkempt alcoholic member of the lower classes (the film is again a warning against the corrupting influence of drink). The class divide is illustrated by the distance that Rover, the loyal family dog, travels in search of the missing baby, from the comfortable middle-class family home in a pleasant leafy suburb, across a river (representing a physical and metaphorical dividing line between the classes), to the plain terraced housing of the working-class district where the dastardly kidnapper lives. After discovering the where-abouts of the baby, Rover retraces his steps to the family home to find the father and the journey is repeated with Rover leading him to the baby. As if the father's class membership was not already apparent from the mise-en-scène of the home, he under-takes the journey dressed ludicrously in top hat and tails, making his presence in the working-class district where the baby is being held even more incongruous. (It is perhaps significant that Hepworth himself plays the father in the film and the middle-class family was in real life his own family.) Once again the mise-en-scène of the attic room, bereft of furniture, with bare rafters and crumbling plaster, emphasises the class opposition in the film. The father's abandonment of the baby's fine clothing to the pathetic figure of the woman, who had earlier been seen wearing a ragged shawl when she stole the baby, is a final gesture of his social superiority.

Both *Buy Your Own Cherries* and *Rescued by Rover* are reaffirming the values of the dominant class in their privileging of the middle-class viewpoint over that of a working-class perspective in the films. But not all films of the time can be said to be performing this hegemonic task. William Haggar was one film-maker who operated outside of the

• Plate 10.3 *Desperate Poaching Affray* (UK 1903)
Images of working-class resistance

302

middle-class social circle of Robert Paul and Cecil Hepworth. He was a showman who earned a living touring the fairgrounds of Wales and the west of England with his travelling theatre, providing entertainment for the mining communities in the region. It was for these communities that he made films when he turned to film-making at the turn of the century, using members of his travelling theatre company to make dramatic films which he knew would be popular with his working-class clientele.

Many of Haggar's films are now lost, even *The Salmon Poachers* (1905) which reputedly sold 480 prints – an indication of its popularity. Like his earlier *Desperate Poaching Affray* (1903) – which has survived – the popularity of *The Salmon Poachers* may be explained partly because it was a chase film, a popular genre with early cinema audiences. But, as with his film *Charles Peace* (1905), about the notorious nineteenth-century criminal, *The Salmon Poachers* may have been popular for ideological as well as generic reasons. Noel Burch has drawn attention to the subversive aspects of these films which may have appealed to a working-class audience for whom hardship and exploitation were common experiences. Burch has described how Haggar's depiction of Charles Peace was designed to encourage audience identification with the criminal by portraying him as:

> a kind of acrobat-clown straight from the popular music-hall (his face is made up in the same way), and the way he ridicules the police, in particular, makes him a character manifestly close to the popular audience – who are also assumed to be quite familiar with the historical Peace's deeds, although he had been executed some fifty years earlier.
>
> (1990: 100)

Haggar's working-class audiences, for whom a spot of poaching may not have been unusual in times of hardship, would also have enjoyed the resolution to *The Salmon Poachers*. In this the poachers, having been apprehended by the police while doing some night-time poaching, outwit their pursuers and make their escape – a resolution which might have seemed quite subversive to the authorities at the time. There is an 'oppositional' element therefore in some of Haggar's films which is not to be found in the work of other film-makers of the time. As Burch notes, 'Authority baffled was a recurrent theme in Haggar's films' (1990: 102).[6]

THE CONCEPT OF NATIONAL CINEMA IN THE 1930S

After the precocious promise that British films had shown in the early years, British cinema went into a decline after 1906, as far as production was concerned, although audiences continued to grow. The decline was exacerbated by the First World War, which enabled Hollywood to achieve a hegemony over European cinema which it has never lost. By the mid-1920s British film production was at such a low ebb that British films comprised only 5 per cent of the films showing in British cinemas, and there was a growing recognition of the need to take action to rescue British cinema from its subservience to Hollywood.

Action was taken in the form of government legislation when the 1927 Cinematograph Films Act introduced a quota system for the British film industry, stipulating that the number of British films being shown by exhibitors in Britain should rise progressively to reach 20 per cent by 1936. In fact, the Act was more successful in stimulating British film production than was anticipated and this target had been reached by 1932. The downside of this was that the American companies responded by investing in British films which were, in the words of Simon Hartog,

> cheap, awful, and just long enough to qualify as feature films under the 1927 Act. The films, which were usually financed at a rate per foot, became known as 'quota films' or 'quota quickies'. By complying only with the letter of the law, the American renters funded the production of hundreds of British films which discredited both British film production and the quota legislation.
>
> (1983: 68)

On the positive side, however, the Act did succeed in stimulating film production and not only gave film personnel a period of sustained employment but brought new talent into the industry. Many of the great names in British cinema of the next twenty or thirty years cut their cinematic teeth on quota pictures in the 1930s. Rather than merely discrediting film production, quota quickies provided young film-makers with the opportunity to learn their craft.

Under the stimulus of the Act, the number of films produced increased from twenty-six feature films in 1925 to nearly 200 in 1935 and 228 in 1937, before a slump resulting from over-investment caused a dramatic fall to seventy-six in 1938. At a time of high unemployment and worldwide recession the British film industry saw a period of unprecedented growth during the ten years that the 1927 Films Act was in force, with more than 1,600 British films being produced and an estimated 7,000 people employed in British studios by 1936.[7]

One of the 'hidden' objectives of the 1927 Act had been a cultural one: to counter the 'Americanisation' of British life resulting from exposure to an ever increasing number of American films. It was hoped that an increase in the numbers of British films would not only be economically advantageous to Britain but would encourage the development of a national film culture reflecting British morality, culture and ideals. That this was an objective of the Act was acknowledged by R.D. Fennelly, a member of the Board of Trade, in 1936:

> By 1925 the depressed state of the British industry was causing general concern. Apart from the purely industrial aspect of the matter it was felt that from the point of view of British culture and ideals it was unwise to allow the United States to dominate the cinemas of this country. At that time nearly every film shown represented American ideas set in an American atmosphere, and the accessories were American houses, American materials, American manufactures, etc. Whatever the position today, cinematograph audiences then were made up of the most impressionable sections of the community, and it was felt to be of the utmost importance for our prestige, for our trade and, it was even asserted, for our morals, that they should see at least some proportion of British films.
>
> (cited in Hartog 1983: 73)

It is difficult today not to see this statement as advocating an injection of British 'high culture' to counteract the 'low culture' of the American cinema. In view of other criticisms current at the time, and subsequently, about the erosion of cultural values represented by Hollywood films this could be seen as part of a reactionary backlash against popular culture.[8]

But the real questions which the statement begs are 'what kind of films?' and 'what kind of culture?' For an answer we must turn to the films themselves, and not just the high profile films of Hitchcock and Korda for which the decade is remembered, but also the popular comedies of the time and those more marginal documentaries, both mainstream and oppositional, which also contributed to what was a *pluralistic* national film culture in the 1930s.

THE POPULAR ENTERTAINMENT CINEMA OF THE 1930S

Let us begin with the dominant British cinema of the time. Apart from Hitchcock, one figure looms large in histories of 1930s British cinema: Alexander Korda. Born in Hungary, Korda came to Britain in 1931 after spells of film-making in Hungary, Germany, America and France. Establishing his own production company, London Films, he received funding

• Plate 10.4 *The Scarlet Pimpernel* (UK 1934)
Celebrating national identity through images of aristocracy

from American companies, initially Paramount and then United Artists, to make British films (an example of the ways in which American companies managed to retain an involvement in British cinema after the 1927 Quota Act). United Artists, unlike Paramount which was one of the 'Big Five' Hollywood companies with its own production studios, was dependent on affiliated production companies like London Films to supply films for the parent company to distribute. UA commissioned Korda to produce three big-budget films which would be acceptable to the American market (quota films were not acceptable because of their low production values and parochial subject-matter). This set Korda on the road to producing the kind of 'international' pictures for which London Films is now remembered. The first of these was *The Private Life of Henry VIII* (1933), starring Charles Laughton. Made on a huge budget, by British standards, of £94,000, the film was British cinema's first big international success, initiating a cycle of lavish historical dramas attempting to repeat its success, a risky strategy that precipitated the financial crisis of 1937. However, the huge success of *Henry VIII* (the film earned over £500,000) enabled Korda, with financial assistance from the Prudential Life Assurance Company, to build big new studios at Denham. Korda followed *Henry VIII* with a number of films focusing on aspects of British history and heritage, all with an eye on the international market as much as the British one.[9]

One of the historical films which followed *The Private Life Of Henry VIII* was *The Scarlet Pimpernel* (1934). This film provides an excellent illustration of the particular definition of 'Britishness' in Korda's films, a definition which is centred upon the life and culture of the upper classes and which is unashamedly patriotic. It emphasises the extent to which Korda, as a middle-class immigrant, wished to demonstrate his credentials to be British through an identification with the middle and upper classes, and with the upper-class gentleman in particular. (Korda became a naturalised British subject in 1936.)

In *The Scarlet Pimpernel* Leslie Howard, so often the embodiment onscreen of the cultured English gentleman, plays the eponymous hero who undertakes to save French aristocrats from the guillotine during the French Revolution. When he is not disguised as the Pimpernel his real identity is the English nobleman Sir Percy Blakeney who adopts an exaggerated foppishness in order to conceal his identity as the Pimpernel. The 'real' Sir Percy, we are led to believe, is the one who recites the John of Gaunt deathbed speech from *Richard II* – 'this earth, this realm, this England' – when he is about to be taken before a French firing squad. But the firing squad has been taken over by the Pimpernel's own men and he therefore lives to utter the final uplifting patriotic sentiment to his wife Marguerite as their ship returns them from France: 'Look, Marguerite . . . England', a line which Korda believed was guaranteed to stir the audience's emotions and get them applauding.[10]

For Korda, national identity equalled the culture of the upper classes. *The Scarlet Pimpernel* not only allowed this definition of national identity to be given expression, but also provided a vehicle for the expression of Korda's own nationalistic patriotism:

> British nationalism surfaces in this contrast between French and English as the French are shown to have lost control of their society. The French revolutionaries are shown to be mean-spirited, inflexible, and above all, bores. By contrast, the Englishman as exemplified by Sir Percy is the consummate image of gallantry and wit in both his public and his private conduct. His scrupulous sense of duty does not stop with his ferreting out of public enemies but extends to his exacting comparable behaviour from his wife. The issue of class is uppermost here in the iconography of

the characters as well as in their behaviour. The film does not question the saving of the aristocrats. It takes for granted that the Pimpernel is doing the right thing, and it portrays, moreover, the superiority of the aristocrats over the plebeians. Not only are the aristocrats more beautiful but they are more cultured. Even in his role as a fop, Sir Percy is able to outsmart his duller colleagues. His greatest weapon is not a lethal instrument but his cleverness and wit. The Pimpernel is related to the protagonist of the films of empire. He is the incarnation of the consummate British gentleman.

(Landy 1991: 130–1)

This obsession with a highbrow interpretation of class and culture in Korda's films is in marked contrast to the working-class comedies, musicals and melodramas which were just as popular in Britain, if not more so, as Korda's more prestigious productions in the 1930s. These films, featuring music-hall and variety stars like Gracie Fields, George Formby and Will Hay, were not targeted at an international market as Korda's films were and usually proved to be far more popular in the regions than in London and the home counties. They were as unashamedly lowbrow as Korda's films were highbrow and offered a mainstream alternative to the kind of national cinema which Korda at London Films and Michael Balcon at Gaumont British were trying to promote.

Gracie Fields' screen debut was in *Sally in Our Alley* (1931). This film is of interest not only because it provides a sharp contrast to the privileging of the upper classes and the aristocracy in Korda's historical films, but for the way in which it engages with class conflict and emphasises a working-class point of view. One sequence in the film illustrates this well. Sally (Gracie Fields) is invited to sing at a high society party by an upper-class lady who hears her singing in the East End coffee shop where Sally works as a waitress. At the party Sally is treated as a source of amusement by the society party-goers and is clearly portrayed as a fish out of water. But the sympathies of the audience are clearly intended to lie with Sally and to see the upper-class characters as patronising and privileged (something which working-class audiences would have had little difficulty in doing, given the level of unemployment and the introduction of the '**means test**' in the year the film was released). Tables are turned, however, when Sally returns to the coffee shop. Here she makes fun of the low-cut dress she was given to wear at the party before delivering an emotional rendition of the title song to the working-class clientele. This scene is comparable to the one at the end of *The Scarlet Pimpernel* which was also designed to stir the emotions of the audience, but it is easier to imagine working-class audiences at the time identifying with Sally (and with Gracie Fields) than with Sir Percy Blakeney – no matter how much star appeal Leslie Howard may have had.

While it would be a mistake to claim that a film like *Sally in Our Alley* is politically 'radical' or 'progressive' in relation to a film like *The Scarlet Pimpernel*, both of these films can be seen to be performing an ideological function for British audiences in the 1930s, the latter by reinforcing the dominant culture and projecting an image of 'Britishness' which was class specific, equating it with the culture of the upper classes, the former by offering a view of an alternative working-class culture and identity. At a time when the working classes were experiencing real poverty and deprivation in a way that the upper classes were not, it seems likely that the films of Gracie Fields and George Formby (who took over from Gracie as Britain's top box-office star in 1938) were just as important in terms of a 'national cinema' in the 1930s as the more high profile

'means test'

A measure introduced in 1931 to assess the eligibility of claimants to benefit after a period of twenty-six weeks of unemployment and calculated on the basis of existing household means as determined by a Public Assistance Committee.

• Plate 10.5 *Sally in Our Alley* (UK 1931)
A celebration of working-class identity and culture

films of Korda and Hitchcock. They certainly had an ideological role to play in countering the representation of the privileged classes in Korda's films by offering alternative, working-class identities and pleasures for what was, after all, the bulk of the cinema-going audience at the time.[11]

THE DOCUMENTARY MOVEMENT IN THE 1930S

In the documentary cinema of the 1930s we can perhaps get closer to the 'reality' of life. This is because the commercial pressures to produce particular kinds of representations, experienced by mainstream commercial cinema, were not present. Within this documentary movement, however, it is possible to identify both 'mainstream' and 'alternative' traditions and, while both traditions are concerned with representations of the working class, they provide different interpretations of working-class life, experience and

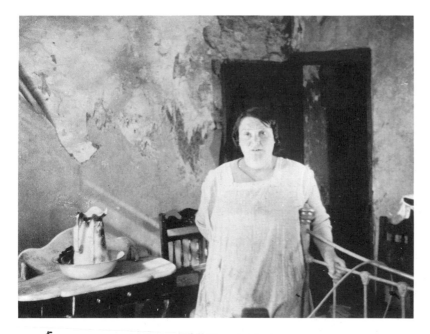

• Plate 10.6 *Housing Problems* (UK 1935)
The real conditions of existence

struggle. A comparison of the films produced by these two different documentary traditions foregrounds the way in which institutional, economic and political determinations
influence the kinds of representations which it was possible to produce outside the
commercial cinema.

The dominant documentary tradition was that associated with John Grierson and the
film-makers he worked with, first, at the Empire Marketing Board Film Unit between
1928 and 1933 and, subsequently, at the General Post Office Film Unit from 1933 until
1939. In spite of the fact that the films he produced were essentially promotional films
financed by various state organisations, Grierson was interested in the educational and
'democratising' possibilities of film. In addition, many of the film-makers working under
his auspices were socialist and interested in the Soviet films that were being screened
in Britain at places like the London Film Society. There was therefore a tension between
the demands of the sponsors of the films and the aesthetic and ideological interests of
the members of the film units, and this resulted in some rather unconventional documentary films.

This tension can be seen in a film like *Housing Problems* (1935) which was sponsored by the gas industry. The film is slightly unusual within the body of work of the
GPO Film Unit in that it eschews the montage style of many of the films produced by
the Unit in favour of a more 'realist' approach. Working-class families are seen talking
in their homes, directly addressing the camera, about the atrocious housing conditions
in which they live, before being filmed in the new apartment blocks to which they were
soon to be relocated. One gets a sense of the film-makers, Edgar Anstey and Arthur
Elton, wanting to make a statement about working-class poverty within a film which
is essentially a propaganda exercise on behalf of the gas industry to extol the virtues

of the new housing over the old slum terraces. As Ian Aitken argues, despite the attempt to expose the real conditions of working-class existence, and to give a voice to working people which they are usually denied in mainstream documentaries,

> *Housing Problems* represented the social problems it examined as fully resolvable, and the film ends with an over-optimistic vision of 'ideal' housing estates, which replace the slums. The final text is a contradictory document, in which criticism of poverty contrasts with the film's final message. Because of this *Housing Problems* has become a paradigm case for those who argued that sponsorship compromised the critical faculties of the documentary film-makers.
>
> (1990: 139)

The contradictions were no less evident in the more 'unconventional' (but more typical) documentaries of the GPO Film Unit. Although the EMB and GPO film-makers were politically of the left, their interest in the Soviet films of the 1920s was as much aesthetic as it was political and this interest manifested itself in the montage style of many of their films. Two of the GPO Film Unit's best-known films, *Coalface* (1935) and *Night Mail* (1936), illustrate this well. Both films combine an aesthetically pleasing montage of images, of the coal industry in the former film and the postal service in the latter, with verse by W.H. Auden and music by Benjamin Britten. But for all their radical, **modernist** credentials at the time, the poetry of Auden and music of Britten have 'high cultural' connotations today that seem at odds with the industrial working-class subject-matter of the films.

modernist

Modernism is a term used to describe developments in twentieth-century art, literature, music, film and theatre which were a conscious reaction against a perceived conservatism in the arts. Modernist art is characterised by experiment and innovation and modernist artists, because of their avant-garde practices, inevitably constitute a cultural elite.

• Plate 10.7 *Night Mail* (UK 1936)
Working-class labour romanticised?

These films are prime examples of Grierson's belief in the 'creative treatment of actuality' in documentary films. However, the aesthetics of the approach merely succeed in romanticising the labour of the workers who are the subjects of the films. No matter how sincere the intentions of the film-makers may have been, the effect is to dehumanise the workers, to portray them as subjects to be observed, studied, pitied or admired. The films put us, as spectators, in the same position as that of their middle-class film-makers; as outsiders looking in on an authentic but intangible working-class reality. In giving us this ideological position they position us (and the audiences of the time) with the dominant culture, rather than allowing us to identify with the workers.

What is being projected in these films is an idea of the nation in which workers from different industries are constructed as part of a national community, with each worker doing his part (in these male-centred films) for the good of the nation. Far from simply documenting or observing the working class in an objective or dispassionate manner, these films romanticise the working class while emptying out all political significance from the work they are doing. There is little or no evidence of wage disputes, unemployment, poverty or the reality of 1930s working-class life in these films. Perhaps this is not surprising, given the state sponsorship which lay behind them. While there is something to be said for the attempt to portray the lives of the working class in a less frivolous and stereotyped manner than in mainstream commercial cinema, the representation of the working class in these films is ultimately subordinated to Grierson's ideological project of portraying a mythical 'national community' and a cohesive 'national culture'. As such, these state-sponsored films could be said to be contributing to the consensus politics of the decade.[12]

OPPOSITIONAL CINEMA IN THE 1930S

There was, however, another tradition of documentary film-making in the 1930s which, until recently, has been paid much less attention than the Griersonian tradition. This was the body of alternative or oppositional film-making which emerged from workers' film groups and film societies in the 1930s. In some ways this tradition stands in the same relationship to the 'mainstream' documentary movement of the time as the working-class entertainment films of Gracie Fields *et al.* stood to the highbrow commercial cinema of the time. As with the lowbrow popular cinema, but much more so here, the workers' documentary films were very much the 'poor' relation to the mainstream documentary tradition. Literally so, since, unlike the state-sponsored documentary films of the EMB and GPO Film Units, the workers' films of the 1930s were produced on very meagre resources. Financed by the workers themselves, with perhaps some support from trade unions or labour organisations, the films were usually shot silent (because the expense of making sound films was prohibitive) on budgets of less than £40. They took the form, initially, of newsreels like *Workers' Topical News No. 1* (1930), a five-minute film which was the first production of the London Workers' Film Society, and which documented the rally and march against unemployment in London in March 1930. Paul Marris' account of this film gives an indication of the 'amateur' production values and political objectives of many of the workers' films produced in the early 1930s:

> The short time – three days – between the event depicted in the film and its first showing indicates how technically unambitious the film is in its construction. Made on 35mm, it is silent, consisting of documentary-style long shots with some closer shots edited together by Ralph Bond. These are probably shown in much

the same order in which they were shot: short series of two or three shots, introduced by title cards that briskly name the items depicted. This topical newsreel
set the basic pattern for many of the films produced within the labour movement
throughout the decade: films that simply sought to record labour movement events,
usually those in which the Communist Party had a leading organisational and
political role.

(1980: 72)

Ralph Bond was a leading figure in the movement. A member of the Communist Party,
he helped to set up the Federation of Workers' Film Societies in October 1929. Its aim
was to co-ordinate and encourage the activities of workers' film societies around the
country in an attempt to build a 'proletarian culture' in opposition to the dominant culture
of the time. The commercial cinema was seen to be responsible, by Bond and others,
for maintaining the hegemony of the ruling classes, and it was considered to be politically expedient to establish an alternative network of production, distribution and
exhibition in order to challenge this hegemony:

The Cinema today is a weapon of the class struggle. So far this weapon has been
the exclusive property of the capitalists. We cannot hope to wrest it completely from
their hands until the relations in society have changed, but we can and must fight
capitalist influences in the Cinema by exposing, in a Marxist manner, how it is used
as an ideological force to dope the workers. That can be done by exhibiting the
films of the only country where the workers are the ruling class, and by making our
own films.

(Bond 1980: 141)

• Plate 10.8 *Hell Unlimited* (UK 1936)
Oppositional film culture in the 1930s

In addition to exhibiting the films of the Soviet Union, workers' film societies set up their own film-making groups to produce newsreels, documentaries and the occasional drama-documentary like *Bread* (1934), a twelve-minute film made by the London Production Group of Kino (a left-wing film distribution company) in collaboration with the Workers' Theatre Movement. *Bread* was clearly influenced by the Soviet montage style which it utilised, together with some stylised camerawork, to tell the story of an unemployed worker who steals a loaf of bread to feed his starving family but who gets caught and is sent to jail. The film ends with documentary footage of the 1934 Hunger March, indicating the action that unemployed workers needed to take in an effort to resolve the problems dramatised in the film.

A similar tactic was used by Ralph Bond in his own *Advance Democracy*! (1938). This eighteen-minute film was sponsored by the Co-operative Society, enabling Bond to give the film slightly higher production values and to make use of sound (*Bread* had been silent). After a narrative exposition dramatising the politicisation of a dockyard worker, drama and documentary come together when the worker is seen participating in the actual May Day celebrations of 1938 (the addition of 'The Red Flag' and other labour movement anthems on the soundtrack bringing the film to a rousing finale).

Perhaps the most radical and impressive film of the movement was *Hell Unlimited* (1936), a fifteen-minute film made by two students at the Glasgow School of Art, Helen Biggar and Norman McLaren, both members of the Communist Party. The conjunction of radical politics and an art school aesthetic resulted in a dynamic film combining stills, animation, graphics, documentary and dramatised footage in an energetic montage. This produces an ambitious political analysis of the factors leading up to the First World War, identifying who profited from it and at whose expense, before addressing itself to the contemporary situation. The film concludes with a section indicating what action needs to be taken to avert another world war in a series of steps culminating with the mass withdrawal of labour.

These examples give some indication of the range of films being produced, on very meagre resources, on the left of the political spectrum in the 1930s. In terms of representation these films (about a hundred or so altogether) constitute a body of work offering alternative class identities to those on offer to working-class audiences within the mainstream commercial cinema of the time. They also offer a radical politics which was simply not in evidence elsewhere. But the effectiveness of these films must be qualified by their restricted availability. They were certainly not seen by the mass of the cinema-going audience in the 1930s and their exhibition was limited to the alternative network based around the established organisations of the labour movement. The documentaries and occasional dramas produced by these workers' film groups constitute the oppositional film culture of the time, an alternative, if marginalised, network of production, distribution and exhibition which offers further evidence of the diversity of British film culture in the period.[13]

NOTIONS OF 'INDEPENDENCE' IN BRITISH CINEMA

Consideration of an 'oppositional' film culture in the 1930s returns us to the question of 'what is a British film?' We now approach this from a different ideological angle, one where we need to ask not 'what makes a film British?', but 'what kind of British film is it?' and 'what does it tell us about British society and British culture?' Clearly, in the 1930s, British cinema comprised a range of different film-making activities for a heterogeneous audience, an audience which was divided by class, culture and politics. On the one hand, there existed a dominant cinema and a dominant culture; on the other, there was an independent cinema and a subordinate working-class culture.

These notions of 'dominance' and 'independence' require some elaboration however before we proceed to consider further aspects of representation in British cinema. The notion of 'independence', in particular, is problematic because of the difficulty of establishing how a cinema, or a film, *can* be 'independent', and what that cinema, or film, is independent of. It also invites the question of how we recognise an independent film, what are its defining characteristics?

The Women's Companion To International Film provides a useful definition which we can take as a starting-point. Here, Sylvia Harvey describes independent cinema as

> the forms of cinema that exist outside of a popular or commercial mainstream film industry. Independent films are usually characterized by a rejection of the aesthetic or ideological norms of the dominant industry, and independent cinema is generally thought of as a marginalized, alternative or oppositional cinema within capitalist societies, fighting for a voice in relation to more economically and socially powerful forms of communication.
>
> (Kuhn 1990: 215)

This definition would exclude both types of popular entertainment film we have been discussing from the 1930s, the highbrow films of Korda and the lowbrow films of Gracie Fields, because they were both, in their different ways, popular, and were both produced within the context of the commercial film industry, albeit at different ends of the scale in financial (as well as cultural) terms. Even though it is possible to argue that the films of Gracie Fields were made independently of American finance by a British production company, this would not make the films 'independent' according to the definition given above because they could not really be said to be rejecting the aesthetic or even the ideological norms of the dominant industry. Rather they were films made within the structures of the commercial cinema to entertain an audience and with a view to making a profit at the box office. This would have been the primary concern of the production company, rather than the ideological objective of questioning the subordination of the working class in a capitalist society at a time of mass unemployment.[14] Furthermore, the films of Fields, Formby and others did attract large audiences and can hardly be described as 'marginalised' or 'alternative' in an institutional sense, even though they may be described as providing a popular alternative to the highbrow films of Korda *et al*.

When we turn to the documentary cinema of the 1930s the films we have been considering fall more readily into the category of 'independent' in both institutional and aesthetic terms; institutionally because they were made and exhibited outside the structures of the mainstream, commercial film industry, and aesthetically because they reject, in different ways, the classic narrative structure and 'entertainment' ethos of the popular mainstream cinema. We need, however, to distinguish between the dominant Griersonian tradition and the subordinate tradition of the workers' film societies. As we have already seen, the fact that the Grierson documentaries were financed by various state organisations immediately raises questions about their ideological independence, even though many of the films can still be described as 'alternative' on the level of aesthetics.

It is the workers' films which conform most fully to the definition of independent cinema given above. Not only did the workers' film groups operate outside the institutional structures of the mainstream commercial cinema, but they also constituted an ideological alternative to the dominant culture of the time, and were oppositional in a political sense, in a way that the EMB and GPO documentaries were not. It is the workers' films of the 1930s that most completely fulfil the criteria of 'independence' in the sense of 'fighting for a voice in relation to more economically and socially powerful forms of communication'.

It is for this reason that independent film-makers and film theorists in the 1970s were interested in looking back and recovering a 'lost' tradition of oppositional film-making, represented by the workers' film groups of the 1930s, a tradition which had been neglected or ignored altogether in mainstream histories of British cinema in the intervening period. Although it is possible to talk about 'mainstream' independent film production in Britain, in the sense of production companies being independent of the major studios, companies or conglomerates (usually American) which control film production, distribution and exhibition worldwide (and which therefore constitute the 'dominant' cinema), 'independence' by this definition does not have the *oppositional* connotations which are at the heart of the definition of independent cinema given by Sylvia Harvey above.

By this definition, as Harvey goes on to discuss, independent cinema constitutes a movement which emerged in the late 1960s, and which 'developed in conjunction with movements for social emancipation' (Kuhn 1990: 215). These oppositional movements (the Campaign for Nuclear Disarmament, the campaign against the war in Vietnam, the women's liberation movement, gay liberation and other civil rights campaigns) were all a response to a breakdown in the social-democratic consensus which had existed in Britain since the capitalist boom of the 1950s had ushered in a period of affluence and improved lifestyles for all social classes. This consensus, which had been presided over by successive Conservative and Labour governments in the postwar period, was eroded during the 1960s, coming to a head in a series of confrontations between students (largely, but not entirely) and police in 1968, in protests against the Vietnam War. These confrontations, an expression of a growing discontent with the ruling order, were followed, in Britain, by a decade of industrial disputes in the 1970s as the capitalist boom of the 1950s collapsed and recession set in. In these circumstances it is not surprising that the oppositional groups that formed part of the new independent cinema in the 1960s and 1970s should look back to an earlier period of oppositional film-making which had emerged in response to a similar capitalist crisis in the 1930s.[15]

It would be wrong, however, to give the impression that the independent cinema which emerged in the late 1960s was born entirely out of, and because of, these circumstances. Even before these political events gave impetus to an oppositional independent cinema there had been moves towards developing an alternative to the mainstream cinema, based upon the example of the 'New American Cinema' of the 1950s and 1960s. This tradition was allied to an avant-garde movement in the arts which was concerned with formal experimentation and modernist aesthetics. It was also intent upon developing alternative structures of production, distribution and exhibition, based upon the 'co-operative' workshop model. In fact, the beginnings of the modern independent cinema movement in Britain can perhaps be dated from the foundation of the London Film-makers' Co-op in 1966 as a centre for film production and exhibition. The development of alternative structures and spaces for making, viewing and discussing films, outside of the established commercial cinema, was central to both the 'aesthetic' and the 'political' wings of the independent sector:

The aspirations, and the political and aesthetic interests of the members of the London Film-makers' Cooperative were in many respects quite different from those of the other production groups discussed above [that is, the 'political' film-making groups such as Cinema Action, the Berwick Street Collective, Amber Films, the London Womens' Film Group and others]. But they did hold in common the project of developing different modes of production, and of achieving a qualitatively different relationship with their audiences. Both the Co-op and the other groups sought, whether through formal and aesthetic means or through political radicalism, to transform the existing practices of cinema, from the point of production, through the processes of distribution and exhibition, to the point of viewing or 'consumption'.

(Blanchard and Harvey 1983: 232)

In the late 1970s members of the independent sector were very active in campaigning for the fourth television channel as an outlet for independent film and video. Although the 'radical' nature of Channel 4 was watered down by the Conservative government that oversaw its introduction, the new channel did, for much of the 1980s, provide a source of finance and an exhibition outlet for film and video work from the independent sector and a wider audience than independent film-makers could ever hope to reach through cinema screenings alone.[16]

This necessarily brief detour through the history and nature of independent cinema in Britain is relevant to our discussion of the ways in which British films represent the nation because independent films, as a consequence of their very 'independence' from the commercial imperatives and constraints of the mainstream film industry, are able to produce different kinds of representations to those produced by the dominant cinema. It is in the independent sector, therefore, that we must look for *different* images of class, gender, sexuality, race, regional and national identity, images that are perhaps not to be found in the mainstream cinema, or which are relatively free of the negative stereotyping that often occurs when the subordinate groups within our society are portrayed in mainstream films.

BRITISH CINEMA IN THE 1980S

While there are a number of moments in British cinema between the 1930s and the 1990s that we could scrutinise for representations of class, gender, race and other identities, the 1980s offer the possibility of considering the representation of different social groups in a range of different types of film, which is comparable to that found in the 1930s. Furthermore, the period offers the opportunity to consider British cinema at a time when the mainstream cinema was struggling to survive in the shadow of a dominant American cinema, and in the absence of government support, and when Channel 4 emerged as a new force to give impetus to the production of different kinds of independent film. Finally, the social context is one which is not dissimilar to that of the 1930s, with high unemployment resulting from a period of recession, and the monetarist policies of a reactionary Conservative government causing a widening of class divisions and the erosion of social and democratic advances made in the postwar period.

Let us begin with what is really the dominant British cinema of the decade, comparable in many ways to the dominant cinema of Alexander Korda in the 1930s: the cycle of nostalgic costume dramas, including *Chariots of Fire* (1981), *A Passage to India* (1985) and *A Room With a View* (1986), invariably looking back to an earlier moment in British history when Britain was still 'Great' (that is, an imperial power possessing an empire).

• Plate 10.9 *Chariots of Fire* (UK 1981)
Representing the nation

This genre of film-making bears the iconographic hallmarks of 'art cinema' perhaps more than a populist commercial cinema (although many of these films have been very successful at the box office) and has more recently been characterised as 'heritage' cinema:

> The heritage cycle and its particular representation of the national past is in many ways symptomatic of cultural developments in Thatcherite Britain. The Thatcher years, of course, coincided with an international capitalist recession that accelerated Britain's decline as a world economic power, but that also saw a growth of multinational enterprises, including the European Community. Inevitably, these processes disturbed traditional notions of national identity, which were further upset by the recognition that British society was increasingly multiracial and multicultural.
>
> (Higson 1993: 109)

The success of *Chariots of Fire* at the 1982 Academy Awards, where it won four awards including the Oscar for Best Picture, brought forth premature claims of a renaissance in British cinema in the early 1980s. This, despite the fact that the film was financed by a combination of American and Egyptian money, and was clearly targeted at an American market as much as a British one – producer David Puttnam being a figure very much in the Alexander Korda mould. There are other similarities between this film and those of Korda, similarities which can be seen in most of the films that fall into this category of heritage cinema: the nostalgic celebration of a moment in British history when Britain still had an empire and was still a world power, a preoccupation with the culture and values of the upper echelons of society and the adoption of high production values in the representation of the period detail and costumes.

Chariots of Fire offers scope for considering a number of aspects of representation:

- representations of *class* – with its portrayal of the British upper-class Establishment contrasting with both the lower-class status of Harold Abrahams and his trainer Sam Massabini and the 'classless' American athletes over whom the British athletes triumph in the 1924 Olympics;
- representations of *gender* – in particular, the emphasis upon masculinity in the display of the athletic male body and the aggressive competition between the athletes;[17]
- representations of *race* – the identities of Abrahams as a Jew of Lithuanian extraction, his Italian–Arab trainer Massabini and the Scottish missionary Eric Liddell all provide potential for religious and racial tension and conflicts which are exploited for their narrative and dramatic potential in the film;
- representations of *sexuality* – the goal of the film to achieve a successful patriarchal resolution involving different kinds of sexual repression: 'not only of women and female desire, but also of male homosexual desire' (Neale 1982: 52);
- representations of *regional identity* – where the introduction and placing of Liddell as Scottish offers a contrast to the 'Englishness' of which we are constantly reminded throughout the film, from the settings to the frequent renditions of Gilbert and Sullivan.

All of these contribute to the representation and construction of *national identity* in the film, providing a good example of how national identity is constituted largely through the combined and interdependent identities of class, gender, race, sexuality and regional identity.

But perhaps the most important factor in this construction of national identity was that the film's release coincided with the outbreak of the Falklands War, an event which was as much an attempt on the behalf of Margaret Thatcher to resurrect the imperial past of 'Great' Britain as it was to protect a British colony from invasion. This historical coincidence gave *Chariots of Fire* a jingoistic resonance – especially in such details as the newspaper headline 'Our boys are back' which greets the Olympic team on their return to England. It is a meaning that was somewhat at odds with the intended message, for the film invites identification with Abrahams and Liddell as anti-Establishment figures and is implicitly critical of the archaic values of the ruling classes. This historical coincidence does, however, illustrate how the meaning of a film is determined, to a large extent, by the circumstances of its consumption, and emphasises the importance of taking into consideration the three contexts indicated earlier in this chapter (p. 297) when reading a film: the circumstances of the different historical moments at which the film is set, produced and consumed. In the case of *Chariots of Fire* the film is set in the early 1920s, produced in 1980/81 – before the outbreak of the Falklands War – whereas its reception (and Academy Awards) coincided with the Falklands War (which broke out in the spring of 1982).

Furthermore, the film has a different ideological resonance when viewed today, looking back upon the legacy of Thatcherism which was in its early days when the film was produced and released. With its emphasis upon the individual enterprise and ambition of Harold Abrahams, who is seen to represent the future whereas the bigoted attitudes of his Cambridge professors represent the values of the past, the film can be seen to be fully in tandem with the ideology of individualism and enterprise central to Margaret Thatcher's Conservative government:

> *Chariots of Fire* remains overtly critical of an England built on rigid class demar-
> cations and aristocratic hauteur, but in its stead it implicitly endorses the Thatcherite
> ethos of a nation based on a meritocracy of the ambitious, the diligent and the
> gifted. In the film's vision, the Establishment's values begin to shift, becoming more
> tolerant of individual difference and comprehending that the future no longer rests
> solely within their control. But the film's idea of a more dynamic, diverse nation, one
> where a man like Abrahams has the chance to succeed, is depicted with as much
> uncritical sentimentality as the Cambridge masters treat their own hierarchical and
> racist vision of Britain. It's a fitting message for a Thatcher-ruled England where the
> traditional class lines give way to individual achievement, usually defined in terms of
> wealth and status.
>
> (Quart 1993: 25–7)

REDEFINING NATIONAL IDENTITY

A British film from the mid-1980s which gives a different perspective on Thatcherism is *My Beautiful Laundrette* (1985), written by a young Asian, Hanif Kureishi, and directed by Stephen Frears. Financed entirely by Channel 4, the film is an example of one kind of independent film production in the 1980s. It is not one that conforms fully to the criteria for independence given by Sylvia Harvey, in terms of a rejection of the aesthetic norms of the dominant industry (the film tells a story in more or less classic narrative fashion), but which does reject the ideological norms of the dominant cinema with its narrative of a young Asian man who opens and manages a laundrette with the assistance of his white, male lover. *My Beautiful Laundrette* was an 'ironic salutation to the entre-preneurial spirit' (Barber 1993: 221) championed by Margaret Thatcher in the 1980s, ironic because the entrepreneurs here are an extended Pakistani family who have taken the Thatcherite ideology to heart and turned the tables on the old colonial order. Thus it is Omar, the young Asian, who employs Johnny (played by Daniel Day-Lewis) to work in his laundrette, while Johnny's white, racist peers wander the streets outside: the new disenfranchised underclass of Thatcher's Britain. Ironic also in portraying a gay relation-ship between Omar and Johnny at a time when the Conservative government was introducing legislation designed to prevent local authorities from 'promoting' homo-sexuality, thus effectively banning all representations which might be seen to be offering gay and lesbian relationships as a viable alternative to the heterosexual nuclear family. The unexpected success of the film at the box office demonstrated the extent to which audiences were not in agreement with such attempts to turn the clock back to a pre-'permissive' age, an age of prejudice, homophobia and repression.

My Beautiful Laundrette ends with the entrepreneurial dreams of the Pakistani com-munity apparently in ruins, relationships (except for that of Omar and Johnny) broken up and a bloody conflict between the white and Asian communities, with Johnny reluc-tantly taking the side of Omar's family against his old mates. The film ends with a series of question marks about the future – questions to which there are no easy answers – and the audience is invited to ask the same questions, and, by implication, to see them-selves as partly responsible for finding a solution to the problems highlighted in the film.

As with *Chariots of Fire*, *My Beautiful Laundrette* offers scope for considering a number

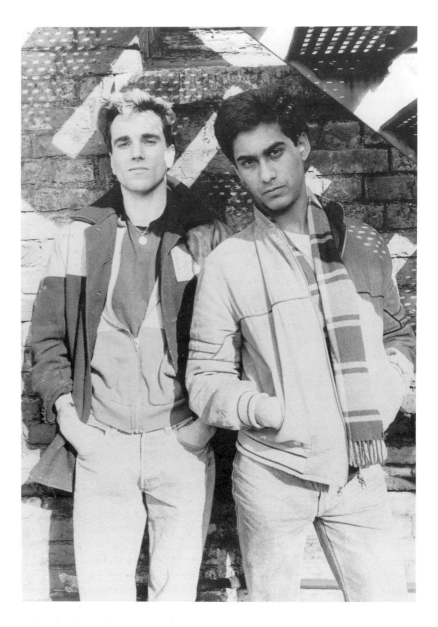

• Plate 10.10 *My Beautiful Laundrette* (UK 1985)
Representing the nation . . . differently

of aspects of representation, with race and sexuality foremost. But again these different aspects of representation come together to inform the construction of an image of national identity which is in ironic contrast to that constructed in other films of the time, films like *Chariots of Fire*, *A Passage to India* and *A Room With a View*, where it is Britain's colonial and imperial heritage that is foregrounded, and ultimately celebrated, because of the 'nostalgic gaze' (Higson 1993: 109) which the films invite (in spite of 'the ironies and social critiques' which may be evident in them). As a made for television film which had a very successful cinema release, *My Beautiful Laundrette* is representative of the real renaissance in British cinema in the 1980s, not the one promised by the success of *Chariots of Fire* at the Academy Awards, but the emergence of a body of low-budget indigenous film-making dealing with the contradictions, conflicts and concerns of contemporary British society, rather than the celebration of an imperial Britain which no longer exists.[18]

Another film that deals with questions of race and national identity in the 1980s is *Handsworth Songs* (1986), made by the Black Audio Film Collective and an example of a film which is firmly in the tradition of the new independent cinema. BAFC was one of a number of film workshops which were set up in the early 1980s, around the time that Channel 4 was nurturing an independent sector which could provide it with material. Film workshops had been set up during the 1970s, following the example of the London Film-makers Co-op, but the arrival of Channel 4 gave new impetus to the sector. This was enhanced by the signing of an agreement, the Workshop Declaration, between the Association of Cinematograph, Television and Allied Technicians (ACTT), Channel 4, the Independent Film-makers Association, the British Film Institute and Regional Arts Associations:

> The Declaration gave accreditation or 'franchise' to those production-based, non-profit-distributing workshops which employed a minimum of four full-time workers and which were also involved in a range of other 'cultural' activities, including distribution, education and exhibition of their own and/or others' work. By recognising the special financial and cultural practices of film and video workshops, the Declaration enabled production (at comparatively low cost) from original and often radical perspectives to reach national as well as regional and local audiences via television – in particular, Channel 4's 'Eleventh Hour' and 'People To People' slots.
>
> *(BFI Film and Television Yearbook* 1988–9: 348)

Where *My Beautiful Laundrette* had been commissioned by Film Four International, on a budget of £650,000, with a view to being screened in the 10 p.m. 'Film On Four' slot on Channel 4, *Handsworth Songs* was made for just £11,000 and was shown in the late-night 'Eleventh Hour' slot. Nevertheless, even a late-night screening on Channel 4 could enable a film like *Handsworth Songs* to reach a much larger audience than it was ever likely to reach from workshop and independent cinema screenings alone, and the film has had an influence, on other film-makers as well as on audiences, which cannot be calculated in terms of viewing figures. With its montage-style approach and mixture of different filmic discourses and modes of address the film departs significantly from the conventional narrative strategy of a more 'mainstream' independent film like *My Beautiful Laundrette*. It thus conforms fully to Sylvia Harvey's definition of an independent film in terms of aesthetics, ideology and its 'oppositional' nature:

> Variously described as a 'documentary' and a 'film essay' on race and civil disorder in Britain today, *Handsworth Songs*, as its title suggests, in fact owes more to poetic structures than to didactic exposition. Familiar TV and newspaper reportage is juxtaposed with opaque, elusive imagery, newsreel and archive material is reworked, and

sound is pitted against image to release a multitude of unanswered questions about the underlying causes of 'racial unrest'. The result is a powerful combination of anger and analysis, of lyricism and political strategy, elegy and excavation.

(Cook 1987: 77)

Like *My Beautiful Laundrette*, *Handsworth Songs* offers no resolution, no easy answers to the problems of racial integration and discrimination which it presents. Like *Laundrette*, but far more so, it offers a space for reflection and critical engagement with the issues of politics, representation and identity which the film analyses. But, as Pam Cook points out in her *Monthly Film Bulletin* review, the film is not didactic, its combination of lyrical sounds and images with archive footage and documentary direct address is both contemplative and provocative.

The film adopts a strategy of combining historical archive footage with poetic voice-overs which construct a lament for what the past had promised for immigrant communities. This material is contrasted with the reality for ethnic communities in 1980s Britain, a reality seen in the aftermath of riots in Brixton, Birmingham and Tottenham. This reality is also seen in the juxtaposition of Margaret Thatcher speaking on television about the 'fear of being swamped' by ethnic minorities, juxtaposed with slow-motion footage of a young black man being literally 'swamped' by police who overpower him as he runs down a street trying to evade them. This particular juxtaposition of images, of different discourses, illustrates well the dialectical strategy of creating a new meaning out of two different elements, showing how the film-makers have learnt from previous traditions of 'oppositional' film-making, from Eisenstein to the counter-cinema of Jean-Luc Godard. What is the 'truth' of the situation? Is it really the case that 'people are really rather afraid that this country might be swamped by people of a different culture' as Margaret Thatcher says in the TV interview? Or is the 'truth' that of the young black man as he is 'swamped' by an intimidating police presence on the street? The aesthetic and ideological strategies of *Handsworth Songs*, utilising but going beyond the dialectical strategies of previous oppositional cinema, indicate a determination to find new ways of addressing the problems of black communities in the 1980s. As John Akomfrah wrote in a manifesto for the Black Audio Film Collective in 1983, they were conscious of a need to evaluate the

> available techniques within the independent tradition and to assess their pertinence for black cinema. In this respect our interest did not only lie in devising how best to make 'political' films, but also in taking the politics of representation seriously.
>
> (cited in Diawara 1993: 151)

And as Manthia Diawara observes:

> By adding the dimension of the 'politics of representation' to their agenda, Black Audio problematized the whole notion of black people's 'relation to images'. They demonstrated that the issue of representation was not resolved by simply shifting from negative images to positive images. Positive images, they believed, were as embedded in stereotypes as negative images, and only a politics of representation could account for the filmmaker's relation to the images that he or she arranged on the screen.
>
> (1993: 151)

• Plate 10.11 *I'm British But . . .* (UK 1989)
Redefining national identity

These quotes draw attention to the importance given to theory in the independent cinema
of the 1970s and 1980s. Making 'political' films for many film-makers was simply not
enough; it was equally important to understand what sense audiences made of them,
which required a theoretical engagement with questions of representation and stereotyping, with the development of new strategies for addressing the audience. In some
cases this resulted in the production of films which were deliberately challenging, often
too challenging for audiences, who sometimes found the level of engagement with a
'politics of representation' impenetrable.

While *Handsworth Songs* is challenging, providing no straightforward narrative and no
easy solutions, it cannot be said to be impenetrable. Instead it offers pleasures as well

as analysis and attempts to engage the audience on a number of different levels and in a number of different ways: being about black British history and oppression, but at the same time about the *representation* of this history and this oppression, both in the media and in the film itself.

A more 'orthodox' black British independent film, but one which foregrounds questions of race, regional and national identity in an equally intriguing manner, is *I'm British But . . .* (1989), a thirty-minute documentary directed by Gurinder Chada, who went on to direct the feature film *Bhaji on the Beach* (1993). *I'm British But . . .* like *My Beautiful Laundrette* and *Handsworth Songs*, investigates the **diaspora** by focusing on four British Asians, the sons and daughters of Asian immigrants who settled in the four countries of the United Kingdom. In doing so it offers an interesting new dimension on representations of race, regional and national identity, for the four Asian Brits express their feelings about being British, but of Asian descent, in dialects that are unmistakably English, Welsh, Scottish and Irish.

This problematises not only the question of racial identity, but also, with its emphasis upon the regional identity of these four Asians, the question of national identity. As one of the interviewees says, for her, 'nationality is an outdated concept', and they all see themselves as 'British' rather than Asian, and, more specifically, as English, Welsh, Scottish and Irish Asians, rather than simply as 'British Asians' or 'Asian Brits'. Furthermore, they talk about their relationship to both British culture and Asian culture and the film explores the ways in which, for diasporic cultures, British culture is a hybrid of different cultures: British, Asian, African, etc.

What emerges in *I'm British But . . .*, as it does also in *My Beautiful Laundrette* and *Handsworth Songs*, is the notion of diasporic culture and identity as what Manthia Diawara describes as a 'third space': 'By third space I mean the familiar notion of hybrid spaces that combine the colors and flavours of different localities, and yet declare their specificity from each of these localities' (1993: 157). British national identity, in this context, is defined as unequivocally multiracial and multicultural. Films like *My Beautiful Laundrette, Handsworth Songs* and *I'm British But . . .* can be seen to be participating in a process of redefining 'outdated' notions of nationality and national identity, and they offer invaluable material for engaging with, debating and helping to change these outdated notions.

diaspora

the dispersal of ethnic communities around the world.

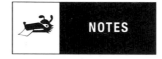

NOTES

1   Source of financial information is *BFI Film and Television Handbook 1993*. Published annually this is an indispensable reference book for information on British film production, distribution and exhibition.

2   For further reading on the concept of National Cinema see McIntyre 1985; and Higson 1989 and 1995. For more on the cinemas of Scotland, Ireland and Wales see McArthur 1982; Rockett, Hill and Gibbons 1987; Hill, McLoone and Hainsworth 1994; and Berry 1994.

3   For further reading on ideology and hegemony see the relevant sections in Williams 1976; O'Sullivan *et al.* 1994; Cormack 1992; Turner 1992; and Storey 1993.

4   For more on stereotyping see Dyer 1979.

5   In *What Do Those Old Films Mean?: History, Cinema, Society – Great Britain 1900–1912*, transmitted on Channel 4 in 1985.

6   Haggar's *Desperate Poaching Affray*, although it does not have the radical resolution of *The Salmon Poachers*, can be found on volume 1 of *Early Cinema: Primitives and Pioneers*, a two volume compilation of early cinema material available from the British Film Institute. The tapes also include *Buy Your Own Cherries* (vol. 1) and *Rescued by Rover* (vol. 2). For further reading on early British cinema see Low and Manvell 1948; Chanan 1980; and Burch 1990.

7   See Wood 1980 and 1986, and the appendix to Curran and Porter 1983 for statistical information on the British film industry. For further reading on British cinema in the 1930s see Richards 1984; Low 1985; and Ryall 1986. For more on unemployment and the social context see Stevenson 1984, especially ch. 10.

8   On the other hand, the statement strikes a chord with those arguments against the cultural hegemony of Hollywood today, especially in relation to the GATT (General Agreement on Tariffs and Trade) talks of 1993 which saw a battle fought out between Europe (and the French film industry in particular) and America over the extent to which European cinema (and European culture) should be protected from the pervasive influence of American culture as manifested in the Hollywood films which dominate the cinema screens of Europe.

9   Financial details come from the chapter on 'Film Finance in the 1930s', in Dickinson and Street 1985: 76–88.

10 It is worth noting that, although he is not credited with the direction of *The Scarlet Pimpernel*, Alexander Korda did direct much of the film after he removed the American director Rowland Brown from the picture for making it 'too grim and gory' (Richards 1984: 236). The film was completed by Harold Young who received sole directorial credit.

11 For more on the films of Gracie Fields and George Formby see Richards 1984 (chs 10 and 11) who also considers the careers of more 'middle-class' stars such as Jessie Matthews, Robert Donat and Leslie Howard. Richards, like Aldgate 1983, argues, however, that these films contributed to re-inforcing the status quo in the 1930s by promoting a consensual politics, an argument which both Aldgate and Richards put forward in relation to what is probably Fields' best known film, *Sing As We Go* (1934), and with detailed reference to the 'political' role of the British Board of Film Censors in the 1930s.

12 See Colls and Dodd 1985 for an interesting discussion of the ideological role of the Griersonian documentary from 1930–45.

13 For further reading on the workers' film movement of the 1930s see Ryan 1983; Hogenkamp 1986; Jones 1987; and Macpherson 1980.

14 Had such a project been undertaken it would almost certainly not have got past the censors at the time. See Jeffrey Richards' account of the censorship of *Love on the Dole* in the 1930s (Richards 1984: 119–20)

15 For further reading on the postwar social/historical context see Marwick 1990.

16 For further reading on independent cinema see Stoneman and Thompson 1981; Ellis 1982; Harvey 1982; Blanchard and Harvey 1983; Whitaker 1985; Harvey 1986; and Lant 1993.

17 For Steve Neale, masculinity is 'the determining focus around which race, religion, class and nationality are themselves articulated and defined' in *Chariots of Fire* (1982: 47–8).

18 For more on British cinema in the 1980s see Friedman 1993, which contains a useful, if uneven, collection of essays covering a number of aspects of British cinema in the period.

FURTHER WORK

This chapter has only been able to touch on certain aspects of how British cinema represents the nation. The intention has been to provide a framework for exploring representations of class, race and other identities, and to demonstrate this by looking at how a range of different films have represented the nation at three different moments: the early years, pre-1910, when British cinema was still in its infancy, the 1930s, and the 1980s. The same approach could be used for a number of other moments in the history of British cinema: the Second World War is a particularly rich period for exploring representations of class, gender and national identity; the period from 1956–63, with its preoccupation with notions of social realism, offers scope for exploring a number of aspects of representation, especially class, gender, race, sexuality and regional identity; while the 1960s offers the opportunity of a different perspective on all of these, plus national identity too, in films as different as the James Bond series and the *Carry On*'s. A comparative analysis of films made in different periods would be equally rewarding, as this would enable historical changes to be taken into consideration in the representation of particular social groups or identities.

I have tried to emphasise the importance of situating the analysis of specific films within their social, cultural and institutional contexts and of taking into consideration the different circumstances of the production and reception of the films. The extent to which this has been possible here has been limited, but it is hoped that the advantages of doing this have been demonstrated.

Finally, the explosion of critical interest in British cinema in recent years should be acknowledged and the extent to which this chapter has been informed by these writings is indicated in the extensive list of references in the bibliography. A short list of further reading and viewing is given below.

FURTHER READING

Barr, Charles (ed.), *All Our Yesterdays*, London: British Film Institute, 1986.

—— *Typically British*, London: British Film Institute, 1996.

Curran, James and Porter, Vincent (eds), *British Cinema History*, London: Weidenfeld and Nicolson, 1983.

Friedman, Lester (ed.), *British Cinema and Thatcherism*, London: University College London, 1993.

Gledhill, Christine and Swanson, Gillian (eds), *Nationalising Femininity*, Manchester: Manchester University Press, 1996.

Higson, Andrew (ed.), *Dissolving Views: Key Writings on British Cinema*, London: Cassell, 1996.

Hill, John, *Sex, Class and Realism: British Cinema 1956–1963*, London: British Film Institute, 1986.

Landy, Marcia, *British Genres: Cinema and Society, 1930–1960*, Princeton, NJ: Princeton University Press, 1991.

Lant, Antonia, *Blackout: Reinventing Women for Wartime British Cinema*, Princeton NJ: Princeton University Press, 1991.

Murphy, Robert, *Realism and Tinsel: Cinema and Society in Britain 1939–49*, London: Routledge, 1989.

—— *Sixties British Cinema*, London: British Film Institute, 1992.

Park, James, *British Cinema: The Lights That Failed*, London: Batsford, 1990.

Taylor, Philip (ed.), *Britain and the Cinema in the Second World War*, London: Macmillan, 1988.

Young, Lola, *Fear of the Dark: 'Race', Gender and Sexuality in the Cinema*, London: Routledge, 1996.

FURTHER VIEWING

The following chronological list gives a selection of films that can be used for exploring more than one aspect of representation in British cinema.

Sing As We Go (1934): class, gender, regional identity.

Sanders of the River (1935): class, race, national identity.

Pygmalion (1938): class, gender.

Love on the Dole (1941): class, gender, regional identity.

In Which We Serve (1942): class, gender, regional/national identity.

Millions Like Us (1943): class, gender, regional/national identity.

Brief Encounter (1945): class, gender, sexuality.

Room at the Top (1958): class, gender, sexuality, regional identity.

Sapphire (1959): race, sexuality.

Saturday Night and Sunday Morning (1960): class, gender, sexuality, regional identity.

Flame in the Streets (1961): class, gender, race, sexuality.

A Taste of Honey (1961): class, gender, sexuality, regional identity.

Victim (1961): class, sexuality.

Goldfinger (1964): class, gender, race, sexuality, national identity.

Kes (1968): class, regional identity.

Carry On at Your Convenience (1971): class, gender, sexuality.

The Long Good Friday (1979): class, gender, regional/national identity.

Babylon (1980): race, national identity.

Maeve (1981): gender, regional/national identity.

Local Hero (1982): regional/national identity.

The Ploughman's Lunch (1983): class, gender, national identity.

High Hopes (1988): class, gender, national identity.

Young Soul Rebels (1991): race, sexuality, national identity.

Bhaji on the Beach (1993): gender, race, sexuality, national identity.

Chapter 11

The Soviet montage cinema of the 1920s

Mark Joyce

■ The Soviet montage cinema of the 1920s

INTRODUCTION: WHY STUDY THE SOVIET CINEMA?

> As the lights went up at the end an emotion-charged silence reigned, broken only when Lunacharsky [the Soviet Union's Commissar for Education] jumped on his chair and began an enthusiastic speech: 'We've been witnesses at an historic cultural event. A new art has been born. . . .'[1]

Anatoli Lunacharsky's response to Sergei Eisenstein's 1925 film *Battleship Potemkin* acknowledges the importance of a new wave of film-making. The films made by the Soviet directors of the 1920s are considered by many as the most innovative and exciting to have been produced in the history of the cinema. The names of these film-makers, such as Eisenstein, Pudovkin, Vertov and Kuleshov, are far from forgotten and a number of the films and directors from this period consistently score highly in *Sight and Sound*'s critics/directors choice of best ten films and directors.

This decade of intensive experimentation with film-form produced techniques that have subsequently been widely emulated. In addition, the theoretical debates formulated by these film-makers are still relevant today. For these reasons the **Soviet cinema** of the 1920s merits detailed analysis.

HISTORICAL BACKGROUND

The Soviet film-makers of the 1920s reflect the **ideology** (the values and beliefs) and politics of the society in which they were produced. The early 1920s marked the end of a period of civil unrest, the causes of which lay in the great divide that separated wealthy landowning Russians from the peasants and workers.[2] For centuries Russia had been governed by the single figure of the autocratic Tsar who had absolute powers. The Russian serfs were not granted freedom from slavery until 1861; this liberation, however, did not mean improved conditions, as they continued to live an existence of appalling poverty. Attempts had been made prior to the revolution of October 1917 by various factions to undermine the Tsarist regime, all of which were unsuccessful. A wave of revolutionary activity in 1905 included a mutiny by Russian sailors at Odessa which formed the basis for Sergei Eisenstein's 1925 film *Battleship Potemkin*.

The First World War (1914–18) eventually proved to be disastrous for Tsar Nicholas II as it consumed vast amounts of money and resources that were sorely needed at home. It was also unpopular with the Russian people as the reasons for fighting were unclear. The peasants and the workers were the worst hit by the impact of the war, either being killed on the front or starving at home as supplies became depleted. The landowning rich were protected by their wealth and were able to continue in their existing lifestyle.

These conditions provided the catalyst for the revolution of 25 February 1917 which resulted in the formation of a liberal provisional government led by Alexander Kerensky and later supported by Menshevik and Socialist Revolutionary factions. This caused Nicholas II to abdicate on 4 March. The provisional government decided to continue the war, and for many (especially V.I. Lenin who was in hiding in Zurich) it appeared that the new government was in effect continuing the policies of the Tsarist order.

On 25 October 1917 the Bolsheviks, taking advantage of a situation of confusion and competition between the various factions, seized power by storming the Winter Palace.[3]

Soviet cinema

This will refer to films made in the Soviet Union between October 1920–91, although for the purposes of this chapter most Soviet films discussed will be confined to the 1920s.

ideology

There are two key definitions of this term, one provided by the German nineteenth-century philosopher Karl Marx, the other by the French twentieth-century Marxist philosopher Louis Althusser, drawing upon Marx's original ideas.

For Marx, ideology was the dominant set of beliefs and values, existent within society, which sustained power relations. For Althusser, ideology was the representations and images which reflect society's view of 'reality'. Ideology thus refers to 'the myths that a society lives by'.

The new Bolshevik government agreed to Germany's demands for control of areas of land previously under Russian administration, and pulled out of the war. Almost immediately, however, a fierce civil war broke out between the Bolsheviks (known as the Reds) and those still loyal to the Tsarist regime (known as the Whites).[4]

By 1920 it was clear that the Bolsheviks had seized ultimate control of the country. The new Soviet government under the leadership of V.I. Lenin was faced with the task of convincing the population of Russia of the evils of the Tsarist regime and the positive points of the new Communist one.

Selected historical dates

1905, Jan.	First revolution (abortive)
	Provides the backdrop for Eisenstein's *Battleship Potemkin*
1914, July	General strike organised by the Bolsheviks
	Outbreak of war and the crushing of the political unrest
	The war was a general disaster for the Russians; low morale and food shortages in the following years led to uprisings in 1917
1917, Feb.	Popular uprisings culminating in the overthrow of the Tsar, and the setting up of a provisional government
1917, Oct.	The Bolsheviks overthrow the provisional government and seize political power
1918–21	Civil war between White and Red factions, as well as fighting of hostile troops sent from abroad in an attempt to restore the power of the Tsar. The continued fighting led to the destruction of trade, agriculture, industry and film production
1922–8	NEP (New Economic Policy) adopted by Lenin. A brief return to controlled forms of capitalism to help to rebuild the shattered economy
1922–3	Soviet feature film production resumes
1924	Sergei Eisenstein's *Strike* completed
1927	The tenth anniversary of the October Revolution. A number of films are made to mark the occasion including:
	October (Eisenstein)
	The End of St. Petersburg (Vsevolod Pudovkin)
	The Fall of the Romanov Dynasty (Esfir Shub)

PRE-REVOLUTIONARY RUSSIAN CINEMA

The nature of the Russian cinema

When discussing the Soviet cinema it is important to have at least an outline of the form and content of its antecedent, for although the majority of the Soviet directors had not made films prior to 1919 they would certainly have been familiar with the

Russian cinema

This will refer to the body of films
made in Tsarist Russia between
1907 and 1919.

mise-en-scène

This literally means 'placed in the
scene' and it includes all elements
that are placed before the camera
such as props, actors, costume,
movement and position of actors,
etc.

montage

Montage comes from the French
word meaning to edit; it means the
assembling of bits of footage to
form a whole. In Film Studies it
usually refers to the style of fast
editing adopted by the Soviet film-
makers of the 1920s.

conventions of the pre-revolutionary cinema. Significantly, for a number of the Soviet directors, this cinema was the antithesis of their new approach to film-making. The **Russian cinema** 1907–17 was in fact markedly different from the Soviet cinema of the 1920s. The majority of the films that are available for viewing today[5] are between thirty-five and seventy minutes long and deal predominantly with the lives of the upper classes, quite frequently centring on their relationship with servants and/or the working class. Their subject-matter, plot and preoccupations are often melodramatic; unfaithful husbands and wives, psychological states of mind and death predominate. The form of the films is also different, comprising slow-moving scenes containing a limited number of shots, with an emphasis on the **mise-en-scène** and in particular the expressions of the actors. A key director working in this period is Evgeny Bauer, who produced a large number of films including *After Death* (1915), *A Life for a Life* (1916) and *The King of Paris* (1917).[6]

The Russian Revolution of October 1917 and the civil war that followed had a devastating effect on the Russian film industry, which was almost completely destroyed. Very few of the Russian directors and stars remained in Russia after 1919, the majority having fled to Paris where they continued production.[7] Initially it would seem that the Russian cinema had little in common with the Soviet cinema that followed, and there appears to have been a clear break in terms of style between the two cinemas after the revolution. The figure of Yakov Protazanov, however, provides an interesting example of a film-maker who made films between 1911–43.[8] His key films from the pre-revolutionary era include, *The Queen of Spades* (1916) and *Satan Triumphant* (1917); these all conform to the conventions of the Russian cinema outlined earlier. His best-known film of the 1920s is *Aelita* (1924), a fantasy concerning a revolution on Mars. Protazanov was more concerned with mise-en-scène than with creating new meanings by juxtaposing images. A study of his films reveals that the Tsarist cinema continued into the Soviet **montage** era and was by all accounts successful with the public.[9]

Russian cinema audiences and imported films

That Russian films had moderate success with native audiences is not surprising. What is significant, however, is that before the revolution the most popular films with Russian audiences were imported from America, France and Germany. The first Russian film studio was not set up until 1907[10] and this can partly account for the success of these foreign films as audiences had grown accustomed to watching them. In the 1910s when native films vied for audiences with imported films, foreign ones were clearly the more successful and were perceived by Russian audiences as being more entertaining and having higher production values than Russian films.

SOVIET CINEMA AND IDEOLOGY: FILM AS AGENT OF CHANGE[11]

The October revolution was the first successful revolution made in the name of Karl Marx (1818–83). For Marx, the key fact about any society was how it produced its livelihood. He saw capitalism as an economic system, which, just like every other previous economic system, was based on exploitation. In capitalism the class with power was the bourgeoisie, the owners of the means of production, and the class subject to their power was the proletariat or working class. In addition, the bourgeoisie's economic strength was protected by the state and sustained by ideology. However, as capitalism developed, the workers, who survived by selling their labour for wages, would be squeezed more and more as competition between capitalists intensified. At the same time they would become aware that they would have everything to gain by replacing an economic system based on the ownership of private property with one based on the non-exploitative communal ownership of productive property. This awareness, or class-consciousness, would eventually produce a revolution. The October Revolution was seen as such a proletarian revolution in Russia and was celebrated as such by the films of the key Soviet film-makers of the 1920s.

The revolution, however, was only the beginning of a process of radical social change, called the era of 'the dictatorship of the proletariat' because it involved the proletariat, or in this case its representatives, the Bolshevik Party, establishing its dominance. V.I. Lenin writing in *Pravda* outlined the situation:

> Theoretically, there can be no doubt that between capitalism and communism there lies a definite transition period which must combine the features and properties of both these forms of social economy. This transition period has to be a period of struggle between dying capitalism and nascent communism – or, in other words, between capitalism which has been defeated but not destroyed and communism which has been born but is still very feeble.[12]

The transition to communism referred to by Lenin would have been a monumental task at the best of times, but the Bolsheviks had seized control of a country whose industry and agriculture were relatively underdeveloped. Also they had to confront internal and external opposition, civil war and famine. In such a situation artists and film-makers were perceived as having a special role as proponents of **propaganda cinema**. Lenin declared in 1922 that 'of all the arts, for us the cinema is the most important'.[13] Prior to this, trains highly decorated with Soviet flags and paintings had been sent into the countryside in an attempt to educate and inform the peasants.[14] Short agitational films called *agitki* were made. Pre-revolutionary newsreels and foreign fiction films were also shown, with a Soviet commentator giving a 'new' reading to the material. Later most of the energy went into the making of new feature films that reflected the ideals of the new regime. Anatoli Lunacharsky (the People's Commissar for Education) had stated in 1924:

propaganda cinema
This is a term used pejoratively with reference to any film that consciously attempts to persuade an audience towards certain beliefs and values.

> There is no doubt that cinema art is a first-class and perhaps even an incomparable instrument for the dissemination of all sorts of ideas. Cinema's strength lies in the fact that, like any art, it imbues an idea with feeling and with captivating form but, unlike the other arts, cinema is actually cheap, portable and unusually graphic. Its effects reach where even the book cannot reach and it is, of course, more powerful than any kind of narrow propaganda. The Russian Revolution, which is extremely interested in exercising the broadest possible influence on the masses, should long since have turned its attention to cinema as its natural instrument.[15]

The enthusiastic, young, educated film-makers, who attempted to fulfil Lunacharsky's ideal of revolutionary cinema, responded by making innovative films, revolutionary both in content and in form.

ECONOMICS OF THE SOVIET FILM INDUSTRY

The pre-revolutionary Russian film industry had previously imported its film stock from abroad, and during the civil war most of the Russian film-makers had fled to White-held areas (or abroad) taking their equipment with them. The reality facing the film-makers of the newly formed state was that there was little in the way of film stock or equipment.[16]

The Soviet government initially attempted to ban the showing of all American and European films, as they were concerned about the public being exposed to films that reflected the values of capitalist societies. The Soviets had little option, however, but to show these films as they had no native film industry to produce their own. The cinema was seen by the new government as a means of keeping the public entertained at a time of hardship and general civil unrest.

From a western perspective it is easy to underestimate the importance of imported films in the Soviet Union in the 1920s. Denise Youngblood (1985: 944–71), in *Movies for the Masses*, states that 'Foreign films accounted for almost two-thirds of the titles screened in the twenties. . . . Nearly as many American as Soviet films were shown in this period'. She continues: 'Sovkino's head, K. M. Shvedchikov, claimed in 1927 that Sovkino would be bankrupt were it not for the success of its import policy.'[17]

The 1920s could be characterised as a period in which American and European narrative films were in effect directly subsidising the dramatic experimentation with film-form undertaken by the Soviet film-makers.

Innovation and experimentation frequently come from a lack. In the Soviet Union the lack of film stock (and even film cameras) meant that certain groups of film-makers worked on re-editing existing films (often European/American films and old Russian newsreels) to make them conform to the values of the Soviet state. Other film-makers experimented with creating films from the small amount of negative available, which often only came in short lengths. Out of this experimentation came Soviet montage cinema.

FORM: MONTAGE

The roots of Soviet montage

The innovative use of montage in film by the Soviet film-makers had its roots in art forms such as painting, literature and music from pre-revolutionary Russia. David Bordwell in 'The Idea of Montage in Soviet Art and Film'[18] states that by 1910 a group of Russian painters had already experimented extensively with 'montage': 'the Russian futurists declared that conventional art must be destroyed and that a new art, appropriate to the machine age, must be created. Hence the Futurists took their subjects from modern life and exploited a technique of shocking juxtapositions.' Poetry too, in particular that of Mayakovsky,[19] was also 'shattering words and reassembling them into brutal images'.

The question needs to be asked: why didn't the Russian film-makers of the 1910s experiment with montage earlier? This lack of explicit montage experiment in the Russian cinema compared to that taking place in other art forms can perhaps be attributed to economics. The crucial difference between film and many of the other arts at the time was that the small groups of experimental artists, writers and musicians were often privately funded by rich patrons. The film industry, however, was not.[20] The revolution of October 1917 provided the right conditions for experimentation with film to take place. It is ironic that this experimentation had its roots in the elitist art forms of pre-revolutionary Russia.

The Kuleshov effect and its consequences

The montage technique is based on the theory that when two pieces of film are placed side by side the audience immediately draws the conclusion that the two shots must be directly related in some way. In other words, the audience try to create meaning by combining the two separate images. The experimentation along these lines by Lev Kuleshov, a young Soviet film-maker, culminated in what became known as the Kuleshov effect. Vsevolod Pudovkin outlined the experiment in a lecture given at the London Film Society in February 1929:[21]

> Kuleshov and I made an interesting experiment. We took from some film or other several close-ups of the well-known Russian actor Mosjukhin. We chose close-ups which were static and which did not express any feeling at all – quiet close-ups. We joined these close-ups, which were all similar, with other bits of film in three different combinations. In the first combination the close-up of Mosjukhin was immediately followed by a shot of a plate of soup standing on a table. It was obvious and certain that Mosjukhin was looking at this soup. In the second combination the face of Mosjukhin was joined to shots showing a coffin in which lay a dead woman. In the third the close-up was followed by a shot of a little girl playing with a funny toy bear. When we showed the three combinations to an audience which had not been let into the secret the result was terrific. The public raved abut the acting of the artist. They pointed out the heavy pensiveness of his mood over the forgotten soup, were touched and moved by the deep sorrow with which he looked on the dead woman, and admired the light, happy smile with which he surveyed the girl at play. But we knew that in all three cases the face was exactly the same.

Kuleshov carried out further experiments using editing in which he cut together separate shots of a walking man, a waiting woman, a gate, a staircase and a mansion.[22] When the shots were combined the audience assumed that the different elements were present at the same location. Kuleshov had discovered the cinema's ability to link entirely unrelated material into coherent sequences. He termed the technique 'creative geography'.

Kuleshov's discoveries about the nature of the cinema medium provided a number of film-makers with a new set of ideas about how film could manipulate and deceive an audience. Perhaps the most vital consequence of the Kuleshov effect, however, for later directors, was its recognition that the audience were not merely passive recipients.

Soviet montage cinema

In the 1920s a number of the film-makers carried out further experiments with editing techniques along the same lines as Kuleshov. It was discovered that when two shots were joined together meaning could be made by emphasising the difference between shots, that is, instead of trying to cover up graphic dissimilarities between shots, as in the **Hollywood cinema**, the difference could be emphasised and indeed become the main way in which meaning could be created. This 'montage' cinema which demanded that audiences continually searched for the meanings created by the **juxtaposition** of two shots can thus be seen as **alternative** to the continuity editing-based Hollywood

Hollywood cinema

In the classical Hollywood cinema the editing is designed to be 'invisible'; it is intended to allow the audience closer views and to see the point of view of different characters. The editing is used essentially to clarify what is taking place in the narrative. This type of editing had become dominant in Hollywood film-making by approximately 1920.

juxtaposition

In Film Studies this usually refers to two different shots that have been joined together to make a contrast.

alternative

Alternative cinema is defined with reference to dominant; it is an alternative (both economically and formally) to the dominant form. In any study concerning an 'alternative' cinema, the films would not only have to be examined in their own right, but also compared to the contemporary dominant Hollywood cinema. A number of questions might have to be posed when analysing these alternative films: in what ways is this group of films different to the dominant cinema at the time?

What are the possible reasons for this difference: cultural? economic? social? political? Could this 'alternative' way of making films have itself turned into the dominant cinema given the right conditions? The Soviet cinema of the 1920s, when compared to the Hollywood cinema of the same time, certainly could be regarded as alternative. In other words it offered a style of film-making that was radically different to the mass of films that were being produced in America.

dialectical

This is difficult term to define, having many different meanings. The Collins English Dictionary (2nd edn, 1986), for example, defines dialectic as 'disputation or debate, esp. intended to resolve differences between two views rather than to establish one of them as true'. The crucial factor to grasp, however, in the context of Eisenstein's thinking is the notion of change and the creation of a new order. Eisenstein would have defined dialectic with reference to Marxist philosophy, which believed that society was contradictory and in need of change.

cinema. One of the Soviet film-makers who developed this idea into both a theory and a practice of film-making was Sergei Eisenstein.

Eisenstein believed that maximum impact could be achieved if shots in a scene were in conflict. This belief was based on the general philosophical idea that 'existence' can only continue by constant change. In other words, everything surrounding us in the world is as a result of a 'collision' of opposite elements. The existing world is itself only in a temporary state until the next collision of elements produces a completely new state. It is only through this 'collision' that change can be effected. This method of creating meaning from such collision of opposites is termed **dialectical**. When applying this idea to film, Eisenstein proposed the view that when two shots are combined a completely new meaning is formed. For example, shot A combined with shot B does not produce AB but the new meaning C. The formulation can also be presented as: thesis + anti-thesis = synthesis.

Vsevolod Pudovkin, another key Soviet film-maker, was opposed to the theoretical ideas of Eisenstein although they both used innovative forms of montage in their films. Pudovkin, like Kuleshov, believed that shots could be likened to bricks in the sense that they could be used as building blocks to construct a scene. Pudovkin then did not see his shots as being in conflict. In Pudovkin's formulae shot A + shot B = **AB** rather than C. Pudovkin aimed at linkage rather than conflict in his scenes.

The montage technique was not only confined to fiction film-making. Soviet documentary film-makers such as Dziga Vertov and Esfir Shub used montage extensively in a range of films in the 1920s including Vertov's well-known *The Man With a Movie Camera*. For Vertov much of the power of cinema came from its ability to mechanically record events that took place before the camera, but he also ensured that the audience was made aware of the constructed nature of his films. His films are a whirlwind of conflicting shots which disavow conventional ideas of narrative.

The montage technique for the majority of the Soviet film-makers could also provide sequences with a sense of rhythm and momentum, which could be used to increase or decrease the speed of the action. Eisenstein, for example, frequently increases his rate of cutting prior to the climax of a scene. Violent actions could also be emphasised by using a succession of short conflicting shots from different viewpoints. Montage, the film-makers discovered, could further be used to either compress or expand time, which could heighten the effect of certain actions or events.

Four different types of film montage[23]

The first two categories of montage outlined below are frequently, although not exclusively, used in Soviet film; the last two categories deal with montage techniques that are often to be found in mainstream films:

- Intellectual montage (also called dialectical montage or discontinuity editing)
- Linkage editing (also known as constructive editing)
- Hollywood montage
- Fast cutting

Intellectual montage

In this type of editing, shots are placed together to emphasise their difference. They are in 'collision' with each other. For example, in *October* a shot of a mechanical golden peacock is placed next to a shot of a man (the peacock does not form part of the world of the film, that is, it is **non-diegetic**). The audience draw the conclusion that the man is vain. In this type of editing the audience are not passive as they play an active part in producing meaning from the film.

Linkage editing

Mainly used by Pudovkin, who proposed a theory of montage based on this principle. In linkage editing individual shots are used to build up scenes. The shots are not in collision with each other, but are used as fragments or parts of a whole scene. The technique can be seen in *The Mother* and *The End of St. Petersburg*.

Hollywood montage

Is often used to show a quick succession of events over a period of time. For example, in *Raging Bull* (1980) Martin Scorsese shows the successful career of the boxer Jack La Motta by combining shots (mostly still photographs) taken from a number of different fights interspersed with home movie footage of La Motta's home life. The shots are clearly intended to flow into each other rather than to be in conflict. The music played on the soundtrack over the images reinforces the sense of continuity.

Fast cutting

In which editing is used primarily to build suspense or tension. For example, in the gunfight at the climax of *The Good, the Bad and the Ugly* (1966), Sergio Leone creates a dramatic effect by using a combination of music, tighter and tighter close-ups of the three characters and a shortening of shot length.

non-diegetic

Refers to any elements that remain outside the world of the film such as voice-overs, credits and mood setting music that does not directly originate from the world of the film.

Statistical analysis of Soviet films

Soviet films, because of the use of the montage technique, contain many more shots than Hollywood films of the same period. David Bordwell[24] claims that the Soviet films of the 1920s contain on average between 600–2,000 shots, whereas the films made in Hollywood between 1917 and 1928 contain on average 500–1,000 shots. He further suggests that Hollywood films had an average shot length of five to six seconds and the Soviet films had an average shot length of two to four seconds. The comparison provides concrete evidence of the unique nature of the editing used in the Soviet films in this period.

OTHER FEATURES OF THE SOVIET MONTAGE CINEMA

Aside from editing, these films have other features which separate them from the **dominant** Hollywood cinema. In keeping with a Marxist analysis of society, plots frequently do not centre on the individual; for example, in Eisenstein's *Strike*, *October* and *Battleship Potemkin*, individual heroes are replaced by a mass of people. The only characters that are individuated are those that wield power or have wealth. Events in the narrative therefore are not motivated by individuals. Films such as Pudovkin's *The Mother* and *The End of St. Petersburg* and Dovzhenko's *Earth* do have central characters, but it is made clear that these characters are representative of the masses. The audience is not interested in the details of the heroes, only what they represent. A number of the Soviet film-makers (including Eisenstein and Pudovkin) also used

dominant

Dominant cinema in Film Studies is assumed to be Hollywood. The term dominant refers both to economic strength and also to the dominant form or convention, which is realism.

non-actors to play key parts, believing that the external appearance of the character was vital to the performance. This idea is termed 'typage'.

The montage style also means that Soviet cinema relies more heavily on the use of the close-up than Hollywood cinema. Not only are there more shots overall in a scene, but a greater proportion of them are close-ups. A number of Soviet films also rely on high levels of **symbolism** to achieve their aims. The audience must be culturally and politically aware to be able to decode the messages that are being presented. In Eisenstein's *October*, for example, great demands are made on the audience to create a 'reading' of the film which does justice to Eisenstein's political thinking. It may seem that many of the film-makers ran the risk of making films that were not understood by their audience.

Several of the montage film-makers combined the montage principle with other techniques that they believed would revitalise the cinema. Lev Kuleshov, for example, placed great emphasis on the gestures and movement of actors. FEKS (Factory of the Eccentric Actor), formed by film-makers Grigori Kozintsev and Leonid Trauberg, had similar concerns about the role of the actor, but also paid great attention to mise-en-scène.

THE KEY SOVIET MONTAGE FILM-MAKERS OF THE 1920S

....

Fiction
Lev Kuleshov

Sergei Eisenstein

Vsevolod Pudovkin

FEKS (Kozintsev and Trauberg)

Alexander Dovzhenko

....

Documentary
Dziga Vertov

Esfir Shub

....

A film directed by Eisenstein probably provided most viewers' first experience of Soviet montage. The history of the Soviet cinema of the 1920s, however, involves more than the work of this one director. In this section, although the work of Eisenstein is discussed in detail, the vital importance of Eisenstein's contemporaries is recognised by analysing the work of directors such as Kuleshov, Pudovkin, Kozintsev and Trauberg, Dovzhenko, Vertov and Shub.

Lev Kuleshov (1899–1970)
Shortly after the revolution, Kuleshov was recruited as a teacher by the State Film School where he set up an experimental film workshop. Kuleshov and his students carried out a number of experiments related to editing, partly inspired by a lack of raw film stock. One of these experiments included re-editing D.W. Griffith's *Intolerance* (1916), a film

symbolism

In film this is a means by which film-makers can assign additional meanings to objects/characters. For example, in Dovzhenko's *Earth* and Eisenstein's *Old and New* the tractor is a symbol of progress.

key films

Engineer Prite's Project (1918)

The Extraordinary Adventures of Mr. West in the Land of the Bolsheviks (1924)

The Death Ray (1925)

By The Law (1926)

that had impressed Kuleshov because of its innovative use of editing. The experiments resulted in the formation of a number of principles of film-making that the group adopted. The underlying belief for Kuleshov was that 'Film-art begins from the moment when the director begins to combine and join together the various pieces of film.'[25] Kuleshov's ideas about how editing should work are similar to those of Pudovkin in that his shots, rather than being in conflict, can be seen as blocks out of which a scene can be constructed. Significantly, Kuleshov's students included Vsevolod Pudovkin and for a brief time Sergei Eisenstein. In Eisenstein's films and theoretical writing the influence of Kuleshov can clearly be seen.

Kuleshov's experimentation was not confined to editing, however, but also involved acting. He believed that theatre-trained actors, in particular those from the Moscow Arts Theatre[26] were not suitable for the cinema. He also rejected the idea of using non-actors or 'types' chosen for their visual suitability for a role. He set up an acting laboratory dedicated to developing a style of acting tailored specifically to the requirements of the cinema and he carefully recruited would-be film actors who were 'endowed with natural beauty, good health, and the ability to show expediency and purpose on the screen without "acting" or "recreating," unaided by makeup, wigs, and props, of course'.[27]

The techniques that Kuleshov adopted emphasised gesture and movement, the exact nature and timing of which had been practised rigorously in rehearsals. This style of acting was combined with great attention to the composition and framing of each shot to give maximum impact to the action. Kuleshov's opportunity to apply the principles that he had developed came in 1924 when he was assigned valuable imported film stock to direct the first feature film of the film school: *The Extraordinary Adventures of Mr. West in the Land of the Bolsheviks*.

☐ CASE STUDY 1: LEV KULESHOV, *THE EXTRAORDINARY ADVENTURES OF MR. WEST IN THE LAND OF THE BOLSHEVIKS* (1924)

The film is an action-comedy which uses satire to expose the false attitudes and beliefs about the Soviet Union that many in the West held. The action is centred on the fate of Mr West, an American visitor to the USSR, whose view of the Bolsheviks as savages is formed by reading the *New York Times*. Mr West falls into the hands of a group of petty criminals who frighten him into parting with his dollars by dressing up to look like the Bolsheviks that Mr West had seen in his paper. At the climax he is rescued by a 'real' Bolshevik who uncovers the deception. Mr West's stereotypical views of the Bolsheviks are dismantled and he sends a radio message to his wife telling her to hang Lenin's picture in the study.

The montage technique used in *Mr. West* is largely based on a system of close-ups of the actors that emphasise facial expressions. Kuleshov frequently cuts from an action to a close-up reaction shot of a character's face. He starts the film with a separate shot of Mr West juxtaposed with another of his wife; it is only later that we see them together. Later in the film Kuleshov cuts between a shot of the 'real' Bolshevik and Mr West standing on a balcony and another shot of marching Soviet troops taken at a different place and time (the film stock is markedly different). Kuleshov is here using his technique of creative geography to make the audience construct a location in their minds that does not actually exist. The film also fulfils Kuleshov's ideas concerning

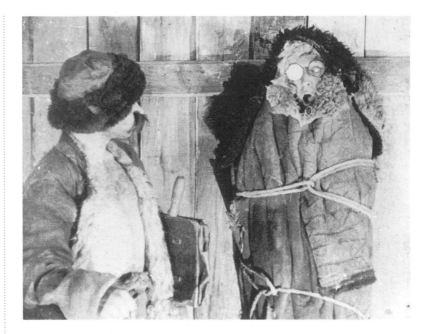

• Plate 11.1 *The Extraordinary Adventures of Mr. West in the Land of the Bolsheviks* (1924)
Mr West is duped by the false Bolsheviks

acting. The movements of the actors are stylised and precise and it is clear that attention has been paid to even the smallest action. The comical nature of the action and a plot based on individual characters meant that the film was popular with audiences.[28]

key films

Strike (1924)
Battleship Potemkin (1925)
October (1927)
Old and New (1929)

Sergei Eisenstein (1898–1948)[29]

Eisenstein, as his age might indicate (he was just 26 when he completed *Strike*), did not emerge from the context of the pre-revolutionary Russian cinema. Prior to his film-making career, he had experimented with a number of different art forms, including the theatre. In this experimentation, the principles of his work in film may be found. In 1923 Eisenstein produced a version of a play by Alexander Ostrovky,[30] in which he attempted to communicate the messages of the play to the audience using a series of shocks which Eisenstein termed 'attractions': 'Emotions were expressed through flamboyant physical stunts . . . at the finale, fire-crackers exploded under spectators' seats . . . [he] explained that the theatre could engage its audience through a calculated assembly of "strong moments" of shock or surprise.'[31]

Eisenstein quickly abandoned experimentation with the theatre and turned to the more popular and accessible medium of film to which he rigorously applied his theatrical principle of 'montage of attractions'.

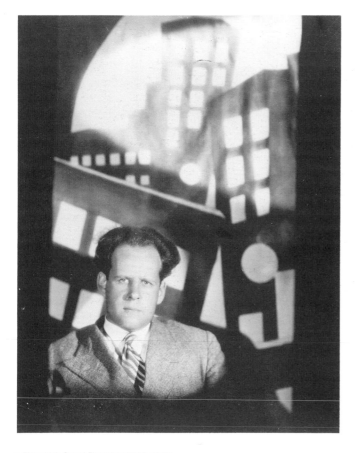

• Plate 11.2 Sergei Eisenstein (1898–1948)

☐ CASE STUDY 2: SERGEI EISENSTEIN, *STRIKE*; *BATTLESHIP POTEMKIN*; *OCTOBER*; *OLD AND NEW*

Strike (1924)

Strike was the first of a proposed series of eight films[32] made by the Moscow Theatre of the Proletkult, under the general subheading 'Towards the Dictatorship of the Proletariat'. *Strike* is about the repression of a group of factory workers involved in an industrial dispute, which ends with the massacre of the strikers and their families by government forces. The six-part structure of 'Strike' – 1 'All Quiet at the Factory', 2 'The Immediate Cause of Strike', 3 'The Factory Stands Idle', 4 'The Strike is Protracted', 5 'Engineering a Massacre', 6 'Slaughter' – is partly due to Eisenstein's theatrical background, but it would also have been vital for the film to be contained on single reels as many cinemas had only one projector.

The plot of *Strike*, as in Eisenstein's later films *Battleship Potemkin* (1925) and *October* (1927), is not told using individual characters as heroes. Instead, any character that is individuated is deemed to be 'bad' or corrupt. The grotesque factory-owner, for example,

• Plate 11.3 *Strike* (1924)
Mounted police enter the factory district

is shown completely isolated in a vast office. The workers themselves, however, are seen usually as a group with no one individual standing out to play the role of leader. In Part 3 these ideas are combined. The scenes depicting the four stockholders of the factory carelessly deciding the future of the strikers are intercut with images of strikers being attacked by mounted police; the individual concern of the capitalists contrasts with the collective concern of the masses. The effect of this montage is dramatic as parallels can immediately be drawn by the viewer between, for example, the dishonesty, greed, deviousness and wealth of the management and the poverty and honesty of the workers. The political implications of this are obvious. Eisenstein, through montage, is seeking to persuade his audience towards a certain view.

The methods applied by Eisenstein in *Strike* are derived in part from a rebellion against what Eisenstein termed the 'Bourgeois Cinema' that was still the main form of entertainment in post-revolutionary cinemas. Eisenstein explains how this cinema was rejected in favour of his own approach: 'We brought collective and mass action onto the screen, . . . our films in this period made an abrupt deviation – insisting on an understanding of the masses as hero.'[33]

In terms of the Hollywood cinema it is not difficult to imagine how the plot of *Strike* could have been adapted into a mainstream film: the story of one individual's fight against authority. The comparison may be trite, but it does emphasise the difference in approach and purpose between the two different modes of representation. Eisenstein's decision not to use individual heroes is of course deliberate; the film registers a political ideology that enshrines the notion of collective strength.

In *Strike* Eisenstein applies his principle of 'montage of attractions' to the editing. He believed that by creating visual 'jolts' between each cut, the viewer was to be 'shocked' into new awarenesses. In most sequences this approach involves juxtaposing shots that are in conflict with each other in some way, either cutting between different actions taking place in a scene or emphasising the importance of certain actions or events by fragmenting them into a number of shots taken from different viewpoints. At various points in *Strike* Eisenstein juxtaposes shots which need to be interpreted by the audience. One of the best examples of this type of 'intellectual' montage is in the last part of the film 'Slaughter', in which Eisenstein juxtaposes a non-diegetic image of a bull being slaughtered with the shots of the factory workers being systematically butchered by government forces. The formula mentioned earlier can be applied: shot A (massacre of the workers) + shot B (Bull being slaughtered) = NEW MEANING C (that the workers are being killed cold-bloodedly like animals in a slaughter-house). It is the audience that is creating meaning here from the juxtaposition of the shots, thus becoming active political interpreters.

Battleship Potemkin (1925)

Eisenstein's second film *Battleship Potemkin* is based on the true story of a mutiny that took place on board the Potemkin in 1905.[34] As in *Strike*, *Battleship Potemkin* is split into a number of distinct parts: 1 'Men and Maggots', 2 'Drama on the Quarter Deck', 3 'Appeal from the Dead', 4 'The Odessa Steps', 5 'Meeting the Squadron'.

The central scene of the film, 'The Odessa Steps', consisting of parallel lines of soldiers marching down the steps leading to the harbour systematically shooting the onlookers, provides a vivid example of the effectiveness of Eisenstein's montage technique.[35] A close examination of the sequence reveals that Eisenstein by using montage to repeat certain key events has expanded time.[36] The effect is to heighten the horrific nature of the slaughter as well as to hold the audience in suspense as the pram finally begins its descent. The furious and shocking climax to the scene demonstrates how Eisenstein is able to use montage to manipulate audience expectations and to shock with violent juxtapositions and graphic images.

• Plate 11.4 *Battleship Potemkin* (1925)
Drama on the quarter-deck (the firing squad)

• Plate 11.5 *Battleship Potemkin* (1925)
The Odessa Steps

• Plates 11.6, 11.7 and 11.8
Battleship Potemkin (1925)
Immediately after the massacre on
the Odessa Steps, the sailors on the
battleship take their revenge by
shelling the headquarters of the
generals. As part of this sequence
Eisenstein juxtaposes three images
of stone lions in different stages of
awakening as a symbol of the
awakening of the Russian people to
political ideas and action

In the last part of the film in which the sailors aboard the Potemkin are nervously anticipating an attack by the rest of the Russian fleet, Eisenstein builds up tension by increasing the number of cuts in a montage finale that maintains a consistently high rate of shots per minute. The scene provides an excellent example of the way in which montage could be used to create an event that did not exist as a whole, as according to Eisenstein the shots of the 'Russian' squadron were taken from 'old newsreels of naval manoeuvres – not even of the Russian Fleet'.[37] It also reveals how montage can be used for rhythmic effect as the fast cutting between the different elements gives the scene a sense of urgency which would be impossible to achieve using any other method.

The opposition of critics at the time ironically stressed the difficulties of understanding *Potemkin*'s experimental form; ironic because it was through film form that Eisenstein hoped to make his political points. It was also declared that *Potemkin* was pitched far above the intellectual level of most peasants, a damning indictment for any propaganda/revolutionary piece. However, although *Potemkin* was not successful as a piece of popular propaganda, it did, like *Strike* before it, mark a major step in the progress of revolutionary cinema. It also represented the first film that gave recognition and acclaim to Soviet cinema. The claim that the experimental nature of *Potemkin* was not solely to blame for its unpopularity, and that it was badly let down by Sovkino's methods of distribution, is a view that should certainly be considered.

October (1927)

October, made for the Tenth Anniversary celebrations of the Russian Revolution, depicts the build up to the October Revolution ending with the storming of the Winter Palace by the Bolsheviks. It is considered the most experimental of Eisenstein's films especially in its increased use of 'intellectual montage', which demands that the audience think critically and constructively about important political issues. A demonstration of this type of montage can be found in the scene in which both Kerensky and General Kornilov are depicted as Napoleons. By intercutting between the two men and the plaster cast figures of Napoleon, Eisenstein effectively exposes both the vanity and essentially the lack of any power within the characters themselves to form a separate identity.[38] Eisenstein's 'intellectual' montage also involves **diegetic** material. For example, early in the film, shots of a soldier cowering in a trench are juxtaposed with low-angle shots of a vast cannon being unloaded elsewhere. The combination of shots initially points to the soldier being physically crushed, but then swiftly the assumption is reached that the war is oppressive, degrading and without purpose for the ordinary troops.

diegetic

This refers to elements of a film that originate directly from within the film's narrative. For example, a popular song that is being played on the soundtrack would be diegetic if it was clear that it was coming from a source within the world of the film such as a car radio.

• Plate 11.9 *October* (1927)
Lenin's arrival at the Finland Railway Station

• Plate 11.10 *October* (1927)

Eisenstein also combines montage techniques with visual puns and symbolism for political effect. At one point, in order to degrade the power of the church, he swiftly cuts from the image of one deity to another, starting with a magnificent statue of Christ, and ending up with a primitive wooden idol, demonstrating that all religions essentially worship crude man-made objects. Eisenstein's use of such techniques was considered by many to be obscure, inaccessible in their meaning and elitist. Victor Shklovsky, writing in *Novyi Lef* in 1927, records the responses of a man connected with the cinema:

> After viewing some Eisenstein sequences a man who is intelligent and conversant with cinema said to me, 'That is very good. I like that a lot but what will the masses say? What will the people we are working for say?' What can you say to that?[39]

Indeed, an examination of contemporary criticism of *October* reveals that far from being popular among Soviet audiences, the film was met with derision and apprehension.

Old and New (1929)

The adverse reaction to *October* prompted Eisenstein to produce *Old and New*, a film more readily understood by audiences. Despite employing a number of the techniques used in *October*, Eisenstein presents them in a simplified form. Juxtapositions, for example, are more obvious and on a less symbolic level.

The narrative of *Old and New*, concerned with the collectivisation of agriculture, is, unlike Eisenstein's previous films, bound together by a central character or heroine

• Plate 11.11 *Old and New* (1929)
The new tractor is eventually delivered to Martha's co-operative

'Martha'. Despite its more conventional narrative form the film contains one of Eisenstein's most effective montage sequences in which a cream separator is delivered to the collective farm. The new machine is eyed suspiciously by the peasants as milk is poured into it. In an ever-quickening flow of images, Eisenstein cuts between the glittering, spinning parts of the machine, the changing faces of the peasants and non-diegetic shots of fountains of water which symbolise the future flow of cream from the separator. The film is fascinating to study in the context of Eisenstein's earlier work and marks an attempt to address problems of understanding associated with *October*.

Vsevolod Pudovkin (1893–1953)

> Editing is the language of the film director. Just as in living speech, so, one may say, in editing: there is a word – the piece of exposed film, the image;
> a phrase – the combination of these pieces.[40]

(Pudovkin)

Pudovkin believed that the power of cinema comes from editing. In the above quotation he claims that a 'shot' (or image) which is the equivalent of the single word in language has very limited meaning. However, when a number of words are combined together they form a 'phrase' which is dense with meaning. Pudovkin's equivalent of a 'phrase' was a number of shots edited together. He went further to support his claim by contending that:

key films

The Mother (1926)
The End of St. Petersburg (1927)
Storm Over Asia (1928)

every object, taken from a given viewpoint and shown on the screen to spectators, is a *dead object*, even though it has moved before the camera. . . . Only if the object be placed together among a number of separate objects, only if it be presented as part of a synthesis of different separate visual images, is it endowed with filmic life.[41]

It would seem initially that Pudovkin's theoretical position regarding the effectiveness of editing was in tandem with his contemporary Eisenstein. There are, however, important differences in the specific way each director thought editing should be used.[42] Pudovkin did not agree with Eisenstein's system of montage, which created visual 'jolts' between cuts. Instead, Pudovkin believed greater impact could be made by linking shots in a constructive way. Shots were to be used as individual building blocks, made to fit together exactly. Though seemingly theoretically opposed to Eisensteinian montage, Pudovkin made extensive use of devices such as 'intellectual montage' in *The Mother* and *The End of St. Petersburg*. Pudovkin's juxtapositions, however, are much less symbolic, more clearly related to the diegetic world of the film and less intent on creating conflict than those of Eisenstein. Leon Moussinac, a French historian, summed up the differences between the two directors: 'An Eisenstein film resembles a shout, a Pudovkin film evokes a song.'[43]

Pudovkin, like Eisenstein, cast according to 'type' and was concerned about the problem of 'stagey acting'. He stated:

I want to work only with real material – this is my principle. I maintain that to show, alongside real water and real trees and grass, a property beard pasted on the actor's face, wrinkles traced by means of paint, or stagey acting is impossible. It is opposed to the most elementary ideas of style.[44]

Unlike Eisenstein, however, Pudovkin uses individual characters that are cast in the role of hero or heroine to carry the narrative, and although he discouraged the use of professional actors some of his lead parts were played by professional actors of the Moscow Arts Theatre.[45]

CASE STUDY 3: VSEVOLOD PUDOVKIN, *THE MOTHER*; *THE END OF ST. PETERSBURG*

The Mother (1926)

The scenario for Pudovkin's *The Mother* is based on the earlier play by Gorky of the same name. The plot is concerned with the political awakening of a mother after she betrays her son to the police, in the belief that he will be dealt with justly. The action is set (as in *Battleship Potemkin*) in the revolutionary context of 1905, with strikes, mass protests and a final brutal massacre of the workers.

With its focus on individuals, the film offers an interesting contrast to Eisenstein's approach to revolutionary cinema. In *The Mother*, the role of the individual is reinstated and emphasised. The mass struggle is thus registered through the lives and fates of separate characters involved in that struggle. It is important to note that the individual characters are not highlighted in such a way that the general struggle itself becomes obscured. The audience is encouraged to make connections between individual fate and

• Plate 11.12 *The End of St. Petersburg* (1927)
One of Pudovkin's central characters, a young peasant boy, is seen here demanding justice from the authorities

the fate of the masses. Pudovkin is thus using individual characters to make his political points, believing that the audience would be able to relate better to separate identities than to an anonymous mass.

Pudovkin's use of 'linkage' editing (shot A + shot B = AB) can be illustrated in the trial scene mid-point in the film. The scene is composed of a large number of shots which tend to centre on single or pairs of characters. The fragmentation allows Pudovkin to draw direct comparisons between, for example, the uninterested and uncaring attitude of the judges, the accused Pavel, his mother and several of the gossiping onlookers. Close shots of the soldiers guarding the courthouse are also inserted in order to demonstrate that 'justice' is being upheld by a substantial force. Pudovkin clearly reveals the judges to be vain and self-interested by highlighting their overriding concern with attire and pictures of horses, rather than the proceedings of the trial. If the same scene had been shot by Eisenstein the vanity of the judges might have been indicated in a similar way to that of Kerensky in *October* (that is, juxtaposing him with a shot of a peacock).

The End of St. Petersburg (1927)

Made to celebrate the Tenth Anniversary of the October Revolution, *The End of St. Petersburg*, based on André Bely's 1916 symbolist novel *Petersburg*,[46] also uses individual characters to deal with the events preceding the revolution. One is a young peasant boy who has come to St Petersburg to seek work, as his family can no longer support him at home. Despite initial involvement with strike-breakers, the boy quickly becomes aware of the corruption and injustice of the Tsarist regime. His political awakening, however, lands him in prison and then he is forced to volunteer into the Tsar's army, where he is exposed to the horrors of trench warfare.

Using montage, Pudovkin draws a contrast between the suffering of the soldiers who are fighting for the Tsar and the greed of those who are benefiting financially from the war. Horrific images of dying soldiers in mud at the front-line trenches are intercut with scenes at the St Petersburg stock market. As the fighting gets worse and worse at the front, the higher the value of the shares becomes – thereby enforcing the point that people are making money out of suffering. The old order, by supporting and being supported by the stock market, is seen to be inhumane and preoccupied with the wrong values – the acquisition of wealth at whatever cost. Pudovkin at one point intercuts between the image of a soldier slashing ferociously at an opponent with his bayonet and the image of a stock market figure frenetically dealing at the stock exchange. He thus likens the barbarities of war to the barbarity inherent in the centre of the capitalist structure. Earlier Pudovkin intercut between the images of death at the front and the words 'In the name of the Tsar, the fatherland, and the capital'. This is clearly ironic as the soldiers have no idea what they are fighting for – certainly not for the Tsar.

In the final part of *The End of St. Petersburg*, in the storming of the Winter Palace sequences, Pudovkin intercuts the images of the advancing Bolsheviks with both fast-moving clouds and crashing waves. This emphasises the power and inevitability of the revolution – revolution is unstoppable. Earlier in a Bolshevik's speech at the Lebedev factory, images of slowing down machinery are intercut with the speaker to point to the power of his words upon the workers.

key films

The Adventures of Oktyabrina
(1924)

The Cloak (1926)

The New Babylon (1929)

Eccentrism of the FEKS: Grigori Kozintsev and Leonid Trauberg

FEKS (Factory of the Eccentric Actor), formed in December 1921 by a small group of theatre actors and directors, shared the common aim of reforming the traditional theatre and incorporating into their experimental work elements of the circus, music hall and puppet theatre. On 9 July 1922 FEKS published a manifesto which stated their aims as a group.[47] The poster shown on p. 352 shows just a small sample of the material contained within the manifesto.

The extract makes it clear that FEKS valued the bold, dynamic and popular elements of circus and cinema posters. It was with these elements that they proposed to revitalise the theatre. Two of the founding members of the group, Grigori Kozintsev and Leonid Trauberg, became interested in the cinema, making a number of short experimental films between 1924 and 1927, including *The Adventures of Oktyabrina* (1924) and *The Cloak* (1926). The films primarily emphasised the artificial nature of the mise-en-scène and the stylised nature of the acting rather than the editing.

Kozintsev and Trauberg are perhaps best known for their 1929 film, *The New Babylon*, based on the events building up to the Paris Commune of 1871. As in their previous films, artificial mise-en-scène combined with stylised acting were employed, but also extensive use was made of camera movement. At one point in the film the camera moves swiftly enough to blur the image, thus conveying the sense of confusion present in the scene. The response to the film was unfavourable, as audiences failed to understand its form.

• Plate 11.13 *The New Babylon* (1929)

□ CASE STUDY 4: ALEXANDER DOVZHENKO (1894–1956),[48] *ARSENAL* (1929), *EARTH* (1930)

Inspired by the creative and political possibilities of film, Dovzhenko had approached the Odessa film studio in 1926. At this point he had little knowledge of cinema, but within a few years he had made an outstanding contribution to Soviet revolutionary cinema with films such as *Arsenal* and *Earth* which, in addition to revolutionary fervour, displayed poetic qualities and provided a demonstration of his love for the Ukraine and its people.

Arsenal surveys the devastating impact of the First World War and the political struggles between the Social Democrats and the Bolsheviks during 1917. The opening sequences of *Arsenal* exemplify Dovzhenko's approach to film-making. There is little camera movement or use of establishing shots and, overall, there is less concern

WE
CONSIDER ART AS A TIRELESS RAM SHATTERING THE HIGH WALLS OF HABIT AND DOGMA

———

But we also have our own ancestors!
and lots of them

———

The brilliant creators of cinema posters, circus posters, music hall posters. Unknown designers of pulp thrillers who exalt the exploits of the King of the detectives or adventurers. In using your art, more magnificent than a clown's red nose, we spring up as if from a trampoline to perform our intrepid Eccentric somersault!
Only the poster has escaped the pernicious scalpel of analysis and the intellect. Subject and form are indivisible, but what do they sing of?

Danger, Audacity, Violence, Pursuit, Revolution, Gold, Blood, Laxative pills, Charlie Chaplin, Catastrophes on land, sea and in the air. Fat cigars, Prima donnas of the operettas, Adventures of all sorts, Skating rinks, Tap shoes, Horses, Wrestling, Torch singers, Somersaults on bicycles and all those millions and millions of events which make splendid our Today!

THE 200 VOLUMES OF GERMAN EXPRESSIONISM DO NOT OFFER THE EXPRESSIVITY OF ONE SOLE

CIRCUS POSTER!!!

• Plate 11.14 *Earth* (1930)

with a conventional rendering of space and time than with the emotional impact of the flow of images. In these opening and further sequences Dovzhenko reveals the loss and impoverishment of the people as well as the unthinking callousness of the social order.

Arsenal shows that Dovzhenko is not concerned with personalised conflict between individuals, but with the ongoing struggle between opposing social forces. This concern is pursued further in *Earth* which deals with class struggle in the countryside, although like *Arsenal* it features a strong attractive male hero, Vasil. The latter is the operator of the tractor which will allow the collective farm to effectively rid the village of the self-seeking and more prosperous peasants, the kulaks. In the end Vasil is shot by Khoma, the son of a kulak, although what he stands for will not be defeated. Vasil's father, hitherto hostile to the young revolutionaries of the village, commits himself to the cause of collectivisation and rejects a religious burial in favour of the village youth singing songs about the new life to come. The film, then, presents a strong case for the recently instigated policy of the collectivisation of agriculture. Commentators on the film, however, have argued that the formal and poetic qualities of the film actually undermine the political message. Denise J. Youngblood, for example, states that,

> Dovzhenko's *Earth* (1930) is a much more curious example of the collectivisation film – the politically correct story of a handsome young village Party activist murdered by an evil and dissolute *kulak* opposed to collectivisation is undercut by a deeply subversive subtext related to its form. The lyrical imagery and slow rhythms of this film, totally unlike Eisenstein's, belie the purported theme and in effect serve as a paean to a way of life soon to be no more.[49]

The opening sequence in which Vasil's grandfather dies would certainly seem to bear out this interpretation. He dies contented, his last act being to enjoy a pear, a product of the fruitful Ukrainian earth. Next to him a baby plays and a boy eats an apple, while the adult members of the family await the inevitable. This portrait of pastoral abundance and peacefulness with its allusions to the cycle of life and death seem to undermine the necessity for revolutionary change, but it is made clear by the old man's friend Petro that his has been a life of hard work – '75 years behind a plough'.

Dziga Vertov (1896–1954)

Dziga Vertov[50] (pseudonym of Denis Kaufman) was interested in the idea that the film camera had the potential to capture 'truth'; the camera could be seen simply as a mechanical device that was capable of recording the world without human intervention. Vertov led a group of film-makers called Kinoki (cinema-eye) who stated in their 1923 manifesto:

> I am the Cine-Eye. I am the mechanical eye.
> I the machine show you the world as only I can see it.
>
> I emancipate myself henceforth and forever from human immobility. *I am in constant motion.* I approach objects and move away from them, I creep up on them, I clamber over them, I move alongside the muzzle of a running horse, I tear into a crowd at full tilt, I flee before fleeing soldiers, I turn over on my back, I rise up with aeroplanes, I fall and rise with falling and rising bodies.[51]

Vertov believed that the fiction film could not be used to reveal the 'truth' about a society. His films were based on documenting events around him; nothing should be artificially set up or staged for the camera. In 1922 Vertov had stated: 'WE declare the old films, the romantic, the theatricalised etc., to be leprous.'[52]

Vertov's techniques were based on experimentation caused by the general scarcity of film stock and also, when available, the short lengths of the negative film. His experiments included using old newsreels as part of his films, and he found that new meanings could be created by the conflict produced by the old material and the new. Vertov soon discovered that the conflicts produced by montage were a vital element in the construction of meaning in his films.

Perhaps one of the most interesting features of Vertov's films is that great effort is taken to ensure that the audience is made aware of cameraman, editor and the whole process of producing a film. In *The Man With a Movie Camera,* for example, Vertov shows the cameraman shooting the scenes that we see before us, and later we see shots of this same film being edited. This technique of acknowledging the nature of the film-making process can be linked to documentary film-making practice in the 1970s and 1980s (in the films of Emile de Antonio and Jean-Pierre Gorin, for example) which went against the **fly-on-the-wall** practice and attempted to show the presence of the film-crew and camera and the fact that the audience are watching a manufactured film rather than 'reality'. This style of film-making which draws attention to its own process is often termed 'self-reflexive'.

fly-on-the-wall

This is a term associated with a style of documentary film-making which attempts to present events to the audience as though the presence of the camera and film crew had not influenced them in any way.

Esfir Shub (1894–1959)

Esfir Shub is an interesting female figure in a period of film-making dominated by men. She was initially employed by the Soviet government to re-edit foreign films to make them conform to the ideology of communism. Shub also re-edited old Tsarist newsreels to show the corrupt nature of the old order. Shub's practice of reassembling parts of existing films culminated in the adoption of the montage technique.

key films

The Fall of the Romanov Dynasty (1927)
The Great Road (1927)
The Russia of Nicholas II and Lev Tolstoy (1928)

☐ CASE STUDY 5: ESFIR SHUB, *THE FALL OF THE ROMANOV DYNASTY* (1927)

Shub's first feature-length film, *The Fall of the Romanov Dynasty*, constructed entirely from old newsreels, was made to celebrate the Tenth Anniversary of the October Revolution and it is claimed that 60,000 metres of film had to be examined in order to finish the project.[53] Shub provides new commentary on existing material by inserting intertitles between shots. By juxtaposing sequences of shots from different newsreels she also makes the audience draw new conclusions about the material. For example, she contrasts shots of an aristocratic gathering with shots of workers digging ditches. The intertitle reads 'by the sweat of your brow'. The intertitles and the juxtaposition of the images encourage the audience to assign an aberrant decoding to the original shots. In other words, the audience can deliberately 'misread' the images. Shub uses images which emphasise the pomp and splendour of Tsarist Russia, which in the context of the film look absurd and out of place; the audience is forced to be critical of this obvious display of wealth.

Although the film in principle uses montage in a similar way to Eisenstein or Pudovkin (in particular the way in which the audience are placed as active participants in the text) Shub does not make use of its rhythmic possibilities. Although the pace of the film is on the whole sedate it does put its political messages across in a powerful and convincing way. Recently, there has been a call for a re-evaluation of Esfir Shub by Graham Roberts who claims that Shub's contribution to the Soviet cinema has been undervalued.[54]

AUDIENCE RESPONSE

Viewers in the West may possibly already have an idea of the nature of the Soviet cinema after seeing extracts from films discussed previously such as Sergei Eisenstein's *Battleship Potemkin* or *October*. They may have wondered how many films such as these were made and how they were received by Soviet audiences that had only a few years previously gone through the upheaval of civil war. They may have pitied or even envied the Soviet cinema-goer – were these the only films that the Soviet cinema-goer could see on a Friday night? How could a largely uneducated population have coped with sophisticated material like this?

Recent research into the Soviet cinema of the 1920s has encouraged new ideas. In the past, attention has focused on a number of key directors such as Pudovkin, Eisenstein and Vertov, whose films in the Soviet Union and later in the West were received with critical acclaim. We must examine, however, new evidence that points to the fact that Russian audiences were far more likely to be watching the Soviet 1920s equivalent of *Jurassic Park* than the likes of *Battleship Potemkin*, *Strike* and *October*.

355

Richard Stites, in *Russian Popular Culture: Entertainment and Society since 1900*, reveals that the majority of Soviet directors were making mainstream films that were conventional in form and content. The montage film was the exception rather than the rule:

> The most popular movie genres of the revolutionary period were the same as the foreign and pre-revolutionary Russian ones: costume drama, action and adventure, literary works adapted for the screen, melodramas, and comedy. Those who patronized them were not merely the *nepmanskaya auditoriya*, that is the bourgeoisie, alleged to be addicted to lurid sex films. Working-class clubs sponsored by the Communist Party also had to show some entertainment films or risk losing their audience.[55]

Soviet audiences also favoured foreign films which were imported in large numbers thoughout the 1920s.

But why were the Soviet propaganda films relatively less successful? Why would audiences rather see foreign and conventional Soviet genre films? Were foreign films perceived as being more exciting or exotic? Denise Youngblood, in *Movies for the Masses*, cites an interview conducted in 1929 with a Soviet cinema manager that recorded audience response:

> He noted that 'the public watched [Dovzhenko's *Arsenal*] with great difficulty,' and that attendance dropped to 50 percent of normal when his theatre screened *New Babylon*, Kozintsev and Trauberg's famous picture about the Paris Commune. Asked about the reaction to Vertov's *The Man with the Movie Camera*, he replied sarcastically, 'One hardly need say that if *New Babylon* didn't satisfy the spectator's requirements and "lost" him, then *The Man with the Movie Camera* didn't satisfy him either.'[56]

The problem is clear. The Soviet propaganda films that were intended for the masses, from the illiterate peasant upwards, simply were not being understood by Soviet audiences, whereas the clear hero-led narrative structure of the foreign and Soviet genre films were far more straightforward and appealing. It is well documented that the American version of *Robin Hood* proved more successful in Soviet cinemas on all counts. The film-makers involved in Soviet propaganda production although committed to the ideals of communism were also committed to experimenting with film form. The experimentation in this case clearly did not culminate in a popular cinema that appealed to the masses.

THEORETICAL DEBATES: MONTAGE VS REALISM

The montage technique has been widely acknowledged as a powerful means of expression and to many cinema theorists 'montage' is the essence of cinema. The technique, however, does have its opponents, among them the French film critic and theorist André Bazin.[57] Bazin was concerned with the cinema's ability to record 'reality'. He saw in cinema a means of capturing a record of events before the camera with minimum mediation. Bazin regarded the montage cinema of the Soviets (among others) as essentially non-realist as scenes could be manipulated and altered in many different ways. He claimed that the audience of montage cinema was essentially passive,[58] as the director forced the audience towards certain meanings.

Bazin saw montage cinema as being in direct opposition to a style of film-making associated with realism. Realism is a term often associated with the Hollywood cinema, but Bazin used it to refer to a style of film-making adopted by certain film-makers such as Jean Renoir, a French director, who felt that the power of cinema came not from editing, but from mise-en-scène. The realists, unlike the montage film-makers, took great pains to hide the artificial constructed nature of film. The long take, for example, was frequently used as it made editing unnecessary. The use of the long take supported the claim that what was being watched was unmediated and therefore more 'realistic'. Bazin cited further devices that could enhance the 'reality' of a scene, such as the use of deep-focus, wide-angle lenses, the long shot and a highly mobile camera which all meant that the film-maker could preserve real time and space in individual scenes.

POSTSCRIPT TO THE 1920S

The 1930s and after: the decline of experimentation in the Soviet cinema

In the 1930s the Soviet authorities, under the guidance of Stalin, reacted to the unpopularity of many of the Soviet films by issuing strict guidelines on how films should be made. This set of 'rules', essentially demanding hero-led narratives and concerned with realistic subject-matter, was termed 'Socialist Realism'. The head of the Soviet film industry outlined why such a policy was necessary in 1933: 'A film and its success are directly linked to the degree of entertainment in the plot . . . that is why we are obliged to require our masters [the film-makers] to produce works that have strong plots and are organised around a story-line.'[59]

The policy of 'Socialist Realism' was combined with a complete ban on imported foreign films. By removing these positive representations of capitalism Stalin had also effectively made the Soviet film industry a monopoly; audiences could either see Soviet films or not see any films at all.

The direct interest that the Soviet state took in the film industry reveals its perceived importance, but also had drastic consequences for many of the directors. It was noted by the authorities, for example, that several of these directors were not actually Communist Party members. (This might explain perhaps why they were more interested in form or technique than making positive films about communism that were easy to comprehend.) The film-makers of the 1920s discussed in this chapter were mostly not successful in the 1930s and 1940s. Eisenstein, for example, continued to make films, but the majority were either suppressed or had their funding withdrawn.

However, the decline of montage cinema could possibly be the consequence of another factor: technology. In October 1929 the first Soviet sound films were released and with this advance in cinema technology came the almost immediate downfall of film-making practices that relied on either complex camera movement or rapid editing, as sound cinema initially required non-movable cameras and fixed microphones in order to record dialogue.

The legacy of the Soviet cinema: its influence on modern cinema[60]

The impact of the Soviet films of the 1920s on the analysis of film and film-making itself was immediate and continues to this day. The films, however, have not so much provided a model for successive film-makers as been an inspiration for their work. The British Documentary Movement of the 1930s, for example, was influenced by Soviet montage as well as impressed by the idea that films could be a force for education. The film-makers in this movement, however, did not conceive of films having a revolutionary role or even the role of questioning contemporary inequalities. Other film-makers have been inspired by the Soviet cinema because of its rejection of the forms and conventions of the dominant Hollywood entertainment cinema. Jean-Luc Godard, for example, demanded that audiences participate in the construction of meaning in his films and so engage directly with social and political questions. The achievements of Eisenstein continue to impress film editors as well as contemporary film directors. The editor, Ralph Rosenblum, for example, states in his discussion of *Battleship Potemkin* that 'Although the movie is filled with stunning moments, the massacre on the Odessa steps outweighs them all; it remains for editors everywhere the single most intimidating piece of film ever assembled.'[61]

Direct references to Eisenstein's films are numerous, ranging from Bernardo Bertolucci's subtle allusions to *Strike* in his *Tragedy of a Ridiculous Man* (Italy/US 1981) through Brian de Palma's opportunistic reworking of the Odessa Steps sequence in *The Untouchables* (US 1987)[62] to Zbigniew Rybczynski's use of the same sequence in *Steps* (US/UK/Poland 1987)[63] in order to satirise cultural attitudes including the veneration of *Battleship Potemkin* as a work of art.[64] Dovzhenko's influence has not been a direct political one, but the films of Andrei Tarkovsky, at one time a pupil of Dovzhenko, and a film like *My Childhood* by the Scottish film-maker Bill Douglas, exhibit a similar emotional intensity.

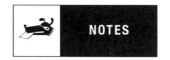

NOTES

1 Quoted in Yon Barna, *Eisenstein,* London: Secker & Warburg Ltd., 1973, p. 102.

2 The term peasants is used to describe those who worked on the land in the country and the term workers describes those who worked within cities.

3 This was a planned attack by a relatively small force, not a mass uprising as chronicled by Eisenstein in his 1927 film *October.*

4 An unusual account of this period told from the point of view of the White side can be found in Mikhail Bulgakov's 1926 novel, *The White Guard* (available in UK as a Flamingo paperback).

5 The British Film Institute have released a number of early Russian films on video (in ten volumes).

6 See list of selected Russian films in Further viewing.

7 The history of what happened to the migrant Russian film-makers and stars is an area worthy of study in its own right.

8 Protazanov was not in the Soviet Union for the full duration of this period; he emigrated briefly to Paris in 1920–3.

9 For more information on Protazanov see Ian Christie and Julian Graffy, (eds), *Yakov Protazanov and the Continuity of Russian Cinema*, London: British Film Institute/NFT, 1993. For more information on the Russian cinema see: Jay Leyda, *Kino*, London: George Unwin & Allen, 1960; and Paolo Usai, Lorenzo Codelli, Carlo Montanaro and David Robinson (eds), *Silent Witnesses*, London: British Film Institute, 1989.

10 The first Russian studio was set up by Drankov in 1907.

11 The first half of 'Soviet Cinema and Ideology: Film as Agent of Change' by Danny Rivers (Film Studies Lecturer, West Kent College).

12 V.I. Lenin, in *Pravda*, no. 250, 7 November 1919. Reprinted in *Lenin: Economics and Politics in the Era of the Dictatorship of the Proletariat*, Moscow: Progress Publishers, 1978, p. 3.

13 The context of this remark can be found in Leyda, *Kino*, p.161.

14 The Museum of the Moving Image (MOMI) has recreated the cinema carriage of an Agit Train complete with commentator, although the Soviet films being shown are from the period 1924–30.

15 Richard Taylor and Ian Christie (eds), *The Film Factory: Russian and Soviet Cinema in Documents, 1896–1939*, London: Routledge, 1988, p.109.

16 The civil war also resulted in trade barriers being set up which prevented the importation of film stock and cinema equipment into the Soviet Union. This had a dramatic effect on the film industry as the Soviet Union initially had no means of producing its own film stock and lenses.

17 Denise Youngblood, *Movies for the Masses*, Cambridge: Cambridge University Press, 1992, p. 51.

18 *Cinema Journal*, vol. 11, no. 2, 1972.

19 Vladimir Vladimirovich Mayakovsky (1893–1930).

20 The team effort involved in the production of a feature film would clearly cost a great deal more than an individual artist producing a painting. The Russian film industry, although economically successful, needed to produce films that would appeal to a wide audience. The desire to experiment with film form, when the existing genres were popular, was therefore limited.

21 From, Vsevolod Pudovkin, 'Types instead of Actors', in his *Film Technique and Film Acting*, London: Gollancz, 1929.

22 The mansion was in fact The White House.

23 Adapted from Bruce Kawin, *How Movies Work*, London: Collier Macmillan, 1987, pp. 99–101.

24 David Bordwell, *Narration in the Fiction Film*, London: Routledge, 1986 (Bordwell uses a technique pioneered by Barry Salt in his article 'Statistical Style Analysis of Motion Pictures', *Film Quarterly*, vol. 28, no. 2, winter 1974–5).

25 Quoted by Pudovkin at a lecture given at the London Film School in 1929.

26 The Moscow Arts Theatre under the direction of Konstantin Stanislavski developed a method of acting which required the actor to attempt to 'become' the character.

27 Quoted in Neya Zorkaya, *The Illustrated History of Soviet Cinema*, New York: Hippocrene Books, 1989, p. 52.

28 This can be inferred from the fact that Goskino made thirty-two prints of the film.

29 For fuller details and a chronology of the life of Eisenstein see David Bordwell, *The Cinema of Eisenstein*, Cambridge, Mass.: Harvard University Press, 1993.

30 A well-known Russian playwright (1823–86).

31 David Bordwell, *The Cinema of Eisenstein*, p. 6.

32 The other seven films were never made.

33 Quoted at further length in *Kino*, p. 181.

34 Eisenstein bends historical fact in the film as the sailors on board the Potemkin, instead of persuading the Russian fleet to join the struggle, were captured and the mutiny suppressed.

35 The scene has been much copied by recent film-makers: see the section on the 'Legacy of the Soviet cinema: its influence on modern cinema', on pp. 357–8.

36   See Bordwell, *The Cinema of Eisenstein*, p. 74 for an excellent analysis of the sequence.

37   Quotation cited by Leyda in *Kino*, p. 195. Leyda also points out that the same sequence caused 'an anxious debate in the German Reichstag on the size of the Soviet Navy'.

38   Bordwell, in *The Cinema of Eisenstein*, p. 85, claims that the peacock could be seen as a diegetic image as it forms part of the treasures contained within the Winter Palace. Yuri Tsivian, in 'Eisenstein's *October* and Russian Symbolist Culture', in Ian Christie and Richard Taylor (eds), *Eisenstein Rediscovered*, London: Routledge, 1993, puts forward the view that 'Eisenstein was hoping to attain the effect of Kerensky entering the peacock's asshole.'

39   Taylor and Christie, (eds), *The Film Factory*, p. 182.

40   Quoted in V. Perkins, *Film As Film*, London: Penguin, 1972, p. 21.

41   ibid., p. 22.

42   Pudovkin's films like those of Eisenstein were also based on a body of theoretical writing.

43   Quoted by Richard Taylor, *The Politics of the Soviet Cinema 1919–1929*, Cambridge: Cambridge University Press, 1979, p. 142.

44   Lecture given by Pudovkin at the London Film Society, 1929.

45   The theatre was founded in 1898 by Konstantin Stanislavski and Vladimir Nemirovich-Danchenko.

46   Published in the UK by Penguin (London, 1983).

47   The manifesto was reprinted in 1992 in a limited edition of 500 copies by Aldgate Press, London.

48   Section on Dovzhenko written by Danny Rivers (West Kent College).

49   *Movies for the Masses*, p. 169.

50   Vertov in Russian is derived from the Russian word for 'rotation' and was thus a reflection of his approach to the arts.

51   Quoted in Taylor and Christie (eds), *The Film Factory*, p. 93.

52   ibid., p. 69.

53   Soviet montage cinema tended to put the stress on the importance of the director (auteur) and work in post-production, rather than scriptwriting and the screenplay. This became a source of dispute in the 1920s when there was greater concern with efficiency and a more elaborate division of labour. See Kristin Thompson's 'Early Alternatives to the Hollywood Mode of Production', *Film History: An International Journal*, vol. 5, no. 4, December 1993.

54   See 'Esfir Shub: A Suitable Case For Treatment', *Historical Journal of Film, Radio and Television*, vol. 11, no. 2, 1991.

55   Richard Stites, *Russian Popular Culture: Entertainment and Society since 1900*, Cambridge: Cambridge University Press, 1992, p. 56.

56   *Movies for the Masses*, pp. 18–19.

57   Bazin was also editor of the French film journal *Cahiers Du Cinema*.

58   Eisenstein rigorously opposed this view claiming that the audience for his films played an active part in the text.

59   The head of Sovkino at this time was Boris Shumyatsky. The quotation is taken from Richard Taylor, 'Boris Shumyatsky and the Soviet Cinema in the 1930s: Ideology as Mass Entertainment', *Historical Journal of Film, Radio and Television*, vol. 6, no.1, 1986, p. 43.

60   This section was written by Danny Rivers (West Kent College).

61   From Ralph Rosenblum and Robert Karen, *When The Shooting Stops . . . The Cutting Begins: A Film Editor's Story*, New York: Da Capo Press, 1979.

62   A statistical analysis of both scenes in terms of shot length/shot type reveals that they are also very similiar in form.

63   A co-production of KTCA-TV Minneapolis and ZBIG Vision Ltd in association with Channel 4 London.

64   Woody Allen in *Love and Death*, (US 1975) also makes reference to this sequence.

 FURTHER READING

Emboldened references indicate the key texts.

Books

Aumont, Jacques, *Montage Eisenstein*, London: British Film Institute, 1987.

Barna, Yon, *Eisenstein*, London: Secker & Warburg, 1973.

Barron, Stephanie and Tuchman, Maurice (eds), *The Avant-Garde in Russia, 1910–1930: New Perspectives*, Los Angeles: Los Angeles County Museum of Art, 1980.

Birkos, Alexander, *Soviet Cinema: Directors and Films*, Hamden, Conn: Archon, 1976.

Bordwell, David, *The Cinema of Eisenstein*, Cambridge Mass.: Harvard University Press, 1993.

Christie, Ian and Gillett, John (eds), *Futurism/Formalism/FEKS: 'Eccentrism' and Soviet Cinema 1918–1936*, London: British Film Institute (Film Availability Services), 1978.

Christie, Ian and Graffy, Julian (eds), *Yakov Protazanov and the Continuity of Russian Cinema*, London: British Film Institute/NFT, 1993.

Christie, Ian and Taylor, Richard (eds), *Eisenstein Rediscovered*, London: Routledge, 1993.

Dickinson, Thorold and de la Roche, Catherine, *Soviet Cinema*, London: The Falcon Press, 1948.

Eisenstein, Sergei, *Notes of a Film Director*, New York: Dover Publications, 1970.

—— *The Film Sense*, London: Faber & Faber, 1986.

Film scripts of *The Mother*, *Earth* and *Battleship Potemkin* have been published by Simon & Schuster, New York, 1973.

Goodwin, James, *Eisenstein, Cinema and History*, Urbana and Chicago: University of Illinois Press, 1993.

Kenez, Peter, *Cinema and Soviet Society, 1917–1953*, Cambridge: Cambridge University Press, 1992.

Kepley, Vance, Jr, *In the Service of the State: The Cinema of Alexander Dovzhenko*, Madison: University of Wisconsin Press, 1986.

Lawton, Anna, *The Red Screen: Politics, Society, Art in Soviet Cinema*, London: Routledge, 1992.

Leyda, Jay, *Kino: A History of the Russian and Soviet Film* (3rd edn), London: George Allen & Unwin, 1983.

Marshall, Herbert, *Masters of the Soviet Cinema*, London: Routledge & Kegan Paul, 1983.

Michelson, Annette (ed.), *Kino Eye: The Writings of Dziga Vertov*, Berkeley: University of California Press, 1984.

Petric, Vlada, *Constructivism in Film: The Man with the Movie Camera – A Cinematic Analysis*, Cambridge: Cambridge University Press, 1987.

Schnitzer, Luda and Martin, Jean and Marcel (eds), *Cinema in Revolution*, London: Secker & Warburg, 1973 (reprinted by New York: Da Capo Press, 1987).

Stites, Richard, *Russian Popular Culture: Entertainment and Society since 1900*, Cambridge: Cambridge University Press, 1992.

Taylor, Richard, *Film Propaganda: Soviet Russia and Nazi Germany*, London: Croom Helm, 1979.

—— *The Politics of the Soviet Cinema, 1917–1929*, Cambridge: Cambridge University Press, 1979.

—— (ed.), *S.M. Eisenstein: Writings 1922–1934*, Selected Works vol. I, London: British Film Institute, 1988.

—— (ed.), *Beyond the Stars: The Memoirs of Sergei Eisenstein*, Selected Works vol. IV, London: British Film Institute, 1995.

Taylor, Richard and Christie, Ian (eds), *The Film Factory: Russian and Soviet Cinema in Documents, 1896–1939*, London: Routledge, 1988.

—— (eds), *Inside the Film Factory: New Approaches to Russian and Soviet Cinema*, London: Routledge, 1991.

Taylor, Richard and Glenny, Michael (eds), *S.M. Eisenstein: Towards a Theory of Montage*, Selected Works vol. II, London: British Film Institute, 1994.

Tsivian, Yuri, *Early Cinema in Russia and its Cultural Reception*, London: Routledge, 1994.

Usai, Paolo, Codelli, Lorenzo, Montangro, Carlo and Robinson, David (eds), *Silent Witnesses: Russian Films 1908–1919*, London: British Film Institute, 1989.

Youngblood, Denise, *Soviet Cinema in the Silent Era, 1918–1935*, Ann Arbor, Mich.: UMI Research Press, 1985.

—— *Movies for the Masses: Popular Cinema and Soviet Society in the 1920s*, Cambridge: Cambridge University Press, 1992.

Zorkaya, Neya, *The Illustrated History of Soviet Cinema*, New York: Hippocrene Books, 1989.

Chapters in books

Bordwell, David, *Narration in the Fiction Film*, London: Routledge, 1990, pp. 234–73.

Cook, Pam, *The Cinema Book*, London: British Film Institute, 1985, pp. 34–6 and 218–19.

Dudley, Andrew, *The Major Film Theories: An Introduction*, Oxford: Oxford University Press, 1976, chs 3 and 4, pp. 42–101.

Giannetti, Louis, *Understanding Movies*, 6th edn, Englewood Cliffs, NJ: Prentice Hall, 1993, pp. 135–47 and 373–83.

Giannetti, Louis and Eyman, Scott, *Flashback: A Brief History of Film*, 2nd edn, Englewood Cliffs, NJ: Prentice Hall, 1991, pp. 82–90.

Gomery, Douglas, *Movie History: A Survey*, Belmont, Calif.: Wadsworth, 1991, pp. 135–60.

Henderson, Brian, 'Toward a Non-Bourgeois Camera Style', in Nichols, Bill (ed.), *Movies and Methods*, Berkeley, University of California Press, 1976, pp. 422–38.

Kawin, Bruce, *How Movies Work*, London: Collier Macmillan, 1987, pp. 264–75.

Kenez, Peter, *The Birth of the Propaganda State: Soviet Methods of Mass Mobilization 1917–1929*, Cambridge: Cambridge University Press, 1985, ch. 9, pp. 195–219.

Robinson, David, *World Cinema 1895–1980*, London: Methuen, 1981, pp. 123–42.

Thompson, Kristin and Bordwell, David, *Film Art: An Introduction*, 4th edn, New York: McGraw-Hill, 1993, pp. 466–9.

—— *Film History: An Introduction*, New York: McGraw-Hill, 1994, pp. 128–55.

Tudor, Andrew, *Theories of Film*, London: Viking Press and Secker & Warburg, 1973, pp. 25–58.

Articles

Bordwell, David, 'The Idea of Montage in Soviet Art and Film', *Cinema Journal*, vol. 11, no. 2, 1972.

Christie, Ian, 'From the Kingdom of Shadows', in catalogue to *Twilight of the Tsars*, Hayward Gallery, 1991.

Hartsough, Denise, 'Soviet Film Distribution and Exhibition in Germany, 1921–1933', *Historical Journal of Film, Radio and Television*, vol. 5, no. 2, 1985.

Historical Journal of Film, Radio and Television, vol. 11, no. 2, 1991. A special issue centred on new research into Soviet cinema including: Tsivian, Yuri, 'Early Russian Cinema and its Public'; Yangirov, Rashit, 'Soviet Cinema in the Twenties: National Alternatives'; Youngblood, Denise, ' "History" on Film'; Yampolsky,

Mikhail, 'Reality at Second Hand'; Listov, Viktor, 'Early Soviet Cinema: The Spontaneous and the Planned, 1917–1924'; Roberts, Graham, 'Esfir Shub: A Suitable Case for Treatment'.

Kepley, Vance, Jr, 'The Origins of Soviet Cinema: A Study in Industry Development', *Quarterly Review of Film Studies*, vol. 10, no. 1, 1985.

Kepley, Vance, Jr and Kepley, Betty, 'Foreign Films on Soviet Screens 1922–1931', *Quarterly Review of Film Studies*, fall 1979.

Screen, vol. 12, no. 4, winter 1971–2. A special issue centred on Soviet film of the 1920s including translations from: LEF, Novy LEF, Brik, Kuleshov, Shklovsky, Vertov, Mayakovsky Film Scenarios.

Stites, Richard, 'Soviet Movies for the Masses and Historians', *Historical Journal of Film, Radio and Television*, vol. 11, no. 3, 1991.

Thompson, Kristin, 'Early Alternatives to the Hollywood Mode of Production', *Film History: An International Journal*, vol. 5, no. 4, December, 1993.

 **FURTHER VIEWING**

Selected Russian films of the 1910s

V = available on video

16mm = available to hire on 16mm

Where neither one is listed, the film is not available to buy or rent.

1908	*Sken'ka Razin*, Drankov (V)
1909	*A Sixteenth-Century Russian Wedding*, Goncharov (V)
1910	*The Queen of Spades*, Petr Chardynin (V)
	Rusalka/The Mermaid, Goncharov (V)
	The House in Kolomna, Petr Chardynin (V)
1912	*The Brigand Brothers*, Goncharov (V)
	The Peasants' Lot, Vasilii Goncharov (V)
1913	*Twilight of A Woman's Soul*, Evgeny Bauer
	Merchant Bashkirov's Daughter, Larin (V)
1914	*The Child of the Big City*, Evgeny Bauer (V)
	Silent Witnesses, Evgeny Bauer (V)
1915	*After Death*, Evgeny Bauer
	Daydreams, Evgeny Bauer (V)
	Happiness of Eternal Night, Evgeny Bauer
	Children Of The Age, Evgeny Bauer
1916	*The 1002nd Ruse*, Evgeny Bauer (V)
	The Queen of Spades, Yakov Protazanov (V)
	Antosha Ruined by a Corset, Eduard Puchal'ski (V)
	A Life for a Life, Evgeny Bauer (V)
1917	*Satan Triumphant*, Yakov Protazanov
	The King of Paris, Evgeny Bauer
	Grandmother of the Revolution, Svetlov
	The Revolutionary, Evgeny Bauer
	For Luck, Evgeny Bauer (V)

1918   *Jenny the Maid*, Yakov Protazanov

Still, Sadness, Still, Petr Chardynin

Little Ellie, Yakov Protazanov

Selected Soviet films of the 1920s–40s

1922–5 *Film-Truth*, Dziga Vertov (a series of newsreels)

1924   *The Extraordinary Adventures of Mr. West in the Land of the Bolsheviks*, Lev Kuleshov (16mm)

Strike, Sergei Eisenstein (V, 16mm)

Aelita, Yakov Protazanov (16mm)

Kino-Eye, Dziga Vertov

Cigarette-Girl from Mosselprom, Yuri Zhelyabuzhsky

1925   *Battleship Potemkin*, Sergei Eisenstein (V, 16mm)

The Death Ray, Lev Kuleshov

1926   *The Mother*, Vsevolod Pudovkin (V, 16mm)

A Sixth of the World, Dziga Vertov (16mm)

1927   *The End of St. Petersburg*, Vsevolod Pudovkin (V, 16mm)

October, Sergei Eisenstein (V, 16mm)

The Fall of the Romanov Dynasty, Esfir Shub (V, 16mm)

The Great Road, Esfir Shub

1928   *Storm Over Asia*, Vsevolod Pudovkin (V, 16mm)

The Russia of Nicholas II and Lev Tolstoy, Esfir Shub

1929   *The New Babylon*, Grigori Kozintsev and Leonid Trauberg (V)

Old and New or *The General Line*, Sergei Eisenstein (V, 16mm)

The Man With a Movie Camera, Dziga Vertov (16mm)

Arsenal, Alexander Dovzhenko (V, 16mm)

Turksib, Victor Turin

Ranks and People, Yakov Protazanov

1930   *Earth*, Alexander Dovzhenko (V, 16mm)

Enthusiasm, Dziga Vertov (16mm)

1934   *Chapayev*, Sergei and Georgy Vasiliev (V)

1935   *The Youth of Maxim*, Grigori Kozintsev, and Leonid Trauberg (16mm)

Aerograd, Alexander Dovzhenko

1936   *We from Krondstadt*, Yefim Dzigan (V)

Alexander Nevsky, Sergei Eisenstein (16mm)

1945   *Ivan The Terrible: Part I*, Sergei Eisenstein (V, 16mm)

1946   *Ivan The Terrible: Part II*, Sergei Eisenstein (V, 16mm)

Availability of Russian/Soviet films

Soviet/Russian films are easily obtained both on video and for hire on 16mm. Most of the key 1920s Soviet films have been released on video by **Hendring** and can also be hired on 16mm from the BFI at a relatively low cost (on average £25.00 plus delivery). For more information about hiring films see the BFI's films for hire catalogue, *Films on Offer*. A large number of the Russian films of the 1910s are also available (released by the BFI) as a set of ten videos.

Chapter 12

An introduction to Indian cinema

Asha Kasbekar

■ An introduction to Indian cinema

INTRODUCTION

India produces over 900 films a year, making it the world's largest film-producing nation. These films are viewed not just within the country, where they constitute the most important cultural activity, but in all of South Asia (Pakistan, Bangladesh, Sri Lanka), Africa (including the Maghreb countries of North Africa), South America, Eastern Europe and Russia. These films are also imported into all major European cities with a sizeable population of people of Asian and African descent.

The popular Indian film is radically different in narrative form and content to the Hollywood model of entertainment. Consequently, it offers its audiences an alternative to Hollywood, and one that is more in keeping with concerns particular to developing countries. Critical studies on Indian cinema, both in India and abroad, have been confined to just a handful of books and articles, and most of these have tended to concentrate on the work of 'art' film directors such as the internationally-renowned Satyajit Ray. This emphasis on highbrow art films tends to distort the understanding of Indian cinema, where the bulk of films are low-brow, mass-produced for multi-cultural audiences from varied linguistic backgrounds within India.

Although there is a tendency to refer to Indian cinema as if it were a cohesive whole, it is in fact fragmented into many regional film-producing centres, scattered all over the country. India has sixteen official languages and films are made in all the regional languages, with even an occasional film in classical Sanskrit. Hindi, the national language, is spoken in a variety of dialects by about 40 per cent of the population, and is broadly understood in most of the northern and central states. About 200 Hindi films are made each year in Bombay and are distributed throughout the country. Although Madras, the other film-making centre, makes more films a year in the regional languages of Tamil and Telugu, language barriers prevent it from challenging Bombay's national, and international, distribution network.

This chapter on Indian cinema will concentrate on the popular Hindi film. It will consider its narrative structure and formal conventions, both of which are in fact common to regional films as well, before embarking on a brief account of its historical evolution. This is so that the reader may bear in mind the unique nature of the cinematic experience while understanding the particular historical factors that have moulded it. It will also highlight certain directors from the popular as well as the elite 'art' cinema, and briefly examine their individual contributions.

THE NARRATIVE STRUCTURE

Popular Hindi cinema incorporated many of the formal conventions of the popular theatres, both rural and urban, that flourished in 1896 when the first foreign films began to be screened in the country. As a result the narrative structure does not follow the classic codes of Hollywood. Instead it has a loose storyline that is fragmented by frequent digressions into sub-plots and song and dance sequences. The audience is usually familar with the main plot because it is often a reworking of a previously successful film. Often it contains deep mythological resonances that are easily accessible to them. The films indulge in highly emotional scenes that are played out with tumescent rhetoric in grand, declamatory style. The comic sub-plots, the overstated emotions and the song and dance sequences, all of which are held together by the thin thread of a main story-line, result in films that would be considered 'nightmarishly long' by western audiences. However, for those initiated into the pleasures of the popular Hindi film, the two hours and forty-five minutes that any viewing demands is a very satisfying and cathartic experience, where not only are the anxieties of its audiences clearly identified, but fantasies to escape from those very anxieties are also provided.

Plot

As in Hollywood, the most favoured theme of the Hindi film is that of romance. A hand-some man, usually poor, but hard-working and honest, accidentally meets a rich and beautiful young woman. The two fall in love, but the young woman's father refuses to let them entertain any thoughts of marriage (the man's poverty, a prior marriage arrange-ment with the father's business partner's son or a feud between the two families being the most common reasons), and the two lovers are separated. However, when the young man saves the father's life, or shows the business partner to be a scheming crook intent on defrauding the credulous father, the father acknowledges his error of judgement and the young man is welcomed into the family fold.

Family relationships

Another recurring theme deals with family relationships. In the 1950s it featured the strains and pressures of modern life on the traditional, extended ('joint') family struc-ture, where three generations of the same family usually live under the same roof. In such films, the initial domestic harmony is threatened by the arrival of a new, western-ised daughter-in-law who refuses to respect the family hierarchy and nearly causes the family to break up. The crisis is then resolved through some supreme sacrifice on the part of one family member (usually the hero), who makes the young bride see the error of her ways.

By the 1970s, the family relationships theme evolved into 'lost and found' sagas, where two brothers become separated at birth, either because of a natural disaster (floods, tidal wave, earthquake) or an accident (usually involving trains). The two grow up in the same city (invariably Bombay), and one becomes a police officer while the other becomes a good-hearted gangster. When it falls to the police officer to shoot the gangster in the line of duty, kinship is suddenly recognised (a birthmark, a pendant, a long-lost sepia-coloured photograph) and the two brothers are united. Together they then embark on a mission to capture some other arch-criminal.

Family relationships are crucial to popular Hindi film regardless of its genre. Often, it is an individual character's response to family duties and responsibilities that defines his or her virtue or villainy. Thus in the 'lost and found' plot lines it is the gangster brother's longing for his family, in particular his mother – a longing that is expressed with poignant emotion and reiterated at critical dramatic junctures in the narrative – that reassures the audience of his inherent goodness. By the same token, a villain is one who completely disregards the sanctity of family relationships, and, by doing so, ensures that he is morally irredeemable.

Such romantic, family-related plot lines are completely familiar to the audiences. As Ashis Nandy points out:

> The Bombay film-story does not generally have an unexpected conclusion, it only has a predictable climax. It bases its appeal not on the linear development of a story line but on the special configuration which the film presents of many known

elements or themes derived from other movies, or, as Sudhir Kakar suggests, from familiar traditional tales.

(Nandy 1981: 90)

In the different forms of popular Indian theatre, such as the 'Ram Lila', episodes from the Indian epics are performed to audiences who are completely familiar with the stories, and who take pleasure in the familiarity of these myths and legends as well as in the visual spectacle of these performances. Since the plot is usually familiar to the audience, the interest lies in '*how* things will happen rather than *what* will happen next' (Thomas 1985: 130; emphasis in original). The familiar narrative then serves to provide openings for the exploration of emotions, songs and spectacle. Unlike the Hollywood film, it does not develop in a linear fashion with events arranged 'in a relationship of cause and effect'.

Whatever the plot, the central conflict involves notions of 'good' and 'evil' in which the Hindu concept of *dharma* (duty), kinship ties and social obligations play a crucial role (Thomas 1985: 125). The action is set in a fictional world that is not governed by spatial and temporal verisimilitude. This does not mean that in the fictional world constructed by the film, time and space relations are completely 'unmotivated', but that the popular Hindi film is not committed to a 'realist aesthetic', and consequently it does not construct the fictional world as an authentic 'slice of life'. Instead it constructs a system that has its own logic, and where 'realism' is sacrificed to the advantage of other considerations, the most of important of all being that of emotion.

Emotion

The affective principle is considered to be of very great importance to the cinematic experience and for a film to succeed at the box office it must be able to 'move' the audience, to reach out and 'touch their hearts'. Such emphasis on emotion finds its origins in the conventions of the classical Indian theatre as documented in the *Natyashastra* (*c*. second century AD), a scholarly treatise on the performing arts. According to Bharata, to whom this work is attributed, drama is played for the amusement of the audience through the use of stylised acting methods in order to convey eight basic emotions (**bhava**): love, humour, energy, anger, fear, grief, disgust and astonishment. These emotions are conveyed by playing their causes and their effects, so that the audiences watching the enactment experience the aesthetic essence of the eight corresponding sentiments (**rasa**) – the erotic, comic, heroic, furious, apprehensive, compassionate, horrific and marvellous (Warder 1975: 172). Based on the *rasa*, Bharata then outlined an elaborate theory of aesthetics in the performing arts.

Although the classical stage declined many centuries ago, its dramatic codes were inherited and deployed, albeit in a less refined form, by the various regional and 'folk' theatres throughout the land. The same aesthetic traditions were also incorporated into the popular urban theatres in the nineteenth century, such as the Parsi Theatre (so called because the theatres were often owned by Parsis, a distinct ethnic group of Persian origin) in Bombay and Calcutta, and later were incorporated into the newly arrived form of entertainment – the cinema. By adapting traditional aesthetics to a modern form of entertainment, the Indian cinema not only maintained an unbroken link with its historical past, but it also made itself immediately accessible to the people as a mass entertainer.

The exploration of many, and sometimes even all, of the eight emotions, identified by Bharata, within a single film has led the Bombay film to be referred to as '*masala*'

bhava

The eight basic emotions – love, humour, energy, anger, fear, grief, disgust, astonishment.

rasa

The eight sentiments which correspond to the emotions – erotic, comic, heroic, furious, apprehensive, compassionate, horrific, marvellous.

masala movie

Spicy Indian movie overloaded with emotion.

(as in Indian spices) movies. However, it is not enough to just convey these emotions through the various sub-plots and songs – they must also be powerfully overstated. Melodramatic overstatement is a 'crucial stylisation of the Bombay film' for it strives to be 'convincing as a spectacle by exaggeration' (Nandy 1981: 90). Nandy also cites the case of a disgruntled critic who complained that whenever a clock strikes in Indian films, it always strikes twelve! (Nandy 1981: 90).

Song

Even more important than emotion in the popular film is the presence of songs. Each film has about six to eight songs, although one early film, *Indrasabha*, is said to have contained seventy-one songs! (Kabir, 1991: 1). Critical studies of popular Indian cinema tend to concentrate on the structural complexities of film plots and often ignore the extra-narrative texts that are provided by the songs. However, the plot of a film is deliberately engineered so as to provide openings for a song and dance number at regular intervals.

The use of song and dance was already established in classical theatre, and Bharata in the *Natyashastra* considered **sangeeta** – that is, song, instrumental music and dance – to be an essential feature of the dramatic performance. The tradition has continued in popular theatre, where, even today, the song and dance numbers are the only sequences that are composed and rehearsed by the actors, the rest of the performance – the dialogue and witty repartees – being often improvised.

sangeeta

Combination of song, instrumental music and dance.

In popular cinema, attempts by established directors to present 'songless' films resulted in box-office disasters, and the importance accorded to songs in cinematic entertainment can be gauged by the important billing the 'music director' (the composer and arranger of music) and the lyricist are given in the credits. Their names also appear alongside those of the producer and director on billboard hoardings, posters and other film publicity materials.

The first talkie, *Alam Ara* (A. Irani, 1931), was a direct transfer from the stage of the Parsi Theatre and included many songs. The success of *Alam Ara*, and in particular of its songs, meant that the form of the musical drama set the trend for the future of Indian films. According to film historians Barnouw and Krishnaswamy:

> The Indian sound film, unlike the sound film of any other land, had from its first moment seized exclusively on music–drama forms. In doing so, the film had tapped a powerful current, one that went back some two thousand years.
>
> (1980: 69)

The development of song and dance

During the silent era, film screenings were accompanied by live music played by a small group of musicians. Imported films had western musical accompaniment (usually on a piano), whereas Indian films had Indian musical accompaniment. In rural areas, special narrators would explain the 'title cards' and elaborate on the intricacies of the plot. Sometimes they even provided their own sound effects (such as the sound of galloping horses or, for the more dramatic scenes, the crash of thunder).

The songs in the early talkies were based on melodies borrowed from folk and classical traditions. Sound technology in the early 1930s was primitive. The microphones used for sound recording had to be stationary in order to reduce noise disturbances, and thus restricted the physical movements of the actors (Skillman 1986: 134). Early sound recordists recall the difficult circumstances under which songs were performed for the camera. One technique was to bury the camera under mattresses and covers in order to muffle its whirring noise. Then a single microphone would be directed at the actor/singer while a small number of musicians sat outside of the camera frame to provide the accompaniment. The placing of the single microphone meant that the actor could not move without upsetting the balance between voice and musical accompaniment, and the scene had to be shot in a single take with the actor/singer standing stiffly, rooted in one spot (Kabir 1991: 1). Musicians and even orchestras were hidden behind the surrounding trees and bushes which soon became crucial fixtures during song and dance sequences. Sometimes the musicians were even suspended from branches in order to be close enough for the singer to hear the notes clearly. These sylvan surroundings, which began as a technical necessity, have today become a clichéd convention of the popular film song, even though they have long outlived their usefulness, and the actor's tendency to 'run around trees' during a song is regularly satirised in the elite press.

The overwhelming importance of song resulted in the industry preferring to employ singers, even if they could not act, rather than actors who could not sing. But in 1935, music director R.C. Boral discovered that if he pre-recorded the songs with good singers, then non-singing actors could be made to lip-synchronise on screen during the song (Skillman 1986: 135). The practice became known as '**play-back**' and is today a standard feature of popular Indian cinema.

'Play-back' liberated the actor's dance movements, and the filming of the song and dance routine is referred to as a '**song picturisation**'. Soon singers became celebrities in their own right. Lata Mangeshkar, who recently retired after nearly half a century of 'play-back' singing, has over 25,000 songs to her credit.

Most songs last about five minutes. According to composer Bhaskar Chandavarkar, these songs started out being three and a half minutes long because

> the 78 r.p.m. was the only recording format available till other means of sound recording came to be invented and the film magazine would not allow very lengthy sequences to be filmed without a break. These factors made it necessary to have songs of about 3½ minutes neatly cut into 3 stanzas along with the opening 'mukhra' – the catch words. The three stanzas were again neatly interspersed with musical interludes. These features became so popular that songs which were not recorded for films also emulated them.
>
> (Chandavarkar 1985: 249)

The arrival of the 33⅓ long-playing disc-recording developed in the 1950s enabled music directors to compose longer songs and by the 1970s the average film song was about five minutes long and in stereo (Skillman 1986: 142).

Today the film song has a life beyond the screen. They are played over loud speakers on national holidays and religious festivals. At weddings the band invariably belts out the current favourites. Beggars, singing in the streets and on trains, have incorporated them into their repertoire. Even the 'folk' theatres, that once inspired film music, have now abandoned their original songs for the film versions of the same. Radio stations entirely devoted to film songs abound, and television programmes that provided a compilation of song and dance sequences from different films were popular in India long before music videos and MTV were devised.

play-back

Pre-recording of songs with good singers and with non-singing actors lip-synchronising on screen.

song picturisation

Filming of a song and dance routine.

• Plate 12.1 Raveena Tandon and Akshay Kumar in Rajiv Rai's *Mohra*

Spectacle

The song and dance numbers are devised as visually spectacular sequences. Traditional forms of entertainment placed great emphasis on spectacle and used elaborate masks (or stylised make-up), ornate costumes and decorative head-dresses. Indian cinema, having incorporated their aesthetic conventions, places similar importance on spectacular visual display, particularly in the song and dance sequences, and uses grand settings (palaces or breathtaking landscapes) and glittering costumes which often have little bearing on the actual story. In *Mughal-e-Azam* (K. Asif, 1960), an extravagant historical costume drama that is alleged to have taken fifteen years to complete, the crucial moment of the film is constructed around a song and dance number, and choreographed in a specially constructed 'Hall of Mirrors' (*Sheesh Mahal*), in such a manner that the danceuse is reflected in miniature in every piece of mirror in the hall. Although not every film can afford to achieve such dazzling brilliance, sumptuous visual effects are eagerly sought after by film directors.

Love songs are central to the popular Hindi film and they are often contrived as 'dream sequences'. During such flights into fantasy the unities of time and space are completely disregarded. The 'song picturisations' strive for maximum visual effect,

• Plate 12.2 Madhuri Dixit and Kumar Gaurav in Aryam Films *Phool*

and each stanza of the song reveals a different panoramic setting and yet another gorgeous costume. The film industry's penchant for such opulent pageantry has resulted in it being regularly condemned by the cultural elite as 'dream merchants' peddling 'escapist fantasies'.

Functions of the song

In addition to the aural and visual pleasures that the song offers its public, it also fulfils a more delicate social function. In a conservative society that frowns on romantic liaisons, and where marriages are arranged within caste groupings (*jatis*), any verbal declaration of love and sexual desire between man and woman risks causing embarrassment. By transferring such declarations into song and distancing the emotions by putting them in the realm of fantasy or dream, the family watching the film together (a common practice in India) is spared any possible awkwardness.

The song also links disparate elements of the usually complicated plot and sub-plots, thus ensuring some coherence in the theme. It also offers a commentary on Life, Fate and Destiny and even provides an escape from an overwrought emotional scene. More importantly, the song functions as a bridge between tradition and modernity (Skillman 1986: 143). Pressure on music directors to come up with six to eight songs for each film has resulted in rampant pilfering from all musical sources and particularly western pop music. While early films drew on Indian classical and folk traditions, by the 1950s music directors began seeking inspiration from western sources. Not only were western instruments incorporated into ever-growing orchestrations, but blatant copies of rock 'n' roll, samba and even western classical symphonies set to Indian lyrics became common-place. A guitar-strumming Elvis, a disco-dancing John Travolta, a break-dancing Michael Jackson and many other icons of western culture have all been reproduced on the Indian screen. Such 'hybridisation' of film music, although distasteful to the purists, has provided a cultural filter through which the latest musical trends have been made accessible to the Indian public.

Stars

Along with the spectacular song and dance sequences, and the emotional excess indulged in during scenes of dramatic intensity, the next most important features of the popular Indian film are the stars or 'superstars' (as they have been proclaimed by the well-oiled publicity machinery). The stars earn fabulous sums of money that could easily compare with their counterparts in Hollywood. Male stars are always paid more than female stars. So familiar are their faces to the public that they do not need to be ident-ified by name either on the posters or on the huge hand-painted billboards that dominate the skyline of all major Indian cities.

The actors and actresses work several shifts a day on different films, and getting 'dates' for a major star is a serious problems for film-makers. Gossip magazines provide an inexhaustible supply of stories about their extravagant lifestyles and their unconventional sex life. They are seldom sued by the stars implicated in the gossip, and often the revelations are made to coincide with an important release to help boost attendance in cinemas. Many stars of the 1960s and the 1970s have been successful in pushing their offspring into films, creating a second generation of stars within certain families. A growing number have been able to pursue a successful career in politics after retiring from films. A few have tried to find fame and fortune in Hollywood but with little success.

Genre

Indian films have their own genres that do not always correspond with western generic classifications (Thomas 1985: 120). Since every film is a 'musical' as well as a 'melo-drama', genre is determined by the dominant emotion in the assortment on offer within a particular film. Most films have a romantic plot in which family relationships are crucial to the drama, thus a film is described as a 'romance' if family relationships are not as important in the film as the love interest, and a 'family drama' if family relationships are given greater prominence than romance. Additionally there are 'mythological' films that usually recount myths or legends from the two great Hindu epics, the *Ramayana* and the *Mahabharata*, while 'devotional' films (both Hindu and Muslim) explore divine interventions and miracles or recount the lives of saints, or involve a pilgrimage to holy shrines and rivers, because such viewings of sacred sites (even on celluloid) are con-sidered to shower blessings on the viewer.

The 'social' is an extended generic classification and refers to any film with a socially uplifting message. It can cover themes of economic exploitation, the evils of the caste system, child marriages, each of which is often placed within a romantic plot. The subgenre of the 'Muslim social' indicates a romance set in a Muslim community and in which Muslim lifestyles are exotically exaggerated. There are a few 'horror' films that feature supposedly *Tantric* rituals and other black magic practices. 'Suspense dramas' make very rare appearances on the screen because the public's need to know the plot in advance is a decided disincentive.

Formula

A film that has a familiar plot and contains romance, dramatic family relationships and an epic struggle between the forces of 'good' and 'evil', themselves determined by traditional concepts of 'duty' (*dharma*) and family obligations, and is enacted by stars and embellished by several spectacular song and dance numbers, is referred to as a 'formula' film. The director's skill lies not just in deploying the different components of the 'formula' but in presenting them in innovative ways so that they appear new and different with each film.

It is this elusive perfection of balance between the different components of the 'formula', this magical combination of the emotional, the visual and the musical ingredients, that holds the key to a box-office success so crucial to the industry. The fact that out of the approximately 200 films produced in Hindi each year, only 5 to 10 per cent are commercially successful, shows that Indian audiences are mercilessly discerning in their assessment of the films on offer. Fifteen to twenty per cent of the films manage to break even, while the rest lose money. A successful film can reap huge financial rewards for the distributors, catapult new actors and actresses into instant stardom or double a star's rates and, as approving audiences flock to the cinemas (estimated at 90 million a week throughout India) to view the film not once but several times, can immediately activate a thriving black market for tickets outside the cinemas.

HISTORY OF THE POPULAR HINDI FILM

The Lumière Brothers opened their cinematograph to the public on 28 December 1895 in Paris. Six months later their emissary, Maurice Sestier, *en route* to Australia to exhibit a collection of short films, stopped off in Bombay. The first screenings of these Lumière films took place in Bombay at Watson's Hotel for an audience consisting largely of British residents in India, some Europeans and a few Anglicised Indians. The response from the English-language press was so unexpectedly enthusiastic that further screenings were quickly programmed, and later, to accommodate the even bigger crowds that showed up, the screenings were moved to the much larger Novelty Theatre.

A cinema audience had suddenly been created and from 1897 onwards there was a regular inflow of films, imported from Britain, France, USA, Italy, Denmark and Germany. The British residents in India as well as the Indians soon began to import filming equipment and to make their own films. These short features consisted of comic gags, operas, sports events and other documentaries about local events (Barnouw and Krishnaswamy 1980: 8). By 1902, a network for the distribution and exhibition of films within India and South-East Asia had been put in place by several Indian entrepreneurs.

The silent films

The first feature-length Indian feature was called *Raja Harishchandra*. Made in 1912 by D.G. Phalke, it was about a famous king from Hindu mythology, named Harishchandra, who was willing to sacrifice all his worldly possessions in his pursuit of Truth. The film was 3,700 feet long, and when screened with a hand-cranked projector lasted about fifty minutes. It is said that the inspiration for this film came from *Life of Christ* (Gaumont, 1906) that was being screened in Bombay as a Christmas feature in 1910. Phalke was so impressed by the special effects used to show the miracles performed by Christ, that he went to see it again, this time taking his wife with him and borrowing money from his neighbours for the transport and tickets (Barnouw and Krishnaswamy 1980: 11). Film historian B.V. Dharap cites an article written by Phalke in November 1917 in which Phalke states:

> While the *Life of Christ* was rolling fast before my physical eyes, I was mentally visualising the Gods, Shri Krishna, Shri Ramachandra, their Gokul and their Ayodhya. I was gripped by a strange spell. I bought another ticket and saw the film again. This time I felt my imagination taking shape on the screen. Could this really happen? Could we, the sons of India, ever be able to see Indian images on the screen?
>
> (Dharap 1985: 35)

Phalke, a graduate of an art school and one-time draughtsman and photographer at the Archaeological Department, had given up his job to join the struggle for freedom from British colonial rule. After seeing the *Life of Christ*, he liquidated his possessions, journeyed to London and bought himself some film-making equipment. On returning to India he enlisted the help of his wife and made India's first film feature – *Raja Harishchandra*. It met with phenomenal success. Phalke, also an amateur magician, had incorporated the techniques of Georges Méliès, famed for his special effects. These techniques lent themselves easily to the miracles and divine interventions that abound in stories from Hindu mythology. Suddenly the mythological kings and sages, that were so familiar, came alive before the very eyes of the cinema audiences and Hindu legends began to acquire an unprecedented allure.

After the success of *Raja Harishchandra*, Phalke moved to Nasik, bought a huge house and set up the nation's first studio. All the actors lived and worked in Phalke's family home. Initially the actors were all male because acting, as a profession, was considered no better than prostitution. Even prostitutes, unsure of the new form of entertainment, declined to participate. (It was only a decade later that women agreed to act in films. At first the actresses were from the Anglo-Indian community, who were despised by 'respectable' society. They assumed Hindu names to make themselves acceptable to the film-going public.)

Phalke's acting team went on to make at least two silent films a year. The stories were usually drawn from Hindu mythology which made them instantly accessible to a nation familiar with the myths and legends. Phalke had started a national culture and a lucrative industry. Sadly he died in 1944, a destitute and forgotten man. It was only several decades after his death that his contribution was officially recognised and he was hailed as the 'Father of Indian cinema'.

Meanwhile, others entered the field, and soon historical and social themes began to be introduced to the screen. Audiences seemed to prefer locally-made films to the European and American imports. Between 1912 and 1934 1,279 silent films were made in the country (Wadia 1985: 21). Most of these have perished, but the few that have survived are preserved at the Film Archives in Pune.

The age of sound

The arrival of sound was to prove a serious problem for the film industry. India, with its linguistic diversity, would need to make films in different regional languages which would mean the fragmentation of a vast national market into smaller regional, and consequently commercially less lucrative, ones. *Alam Ara* (A. Irani, 1931), the first talkie, was made in Bombay in Hindi, the national language. Ever since, the Bombay-based film industry, which makes films in Hindi, has dominated film production in India.

The advent of sound necessitated the construction of sound studios and indoor shooting. Several studios were constructed in the major cities of India, and Lahore (now in Pakistan), Bombay, Calcutta and later Madras became important film centres. By the end of the 1930s there were nearly a hundred studios, big and small, involved in film production. Of these there were three that were to greatly influence the future development of the Indian cinema.

New Theatres

In 1931, B.N. Sircar, an engineer who had completed the construction of a brand new theatre, decided to build a film theatre for himself in Calcutta. He equipped it with a first-class studio and provided the talented group of Bengalis he had gathered around him with all the resources necessary for creative film-making. This was the start of New Theatres. One director to achieve fame and recognition soon after the studio was set up was Debaki Bose. His first success was *Chandidas* (1932) based on the life of the eponymous sixteenth-century poet–saint. Bose's liberal use of music and song blended well with the requirements of the religious theme. His later films for New Theatres were also on religious or mythological themes, the most famous being *Puran Bhagat* (1933) and *Seeta* (1934). *Seeta* was the first ever Indian film to be screened at an international festival.

However, the greatest sensation to emerge from New Theatres was P.C. Barua, an Assamese prince whose production of *Devdas* (1935), based on a novel by the renowned literateur Sarat Chandra Chatterjee, was to overwhelm the nation. Made in Bengali and in Hindi, it told the tragic tale of Devdas, a man who takes to drink and drowns his sorrows in melancholic songs when the woman he loves is married off to another by her parents. Indeed, so moving were these soulful songs and the tragic resolution that 'virtually a generation wept over Devdas' (Barnouw and Krishnaswamy 1980: 80). P.C. Barua, who directed both versions but starred in only the Bengali version, also died of drink (but not melancholy) at the age of 48.

Most of the later films made by New Theatres were drawn from literary sources, thus the audience began to associate the studio's productions with sophisticated, high calibre and intellectual music–dramas.

Prabhat Studios

Competition to New Theatres in Calcutta was to come from Prabhat Studios in Pune. First established in Kolhapur in Maharashtra State in 1929, the studio shifted to Pune in 1933. Like New Theatres, Prabhat too began by making mythological and devotional films. The most influential personality to emerge from this studio was V. Shantaram. His first film, made in Marathi (the regional language), was *Ayodhyache Raja* in 1932 and it told the story of the same King Harishchandra that had made Phalke famous. In 1936, Shantaram's associates S. Fatehlal and V.G. Damle made a devotional film on Tukaram, a seventeenth-century poet–saint. Called *Sant Tukaram*, it was the first Indian film to win an international award at the Venice Film Festival and it is still considered one of the finest Indian films ever made.

Shantaram, however, moved away from mythological themes and began to explore social issues. His most famous films dealt with the abuses of arranged marriages (*Duniya Na Mane* in 1937) and Hindu–Muslim animosity (*Padosi* in 1941). Soon Prabhat became known nationwide for its 'social' films. Not only were the films ideologically bold for the times, they were also innovative in their use of camera, music and song and would greatly influence later directors who began as apprentices at the studio.

Bombay Talkies

The other major studio in the 1930s was Bombay Talkies which was set up by Himansu Rai. Rai had worked in Britain and Germany, but the economic depression and the subsequent rise of fascism forced him and his actress wife, Devika Rani, to return to India. Devika Rani, who had trained in London, met Rai and worked with him in Germany where she had the opportunity to watch Fritz Lang, G.W. Pabst and Marlene Dietrich at work (Barnouw and Krishnaswamy 1980: 97). Returning to Bombay with a few German technicians, they set up Bombay Talkies, and proceeded to make three films a year. These were usually sophisticated romances in Hindi and were directed by Rai with Devika Rani as the leading actress. Occasionally they made a film with a social message that reflected the nationalism of the time. One such film was *Achhut Kanya* (1936) which explored the doomed relationship between a high caste Brahmin man and a woman from an 'untouchable' caste.

Rai ran his studio with an authoritarian paternalism. He would recruit only university graduates, and all recruits were given equal status regardless of whether they were actors or technicians. They received a monthly salary and worked fixed hours. They were provided with a canteen, health-care facilities and free education for the children. Film historians Barnouw and Krishnaswamy write:

> It was known that at Bombay Talkies all company members, of whatever caste, ate together at the company canteen. It was even said that top actors, on occasion, helped clean floors. . . . All this was part of the legend and role of Bombay Talkies.
>
> (1980: 103)

Many film directors, who were to find fame and fortune in independent India, received their early training at this studio.

In addition to these three major studios, other smaller studios (or 'banners', as they were called) included Minerva Movietone, built around the personality of Sohrab Modi, the Laurence Olivier of India, which specialised in grand productions based on historical subjects; Wadia Movietone which specialised in stunt films starring the female stunt artiste Nadia. Of Welsh and Greek origin, Nadia amazed her audiences with her daring exploits which often included dramatic rescues from moving trains, runaway cars or wild horses, cheaper imitations of which were reproduced by lesser companies.

The end of the studios

The 'studio era' was an exciting period in the development of Indian cinema. It laid the foundations for a powerful nationwide industry, trained a whole generation of actors, directors and technicians and created a discerning but enthusiastic audience all over the country. The outbreak of the Second World War was to drastically change the film industry. The war, in which India was an unwilling partner, necessitated an expansion of defence-related industries within the country. Rapid industrialisation brought in new money for investment in films. The reduced marine traffic between Britain and India led to a scarcity in essential commodities, and black marketeering flourished. This untaxed (or 'black') money found its way into films and established a covert relationship between money laundering and film finance, a relationship that continues to thrive even today.

With large amounts of extra cash, new independent producers entered the market. Not wishing to be encumbered with the overheads of a studio and staff, they began to entice actors, musicians, singers and technicians away from the studios for large sums of money. Actors discovered that they could command huge fees for a single film and the producers realised that by promoting the image of an actor as a 'star' they could woo large audiences. Within a decade, the studios, with their high overheads including maintenance of the studios as well as monthly salaries to actors regardless of whether they made films or not, ran into financial difficulties and many, like Bombay Talkies, were soon reduced to renting out their studios to the new breed of independent producers, before being forced to close down completely.

The struggle for independence

The late 1930s onwards was a period of intense political activity that continued until India gained independence from Britain on 15 August 1947. The struggle for freedom from colonial rule, led by Mahatma Gandhi, resulted in strict British censorship of Indian films. Political films that overtly reflected the growing nationalist spirit were subject to close scrutiny. Any film that brought into contempt 'soldiers wearing His Majesty's uniform, Ministers of Religion, Ministers of the Crown, Ambassadors and official representatives of foreign nations, the police, the judges or civil servants of Government' was banned (Shah 1981: 234). But films that dealt with social reform did not challenge British authority. In fact, they promoted the 'civilising' role that the British liked to believe they played in India. Concerned about their financial investments, which would suffer if their films were to be banned, film-makers opted to entertain the Indian public with heady romances or social dramas.

Some film-makers, however, responded to these political strictures by deliberately creating an Indian character who caricatured British mannerisms. Wearing a tailored suit and carrying a hat, he was ridiculed as either a villain or a buffoon who constantly berated the Indians as 'damn fools'. The nationalist hero, in traditional Indian attire, usually got the better of him.

As the fervour for independence increased, some directors responded to the mood of the nation by slipping in patriotic images. For instance, in *Anmol Ghadi* (Mehboob, 1945) a character opens a magazine, the cover of which carries the picture of Subhash Chandra Bose, founder of the outlawed Indian National Army. In courtroom dramas, it was a picture of Mahatma Gandhi that hung on the wall, instead of a picture of the British monarch. The censors lost no time in removing these images. Barnouw and Krishnaswamy write:

> Film producers now took to the casual introduction of Congress symbols into films. On the wall, in the background, one would see the Gandhian motif, the spinning wheel, signifying defiance of the economic pattern of empire. In a store there would be a calendar with Gandhi's portrait; in a home, a photograph of Nehru; on the sound track, the effect of a passing parade, with few bars of a favourite Congress song. Often such symbols had no plot reference; but in theatres they elicited cheers. As war began, British censors ordered the scissoring of such shots. After 1942, when Gandhi was again imprisoned – along with a number of other Congress leaders – no photograph of Gandhi was allowed on screen, no matter how incidentally.
>
> (1980: 124)

In *Kismet* (G. Mukerjee, 1943), a crime thriller, a rousing song asks the Germans and Japanese to leave India alone. However, the 'song picturisation' leaves no one in doubt as to which foreign power is being implied in the lyrics. In Calcutta alone *Kismet* ran for three and a half years at one theatre.

The pre-independence years also saw the revival of historical and mythological themes as metaphors for the political struggle. In *Sikander* (Sohrab Modi, 1941), a brave Indian ruler fights back Alexander the Great's bid to conquer India. In *Ram Rajya* (Vijay Bhatt, 1943) the epic battle between Lord Rama and Ravana, a struggle between 'good' and 'evil', came to signify India's struggle against the British. Having captured the belligerent mood of the nation, these films proved to be box-office hits.

During the Second World War, the British government introduced a quota system to distribute scarce raw film stock. In order to qualify for the quota, film-makers were required to devote at least one film out of every four films made to promoting the 'war effort' (Barnouw and Krishnaswamy 1980: 130). These films were very rarely popular with the Indian public. Director V. Shantaram found that one way to circumvent the requirements of the British government was to make an anti-Japanese film set in China. *Dr. Kotnis Ki Amar Kahani* (1946), about an Indian doctor who helps the Chinese communist forces fight the Japanese, was perhaps the only 'war effort' film to find favour with the public.

Independence and after

India became independent in 1947. The film industry celebrated by immediately making films about those who had martyred themselves for the cause of liberty, such as *Shaheed* (R. Sehgal, 1948). But the celebrations were marred by the nightmare of partitioning the country into a secular India and an Islamic Pakistan. Millions of Hindus and Muslims crossed the new frontiers and arrived as refugees in the country of their choice. Many Punjabi Hindu film-makers, musicians, lyricists and technicians, who had worked at the studios in Lahore (now in Pakistan), made their way to Bombay and within a decade began to influence film-making there. Calcutta lost a substantial proportion of its audience when East Bengal became East Pakistan (today Bangladesh). As the studios in Calcutta began to flounder, many who had worked and trained at New Theatres moved to Bombay. The decline of Lahore and Calcutta as centres of film-making established Bombay as the film capital of India and it was unofficially christened '**Bollywood**'.

'Bollywood'

Bombay, the film capital of India.

If the film producers were expecting a comprehensive liberalisation of censorship after independence, they were sorely disappointed. The Indian censors had begun to show that they were even stricter than their colonial predecessors. 'Sexual immorality' was to be avoided at all costs. Censorship guidelines quoted in the *Journal of the Bengal Motion Picture Association* in May 1949 advised:

> Illegal forms of sex relationship, such as free love, companionate marriage or virgin motherhood, shall not be permitted. Adultery or illicit sex relationship, if necessary for the plot, shall not be justified nor presented attractively. Kissing or embracing by adults, exhibiting passion repugnant to good taste shall not be shown.
>
> (cited in Shah 1981: 246)

Denied the chance to explore desire, the songs sang about it and, at the crucial moment when the lovers' lips came close to kiss, the camera turned away abruptly to show a pair of love birds, a garden of roses or a gushing fountain. Recently the ban on kissing was finally lifted by the censors, but directors still prefer to employ

• Plate 12.3 Akshay Kumar and Raveena Tandon in Trimurti Film's *Mohra*, produced by Gulshan Rai and directed by Rajiv Rai

the stratagems evolved over the decades to display passion. Besides, the actresses are still reluctant to kiss their male partners on screen.

The 'golden age' of Hindi cinema

Enthusiasm for the new republic gave fresh impetus to film production in the country. As talented writers, musicians, lyricists, actors, directors and technicians found their way to Bombay, the combination of such varied talent led film historians to refer to the 1950s as the 'golden age' of Hindi cinema.

Four directors were to dominate the decade: Mehboob Khan, Raj Kapoor, Bimal Roy and Guru Dutt. All four had served their apprenticeship in the major studios and all four showed themselves to be influenced by the major film movements in the West. These influences they managed to incorporate into the conventions of song, dance, melodrama and spectacle that had by now become well-established within the popular Hindi film. Their works also reflect the changes within a country that had now embraced industrialisation, agrarian reforms and Nehru's socialism.

☐ CASE STUDY 1: MEHBOOB KHAN (1904–64)

In a recent biography, Mehboob Khan has been compared to Hollywood's Cecil de Mille. However, in his early films Mehboob brought to the screen his own brand of Marxist–Islamic ideology. His two main concerns were poverty and the tragedy of women under patriarchy. His early film, *Roti* (1942), is a stark denunciation of capitalism and man's incurable greed.

Of very humble origins, Mehboob began as an 'extra' before working his way up to direction and production. His early films show Eisenstein's formalist influence, and only in his later films does he reveal the spectacular flourish of Cecil de Mille. Mehboob's most famous work is *Mother India* (1957), the status of which has been compared to that of *Gone With the Wind* in Hollywood. A remake of his earlier film *Aurat* (1940), it tells of a peasant woman's struggle to keep alive her children in the face of famine without sacrificing either her virtue or her self-respect. The story takes place against a background of the nation's transition from primitive farming to modern mechanised agriculture. While the denunciation of exploitation of peasants is robust, the production itself is very lavish and extravagant. Some of his other films, *Najma* (1942), *Andaz* (1949) and *Anmol Ghadi* (1945), explore the claustrophobic world of women, and the tragedy of those who try and escape it. An ardent supporter of Nehru's socialistic programmes, Mehboob's own death occurred one day after Nehru died.

☐ CASE STUDY 2: RAJ KAPOOR (1926–88)

The Kapoor family hold a very special place in Indian cinema and in the hearts of movie-goers. Raj Kapoor, son of the famous stage and film actor Prithviraj Kapoor, trained with the Bombay Talkies before being given the opportunity to direct his first film *Aag* (1948) at the age of 22. Handsome with unusual blue eyes, he showed his early influences to be Hollywood actors such as Ronald Coleman, Clark Gable and Charlie Chaplin. His early films tackle issues of unemployment and homelessness – serious themes that he presented, not with didacticism, but with entertaining music and audacious love scenes. With the success of *Awara* (1951), which became an instant hit in the USSR and was alleged to be one of Chairman Mao Zedong's favourite films, and *Shri 420* (1955), in which he assumed a tragi-comic Chaplinesque persona, Kapoor established himself as superb entertainer of the masses.

Raj Kapoor acted in over seventy films in his lifetime and produced about seventeen features. He often played the common man seeking to survive the problems of rapid industrialisation and unemployment. In his later films he was to exploit the theme of sexual corruption, but with increasingly erotic imagery, as in *Sangam* (1964), *Satyam Shivam Sundaram* (1978) and *Ram Teri Ganga Maili* (1985). His younger brothers, Shammi Kapoor and Shashi Kapoor, also became highly successful film stars, and his son Rishi Kapoor is still popular with audiences. With granddaughter Karishma Kapoor now established as an actress, the Indian audiences have seen four generations of the Kapoor family in stellar roles.

CASE STUDY 3: BIMAL ROY (1902–66)

Son of a rich landowning family, Bimal Roy moved from New Theatres in Calcutta to the film industry in Bombay. His first film in Hindi, *Do Bigha Zamin* (1953), shows the stylistic influence of the Italian neo-realists, and in particular Vittorio de Sica's classic *Bicycle Thieves* (1948). *Do Bigha Zamin* tells the tragic tale of the small farmer forced off his land by big business and eventually reduced to a migrant worker seeking employment in the city. Roy's most memorable commercial successes were *Madhumati* (1958) and *Sujata* (1959), both of which revealed his ability to integrate his personal political ideology with the requirements of the box office. A committed opponent of the *zamindari* system of landownership, the tyrannical landlord frequently appears as the villain in his films.

CASE STUDY 4: GURU DUTT (1925–64)

No other popular film director has attained the cult status accorded to Guru Dutt. A trained dancer, he served as an apprentice at Prabhat before being given a chance to direct a film. As his repertoire of films reveals, Dutt experimented with a different genre in each new film. What is striking about his art is his unusually dynamic use of camera and his highly innovative style of 'song picturisation'. Like Raj Kapoor, Guru Dutt acted in many of the films that he directed. His greatest film success came in with *Pyaasa* (1957), which told the tale of a neglected poet, traumatised by society's obsession with money and by the moral corruption that lies behind the respectability of the middle classes. The film has a powerful mystical undercurrent, and the material and spiritual are juxtaposed within the poet's world.

In *Kaagaz Ke Phool* (1959), Dutt pays homage to the studios of the 1930s and in particular to P.C. Barua. In the film a respected director finds that his domestic problems begin to take a toll on his work, and he succumbs to drink and degradation. The film flopped at the box office. A disappointed Dutt committed suicide at the age of 39.

All the four directors mentioned above explored new, exciting themes while honouring the conventional demands of the box office. With great actors like Dilip Kumar, Dev Anand, Raj Kapoor, actresses such as Nargis, Meena Kumari and Madhubala, music directors such as Naushad Ali, Salil Chaudhary and Ravi, lyricists like Sahir Ludhianvi, Majrooh Sultanpuri and Shakeel Badayuni, never again was such a glittering array of talent to be assembled at one time in the Hindi film industry.

Colour and the triumph of romance

Although Mehboob's *Aan* (1952) was the first colour film in India (it was in technicolour and processed in Europe), colour processing equipment was not imported into India until the early 1960s. Colour photography raised production costs and at first only a few crucial scenes in some major productions were shot in colour. Colour lent itself easily to the need for spectacle and in *Mughal-e-Azam* (1960), the famed dance in the 'hall of mirrors' was one of the few scenes in colour, while the rest of the film was shot in black and white.

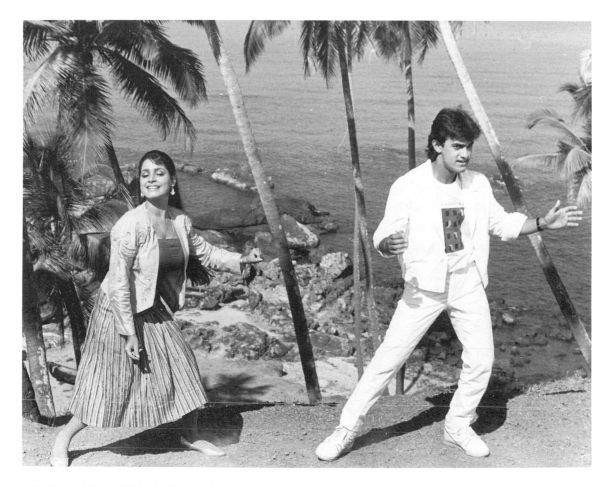

• Plate 12.4 Aamir Khan and Neelam in *Afsana Pyar Ka*

Colour also provided tremendous scope for outdoor shooting in scenes of romance. The magnificent landscape in Kashmir or the 'hill stations' at the foothills of the Himalayas brought home to the predominantly urban audiences the majestic beauty of certain regions of India. Film plots were accordingly adjusted to provide scope for such visual delights. For example, in *Jungalee* (S. Mukherjee, 1961), a romantic comedy, the protagonist undertakes a trip to Kashmir where he meets a beautiful woman and falls in love, which then provides the excuse for many love songs set in the snow-covered mountains of the region before the two return to Bombay. When most areas of scenic beauty in India were exhausted, producers began to go abroad in search of new and exotic locations. Film titles like *Love in Tokyo* (1966), *Singapore* (1960), and *Around the World on Eight Dollars* (1967), clearly revealed the producers' intentions to the audiences.

The 1960s was a decade of romance. With the memories of colonial rule now dimmed by the passage of time, it became acceptable to present the hero with a veneer of westernisation. The villain, however, continued to be presented as an over-westernised creature, a caricature devised during colonial rule, in order to circumvent censorship.

The difference is that today he functions as a symbol, not of British colonialism, but of an un-Indian 'unwholesomeness', of an immoral and decadent 'Other' against which the Indian identity can be defined.

Writing on the subject of Indian identity, Thomas states:

> Since it first emerged in the context of colonial India's fight for independence, Indian cinema, for a number of reasons, has been concerned with constructing a notion of Indian cultural and national identity. This has involved drawing on concepts such as 'tradition'. But a chaste and pristine India has also been constructed by opposing it to a decadent and exotic 'other', the licentious and immoral 'West', with the films' villains invariably sporting a clutter of signifiers of 'Westernisation': whiskey bottles, bikini-clad escorts, or foreign limousines.

(1989: 11)

The westernised (but not over-westernised) hero, for example Shammi Kapoor, star of several lively romances in the 1960s, who in unabashed imitation of Elvis strutted across the screen sporting a quiff and strumming a guitar, came to epitomise 'modernity' as part of a quest for a modern national identity in post-colonial India. (For a discussion of the images of Elvis in Indian cinema see Rai 1994: 51–77.)

The angry young man

The romance of the 1960s was to change dramatically with the arrival of a new team of screenwriters. Salim Khan and Javed Akhtar replaced the anodyne romantic hero with a new 'angry young man'. In their first commercial success, *Zanjeer* (Prakash Mehra, 1973), the new hero was inspired by Clint Eastwood in *Dirty Harry* (Don Seigel, 1971). He was lean, mean and angry, more prone to fight than burst into melancholic songs. This image of the introverted avenger, mostly popularised on screen by actor Amitabh Bachchan, was to dominate the hearts and minds of the cinema-going public for the next fifteen years. Although songs were not entirely dispensed with, these films placed less emphasis on songs and dances and, in many instances, substituted them with colourful, bone-crunching fight sequences. The prioritisation of action over romance led inevitably to the presentation of violence as gory 'spectacle'.

Technology borrowed from Hollywood gave cinematographers greater scope to offer 'realistic' violence (blood spurts, neck breaks, etc.). A new function, that of the **fight composer**, who choreographed spectacular fights in which incredible acts of valour and heroism were enacted, was created and was given an important billing in the film credits. The romantic heroes of the 1960s found themselves nudged aside by actors who could perform audacious stunts.

One way of cashing in on the new demand for 'violence as spectacle' was to increase the number of 'villains' in a film, which in turn necessitated a proliferation of heroes to combat these villains. 'Multi-starrers' became a generic term in the 1970s, particularly after the unparalleled success of a spectacular multi-starrer 'curry western', *Sholay* (Ramesh Sippy, 1975). The new 'superstars' as they became known, thanks to the film publicists, were paid enormous sums of money, and more importantly began to exercise control over different aspects of the film. Screenplays, songs and dialogues began to be rewritten to suit the whims of the superstars.

fight composer

Individual who choreographs spectacular fights in Indian movies.

Film journalism

The 1970s also saw a proliferation of new film magazines. Until that time, staid film trade journals such as *Trade Guide*, or *Screen* informed the public about new releases and industry figures. In 1971, a new fortnightly called *Stardust* was launched. Its racy style and sleazy revelations about the private lives of the stars met with unprecedented success. Written in irreverent semi-literate English, with frequent and deliberate lapses in colloquial Hindi (transliterated into English), it was to change the face of film journalism. It bred a whole new generation of women gossip writers, and spawned innumerable magazines that tried to copy the subversive style. So successful was this Indian–English style of writing that soon even established journals began to include a page on 'shocking' revelations. Today *Stardust*'s unique idiom has become *de rigueur* in Indian journalism and is even sometimes used in political reporting.

Associations

In the 1960s the chaotic world of the film industry began to organise itself into unions and associations. Producers formed the Indian Motion Picture Producers Association (IMPPA) to deal with government bureaucracy. The 'extras', too, formed themselves into a union called the Junior Artistes Association, which demanded that they be referred to henceforth as 'junior artistes' and not 'extras'.

There were three main categories of junior artistes – 'ordinary', 'decent' and 'super decent' with a sliding scale of remuneration according to category (Barnouw and Krishnaswamy 1980: 171). The clothes and footwear are provided by the junior artistes themselves, the only exceptions being made in the case of costume dramas. In addition, men in the 'decent' and 'super decent' categories are required to arrive on the sets with decently shaven faces.

'Art' cinema and the 'parallel' film movement

While many bemoaned the demise of the romance and the rise of violence in the newer films, the 1970s also signalled the establishment of **'art'** or **'parallel'** cinema, that tried to offer an alternative to the commercially driven 'formula' films. Dispensing with stars, songs and spectacle, in favour of serious themes, these films adopted the classic codes of western narrative cinema, with a linear narrative set in a fictional world of spatial and temporal verisimilitude. This move towards realism had already been started by Satyajit Ray in 1955.

'art' or 'parallel' cinema

Serious, realistic film with a linear narrative which offers an alternative to the 'formula' film. Pioneered by Satyajit Ray

□ CASE STUDY 5: SATYAJIT RAY (1921–92)

Satyajit Ray, the most famous Indian director abroad, brought to the Indian cinema a respectability and status that it had never known before. Born in Calcutta in 1921, he studied for some time under Nobel laureate Rabindranath Tagore at Shanti Niketan. A young copywriter with an advertising firm, Ray had the opportunity to watch Jean Renoir at work on *The River*. Inspired by him, but with no actual experience of film-making, Ray bought the rights to a Bengali novel, *Pather Panchali* by Bibhutibhushan Banerji, and wrote a complete screenplay for it. Finding a producer was to prove very difficult. Dismayed that the film was to have no songs and dances, producers turned it down. In desperation Ray sold most of his belongings and managed to shoot a few scenes. When the money ran out, as it soon did, he turned to the state government of West

Bengal who, surprisingly, agreed to finance the film. This, as many historians have declared, was the best investment ever made by a government body in an artistic field.

Shot on a very tight budget and in natural surroundings, and with a musical score by Ravi Shankar, *Pather Panchali* (1955) is a simple document of extreme realism and great visual beauty on the childhood of a young boy named Apu. It met with great success in West Bengal and when it was entered at the Cannes Film Festival as an official entry from India, it was voted the 'best human document', and marked the debut of a brilliant career. The film also set a new record for the 'longest running film at New York's Fifth Avenue cinema'. Ray followed *Pather Panchali* with two more films, *Aparajito* (1956) and *Apur Sansar* (1959), on Apu, the central character, to complete what has become known as the Apu Trilogy.

The greatest influences on Ray were undoubtedly the Italian neo-realists from whom he learnt to make film on shoestring budgets. Working mostly in Bengali, he kept tight artistic control over his films and with each film experimented with a new genre. Ray even made one foray into the commercial cinema of Bombay with *Shatranj Ke Khilari* (*The Chess Players*, 1977), in Hindi, which used for the first time leading film actors from Bombay. Whatever the genre – comedy, literary adaptations, adventure, musical fantasy – Ray's view of the world would always remain distinctive.

The establishment of the Film and Television Institute of India (FTII) in 1961 and the Film Archives in 1964 encouraged the development of an alternative kind of cinema that had already been started by Satyajit Ray. An institute that provided professional training in the different branches of film-making led to a growing number of qualified actors, directors and technicians, some of whom were absorbed into the mainstream popular cinemas in Hindi and the regional languages. Others wished to experiment with alternative forms of cinematic expression. However, raising funds for such experimental work was nearly impossible. A few opportunities for the financing of films were provided by the government-funded Film Finance Corporation (FFC), which has since been incorporated into the National Film Development Corporation (NFDC). The erstwhile FFC offered financing for low-budget films in order to provide new talent with an opportunity to pursue ideas without the compromises that would have been demanded by the box office.

It was under these circumstances that director Mani Kaul made the experimental film *Uski Roti* in 1970, which tells a simple tale about a young woman Balo who walks several kilometres each day to deliver her lorry-driver husband his midday meal. One day she is delayed and she fears that her husband will leave her forever. The film not only challenged the conventional codes of popular film narrative, but it also eschewed 'realism' for a more expressionistic style of narration. The success of such experiments by Mani Kaul, Kumar Shahani (*Maya Darpan*, 1972) and other graduates of the Film Institute began the Indian 'new wave', even though their films never found general release and were restricted to the film club circuit.

Directors such as Shyam Benegal, who also abandoned the popular conventions of song, dance and spectacle, pursued a less experimental kind of cinema and chose the western traditions of a linear narrative and the 'realist aesthetic'. Coming to cinema from the world of advertising, Benegal's first film, *Ankur* (1974), treated the theme of rural exploitation by the landed classes. He brought a western sophistication to Indian themes, making his films appealing not just to the western-educated intellectual and cultural elite of India but also to the western critics, who were looking to find a cinema in India that they could appreciate and, more importantly, understand. Benegal's films are regularly screened at film festivals in Britain, France and the United States.

Other kinds of films were made by directors such as Basu Chatterji and Basu Bhattacharya, who worked within the constraints of the popular Hindi cinema using songs and dances, but toned down its emotional and spectacular excesses and replaced the implausible film plots with more realistic stories. Theirs was not a world of separated twins, reunited by the chance meetings, but a world of writers, lecturers and retired postmasters coming to terms with life. Even the songs were given 'realistic' motivations (for example, a record, a radio broadcast), and, on the whole, they offered a more refined form of entertainment for the middle classes.

The cinema in the 1970s could thus be divided into four main categories:

1   the mainstream popular film with its songs, dances, spectacle, familiar plot and over-wrought emotion;
2   the emotionally restrained and 'sober' stories told with an attempt at a realistic narrative, without dispensing with songs and dances;
3   the 'realist–representational' film with a narrative linearity that completely dispensed with songs and the other ingredients of popular cinema as in the works of Shyam Benegal, Govind Nihalani and others; and
4   the 'art' films in which directors such as Mani Kaul and Kumar Shahani experimented with the formal devices of cinema itself.

THE DISTRIBUTION NETWORK

The Indian 'new wave' could never combat the sheer volume of production and the extensive distribution network of the popular Hindi cinema. For distribution purposes, the market was, and continues to be, divided into 'territories', which coincide with the provinces that existed in pre-independence India. Each territory has its own distributor, who works in conjunction with the exhibitors, that is, those who own or have access to film theatres within that territory. Unfortunately, there are only about 15,000 cinemas in all of India, most of which are concentrated in the major towns and cities, while tents or temporary structures are usually deployed in the rural areas and the more remote villages. The combined annual production of over 900 films in the different regional languages results in a chronic shortage of outlets for exhibition, and some films fail to ever make it to the screen.

The distributors enter into agreements with the different exhibitors. The latter explain to the distributors what has met with approval from the audiences – a particular song, a particular dance sequence or a certain emotional scene, etc. All this information in based on audience reactions to the film as a whole as well as to individual scenes, as gauged by the exhibitor attending public screenings, and also from the box-office returns. Armed with this information, the distributors in turn contact producers and book future films. Often the booking fee is paid in advance, well before the film has commenced shooting. This means that distributors are able to indicate their preferences for certain stars, music directors and the kind of film that will eventually be made. Sometimes a particular star may be extremely popular with audiences in Calcutta, but less so in Bombay. In this case, the distributors from the Bengal territory must be able to raise enough funds as advance payment to make it attractive enough for producers to cast their preferred actor in a film. Films are thus part-financed by advances paid by distributors.

The scarcity of cinemas gives both exhibitors and distributors the right to dictate the kind of film that is to be produced, and the refusal to produce the kind of film demanded may result in a producer not finding a venue for his film at all. In the 1980s, recording companies also began to finance films and bought up copyrights to the film songs, long before they were even composed. According to trade journals, the growth in the sale of music audio-cassettes, of which film songs alone account for three-quarters of the total sales of a company, has made investment in films a profitable business for the recording companies (Chandra 1993: 52).

Under such financial arrangements, the low-budget 'art' film producers often cannot find a theatre that is willing to exhibit their film. In fact, many films financed by the NFDC or other quasi-government bodies have never been screened, and many directors find it easier to show their work overseas, usually during film festivals, than in India.

SATELLITE TELEVISION

By the 1980s, Hindi cinema began to feel the effects of the video boom. Big budget productions, in particular, were unable to get a reasonable return on their investment. Besides, the smaller video screen did not do justice to the extravagant spectacle. Video piracy forced producers to release their films in all territories at the same time (whereas earlier they were staggered so as to recover the investment over three to four years), and in some cases to release the film and the video simultaneously.

In January 1991, satellite broadcasting from Hong Kong by STAR (Satellite Transmission for Asian Region), now owned by Rupert Murdoch, began a media revolution. Hitherto Indian television (Doordarshan), controlled by the government of India, measured out the kind of entertainment seen as being suitable by bureaucrats from their offices in the Ministry of Information and Broadcasting. The satellite invasion has forced the government to loosen its hold on the media, and has put considerable pressure on the popular Hindi cinema too. So far, the flexible structure of the narrative has allowed it to absorb the foreign influences and the song and dance numbers have begun to show the influence of American music videos as seen on the MTV channel.

THE INFLUENCE OF HOLLYWOOD

Although Indian cinema has a different narrative structure from that of western cinema, the influence of Hollywood and, before that, of European cinema, has always been apparent. As seen in the section on the historical development of Indian cinema, the first Indian film was inspired by Gaumont's *Life of Christ*. Later, during the studio era, European film movements also had a stylistic effect on Hindi films. Thus German expressionism, Italian neo-realism, Soviet formalism were incorporated into the quintessential Indian popular narrative. As Barnouw and Krishnaswamy point out, many of Wadia Movietone's 'stunt' films in the 1930s, starring 'Fearless Nadia', were inspired by Douglas Fairbanks, Pearl White and Eddie Polo. According to them:

> The American Eddie Polo, now almost forgotten in the United States, was among the most popular film heroes in India in the early 1920s. In 1927 a headmaster of a high school in Hyderabad, Sind, told the Indian Cinematograph Committee: 'I once asked my class of 50 boys what was their ambition in life. Five boys wrote, "To be Eddie Polo".'
>
> (Barnouw and Krishnaswamy 1980: 110)

The most significant influence of Hollywood has been the use of new technologies in sound recording, colour processing and, most important of all, the special effects. Mannerisms, sartorial styles and swaggers, too, have been endlessly reproduced, even though the content of the Hindi film still remains traditionally Indian. In the 1950s, Raj Kapoor popularised the Charlie Chaplin look, while in the 1960s, Shammi Kapoor brought Elvis to the popular screen. Amitabh Bachchan's 'angry young man' was inspired by Clint Eastwood in *Dirty Harry*.

Sometimes scenes from Hollywod films are copied into a Hindi film, and, on occasion, entire films are 'borrowed' not once but even twice! For example, the Oscar-winning Hollywood film *It Happened One Night* (Frank Capra, 1934) became *Chori Chori* (A. Thakur) in 1956 and *Dil Hai Ke Manta ‹Nahin* (Mahesh Bhatt) in 1991.

However, whenever a Hollywood film is remade in India it has to be recast in the Indian mould, that is, emotions have to be overstated, songs, dances and spectacle have to be added, family relationships have to be introduced if they do not exist in the original, traditional moral values such as *dharma* (duty) must be reiterated and female chastity must be eulogised. Only then will the film find success at the box office.

CONCLUSION

By evolving its own narrative style, popular Hindi cinema offers the Indian audiences an alternative to Hollywood. It challenges American cultural hegemony not just in India but, through the export of its films, in developing countries as well. The fragmented narrative structure gives the films great flexibility and allows the integration of new influences while maintaining links with ancient traditions. Images of westernisation allow the films to tackle issues surrounding modernity and national identity. The songs, through their energetic and unabashed dance movements and sometimes bawdy lyrics, provide the audience with emotional and sexual release, while at the same time the plot reinforces society's conservative moral values.

Indian cinema currently finds itself under threat from satellite television. However, the flexible narrative structure that it has inherited and which has helped it survive foreign competition will undoubtedly help it survive the threat of new technology and maintain its position as the single most important cultural activity in India.

RECOMMENDED VIEWING

Videos available with English subtitles

Awaara (*The Vagabond*, 1951) Black and white, 170 minutes. Producer: R.K. Productions. Director: Raj Kapoor. Script: K.A. Abbas and V.P. Sathe. Camera: Radhu Karmarkar. Lyrics: Hasrat Jaipuri. Music: Shankar–Jaikishen. Cast: Raj Kapoor (Raju), Nargis (Rita), Prithviraj Kapoor (Raju's father), Leela Chitnis (Raju's mother), Shashi Kapoor (young Raju), K.N. Singh (Jaggu).

Story: Raju, a crook, does not know that his father is Judge Raghunath. The judge had banished his pregnant wife from his house because she had been abducted by the criminal Jaggu, and although she was returned unharmed, he suspects that she has been 'dishonoured'. Raju's childhood friend Rita (coincidentally the judge's protégée) makes Raju give up his life of crime, but Raju kills Jaggu and is sent to prison. A loving Rita and a penitent father await his release.

Deewar (*I'll Die for Mama*, 1975) Colour, 174 minutes. Producer: Gulshan Rai. Director: Yash Chopra. Script: Salim–Javed. Camera: Kay Gee. Lyrics: Sahir Ludhianvi. Music: R.D. Burman. Cast: Shashi Kapoor (Ravi), Amitabh Bachchan (Vijay), Neetu Singh, Nirupa Roy, Parveen Babi.

Story: Ravi and Vijay are two brothers, who move to the city with their mother after their father abandons them. In order to provide his mother with a decent life, Vijay takes to a life of crime and very quickly becomes fabulously rich. His brother Ravi prefers the path of righteousness and joins the police force. The two brothers confront each other, and when it becomes Ravi's duty to shoot Vijay, he does so. Vijay dies in his mother's arms.

Madhumati (1958) Black and white, 163 minutes. Producer/director: Bimal Roy. Story: Ritwick Ghatak. Dialogue: Rajinder Singh Bedi. Camera: Dilip Gupta. Lyrics: Shailendra. Music: Salil Choudhary. Cast: Dilip Kumar (Devenandra/Anand), Vyjayanthimala (Madhumati), Johnny Walker, Pran (Ugra Narain), Jayant, Tiwari.

Story: Devendra, an important official, and his colleague are on an official tour of a distant region when they find they have to seek shelter in an abandoned mansion. At night, Devendra awakes and slowly begins to remember a previous incarnation, and his connection with this mansion. In that life he is Anand, a manager of a timber estate who meets and falls in love with a tribal woman called Madhumati. Landowner Ugra Narain who is also Anand's employer tries to rape Madhumati, but she kills herself. Anand brings him to justice, but dies soon after. When the flashback ends, Devendra rejoins his family and finds that his wife is none other than the reincarnation of Madhumati.

Mother India (1957) Colour, 190 minutes. Producer: Mehboob Productions Ltd. Director: Mehboob Khan. Script: V. Mirza, Ali Raza. Camera: Faredoon Irani. Lyrics: Shakeel Badayuni. Music: Naushad. Cast: Nargis (Radha), Sunil Dutt (Birju), Raaj Kumar (Shyamu), Rajendra Kumar (Ramu), Kanhaiyalal (Sukhilala).

Story: Radha is left destitute by her husband Shyamu, when he loses his arms in a farming accident. She struggles to bring up her starving children and fights off the sexual advances of the moneylender Sukhilala, to whom their land is mortgaged and who is willing to write off her debt if she sleeps with him. Driven to do the unthinkable, her virtue is saved in time thanks to divine intervention. She finds they can survive without Sukhilala's financial assistance. Her sons grow up, but the debt still remains unpaid thanks to Sukhilala's fraudulent accounting. One day Birju kills Sukhilala and abducts his daughter, but mother Radha shoots her son dead in order to preserve the honour of all womankind.

FURTHER VIEWING

The Bollywood Story (1989) A two-part documentary on the Bombay film industry produced for Channel 4. It provides a historical study of Indian cinema and highlights the salient features of its cinematic conventions.
The Peacock Screen (1991) A four-hour documentary on popular Hindi cinema produced for Channel 4 that combines a historical survey of the industry with a debate on the subject. It contains interviews with many important personalities from the Bombay cinema as well as 'art' film world.
Raj Kapoor – The Living Legend (1988) A documentary on the life and work of Raj Kapoor, directed by Simi Grewal and co-produced by Channel 4.

In Search of Guru Dutt (1989) A documentary on Guru Dutt produced and directed by Nasreen Munni Kabir for Channel 4. It contains interviews with Dutt's family and associates and excerpts from his major works.

Lata in Her Own Voice (1990) A six-part documentary on the singing legend Lata Mangeshkar, produced and directed by Nasreen Munni Kabir for Channel 4. It provides an insight into the workings of the Hindi film industry.

Videos of Hindi films are available from: Tip Top Video, 4, Coronet Parade, Ealing Road, Wembley, London HAO 4AY. Telephone: 0181 903 0605.

Chapter 13

New German Cinema

Julia Knight

■ New German Cinema

INTRODUCTION

New German Cinema is a term that is usually applied to a loose grouping of films that were made in the Federal Republic of Germany (what was then West Germany) during the 1960s, 1970s and early 1980s. Unlike film movements such as Italian neo-realism or Soviet cinema of the 1920s, however, its films have resisted clear generic delineation. Although critics have attempted to identify common elements by examining the film-makers' motivating concerns and the conditions of production, the films themselves can be most easily characterised as a body of work marked by its stylistic and thematic diversity. Nevertheless, the New German Cinema has firmly established itself on the international film scene, and a handful of its directors – especially Wim Wenders (born 1945), Rainer Werner Fassbinder (born 1945), Werner Herzog (born 1942) and more recently Edgar Reitz (born 1932) – have become extremely well known.

In Britain and the US awareness of the New German Cinema began to grow during the mid-1970s. In February 1976, for instance, the US magazine *Newsweek* ran an article entitled 'The German Film Renaissance'; a few months later the BBC featured the new cinema in an *Omnibus* report called 'Vigorous Signs of Life'; and by 1978 *Time* magazine described it as 'the liveliest in Europe' (Clarke 1978). These early accounts tended to suggest that this new phase in the history of German cinema had been brought into being solely through the endeavours of a small number of talented and dedicated young directors. Consequently, many observers focused on the personalities of the new directors, discussing them as creative geniuses, 'artists with something to say' (Eidsvik 1979a: 174) and examined the films almost exclusively in terms of their directors' personal visions. Thus, in Britain and America the New German Cinema was, to start with, discussed predominantly as a 'cinéma des auteurs'. And this approach was also adopted in the first major British and US studies of West Germany's new cinema, all of which dealt with no more than six or seven (male) film-makers at most.[1]

• Plate 13.1 Wim Wenders (b. 1945)

• Plate 13.2 Rainer Werner Fassbinder (1945–82)

To a certain extent this is unsurprising since there is a broad degree of general acceptance, within mainstream film criticism at least (such as that found in the major daily newspapers, glossy lifestyle magazines and Barry Norman's weekly television programme on BBC1), of the idea of a director as the 'auteur' or 'author' of his or her film – hence we talk about Ridley Scott's *Thelma and Louise* (1991) or Mira Nair's *Mississippi Masala* (1991), as well as Werner Herzog's *Fitzcarraldo* (1980–1). Furthermore, it has not been uncommon to discuss European cinema in particular in this manner as it has frequently been characterised as an **'art' cinema** in order to distinguish it from the more commercially orientated Hollywood product.

However, irrespective of the context, **auteurism**, as it is termed, can only ever give us an extremely limited understanding of how and why a particular cinema move-ment or body of films has come into existence. As the name 'New German Cinema' suggests, the cinema under discussion here is also a *national* cinema and any con-sideration of it purely in terms of its directors neglects the specific social, political and economic conditions in West Germany which also helped shape the New German Cinema. This is not to deny that the directors that have come to be most closely associated with that cinema are highly talented film-makers, but rather to assert that it is crucial to consider a number of other factors and issues *as well* if we are to achieve a fuller and more adequate understanding of how the New German Cinema emerged and why it took the form it did.

THE AMERICAN LEGACY

West German cinema in the 1950s

To start with, it is necessary to examine the way in which the West German film industry developed during the 1950s since this set the essential preconditions for the emergence

'art' cinema

A term usually applied to films where the director has clearly exercised a high degree of control over the film-making process and thus the films can be viewed as a form of personal expression.

auteurism

A critical approach to the study of film which identifies the director as responsible for whatever the viewer finds of thematic, stylistic or structural interest in a single film or across a body of work by one director.

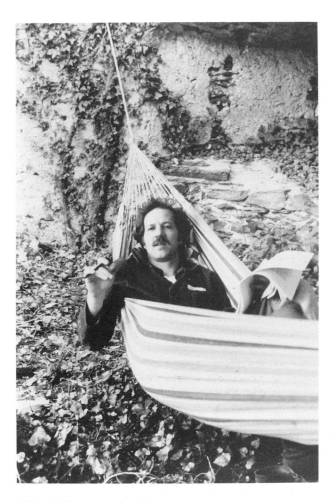

• Plate 13.3 Werner Herzog (b. 1942)

of the New German Cinema in the 1960s and 1970s. At the end of the Second World War the western Allies had felt it was vital to 're-educate' the German people in order, first, to 'de-Nazify' Germany and, second, to build up the western zones of Germany as a buffer to the Soviet influence in eastern Europe. American films were quickly identified as an effective way of disseminating western notions of freedom, democracy and capitalist enterprise.[2] Before the American distributors agreed to send their films to West Germany for this purpose, however, they insisted they should be allowed to transfer any profits made in Germany back to America. Since the German market had been closed to America during the war, once this condition had been met Hollywood had an enormous backlog of films which could then be poured into the western zones. And as these were films that had already gone into profit in their home and other overseas markets, they could also be made available at prices which undercut any European competitors. This in turn enabled American companies to easily achieve a position of economic dominance in Germany by the beginning of the 1950s.

The American film industry was, of course, keen to protect this lucrative new market. Measures were therefore taken to prevent the imposition of an import quota on American films (a safeguard which was introduced by other European countries after the war to protect their own film industries) and American companies remained free to flood the German market with Hollywood films. The Allies also dismantled the remnants of the Nazi film industry, which had been centralised and state-controlled through a giant conglomerate, UFA. Decartelisation laws were passed which broke up the UFA conglomerate and separated out the various production, distribution and exhibition branches of the industry, and only small independent production companies were licensed. The aim was to permit an indigenous film industry to develop, but at the same time to ensure it remained on a small scale and thus unable to threaten America's monopoly of the German market.

This pursuit by the Americans of their own political and economic interests had significant consequences for the new West German film industry. As the German industry was forced to remain small scale, it failed to attract any substantial investment. This was compounded as the country's general economic recovery got underway, since other industries prospered and offered far safer investment prospects than the high risk area of film production. In other countries like Britain and France, American distributors became investors in indigenous film production as their profits had to remain in those countries, but in West Germany, as American companies were allowed to transfer their profits back to the US, they had little incentive to invest in West German production.

This overall lack of investment meant that German films had to be produced relatively cheaply, making them unable to compete with the expensively produced, spectacular Hollywood product. As a result, indigenous production was quickly directed towards catering expressly for the specific tastes of German audiences and mostly comprised **Heimatfilme** or homeland films which depicted simple country life in a rural Germany, adventure films based on popular German novels, historical films set in imperial Austria, together with romantic adventures and comedies set in picturesque locations. However, this overwhelming orientation towards the home market rendered German films on the whole unsuitable for export. This meant that films had to try and break even on national box-office receipts alone, which ensured production remained low-budget and resulted in a national cinema marked by correspondingly low production values. Compared with the Hollywood product German films looked decidedly provincial – 'drab' and 'shoddy' were adjectives used by some critics – and did little for the reputation of West German cinema abroad. Other commentators noted the cinema's preference for 'escapist' films and one foreign critic was moved to observe that the 'events of the Thirties and Forties are either ignored or treated as something remote, regrettable, and faintly unmentionable' (quoted in Sandford 1980: 156).

The fact that the German cinema which emerged in the 1950s can be characterised by its orientation towards 'escapist' entertainment and by its refusal to deal with the Nazi past is, for a number of reasons, hardly surprising. To start with, under the Nazi regime the film industry had been tightly controlled by the Ministry for Propaganda and Popular Enlightenment which had been headed up by Joseph Goebbels. When the Nazis came to power in 1933 Goebbels had quickly identified the propaganda potential of cinema and had informed the industry that he wanted film to be used in support of the new regime. Goebbels' ministry controlled the department which licensed every film before it could go into production, decided whether completed films could be released and even selected film personnel in the case of particularly important productions. Gradually all film companies came under state control and by 1942 the

Heimatfilme

A German term which can be loosely translated as 'homeland films' and was coined to delineate a film genre which depicted simple country life in a rural Germany.

whole industry had been centralised via the UFA conglomerate. Consequently, for many the cinema (and indeed other areas of cultural production) had become tarnished with the brush of Nazism, and this bred a distrust of all but the most innocuous seeming German films.

At the same time, given the traumas and upheaval of the war, followed by the division of Germany which exiled many people from their families and former homes, the 'escapism' of such films proved extremely popular with German audiences and in fact precipitated a brief boom for the industry during the mid-1950s.

Furthermore, although UFA was closed down, most of the directors, writers, actors, cameramen and technicians who had worked in the Nazi film industry were re-employed after the war. This was partly because those directors who had opposed the Nazi regime – such as Fritz Lang, Billy Wilder, Ernst Lubitsch and Douglas Sirk – had fled the country when the Nazis came to power. But also, with the escalation of the Cold War, the recruitment of ex-Nazis was considered distinctly preferable to the risk of communist infiltration. Consequently, the new West German film industry was effectively run by the old UFA generation which only further impeded any chance of the German cinema experiencing a cultural rebirth in the West after the war.

The fight for survival

There were a few notable exceptions to the general 'escapist' trend. Bernard Wicki's *Die Brücke/The Bridge* (1959), for instance, became a classic anti-war film, while Wolfgang Staudte's *Rosen für den Staatsanwalt/Roses for the Prosecutor* (1959) attracted similar attention for addressing the fact that former Nazi officers had obtained positions of power in the new Federal Republic of Germany. But these exceptions could not prevent what became a steady decline in the international standing of West German film. As the 1950s progressed and television started to take off, production figures and box-office receipts also began to decline, and gradually cinemas started to close (as in the rest of Europe and in the US).

Thus, by the end of the 1950s the Allies' handling of the film industry in Germany had left West German cinema economically vulnerable and artistically impoverished. It had in fact become apparent as early as the mid-1950s that, if the German cinema was to survive this American legacy, government intervention would be necessary. Representatives from the industry began to lobby parliament and by the end of the 1950s criticism of West German cinema was being voiced from a number of quarters. In 1959 two young film-makers, Haro Senft and Ferdinand Khittl, campaigned to highlight the need to improve the quality of films and to provide grant aid for film projects. Two years later film critic Joe Hembus condemned the industry's 'factory-like production system where standardised models are turned out on an assembly-line' (quoted in Johnston 1979–80: 72). And in 1961 the organisers of the Venice Film Festival rejected all the West German entries, while at home the Federal Film Prize given annually by the Federal Ministry of the Interior (**BMI**) went unawarded for best feature film, best director and best screenplay because none were considered to be of sufficient quality.

In 1962 a group of twenty-six film-makers, writers and artists, spearheaded by Alexander Kluge (born 1932) and including Ferdinand Khittl, Edgar Reitz and Haro Senft, added their voices to this escalating condemnation of West German film. They drew up and published what has become known as the **Oberhausen Manifesto**, in which they also argued that given the opportunity they could create a new kind of film which would breathe life into the dying German cinema:

BMI

The Federal Ministry of the Interior which awards the annual Federal Film Prize and was initially responsible for funding the Kuratorium junger deutscher Film.

Oberhausen Manifesto

A manifesto drawn up and signed by twenty-six film-makers, writers and artists at the 1962 Oberhausen Film Festival to campaign for access to the means of feature film production.

• Plate 13.4 Alexander Kluge (b. 1932)

The collapse of the conventional German film finally removes the economic justification from a mentality which we reject. The new German film thereby has a chance of coming to life.

In recent years German short films by young authors, directors and producers have received a large number of prizes at international festivals and have won international critical acclaim. These works and their success shows that the future of the German film lies with those who have demonstrated that they speak a new film language.

In Germany, as in other countries, the short film has become a training ground and arena of experimentation for the feature film.

We declare our right to create the new German feature film.

This new film needs new freedoms. Freedom from the usual conventions of the industry. Freedom from the influence of commercial partners. Freedom from the tutelage of other groups with vested interests.

We have concrete ideas about the production of the new German film with regard to its intellectual, formal and economic aspects. We are collectively prepared to take economic risks.

The old film is dead. We believe in the new.

Eventually the government responded to this mounting criticism by setting up the first film subsidy agency, the **Kuratorium junger deutscher Film** (Board of Young German Film). Launched in 1965 by the BMI, the Kuratorium was given a brief to promote the kind of film-making demanded by the Oberhausen Manifesto signatories and to 'stimulate a renewal of the German film in a manner exclusively and directly beneficial to the community' (quoted in Dawson 1981: 16). Kuratorium funding took the form of

Kuratorium junger deutscher Film

The Board of Young German Film which was the first film subsidy agency, set up by the BMI in 1965. Its brief was and remains to fund first feature films only.

interest-free production loans for *first* feature films only, which meant that for the first time young, new film-makers who had been unable to gain access to the commercial film industry had a real chance to break into feature film production.

Initially the Kuratorium was very successful in fulfilling its brief. Within two years twenty-five films had been produced with Kuratorium funding. Four of these were the first features of Oberhausen signatories Alexander Kluge (*Abschied von gestern/Yesterday Girl*, 1965–6), Hans Jürgen Pohland (*Katz und Maus/Cat and Mouse*, 1966), Edgar Reitz (*Mahlzeiten/Mealtimes*, 1966) and Haro Senft (*Der sanfte Lauf/The Gentle Course*, 1967). A further two – *Professor Columbus* by Rainer Erler (1967) and *Tätowierung/Tattooing* by Johannes Schaaf (1967) – were produced by signatory Rob Houwer. In direct contrast to the commercial industry, the contractual arrangements governing the Kuratorium loans allowed film-makers to retain total artistic control over their work, and as a result most of these films broke with the conventions of mainstream cinema, varying from episodic and experimental narratives to highly avant-garde pieces (see pp. 407–8 for a discussion of Kluge's *Yesterday Girl*).

Some of these films also enjoyed unprecedented critical acclaim. Kluge's *Yesterday Girl* won several awards, including the Silver Lion at the 1966 Venice Film Festival, while the following year Reitz's *Mealtimes* received the Best First Feature Award. This success also seemed to mark the beginning of an upturn in the fortunes of West German cinema generally. Non-Kuratorium financed films by other new directors were well received at Cannes in 1966, especially Ulrich Schamoni's *Es/It* (1965), Volker Schlöndorff's *Der junge Törless/Young Törless* (1966), which received the International Critics Prize, and Jean-Marie Straub and Danièle Huillet's *Nicht Versöhnt/Not Reconciled* (1965). Back in Germany Peter Schamoni's *Schonzeit für Füchse/Closed Season for Foxes* (1966) won a Silver Bear at the Berlin Film Festival, and between 1967 and 1969 three Kuratorium films and three further films by new young directors also won Federal Film Prizes.

Not only did these films offer a radical departure from mainstream cinema at a formal level, they also dealt with contemporary concerns in a way that contrasted sharply and refreshingly with the 'escapist' nature of the German cinema of the 1950s. For instance, *It* by Schamoni (born 1939) addressed the question of abortion at a time when it was still illegal in Germany, while *Young Törless* by Schlöndorff (born 1939) used the story – adapted from a Robert Musil novel originally published in 1906 – of a young boy's experience of two fellow pupils at a boarding school torturing a Jewish boy to raise questions about the Nazi past. According to Edgar Reitz, 'The press was unbelievably positive. And when the first films came out, there was a degree of public interest which has never been matched since' (quoted in Dawson 1981: 17).

Consequently, the setting up of the Kuratorium and this first batch of critically acclaimed films clearly appeared to many observers to have brought about 'a renewal of the German film', and this point is often taken to mark the start of what has become known as the New German Cinema. While this may be true in one sense – since that was when the first films were made – the fact that it was possible for those films to be made at all was largely a result of the growing body of criticism that was being directed at the West German cinema in the late 1950s and early 1960s. And the origins of this criticism stemmed from the Allies' handling of the film industry after the Second World War which was motivated by political and economic self-interest.

THE DEVELOPMENT OF THE FILM SUBSIDY SYSTEM

Production funding: problems and solutions

However, this renewal of the German film was almost extremely short-lived. Having made their first feature films, the new directors became ineligible for further Kuratorium funding and were faced with limited possibilities for financing subsequent films. If they had not been fortunate enough to win a Federal Film Prize which carried a cash award for future production work, they were forced to turn to the diminishing commercial sources. Furthermore, the Kuratorium was dependent on the repayment of its loans from box-office receipts to provide the financing for further film projects. But, although the first batch of films had been well received, they did not do well enough in the cinemas to fully repay their loans, leaving the subsidy agency with rapidly diminishing funds.

At the same time, however, the commercial sector viewed Kuratorium-funded films as unfair competition. In a market where it was increasingly difficult to produce films on a commercial basis, young film-makers were being given money to make whatever films they liked. The film industry therefore started to lobby the German government, demanding that any film subsidies should be directed towards helping the commercial sector get back on its feet, and was successful in bringing about a more commercially orientated revision of film policy. In December 1967 a new Film Development Act (**FFG**) was passed which raised a levy on every cinema ticket sold in the Federal Republic to provide funding for film production, and the Film Development Board (**FFA**) was set up to adminster these funds. In complete contrast to the Kuratorium's promotion of first-time feature film directors, FFA funding was awarded to any film project as long as the producer's *previous* film had grossed a certain amount at the box office during the first two years of its release. Consequently, first-time directors were not eligible for FFA funding, and unfortunately most of the new films had not done well enough at the box office to trigger the FFA funding mechanism.

As a result, by the beginning of the 1970s Germany's promising new cinema appeared to have been almost squeezed out of existence. It also quickly became apparent that the FFG was actually failing to stimulate the economic revival of the industry. The retroactive nature of the FFA funding encouraged the production of tried-and-tested formula films which gave rise to a cinema of 'unparalleled mediocrity' (Phillips 1984: xviii), consisting primarily of sex films and lowbrow classroom comedies. This drove significant segments of the cinema audience away and resulted in further cinema closures.

Ironically, it was television that initially ensured the continuing existence of the new German film. In the Federal Republic there were ten broadcasting companies – nine regional ones which constituted the national network of the first channel (ARD) and the regional networks of the third channel, and Zweites Deutsches Fernsehen (ZDF) which broadcast the second national channel. These were public corporations and produced relatively few programmes themselves, commissioning commercial companies or freelance independents to produce the rest. Consequently, television represented an enormous source of potential funding for the new directors, and by the early 1970s they were increasingly turning to television companies to find financing for their film projects.

To start with, film-makers were commissioned on a fairly arbitrary and ad hoc basis, but in 1974 the role of television within West German cinema was formalised via a **Film and Television Agreement**. This was drawn up between the FFA and the ARD and ZDF

FFG

The Film Development Act which was passed in 1967 to raise a levy on every cinema ticket sold in West Germany to provide funding for film production.

FFA

The Film Development Board which was set up to administer the funds raised by the FFG.

Film and Television Agreement

An agreement made in 1974 between the FFA and the first and second West German television networks which set up a film production fund.

television networks, and committed the television corporations to providing DM34 million over a five-year period for film production. Productions funded by this scheme were guaranteed a theatrical release before being broadcast on television, and further funds were given to the FFA to fund the development of film projects.

And as the 1970s progressed the film subsidy system was expanded and developed, gradually improving the funding options available. As the shortcomings of the FFG became apparent, the act underwent successive revisions which, for instance, ensured that pornographic and low-quality films could not qualify for subsidies and permitted the FFA to make discretionary cash awards to 'good entertainment films' which had fulfilled certain audience attendance criteria. The Board also introduced project funding which could be awarded to any project that seemed likely 'to improve the quality and profitability of the German film' (quoted in Pflaum and Prinzler 1983: 99), irrespective of a producer's previous work. In 1977 the Länder (states) who had taken over responsibility for the Kuratorium agreed to increase its funding. And in the same year the city of Berlin pioneered the idea of regional funding, which was designed both to encourage film-makers to bring work to that region and to promote productions of particular cultural and political interest to the city. Over the next four years Bavaria, Hamburg and North Rhine–Westphalia also introduced regional funding schemes.

Distribution and exhibition

However, it had become apparent very early on that if 'a renewal of the German film' was to take place, it was not enough simply to address the production sector: the distribution and exhibition sectors of the industry also needed subsidy support. Since the distribution sector was largely under American control,[3] the new directors had no guarantee that their films would get taken into distribution and hence get into cinemas.[4] Thus, as the film subsidy system developed increasing attention was paid to these areas, with the BMI, the FFA and the Kuratorium all channelling some of their funding into distribution and exhibition from 1970 onwards.

For example, in April 1970 the BMI started offering financial subsidies to cinemas which had screened what was referred to as a 'suitable quota' of 'good' German films. And from December 1976 it introduced awards for companies that had released quality rated or state subsidised German films.

Kuratorium funding enabled a small production company called Basis-Film to take on the distribution of their first film, *Liebe Mutter, mir geht es gut/Dear Mother, I'm OK* (1972), when no existing distributor showed any interest in releasing the film. Made by Christian Ziewer (born 1941) and the first in a series of so-called *Arbeiterfilme* (worker films), the film is about a mechanic who through losing his job gradually comes to understand the social and political conditions that prevent workers like himself from improving their situation. Filmed in a very detached, static and analytical style, the film proved too demanding for commercial distributors and cinemas. Their experience with this film made Basis recognise the need for a company that specialised in distributing the less commercially orientated, more socially critical films that many of the new young directors were making. They set up their own distribution wing, Basis-Film Verleih (Basis Film Distributor), in order to help build up audiences for such films – often among trade union organisations, factories and educational institutions – and frequently supplied background material to accompany the film and inform any after-screening discussions, or arranged for directors to attend screenings.

At the same time a group of thirteen film-makers also took their own initiative – among them Wenders, Fassbinder and Thomas Schamoni (born 1936) – and founded Filmverlag

• Plate 13.5 Margarethe von Trotta (b. 1942)

der Autoren (Film Publishing House of the Auteurs). As with Basis, Filmverlag was originally set up as a (collectively run) production company, but it quickly moved into and prioritised distribution. However, in contrast to Basis, Filmverlag identified a need to actively promote the new German films to national and international cinema audiences.

A coming of age

As revisions to the film subsidy system during the 1970s began to substantially improve production opportunities, as well as distribution and exhibition possibilities, the New German Cinema gradually began to reassert itself. By 1977–8 half of the feature films being made were deemed to belong to the new cinema. Few were in fact box-office successes,[5] but they won renewed international acclaim for German cinema. Among those that attracted particular attention were Volker Schlöndorff and Margarethe von Trotta's *Die verlorene Ehre der Katherina Blum/The Lost Honour of Katherina Blum* (1975), based on a Heinrich Böll novel of the same name about a woman who becomes involved with a man wanted by the police, Wim Wenders' *Im Lauf der Zeit/Kings of the Road* (1976) about the friendship between two men, American cultural imperialism, present-day divided Germany and cinema itself, *Das zweite Erwachen der Christa Klages/The Second Awakening of Christa Klages* (1977) by von Trotta (born 1942) about a woman who commits a bank robbery, Fassbinder's *Die Ehe der Maria Braun/The Marriage of Maria Braun* (1978) about a woman who has to survive on her own in postwar Germany, and Schlöndorff's *Die Blechtrommel/The Tin Drum* (1979), based on Günter Grass' novel of the same name about a young boy growing up in Germany during and after the Second World War. When *The Tin Drum* won the highly coveted American Oscar for the best foreign film in 1980, one British critic was moved to comment that the New German

• Plate 13.6 *Die Blechtrommel/The Tin Drum* (Volker Schlöndorff, 1979)

Cinema was 'one of the most remarkable, enduring, and promising developments in the cinema of the 1970s' (Sandford 1980: 6).

Thus, the criticism of the West German cinema in the late 1950s and early 1960s eventually precipitated the development of a whole system of public subsidies which *in turn* facilitated the emergence of a critically acclaimed new cinema by the end of the 1970s. Although the country undoubtedly produced some very talented film-makers, their work would not have been possible without the financial support offered by the various subsidy agencies. And taken together, this complex network of film subsidies can be best understood as a much-needed institutional initiative that was designed to promote and develop a national cinema that was both culturally motivated and economically viable.

THE ARTISANAL MODE OF PRODUCTION

Although the film subsidy agencies were clearly concerned with promoting the economic revival of German cinema, in order to stimulate a cinema that was culturally motivated as well the philosophy behind much of the subsidy system deliberately promoted a mode of production that is more usually associated with the arts, that is one that recognises *individual* authorship and creativity. Many of the ideas informing the network of subsidies were most clearly articulated and theorised by one of the Oberhausen Manifesto signatories, Alexander Kluge.

In his writings and campaigning work, Kluge developed and promoted the notion of an **Autorenkino**, which roughly translated means 'cinema of auteurs'. Although the German concept of *Autor* differs slightly from the French *auteur*, both terms identify the director as a film's creator and regard a film as an expression of that creator's personality. This approach to cinema was already evident in the Oberhausen Manifesto: since Kluge and the other signatories insisted on freedom from economic and vested interests, they were basically opposing industrial modes of production and demanding the freedom of expression normally associated with 'artistic' production. In subsequent writings, Kluge developed the idea of the director as *Autor* by contrasting the new German film with what he termed a *Zutatenfilm* (recipe film). The 'recipe film' was a typical industry product, made up of ingredients such as stars, ideas, directors, technicians and scriptwriters which the producer simply went out and purchased according to requirements (Johnston 1979–80: 72). In contrast, the new directors would bring something personal to their films, making the new German film much more than just the sum of its parts.

During the 1960s Kluge developed these ideas, together with Edgar Reitz, into a coherent education programme at a private college in Ulm. There they developed a course which offered film-makers an all-round film education, familiarising them with all areas of production. Instead of becoming specialists trained in a particular area, such as camera, scriptwriting, editing or direction in readiness for an industrial context, students would become *Filmautoren* – that is, directors who exercised a far greater degree of authorial control than industrial production methods normally permitted and who could consequently use film as a medium for personal expression.

The lobbying efforts of Kluge and others helped ensure that the concept of an *Autorenkino* informed the framework of the first film subsidy agency, the Kuratorium. In his account of its work, Norbert Kückelmann explains that 'according to the fundamental Oberhausen principle the filmmaker was to have autonomy in giving shape to his film idea . . . he was to retain control over the direction and entire production process' (quoted in Knight 1992: 55). Thus the Kuratorium clearly identified the director as a film's author and endeavoured to guarantee his or her independence, implying that film-making is an act of personal expression and hence an art form.

However, the institutional sanctioning of the *Autorenkino* principle was not due solely to the efforts of Kluge and his colleagues. Their campaigning coincided with 'a political will to see film acquire the status of "Kultur"' (Elsaesser 1989: 28) and the desire to use film as a means for promoting German culture as a 'manifestation of national identity' (quoted in Elsaesser 1989: 29), both at home and abroad. Although the film subsidy system was undeniably shaped by economic considerations, it was equally determined by an institutional belief that just like the fine arts, literature and music, film should also be regarded as an art form. Thus, the Kuratorium was in fact modelled on forms of patronage and commission that are traditionally associated with the fine arts. And as the subsidy system evolved most of the agencies also identified the director as a film's author.

The concrete result of this was that the contractual arrangements between the funding bodies and directors encouraged film-makers to take on more than just a directorial role, resulting in film-makers often becoming their own scriptwriters and/or producers

Autorenkino

A concept, loosely translated as a 'cinema of authors', promoted by Alexander Kluge while campaigning for the production funding, and developing the film education necessary to produce a culturally motivated cinema. According to this concept the director is to be regarded as a film's creator and the film can be regarded as an expression of that creator's personality.

as well as taking many of the artistic, casting, editing and organisational decisions. Hence, film-makers were not only given institutional recognition as 'artists', but were usually in a position to exercise a large degree of creative control over their films. This, of course, meant that the cinema could be easily and readily discussed as a 'cinema des auteurs', which in turn helped obscure the other factors that had contributed to bringing it into existence.

artisanal mode of production

A term used to describe the way in which most New German Cinema films were made with such small budgets and minimal production teams that film-making was considered by some to be more like practising a craft than engaging in a technological process.

At the same time, the subsidy system and the resultant **artisanal mode of production** encouraged the development of a small, team-based 'cottage industry'. Compared to the size of investment normally associated with film production in the commercial sector or even the 'quality' art-house cinema, the loans and subsidies handed out by the various film promotion agencies were usually extremely small. During the 1970s film-makers were often producing feature films for between DM80,000 and DM200,000, while Italian or French directors might be working with a budget of at least DM800,000. When it was first set up, the *maximum* loan the Kuratorium could offer was DM300,000. As a contemporary writer observed: 'It is like trying to build a Rolls-Royce with money that is just enough to put together a bicycle' (quoted in Elsaesser 1989: 25).

Given the inadequate levels of funding, and since the funding agencies actively encouraged film-makers to take on a greater degree of responsibility, directors were more or less forced to work in small teams – without the luxury of, say, a production manager or extra people for props, costumes or make-up – if they were to realise their projects. However, working in small teams allows the development of much closer collaboration, and film-makers frequently worked with the same people time and again. Wenders often collaborated with writer Peter Handke and cameraman Robby Müller, Fassbinder with actress Hanna Schygulla, and Herzog with editor Beate Mainka-Jellinghaus. Margarethe von Trotta either co-wrote, co-directed and/or acted in many films made by her then husband Volker Schlöndorff, while Jean-Marie Straub (born 1933) and Danièle Huillet (born 1936) shared the writing and directing credits on most of their films.

Although film-makers argued they needed larger subsidies if they were to produce a 'quality' national cinema, the artisanal and team-based mode of production allowed a far greater degree of experimentation to take place than would have been possible in a conventional commercial context. And this freedom to experiment has, of course, contributed to the enormous stylistic and thematic diversity that is a mark of the films that have been designated as belonging to the New German Cinema. But that said, the mode of production – as dictated by the subsidy agencies – nevertheless gave the cinema a clearly identifiable character.

THE QUEST FOR ALTERNATIVE IMAGES AND COUNTER-REPRESENTATIONS

Formal experimentation and contemporary issues

In the early years of the New German Cinema, much of the experimentation that took place was at an extreme formal level. For instance, Straub and Huillet's *Not Reconciled* (1965), which is based on a Heinrich Böll novel entitled *Billiards at Half Past Nine*, completely does away with the book's chronology and instead intermeshes simultaneously the present, the Nazi era and that of the First World War. Indeed, some of the early films have been characterised by the way they seem to operate 'outside any recognisable tradition of film-making either commercial or avant-garde' (Elsaesser 1989:

• Plate 13.7 *Abschied von Gestern/Yesterday Girl* (Alexander Kluge, 1965–6)

25). To a certain extent, this kind of experimentation can be viewed as arising out of necessity: small budgets meant it was impossible to make feature films according to the conventions of commercial cinema. Therefore, rather than trying to produce pale imitations, film-makers were forced to try and find completely different ways of working altogether. But as the Oberhausen Manifesto openly declared, many film-makers also *wanted* to break with the 'old cinema' and to develop a new film language in order to inject the German cinema with new life.

Kluge's approach to film-making, for instance, can probably be best described as 'Brechtian' (and his films have also been compared to those of French new wave director Jean-Luc Godard). Like Brecht's epic theatre, Kluge's films are designed to discourage viewers from identifying with the fictional characters, to challenge people's usual forms of perception and to stimulate a questioning attitude towards their surroundings rather than provide reassurance. This is very evident in his first feature film, *Yesterday Girl* (1965–6).

☐ CASE STUDY 1: *YESTERDAY GIRL*

This was filmed in black and white and based on the real-life story of a young Jewish woman, Anita G, who comes to West Germany from what was then the GDR (East Germany) with virtually nothing in an attempt to make a new life for herself. In a highly episodic and impressionistic narrative, the film follows Anita through a number of unsuccessful jobs, a couple of attempts to steal and a series of unhappy affairs which end with her becoming pregnant. Unable to support herself, she wanders the streets with her suitcase and finally turns herself over to the police.

In order to break up the narrative, Kluge incorporates intertitles to subdivide the film and comment on events. Verbal commentary, direct address to camera by characters and old photos are also intercut to illustrate and invite reflection upon the narrative sequences. And the events that constitute the narrative are only shown obliquely – we see only the court proceedings against Anita that result from a theft, not the theft itself, nor where it took place or its discovery; we are given only a brief indication that Anita is having an affair, never how or why it started. These filmic devices give the film a very disjointed feel, something that is compounded by the use of music on the soundtrack which is often inappropriate to the visual images it accompanies. This means the viewer has to take a very active role in constructing the film's meaning and can precipitate a more analytical consideration of the issues and ideas raised by *Yesterday Girl*.

Since the filmic devices employed by Kluge discourage us from identifying with Anita as a psychologically-rounded individual, she becomes a powerful signifying element. As a Jew who leaves the GDR, she acts as a reminder both of the Nazi persecution of the Jews and of the communist rejection of capitalism. Thus, through the character of Anita the film links together questions of German history and the contemporary situation of postwar divided Germany, suggesting the inseparability of past and present. Although Anita tries to escape her personal history by moving to West Germany, she fails miserably to make a new life for herself. Just as she would have failed to fit into Nazi Germany and has failed to fit into East Germany, so she fails to integrate into West German life. In terms of both her past and present, Anita is 'an unwanted outsider' (Sandford 1980: 21) – that is, she cannot escape her past. Her specific situation is, however, peculiarly German, and thus Kluge's film can be understood as a film about Germany, one that suggests that while people may wish to forget the Nazi past, it nevertheless is and will remain an essential precondition of the present socio-political situation.

As is evident from this analysis of *Yesterday Girl*, the desire to develop a new film language extended beyond pure formal experimentation to include questions of content as well (although in many ways the two are, of course, indivisible). As already discussed, German cinema of the 1950s had been characterised by its 'escapism', especially in its refusal to address recent history and contemporary concerns. So, for instance, a classic *Heimatfilme* from the mid-1950s, Harald Reinl's *Die Fischerin vom Bodensee/The Fisherwoman from Lake Constance* (1956) shows people living in harmony with their surroundings with no evidence of war damage or postwar reconstruction. For the new generation of film-makers who were all born around the time of the Second World War and grew up in a postwar divided Germany, such films were a blatant denial of the realities of contemporary German life. If there was to be a renewal of German cinema, then its films had necessarily to tackle contemporary issues or demonstrate at least some contemporary relevance.

As the new cinema developed, film-makers addressed many issues of contemporary relevance via a number of different styles and genres. Although it is not possible to undertake a comprehensive study here, the films can be characterised as an endeavour to represent a reality that previously had been largely excluded from German cinema – rather than through any shared aesthetic concerns or stylistic similarities – and thus they have been described as 'the quest for alternative images and counter-representations' (Rentschler 1984: 4).

The *Gastarbeiter*

Both Fassbinder and Helma Sanders-Brahms, for instance, address the presence of **Gastarbeiter** (guest workers) in West Germany in a number of their films: Fassbinder in *Katzelmacher* (1969), *Wildwechsel/Wild Game* (1972) and *Angst essen Seele auf/Fear Eats the Soul* (1973), and Sanders-Brahms in *Die industrielle Reservearmee/The Industrial Reserve Army* (1971) and *Shirins Hochzeit/Shirin's Wedding* (1975).

Gastarbeiter

The term used for the foreign labour that the West German government started to import from Turkey and southern Europe in the 1950s to help sustain its industries.

• Plate 13.8 *Katzelmacher* (Rainer Werner Fassbinder, 1969)

When the Federal Republic started to enjoy economic prosperity in the 1950s it became necessary to import foreign labour – mostly from Turkey, although also from the former Yugoslavia, Italy and Greece – in order to sustain its industries. These *Gastarbeiter* were regarded by successive German governments as temporary labour and in theory could be sent home if unemployment among Germans ever became acute. However, due to the lack of a comprehensively formulated policy, many *Gastarbeiter* remained in West Germany, often establishing their families and raising their children there. Once West Germany's 'economic miracle' began to wane in the 1960s, the country

• Plate 13.9 *Shirin Hochzeit/Shirin's Wedding* (Helma Sanders-Brahms, 1975)

was faced with a growing, semi-permanent non-German population who needed education, housing and other resources, but were themselves no longer needed by their host society and thus increasingly prone to racist attack.

The above-mentioned films tackle the *Gastarbeiter* issue in different ways, but they all draw attention to their presence in West Germany. Sanders-Brahms' *Shirin's Wedding*, for example, is the moving story of a young Turkish woman who goes to Germany in search of the man she is betrothed to. By focusing on Shirin's attempts and ultimate inability to survive in the Federal Republic, the film acts as an observation on the meeting of two alien cultures. In contrast, Fassbinder's films are less concerned with exploring the experiences of the *Gastarbeiter* themselves, tending instead to concentrate on exposing the roots of some of the attitudes towards them.

Katzelmacher – a Bavarian term of abuse for immigrant workers – for instance, revolves around a group of directionless young couples who live in a suburban block of flats. With little to interest or motivate them, the arrival of a Greek *Gastarbeiter*, Jorgos, unleashes what critics saw at the time as the fascist tendencies that were still latent in West German society. As the women gradually become curious about Jorgos it arouses the jealousies of their respective male partners. The situation starts to become antagonistic, with the men getting increasingly violent towards 'their' women and eventually beating up Jorgos. A very stylised film, *Katzelmacher* thereby suggests that any perception that the *Gastarbeiter* were unwelcome in West Germany had as much, if not more, to do with attitudes that already existed within German society as with the economic situation that developed after their arrival.

Terrorism

During the 1970s a number of film-makers also turned their attention on the increasing terrorist activity that was disrupting German life. The origins of West German terrorism stem largely from the country's political situation in the late 1960s. In 1966 the Federal Republic's two main political parties had been forced to govern by coalition. The conservative nature of this coalition and the fact that it possessed an overwhelming majority in parliament led to the growth of an extra-parliamentary opposition movement. This opposition movement found its most ardent supporters among left-wing students who were disappointed at how little social change had been effected since the end of the war. They were, for instance, extremely critical of the fact that ex-Nazis, such as the then Chancellor, Georg Kiesinger, had been able to rise to prominent positions in the new Federal Republic. Student protest of this kind was, of course, not confined to Germany, but swept across Europe and America in 1968, opposing in particular America's involvement in Vietnam.

As the 1960s came to a close, however, the student movement in Germany collapsed and a small number of left-wing extremists turned to violence in order to try and bring about concrete changes. Sporadic terrorist acts such as bombings, bank robberies and arson attacks started in 1968. A couple of years later, terrorist Andreas Baader met a journalist called Ulrike Meinhof, and together they set up the Baader–Meinhof terrorist group, which later became known as the **Red Army Faction** (RAF). Although Baader and Meinhof were both arrested in 1972 – together with fellow terrorist Gudrun Ensslin – other RAF members escalated terrorist attacks throughout the 1970s. The government took increasingly repressive actions to try and curb the attacks, but largely without success. Events came to a head in autumn 1977 when, after a spate of terrorist activity involving the kidnapping and killing of a prominent industrialist and former Nazi, Hans Martin Schleyer, and an aeroplane hijacking, three imprisoned terrorists (Baader, Ensslin and Carl Raspe) were found dead in their prison cells.

Several films were made which directly or indirectly addressed the issues raised by the terrorist activity and the state's response to it. The combined incidents of autumn 1977, in particular, had a profound effect on the new generation of film-makers, and Fassbinder, Kluge, Edgar Reitz, Volker Schlöndorff and a few others decided to produce a collectively made film about these events, *Deutschland im Herbst/Germany in Autumn* (1978). Each contributing director made a segment – and all are widely differing in terms

Red Army Faction

A West German terrorist group set up by Andreas Baader and Ulrike Meinhof in 1970.

• Plates 13.10 and 13.11 *Deutschland im Herbst/Germany in Autumn* (Fassbinder/Kluge/Edgar Reitz/Volker Schlöndorff *et al.*, 1978)

• Plate 13.12 *Das zweite Erwachen der Christa Klages/The Second Awakening of Christa Klages*
(Margarethe von Trotta, 1977)

of style and approach – which presented his or her response to the events, and the
film is introduced by a short text which states: 'Once atrocity has reached a certain
point, it does not matter who committed it, it should just stop.' In his contribution, for
instance, Fassbinder reflects on the events in a staged conversation with his mother;
Schlöndorff collaborated with writer Heinrich Böll to produce a short drama about the
cancellation of a television broadcast of Sophocles' *Antigone* because its themes of
violence and resistance would be too inflammatory; while Kluge invented the character
of Gabi Teichert, a history teacher, who uses a spade to literally dig for the roots of
German history.

Margarethe von Trotta has also repeatedly returned to terrorist-related themes in her
films. In *Die verlorene Ehre der Katherina Blum/The Lost Honour of Katherina Blum*
(1975), co-directed with Volker Schlöndorff and based on a Heinrich Böll novel of the
same name, she explores what happens to a young woman at the hands of the authorities and the press after she unwittingly becomes involved with a man wanted by the
police. Her next feature film, *Das zweite Erwachen der Christa Klages/The Second
Awakening of Christa Klages* (1977), is based on the true life-story of a woman who
robbed a bank to try and keep open a child-care centre threatened with closure. The
director made *Die bleierne Zeit/The German Sisters* (1981) after she met Christiane
Ensslin, the sister of dead terrorist Gudrun Ensslin. The film focuses on the relationship
between two sisters, Marianne and Juliane, who are loosely based on the Ensslin sisters.
Although we see nothing of Marianne's actual terrorist activities, through the eyes of
Juliane we learn how Marianne has left her family to join a terrorist group, is eventually
arrested and finally dies in prison. Initially Juliane is unsympathetic to her sister's politics,
but on witnessing the inhumane way Marianne is treated in prison and by remembering
their childhood together she increasingly comes to understand her sister's actions.

Feminism

At the same time, the work of Margarethe von Trotta is also part of a vibrant women's cinema that emerged as part of the New German Cinema. In Germany, women's film-making was closely connected with the development of the contemporary women's movement, and the main impetus for the movement came from the student protest movement discussed above. Although the student movement was concerned with bringing about social change, its male leaders failed to acknowledge the oppression of women. Eventually, student film-maker Helke Sander (born 1937) delivered a stinging attack on her male colleagues during the Socialist German Students Union annual conference in 1968, and in the wake of her speech women's groups began to be set up throughout the country to campaign for women's rights. Although it took several years for it to gain momentum, the growing women's movement gradually raised awareness of such issues as child-care, abortion, violence against women and discrimination in the workplace.

Some feminist activists also drew attention to the way in which women are so often excluded from the public domain, and thus their stories are rarely told, their experiences rarely acknowledged. Although relatively few women film-makers actively participated in the women's movement, its consciousness-raising aims fostered a new women's cinema that was concerned with representing the authentic experiences of women. The majority of films that made up this cinema explored or were based on the lives of actual women. Several film-makers simply turned their cameras on women in their own circle of friends and acquaintances to produce imaginative and experimental documentaries. For example, in her film *Ein gar und ganz verwahrlostes Mädchen/A Thoroughly Demoralized Girl* (1977) Jutta Brückner (born 1941) documents a day in the life of her friend Rita

• Plate 13.13 *Die allseitig reduzierte Persönlichkeit/The All-round Reduced Personality – Redupers* (Helke Sander, 1977)

• Plate 13.14 *Deutschland, bleiche Mutter/Germany, Pale Mother* (Helma Sanders-Brahms, 1979–80)

Rischak and her attempts to improve herself, while Elfi Mikesch (born 1940) made *Ich denke oft an Hawaii/I Often Think of Hawaii* (1978) about her neighbour Ruth, a deserted wife and mother of two children. Other films – such as those of von Trotta mentioned above – were based on the documented lives of actual women.

However, some directors turned to their own experiences and produced auto-biographical feature films. Among these are Helke Sander's *Die allseitig reduzierte Persönlichkeit/The All-round Reduced Personality – Redupers* (1977), Helma Sanders-Brahms' *Deutschland, bleiche Mutter/Germany, Pale Mother* (1979–80), Jutta Brückner's *Hungerjahre/Years of Hunger* (1980), Jeanine Meerapfel's *Malou* (1980) and Marianne Rosenbaum's *Peppermint Frieden/Peppermint Freedom* (1983). Although each film adopts a different approach to its subject-matter, in many of them the directors look back to their childhoods, their experiences of growing up in the 1950s and the lives of their parents. Others are more contemporary. In *Redupers*, for instance, Sander explores her own experiences of being a working single mother through the fictional character of Edda Chiemnyjewski, a freelance photographer who desperately tries to balance her commitments as a mother with her need to earn a living.

An important dimension of these films is the desire to put on screen those particular aspects of women's lives that have usually been marginalised by or excluded from mainstream cinema. In the opening scenes of *Redupers*, therefore, we see Edda picking up her young daughter to say goodbye before she leaves for work. The girl clings on to Edda's scarf and refuses to let go. In despair Edda takes off the scarf and rushes out of the flat. This 'tug-of-war' between mother and daughter confronts the viewer with what is so frequently ignored – the difficulties that many women face in trying to combine a career and motherhood.

American imperialism and popular culture

A number of other contemporary issues have been addressed within the New German Cinema, but what the cinema has probably become most well known for outside Germany has been its exploration of America's role in postwar Germany and its 'remembering' of the Nazi past. As US armed forces took up occupation of West Germany after the war, they brought with them American culture in all shapes and forms. The trappings of American life became so commonplace that film-maker Wim Wenders and others have referred to the 'Americanisation' of West Germany (Sandford 1980: 104). Indeed, in his film *Im Lauf der Zeit/Kings of the Road* (1976) Wenders has one of the characters observe: 'The Yanks have colonized our subconscious.' Initially this seemed to be welcomed by many Germans – when Hollywood films reappeared in the cinemas, for instance, Germans literally *flocked* to see what they had been missing. In a sense this is hardly surprising, but Wenders has argued that the reason Germans embraced American culture so readily had more to do with trying to blot out the unpleasant memory of Nazism: 'The need to forget 20 years created a hole, and people tried to cover this . . . by assimilating American culture' (quoted in Sandford 1980: 104). At the same time, however, in a postwar *divided* Germany, many Germans also simply lacked any clear

• Plate 13.15 *Im Lauf der Zeit/Kings of the Road* (Wim Wenders, 1976)

• Plate 13.16 *Der amerikanische Freund/The American Friend* (Wim Wenders, 1976–7)

sense of what it meant to be German which compounded the embracing of American popular culture.

Thus, for the new generation of directors who had all grown up in postwar Germany, American culture was very much part of everyday life. It is unsurprising therefore that a number of their films explore the experience of being caught between two cultures. Different film-makers have focused on different aspects of this experience, but several have highlighted the influence of Hollywood cinema by drawing on the conventions of American films while dealing with specifically German subject matter. Fassbinder, for instance, made three films which are all set in the criminal underworld of Munich but which also play with the conventions and plots of the Hollywood gangster genre: *Liebe ist kälter als der Tod/Love is Colder Than Death* (1969), *Götter der Pest/Gods of the Plague* (1970), *Der amerikanische Soldat/The American Soldier* (1970). Later, he also turned his attention to Hollywood melodramas, especially those directed by Douglas Sirk, such as *Written on the Wind* (1956) and *Imitation of Life* (1959). Sirk's films attracted critical praise in the 1970s for the way in which they exposed the underlying tensions present in 1950s American society. During the late 1970s and early 1980s Fassbinder made a number of films, such as *Lili Marleen* (1980) and *Lola* (1981), which drew on

417

the style of Sirk's films and the conventions of melodrama to explore German society.

However, although the Americans had been greeted as saviours in 1945, by the time Wenders, Fassbinder and others were starting to make films attitudes towards the American presence in West Germany – particularly among the younger generation – were also becoming more ambivalent. As the student movement protested against America's involvement in Vietnam it highlighted what many now began to perceive as America's equally imperialist role in West Germany.

This ambivalence towards the 'Americanisation' of West Germany is particularly evident in many of Wenders' films, including *Der amerikanische Freund/The American Friend* (1976–7). Based on the Patricia Highsmith novel, *Ripley's Game*, the film centres on a friendship that develops between Ripley, a crooked American art-dealer (played by Dennis Hopper) living in Hamburg, and Jonathon, a German picture framer suffering from a terminal illness. At Ripley's instigation, Jonathon carries out two murders in return for a sizeable payment so that he can leave his family well provided for after his death.

The film clearly owes much to Hollywood cinema – Ripley dresses and behaves like the hero from a latter-day western; in addition to the casting of Dennis Hopper, American directors Samuel Fuller and Nicholas Ray both have small cameo roles; and the second murder which takes place on a train is very reminiscent of several Hitchcock films. And the fact that Wenders chose to cast Hopper, Fuller and Ray suggests a fascination on his part with American films. At the same time, however, much of the narrative detail suggests a deep mistrust of America's motives for remaining in Europe. It is Ripley who for his own ends leads Jonathon into a life of crime, which ultimately results in Jonathon's premature death. And Ripley is only in Hamburg in order to use the German art market to circulate forged paintings. There is also a suggestion that the Americans are making money out of the German porn industry. Thus the film can be viewed as giving expression to a love–hate relationship with the American role in West German life.

German history

The New German Cinema directors have also participated in the country's so-called 'remembering' of its Nazi past. As already mentioned, after the war there had been a desire to forget the Nazi past, and during the 1950s it had simply not been a subject for public discussion. As Margarethe von Trotta has observed: 'We felt that there was a past of which we were guilty as a nation but we weren't told about in school. If you asked questions, you didn't get answers' (quoted in Knight 1992: 141). During the late 1970s, however, for a number of reasons – especially the events of autumn 1977 (discussed on p. 411) and the broadcast of the American television series *Holocaust* on West German television in 1979 – the Germans finally began to 'remember' and deal with their recent history. Unsurprisingly, this act of 'remembering' had an impact on cinema, and by the early 1980s a number of directors had endeavoured to explore the Nazi past in a way that had not been attempted before.

Some of the films that have been singled out for attention in this connection are *Hitler – ein Film aus Deutschland/Hitler, a Film from Germany* (1977) by Hans Jürgen Syberberg (born 1935), Rainer Werner Fassbinder's *Die Ehe der Maria Braun/The Marriage of Maria Braun* (1978), Alexander Kluge's *Die Patriotin/The Patriot* (1979), Helma Sanders-Brahms' *Deutschland, bleiche Mutter/Germany, Pale Mother* (1979–80) and Edgar Reitz's sixteen-hour television epic *Heimat/Homeland* (1984). Rather than being about historical events, these stylistically very different films tried to explore how the German people had experienced the Hitler era as a lived reality. To do this the films tended to concentrate on the telling of *personal* stories. For instance, Fassbinder's film follows

• Plate 13.17 *Hitler – ein Film aus Deutschland/Hitler, a Film from Germany* (Hans Jürgen Syberberg, 1977)

one woman's struggle to survive during the immediate postwar period when her husband at first fails to return from the war and then ends up in prison for murder, while the film by Sanders-Brahms (born 1940) examines how her parents, neither of whom were party members, survived during wartime but could not come to terms with postwar life.

Since the films focus on personal stories, political events become more of a back-drop to or an intrusive element in people's private lives, or in some cases are virtually

• Plate 13.18 *Die Ehe der Maria Braun/The Marriage of Maria Braun* (Rainer Werner Fassbinder, 1978)

excluded altogether. Reitz's *Heimat*, for instance, traces the lives and fortunes of two families in a small village from 1919 to 1982. Set in an isolated rural location, the village seems far removed from any of the political realities of the twentieth century. In the episodes that deal with the Nazi era the persecution of the Jews is barely mentioned, and the villagers main contact with Nazism is when three Nazi dignitaries pass through for a brief visit. Although the son of one family does become a Nazi officer he is represented as being too young and naive to fully understand what he is getting involved in.

Consequently, the films act as a powerful counter-balance to populist representations of Germany's history – such as *Holocaust* – which usually deal *exclusively* with the atrocities committed under the Nazi regime, public figures and resistance fighters. Although such a balance is undoubtedly necessary, and while the films may be a more accurate representation of how many Germans did actually experience Hitler's Third Reich, they conveniently avoid any exploration of who should bear responsibility for the Nazi atrocities. Thus the films have also been viewed as 'revisionist' – that is, it has been suggested that they also 'rewrite' German history in a manner that is more palatable to the Germans.

• Plate 13.19 *Heimat/Homeland* (Edgar Reitz, 1984)

A question of German identity?

As is evident, a consideration of the sociopolitical context within which the film-makers were working is of crucial importance to an understanding of the films they made. This clearly marks the New German Cinema as a specifically *national* one – that is, one which was shaped as much, if not more so, by the nationally prevailing circumstances and conditions as it was by the creative talent of individual film-makers. But the fact that a significant number of the films are effectively exploring the experience of being German in a postwar western society also suggests a deep concern with questions of national identity. Although film and television generally (among other things) help give us or express a sense of national identity, these films are also very much a product of the way in which concerns within West German society shifted during the 1970s from steadfastly denying the Nazi past, from consuming American culture and allowing others to represent German history for them (as with the American series *Holocaust*), to trying to evolve a self-determined German identity. In a sense, the films are indicative of a desire on the part of West Germans to finally reassert themselves as German.

SPONSORSHIP OR CENSORSHIP?

As the film subsidy system developed, it had quickly become apparent that the new directors were far from free of vested interests. Since the New German Cinema had not achieved wide commercial success, it had remained completely dependent on public money for its existence. State support may have helped produce an internationally acclaimed cinema, but it had also been responsible for political and artistic censorship.

Although the funding agencies promoted film as an art form, the economic rationale underlying their guidelines often determined whether funds were awarded or not. In 1978 Wilhelm Roth of the FFA project commission observed that 'the main discussion that takes place . . . is always about whether or not the film will be successful at the box-office' (quoted in Knight 1992: 37). Thus, the formal experimentation that characterised many of the early New German Cinema films gradually began to disappear and the cinema became predominantly one of narrative-based feature films.

Projects that addressed politically sensitive issues or were socially critical in some way also often failed to find funding. In 1975, for instance, Fassbinder submitted a proposal to the FFA entitled *Der Müll, die Stadt und der Tod/The Garbage, The City and Death*. Based on a Gerhard Zwerenz novel, Fassbinder had originally written it as a play which examined some of the negative aspects of capitalism. However, he was accused of anti-Semitism and the play was never staged. The FFA felt that the racist implications persisted in the film project and refused funding. Kluge was even told that he would have to give back his subsidy after making *Gelegenheitsarbeit einer Sklavin/Occasional Work of a Female Slave* (1973) because discrepancies were noticed between his original proposal and the finished film. It has been suggested that this was an attempt to censure the critical stance the film took on the existing anti-abortion laws (*New German Critique* 1981–2: 23). With the rise of the women's movement many women film-makers also wanted to make films dealing with so-called 'women's issues', but found it difficult to even attract funding in the first place. Helke Sander tried to make a film about menstruation, but the funding agencies 'were so disgusted . . . they didn't even want to deal with the topic' (Silberman 1982: 48).

Furthermore, in West Germany representatives of the various political parties sat on the boards of all the television corporations and were therefore in a position to exercise censorship powers. In 1980, for instance, members of the right-wing CDU/CSU blacklisted *Der Kandidat/The Candidate*, a film about the CSU politician Franz-Josef Strauss made by a group of directors which included Kluge and Schlöndorff. The following year Helga Reidemeister reported that she had received rejections from nine television companies when she was trying to raise funding. It was for a film about Carola Bloch, a Jewish political activist who joined the German Communist Party in the 1930s

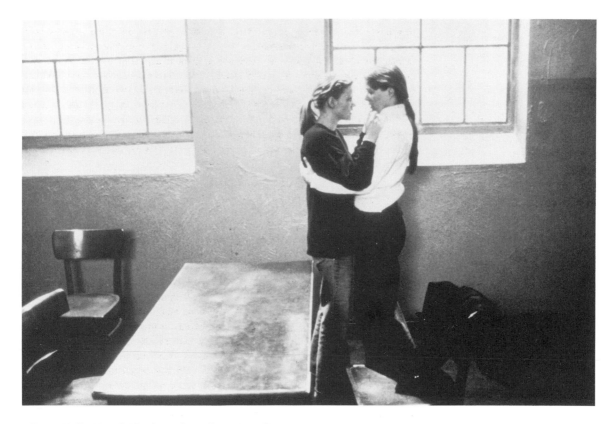

• Plate 13.20 *Die bleierne Zeit/The German Sisters* (Margarethe von Trotta, 1981)

and lived in East Germany after the war. According to Reidemeister, 'the problem is Carola's past as a CP member, something I can't and don't want to conceal' (in Silberman 1982: 48).

Such censorship reached an unprecedented peak in the mid- to late 1970s. As terrorist activity had escalated during the 1970s, it resulted in increasing intolerance of dissident viewpoints. Measures were introduced to prevent political extremists from entering the civil service and to prohibit the advocating or approval of criminal deeds in public. And leftist bookshops, printers and news services were subjected to repeated investigations, with arrests and confiscation of material not uncommon. Consequently, by 1977 many people felt West Germany had become a police state in which it was impossible to express oppositional viewpoints.

As a result film funding agencies became even more conservative, avoiding any projects that could be construed as politically radical, controversial or socially critical. This meant that if film-makers wanted to directly address politically sensitive issues such as terrorism they had to seek other sources of funding. And the collectively-made *Deutschland im Herbst/Germany in Autumn* (1978) was in fact made through private investment.

The effects on state-subsidised film-making were twofold. First, it exacerbated a tendency for German film-makers to draw on literary sources. Since funding agencies demanded that proposals be accompanied by finished scripts, the system already encouraged producers to undertake literature adaptations. However, in 1976–7 political conservatism produced what was viewed as a 'literature adaptation crisis'. In those years there was not only an overwhelming number of literature-based films, but most were adaptations of nineteenth-century classics which appeared to have little or no contemporary relevance.

On the other hand, censorship gave rise to what has been described as a passion for 'oblique approaches and microcosmic case histories' (Dawson 1979: 243). This is particularly evident in films such as Margarethe von Trotta's *Das zweite Erwachen der Christa Klages/The Second Awakening of Christa Klages* (1977) and *Die bleierne Zeit/The German Sisters* (1981). Although both films allude to terrorism, they do not overtly examine terrorist politics. Some critics have suggested that the approaches of such films are so oblique that they have little contemporary relevance. According to Charlotte Delormé, for instance, 'if *The German Sisters* were really what it purports to be, it would not have received any support, distribution or exhibition' (quoted in Knight 1992: 41). Others, however, have argued that it subtly explores the contemporary social problems and their connections to Germany's past through the experiences of individual protagonists.

Thus, developments during the 1970s appeared to threaten the existence of Germany's new cinema for a second time. Although the apparent crisis had passed by the end of the decade, many film-makers came to view the film subsidy system as something of a mixed blessing. Without doubt it had played an absolutely crucial role in making the New German Cinema possible, but at the same time the subsidy system had limited the scope of that cinema. Not only had the funding agencies promoted one particular mode of production, they had also helped to shape the cinema's narrative-based style and to circumscribe its subject matter.

CONCLUSION

By the mid-1980s innumerable critics had pronounced the demise of the New German Cinema. This was partly due to the fact that many of the directors that had been most closely associated with it had moved abroad. Herzog, Schlöndorff, von Trotta, Wenders, Straub and Huillet, for instance, had either spent periods working in other countries or had actually emigrated. Furthermore, Fassbinder, who was by far the most prolific of the cinema's directors – making over twenty feature films and numerous television productions in just over ten years – had died in 1982.

However, the same year also saw the end of seventeen years of Social Democrat rule when elections returned the right-wing CDU/CSU union to power. This had far-reaching consequences for the film sector since the ultra-conservative Friedrich Zimmermann became Minister of the Interior. Under his guidance film policy was revised to clearly favour commercial projects over any form of artistic experimentation. Within his own ministry Zimmermann assumed absolute control over how funds were administered, and much of the work that characterised the New German Cinema quickly became a casualty of his approach.

At the same time, the cost of producing films rose so dramatically during the 1980s that national funding initiatives alone were frequently inadequate. As a result film-makers had increasingly to turn to other countries to find co-funding or to apply to the new pan-European agencies to help meet the shortfall. In order to meet the criteria of such funders, however, film projects are often required to demonstrate a broader European appeal. Consequently, it becomes increasingly difficult to view the films funded in such a manner as part of a specifically national cinema.

Thus, just as a set of historically specific circumstances and conditions had brought the New German Cinema into being, another set of historically specific circumstances meant that much of what made the cinema distinctive disappeared. So, far from being solely the product of a small number of creative geniuses, a 'cinema des auteurs', the New German Cinema has to be understood as a national and historically specific phenomenon. And in a sense, the reason it was able to establish itself so decisively on the international scene, especially in Britain and America, is equally historically specific. During the 1970s, the auteurist approach to cinema had gained enormous sway within the field of film studies on both sides of the Atlantic. Since the *Autorenkino* principle informing much of the subsidy system and the cinema's artisanal mode of production meant that the films readily lent themselves to being discussed as the work of creative geniuses, the New German Cinema was easily valued, if inadequately understood, as a 'cinéma des auteurs'.

NOTES

All references for works cited in the notes section can be found in the bibliography.

1   See, for instance, *Literature/Film Quarterly* 1979; Sandford 1980; *Wide Angle* 1980; Corrigan 1983; and Franklin 1986.

2   In a famous speech, for instance, Spyros Skouras, head of Twentieth-Century Fox, declared that American films were a potential means of 'indoctrinating people into the free way for life and instil[ling] in them a compelling desire for freedom' (quoted in Knight 1992: 26).

3   According to Elsaesser 1989: 15, by the early 1970s there was not a single commercial distributor which was not American controlled.

4   According to Rentschler 1984: 46, 'in April 1970 it was reported that nineteen Young German films could not find a distributor'.

5   Indeed, the New German Cinema directors were not without their critics at home. Eckart Schmidt, for instance, declared in *Deutsche Zeitung* in September 1977:

> Film-makers like Kluge, Herzog, Geissendörfer and Fassbinder, all of whom have collected subsidies more than once, and who despite such public funding are incapable of directing a success, should in future be barred from receiving subsidies. Film subsidy is no pension fund for failed film-makers.
>
> (quoted in Elsaesser 1989: 37)

FURTHER READING

Corrigan, T., *New German Film. The Displaced Image*, Bloomington and Indianapolis: Indiana University Press, revised edition, 1994.

Elsaesser, T., *New German Cinema: A History*, Basingstoke: Macmillan/British Film Institute, 1989.

Franklin, J., *New German Cinema*, London: Columbus, 1986.

Hartnoll, G., and Porter, V. (eds), *Alternative Filmmaking in Television: ZDF – A Helping Hand*, Dossier 14, London: British Film Institute, 1982.

Kaes, A., *From 'Hitler' to 'Heimat'. The Return of History as Film*, Cambridge, Mass. and London: Harvard University Press, 1989.

Knight, J., *Women and the New German Cinema*, London and New York: Verso, 1992.

McCormick, R., *Politics of the Self*, Oxford: Princeton University Press, 1991.

Pflaum, H.G. and Prinzler, H.H., *Cinema in the Federal Republic of Germany*, Bonn: Inter Nationes, 1993.

Phillips, K. (ed.), *New German Filmmakers*, New York: Frederick Ungar, 1984.

Rentschler, E., *West German Film in the Course of Time*, Bedford Hills, NY: Redgrave, 1984.

—— *German Film and Literature. Adaptations and Transformations*, New York and London: Methuen, 1986.

Rentschler, E. and Prinzler, H.H. (eds), *West German Filmmakers on Film*, New York: Holmes & Meier, 1988.

Sandford, J., *The New German Cinema*, London: Eyre Methuen, 1980.

Wenders, W., *Emotion Pictures*, Faber & Faber: London, 1989.

FURTHER VIEWING

Aguirre, der Zorn Gottes/Aguirre, Wrath of God (W. Herzog, 1972)

Alice in den Städten/Alice in the Cities (W. Wenders, 1973)

Die Angst des Tormanns beim Elfmeter/The Goalie's Fear of the Penalty Kick (W. Wenders, 1971)

Angst essen Seele auf/Fear Eats the Soul (R.W. Fassbinder, 1974)

Die Artisten in der Zirkuskuppel: Ratlos/Artists at the Top of the Big Top: Disorientated (A. Kluge, 1967)

Die Berührte/No Mercy No Future (H. Sanders-Brahms, 1981)

Bildnis einer Trinkerin/Ticket of No Return (U. Ottinger, 1979)

Die bitteren Tränen der Petra von Kant/The Bitter Tears of Petra von Kant (R.W. Fassbinder, 1972)

Das Boot/The Boat (W. Petersen, 1981)

Chronik der Anna Magdalena Bach/Chronicle of Anna Magdalena Bach (J.-M. Straub and D. Huillet, 1968)

Die dritte Generation/The Third Generation (R.W. Fassbinder, 1979)

Fontane Effi Briest/Effi Briest (R.W. Fassbinder, 1974)

Himmel über Berlin/Wings of Desire (W. Wenders, 1987)

Jeder für sich und Gott gegen alle/The Enigma of Kaspar Hauser (W. Herzog, 1974)

Ludwig – Requiem für einen jungfräulichen König/Ludwig – Requiem for a Virgin King (H.J. Syberberg, 1972)

Schwestern oder die Balance des Glücks/Sisters or the Balance of Happiness (M. von Trotta, 1979)

Stammheim (R. Hauff, 1986)

Strohfeuer/A Free Woman (V. Schlöndorff, 1972)

Der subjektive Faktor/The Subjective Factor (H. Sander, 1980)

A wide range of New German Cinema Films can be hired from: Glenbuck Films, British Film Institute, 21 Stephen Street, London, W1P 1PL. Telephone: 0171 957 8938, fax: 0171 580 5830.

A selection of films by Wenders, Fassbinder and Herzog are also available on video.

GLOSSARY OF KEY TERMS

alternative cinema provides an alternative to the codes and conventions of mainstream, narrative cinema, often both thematically and visually. Alternative cinema is defined in reference to the dominant form at the time. Any study concerning 'alternative' cinema films would not only have to examine them in their own right, but also compare them to the contemporary dominant Hollywood cinema. For example, the Soviet cinema of the 1920s was 'alternative' to the Hollywood cinema of the same time.

anthropomorphism The tendency in animation to present creatures with human characteristics. This can redefine or merely draw attention to characteristics which are taken for granted in live-action representations of human beings.

art cinema A term usually applied to films where the director has clearly exercised a high degree of control over the film-making process and thus the films can be viewed as a form of personal expression. The Swedish director, Ingmar Bergman, often writes (and publishes) the screenplay and works closely with key actors who appear frequently in his films.

artisanal mode of production A term used to describe the way in which most New German Cinema films were made with such small budgets and minimal production teams that film-making was considered by some to be more like practising a craft than engaging in a technological process.

auteur An individual, inevitably the director, whose contribution to a film's style and theme is considered so significant that he or she can be considered the 'author' of the film despite the fact that a film's production is dependent on a large number of people with specific skills and talents working collaboratively. An auteur establishes his or her identity across a body of films which can be seen to bear a distinctive 'signature' (compare with **metteur-en-scene**)

auteurism A critical approach to the study of film which identifies the director as responsible for whatever the viewer finds of thematic, stylistic or structural interest in a single film or across a body of work by one director; for example, the films of Hitchcock, Ford and Scorsese.

autorenkino A concept, loosely translated as a 'cinema of authors', promoted by Alexander Kluge while campaigning for the production funding and the development of film education necessary to produce a culturally motivated cinema. According to this concept, the director is to be regarded as a film's creator and the film can be regarded as an expression of that creator's personality.

avant-garde cinema The practice of innovative and inventive use of the cinematic form outside the codes and conventions of mainstream film-making (that is, classical Hollywood narrative). It is essentially non-narrative in structure and often intellectual in content. It is often self-conscious and frequently makes use of devices such as cuts to the camera crew, talking to the camera and scratching on film. For example, the films of Peter Wolten, Laura Mulvay and Jean-Luc Godard.

BBFC British Board of Film Classification responsible for *both* classification and censorship of film shown in the UK.

bhava The eight basic emotions in Indian cinema – love, humour, energy, anger, fear, grief, disgust, astonishment.

BMI The Federal Ministry of the Interior in Germany which awards the annual Federal Film Prize and was initially responsible for funding the Kuratorium junger deutscher Film.

'Bollywood' Bombay, the film capital of India.

bricolage The putting together of features from different genres and styles, self-consciously and usually playfully. This is seen as one of the principal characteristics of **postmodernism**.

character animation Many cartoons and more sophisticated animated films are still dominated by 'character' or 'personality' animation, which attempts to present human traits in an expressive form that directs attention to the detail of gesture and the range of human emotions and experience.

close-up Normally defined as a shot of the head from the neck up.

condensation The compression of a set of narrative or aesthetic agendas within a minimal structural framework.

conjuncture A combination of events – social, political, economic – occurring at a particular historical moment.

deconstruction All forms of communication, including films, are made up of **structures** – narrative structures, generic structures, etc. Deconstruction is a critical activity which involves dismantling these structures in order to better understand how the film functions as, for example, a source of pleasure, an aesthetic artifact, an instrument of ideology.

diegetic Refers to elements of a film that originate directly from within the film's narrative. For example, a popular song that is being played on the soundtrack would be diegetic if it was clear that it was coming from a source within the world of the film, such as a car radio. **Non-diegetic** refers to any elements that remain outside the world of the film, such as voice-overs, credits and mood-setting music that does not directly originate from the world of the film.

distribution A division concentrating on the marketing of film, connecting the producer with the exhibitor by leasing films from the former and renting them to the latter.

dominant cinema In Film Studies, this is assumed to be Hollywood. The term dominant refers not only to economic strength but also to the dominant form or convention, which is realism.

drama-documentary Any format which attempts to recreate historical or typical events using performers, whether actors or not.

economic presentation All the components are designed to help us read the narrative. An examination of the first few minutes of almost any mainstream fictional film will reveal a considerable amount of information about characters, their social situation and their motivation.

embourgeoisement A sociological term describing the adoption of middle-class (bourgeois) values and attributes by members of the working class as a result of increased affluence.

establishing shot A shot using distant framing, allowing the viewer to see the spatial relations between characters and the set.

exclusive run A film is only screened in one movie theatre.

Exhibition A division of the film industry concentrating on the public screening of film.

feminism A concept based on the belief that we live in a society where women are still unequal to men; that women have lower status than men and have less power, particularly economic power. Feminists argue that the media reinforces the status quo by representing a narrow range of images of women; for instance, woman as carer, as passive object, as an object of desire. Many feminists argue that the range of representations for both male and female is limited and slow to change. In recent years, feminism has become fragmented and it is difficult to argue that feminism is a complete area of study; but gender and power relations in society can be seen as central to feminist thinking. For an interesting discussion of this area, see *Feminist Media Studies*, Liesbet van Zoonen (1994).

FFA (Germany) The Film Development Board, which was set up to administer the funds raised by the FFG.

FFG (Germany) The Film Development Act which was passed in 1967 to raise a levy on every cinema ticket sold in West Germany, to provide funding for film production.

fight composer Individual who choreographs spectacular fights in Indian movies.

Film and Television Agreement An agreement made in 1974 between the FFA and the first and second West German television networks, which set up a film production fund.

first run Important movie theatres would show films immediately upon their theatrical release or their 'first run'. Smaller, local theatres would show films on subsequent runs, hence the terms 'second run', 'third run', etc.

fly-on-the-wall A term associated with a style of documentary film-making which attempts to present events to the audience as though the presence of the camera and film crew had not influenced them in any way.

Gastarbeiter The term used for the foreign labour that the West German government started to import from Turkey and southern Europe in the 1950s to help sustain its industries.

gay A description of strong, positive, sexual love and attraction between members of the same sex, used by extension to describe cultural products, such as film and video concerned with similar themes. Mainly referring to males, it can also be used for any person.

gender A name for the social and cultural construction of a person's sex and sexuality. Gender, sex and sexuality can overlap but are by no means an exact match; it is this 'mis-match' which has generated a fascinating body of film production and criticism.

genre A category or type of film which is often identifiable by a repeated pattern of iconography (props, costume, setting); for example, the western or science fiction genres. However, many genre films cannot be identified by their 'look' – comedy and melodrama, for instance. It may be more useful to analyse the narrative conventions of different genre as a means of understanding film. Steven Neale in his book *Genre* (BFI 1980, p.19) says 'Genres are not to be seen as forms of textural codification but as systems of orientations, expectations and conventions that circulate between industry, text and subject.' Genre is part of the 'mental machinery' which links those who work in Cinema to its consumers.

hegemony A concept developed by the Italian political thinker, Antonio Gramsci, to explain the process by which the dominant classes or groups in a nation maintain power over subordinate classes or groups. Hegemony can be achieved by coercion through 'repressive' state institutions like the police, the penal system, the army, or it can be achieved by consent, operating *ideologically* through the institutions of civil society; for example, the media, the family, the education system. Ideology is therefore central to the maintenance of hegemony in capitalist societies.

Heimatfilme A German term which can be loosely translated as 'homeland films' and was coined to delineate a film genre which depicted simple country life in rural Germany.

high angle A shot from a camera held above characters or object, looking down at them.

Hollywood cinema In the classical Hollywood cinema, the editing is designed to be 'invisible'; it is intended to allow the audience to become immersed in the film and to see the point of view of different characters. The editing is used essentially to clarify what is taking place in the narrative. This type of editing had become dominant in Hollywood film-making by approximately 1920.

homoerotic A description of a text – prose, poem, film, painting, photograph, etc. – conveying an enjoyable sense of same-sex attraction.

homosexual A word used to name and describe a person whose main sexual feelings are for people of the same sex. It is mainly, but not exclusively, used in reference to males.

iconic The iconic is defined by the dominant signs which signify a particular person or object – Chaplin, for example, would be defined by his bowler hat, a moustache, a cane and some old boots, while Hitler would be defined by a short parted hairstyle and a small moustache. In the case of **genre**, the iconography is repeated across a body of films.

ideology A set of ideas and attitudes held so much in common by most members of a society that they are seen as part of the natural order. Ideology can be highly visible, as in 'racist ideology' or 'sexist ideology', where the racist or sexist beliefs of individuals are self-evident; it can also be 'invisible' in the sense that it is something we take for granted in our everyday lives. Ideology permeates social institutions such as the media, education and the family but we are often not conscious of it because of the manner in which ideology 'naturalises' values and beliefs, making them seem like 'common sense'.

identification The process of identification allows us to place ourselves in the position of particular characters, either throughout or at specific moments in a movie. The devices involved include subjectivity of viewpoint (we see the world through their eyes), a shared knowledge (we know what and only what they know), and a sharing in their moral world, largely through narrative construction.

Imax Similar to the **Omnimax**, though the imax covers a narrower vertical field of vision, the image of which is projected on to a large, horizontally curved surface.

impersonation The conscious alteration of self in order to 'become' someone quite different for the purpose of a performance (compare with **personification**).

IMR The Institutional Mode of Representation is a broad categorisation of systems of film form and narrative characterising mainstream cinema from around 1915 onwards. It was perceived as replacing the Primitive Mode of Representation (a set of conventions used in early film between 1895 and 1905) as a gradual process in the first twenty years of cinema.

independent cinema may be divided into two areas. First, independent mainstream cinema, produced by companies such as Hand-Made Films, which aim to compete with the big studios, although without any large financial back-up, and find it difficult to survive. Second, the term is used to describe film-making outside the mainstream sector; for instance, film workshops, avant-garde film, feminist film. The boundaries between these two areas are not always clear and they may overlap.

intertextuality The explicit or implicit way in which a (film) text relates to other film texts, thereby increasing its range of meanings through association.

juxtaposition In Film Studies, this usually refers to two different shots that have been joined together to make a contrast.

kinetograph Edison's first movie camera.

Kuratorium junger deutscher Film The Board of Young German Film, which was the first film subsidy agency, set up by the BMI in 1965. Its brief was, and remains, to fund first feature films only.

lesbian A word used to name and describe a woman whose main sexual feelings are for other women. Coined as a medical term in the late nineteenth century, the word has been invested, post-Stonewall, with new ideas of openness and liberation. It can also be used to describe cultural products, such as film and video, dealing with lesbian themes.

lightbox A type of drawing desk used by animators working with traditional drawn techniques. Basically, a box with a light source in it; the sloped drawing surface has a panel of either frosted glass or perspex. This allows the animator to view a number of drawings superimposed over one another. **Electronic lightbox** A concept whereby the drawings are made directly within a computer environment through the use of a touch-sensitive screen and stylus. Similar to a conventional lightbox, it uses advanced computer animation technology which enables instant recording of imagery.

low-key image Light from a single source producing light and shade.

magic lantern An early form of slide-projector usage. More advanced models used three separate lenses and were capable of optical effects such as dissolves and mixes. Some slides were capable of achieving simple animation sequences.

mainstream Feature-length narrative films created for entertainment and profit. Mainstream is usually associated with Hollywood, regardless of where the film is made.

Marxist theory This argues that those who have the means of production have control in a capitalist society. The dominant class has control of the means of production and an interest in perpetuating the dominant ideology. More recently, exponents of Althussian Marxism, particularly post-1968, have argued that mainstream narrative cinema reinforces the capitalist system and that a revolutionary cinema is needed to challenge the dominant ideology.

'masala' movie A spicey Indian movie overloaded with emotion.

'means' test A measure introduced in 1931 in the UK to assess the eligibility of claimants to benefit after a period of twenty-six weeks of unemployment, and calculated on the basis of existing household means as determined by a Public Assistance Committee.

mediation A key concept in film and media theory, it implies that there are always structures, whether human or technological, between an object and the viewer, involving inevitably a partial and selective view.

metamorphosis The ability of one creature or object to make the transition into another form by the manipulation of the material in which they were created; that is, pencil-drawn characters, by a reduction into line and colour, may be re-formed into another shape. Similarly, clay may change from one form into another by first degenerating into a mass before being moulded into a new form.

metteur-en-scène A director, often admired for the competence of his or her work, who lacks the recurring and distinctive 'signature' that would grant the status of **auteur**.

mise-en-scène A theatrical term usually translated as 'staging' or 'what has been put into the scene'. In film, mise-en-scène refers not only to sets, costumes and props but also to how the scene is organised, lit and framed for the camera. Mise-en-scène is one way of producing meaning in films which can be straightforward and extremely complex, depending upon the intentions and skill of the director (the **metteur-en-scène**).

modernist Modernism is a term used to describe developments in early twentieth-century art, literature, music, film and theatre which were a conscious reaction against a perceived conservatism in the arts. **Modernist art** is characterised by experiment and innovation and modernist artists, because of their avant-garde practices, inevitably constitute a cultural elite. Filippo Marinetti and Man Ray were modernist artists. A **modernist device** is any device which undercuts the invisible telling of the story. It draws attention to itself and makes us aware of the construction of the narrative.

montage This comes from the French word meaning to edit. It means the assembling of bits of footage to form a whole. In Film Studies it usually refers to the style of fast editing adopted by the Soviet film-makers of the 1920s.

MPAA The Motion Picture Association of America administers the classification (ratings) system in the US.

multiple run The term given to the procedure where a film is shown simultaneously at a number of cinemas.

'New' Hollywood A term used to refer to Hollywood since the collapse of the **studio system**, and characterised by the way film production is dominated by freelance talent brought together in one-off deals.

noise In the film industry, it refers to any barrier to successful communication.

NRA The National Recovery Administration programme was a 1930s government programme designed to rescue the American economy from the Great Depression and was commonly known as the 'New Deal'.

Oberhausen Manifesto A manifesto drawn up and signed by twenty-six film-makers, writers and artists at the 1962 Oberhausen Film Festival, West Germany, to campaign for access to the means of feature-film production.

oligopoly A state of limited competition between a small group of producers or sellers.

Omnimax A specialist format of cinematography requiring specific recording and projection equipment and facilities. It enables the recording of images in a far greater lateral and vertical field of vision. The aim is to achieve the projection of images on to a concave surface that extends into and beyond the peripheral field of human vision.

paradigm The common sense range of alternatives which will fit into a particular 'slot' within a **structure**: in verbal communication one might describe a house as large, grand, imposing, but it would be only appropriate in, say, poetic communication to describe it as 'fat' or 'obese'; in visual communication one might place on the head of a modern soldier a helmet or a beret but not a native American head-dress, unless some comic or satiric effect was being sought.

'parallel' or 'art' cinema Serious, realistic film with a linear narrative which offers and alternative to the 'formula' film in India. Pioneered by the director Satyajit Ray.

patent pool An association of companies operating collectively in the marketplace by pooling the patents held by each individual company.

patriarchal society A society in which it is men who have power and control. Women are generally disadvantaged and have lower status.

personification The exploitation of physical features to embody a particular character type. Traditionally Hollywood **stars** have personified types rather than engaged in the act of **impersonation**.

Phenakistoscope Invented by Belgian physicist Joseph Plateau in 1832, it is an optical device consisting of a disk with slots cut into its edge. When rotated, images on one side could be viewed with the aid of a mirror; the resulting stroboscope images gave the illusion of movement.

pixillation The extreme editing of rehearsed and deliberately executed 'live-action' movement to create the illusion of movement impossible to achieve by naturalistic means; that is, figures spinning in mid-air or skating across grass.

play-back The pre-recording of songs with good singers and with non-singing actors lip-synchronising on screen.

polysemic Having many potential meanings which are available for decoding by the spectator.

postmodern A term used to describe many aspects of contemporary cultural production from architecture to music. Characteristics include eclectic borrowing from earlier styles (see **bricolage**) to produce witty new combinations. Postmodernism involves the playful manipulation of **paradigms** and the explotation of **intertextuality**.

poststructuralist The critical movement away from an emphasis on the film text and the 'machinery' of Cinema to an emphasis on the spectator's decoding of the text in order to create meaning. This represents a rejection of some aspects of the deterministic Marxist/Freudian theories at the heart of **structuralism** while still recognising that the spectator is himself or herself 'determined' by a range of factors (compare with **structuralist**).

Praxinoscope An advanced version of the Zoetrope which was invented by the Frenchman Emile Reynaud in 1878. Utilising mirrors and its own discrete light source, it was the forerunner of Reynaud's Thèatre Optique.

Production The division in a film company which is concentrated on the making of a film.

propaganda cinema A term used pejoratively with reference to any film that consciously attempts to persuade an audience towards certain beliefs and values.

proto-animation Early live-action cinema which demonstrated certain techniques preceding their conscious use as a method in creating 'animation'. A term used largely in referring to stop-motion, mixed-media and the use of dissolves to create the illusion of metamorphosis in early 'trick' films.

psychoanalytic theory A system of ideas based on the theories of Freud and, more recently, Lacan. Feminists argue that aspects of psychoanalysis are questionable because they are based on patriarchal assumptions that the woman is inferior to man. Freud found female sexuality difficult and disturbing. Lacan argues that the mother is seen as lacking by the child because she has no phallus. Uncertainty about the role of the female in psychoanalytic theory has been picked up on by a number of feminists such as Mulvey, De Lauretis and Modleski, who question the inevitability of Freud and Lacan's theories which emphasise the importance of the phallus, penis envy and patriarchal supremacy.

rasa In India, the eight sentiments which correspond to the emotions – erotic, comic, heroic, furious, apprehensive, compassionate, horrific, marvellous.

reading a film Although films are viewed and heard, the concept of 'reading' a film implies an active process of making sense of what we are experiencing.

realism Live-action cinema has inspired numerous debates about what may be recognised as 'realism'; that is, what may be considered as the most accurate representation of what is 'real' in the recording of the concrete and tangible world. Clearly, the animated form itself resists realism and prioritises 'fantasy'. Disney, however, still aspired to **hyper-realism** in his films, by making his characters correspond as closely as possible to the 'real' world in their movement and context, while allowing for fantasy elements in character and narrative.

reappropriation The process whereby a previously oppressed group takes a negative term and turns it around to invest it with new meanings of power and liberation. Examples include 'black', 'virago' and 'queer'.

Red Army Faction A West German terrorist group set up by Andreas Baader and Ulricke Meinhof in 1970.

reduced animation Animation may be literally the movement of one line which, in operating in time and space, may take on characteristics which an audience may perceive as expressive and symbolic. This form of 'minimalism' constitutes reduced animation which takes as its premise that 'less is more'.

Animation is created at its sparest level to suggest more to its audience. This may enable the film to work in a mode which has an 'intensity of suggestion'.

representation The media *re*-presents information to its audience, who are encouraged by the mainstream media to see its output as a 'window on the world', as reflecting reality. Yet the process of representing information is highly complex and highly selective. Many feminists argue, for instance, that the way notions of gender are represented by the media perpetuates and reinforces the values of patriarchal society: men tend to take on strong, active roles while women are shown as passive and relying on their attractiveness. Representation often makes use of stereotypes because they are a shorthand, quick and easy way of using information. It could be argued that the media production process encourages the use of stereotypes because of the pressure of time and budget. Many feminists point out that because so few women hold key positions in the media hierarchies representations of women are bound to be from a male perspective.

Russian cinema The body of films made in Tsarist Russia between 1907 and 1919.

signifier A sign – verbal, visual or aural – which contains meaning. Signs usually function in combination with other signs according to rules of combination in order to produce complex meaning (see **iconography**, **paradigm**, **polysemic**, **syntagm**).

star A star embodies a set of meanings which derive less from the character role the star plays within a particular film than the identity (persona) which pre-exists the film. To this extent a star can be considered as similar to a **genre**, bringing 'systems of orientations, expectations and conventions that circulate between industry, text and subject'. Defining 'star quality' is difficult – but it is clear that it is contained less in the skills and talents possessed by the individual than in their physical being. A star has a particular capacity for mobilising the fantasies of the audiences. As a **signifier**, the star contains meanings which carry a particular force at the historical moment of their stardom.

structuralist A critical approach dominant in the 1970s when much film theory was first formulated. It is characterised by an emphasis on the structures of the film and the operation of cinema in rendering the spectator passive and hence vulnerable to emotional and ideological manipulation (compare with **post-structuralist**).

studio system A term used to describe the production system of Hollywood during its 'classic' period from the late 1920s until the mid-1950s and characterised by contracted talent and 'factory-line' production (compare with **'New' Hollywood**).

syntagm The rule of combination working within a visual, verbal or aural communication structure. **Paradigms** function within such rules of combination.

BIBLIOGRAPHY

CHAPTER 2: CINEMA AS INSTITUTION

Algate, A. and Richards, J., *Britain Can Take It*, London: Basil Blackwell, 1986.

Allen, R. and Gomery, D., *Film History: Theory and Practice*, New York: Newbery Award Records, 1985.

Andrew, N., 'The Censors Who Are Fighting a Losing Battle', *Financial Times*, 5 September 1993.

Austin, B., *Immediate Seating: A Look at Movie Audiences*, Belmont, Calif.: Wadsworth Publishing Company, 1989.

—— 'Home Video: The Second-Run "Theater" Of The 1990s', in T. Balio (ed.), *Hollywood in the Age of Television*, Boston: Unwin Hyman, 1990.

Balio, T. (ed.), *The American Film Industry*, Madison: University of Wisconsin Press, 1976, see especially sections 1–4.

—— (ed.), *Hollywood in the Age of Television*, Boston: Unwin Hyman, 1990.

Barr, C. (ed.), *All Our Yesterdays*, London: British Film Institute, 1986.

Bernstein, I., *Hollywood at the Crossroads: An Economic Study of the Motion Picture Industry*, Los Angeles: Hollywood Film Council, 1957.

Biskind, P., 'Going For Broke', *Sight and Sound*, October 1991.

Bordwell, D., Staiger J. and Thompson, K., *The Classical Hollywood Cinema*, London: Routledge & Kegan Paul, 1985.

Buscombe, E., 'Walsh and Warner Bros', in P. Hardy (ed.), *Raoul Walsh*, Edinburgh: Edinburgh Film Festival, 1974.

Campbell, R., 'Warner Bros in the 1930s: Some Tentative Notes', *The Velvet Light Trap*, no. 1, June 1971.

Champlin, C., 'What Will H. Hays Begat', *American Film*, vol. 6, no. 1, October 1980.

Christie I. (ed.), *Powell Pressburger and Others*, London: British Film Institute, 1978.

Conant, M., 'The Impact of the Paramount Decrees', in T. Balio (ed.), *The American Film Industry*, Madison: University of Wisconsin Press, 1976.

Daly, D., *A Comparison of Exhibition and Distribution Patterns in Three Recent Feature Motion Pictures*, New York: Arno Press, 1980.

Deschner, D., 'Anton Grot: Warners Art Director 1927–1948', *The Velvet Light Trap*, no. 15, 1975.

'Dialogue on Film', an interview with Richard Zanuck and David Brown, *American Film*, vol. 1, no. 1, October 1975.

Dibie, J., *Aid for Cinematographic and Audio-Visual Production in Europe*, London: John Libbey & Company, 1993.

Docherty, D., Morrison, D. and Tracey, M., *The Last Picture Show?*, London: British Film Institute, 1987.

Eckert, C., 'The Carole Lombard in Macy's Window', *Quarterly Review of Film Studies*, vol. 3, no. 1, 1978, pp.1–12.

Falcon, R., *Classified! A Teacher's Guide to Film and Video Censorship and Classification*, London: British Film Institute, 1994.

Fellman, N. and Durwood, S., 'The Exhibitors: Show and Teller Time', in W. Bluem and J. Squire (eds), *The Movie Business*, New York: Hastings House, 1972.

Ferman, J. and Phelps, G., *Memorandum on the Work of the British Board of Film Classification*, London: BBFC, 1993a.

—— *A Student's Guide to Film Classification and Censorship in Britain*, London: BBFC, 1993b.

Frankel, M. and Wall, C. *et al.*, 'Wiring the World', *Newsweek*, 5 April 1993, pp. 28–33.

Fulton, A. R., 'The Machine', in T. Balio (ed.), *The American Film Industry*, Madison: University of Wisconsin Press, 1976.

Gomery, D., *The Hollywood Studio System*, London: Macmillan, 1986.

—— *Shared Pleasures*, London: British Film Institute, 1992.

Gordon, D., 'Why the Movie Majors are Major', in T. Balio (ed.), *The American Film Industry*, Madison: University of Wisconsin Press, 1976.

Gottlieb, C., *The Jaws Log*, New York: Dell Publishing, 1975.

Handel, L., *Hollywood Looks at its Audience*, Urbana: University of Illinois Press, 1950.

The Independent on Sunday, 'The Hard Sell', 'The Sunday Review', 11 July 1993.

Jowett, G. and Linton, J., *Movies as Mass Communication*, Newbury Park, Calif.: Sage Publications, 1989.

Kent, N., *Naked Hollywood*, London: BBC Books, 1991.

Koenig, P., 'Steve's World, and Our Own', *The Independent on Sunday*, 'Sunday Review' 21 February 1993.

Leff, L. and Simmons, J., *The Dame in the Kimono*, New York: Grove Weidenfeld, 1990.

Merritt, R., 'Nickelodeon Theaters 1905–1914', in T. Balio (ed.), *The American Film Industry*, Madison: University of Wisconsin Press, 1976.

Perry, N., 'Will Sony Make it in Hollywood', *Fortune*, 9 September 1991.

Petley, J., 'Cinema and State', in C. Barr (ed.), *All Our Yesterdays*, London: British Film Institute, 1986.

Randall, R., 'Censorship: from *The Miracle* to *Deep Throat*', in T. Balio (ed.), *The American Film Industry*, Madison: University of Wisconsin Press, 1976.

Robertson, J., *The British Board of Film Censors: Film Censorship in Britain, 1896–1950*, Beckenham: Croom Helm, 1985.

Roddick, N., *A New Deal in Entertainment*, London: British Film Institute, 1983.

Roth, M., 'Some Warners Musicals and the Spirit of the New Deal', in R. Altman (ed.), *Genre: The Musical*, London: BFI/Routledge & Kegan Paul, 1981.

Sheinfeld, L., 'The Big Chill', *Film Comment*, vol. 22, no. 3, May/June 1986.

Staiger, J., 'Combination and Litigation', in T. Elsaesser (ed.), *Early Cinema*, London: British Film Institute, 1990.

Sunday Telegraph, 'The Empire Fights', *Sunday Telegraph*, 4 July 1993, Review, p. 2.

Taylor, C., 'Marks the Spot', *Sight and Sound*, vol. 60, no. 1, Winter 1990–1

CHAPTER 5: GENRE, STAR AND AUTEUR

Overview

Belton, John, *American Cinema/American Culture*, New York: McGraw Hill, 1994.

Collins, Jim, Radner, Hilary, Preacher, Ava and Collins, S. (eds), *Film Theory Goes to the Movies*, New York: AFI/Routledge, 1993 (particularly ch. 4, Dudley Andrews, 'The Unauthorized Auteur Today' and ch. 16, Jim Collins 'Genericity in the Nineties').

Maltby, Richard and Craven, Ian, *Hollywood Cinema*, Oxford: Blackwell, 1995.

Two books which provide excellent contextual accounts of the studio system and the 'new' Hollywood respectively are:

Schatz, Thomas, *The Genius of the System: Hollywood Filmmaking in the Studio System*, New York: Pantheon, 1988.

and

Hillier, Jim, *The New Hollywood*, London: Studio Vista, 1993.

Strongly recommended as an introduction to the theories referred to in this chapter is a book focusing not on film but on television:

Fiske, John, *Television Culture*, London: Routledge, 1987.

Other well-known books which offer a theoretical overview of the principal topics of this chapter include:

Cook, Pam, *The Cinema Book*, London: BFI, 1986.

Ellis, John, *Visible Fictions* (rev. edn), London: Routledge, 1992.

Lapsley, Robert and Westlake, Michael, *Film Theory: An Introduction*, Manchester: Manchester University Press, 1988.

Turner, Graeme, *Film as Social Practice* (2nd edn), London: Routledge, 1993.

A very good example of the kind of study which takes the study of Hollywood cinema from textual to cultural analysis is

Traube, Elizabeth G., *Dreaming Identities: Class, Gender and Generation in 1980's Hollywood Movies*, Boulder, Colo.: Westview Press, 1992.

Structuralism and semiotics

For a useful introduction see ch. 3 of

Morgan, John, and Welton, Peter, *See What I Mean – An Introduction to Visual Communication*, London: Edward Arnold, 1986.

or chs 3–7 of,

Fiske, John, *Introduction to Communication Studies* (2nd edn), London: Routledge, 1990.

For more advanced discussion see:

Gaines, Jane (ed.), *Classical Hollywood Narrative: The Paradigm Wars*, Durham, NC: Duke University Press, 1992.

Stam, Robert, Burgoyne, Robert and Flitterman-Lewis, Sandy, *New Vocabularies in Film Semiotics*, London: Routledge, 1992.

Wollen, Peter, *Signs and Meaning in the Cinema*, London: Secker & Warburg, 1972.

And for an eloquent (and sometimes persuasive) rejection of much of the standard film theory of the last twenty-five years:

Carroll, Noel, *Mystifying Movies*, New York: Columbia University Press, 1988.

Genre

Altman, Rick, (ed.), *Genre – The Musical*, London: Routledge, 1981, (particularly Richard Dyer, 'Entertainment and Utopia').

—— *The American Film Musical*, London: BFI, 1989.

Cawelti, John G., *Adventure, Mystery and Romance*, Chicago: University of Chicago Press, 1976.

Feuer, Jane, *The Hollywood Musical* (2nd edn), London: Macmillan, 1993.

McConnell, Frank, *Storytelling and Mythmaking*, New York: Oxford University Press, 1979.

Neale, Stephen, *Genre*, London: BFI, 1980.

Schatz, Thomas, *Hollywood Genres: Formulas, Filmmaking and the Studio System*, New York: McGraw Hill, 1981.

Stars

Dyer, Richard, *Stars*, London: BFI, 1979.

—— *Heavenly Bodies – Film Stars and Society*, London: BFI/Macmillan, 1987.

Gledhill, Christine (ed.), *Stardom – Industry of Desire*, London: Routledge, 1991 (particularly ch. 13, Barry King, 'Articulating Stardom', ch. 15, Andrew Britton, 'Stars and Genre', and ch. 16, Christine Gledhill, 'Signs of Melodrama').

Hinson, Hal, 'Some Notes on Method Actors', *Sight and Sound*, vol. 53, no. 3, summer 1984 (worth seeking out for the comparative study of Brando and De Niro).

A very witty and wide-ranging study of the relationship between stars and movie-goers is:
Basinger, Jeanine, *A Woman's View – How Hollywood Spoke to Women, 1930–1960*, London: Chatto & Windus, 1994.

Biographies
There are many popular biographies available; the following are indicative rather than particularly recommended:
Agan, Patrick, *Robert De Niro – the Man, the Myth and the Movies*, London: Hale, 1989.
Anderson, Christopher, *Citizen Jane – The Turbulent Life of Jane Fonda*, London: Virgin Books, 1990.
Leigh, Wendy, *Liza Minnelli*, London: New English Library, 1993.

Auteur
Caughie, John (ed.), *Theories of Authorship, A Reader*, London: Routledge, 1981.
Kolker, Robert, *A Cinema of Loneliness: Penn, Kubrick, Scorsese, Spielberg, Altman*, (rev. edn), Oxford: Oxford University Press, 1988.
Sarris, Andrew, *The American Cinema: Directors and Directions 1928–1968*, New York: Dutton, 1968.
Thompson, David and Christie, Ian (eds), *Scorsese on Scorsese*, London: Faber, 1989.

New York, New York
Particularly useful are two articles in *Movie*, vol. 31–2, winter 1986:
Cooke, Lez, '*New York, New York* – Looking at De Niro'.
Lippe, Richard, '*New York, New York* and the Hollywood Musical'.

CHAPTER 8: WOMEN AND FILM
Agosterios, V., 'An Interview with Sally Potter' *Framework*, no. 14, 1979.
Arthur, J., 'Technology and Gender', *Screen*, vol. 30, 1989, pp. 40–59.
Auty, M. and Roddick, N. (eds), *British Cinema Now*, London: British Film Institute, 1985.
Banner, L., *Women in Modern America*, New York: Harcourt, Brace, Jovanovich, 1984.
Berger, J., *Ways of Seeing*, London: Penguin, 1972.
Bergstrom, J., 'Rereading the Work of Claire Johnston', in C. Pentley (ed.), *Feminism and Film Theory*, London: Routledge/British Film Institute, 1988.
Betterton, R., *Looking On: Images of Femininity in the Visual Arts and the Media*, London: Pandora, 1987.
Brundsen, C. (ed.), *Films for Women*, London: British Film Institute, 1986.
Burns, M., 'Women in Focus', *In Camera*, spring 1992, pp. 3–5, 17–19.
Cook, P., *The Gold Diggers*, *Framework*, vol. 24, 1981.
—— (ed.), *The Cinema Book*, London: British Film Institute, 1985.
Cook, P. and Dodd, P. (eds), *Women and Film: A 'Sight and Sound' Reader*, London: Scarlet Press, 1993.
De Lauretis, T., 'Guerilla in the Midst – Women's Cinema in the 1980s', *Screen*, vol. 31, no. 1, 1990.
Donald, L. and Scanlon, S., 'Hollywood Feminism? Get Real!!', *Trouble and Strife*, vol. 25, winter 1992, pp. 11–16.
Dove, L., 'Feminist and Left Independent Filmmaking in England', *Jump Cut*, vol. 10–11, 1976.
Ehrenstein, D., 'Out of the Wilderness', *Film Quarterly*, vol. 47, no. 1, 1993, pp. 2–7.
Fitzgerald, T., 'Now About These Women', *Sight and Sound*, summer 1989.
Florence, P., 'A Conversation With Sally Potter', *Screen*, vol. 34, no. 3, autumn 1993, pp. 275–84.
Friedan, B., *The Feminine Mystique*, London: Penguin, 1963.

Gledhill, C., 'Some Recent Developments in Feminist Criticism', in S. Mast and M. Cohen (eds), *Film Theory and Criticism*, Oxford: Oxford University Press, 1985.

Greer, G., *The Female Eunuch*, London: Flamingo, 1971.

Haskell, M., *From Reverence to Rape*, London: New English Library, 1973.

Heck-Rabi, L., *Women Filmmakers – A Critical Reception*, Scarecrow Press, 1984.

Johnston, C., 'Women's Cinema as Counter Cinema', *Screen Pamphlet*, no. 2, 1973.

—— 'The Subject of Feminist Film Theory/Practice', *Screen*, vol. 21, no. 2, 1980.

Kaplan, E.A., *Women and Film: Both Sides of the Camera*, London: Methuen, 1983.

Kuhn, A., *Women's Pictures*, London: British Film Institute/Routledge & Kegan Paul, 1982.

Lapsley, R. and Westlake, M., *Film Theory: An Introduction*, Manchester: Manchester University Press, 1988.

Lehman, P. and Maynes, J., 'An Interview with Susan Clayton', *Wide Angle*, vol. 6, no. 3, 1981, p. 72.

Lovell, T., *Pictures of Reality: Aesthetics, Politics and Pleasure*, London: British Film Institute, 1983.

—— 'That Was The Workshop That Was', *Screen*, vol. 31, no. 1, 1990, pp. 102–8.

Mast, S. and Cohen, M. (eds), *Film Theory and Criticism*, Oxford: Oxford University Press, 1985.

Maynard, M., 'Current Trends in Feminist Theory', *Social Studies Review*, vol. 2, no. 3, 1987.

Millet, K., *Sexual Politics*, London: Virago, 1977.

Modleski, T., *The Women Who Knew Too Much*, London: Methuen, 1988.

Muir, A.R., 'The Status of Women Working in Film and Television', in L. Gammon (ed.), *The Female Gaze*, London: The Women's Press, 1988.

Mulvey, L., 'Visual Pleasure and Narrative Cinema', *Screen*, vol. 16, no. 3, 1975.

—— *Framework*, vol. 10, nos 6–7, p. 7, 1977.

—— 'Film, Feminism and the Avant-Garde', 1979.

—— 'Afterthoughts on Visual Pleasure and Narrative Cinema', *Framework*, vol. 6, nos 15–17, 1981.

—— *Visual and Other Pleasures*, London: Macmillan, 1989.

Murphy, J., 'A Question of Silence', in C. Brundsen (ed.), *Films for Women*, London: British Film Institute, 1986.

Nicholls, B. (ed.), *Movies and Methods*, vol. 1, University of California Press, 1976.

Penley, C. (ed.), *Feminism and Film Theory*, London: Routledge/British Film Institute, 1988.

Pilcher, J., 'I'm Not a Feminist, But . . .', *Sociology Review*, November 1993, p. 4.

Pilling, J. (ed.), *Women and Animation: A Compendium*, London: British Film Institute, 1992.

Pollock, G., *Vision and Difference*, London: Routledge, 1988.

Pollock, G. and Parker, R., *Old Mistresses*, London: Routledge & Kegan Paul, 1981.

Slide, A., *Early Women Directors*, A.S. Barnes, 1976.

Smith, S., *Women Who Make Movies*, Hopkinson and Blake, 1975.

Zoonen, L., *Feminist Media Studies*, London: Sage, 1994.

CHAPTER 9: LESBIAN AND GAY CINEMA

Babuscio, Jack, 'Camp and Gay Sensibility', in Richard Dyer (ed.), *Gays and Film*, London: British Film Institute, 1977. An essay which presents pioneering insights.

Bad Object Choices (ed.), *How Do I Look? – Queer Film And Video*, Seattle: Bay Press, 1991. Queer theory investigates the process of looking; at Asians in pornography, Dorothy Arzner, skinheads, safe sex, history and photo images of blacks.

Burston, Paul and Richardson, Colin (eds), *A Queer Romance – Gay Men, Lesbians and Popular Culture*, London: Routledge, 1995. Essays on spectatorship and genre along with contributions by film-makers Monika Treut and Bruce LaBruce.

Cook, Pam and Dodd, Philip, *Women and Film – A Sight and Sound Reader*, London: British Film Institute, 1993. An excellent section entitled 'Queer Alternatives' contains B. Ruby Rich's essay on queer cinema,

Pratibha Parmar's response, Amy Taubin's lively criticisms and an essay on Monica Treut.

Creekmur, Corey R. and Doty, Alexander (eds), *Out in Culture – Gay, Lesbian and other Queer Essays on Popular Culture*, Durham NC and London: Duke University Press, 1995. This volume contains Robin Wood's seminal essays on gay film criticism and Hitchcock, along with a variety of useful material on many films mentioned in this chapter.

Dyer, Richard, 'Pasolini and Homosexuality', in P. Willemen (ed.), *Pier Paolo Pasolini*, London: British Film Institute, 1977. A key perspective on this major twentieth-century film-maker and writer.

—— 'Resistance Through Charisma: Rita Hayworth and Gilda', in Ann E. Kaplan (ed.), *Women in Film Noir*, London: British Film Institute, 1978. A case study in homoerotic subtext.

—— 'Rejecting Straight Ideals; Gays in Film', in Peter Steven (ed.), *Jump Cut – Hollywood, Politics and Counter-Cinema*, Toronto: Between The Lines, 1985.

—— *Heavenly Bodies – Film Stars and Society*, Basingstoke: Macmillan, 1987 especially 'Judy Garland and Gay Men'. This essay on gay spectatorship includes a lucid application of camp as a critical concept.

—— *Now You See It: Studies in Lesbian and Gay Film*, London and New York: Routledge, 1990. A detailed, rewarding academic study, mainly of early German film, Genet and developments in America.

—— *The Matter of Images – Essays on Representation*, London: Routledge, 1993. Dyer illustrates the power and complexity of images across a range of films, including film noir, *Victim*, *Papillon* and *A Passage To India*.

—— 'Rock – the Last Guy You'd Have Figured?', in Pat Kirkham and Janet Thumin (eds), *You Tarzan – Masculinity, Movies and Men*, New York: St Martin's Press, 1993b.

Gever, Martha, Greyson, John and Parmar, Pratibha (eds), *Queer Looks – Perspectives on Lesbian and Gay Video*, Toronto: Between The Lines, 1993. A wealth of new insights, including a look at gay punk video-maker Bruce LaBruce, new interpretations of Fassbinder's films and a superb essay by Thomas Waugh on gay spectatorship.

Giles, Jane, *The Cinema of Jean Genet – Un Chant D'Amour*, London: British Film Institute, 1991. This look at Genet's production and influence in film includes an illustrated script of *Un Chant d'Amour*.

Hadleigh, Boze, *The Lavender Screen – the Gay and Lesbian Films*, New York: Citadel Press, 1993. Good illustrations and some lively insights.

Jarman, Derek, *Dancing Ledge*, London: Quartet, 1984. The critically acclaimed artist's account of his formative years, which cover the making of *The Angelic Conversation*, *Sebastiane* and *Jubilee*. The first of a number of fascinating writings he produced, which includes books to accompany *Caravaggio*, *War Requiem* and *Edward II*.

Julien, Isaac and McCabe, Colin, *Diary of a Young Soul Rebel*, London: British Film Institute, 1991. The script of this lively film, along with an introduction and interview which throw light on its director's fascinating insights into race and sexuality.

Kirkham, Pat and Thumin, Janet (eds), *You Tarzan – Masculinity, Movies and Men*, London and New York: Lawrence & Wishart and St Martin's Press, 1993. Contains Richard Dyer's essay on the star image of Rock Hudson. An inspiring set of essays to investigate the construction of masculinity in, for example, Clarke Gable films.

Kureishi, Hanif, *My Beautiful Laundrette and the Rainbow Sign*, London: Faber & Faber, 1986. The script of this noted film, along with scriptwriter Kureishi's articulate essay on its themes of sexuality, race and Britishness.

Marshall, Stewart, 'The Contemporary Political Use of Gay History – The Third Reich', in Bad Object Choices (ed.), *How Do I Look? – Queer Film and Video*, Seattle: Bay Press, 1991.

Mayne, Judith, 'The Critical Audience', in her book *Cinema and Spectatorship*, London and New York: Routledge, 1993. An informed critical overview of lesbian spectatorship.

—— *Directed by Dorothy Arzner*, Bloomington: University of Indiana Press, 1994. The first detailed critical work on the life and films of this neglected Hollywood auteur.

Merck, Mandy, '"Lianna" and the Lesbians of Art Cinema' in Charlotte Brunsdon (ed.), *Films for Women*,

London: British Film Institute, 1986. See also Mandy Merck's essay on *Desert Hearts*, in M. Gever, J. Greyson and P. Parmar (eds), *Queer Looks – Perspectives on Lesbian and Gay Video*, Toronto: Between The Lines, 1993.

Mulvey, L., 'Visual Pleasure and Narrative Cinema', in C. Penley (ed.), *Feminism and Film Theory*, London: British Film Institute, 1988 (also in L. Mulvey, *Visual and Other Pleasures*, Bloomington: University of Indiana Press, 1989; and B. Nichols (ed.), *Movies and Methods*, vol. 1, Berkeley: University of California Press, 1985).

Murray, Raymond, *Images in the Dark – an Encyclopedia of Gay and Lesbian Film and Video*, Philadelphia: TLA Publications, 1994. A comprehensive and illuminating book. It has a refreshingly international outlook, covering mainstream and independent film. There are separate sections on queer, lesbian, gay male and transgender interest and on camp.

Parkerson, Michelle, 'Birth of a Nation: Towards Black Gay and Lesbian Imagery in Film and Video, in *Queer Looks – Perspectives on Lesbian and Gay Film and Video*, Toronto: Between The Lines, 1993.

Pilling, J. and O'Pray, M. (ed.), *Into the Pleasure Dome – the Films of Kenneth Anger*, London: British Film Institute, 1989. A useful set of essays on this influential talent.

Russo, Vito, *The Celluloid Closet – Homosexuality in the Movies*, New York: Harper & Row, 1987. The classic introduction to this area.

Sontag, Susan, 'Notes on Camp', in her *Against Interpretation and Other Essays*, New York: Anchor Books, 1980 (also in S. Sontag, *The Susan Sontag Reader*, London: Penguin, 1983).

Steven, Peter (ed.), *Jump Cut – Hollywood, Politics and Counter Cinema*, Toronto: Between The Lines, 1985. Useful essays include viewpoints on lesbian spectatorship, Richard Dyer on stereotyping and Jan Oxenberg.

Stewart, Steve, *Gay Hollywood – Film and Video Guide*, Companion Publications, 1993. A handy reference volume, available from the NFT bookshop or on order.

Taubin, Amy, 'Queer Male Cinema and Feminism', in Pam Cook and Philip Dodd (eds), *Women and Film – A Sight and Sound Reader*, London: British Film Institute, 1993.

Tyler, Parker, *Screening the Sexes: Homosexuality in the Movies*, New York: DeCapo, 1993. The original pioneering survey, with a new introduction by Andrew Sarris. The breadth and richness of the material Tyler covers, and the insights he presents, make this 1972 text of continuing value.

Weiss, Andrea, 'A Queer Feeling When I Look at You: Hollywood Stars and Lesbian Spectatorship in the 1930s', in Christine Gledhill (ed.) *Stardom: Industry of Desire*, London and New York: Routledge, 1991. A valuable contribution to star study.

—— *Vampires and Violets – Lesbians in Film*, Harmondsworth: Penguin, 1993. Key films and the main debates clearly presented.

White, Patricia, 'Female Spectator, Lesbian Spectator: the Haunting', in Diana Fuss (ed.), *Inside/Out: Lesbian Theories, Gay Theories*, New York and London: Routledge, 1991. A useful individual case study applying ideas of spectatorship.

Wilton, Tamsin, *Immortal Invisible – Lesbians and the Moving Image*, New York and London: Routledge, 1995. A collection of essays which investigates lesbian viewing and production. It includes contributions on *Desert Hearts* and *Salmonberries* along with interpretations of *Aliens* and other mainstream films.

Wood, Robin, 'Responsibilities of a Gay Film Critic', in Bill Nichols (ed.), *Movies and Methods*, vol. 2, Berkeley: University of California Press, 1985. Wood's seminal essay of the late 1970s outlines his critical stance and provides re-readings of some of his work on Renoir, Bergman and Hawks.

—— *Hitchcock Revisited*, London: Faber & Faber, 1989. This volume includes Wood's original auterist essays on Hitchcock with challenging new reinterpretations in the light of gay critical perspectives.

CHAPTER 10: BRITISH CINEMA

Aitken, Ian, *Film and Reform: John Grierson and the Documentary Film Movement*, London: Routledge, 1990.

Aldgate, Anthony, 'Comedy, Class and Containment: The British Domestic Cinema of the 1930s', in James Curran and Vincent Porter (eds), *British Cinema History*, London: Weidenfeld & Nicolson, 1983, pp. 257–71.

Aldgate, Anthony and Richards, Jeffrey, *Britain Can Take It: The British Cinema in the Second World War*, Oxford: Blackwell, 1986.

Armes, Roy, *A Critical History of the British Cinema*, London: Secker & Warburg, 1978.

Auty, Martyn and Roddick, Nick (eds), *British Cinema Now*, London: British Film Institute, 1985.

Barber, Susan Torrey, 'Insurmountable Difficulties and Moments of Ecstasy: Crossing Class, Ethnic and Sexual Barriers in the Films of Stephen Frears', in Lester Friedman (ed.), *British Cinema and Thatcherism*, London: University College London, 1993, pp. 221–36.

Barr, Charles (ed.), *All Our Yesterdays*, London: British Film Institute, 1986.

—— *Ealing Studios*, rev. edn, London: Studio Vista, 1993 (first published 1977).

Barr, Charles and Frears, Stephen, *Typically British*, London: British Film Institute, 1995.

Berry, Dave, *Wales and Cinema: The First Hundred Years*, London: British Film Institute, 1994.

Betts, Ernest, *The Film Business: A History of British Cinema 1896–1972*, London: Allen & Unwin, 1973.

Blanchard, Simon and Harvey, Sylvia, 'The Post-War Independent Cinema: Structure and Organization', in James Curran and Vincent Porter (eds), *British Cinema History*, London: Weidenfeld & Nicolson, 1983, pp. 226–41.

Bond, Ralph, 'Labour and the Cinema: A Reply To Huntly Carter', in Don Macpherson (ed.), *Traditions of Independence: British Cinema in the Thirties*, London: British Film Institute, 1980, pp. 140–1 (first published in *The Plebs*, August 1931).

Burch, Noel, *Life To Those Shadows*, London: British Film Institute, 1990, pp. 80–108.

Burrows, Elaine (ed.), *British Cinema Source Book*, London: British Film Institute, 1995.

Chanan, Michael, *The Dream That Kicks*, London: Routledge, 1980.

Colls, Robert and Dodd, Philip, 'Representing the Nation: British Documentary Film, 1930–45', *Screen*, vol. 26, no. 1, 1985, pp. 21–33.

Cook, Pam, 'Handsworth Songs', *Monthly Film Bulletin*, vol. 54, no. 638, 1987, pp. 77–8.

Cormack, Mike, *Ideology*, London: Batsford, 1992.

Curran, James and Porter, Vincent (eds), *British Cinema History*, London: Weidenfeld & Nicolson, 1983.

Dewe Mathews, Tom, *Censored: The Story of Film Censorship in Britain*, London: Chatto & Windus, 1994.

Diawara, Manthia, 'Power and Territory: The Emergence of Black British Film Collectives', in Lester Friedman (ed.), *British Cinema and Thatcherism*, London: University College London, 1993, pp. 147–60.

Dick, Eddie (ed.), *From Limelight to Satellite: A Scottish Film Book*, London: British Film Institute/Scottish Film Council, 1990.

Dickinson, Margaret and Street, Sarah, *Cinema and State*, London: British Film Institute, 1985.

Dixon, Wheeler Winston (ed.), *Re-Viewing British Cinema, 1900–1992*, New York: State University of New York Press, 1994.

Docherty, David, Morrison, David and Tracey, Michael, *The Last Picture Show?*, London: British Film Institute, 1987.

Durgnat, Raymond, *A Mirror For England*, London: Faber, 1970.

Dyer, Richard, 'The Role Of Stereotypes', in Jim Cook and Mike Lewington (eds), *Images of Alcoholism*, London: British Film Institute, 1979, pp. 15–21. (Also in Richard Dyer, *The Matter of Images: Essays on Representation*, London: Routledge, 1993, pp. 11–18.)

—— 'Taking Popular Television Seriously', in David Lusted and Phillip Drummond (eds), *TV and Schooling*, London: British Film Institute, 1985, pp. 41–6.

Ellis, John, 'Television, Video and Independent Cinema', in Simon Blanchard and David Morley (eds), *What's This Channel Four?*, London: Comedia, 1982, pp. 145–50.

Eyles, Allen, *ABC: The First Name in Entertainment*, London: British Film Institute, 1993.

—— *Gaumont – British Cinemas*, London: British Film Institute, 1995.

Friedman, Lester (ed.), *British Cinema and Thatcherism*, London: University College, London, 1993.

Harper, Sue, *Picturing the Past: The Rise and Fall of the British Costume Film*, London: British Film Institute, 1994.

Hartog, Simon, 'State Protection of a Beleaguered Industry', in James Curran and Vincent Porter (eds), *British Cinema History*, London: Weidenfeld & Nicolson, 1983, pp. 59–73.

Harvey, Sylvia, 'New Images For Old? Channel Four and Independent Film', in Simon Blanchard and David Morley (eds), *What's This Channel Four?*, London: Comedia, 1982, pp. 157–62.

—— 'The "Other Cinema" in Britain: Unfinished Business in Oppositional and Independent Film, 1929–1984', in Charles Barr (ed.), *All Our Yesterdays*, London: British Film Institute, 1986, pp. 225–51.

Higson, Andrew, 'The Concept of National Cinema', *Screen*, vol. 30, no. 4, 1989, pp. 36–46.

—— 'Re-presenting the National Past: Nostalgia and Pastiche in the Heritage Film', in Lester Friedman (ed.), *British Cinema and Thatcherism*, London: University College London, 1993, pp. 109–29.

—— *Waving the Flag: Constructing a National Cinema in Britain*, Oxford: Oxford University Press, 1995.

Hill, John, *Sex, Class and Realism: British Cinema 1956–1963*, London: British Film Institute, 1986.

—— 'The Issue of National Cinema and British Film Production', in Duncan Petrie (ed.), *New Questions Of British Cinema*, London: British Film Institute, 1992, pp. 10–21.

Hill, John, McLoone, Martin and Hainsworth, Paul (eds), *Border Crossing*, London: British Film Institute/ Institute of Irish Studies, 1994.

Hogenkamp, Bert, *Deadly Parallels: Film and the Left in Britain 1929–1939*, London: Lawrence & Wishart, 1986.

Hurd, Geoff (ed.), *National Fictions*, London: British Film Institute, 1984.

Hutchings, Peter, *Hammer and Beyond*, Manchester: Manchester University Press, 1993.

Jones, Stephen G., *The British Labour Movement and Film, 1918–1939*, London: Routledge, 1987.

Kuhn, Annette, with Radstone, Susannah (eds), *The Women's Companion To International Film*, London: Virago, 1990.

Kulik, Karol, *Alexander Korda*, London: W.H. Allen, 1975.

Landy, Marcia, *British Genres: Cinema and Society, 1930–1960*, Princeton, NJ: Princeton University Press, 1991.

Lant, Antonia, *Blackout: Reinventing Women for Wartime British Cinema*, Princeton, NJ: Princeton University Press, 1991.

—— 'Women's Independent Cinema: The Case of Leeds Animation Workshop', in Lester Friedman (ed.), *British Cinema and Thatcherism*, London: University College London, 1993, pp. 161–87.

Lovell, Alan and Hillier, Jim, *Studies In Documentary*, London: Secker & Warburg/British Film Institute, 1972.

Low, Rachel, *The History of the British Film 1914–1918*, London: Allen & Unwin, 1950.

—— *The History of the British Film 1918–1929*, London: Allen & Unwin, 1971.

—— *Film-Making in 1930s Britain*, London: Allen & Unwin, 1985.

Low, Rachel and Manvell, Roger, *The History of the British Film 1896–1906*, London: Allen & Unwin, 1948.

McArthur, Colin, *Scotch Reels*, London: British Film Institute, 1982.

McFarlane, Brian (ed.), *Sixty Voices: Celebrities Recall The Golden Age of British Cinema*, London: British Film Institute, 1992.

McIntyre, Steve, 'National Film Cultures – Politics and Peripheries', *Screen*, vol. 26, no. 1, 1985, pp. 66–76.

Macnab, Geoffrey, *J. Arthur Rank and the British Film Industry*, London: Routledge, 1993.

Macpherson, Don (ed.), *Traditions of Independence: British Cinema in the Thirties*, London: British Film Institute, 1980.

Marris, Paul, 'Politics and "Independent" Film in the Decade of Defeat', in Don Macpherson (ed.) *Traditions of Independence: British Cinema in the Thirties*, London: British Film Institute, 1980, pp. 70–95.

Marwick, Arthur, *British Society Since 1945*, London: Penguin, 1990.

Murphy, Robert, *Realism and Tinsel: Cinema and Society in Britain 1939–49*, London: Routledge, 1989.

—— *Sixties British Cinema*, London: British Film Institute, 1992.

Neale, Steve, '"Chariots of Fire", Images of Men', *Screen*, vol. 23, nos 3–4, 1982, pp. 47–53.

Oakley, Charles, *Where We Came In*, London: Allen & Unwin, 1964

O'Brien, Margaret and Eyles, Allen (eds), *Enter The Dream House*, London: British Film Institute, 1993.

O'Sullivan, Tim, Hartley, John, Saunders, Danny, Montgomery, Martin and Fiske, John, *Key Concepts in Communication and Cultural Studies*, London: Routledge, 1994.

Park, James, *Learning to Dream: The New British Cinema*, London: Faber & Faber, 1984.

—— *British Cinema: The Lights that Failed*, London: Batsford, 1990.

Perry, George, *The Great British Picture Show*, London: Paladin, 1975.

Petrie, Duncan, *Creativity and Constraint in the British Film Industry*, London: Macmillan, 1991.

—— (ed.), *New Questions of British Cinema*, London: British Film Institute, 1992.

Pirie, David, *A Heritage of Horror: The English Gothic Cinema 1946–72*, London: Gordon Fraser, 1973.

Quart, Leonard, 'The Religion of the Market: Thatcherite Politics and the British Film of the 1980s', in Lester Friedman (ed.), *British Cinema and Thatcherism*, London: University College London, 1993, pp. 15–34.

Richards, Jeffrey, *The Age Of The Dream Palace*, London: Routledge, 1984.

Richards, Jeffrey and Aldgate, Anthony, *Best of British: Cinema and Society 1930–1970*, Oxford: Blackwell, 1983.

Richards, Jeffery and Sheridan, Dorothy (eds), *Mass Observation at the Movies*, London: Routledge, 1987.

Robertson, James C., *The Hidden Cinema: British Film Censorship in Action, 1913–1975*, London: Routledge, 1989.

Rockett, Kevin, Hill, John and Gibbons, Luke, *Cinema and Ireland*, London: Croom Helm, 1987.

Ryall, Tom, *Alfred Hitchcock and the British Cinema*, London: Croom Helm, 1986.

Ryan, Trevor, '"The New Road To Progress": The Use and Production of Films by the Labour Movement, 1929–39', in James Curran and Vincent Porter (eds), *British Cinema History*, London: Weidenfeld & Nicolson, 1983, pp. 113–28.

Stevenson, John, *British Society 1914–45*, London: Penguin, 1984.

Stoneman, Rod and Thompson, Hilary (eds), *The New Social Function of Cinema*, London: British Film Institute, 1981.

Storey, John, *Cultural Theory and Popular Culture*, London: Harvester Wheatsheaf, 1993.

Taylor, Philip (ed.), *Britain and the Cinema in the Second World War*, London: Macmillan, 1988.

Threadgall, Derek, *Shepperton Studios*, London: British Film Institute, 1994.

Turner, Graeme, *British Cultural Studies*, London: Routledge, 1992.

Walker, Alexander, *National Heroes: British Cinema in the Seventies and Eighties*, London: Harrap, 1985.

—— *Hollywood, England: The British Film Industry in the Sixties*, London: Harrap, 1986.

Walker, John, *The Once and Future Film: British Cinema in the Seventies and Eighties*, London: Methuen, 1985.

Whitaker, Sheila, 'Declarations of Independence', in Martyn Auty and Nick Roddick (eds), *British Cinema Now*, London: British Film Institute, 1985, pp. 83–98.

Williams, Raymond, *Keywords*, London: Fontana, 1976.

Wood, Linda, *British Film Industry*, London: British Film Institute, 1980.

—— *British Films, 1927–1939*, London: British Film Institute, 1986.

CHAPTER 12: AN INTRODUCTION TO INDIAN CINEMA

Armes, Roy, *Third World Film-Making and the West*, Berkeley: University of California Press, 1987.

Barnouw, Eric and Krishnaswamy, S., *Indian Film*, New York: Oxford University Press, 1980.

Bhattacharya, Rinki, *Bimal Roy – A Man of Silence*, New Delhi: Indus, 1994.

Chakravarty, Sumita, 'National Identity and the Realist Aesthetic: Indian Cinema of the Fifties', *Quarterly Review of Film and Video*, vol. 11, 1989, pp. 31–48.

Chandavarkar, Bhaskar, 'Indian Film Song', in T.M. Ramachandran (ed.), *70 Years of Indian Cinema*, Bombay: CINEMA India-International, 1985.

Chandra, Anupama with Shetty, Kavita, 'Hitting the Right Notes', *India Today*, 30 November 1993, pp. 52–3.

Dharap, B.V., 'Dadasaheb Phalke: Father of Indian Cinema', in T.M. Ramachandran (ed.), *70 Years of Indian Cinema*, Bombay: CINEMA India-International, 1985.

Dissanayake, Wimal and Sahai, Malti, *Raj Kapoor's Films: Harmony of Discourses*, New Delhi: Vikas, 1988.

George, T.J.S., *The Life and Times of Nargis*, New Delhi: Indus, 1994.

Kabir, Nasreen Munni, 'Indian Film Music', unpublished monograph, 1991.

Micciollo, Henri, *Guru Dutt*, Paris: L'Avant-Scene du Cinema, 1979.

Mishra, Vijay, 'Towards a Theoretical Critique of Bombay Cinema', *Screen*, vol. 26, nos 3–4, 1985, pp. 133–46.

—— 'The Actor as Parallel Text in Bombay Cinema', *Quarterly Review of Film and Video*, vol. 11, 1989, pp. 49–67.

Nandy, Ashis, 'The Popular Hindi Film: Ideology and First Principles', *India International Centre Quarterly*, vol. 8, no. 1, 1981, pp. 89–96.

Passek, Jean-Loup (ed.), *Le Cinéma Indien*, Paris: Centre Georges Pompidou/l'Equerre, 1983.

Pfleiderer, Beatrix and Lutze, Lothar, *The Hindi Film: Agent and Re:Agent of Cultural Change*, New Delhi: Manohar, 1985.

Rai, Amit, 'An American Raj in Filmistan: Images of Elvis in Indian Films', *Screen*, vol. 35, no. 1, 1994, pp. 51–77.

Rangoonwalla, Firoze, *Indian Cinema: Past and Present*, New Delhi: Clarion, 1982.

Ray, Satyajit, *Our Films, Their Films*, Bombay: Orient Longman, 1976.

Rueben, Bunny, *Mehboob – India's De Mille*, New Delhi: Indus, 1994.

Robinson, Andrew, *Satyajit Ray: The Inner Eye*, London: André Deutsch, 1989.

Shah, Panna, *The Indian Film*, Westport, Conn.: Greenwood Press, 1981.

Skillman, Terri, 'The Bombay Hindi Film Song', in *Yearbook for Traditional Music 1986*, New York: International Council for Traditional Music, 1986, pp. 133–44.

Thomas, Rosie, 'Indian Cinema: Pleasures and Popularity', *Screen*, vol. 26, nos 3–4, 1985, pp. 116–31.

—— 'Sanctity and Scandal in Mother India', *Quarterly Review of Film and Video*, vol. 11, 1989, pp. 11–30.

Vasudev, Aruna, *The New Indian Cinema*, Delhi: Macmillan, 1986.

Vasudevan, Ravi, 'The Melodramatic Mode and Commercial Hindi Cinema', *Screen*, vol. 30, no. 3, 1989, pp. 29–50.

Wadia, J.B.H., 'The Indian Silent Film', in T.M. Ramachandran (ed.), *70 Years of Indian Cinema*, Bombay: CINEMA India-International, 1985.

Warder, A.K., 'Classical Literature', in A.L. Basham (ed.), *A Cultural History of India*, Oxford: Oxford University Press, 1975.

Books published in India can be ordered from: Books from India, 45 Museum Street, London WC1A 1LR. Telephone: 0171 405 3784.

INDEX